Philosophy
For A-level Year 2

Metaphysics of God and Metaphysics of Mind

Daniel Cardinal
Gerald Jones
Jeremy Hayward

Acknowledgements

The Publishers would like to thank the following for permission to reproduce copyright material.

Text credits: pp.47, 160, 164, 262 & 329 (Anth 1.22) A.J. Ayer, *Language, Truth and Logic*, Dover Publications, 1980. Reprinted with permission; **pp.71, 76 & 323 (Anth 1.9)** Reproduced with permission of author, Richard Swinburne; **pp.132, 139, 148 & 328 (Anth 1.20)** John Hick, *Evil and the God of Love*, Fontana, 1968, p.3, p375, p293: Reproduced with permission of SpringerNature; **pp.188, 214, 330 (Anth 2.2) & 331 (Anth 2.6)** David Chalmers: Reproduced with permission of John Wiley & Sons; **pp.210, 249, 287, 288, 332 (Anth 2.9), 335 (Anth 2.19) & 337 (Anth 2.23)** Churchland, Patricia, *Brain-Wise: Studies in Neurophilosophy*, pp.22–130 [approx. 1,000-word excerpt], © 2002 Massachusetts Institute of Technology, by permission of The MIT Press; **pp.220, 260, 332 (Anth 2.7) & 334 (Anth 2.14 & 2.15)** F. Jackson: Reproduced with permission of Oxford University Press; **pp.231, 236, 241 & 333 (Anth 2.11)** Anita Avramides: With the permission of the Principal, Fellows and Scholars of Hertford; **pp.235, 242, 244, 269, 330 (Anth 2.3), 333 (Anth 2.10 & 2.12) & 335 (Anth 2.17)** Gilbert Ryle: With the permission of ROUTLEDGE; **pp.263, 264, 267, 268, 270 & 334 (Anth 2.16)** Carl Gustav Hempel Papers, 1903–1997, ASP.1999.01, Archives of Scientific Philosophy, Archives & Special Collections, University of Pittsburgh Library System; **pp.277, 301, 335 (Anth 2.18), 336 (Anth 2.22) & 337 (Anth 2.24)** Reproduced with permission of Ruth Anna Putnam, wife of Hilary Putnam; **pp.282, 302 & 338 (Anth 2.25)** Ned Block (1978), 'Troubles with Functionalism', in C.W. Savage (ed.), *Perception and Cognition*, University of Minnesota Press, pp.261–325 (at pp.265, 293): Reproduced with permission of University of Minnesota Press; **pp.285, 288, 291, 293, 294 & 332 (Anth 2.8)** Paul M. Churchland, 'Eliminative Materialism and Propositional Attitudes', LXXVIII, 2 (February 1981): pp.67–90 (at pp.67, 70, 72–3, 74, 89–90): Reproduced with permission of Journal of Philosophy; **p.321 (Anth 1.2)** Eleonore Stump and Norman Kretzmann, 'Eternity', LXXVIII, No. 8 (August 1981: 439–440): Reproduced with permission of Journal of Philosophy.

Photo credit: p.86 Rosenwald Collection, Rare Book and Special Collections Division, Library of Congress, Rosenwald 1806.

Every effort has been made to trace all copyright holders, but if any have been inadvertently overlooked, the Publishers will be pleased to make the necessary arrangements at the first opportunity.

Although every effort has been made to ensure that website addresses are correct at time of going to press, Hodder Education cannot be held responsible for the content of any website mentioned in this book. It is sometimes possible to find a relocated web page by typing in the address of the home page for a website in the URL window of your browser.

Hachette UK's policy is to use papers that are natural, renewable and recyclable products and made from wood grown in well-managed forests and other controlled sources. The logging and manufacturing processes are expected to conform to the environmental regulations of the country of origin.

Orders: please contact Hachette UK Distribution, Hely Hutchinson Centre, Milton Road, Didcot, Oxfordshire, OX11 7HH. Telephone: +44 (0)1235 827827. Email education@hachette.co.uk. Lines are open from 9 a.m. to 5 p.m., Monday to Friday. You can also order through our website: www.hoddereducation.com

ISBN: 978 1 5104 0026 9

© Daniel Cardinal, Gerald Jones, Jeremy Hayward 2018

First published in 2018 by

Hodder Education,

An Hachette UK Company

Carmelite House

50 Victoria Embankment

London EC4Y 0DZ

www.hoddereducation.co.uk

Impression number   10 9 8 7 6 5

Year   2022 2021

All rights reserved. Apart from any use permitted under UK copyright law, no part of this publication may be reproduced or transmitted in any form or by any means, electronic or mechanical, including photocopying and recording, or held within any information storage and retrieval system, without permission in writing from the publisher or under licence from the Copyright Licensing Agency Limited. Further details of such licences (for reprographic reproduction) may be obtained from the Copyright Licensing Agency Limited, www.cla.co.uk

Cover image by Barking Dog Art

Illustrations by Tony Randell, Barking Dog Art, Richard Duszczak and Peter Lubach

Typeset in Chaparral Pro Light 11/13pt by Aptara, Inc.

Printed and bound by CPI Group (UK) Ltd, Croydon, CR0 4YY

A catalogue record for this title is available from the British Library.

Contents

Key to features — iv
Introduction — v

Section 1 The metaphysics of God — 1
  1.1 The concept and nature of God — 2
    1.1.1 God's attributes — 6
    1.1.2 Arguments for the incoherence of the concept of God — 17
  1.2 Arguments relating to the existence of God — 30
    1.2.1 Ontological arguments — 38
    1.2.2 Teleological/design arguments — 57
    1.2.3 Cosmological arguments — 91
    1.2.4 The problem of evil — 129
  1.3 Religious language — 152
    1.3.1 The distinction between cognitivism and non-cognitivism about religious language — 156
    1.3.2 The empiricist/logical positivist challenges to the status of metaphysical language — 160
    1.3.3 John Hick's response to Ayer (eschatological verification) — 165
    1.3.4 The *University* debate: Flew, Hare and Mitchell — 168

Section 2 The metaphysics of mind — 185
  2.1 What do we mean by 'mind'? — 185
    2.1.1 Features of mental states — 186
  2.2 Dualist theories — 192
    2.2.1 Substance dualism — 193
    2.2.2 Property dualism — 212
    2.2.3 The issues facing dualism — 231
  2.3 Physicalist theories — 262
    2.3.1 Philosophical behaviourism — 262
    2.3.2 The mind–brain type identity theory — 273
    2.3.3 Eliminative materialism — 285
    2.3.4 Functionalism — 294

Section 3 How to prepare for the exam — 308
Section 4 Anthology extracts — 320
Glossary — 339
Notes — 349
Index — 357

Key to features

▶ ACTIVITY

Activity
A practical task to help you to understand the arguments or concepts under investigation.

Experimenting with ideas
Plays around with some of the concepts discussed; looks at them from different angles.

Quotation
A direct quotation from a key thinker.

Learn More

Learn more
Introduces related ideas or arguments that aren't required by the AS-level specification, but which provides useful additional material.

Anthology extracts
When you see the Anthology icon in the margin of the book then you should refer to the relevant extract in the Anthology extracts section at the end of the book.

Glossary
Words or phrases that appear in CAPITAL LETTERS are key terms and ideas that are explained in the Glossary at the end of the book.

Introduction

Metaphysics: Introduction

What's it all about: life, the universe and everything? Attempting to answer this (quite vague) question is many people's idea of how philosophers fill their typical day. In the novel *The Hitchhiker's Guide to the Galaxy* intelligent pan-dimensional beings build a super computer, Deep Thought, to answer that very question. This causes the philosophers on the planet to go on strike, claiming that the new computer will mean an end to their jobs. (The computer famously concludes that the answer is 42, but that another computer needs to be built to determine exactly what the question is.)

This book is concerned with METAPHYSICS. And although other areas of philosophy (such as ethics) touch on the meaning and purpose of life, it is metaphysics that attempts to give an account of the ultimate nature of reality – of what is really going on.

Metaphysics and change

Metaphysics often involves exploring concepts that we usually take for granted. Consider the everyday concept of change. In metaphysics we might ask 'is change possible?' This might seem an odd question: the evidence in front of your very eyes, as you turn these pages, hoping to find something more interesting or at least a diagram to distract you from all these words, suggests that change is obviously possible. But beneath the surface, the concept of change is not so straightforward. How is it possible for an object to change and yet still be the same object? Consider yourself. Are you the same person as you were yesterday? Are you different? If you are different, then are you a new person or still the same person?

Difficulties with the concept of change were among the earliest recorded philosophical thoughts. The pre-Socratic philosophers (any philosophically minded writer who lived before Socrates) articulated their ideas through a kind of philosophical poetry, as poetry was the main form of writing at the time, and the concept of change was one of their main concerns. The Greek philosopher Parmenides and his star pupil Zeno argued that change was actually impossible and that the real universe is unchanging. It is *quiescent*. Unfortunately no direct words of Zeno survive, but we know of him through the dialogues of Plato and, in particular, Aristotle's book entitled *Physics* which sets out some of Zeno's (now famous) paradoxes, including one you might have come across about Achilles and the tortoise.

Imagine that the speedy Achilles is in a race with a tortoise. The tortoise, being slow, is given a head start. After a minute, a whistle blows and Achilles sets off. At that very moment, the tortoise is somewhere up ahead on the path, let's say 100 metres away at point X (Figure 0.1).

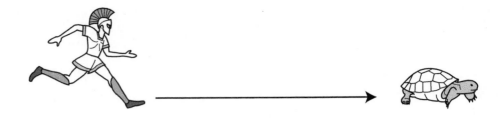

Achilles now   Distance between them = 100 m   Tortoise now at point X

Figure 0.1 Achilles and the tortoise. When Achilles sets off, the tortoise is at point X

It seems an obvious truth that in order to catch the tortoise, Achilles must first reach the point at which the tortoise currently is (point X). However, the tortoise is constantly moving and by the time Achilles arrives at point X our hard-shelled friend will be at a new point – X1, which is now 10 metres in front. Of course, the two competitors are now much closer, so let's magnify the gap between them (Figure 0.2).

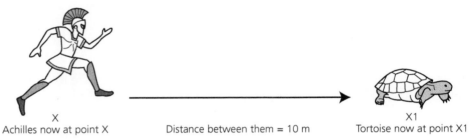

X   X1
Achilles now at point X   Distance between them = 10 m   Tortoise now at point X1

Figure 0.2 Achilles and the tortoise (gap magnified). When Achilles reaches point X, the tortoise is at point X1

Hey presto! After magnification it seems that we are pretty much back where we started. This time, Achilles will need to get to X1 before he can catch the tortoise, but of course, when he arrives the tortoise will have moved forward (to X2). Again, we can magnify this difference and we are back in the same predicament (Figure 0.3).

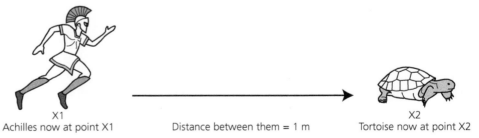

X1   X2
Achilles now at point X1   Distance between them = 1 m   Tortoise now at point X2

Figure 0.3 Achilles and the tortoise (gap further magnified). When Achilles reaches point X1, the tortoise is at point X2

It seems that we can repeat this process infinitely. Achilles constantly has to get to the point where the tortoise has just been, covering smaller and smaller distances but never catching up with the tortoise.

> *In a race, the quickest runner can never overtake the slowest, since the pursuer must first reach the point whence the pursued started, so that the slower must always hold a lead.*
>
> **Zeno recounted by *Aristotle in Physics* VI:9**

▶ **ACTIVITY**

Zeno's paradox arises because his mathematical description of the world undermines our perception of the world, and that there doesn't seem to be a flaw in either the maths or in our perception.

a) Zeno resolves this paradox by arguing that the world as we see it, a world of motion and change, is not what the world is really like, and that the world as described mathematically in the example above is a truer representation. Do you agree? (In other words, does maths give a truer representation of the world than our senses do?)
b) Whether or not you agree, how would you go about solving the paradox?

On the basis of this and several other interesting paradoxes, Zeno concluded that all motion and change is impossible. The appearance of change we see around us is just an illusion. Zeno used reason to take a position on the ultimate nature of reality – a reality beyond the senses. In doing this, Zeno was engaging in metaphysics in its deepest sense. It is worth noting how powerful Zeno's paradoxes were, puzzling philosophers, scientists and mathematicians for two thousand years before they were eventually 'solved' in the early eighteenth century with the invention of differential calculus – a mathematical theorem developed in different ways by both Isaac Newton and also independently by the philosopher Leibniz.

What is metaphysics?

As we outlined in our *Philosophy for A-level Year 1 and AS* textbook (ISBN 9781510400252), metaphysics is one of three broad branches of philosophy, although you have probably already discovered that there is considerable overlap between the three (Figure 0.4).

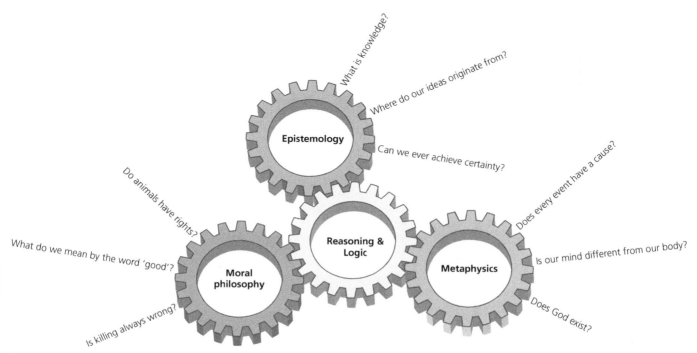

Figure 0.4 The different branches of philosophy

The Philosophy A-level provides an induction into all three branches as well as the methodology of logic and critical thinking. The first year of the A-level explores aspects of epistemology and ethics, whereas the second year examines two issues which come under the loose heading of 'metaphysics': the philosophy of mind and the philosophy of religion. We say that metaphysics is a 'loose' heading because both the meaning of the word and the content it covers are disputed. So far we have described metaphysics as being concerned with ultimate questions about reality/the world, however the origin of the word is something of a riddle.

The word 'metaphysics' originates in the works of Aristotle, although he himself never used the term. One explanation for the etymology of 'metaphysics' is that it was initially the title given to an assortment of essays and tracts by Aristotle, which had no collective name and which the librarian/grammarian Andronicus of Rhodes wanted to compile, in about 70 BCE. So the story goes that Andronicus created the term 'metaphysics' for this collection of works because in his library this collection came after Aristotle's book called *Physics* (which we quoted from above). Hence Andronicus's creation of the portmanteau term 'meta-physics' which broadly speaking means 'after physics'. Others think that the name originates from the subject matter of these assorted essays, in which Aristotle explore such issues as first causes, existence and the nature of mathematical objects – all topics that somehow transcend a discussion of the specific aspects of the physical/natural world: hence 'meta', which can also mean going beyond or transcending, becomes conjoined with 'physics'. Although we do not know the exact origin of the term, we do know that the term stuck to this collection of works by Aristotle, and eventually it came to refer to the philosophical theories and concepts conceived by all sorts of thinkers that went beyond, or transcended, the physical world. Taking Aristotle as their starting point, these metaphysical studies and ideas explore the world as it really is, the world beyond the senses, the fundamental stuff that exists in the world, and how that fundamental stuff operates (see Figure 0.5).

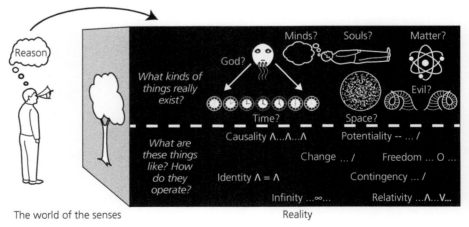

Figure 0.5 In metaphysics philosophers attempt to understand and describe the world beyond the world of the senses – the world as it really is: what kind of things exist, what are they like, how do they behave and operate? Some rationalist philosophers argue that only the use of reason (in contrast to the senses) will enable us to go beyond our senses to answer these questions

Aside from the origin of the word, a bigger philosophical dispute rages as to whether the whole endeavour of metaphysics is even possible. Back in the day, most big questions about reality and existence were matters of philosophical speculation. Where did humans come from? What are stars? Do humans have a soul? Why is there something (a universe) rather than nothing? What holds the moon up? Over time, scientific inventions and discoveries have meant that some of these questions can be given fairly convincing answers. The rest still linger beyond the reach of science and exist as areas that only speculative reason can attempt to answer. For some, the fact that many metaphysical questions continue to elude science/the senses casts a doubt as to whether reason alone is properly equipped to answer them in the first place. Or even whether the questions (and attempted answers) are properly meaningful.

The philosopher David Hume argued these two exact points (you may have covered this in the epistemology unit of the A-level). From an EMPIRICIST perspective, he claimed that reason alone cannot tell us anything new about the world. Further, he argued that words must gain their meaning from our impressions, our sense data of the world. This approach suggests that it is hard, if not impossible, to meaningfully discuss any true nature of reality that might exist beyond our experience of it – there is a 'veil of perception' that we cannot see beyond. But Hume is not alone in his rejection of metaphysics. His sceptical concerns were added to by the philosopher Immanuel Kant in his masterpiece *Critique of Pure Reason*, and in the twentieth century an influential movement called logical positivism dismissed metaphysics as unverifiable and meaningless speculation (see pages 160–5). So, in the last few centuries the very possibility of metaphysics has come under attack (see Figure 0.6).

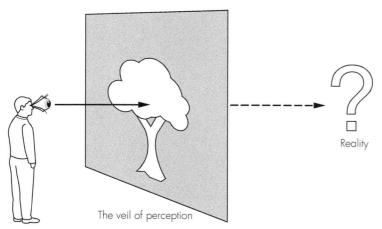

Figure 0.6 Empiricists have argued that, because everything we know is based on sense data, we cannot 'see beyond' the veil of perception – we cannot grasp reality as it might actually be

An alternative way of conceiving the task is to see metaphysics *not* as a way of uncovering the nature of reality, but as an attempt to clear out unhelpful ideas and put our conceptual 'house' in order. This, in turn, may enable science to cross the threshold and unlock the secrets of the universe. This is akin to how John Locke conceived of the role of philosophy – as a kind of preparation for the scientists (in his case, his good friend Isaac Newton):

 it is ambition enough to be employed as an under-labourer in clearing the ground a little, and removing some of the rubbish that lies in the way to knowledge.[1]

This approach was echoed in the last century by Peter Strawson who argued for a 'descriptive' metaphysics, which uses reason and thought experiment to discover, describe and analyse not the world but the deep conceptual schemes that all humans possess. This idea of metaphysics as exploration, not of the world, but of our conceptual understanding of it, is a theme that recurs in several sections of this book. For example, when I conceive of the universe, it seemingly must have a start or first cause. The idea of the universe always existing doesn't appear to make sense to me. But does this thought reveal something about my conceptual framework, or about the nature of reality?

Metaphysics and change revisited

To unpack this discussion of reality versus concepts, let us return to the pre-Socratic philosophers and their obsession with change. In contrast to Parmenides and Zeno, Heraclitus thought that change is ever present – to the extent that the universe is in a constant state of flux. As he famously said:

> *you cannot step twice into the same stream*[2]

The reason Heraclitus claims such a step is impossible, is not just that the water in the stream is constantly changing, but also because the person stepping is constantly changing too. So it is *not* the same person who steps into *not* the same stream.

However, this view raises its own problems. If everything is constantly changing then what, if anything, does it mean to be an object that endures over time? If a boat has its planks changed one at a time, then at what point is it no longer the original boat? Also imagine that the slightly worn planks were stored and eventually turned into an identical boat. Which of the two boats is the original one?

As Heraclitus suggests you, too, constantly change. Your hair grows, new memories are created, you learn new ideas in excellent philosophy books, and so on. You are not exactly the same as yesterday (or even a minute ago). But if *you* are not the same, then who or what is the *you* that is changing? These considerations raise fundamental questions about what we call 'objects'. If the world, as Heraclitus suggests, is really a bumbling mass of energy then what does it mean to be an ever-changing object within this constant flux?

Once again we are engaging in metaphysics. But what kind of metaphysics is this? When we consider the nature of 'object' in general, are we making assertions/claims about the world (which we might term *speculative* metaphysics) or are we trying to establish how our conceptual framework works (which Strawson describes as *descriptive* metaphysics)?

To recap, so far we have seen that metaphysics involves an exploration into the ultimate nature of reality, although the exact character, and even the existence of the subject is disputed. The remainder of this section serves as a very brief introduction to the two areas of metaphysics that are closely examined in the book, and which form the content of Year 2 of the philosophy A-level.

Metaphysics of God

Most people in the world believe in a God (or gods) and most people who don't believe in God, will, at some point in their lives, have pondered whether there is a creator or architect behind the existence of the universe. Engaging in metaphysical speculation about the existence and nature of God is almost part of the human condition!

In the section on the metaphysics of God, we will explore the thoughts, ideas and arguments of some of the greatest philosophers who, like most of us, have looked to the heavens and attempted to find answers. You have already encountered metaphysical positions that refer to God when studying epistemology in your first year. For example, you may remember that Bishop Berkeley believed that the only fundamental 'stuff' (it's a great metaphysical term, 'stuff'!) that existed in the universe were ideas – he was a metaphysical idealist – and that ultimately all ideas depended themselves on the existence of God. You may also remember that Descartes' search for some fundamental certainty in his life also depends on the metaphysical position that God exists, and he provides two *A PRIORI* arguments for God's existence. We explore one of these proofs, his ontological argument, later on (page 45).

The philosophical speculation explored in this book is not restricted to any specific religion or religious belief. General religious beliefs are explored as a way to further understand the ultimate nature of reality. Does the universe have a beginning? Is it designed? Can anything exist necessarily? If God does exist then is his existence eternal, beyond space and time, or everlasting, within space and time? Does evil exist, and if so can it be used to disprove the existence of God? We examine these metaphysical questions before, at the end of the section, we look at A.J. Ayer and those philosophers who reject the whole project of metaphysics as completely meaningless.

So some of the key metaphysical concepts that you will encounter when studying the metaphysics of God are as follows:

Key metaphysical concept	Subsection in which it is discussed	Page number
The existence of God	Throughout Section 1 The metaphysics of God	1–151
The existence of evil	The problem of evil	129–51
Actuality/potentiality	Cosmological arguments: Aquinas' first way (argument from motion)	98–9
Being and existence	Ontological arguments: Norman Malcolm's ontological argument Cosmological arguments: the impossibility of a necessary being	52–5, 124–6
Causation	Design arguments: Hume on causation and constant conjunction Cosmological arguments: Hume's objection to the causal principle	79–82, 120–2
Causes: formal / material / final and efficient	Cosmological arguments: Aquinas' second way (argument from causation)	101–3
Change	The concept and nature of God: God as omniscient Cosmological arguments: the contribution for Plato and Aristotle Cosmological arguments: Aquinas' first way	6–7, 94, 98–101
Contingency and necessity	Ontological arguments: Norman Malcolm's ontological argument Cosmological arguments: Aquinas' third way (argument from contingency)	53–5, 105–8, 112–16
Free will	The concept and nature of God: the compatibility of God's omniscience and free human beings Problem of evil: Free Will defence: St Augustine and Alvin Plantinga	25–7, 140–1
Infinite regress	Cosmological arguments: the possibility of an infinite series	117–19
Personal identity	Religious language: John Hick's response to Ayer (eschatological verification)	166–7
Philosophers of language who aim to debunk metaphysics	Religious language: The verification principle and the metaphysics of God	160–5
Possible worlds and modal metaphysics	Ontological argument: Norman Malcolm's ontological argument The problem of evil: criticism – there are better possible worlds than this one	52–56, 143
Relativity	The concept and nature of God: God as eternal or everlasting	15–17
Space and time	The concept and nature of God: God as eternal or everlasting	10–13
Sufficient reason	Cosmological arguments: Leibniz's argument form the Principle of Sufficient Reason (an argument from contingency)	112–16

Metaphysics of mind

If wondering about the existence of God seems fundamental to the human condition, then so does pondering our souls: whether we have one, if we do have one what happens to it after we die, and how is it that we can be both bodies (who get injured, who fall, who stop working if our brains are removed) and minds (which perceive the beauty and pains of the world). One of the questions we would ask as we examine different cultures past and present is: how much 'mind' is there in the universe? Many societies believe and have believed that minds and spirits were everywhere: in the rivers, trees, wind and even the movements of the stars and planets, that lightning and floods were evidence of the wrath of the gods. Mind-like 'intentions' were often used to explain how the natural world worked, and whole pantheons of gods (the Greeks, the Romans, the Vikings) were used to explain the existence of natural phenomena.

The rise of science slowly displaced the need for 'minds' in our explanation of the universe. It seems we can predict many events (such as storms and eclipses), just by considering matter and fundamental forces. There is no need to use intentions (such as anger, reward or revenge) in our understanding of the natural world. However, the matter is not straightforward when it comes to human beings.

Will we one day be able to explain the behaviour of humans just by reference to matter (brain cells) and laws of biology/chemistry? Most people believe they have a mind which has thoughts, awareness, hopes for the future and intentions. Superficially it would seem that a complete explanation of any human action (for example, someone putting the kettle on) must involve intentions (for example, a desire for a cuppa). An explanation that did not include the intention (desire for a nice cuppa) would be missing something important. But this does not easily fit with the general direction of science. Atoms and cells do not have intentions. They blindly 'follow' laws of nature. So how do we fit 'intentions' into our scientific understanding of the universe? How are we to explain the fact that seemingly inert matter can arrange itself into conscious life forms? Indeed, the very existence of states of awareness is known in philosophy as 'the hard problem' of consciousness.

Just as with the discussion of God above, we can see that the metaphysics of mind soon descends into a discussion of the ultimate nature of reality. Are there two kinds of things in the world – matter and mind? Or just one thing – matter? Or just one thing – mind (as Berkeley thought)? If you believe there is just mind, then how is consciousness possible?

Experimenting with ideas

Think of a green elephant. Now imagine that at that precise moment I froze your brain and proceeded to carve it into very thin slices (sorry about that!). Would I find anything green or anything elephant-like in your brain? Probably not. However, it would seem that you were genuinely thinking about, or picturing, a green elephant in your mind. The question is *where was that thought of a green elephant?*

A   Nowhere. There is no such thing as 'the thought of a green elephant'.
B   It was in my mind. It occupied mind space which is different from physical space.
C   It occurred in my soul, which again is not part of physical space.
D   The thought of the green elephant occurred in my brain, but only looks green and elephanty to the thinker (me). We cannot observe the consciousness of others.

E The language we use to talk about this is all wrong.
F In the future we will be able to locate the thought in terms of the arrangements of neurons. Our understanding of the brain will change so much that we may no longer even talk about 'having thoughts', but may start to talk about having specific brain activity instead.
G None of the above.

We can see that many of these answers have metaphysical importance. If it is the case that there is something akin to mind space that is different from physical space then this has big implications for the ultimate nature of reality. Even if you believe there are just brains but thoughts are only accessible to the thinker – then how is this possible? What sort of thing is consciousness if it is only accessible from one perspective?

There are many areas in the philosophy of mind. Do you have free will, or are you just a complex machine made of atoms each following the laws of nature? Can computers ever think? Are you the same person over time? However, the syllabus focuses solely on this key question of accounting for the human mind. Is there a mind? And what is it?

In addition to consciousness, some of the key metaphysical ideas that you study within the philosophy of mind include:

Key metaphysical concept	Subsection in which it is discussed	Page number
What is 'mind'?	What is the mind?	pp. 185–91
The ultimate nature of the reality	Dualism and physicalism	pp. 192–307
The mind is a kind of substance	Dualism Brain–mind identity theory	pp. 192–261, 273–85
The mind is not a substance	Property dualism, philosophical behaviourism, eliminative materialism, functionalism	pp. 212–13, 262–73, 285–306
The mind as irreducible to matter	Substance and property dualism, behaviourism, eliminativism	pp. 192–281, 262–73, 285–94
The mind as ontologically reducible to matter	Brain–mind identity theory	pp. 273–85
The problem of interaction and nature of the relationship between mind and body	Substance dualism, property dualism, identity theory, functionalism, epiphenomenalism, philosophical behaviourism	pp. 192–231, 246–60, 262–73, 273–85, 294–306
Knowledge of other minds	The problem of other minds, behaviourism, philosophical zombies	pp. 231–45, 213–19, 262–73

A timeline of key figures

In the Year 1 textbook we argued that it is important that as a philosopher you have a broad understanding of history, so that you can understand how ideas and arguments have developed over time, but also so that you can see how ideas and arguments emerge from a particular time or epoch.

In the timeline below (Figure 0.7) we have again divided up western, European thinking into three broad periods: the ancient or classical age, the Middle Ages, and the modern age (which includes a healthy chunk of 'contemporary' philosophers who have been writing in the last fifty years or so). If you compare the two timelines you will see that during the Middle Ages all the philosophers that you study fall into the 'Metaphysics of God' section of the A-level. But this is an exaggeration: it isn't the case that medieval philosophers only contributed to the philosophy of religion; they also contributed to philosophical method

(Okham's razor), to the philosophy of language (the debate about nominalism and universals), to logic (refining and developing Aristotelian logic), and to ethics (Aquinas on Natural Law and virtue ethics). However, in general, the Middle Ages in Europe were a period in which thinkers learnt to read and write, to debate and define, and to interpret the world through the lens of religious thought, so the primary contribution of medieval philosophers has been to theology and the philosophy of religion. The philosophy of mind, on the other hand, exploded as a topic of philosophical analysis in the twentieth century, partly due to the breakthroughs in science, psychology and psychoanalysis, and we weren't able to squeeze into this timeline all the contemporary philosophers that you'll be studying.

Finally, as with the Year 1 timeline, you will notice that in this year 2 timeline there are some giants among the philosophical canon, who straddle both the metaphysics of mind and metaphysics of God. Those highlighted below are Descartes and, once again, Hume, but other philosophers have made equally valuable contributions to both these topics, including Kant, Wittgenstein and A.J. Ayer (those last two we couldn't fit into the diagram!).

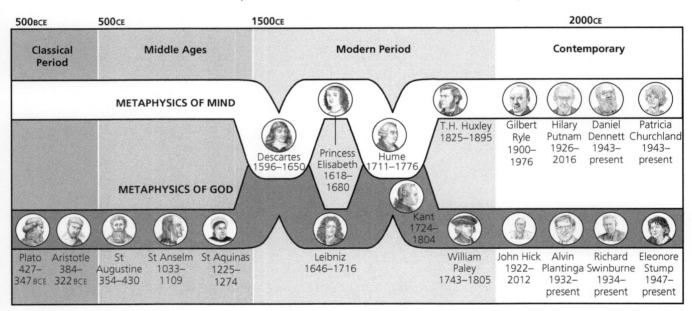

Figure 0.7 Key figures in the history of philosophy you will be studying in the metaphysics of mind and the metaphysics of God

It would be helpful if you could draw your own timeline, with the three periods identified, and add philosophers as you encounter them in your journey through metaphysics.

Section 1 The metaphysics of God

If the stars should appear one night in a thousand years, how would men believe and adore; and preserve for many generations the remembrance of the city of God which had been shown! But every night come out these envoys of beauty, and light the universe with their admonishing smile.[1]

Ralph Waldo Emerson

The observation made by American essayist and thinker Ralph Emerson no longer holds: these days the stars don't come out every night. Light pollution across the developed world (which is where you're likely to be if you're studying A-level Philosophy) prevents us from seeing the stars as our ancestors would have seen them, as an infinite canopy of light and wonder, in which the gods resided. If you are lucky, if on your bucket list is that journey to a remote island in the Pacific Ocean, then once in your life you might see the night sky unveiled, unadorned, unblinking. And it is hard, when looking upwards (or downwards if you're in New Zealand), to avoid having certain thoughts about our own insignificance in relation to the billions of galaxies (each containing billions of stars) of the observable universe. What does this all mean? Why are we here? Where do we come from? What brought all this about? There is a dizzying, existential abyss of meaningless that you are teetering on the edge of when you look at the stars – but this vertiginous abyss of meaninglessness is avoided if, when looking at the infinite universe or thinking about those questions, you see not an abyss but instead a divinity up there in the night sky. And our ancestors did: the Roman gods of Mars, Jupiter and Venus; the Greek constellations of Hercules, and of Zeus (in his form as Taurus, the bull); the Egyptian Sun god Ra; the Moon goddess in religions across the world.

The gods, or God, help answer those questions, rarely asked, but lurking, smothered beneath the routines, habits, pleasures, pains and projects of our everyday life. And these questions are fundamental questions about our universe, about existence, about first causes – metaphysical questions. Believing in God can provide an answer to these questions (God created the universe, God gave us a purpose which we may or may not know, God is the source of all existence and the first cause and creator of the universe).

What particularly excites philosophers is interrogating the beliefs that people have about the world, and it is no surprise that philosophers have had much to say about the belief in God over the last two thousand years. A vast body of philosophical work has built up in western philosophy around the religious traditions of Europe and the Middle East. This philosophy of religion has dealt with questions such as:

- Who is God?
- Can his existence be proved?
- How can God let innocent people suffer so much pain?
- When we talk about God, what meanings do our words have?

In this section on the metaphysics of God we cover three of the most important clusters of issues that theologians and philosophers have debated over the last two millennia.

- The concept and nature of God: Here we look at what philosophers have had to say about the nature of God, the attributes ascribed to God, and whether the concept of God emerging from these attributes is an incoherent concept.
- Arguments relating to the existence of God: Here we look at three of the main attempts by philosophers to prove the existence of God, looking at how philosophical arguments are constructed and the different ways in which it is possible to prove that something exists. We then examine the problem of evil, and how religious philosophers have attempted to reconcile the pain and suffering in the world with the existence of God.
- Religious language: Finally, we examine the meaning of religious language, the ways in which philosophers think we use, understand and make religious statements, and whether metaphysical language (in this case religious language) is even meaningful.

1.1 The concept and nature of God

Any examination into the METAPHYSICS of God must be able to delineate the central concept of that investigation:

- Who or what is God?
- How can God be understood or defined?
- Is the idea of 'God' a coherent one?

The concept under scrutiny in this case is unlike any of those other concepts you have already explored: knowledge, happiness, morality, reason. Examining the concept of God is different in two very important ways: the first is that it is more important to many people than any other philosophical concept. Very little blood has been spilt, very few emotions raised, very few societies oppressed or mobilised for war, because of a strong belief in Kantian (as opposed to utilitarian) ethics or in the empiricist (as opposed to the RATIONALIST) foundations of knowledge.[2] But disagreements about the concept of God have cast a long, bloody shadow over the history of our species.

The second difference is that at a closer glance the concept of God can appear vague, contradictory and without any common core. This is true both for those dispassionately analysing the concept of God (generally philosophers, theologians and slightly drunk first-year undergraduates eager to impress people through their knowledge of the paradox of the stone ... – N.B. don't bother, impressing people in this way doesn't work ... trust us), as well as for those deeply committed to their faith: from Christians who believe in a personal creator to Hindus who believe in multiple gods; from deists who believe in an impersonal first cause to pantheists who believe that all and only the universe is divine. Indeed, thinking about the nature of God ties people up in intellectual knots, and leads to strange, confusing statements – as the quotations below from Blaise Pascal (1623–62) and the Bible illustrate:

It is incomprehensible that God should exist and incomprehensible that God should not exist.[3]
Pascal

God said to Moses: I am what I am.
Exodus 3:13

▶ **ACTIVITY**

1 Write down as many words that you can think of associated with the idea of 'God'.
2 Combine your words with those of your fellow students.
3 Now consider the source of these words or characteristics:
   a) Which you think come from a religious text (for example, the Bible)?
   b) Which come directly from people's experience?
   c) Which come from reason and from the analysis of the concept of God?

Two approaches to investigating the concept and nature of God: revealed theology and natural theology

A promising place to start an investigation into the nature of God is the sacred texts on which religions are based, such as the Torah, the Bible or the Qur'an. These books record the foundations of the religion through the REVELATIONS of certain individuals who it is claimed have had some direct or indirect contact with God, and thus may be best positioned to reveal something of God's nature. This approach to understanding God is called REVEALED THEOLOGY because it trusts sacred texts to reveal religious truths and an understanding of God.

God of Abraham, God of Isaac, God of Jacob, not the God of the philosophers and scholars.
Pascal

In a note found after his death, the seventeenth-century mathematician and philosopher Blaise Pascal distinguishes between 'the God of the philosophers' and the 'God of Abraham, Isaac and Jacob' as revealed in the Bible (Exodus 3:6). The implication of Pascal's words is that if we seek to know and experience God then we should turn to the Bible, and not to those religious philosophers who go far beyond the revelations of the Bible in their quest to understand God. The God of the Bible is a God whose character develops as different facets of God's nature are emphasised at different points in the Bible.[4] Despite this difference in emphasis, there are some attributes that remain fundamental throughout:

- God is *holy* – the object of worship, and worthy of worship, numinous. (Leviticus 11:44, Isaiah 5:16)
- God is the *only* god – this is in stark contrast to the polytheistic religions that existed throughout the world during the time of the Bible's writing. (Isaiah 45:5)
- God is the *creator*. (Genesis 1:1)
- God *intervenes* in his creation. (Joshua 10:13)
- God is a *personal* god – God is loving, just, righteous, vengeful, protective, merciful, gracious, compassionate and so on. (Genesis 1:27, Exodus 15:3, Psalms 103:8, 1 John 4:16ff)

The nature of God as described above will be familiar to many believers, but these features of God have not usually been emphasised in the writings of philosophers. Instead, philosophers have chosen to focus on certain technical attributes of God, which are perhaps a consequence of the God of Abraham being a perfect, holy and unique creator. It is the analysis of these technical attributes that make up the 'God of the philosophers'. Throughout this section, as we analyse the concept of God and look at proofs of God's existence, believers in God might be struck by how different the 'God of the philosophers' is from the God experienced in churches and mosques, in synagogues and temples. One question that might occur to believers while studying the metaphysics of God is: 'Is the God of the philosophers the God I actually worship?'[5] Let us turn now to the God of the philosophers.

Revealed theology is one place in which we can begin to understand God, but an alternative starting point for a *philosophical* investigation into the nature of God would be to look around us at the universe he is said to have created. By analysing the various features of this universe (the types of things that exist, the laws that govern it, human behaviour, and so on) we might hope to establish what God must be like. This second approach is called NATURAL THEOLOGY, because it stresses the possibility of understanding God via human reason and observation alone. The believers who have pursued this rigorous, analytic investigation into the concept of God have done so to understand better the foundations of their belief and the concept at the heart of their belief.

… one God, who is the author of this whole universe … immaterial … incorruptible … who is, in fact, our source, our light, our good.[6]
St Augustine

God is that, than which nothing greater can be conceived.[7]
St Anselm

By the word 'God' I mean a substance that is infinite, independent, supremely intelligent, supremely powerful, and the Creator of myself and anything else that may exist.[8]
René Descartes

A person without a body, present everywhere, the creator and sustainer of the universe, able to do everything, knowing all things, perfectly good … immutable, eternal, a necessary being, and worthy of worship.[9]
Richard Swinburne

Pascal, taking the approach of revealed theology, thought that God was infinitely beyond our comprehension, and he wondered who would dare to think they could know what he was or whether he existed.[10] Despite this, philosophers down the centuries *have* dared to imagine they could tell us something specific about the nature of God, and they have made these claims on the basis of reason and natural theology. The quotations above, which span over a thousand years of religious philosophy, are representative of this theistic philosophical tradition. What these quotations emphasise is God's greatness and perfection. For these philosophers, God is the most perfect and greatest of beings and hence he is supremely good, knowing and powerful; he cannot change and is eternal. At the same time he is the source of all other beings: the creator of the universe.

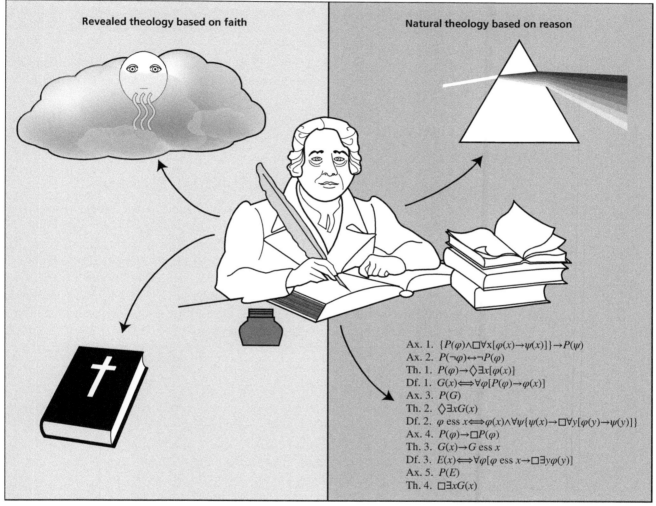

Figure 1.1 The difference between revealed and natural theology. The foundations of revealed theology lie in faith (e.g. accepting the truth of religious beliefs based on spiritual experiences and holy texts); the foundations of the natural theology lie in reason (e.g. demonstrating the truth of religious beliefs based on experience, observation and argument).

There is a tension between the differing approaches of revealed and natural theology: as potential philosophers we are naturally drawn to reason, but as potential believers we cannot put aside faith. The goal of many religious philosophers down the ages has been to resolve the tension between these two.

1.1.1 God's attributes

Here we examine in more detail some of the characteristics that philosophers have ascribed to God, and some of the issues that arise from claiming that God has these characteristics. These concepts have taken on a technical philosophical meaning that has become part of the language of the philosophy of religion – but we should remember that these concepts have their origin both in the work of pre-Christian philosophers such as Plato and Aristotle, as well as in the Bible. Because the writings of philosophers of religion, working in a Christian tradition, can sometimes seem very far removed from the original 'revealed' texts, we have tried to locate the origin of these concepts in specific quotations from the Bible. The specific attributes of God that we examine here are as follows (although we do occasionally refer to other attributes of God, where relevant):

- God as OMNISCIENT
- God as OMNIPOTENT
- God as supremely good (OMNIBENEVOLENT)
- God as either eternal or everlasting

God as omniscient: his infinite knowledge

By the nature of their profession, philosophers place a high value on knowledge, and we shouldn't be surprised to find that religious philosophers consider perfect knowledge to be an aspect of God's perfection. God's omniscience (from the Latin *omni*, 'all', and *scientia*, 'knowing') is illustrated in the Bible by examples, rather than stated explicitly. Psalm 139:4 tells us that 'even before a word is on my tongue, O Lord, thou knowest it altogether' and Hebrews 4:13 says 'nothing in all creation is hidden from God's sight. Everything is uncovered and laid bare before the eyes of him.' However, in some parts of the Bible God's knowledge does not seem to extend so far: 'But the Lord God called to the Man [Adam] and said to him "Where are you?"' (Genesis 3:9).

Philosophers are interested in how far God's omniscience extends. Is God's knowledge only propositional, meaning it involves 'knowing that ...' something is true, such as knowing that the world will come to an end in the year 2999, or that Adam has eaten a forbidden fruit? Does it involve having practical knowledge of how to do things, such as how to ride a bike or create human beings out of clay? If God is INCORPOREAL (that is, he lacks a body) or transcendent (that is, existing outside the universe), then it does not make sense to say that God knows how to engage in physical activity, although a theologian might wish to say that God knows the full set of truths about the activity.[11] Other questions we might wish to ask are 'Can God know what it is logically impossible to know, for example the area of a round square?' and 'Does God know what I'm freely about to do?' We examine the problem of free will and omniscience on pages 25–7.

A more recent philosophical problem with omniscience was identified by Norman Kretzmann (1928–98). He argued in his paper 'Omniscience and Immutability' that there is a contradiction inherent in the claim that a perfect being can be both all-knowing and unchanging (or IMMUTABLE, see page 10). Broadly stated, his argument is this:

1. God isn't subject to change.
2. God knows everything.
3. A being that knows everything, also knows everything in time (that is, in this, our changing world).
4. A being that knows things in time is subject to change.
5. Therefore God is subject to change – which contradicts premise 1 above.

For Kretzmann this problem is highly damaging to the concept of a perfect being, and he controversially suggests that it proves there can be no such thing as a perfect being (that is, no such thing as God). Kretzmann goes on to consider some of the objections to his argument, but he focuses on those objections to statement 4, which is the claim that if God knows everything, and he knows what is going on the changing world, and he knows what is going on in our heads as we change our beliefs in this changing world, then what God knows is changing too. For example, if I know how tall a building is, and then someone adds a mast to it, then what I know has changed. If God knows everything, including what I know, then his knowledge has changed too.

In order to defend the concept of omniscience against attacks such as these, Kretzmann considers the possibility that 'omniscience' may be refined in the same way that philosophers have refined the concept of omnipotence. We shall see in the section below that it is now accepted that omnipotence does not just broadly mean 'can do anything' but that it is now better understood by theologians to mean 'can do anything which it is logically possible for God to do'. This modified explication of omnipotence rules out God having the power to do things that are logically impossible, and even rules out, perhaps, God having the power to do things which then place limits on his power (we explore this idea below in the paradox of the stone). The believer might then argue that we should try to understand omniscience within similar parameters: so, instead of stating 'God knows everything', statement 2 could be amended as follows:

2 a) God knows everything which it is logically possible for God to know and which doesn't limit his knowledge.

If this amendment is successful, then the remaining parts of Kretzmann's argument wouldn't follow (God could still be omniscient, in the revised sense, while not knowing things that would cause him to change). However, Kretzmann does not think that these refinements help avoid the criticism that he has aimed at omniscience. The first part of 2a) states that God only knows what it is logically possible to know, but for Kretzmann that adds nothing to our understanding of omniscience: knowledge (as you remember from your study of epistemology) is of things that are true, and logically impossible things are not true, so *of course* God can only know what is logically possible. What about the second part of 2a)? We shall see in the section below (page 8) that it appears possible to imagine God using his power to limit his power, hence the broad acceptance that omnipotence excludes those things. But Kretzmann says that we can't think of anything that God could know that might limit his knowledge; knowledge of things isn't limiting in the way that power is. There are a number of ways in which I can use my power to limit future use of my power (for example I could lock myself up, or chop my hands off, or row to a desert island and burn my boat). But according to Kretzmann there are no ways in which my knowing something can limit my future knowledge. So Kretzmann concludes that defences of the sort proposed in 2a) do not work against his argument, and his argument against omniscience still stands.

God as omnipotent: his infinite power

The God of Abraham was able to do anything; this is the message behind the countless examples in the Bible of what God could and did do: 'He will not grow tired or weary, and his understanding no one can fathom. He gives strength to the weary and increases the power of the weak' (Isaiah 40:28–30); 'With God all things are possible' (Matthew 19:26); 'For with God nothing is impossible' (Luke 1:37). The power of God to do anything has been termed 'omnipotence' by philosophers (from the Latin *omni*, 'all', and *potens*, 'power') and it takes a central position in God's perfection. But there has long been a question mark over the meaning of omnipotence; can God do literally anything?

There are various ways in which we can try to understand the claim that God is omnipotent. The most obvious, yet most problematic, analysis is that:

a) God can do anything.

Religious philosophers such as the medieval theologian St Thomas Aquinas (1225–74) grappled with the concept of omnipotence hundreds of years ago, attempting to articulate it in a coherent way. When Aquinas asks, 'Is God omnipotent?'[12] he finds an immediate difficulty as all things can be moved and acted upon, yet God is changeless ('immutable') and so there is something God can't do: namely change. There are other, related, problems with formulation a), and in *Summa Contra Gentiles 2:25* Aquinas provides a long list of things that God can't do; for example, he cannot alter what has already happened, or force us to choose something freely. Many theologians agree that God cannot change the laws of mathematics (he cannot, for example, make 2 + 3 = 6), or do what is self-contradictory, such as make something exist *and* not exist at the same time. These examples, and others, have led theologians to amend a) to the more qualified claim that 'If it can be done then God can do it', or, more formally:

anthology 1.1

b) God can do anything which is logically possible.

But even this isn't quite the right formulation, as there are some things that believers agree God cannot do, even though they are logically possible. For example, Aquinas asks whether God can create anything evil, and his reply is no; God cannot sin. Now sinning isn't logically impossible, yet theologians would agree with Aquinas that God is not able to sin. Nor can God act in any other way that goes against his fundamental nature, or which contradicts the other aspects of his perfection (such as his omniscience or immutability). So, as part of an even more nuanced account of omnipotence, religious philosophers may be prepared to offer further modification to their understanding of God's omnipotence:

c) God can do anything which it is logically possible and which does not undermine his perfection.

Theologians, then, have developed a more sophisticated understanding of omnipotence, and one that works alongside other essential perfections of God. But ATHEISTS, such as J.L. Mackie[13] (1917–81), still return to the problem, eagerly pointing out the incoherence of the concept of omnipotence, and hence the incoherence of the idea of God. In the pages below (19–21), we return to some of the main problems emerging from the claim that God is omnipotent when we examine what Mackie calls the 'paradox of omnipotence'. This includes the paradox of the stone (can God create a stone so large that he cannot later move it?) and the paradox of human free will (can God create a being that he later has no control over?).

God as omnibenevolent: his supreme goodness

There are several ways in which philosophers have understood God's supreme goodness (also referred to as his omnibenevolence, or simply benevolence):

- One approach emphasises the account of God's goodness that is found in the Bible, which highlights his love for his creation and in particular for human beings.
- A second approach interprets God's goodness as a type of perfection, influenced by the philosophy of Plato and Aristotle.
- The third way stresses God's goodness in a moral sense, as the source of all value.

These three, and other, approaches are not incompatible, but looking at each of them in turn will help us to understand the different facets of God's supreme goodness.

'O give thanks to the Lord, for he is good, for his steadfast love endures for ever' (Psalm 106:1, and 107, 117, 118, 136, and so on). In the Bible, God's benevolence (from the Latin *bene*, 'good', and *volens*, meaning 'will') is recognisable and familiar to humans. In the Old Testament it is a goodness full of passion, based on righteousness, but carrying with it the consequence of angry retribution to those who disobey him. However, in the New Testament, God's goodness becomes focused through the expression of love and mercy: 'God so loved the world that he gave his one and only Son' (John 3:16); '[God's] mercy extends to those who fear him' (Luke 1:50). It is these more personal aspects of goodness that ordinary, non-philosophical believers may think about when discussing God's goodness. However, theologians themselves have also drawn attention to God's supreme goodness as exemplified through his love. When we come to examine the problem of evil (on page 129) we shall see that one of the reasons why the problem arises is because of the claim that God is loving (why would a loving God allow his creation to include so much pain and suffering?), but paradoxically one of the solutions to the problem of evil also depends upon seeing God as a God of Love[14] who cares deeply about his creation.

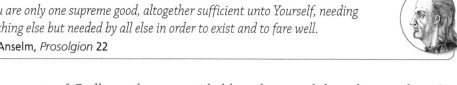

You are only one supreme good, altogether sufficient unto Yourself, needing nothing else but needed by all else in order to exist and to fare well.
St Anselm, *Prosolgion* 22

The account of God's goodness provided by religious philosophers such as St Anselm is more abstract and less personal, and influenced by the two giants of ancient Greek philosophy, Plato and Aristotle. Theologians such as Aquinas (who follow Aristotle's philosophy) view goodness as a form of perfection, meaning that there is no flaw or deficiency and that all the necessary qualities are present. On a mundane level when we say (in Aristotle's sense) that an athlete is good, we are commenting on the level of skill, speed, stamina, strength and other qualities that athletes need to have for high performance. In this sense God's goodness is not just an extra characteristic (to be added to the list, like omniscience or omnipotence), but it is the single property that includes all those other essential characteristics that make God perfect. So saying that

God is supremely good is a way of capturing how complete and perfect God is, containing all the attributes (such as those described by Descartes on page 4) necessary for perfection.

Some philosophers have emphasised the ethical aspects of God's goodness: God is the moral standard and the origin of all moral goodness. On this interpretation God's supreme goodness is seen as the source of all goodness, just as Plato's form of the good is the source for all the other forms. According to philosophers like St Augustine, God's goodness filters down through all of his creation, but all goodness has its origins in God: 'this thing is good and that good, but take away this and that, and regard good itself if you can: so you will see God ... the good of all good'.15 However, there is a problem that arises if God is seen to be the source of all moral goodness – this is known as the EUTHYPHRO DILEMMA, and we examine it on pages 21–5. In its narrower sense, God's goodness could also refer to God's own moral character, and is exemplified in his love, his justice and his wisdom. Even the Bible (in the Book of Job) recognises that God's benevolence has to be reconciled in some way with the horrific pain and suffering that exists in this world. We revisit this in our examination of the problem of evil on page 129.

God as eternal or everlasting: his relationship to time

What is God's relationship to time? The traditional view, drawn from both the philosophy of Plato and Aristotle along with certain passages in the Bible, is that God is eternal. This was understood to mean God exists outside of time, he is timeless, he is ATEMPORAL. But there is an alternative understanding of God's relation with time, which is that God is not timeless (existing outside of time) but that he is everlasting (existing in time but without a beginning or end). We shall look first at the traditional philosophical view of God as eternal, then at the alternative view of God as everlasting, before returning to a modern account of God as eternal.

God as eternal – the traditional view

*You were not, therefore, yesterday, nor will You be tomorrow, but yesterday and today and tomorrow You are.*16
St Anselm

The passage from St Anselm, above, goes on to say that God does not exist yesterday, or today or tomorrow, for these are in time and yet God is absolutely outside of time. Support for the view that God is outside time can be drawn from the opening chapters of the Bible: God in his capacity as creator of the universe (Genesis 1:1–5) must exist outside of the universe in order to create it. So as the universe consists of space and time, God must exist outside of space and time: 'The one who is high and lifted up, who inhabits eternity, whose name is Holy' (Isaiah 57:15). The claim that God exists outside of space leads to attributing to God the property of TRANSCENDENCE; the claim that God exists outside time means also attributing to him the property of ETERNALITY.

Aquinas held the view that God is timeless because it is only by being timeless that God maintains his perfect immutability. God being 'immutable' is another aspect of his nature held to be the case by many theologians. The term 'immutable' is used to refer to things that never change, and cannot change, and as with the previous attributes, the idea of God's enduring, immutable nature has its origins in the Bible. 'They will perish, but you will endure ... you will remain the same and your years will never end' (Psalm 102:26–27); 'For I, the Lord, do not change' (Malachi 3:6). One aspect of God's immutability is that he doesn't change, while for Aquinas another aspect of immutability is that God doesn't consist of different 'parts': his perfection is a single unity (Figure 1.2).

How does a belief in God's immutable nature lead Aquinas to his conclusion that God is atemporal, a being outside of time? The argument draws on similar themes to the one outlined by Kretzmann above (pages 6–7): everything temporal (in time) changes: things fall apart, galaxies and stars are created and destroyed, time moves onward. If God existed temporally, and had relations with this temporal universe, then it would mean that God would change along with the world changing. But God cannot change, he is immutable, therefore he cannot be temporal. Aquinas concludes that God must be eternal, in the sense of atemporal, a being outside of time.

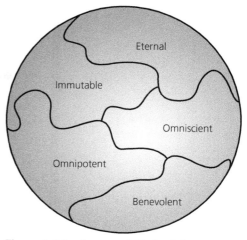

Figure 1.2 For Aquinas, all God's attributes are one

▶ **ACTIVITY**

Rewrite the argument outlined in the paragraph above in a formal way, using clear, numbered statements similar to the formal argument given below on page 12.

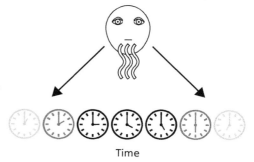

Figure 1.3 God is outside of time

What does it mean to be atemporal, or timeless? Aquinas illustrates how this might be possible by describing the perspectives of two people, one travelling along a busy road, and the other on a hill watching the travellers below. The person on the road cannot see all those people behind him, but the observer on the hill can see everyone simultaneously.[17] In a similar way, all of time is simultaneously present to a timeless God (see Figure 1.3). This timeless or eternal aspect of God mirrors God's position as a transcendent being, existing beyond the universe. Aquinas elsewhere offers another analogy which might also help us understand the difference between eternity and time. An hour, he writes, is part of a day and both can exist simultaneously; in the same way time is a part of eternity, except eternity both exceeds and contains time.

If neither of Aquinas' analogies helps us to imagine what 'seeing time' from the perspective of a timeless being might be like, then this is probably because we have a completely different, and limited, experience of time. The novelist Kurt Vonnegut tries to describe what it might be like to see the world from outside of time in his novel *Slaughterhouse 5*. The Tralfmadorians, a super-intelligent and advanced alien species from the planet Tralfmadore, see the past, present and future simultaneously, and they find it difficult to understand what it must be like to see time in the limited, sequential way that Billy Pilgrim experiences it (Billy is a human whom they've kidnapped for their zoo). This is how the Tralfmadorian guide tries to explain the difference to the visitors at the zoo:

The guide invited the crowd to imagine that they [the Tralfmadorians] were looking across a desert at a mountain range on a day that was twinkling bright and clear. They could look at a peak or a bird or a cloud, at a stone right in front of them ... But among them was this poor Earthling and his head was encased in a steel sphere.

... There was only one eyehole through which he could look, and welded to that eyehole was six feet of pipe ... He was also strapped to a flatcar on rails, and there was no way he could turn his head or touch the pipe ... Whatever poor Billy saw through the pipe, he had no choice but to say to himself, 'That's life.'[18]

Aquinas' view is the classic account of God as an atemporal being. However, in recent years this account has been criticised because it is not in keeping with the nature of God as understood by believers and as described in the Bible (the 'God of Abraham', page 3). There has been a movement since the mid-twentieth century towards the God of Abraham, the god of ordinary believers rather than of scholastic philosophers, and with this movement philosophers have rejected the traditional account of God as timeless, and have sought an alternative more in keeping with their faith. This alternative is to understand God's eternality as everlasting, which we look at in the next section. However, other modern philosophers have sought to revise and update the traditional account of God as eternal, and we return to this modern account on page 13.

God as everlasting

There is a growing modern tradition that queries the classical view that God is atemporal, and looks to an alternative understanding of God's relationship with time, that God is everlasting. A more technical term to describe God as everlasting is 'sempiternal', and both terms mean that he is a being existing throughout time but without beginning and without end. For many believers, a sempiternal God is one who is more obviously capable of a personal relationship with humans and of love for them and the world. This new approach is perhaps more in keeping with the layperson's understanding of God and how he interacts with his creation. The contemporary philosopher Nicholas Wolterstorff (1932–) suggests that an eternal God, existing outside of time, undermines the account of God in the Bible and renders the Bible false or at best a long series of metaphors.[19] After all, if God is eternal, and exists out of time, then it does not seem possible for him to act in the world; in particular, Wolterstorff says that God cannot be the Redeemer if he is outside of time – so God must be everlasting and not timeless.

This tension between the God of Abraham (the God that loves the world and interacts with it, and so must be everlasting) and the God of the philosophers (the God that is immutable and changeless, and so must be atemporal) becomes transparent if we use a more formal, logical, mode of expression as follows:

1. God is atemporal.
2. God interacts with the world [this is an essential tenet of Christianity].
3. The world is temporal.
4. God has a real relationship with the temporal world [from 2 and 3].[20]
5. Any being that has a real relationship with the temporal world is itself temporal.
6. Therefore God is temporal [from 4 and 5].
7. Therefore 1 is false.

The dilemma that a believer faces is this: do you give up on the belief that God is immutable and the creator of space and time (both of which point towards an atemporal God)? Or do you give up on the belief that God is active in the world (which points towards a temporal God)?

There are elements of this argument (for example 2 and 4) that seem to be an essential part of the believer's understanding of God, and which cannot be given up without surrendering certain core beliefs about God. It is critically important that theists do not believe that God is a being who created the world and then removed himself from it (that is DEISM). Instead, a Christian God is understood to be a *personal* God, one who is aware of the pain and suffering in the world, and he is understood to be a *loving* and redeeming God who, because of his love, set about giving humans the opportunity for redemption through the life, then death, then the resurrection of Jesus.

Support for the view that God is everlasting can also be drawn from scriptures. For example, throughout the Old Testament, God is described as without a beginning and without an end (Genesis 21:33, Deuteronomy 33:27, Isaiah 57:15) and, although this is consistent with God being eternal, it is also consistent with the alternative interpretation – namely that God is everlasting: 'Before the mountains were born or you brought forth the earth and the world, from everlasting to everlasting you are God' (Psalm 90:2). In this sense God may be described as always having existed in the past and always going to exist in the future – but he is not eternal (existing outside of time); instead he is everlasting, living alongside and through his creation – which suggests a God who changes.

We might summarise the reasons for a belief in an everlasting (as opposed to a timeless) God as follows:

- An everlasting God is a personal God. (It is hard to see how an atemporal being can be a person.)
- An everlasting God can love his creation, which does involve suffering with the world. (It is hard to see how an atemporal God could have the feeling of love.)
- An everlasting God is closer to the concept of God as written about in the Bible, including God as a being who interacts with the world, and who changes as a result of that interaction.[21]

God as eternal – a modern view

The belief that God is everlasting, rather than timeless, has become the prevailing view among theologians and modern believers who seem to have a more personal, less conceptual relationship with God than philosophers such as St Thomas Aquinas. But the discussion about whether God is timeless (atemporal) or everlasting (and temporal) is not settled, and the debate was sparked again by the influential 1981 article 'Eternity' by Eleonore Stump and Norman Kretzmann.

Learn More

> *Eternity then, is the complete possession, all at once, of illimitable life.*[22]
> Boethius

Their article weaves both a positive and a negative strand together, and is aimed firmly at showing that God is an atemporal, not an everlasting (sempiternal), being. The more positive strand is Stump and Kretzmann's efforts to explain the classic view as espoused by the Roman philosopher Boethius (480–524) that an eternal God is atemporal. The more negative strand is their defence of the concept of 'eternal' against claims made by some philosophers that the concept is incoherent. The two strands of the Stump–Kretzmann article are interwoven as both strands require a clear-sighted account of eternity: a clearer explanation of Boethius' position can be achieved through a robust defence of the concept of 'eternal' against the claim that it is incoherent.

Stump and Kretzmann identify four ingredients in Boethius' definition of eternity. First, anything eternal has *life*; secondly, that it is *illimitable* (beginningless and endless); thirdly, that it is a life of (infinite) *duration*; fourthly, that an eternal being possesses this life of infinite duration all at once (*simultaneously*), which means it is atemporal. We have attempted to illustrate this simultaneity in Figure 1.3 (see page 11).

The incoherence of the classic concept, in which all time is simultaneous for an eternal being, is brought out by Anthony Kenny: 'On St Thomas' view, my typing of this paper is simultaneous with the whole of eternity. Again, on this view, the great fire of Rome is simultaneous with the whole of eternity. Therefore, while I type these words, Nero fiddles heartlessly on.'[23] (See Figure 1.4.) We might express this in more formal terms as follows:

- **(P1):** According to the classic conception of eternity, Rome burning to the ground in 64 CE (while the Emperor Nero allegedly played the lyre) is simultaneous with eternity.
- **(P2):** According to the classic conception of eternity, me typing this sentence now, in 2017, is simultaneous with eternity.
- **(P3):** Intermediate conclusion: Therefore, according to the classic conception of eternity, 64 CE is simultaneous with 2017.
- **(P4):** This is absurd, as the past, present and future cannot be simultaneous with one another.
- **(C):** Therefore the classic concept of eternity is incoherent.

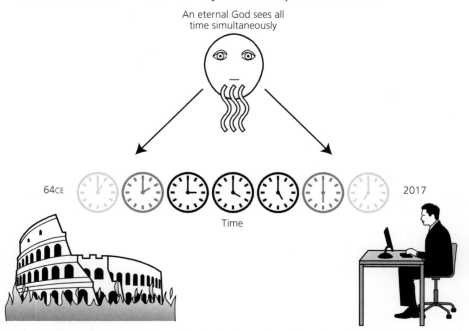

Figure 1.4 An eternal God sees Rome burning in 64 CE and a philosopher writing in 2017 simultaneously

There are various steps and stages that Stump and Kretzmann have to take in order to try to demonstrate that Kenny is wrong, and that eternity is not incoherent, but we shall focus only on a few of the most critical stages in their argument. The first step taken by Stump and Kretzmann is to identify different types of simultaneity so that the concept can accommodate different types of beings (for example, those temporal beings like us, and those atemporal beings like God). They propose that there is a general definition of simultaneity, which is that of things existing or occurring 'at once (together)'. What 'at once' means is different for different types of entities, so when applied to temporal beings, 'at once' means 'at the same time', and when applied to atemporal beings, 'at once' means 'at the same eternal present'. This enables them to describe two different types of simultaneity:

- T-simultaneity (applying to temporal beings like us) = existence or occurrence at the *same time*
- E-simultaneity (applying to eternal beings like God) = existence or occurrence at one and the *same eternal present*

Having made this distinction, the second step for Stump and Kretzmann is to come up with a coherent way of relating what is simultaneous for us (T-simultaneity) with what is simultaneous for God (E-simultaneity). They achieve this by looking towards an analogous situation within Einstein's theory of special relativity (difficult enough to understand in itself, never mind as an analogy with the philosophical concept of eternity!). One corollary of Einstein's theory is the concept of the 'relativity of simultaneity'. According to this concept, whether two unconnected events occur at the same time depends on the frame of reference of the observers: if one of these frames of reference is moving relative to the other, then one observer might see the two events as simultaneous, whereas the other might not. For example, imagine one person is on top of a very fast train (we mean a *really* fast train, one travelling at over half the speed of light), while another person is on the ground – imagine then that lightning suddenly strikes the front and back of the train.

Figure 1.5 illustrates Einstein's idea of the 'relativity of simultaneity'[24]. The ground observer sees the lightning strike the front and back of the train simultaneously (panel A2). But the train observer sees the lightning hit the front of the train first because they are travelling towards that light (panel B2) so quickly that it reaches them first; and they then turn round to see the other lightning strike the back of the train second, as the light takes slightly longer to reach their eyes (panel B3). Each observer has a different frame of reference (one is stationary, one is travelling) and it is these different frames of reference that explain why one observer sees the lightning as simultaneous, whereas the other observer doesn't.

The next step for Stump and Kretzmann is to show how they can use Einstein's idea of frames of reference to throw light onto their own argument. There is an apparent incoherence in saying 'the lightning strikes both did, and did not, occur at the same time' as that is impossible. But this incoherence is resolved within Einstein's theory: the two observers have different frames of reference so to one person the events occurred simultaneously, but to the other person they didn't. A similar approach could be taken to solve the apparent incoherence that Anthony Kenny raised above. Stump and Kretzmann propose that relative to the frame of

A1 An observer on the ground watches a train approach.

A2 The ground observer sees lightning strike the front and back simultaneously.

A3 The train moves onwards.

B1 An observer on top of the train watches as it speeds forwards.

B2 The train observer sees lightning strike the front of the train.

B3 The train observer turns round to see lightning strike the back of the train.

Figure 1.5 Within Einstein's theory it is possible for an event to be seen as simultaneous by one observer, but not as simultaneous by another observer

anthology 1.2

reference of God all events and entities are simultaneous (E-simultaneity), but that relative to the frame of reference to temporal beings like ourselves events happening at the same time are simultaneous (T-simultaneity). So, to God everything is simultaneous, but to us only things that happened at the same time are simultaneous. They go on to propose a new species of simultaneity, which connects E-simultaneity with T-simultaneity, on the rare occasions when what is simultaneous to God is also simultaneous to us. This new species they call 'ET-simultaneity' and it resolves the problem put forward by Kenny by saying that two events or entities are ET-simultaneous if and only if they are both present to an eternal being (from its atemporal reference frame) *and* both are present to a temporal being (from its temporal reference frame).

Stump and Kretzmann hoped to have shown that arguments against eternity, of the sort put forward by Kenny, fail to demonstrate any incoherence in the underpinning concept of simultaneity. They argued that a more nuanced understanding of simultaneity, allowing for different species or types of simultaneity, allowed for events to be simultaneous for beings with different frames of reference. So, from God's atemporal frame of reference me typing this sentence and the Battle of Waterloo happening are E-simultaneous, but from my temporal frame of reference they definitely are not simultaneous (although other things, like my desire to stop writing about Stump and Kretzmann, having done so for what seems like an eternity, are T-simultaneous with me writing this sentence).

'Eternity', the article containing all these ideas, prompted a wide variety of criticism (for example, for their reliance on the Einstein analogy, taken from theoretical physics, at the centre of the argument) but the effect of the article was to put the idea that God is eternal in the sense of atemporal back on the table.

1.1.2 Arguments for the incoherence of the concept of God

We have now looked at the main characteristics of God and sketched some of the problems with these attributes. Several of the issues clustered around each attribute emerge because they don't exist in isolation, but sit alongside other aspects of God's perfection. Once the characteristics are combined with each other, then further contradictions start to emerge, and the question arises as to whether the concept of God, as delineated by these five or so characteristics, is really a coherent concept. Here we examine in more detail some of the arguments to support the claim that the concept of God is incoherent. The arguments that we look at focus on one, or more, of God's attributes:

- The argument arising from God's omnipotence: **the paradox of the stone**
- The argument arising from God's supreme goodness: **the Euthyphro dilemma**
- The argument arising from God's omniscience: **the compatibility of God's omniscience and free human beings**
- The argument arising from God's omnipotence, omniscience and supreme goodness: **the problem of evil**

The idea of 'compossibility' may be helpful in this context: it is taken from the philosophy of Gottfried Wilhelm von Leibniz (1646–1716) and it captures the idea that a number of things (or people, or attributes) can exist as possibilities alongside each other, at exactly the same time, without giving rise to any contradictions.[25] The question is: are God's attributes compossible? In other words, can all these perfections co-exist in the same being at once?

Figure 1.6 shows which attributes, when combined, lead to inconsistencies or contradictions that need to be addressed by the believer. (Obviously these inconsistencies are not a concern for atheists, and can be seen as further evidence that 'God' is not a term that refers to anything in, or out of, the universe.)

	OMNISCIENCE	OMNIPOTENCE	BENEVOLENCE	TRANSCENDENCE	IMMANENCE	ETERNAL	EVERLASTING
OMNISCIENCE	–	–	Problem of evil	Problem of free will	Inconsistent (If God has knowledge of the world he must change.)	Problem of free will	Inconsistent (If God is in time then how can he know the future?)
OMNIPOTENCE		Problem of omnipotence	Problem of evil	Problem of divine action	How could God create the world if he is in the world?	Problem of divine action	How could God create time if he is in time?
BENEVOLENCE			Euthyphro Dilemma	Problem of divine action	Inconsistent (If God is in the world then he is in evil.)	–	–
TRANSCENDENCE				–	Inconsistent (God can't be both in and out of the world.)	–	Inconsistent (If God is outside the world then he is outside of time.)
IMMANENCE					–	Inconsistent (If God is in the world then he is not eternal.)	–
ETERNAL						–	Inconsistent (God can't be both in and out of time.)
EVERLASTING							–

Figure 1.6 Some of the problems associated with the attributes of God

▶ **ACTIVITY**

In the left-hand column opposite are some of the properties attributed to God by believers; in the right-hand column are properties attributed to the universe by believers.

1 Try to think up as many potential problems with the concept of God as you can by combining properties from either column (for example, 2 and D). You may find that a single property is problematic in itself or you may combine three or four properties together to create a problem.

2 How might a believer go about resolving these problems?

Properties of God	Properties of the universe
1 God is omnipotent	A Evil exists in the world
2 God is omniscient	B Humans have free will
3 God is omnipresent	C There is evidence of God in the world
4 God is supremely good	D Humans can have private thoughts
5 God is beyond understanding	E God intervenes in the world
6 God has free will	F The universe is governed by physical laws
7 God defines morality	G The universe exists in space and time
8 God is outside of time	H The universe is made up of matter
9 God acts morally	I The universe had a beginning
10 God is immaterial	J Humans sometimes act immorally

The paradox of the stone

Here we examine in more detail one of the issues with the concept of omnipotence that we have already briefly discussed. The type of question a sceptic might ask about the idea of an all-powerful being is, 'Can such a being create a round square?' or 'Can they make 2 + 2 = 5?' We know that theologians are happy to concede that saying 'God is omnipotent' does not mean that 'God can do anything'; God could still be described as omnipotent, even though he is not able to perform acts that are self-contradictory or logically impossible. Both believers (such as Aquinas) and atheists (such as J.L. Mackie[26]) accept that omnipotence as a concept can be amended along the lines suggested above (page 8) to make it more coherent.

However, there is a more damaging issue that can be found in the idea of omnipotence, and this is the problem of whether an omnipotent being can use its powers to do something that will limit these powers. For example, can God create a stone so large that he cannot move it? This is known as the paradox of the stone, and an early version of this can be found in the work of the medieval Islamic philosopher known as Averroes (also known as Ibn Rushd, 1126–98). Sceptics and atheists argue that the paradox of the stone is a strong indicator that the concept of 'omnipotence' is incoherent and therefore the whole concept of God is undermined.

George Mavrodes gives a more recent version of the paradox, together with his defence of omnipotence. His version starts with the question 'Can God create a stone too heavy for him to lift it?'[27] This question poses a dilemma for the believer as it seems to offer two choices, both of which undermine the claim that God is omnipotent. The first choice is to say that God can create such an unliftable stone, in which case there is something God cannot do (that is, lift such a stone) and he is not omnipotent. The second choice would be to say that God cannot create such a stone. In this case there is also something God cannot do (that is, create such a stone) and he is not omnipotent. So, either way there is something an omnipotent being cannot do. The sceptic is likely to conclude that this is because 'omnipotence' is an incoherent concept, and if so then omnipotence isn't a possible attribute of any being, not even God.

However, Mavrodes thinks that this dilemma fails to undermine the notion of God's omnipotence (in a similar way that not being able to create a round square, and other self-contradictory tasks, also fail to undermine it). His defence explores two possibilities: the possibility that God *is not* omnipotent (which we can call assumption 1) and the possibility that he *is* (assumption 2). Let us look at assumption 1 and apply this to the paradox. If we assume that God *is not* omnipotent then the dilemma simply tells us that a being that isn't omnipotent cannot do certain things (that is, lift a certain stone, or create a certain stone). But this, Mavrodes points out, is a trivial conclusion: if someone is not omnipotent then of course their powers are limited. So the dilemma is insignificant on the basis of assumption 1. He goes on to explore assumption 2: what follows if we assume that God *is* omnipotent, and is a being with the power to do anything (including lift anything)? In this case the original question, 'Can God create a stone too heavy for him to lift?' becomes 'Can a being whose power is sufficient to lift anything create a stone which cannot be lifted by him?'

For Mavrodes this clarification, based on the assumption that God is omnipotent, reveals the task to be a self-contradictory task. Now we have already seen that it is generally agreed that omnipotent beings are not limited in their power by not being able to do self-contradictory things. This takes us back to Aquinas' point that 'It is more appropriate to say that such things cannot be done, than that God cannot do them.'[28] And so Mavrodes concludes that the paradox of the stone proposes a limitation (not being able to lift unliftable stones) that turns out to be no limitation at all, and the doctrine of God's omnipotence remains unaffected by this paradox.

> Learn More
>
> ### Criticism
>
> Another recent philosopher, C. Wade Savage, has argued that the solution proposed by Mavrodes is wrongheaded, and Savage offers a better solution to the paradox.[29] Savage suggests that Mavrodes has presented a version of the paradox (which Savage calls version A) that aims to prove that 'God is not omnipotent'. Proceeding in the way that Mavrodes does will quickly lead to the conclusion that this paradox misses its mark – because assumption 2 asks us to assume that God is omnipotent, and it obviously (and even trivially) then follows, as Mavrodes says, that the task is self-contradictory. But for Savage, version A is not really the main problem, and Mavrodes has been led astray by attacking this version. The paradox of the stone, according to Savage, is not trying to show that 'God is not omnipotent', but instead it is aiming to prove that 'the concept of an omnipotent being is logically inconsistent' and therefore that the existence of an omnipotent being is logically impossible.
>
> Version B, as outlined by Savage, is very general and carefully avoids any reference to 'God'. It begins by offering two possibilities: the first is that a being (X) can create a stone which X cannot lift; the second is that X *cannot* create a stone which X cannot lift. In the first case, X cannot do something (lift the stone) and in the second case X cannot do something (create the stone) and therefore there is at least one thing X cannot do. But if X is omnipotent then X can do anything. Savage then concludes at the end of version B that X is not omnipotent, and that the existence of an omnipotent being is logically

impossible. So it is version B that really needs to be addressed if believers wish to show that existence of God is not logically impossible.

Savage argues that the weakness in the paradox lies in the claim that 'if X cannot create a stone which X cannot lift therefore *there is a task which X cannot do (i.e. create the stone)*'. Savage does not believe that the *second* part of this claim (in *italics*) follows from the first part of this claim; and if he is correct then the rest of the paradox falls apart. His argument is a subtle one, but he asks us to imagine two beings, X and Y. X makes stones and Y lifts stones (it's a boring job, but somebody has to do it). Let us assume that Y can only lift stones that are up to 70 lb. In which case if X cannot create a stone that Y cannot lift (that is, more than 70 lb) then X really does have a limitation on his power. Let us now assume that Y is omnipotent. X can create stones that are 70 lb, 700 lb, 7000 lb, 7 billion trillion lb, and so on, but every stone that X makes Y can actually lift. Savage argues that the fact that X cannot create a stone that Y cannot lift *does not mean that X's power is limited*.

> *If X can create stones of any poundage, and Y can lift stones of any poundage, then X cannot create a stone which Y cannot lift, and yet X is not thereby limited in power.*[30]

The next step that Savage takes is to say that this conclusion holds true even if X and Y are the same person. In which case the fact that X cannot create a stone that X cannot lift does not mean that X is limited in power – and omnipotence is not a logically incoherent concept. Savage concludes that the two possibilities put forward by the paradox are nothing more than the consequences of these two facets (being able to create anything, and being able to lift anything) of God's omnipotence.

The paradox of the stone may seem a trivial, if logically engaging, paradox, but it is essential to philosophers of religion that God's perfections are defended and clarified against such logical attacks. But the atheist may ask other, related questions which are not trivial and do get to the heart of what it is to believe in God. The question 'Can an omnipotent God create something that later he will have no control over?' can be focused on whether God can create a being with genuine free will. This is a more serious problem for the believer since it touches on our own nature and our relationship to God. If God is truly all-powerful, then surely we would not have any power over our own actions. Everything would be under his control. On the other hand, if he were truly all-powerful he should be able to give us power over our own actions. So, once again, either way there is a limitation on his power. We explore further the idea of human free will in relation to God on page 25.

The Euthyphro dilemma

This dilemma was first highlighted by the ancient Greek philosopher, Plato. The usual format for Plato's philosophy was his dramatic dialogues in which his characters, led by Socrates, tried to define and explain a big philosophical idea: justice, love, ethics, courage, knowledge, the soul. The *Euthyphro*, which is one of Plato's earlier dialogues, is no different and it starts with two characters, Euthyphro and Socrates, engaged in conversation at an Athenian court. They quickly turn to the topic of piety, or holiness, as Euthyphro is prosecuting his father for manslaughter (his father allowed a slave to die) and he is very confident that he is doing the right thing and is acting piously. Socrates is surprised at the confidence Euthyphro shows in claiming to know what piety is; after all, piety has a close connection with the rules laid down by God (or gods), and is not easily known. Moreover, Socrates himself is at the court because he is being charged with impiety for corrupting the young people of Athens through his philosophical ideas and debates (a charge on which he would eventually be found guilty and executed). So Socrates engages Euthyphro in a philosophical discussion about what piety is, saying that it will help him in his own court defence.

As is the case in several of Plato's dialogues, Socrates' proffered ignorance of the topic under discussion is a method for revealing that the person who is so certain, and confident in their knowledge of the topic, is actually the ignorant one. And this is true here, as each definition of piety that Euthyphro offers falls apart when Socrates starts to analyse it. Euthyphro's first definition of piety is only an example, not a definition, as Socrates points out. In his second definition Euthyphro says that piety is what is pleasing to the gods, what they love; but Socrates rightly shows that the gods are divided among themselves about what pleases them, and so the same action might be considered both pious and impious according to this definition. Moving towards a third definition, Euthyphro proposes that piety means those things that *all* the gods love, and impiety is what all the gods hate. It is here that Socrates first poses the question that underpins the Euthyphro dilemma:

anthology 1.3

The point which I should first wish to understand is whether the pious (or holy) is beloved by the gods because it is holy, or holy because it is beloved of the gods.
Plato, *Euthyphro*, 10a

We can clarify Socrates' question here: he is asking whether the gods love what is pious (good actions) because it good; or whether the action is good because it is loved by the gods. So is goodness separate from the gods (the first option) or is goodness defined by the gods (the second option)? Socrates points out that these cannot both be true, because if they were then we would arrive at a circular argument: 'The gods love what is good; and what is good? ... It is what the gods love.' At this point both Socrates and Euthyphro agree that the gods love what is pious (good actions) because they are pious; and in agreeing this Euthyphro is being forced to move away from the position that the gods are the most important thing when it comes to morality. We should not be surprised by this as Plato went on to propose in his later dialogues the existence of an external, objective realm, the world of 'forms', which was also the source of universal moral values.

But Socrates' question poses a dilemma that has taken on a significance beyond the one intended by Plato in his original dialogue, and this remains known as the Euthyphro dilemma. Let us now try to understand the Euthyphro dilemma in terms that give it relevance to the philosophy of religion. We have seen that Euthyphro attempts to define morality (piety) as that which is the will of the gods, or, in his phrase, that which is 'dear to God' or 'loved by the gods'. Socrates then raises the question of whether everything that God wills, or commands, must therefore be moral, or whether everything God commands is 'moral' because he is following some external moral authority. The two choices identified by Socrates form a dilemma because they offer two equally unpalatable options to a theist:

1. Every action that God commands us to do (even cruel and despicable ones) is good.
2. Every action that God commands us to do is good because it accords with some other moral authority.

Figure 1.7 The two horns of the Euthyphro dilemma

Let us examine the consequences of following each option, or horn, of the dilemma.

The first 'horn'

The first option assumes that God is the source and standard of all moral goodness, and that whatever he commands will automatically be good. So God could command us to do completely trivial things (such as not stepping on the cracks in the pavement) and these would be morally good. God could even command us to perform cruel, dishonest or unjust acts, which run counter to our moral intuitions. But, according to this interpretation of God's goodness, a believer would be obliged to do these things and they would be morally right because God had commanded them. It is possible to find many examples in the Old Testament of God's commands that seem to us to be morally questionable; for example, the command to Moses to commit acts of genocide while on the journey to Canaan (Deuteronomy 3:2; Numbers 31), or the command given to Abraham to sacrifice his own son Isaac:

> *God tested Abraham and said to him 'Abraham ... Take your son, your only son Isaac whom you love, and go to the land of Moriah and offer him there as a burnt offering.'*
> **Genesis 22:2**

Earlier on in Plato's original dialogue, Socrates asks Euthyphro why we should worship a God who could command us to do horrific acts. But this horn of the dilemma, that is, this interpretation of God's goodness, forces us into a position where any act, however terrible, is good when it is commanded by God. This is a conclusion we might wish to avoid; as Job says:

> *It is unthinkable that God would do wrong, that the Almighty would pervert justice.*
> **Job 34:12**

Criticism

However, Søren Kierkegaard (1813–55) is quite prepared to accept that God may tell us to commit acts that require us to suspend our ethical beliefs, and that we would be obliged to carry out those acts. In *Fear and Trembling*, Kierkegaard defends Abraham's decision to kill his son, on the grounds that God has commanded it as proof of his faith.[31] In doing so Kierkegaard challenges the assumption that ethical values should be placed above all other values. For Kierkegaard there is a higher value, known only by God, and yet we must have faith in God's will if he commands us to perform an apparently unethical act. Such faith cannot be rationally explained, nor supported by evidence, yet faith may, in some situations, require the suspension of our ethical beliefs. It was just so with Abraham: he was, as Kierkegaard says, a 'knight of faith' and was prepared to murder his own son in the faith that he was doing it for some higher purpose or '*telos*'. Kierkegaard refers to this as the 'teleological suspension of the ethical', where the will of God comes above mere ethics.

But Kierkegaard's position is also one that many believers would be uncomfortable with. Both Aquinas and St Augustine believed that God cannot will evil because he is perfectly good, in an ethical sense. It seems tempting to reject an account of moral goodness which implies that God could tell us to do anything and it would by definition be good. In which case, what makes God's commands good?

The first horn of the dilemma throws doubt onto what we could mean by saying God is supremely good. If goodness simply means 'whatever God wills' then saying 'God is good' simply means 'God does whatever God himself wills', which seems to empty the concept of goodness of any meaning. Perhaps we should look to the second horn of the dilemma to better understand God's goodness.

The second 'horn'

We saw in Figure 1.7 that there is a second option, which is the preferred choice of Plato, which states that goodness exists independently of God's will. In this case what makes God good, and everything he says or wills or commands good, is that these conform to some external moral authority. In this case God does not issue commands which then automatically become 'good'; instead God issues commands which are good only insofar as they comply with a moral code that lies beyond God. This approach conforms with Plato's metaphysical theory of forms in which the 'good' has an objective reality discoverable by reason. Philosophers would say that if we agree with the second option then we believe that morality has an objective status, and we would be referred to as realists or cognitivists about religious statements (see page 156). However, for the traditional theist this is a problematic way of accounting for the goodness of God's commands, and it raises a number of other issues:

- Objective morality does not need God. For if moral goodness lies beyond God then we can bypass God if we wish to be moral. In this case God's status as a being worthy of worship is undermined here: why should we worship a God who is bound by the same independent moral rules as ourselves?
- Objective morality limits God's power. If there is a moral law that exists independently of God then God cannot change this and determine for himself what is good and what is bad. His omnipotence is being called into question here, and God cannot command us to do what is morally wrong (for example, instruct Abraham to sacrifice Isaac) and by commanding it make it right.

- Objective morality defines God's benevolence. When we assert that God is supremely good, we are referring to an independent set of moral standards that God conforms to. So isn't it the case that it is those moral standards that are *supremely* good, and not God?

For these reasons, and others, the second horn of the dilemma seems as unacceptable as the first horn for many believers. Plato's dilemma, first proposed in a dialogue over two thousand years ago, remains very much a live issue within the philosophy of religion.

> **Criticism**
>
> However, both horns of the dilemma may be avoided by philosophers who do not locate goodness either in God's will or in God's commands. An alternative theological account of moral goodness can be found in Aquinas' Natural Law ethics. This moral philosophy originates in Aristotle (Aquinas made it his life's work to reconcile Aristotle's philosophy with Christian THEOLOGY) and it sees goodness as related to being good *at* something, or good *for* something. You may remember that this TELEOLOGICAL account of morality looks to function and purpose in order to understand what is good. Aquinas adds to Aristotle's theory by arguing that a universe created by God, and everything in it, will have a function and purpose and it is up to us to determine what these Natural Laws are and then strive to reach our 'good'.
>
> If Aquinas' approach works (and as always in philosophy there are many criticisms that can be made of it) then it avoids the first horn of the Euthyphro dilemma. Having created the world, in line with the Natural Law, God cannot now just arbitrarily 'decide' what is good or bad, as our nature and function (and hence what is good) have already been determined. Aquinas' theory leans towards the second horn of the dilemma by agreeing that the Natural Law is objective, but that it flows from God's omnibenevolent nature. In this way it avoids the claim that morality must exist independently of God.

The compatibility, or otherwise, of God's omniscience and free human beings

We have already looked at one of the problems that arises from claiming that God is omniscient (see pages 6-7). How can we maintain that God knows things in time, when things in time change and so God's knowledge changes, while also maintaining that God is unchangeable (immutable)? Here we look more closely at another issue that emerges from God's omniscience, namely whether it is possible for humans to freely choose an action if God (in his omniscience) already knows what we're going to do.

We explore the concept of free will in more detail when looking at the problem of evil (page 129); the question here is how can we reconcile God's omniscience with human free will? If God really knows everything, then it seems as if he must know the future, and, in particular, he must know what choices we are going to make. But if God knows what action I will perform before I decide to do it, then I cannot have chosen to do otherwise than I did. But if we cannot choose otherwise, then the actions we appear to choose are not really freely chosen at all. I may feel as though I freely choose to do some philosophy rather than watch a movie, but God knew all along that I would do some philosophy. I couldn't have done otherwise than 'choose' philosophy, and so, it seems, this choice was predetermined. It follows that the feeling of free choice is just an illusion.

Anthony Kenny puts forward the problem by asking whether the following two statements are compatible:[32]

1. God knows beforehand everything that men will do.
2. Some actions of people are free.

It appears that these two statements are incompatible, and that one of them must be false. If God knows beforehand what we are going to do, then it is not in our power not to do that thing. This is because knowledge, of any kind, is of what is true, and if God knows my future actions then it must be true that I will do these future actions. There is nothing I can do to prevent it, which firmly suggests that I am not free. So, either God doesn't in fact know what we will do (we give up the first statement) or the actions of people are not free (we give up the second statement).

Now, faced with this dilemma, the believer could surrender their belief in human freedom. Perhaps we are all just robots living out our predetermined lives. But this view of humankind does not sit at all well with the notion that we are responsible for our actions, and with the associated claim, so crucial to most religious systems, that we are accountable to God for our choices. In Christian theology, for example, it is often said that at Judgement Day we will have to account for our actions before Christ, and that if we are found wanting we will be subject to eternal damnation. Now, if I have no genuine choice about the sins I have committed, then I appear to have good reason to feel aggrieved by this arrangement. If God knew I would sin, and made me so that I would sin, then what do my sins have to do with me? If I couldn't help it, why punish me? Surely on this view of human freedom God is the only person responsible for all the crimes of humanity.

Clearly then, denying free will to humans has not been a popular option for believers, since it appears to put the blame for all sin onto God. But neither do believers normally wish to surrender claims to God's omniscience. So how can the problem be resolved?

Kenny highlights one of Aquinas' solutions to this problem, and that is to say that God is eternal and outside of time. This means that for God there is no future or past; or rather, future and past co-exist on a continuum laid out before his gaze. Human actions are not predetermined and we freely choose to act as we do. But, at the same time, God is able to see what actions we do happen to choose. So, just because God knows what I will do, this doesn't mean that I was somehow forced to do it. To explore this thought, consider our own knowledge of what we do. Think back to your decision to read this philosophy book rather than do something even more interesting. You now know that you chose to do some philosophy, because that is exactly what you are doing; but the fact that you *know* that you chose to read some philosophy, does not mean that you did not freely choose to read philosophy. You might have chosen to watch television instead. In the same way, the thought goes, the fact that God can know what our choices will be does not mean that they could not be otherwise. He may know that you will choose to do more philosophy next weekend. But when the choice comes, you are still freely choosing to do philosophy instead of watching television, and it is still true to say that you could, if you wanted, choose to waste away your life watching daytime TV.

According to Aquinas' solution then, God has knowledge of our actions, which to us lie in the future, but which to God are not in the future. So God does not have *fore*knowledge of our actions but he does have knowledge of them, as the point at which he knows them does not lie in the future but in an all-seeing present. However, Aquinas' solution does depend on the claim that God is eternal, and we saw above (page 12) that recently philosophers have argued that God is everlasting, and not eternal, in which case Aquinas' solution is not an option for these philosophers.

The problem of evil

The final and most significant challenge to the concept of God that we examine in this book is the PROBLEM OF EVIL. This is one of the oldest and most pressing concerns faced by the believer. How is it possible that an omnipotent, omniscient and supremely good God allows such horrific pain and suffering to exist within his creation? After all, he knows about it (he is omniscient), he has the power to stop it (he is omnipotent) and he cares about stopping it (he is supremely good). It seems as if God cannot have all the perfections that we ascribe to him, otherwise he would surely do something to stop the suffering of his creatures on Earth. We explore this problem in detail on pages 129–51.

▶ **ACTIVITY**

Consider the problems below. How might a philosophically minded believer respond to each of them?

1. God cannot do what it is logically impossible to do (for example, make a stone so large that he cannot move it). Therefore God is not omnipotent.
2. God cannot create a being whom he can control yet who has genuine free will. Therefore God is not omnipotent.
3. God cannot know what a being with genuine free will is about to do. Therefore God is not omniscient.
4. God has created beings whom he knew would do evil to one another. So, ultimately God is to blame for our wicked acts. Therefore God is not good.
5. God is outside of space and time. Therefore God cannot intervene in the world, and he cannot perform miracles.
6. God is present in the world, existing inside of space and time. Therefore he cannot have created space and time and cannot have created the universe.
7. God is present in the world, existing in all parts of it, including all that is evil and horrific. Therefore God is not perfectly good.
8. Ultimately, the God as described by the philosophers (omnipotent, benevolent, omniscient and so on) cannot possess all the properties they ascribe to him. The very concept of God is an incoherent one, and belief in such a God is irrational.

Summary: The concept and nature of God

One of the skills that you practise when studying philosophy is that of defining or clarifying your terms – trying to be as clear as possible what you *mean* when you are talking about an idea, a concept and in general the thing that you are discussing. This is a difficult skill to develop for a number of reasons.

1 You are normally having to define terms that other people think are significant; so in a way these are second-hand ideas that you are expected to know and think of as 'important'.
2 These terms are generated by philosophers who are often talking about ideas and concepts which you may never have come across in your life before, possibly because these concepts are obscure, or remote from ordinary experience, or possibly because the philosophers have invented these terms themselves because they are trying to describe something new.
3 Dictionaries are not much use when it comes to defining philosophical terms. This is partly because people who compile dictionaries are not philosophers (and so do not know the technical way in which philosophers use words) but partly because philosophers are describing the world in new and different ways, to help them to understand the world. Writers of dictionaries, on the other hand, are just describing how the general population happen to use a term; they are not describing anything new at all.

There are several techniques that you can use to help you to define a term, many of which have been employed since the start of western philosophy by Plato. You can think of lots of examples which illustrate a concept, and try to spot what those examples all have in common. You could look at how philosophers have used the concept in the past, and pull together a definition based on where these different accounts overlap. You could identify some very specific conditions, or criteria or features, which distinguish this concept from other ideas. As a good philosopher you should indicate where people disagree about a concept (where it is a 'contested' term), as it is rare in philosophy that there is full agreement. Many of the activities in this textbook encourage you to practise these techniques, so that eventually you will be able to define your terms with clarity and useful illustrations.

The key metaphysical concept in the philosophy of religion is the concept of 'God' and this needs clarifying before you can begin to try to prove the existence of God, or ask questions about God's relationship with the world (such as why God allows such pain and suffering to exist). Being clear about what we mean by 'God' will help you to address these issues, or at least be clearer about why they are issues in the first place. We have seen that there are two approaches to investigating the nature of God. The first (called 'revealed theology') looks to the revelations of sacred texts and prophets for help in our understanding. The second (called 'natural theology') looks to human observation of the world, combined with reason and analysis, to aid our investigation of the concept of God. It is this second approach that is pursued by philosophers, although philosophers who also have faith will not want to lose sight of the first approach.

By adopting the natural theology approach, philosophers have described God in ways that help them to make sense of the world that God created, and make sense of God as a creator. Some of the key attributes of a God who created the world are that this being must have immense power (omnipotence); immense knowledge (omniscience); must be the source of values (supremely good); and must have an unusual relation with time (be eternal or everlasting). However, when philosophers have gone on to analyse these further concepts in more detail, even those thinkers who are devoutly religious, such as St Aquinas, have quickly realised that these attributes appear to be inconsistent and can lead to paradoxes when combined, or even incoherence if not properly defined. Three of the most important issues that arise when analysing God's attributes are as follows:

1. The paradox of the stone, which questions whether God has 'unlimited' omnipotence; for example, does God have the power to limit his own power?
2. The Euthyphro dilemma, first posed by Plato, which asks what it means to say that God is good; does it mean that literally anything God does is good, or does it mean there is an external standard of goodness which God conforms to?
3. Is the existence of an omniscient God who knows everything (including what you are about to do) compatible with the existence of human beings who have genuine free will (which means you can change what you are about to do)?

You may have found it frustrating that these dilemmas were not easily solved, or that God was not easily defined, or that we did not dismiss some of these ideas at the very beginning because they are obviously wrong, or contradictory, or perhaps even irrelevant (if you are a devout atheist). But unfortunately that is not how philosophy, or any form of careful thinking, works. As a philosopher-in-training you need to adopt a considered approach to defining and analysing terms, to addressing problems that arise internally within these terms, to resolving as best you can criticisms made against these terms. Through this considered approach you will arrive at something you can work with: providing a definition and clarity to a key concept that moves you forward in your thinking about the metaphysics of God.

1.2 Arguments relating to the existence of God

Revision of philosophical proofs

We have seen how philosophers have attempted to analyse *who* God is; now we turn to look at their attempts to prove *that* God is. As we are going to be looking in detail at three of the main arguments for God's existence (ONTOLOGICAL ARGUMENTS, TELEOLOGICAL ARGUMENTS and COSMOLOGICAL ARGUMENTS), it is worth revisiting some of the features of arguments that you hopefully examined in your first year of your Philosophy A-level.

Recalling how arguments are generally structured

You will now know, after a year or more of study, that when philosophers talk about arguments they are not referring to a quarrel, or some kind of personal battle of words involving a denial of everything the other person says, combined with gentle sarcasm and incisive put-downs. An argument, in the sense that philosophers are interested in, consists of one or more statements offered in support of a further concluding statement (you can see examples of these above on pages 6 and 14). The supporting statements, the ones that provide the justification, are referred to as the PREMISES of the argument, and the concluding statement is obviously referred to as the CONCLUSION. There are certain 'argument indicator' words which can help to identify arguments. Thus if a passage contains the words 'and so', 'therefore' or 'hence', then this is a good indication that a conclusion is being drawn and that an argument has been made to support the conclusion. The premises may need to be combined in order to support the conclusion, or they may support the conclusion individually. And the move made between the premise or premises and the conclusion is called an inference.

Premises
⇩ *Inference*
Conclusion

For example:

P1: The world appears well ordered
⇩ *Inference*
C: So, someone must have designed it

P1: The world cannot have appeared out of nothing
⇩ *Inference*
C: So, someone must have created it

Figure 1.8 All proofs or arguments have the same basic structure

The goal of an argument is to convince us of the truth of the conclusion, and so to persuade us to believe it. As the conclusion rests on the supporting premises it is essential that every premise in an argument be true. This means that when constructing, or evaluating, arguments we must pay careful attention to each premise. There are various types of premise which can combine to provide grounds to support the conclusion, for example:

- general observations (for example 'politicians have always done whatever it takes to keep themselves in power')
- statements of fact (for example 'there were only enough lifeboats on the *Titanic* to save half the passengers')
- theoretical assumptions (for example 'everything in the world has a purpose or function')
- definitions (for example 'God is a perfect being')
- HYPOTHETICAL STATEMENTS (for example 'if you eat carrots then you'll be able to see in the dark').

It is helpful to make the premises explicit when evaluating or constructing an argument, so that each one can then be weighed up and considered. As you can see from the Anthology extracts, arguments usually take the form of densely written prose, so you may have to tease out each premise. Many philosophers do this by assigning the premises numbers, and presenting them as a list. This is sometimes called presenting the argument 'formally' or in 'standard form'. Breaking down the arguments in this way can make them easier to understand and evaluate.

Revisiting the logical forms of arguments

> *Demonstration [of God's existence] can be made in two ways: One is through the cause, and is called a priori ... The other is through the effect, and is called a demonstration a posteriori.*[1]
> **Aquinas**

Deductive arguments

Valid arguments are known as deductive or 'deductively valid'. In a DEDUCTIVE ARGUMENT the truth of the premises guarantees the truth of the conclusion, so long as no errors have been made. The key word here is 'guarantee'. With a valid deductive argument, if we accept the premises to be true then we absolutely must accept the conclusion to be true. If, as we have claimed, the goal of an argument is to persuade people to believe its conclusion, then deductive arguments must be a powerful tool; after all, if we can guarantee the truth of a conclusion, we have good reason to believe it. However, this great strength can also appear as a weakness. For deductive arguments cannot establish anything new with their conclusions: they simply reveal what is already contained in the premises. For this reason, they don't really get us beyond what is already known. Another weakness is that, while we can know that the conclusion must follow if the premises are true, we still cannot guarantee that the premises actually are true. Knowing that the conclusion has to follow from the premises is all very well, but it simply passes the buck and we still have to find a way to establish the truth of the premises. To make clearer the strengths and weakness of such arguments, take the following example of a deductively valid argument (an example that has been the staple of dull philosophy books since time immemorial, or at least since Sextus Empiricus in 200CE[2]):

- **Premise 1:** All men are mortal.
- **Premise 2:** Socrates is a man.
- **Conclusion:** Therefore Socrates is mortal.

Here, if we accept the two premises, then the conclusion follows necessarily. The great strength of the argument is that it appears to be impossible to deny the conclusion once we've accepted that the premises are true. We might say that so long as we accept the premises to be true then we can work out the truth of this conclusion in an *A PRIORI* manner, in other words prior to any further experience or fact-finding, simply by teasing out what is implicit in what is already given in the premises. Everything can be done in our heads. However, this also means that we haven't really learnt anything new here. The conclusion says nothing more than was already contained in the premises. Moreover, while we know that Socrates must be mortal *if* he is a man, and *if* all men are mortal, we have still to find a way of establishing that these other facts are actually true. So deductive arguments appear to leave us with further questions to address.

Notice that what makes an argument deductive is the way the premises relate to the conclusion. Deductive arguments are structured in such a way that the truth of the premises is preserved into the conclusion. But this does not mean that the premises have to be true. Take this argument for example:

- **Premise 1:** All cows are green.
- **Premise 2:** Socrates is a cow.
- **Conclusion:** Therefore Socrates is green.

This argument has the same structure as the one we considered above. And so it too must be deductively valid even though the premises are false. This is because what makes it deductive is that the premises give complete support to the conclusion irrespective of whether they are actually true. In other words, if we were to accept that all cows are green and that Socrates is a cow, we would also have to accept that Socrates is green. In technical language, this argument is deductively valid, but unsound. A sound argument is one that has a valid deductive form *and* true premises.

Inductive arguments

INDUCTIVE ARGUMENTS are often contrasted with deductive ones because they strive to reveal something new in their conclusion. This is one of the strengths of such arguments since they promise to enable us to extend our knowledge. However, because this means they have to go beyond the information contained in their premises, they lose the power to guarantee the truth of their conclusions. This means that no inductive argument can be fully valid, and at best their conclusions are only ever probably true, even if the premises are certainly true. Typically, induction occurs where an argument moves from what is known (for example, facts about the past, or particular observations) to what is unknown (for example, speculations about the future, or generalisations). Induction is frequently used in the sciences and social sciences, whenever we move from empirical data to theories about the data. A typical inductive argument might be:

- **Premise 1:** Every raven I've ever seen has been black.
- **Premise 2:** There are ten ravens kept at the Tower of London.
- **Conclusion:** Therefore it is likely that all ten ravens in the Tower are black.

Even if we accept the premises as definitely true, this conclusion does not necessarily follow. This is because there might be whole families of London-born white ravens, which I don't know about, or it might be that for every ten black ravens in a population two of them will be white. Just because I have only ever seen black ravens doesn't establish that they must all be black. Note that, just as with deductive arguments, we still have to accept the premises as true before the argument can be at all convincing.

Another example of an inductive argument is one where we draw a conclusion from a finite set of instances:

1. John 'Stumpy' Pepys used to play drums for rock 'n' roll legends Spinal Tap but he died in mysterious circumstances.
2. Eric 'Stumpy Joe' Childs used to play drums for Spinal Tap but he too died in mysterious circumstances.
3. Peter 'James' Bond used to play drums for Spinal Tap but he eventually died in mysterious circumstances.
4. Mick Shrimpton now plays drums for Spinal Tap.
5. (Conclusion) So it is likely that Mick Shrimpton will one day die in mysterious circumstances.

Here we have observed that these drummers are all similar to each other in one respect (they were members of Spinal Tap), and concluded that the new drummer must be similar to the others in some further respect (he will die in mysterious circumstances). Of course, the conclusion does not follow necessarily from the premises. Mick Shrimpton may be different from the others; he may evade the Grim Reaper of Rock and live to a ripe old age. So, like other inductive arguments, this one cannot establish its conclusion with absolute certainty. Here the strength of the argument will depend on how strong the similarities are between each case of drumming tragedy.

So inductive arguments vary in strength. Here is an example of a rather weak inductive argument:

My team scored while I was in the toilet. So I'd better go to the toilet again – that way we're bound to score!

The fact that my team scored on one occasion when I was out of the room, does not provide good evidence for supposing that these two things will be correlated in the future. This sort of argument just looks like superstition. But if the evidence base is stronger, we may feel more confident about the likelihood of the conclusions we draw. For example:

Every time I leave my bicycle out in the rain, the chain rusts. So if I leave it out in the rain tonight, it's likely my chain will rust.

The strength of this argument depends on how often I have observed the rain–rust correlation, but if it has happened often, then I have good reason to suppose it will happen again. We will be looking later on at the strengths and weaknesses of a particular inductive argument when we come to assess certain versions of the design argument (see page 63).

Abductive arguments

ABDUCTIVE ARGUMENTS are a third type of reasoning you should recall from your Year 1 studies. Abduction is often described as inference to the best explanation. Abductive reasoning usually draws on an inductive understanding of the world, but is distinguished from induction, in part, because of the direction that your reasoning takes you (that is, the direction of the inference). For example:

- A deduction might have the form of: *If A, then B. A is true, so B must be true too*: If it rains on my house, my roof gets wet. It is raining on my house, therefore my roof is wet.
- Inductions too might move from A to B: In the past, when it has been sunny after rain, I have seen a rainbow. Today it has been sunny after rain, so I can expect to see a rainbow.
- In contrast, abductions generally move in the opposite direction from an effect (B) to a possible cause (A): Sherlock Holmes notices the pavements outside 221B Baker Street are wet, and after much pondering, chin-stroking and consideration of all the alternatives, he concludes that this is because it has been raining.

These three different directions are illustrated in Figure 1.9.

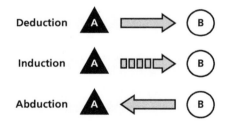

Figure 1.9 The direction of inference in three types of reasoning

Imagine you let yourself into your home. You go straight to the kitchen. No one is there, but you notice that:

- **B** The kettle is boiling.

Your mind immediately wonders what the best explanation for this might be. Did the kettle turn on by itself? Did the cat turn it on by accident? Was it a ghost? However, after brief consideration, you conclude that the best explanation is:

- **A** Someone has recently turned the kettle on.

Here your mind moves from an effect (the kettle being on) to a possible cause. Again, this method is used in science. In trying to understand the natural world, scientists come up with theories which account for or explain what we observe. Why does the Sun rise every morning? There are various possible explanations that have been put forward over time. The ancient Egyptians thought the Sun was a god reborn each morning who sailed his chariot across the sky. The ancient Greek astronomer, Ptolomy, thought the Sun was a fiery disc set in an invisible sphere which rotated around a stationary Earth. These days, most of us accept that the best explanation involves the claim that the Earth turns on its axis every 24 hours.

The key features of abductions are:

- The conclusion is never guaranteed, and an even better explanation is always a possibility.
- Abductions attempt to go from an effect or observation to a possible reason or cause.
- Abductions rely on our current beliefs concerning the way the world normally works.

Because it cannot guarantee the truth of its conclusion, abduction, like induction, is not deductively valid.

ACTIVITY

Read through the following arguments, asking yourself:
1. What is the conclusion of each one?
2. Is the conclusion true?
3. Are the premises (the reasons given for the conclusion) true?
4. Are the arguments inductive, deductive or abductive?
5. Which arguments do you think work, and which do not?
   a) I've split up with every person I've ever been out with, so the relationship I'm in at the moment is bound to end too.
   b) While on the loo, Paul hears a thudding sound near the front door. He concludes that the post has been delivered.
   c) If you don't believe in God you will go to hell. Stuart doesn't believe in God. So Stuart will go to hell.
   d) Philosophers spend much of their time sitting around and thinking, which means their muscles weaken, and so none of them are any good at strenuous exercise such as lifting weights.
   e) Paul says he had a vision of the Virgin Mary in his bedroom last night. Paul is known to be a trustworthy person and so it likely that the Virgin really did appear to him.
   f) It's wrong to kill innocent people. But babies are people too, even when they're in the womb. So it's wrong to have an abortion.
   g) The evil dictator denies he has any weapons of mass destruction. But we know from his denials in the past that he's a liar. So he must have them somewhere, and we should keep looking until we find them.
   h) Amy hears the fire school alarm go off during her maths class. She can't smell any smoke, so reckons it must be a test.
   i) If God exists then he would have created a world without suffering and evil. However, examples abound of terrible suffering and evil in the world. So God cannot exist.
   j) No England football team for the last 50 years has got through to the final of a major competition. So they will obviously fail in the next World Cup.

The strength of an argument's conclusion

As well as paying attention to the formal structure of the argument, we also need to consider the relative strengths of the conclusion. You might like to think of the list of premises as a mathematical sum that 'adds up', or fails to add up, to the conclusion. Different forms of argument (inductive, deductive and abductive) yield different strengths of conclusion. An invalid argument is one where the premises do not add up to the conclusion; in other words, the argument falls short of fully justifying the conclusion. This may be because the argument is flawed or because the argument is an inductive or abductive one – and with inductive or abductive arguments we might only assign the conclusion a varying degree of probability, not certainty.

In contrast, if the premises correctly add up to the conclusion – that is, if by accepting them we are forced to accept the conclusion – then the argument is termed 'valid'. Only deductive arguments can have validity, and where there is a valid deductive argument then this leads to the strongest possible conclusion. However, as with any human calculation, there is always the chance that mistakes have been made, and deductive arguments can be fallacious and go wrong in a wide variety of ways – meaning that the strength of their conclusion is undermined.

So the strength of an argument's conclusion depends on its foundations, its structure and its construction and when you are reading through the arguments for the existence of God you will need to consider all three of these:

1. The argument's foundations:
   - Highlight the main argument indicator words in the passage – indicators of premises, indictors of conclusions and indicators of the progression of the argument.
   - Does the argument have robust premises?
   - What types of premises does it rely on (for example, general observation, facts, assumptions, hypotheticals, intermediate conclusions)?
   - Is each premise true? What evidence is there for each of the premises?
   - Are there any hidden premises, which the philosopher is disguising, or hasn't thought about?
2. The argument's logical form/structure:
   - Is it a deductive argument, which aims for validity, thus guaranteeing the proof of its conclusion?
   - Is it an inductive argument, drawn from strong evidence or observation, thus persuading us of the proof of its conclusion?
   - Is it an abductive argument, looking at an end result and trying to work backwards to its probable cause?
3. The strength of the argument's conclusion:
   - Whatever the form or structure, does the argument commit a FALLACY?
   - If it is deductive then is the conclusion based on a *valid* argument (without flaws in its structure)?
   - If it is deductive then is the conclusion based on a *sound* argument (it has true premises and it is valid)?
   - If it is inductive then is the conclusion based on a *reliable* or *cogent* argument (are the premises true and do they give you good reason to believe in the conclusion)?
   - If it is abductive then is the conclusion the best possible explanation, or are there better alternative explanations?
   - Is the conclusion true?

This framework will come in handy when you are reading the extracts in the Anthology – consider them to be part of the 'argument' lens, which you use when you analyse these extracts.

In addition to the questions above (which can be asked of any argument) there is a further, more specific, question that needs to be asked about the arguments for the existence of God, namely:

- What is the nature of the God that is being assumed or defended by the argument?

This may seem like an odd question to ask – shouldn't the question be 'what is the nature of God that is concluded at the end of the argument', rather than assumed at the beginning? After all (you might think) philosophers should behave like scientists – neutral in relation to the direction that their research is taking them – and so they should start by exploring the reasons and evidence for God's existence/non-existence and see where that takes them. Socrates proposes in the *Republic* that 'we must go wherever the wind of the argument carries us'[3] or as Antony Flew (1923–2010) summarises this:

My whole life has been guided by the principle of Plato's Socrates: Follow the evidence, wherever it leads.[4]
Antony Flew

Flew famously changed his mind about his ATHEISM towards the end of his life, having followed the argument where it led, which for Flew was towards a form of DEISM. But Flew's conversion is a rare one. Many philosophers and many of their arguments you will study in this section begin with a particular conclusion already in mind (usually 'there is a God' or 'there isn't a God') and go about attempting to prove their own beliefs, or at least disprove their opponents' position. So perhaps arguments for or against the existence of God aren't really constructed in order to conclude something new. Instead they could be seen as a rationalisation of belief (providing reasons for some pre-existing belief), as a defence of belief (defending a particular set of beliefs, or undermining a critique made by its opponents) or as an exploration of faith (understanding more deeply what it means to have that set of beliefs).

We have already seen above (pages 3–5) that there is no single interpretation of God, and this is reflected in the proofs of God's existence: different arguments are constructed around different conceptions of God, and we need to ask ourselves, of each argument, what is the nature of God being assumed or defended here? Some of the arguments aim to demonstrate the existence of the 'God of the philosophers' (for example, Aquinas' cosmological arguments), while others aim to defend the existence of the 'God of Abraham' (for example, John Hick's soul-making defence against the problem of evil). Now let us turn first to the ontological proofs for the existence of God.

1.2.1 Ontological arguments

Features of ontological arguments

We can now turn to look at a specific type of proof of the existence of God known collectively as the ontological arguments. There are several different versions of this form of argument which we will examine, alongside various criticisms made of them from the time of St Anselm. We shall also look at modern perspectives on the arguments. But first we look at the key features of an ontological argument, referring to the technical terms outlined above.

- 'Ontology' comes from two ancient Greek words, *on* or *ontos* which means 'being', or 'that which exists', and *logos* which means 'the study of', or 'an account of'. So, ontological (which was the name given by Immanuel Kant to this cluster of related arguments) means 'a study of being' and describes arguments which focus on God's existence as a necessary being.
- Ontological arguments for God's existence are *deductive*, which means that if they are valid, and their premises are true, then the conclusion should follow necessarily. Such arguments, if successful, would clearly represent an incredible achievement for human reason, for they promise to establish God's existence with absolute certainty! However, before we can be certain that they succeed we need to be sure that the premises used in such arguments are true.
- But ontological arguments also claim that their premises are unassailable since they concern only *a priori* definitions and the analysis of concepts, and specifically the analysis of the concept 'God'. Unlike the other arguments for God's existence they do not rely on any empirical observations, or experience of the world. Because they have *a priori* foundations, and proceed deductively, an ontological argument should establish the existence of God with the same degree of certainty as is to be found in mathematics.
- This does mean that the conclusions of ontological arguments, particularly their conclusions about the nature of God, are limited. You have seen (page 32) that the conclusion of deductive argument adds nothing new to the premises, it just teases out, or reveals, or unpacks, what is already contained in the premises. So whatever the nature of God assumed in the premises of a deductive argument will be the nature of God confirmed as existing in the conclusion of the argument.

But how can an argument that proves the existence of something begin from premises that are knowable purely *a priori*? Surely we would need to begin with some experience of the world before we could establish the existence of anything. If we want to know whether there is a black panther living on Bodmin Moor then we examine eyewitness accounts, assess the video footage, carry out autopsies on the savaged lambs and perhaps even recruit thousands of foolhardy students to trawl across the barren hills searching for panther droppings and paw prints.[5] On the basis of the empirical data (the experiences) that we have gathered we then build up a case for, or against, the existence of the beast. So here the proof of the existence of the panther begins with evidence obtained A POSTERIORI. However, the ontological argument claims to be able to establish the existence of something (namely God) without needing to bother with any of this. It can be done completely independently of observation, evidence or experience. How could such a feat be accomplished?

Unpacking concepts

The ontological argument works by analysing the concept of God. This process of analysing a concept can be thought of metaphorically, as 'unpacking' the concept. In other words we must discover all the ideas that are essential elements of the concept. For example, Figure 1.10 illustrates how we might 'unpack' the concept of 'triangle'. We find it contains the following ideas: it is a shape with three sides, the sides are straight lines connecting to form angles, and those internal angles add up to the sum of two right angles.

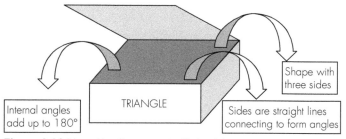

Figure 1.10 Unpacking the concept of 'triangle'

Experimenting with ideas

Unpack each of the following concepts into their component parts (the essential characteristics or ideas that make up each concept).

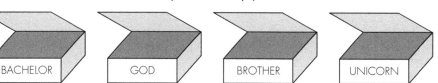

Let us now look at how we might unpack a statement about the world in order to reveal an *a priori* truth. Take the claim that Elvis' mother was female. Without knowing anything about Elvis, his mother or their stormy relationship, we can safely conclude that the claim is true. We do this through unpacking the essential elements of the key term 'Elvis' mother', as shown in Figure 1.11.

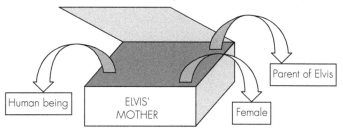

Figure 1.11 Unpacking the concept of Elvis' mother

Our analysis, or unpacking, reveals that 'Elvis' mother' is the human, female parent of Elvis. So we can now see the obvious truth that Elvis' female parent was female.

This statement has a structure similar to the structure of many other claims; for example, that 'terrorists are a threat to national security', or that 'love of money is the root of all evil'. To assist our analysis it is useful to identify two distinct parts of such statements (or PROPOSITIONS):

1. the SUBJECT (the thing the statement is about, for example, 'love of money')
2. the PREDICATE (the properties we are claiming that the subject has, for example, 'is the root of all evil').

ACTIVITY

For each of the following propositions, identify which part is the subject and which the predicate:

1. The Beast of Bodmin Moor is black.
2. Elvis' shoes were blue.
3. The actress loves Prince Harry.
4. Noah counted the animals two by two.
5. The cow jumped over the Moon.
6. Humans could fly too if only they could flap their arms fast enough.
7. God exists.
8. The Earth is about to enter another ice age.
9. Cain's brother was male.
10. This triangle's internal angles add up to 180 degrees.

Once we have identified the subject and the predicate we can then ask whether the claim is true. This usually means gathering empirical evidence. For example, we would need to see Elvis' shoes, or hear from someone who had, before we could determine whether they were blue. And we would need to observe the actress's behaviour in order to work out whether she really loves the prince and isn't just in it for his mother's fabulous jewellery. However, statements 9 and 10 are special cases, as they are both true by definition or ANALYTIC. With a little analysis the predicate (for example, 'was male') can be shown to be already contained in the subject (for example, Cain's male sibling). And saying 'this triangle's internal angles add up to 180 degrees' is very uninformative to people who know what a triangle is: they know it is true by definition. This means that it is possible to know that some propositions are true *a priori* and these do not need any further empirical investigation.

So, to return to the question, one way of justifying a claim *a priori* is to show it is true by definition through analysing the concepts used in the proposition; in other words, to show that the subject already contains within its meaning the property we're claiming that it possesses. With an ontological proof of God's existence a similar process takes place: by analysing, and fully understanding, what 'God' means, we shall see that the proposition 'God exists' is analytically true and hence that God must exist.

St Anselm's ontological argument

Why then has the fool said in his heart, There is no God (Psalm 14.1), since it is so evident, to a rational mind, that thou dost exist in the highest degree of all? Why, except that he is dull and a fool?

St Anselm, *Proslogion*, Chapter 3

St Anselm (1033–1109) is widely credited with inventing ontological arguments in his book the *Proslogion* (or *Proslogium*, meaning 'The Discourse'). He writes in the preface that he was searching for a single proof of God's existence, one that would not only demonstrate that God exists, but also reveal his existence as the supreme good, depending on nothing else. In the *Proslogion* St Anselm offered one famous version of this proof, which we look at below, although he may also have put forward a second proof (see below, page 52). Both proofs rely on the analysis of a particular definition of God; by fully understanding this definition we come to recognise that God must exist.

Although Anselm addresses his proof to God almost as a prayer, it may be easier for us to grasp if we present it in a standard philosophical form: with a list of numbered premises leading to a conclusion.

anthology 1.4

1 God is the greatest possible being (or as Anselm puts it 'that than which nothing greater can be conceived').[6]
2 Even a fool (someone who doesn't believe in God) can understand that God is the greatest possible being.
3 (From Psalms 14 and 53) The fool says there is no God in reality.
4 (From 2 and 3) The fool is convinced that God, the greatest possible being, exists only in his understanding (that is, in his mind) and not in reality.
5 It is greater to exist both in the understanding and in reality, than merely in the understanding.
6 (From 5) The greatest possible being, if it is genuinely the greatest, must exist both in the understanding and in reality.
7 (Conclusion from 1 and 6) Therefore God exists both in reality and in the understanding. Moreover (from 4 and 6), the fool really is a fool, as he is denying the existence of the greatest possible being, that is a being which must exist if it is genuinely the greatest!

Anselm's argument can be made clearer if we take out his passages about the fool. These passages are meant to show that the atheist is guilty of an absurdity; namely, believing that something that must exist (God) doesn't exist! However, Anselm's argument works just as well if we focus only on those parts that prove God exists (and leave out the parts that reveal the fool to be a fool). There are two crucial aspects to Anselm's argument: first his definition of God as the greatest possible being; second his assumption that existing in reality is greater than existing in the understanding or mind. From these two premises it becomes clear why St Anselm believes 'So truly, therefore, thou dost exist, O Lord, my God, for thou canst not be conceived not to exist' (*Proslogion* 3). We can present the essence of Anselm's argument in standard form thus:

1 God is the greatest possible being.
2 It is greater to exist in the understanding and in reality rather than in the understanding alone.
3 Therefore the greatest possible being, God, must exist in the understanding and in reality.

Experimenting with ideas

Who is the greatest? Have a look at the two different scenarios in Figure 1.12 on page 42.

There are two possibilities. Either God, the greatest possible being, exists only in our minds, or he exists in our minds and in reality as well.

1 Which scenario do you think is true? (Which universe do we live in?)
2 Which scenario do you think contains the greater being?
3 Are your answers to 1 and 2 the same? If they are different how can you account for the difference?

Scenario 1: The greatest possible being only exists in people's understanding.

Scenario 2: The greatest possible being exists in people's understanding and in reality.

Figure 1.12 Two possibilities

In scenario 1 people can imagine a powerful being, God, who has created and designed the world, who can perform miracles, who is the source of all morality, and who is omnipotent. Unfortunately, in this scenario, God exists only in people's imagination, and has not really created the world. Compare this with scenario 2 where people can also imagine such a powerful being, except in this scenario the being actually exists, and has in fact created and designed the world, performed a few miracles, and so on. The question St Anselm might ask is: which scenario has described the greater being: scenario 1 or 2? Atheists (Anselm's fools) allege we live in scenario 1, where the greatest possible being exists only in our imagination or understanding. But Anselm's point is that an imaginary greatest possible being cannot be the greatest, because it is possible to conceive of an even greater being, namely one which actually exists and so is actually able to perform miracles and create the world,[7] as in scenario 2. By comparing these two possibilities – a God who is imaginary and a God who really exists – we begin to understand that God, in order to be genuinely the greatest, must exist in reality. Another way of making the point is to consider that a God who didn't exist wouldn't be the greatest possible being, so to be genuinely the greatest he just has to exist.

The exercise above brings out some of the reasons why Anselm thinks it is greater to exist in reality than merely in the understanding. But here is another activity that might also bring out why Anselm's assumption is a plausible one.

Experimenting with ideas

Imagine your perfect partner.
1 Write down all the amazing qualities such a person would have.
2 Now suppose that there is someone, somewhere in the world, who corresponds to your fantasy. Would you rather go out with the real person, or with the purely imaginary one? Why? Why not?

If, in the exercise above, you decided that you'd rather go out with someone who has all the qualities of your perfect partner and actually exists in flesh and blood as well (rather than make do with a perfect but imaginary partner) then it may seem that you are agreeing with Anselm that it is better to exist in reality rather than simply in the mind.

We have seen that Anselm's ontological argument for God's existence springs from his concept of God. By analysing what 'God' means (the greatest possible being), Anselm comes to realise that he must exist, because he is the greatest, and that those who deny his existence don't really understand the kind of being he is. Some philosophers have argued that there is a second ontological proof within Anselm's writings, and we return to examine this below on page 52.

Experimenting with ideas

The philosopher Arthur Schopenhauer (1788–1860) referred to the ontological argument as a 'sleight of hand trick' and 'a charming joke', and the argument strikes many people as suspicious in some way. Have a look at each premise and each step in Anselm's argument: where, if anywhere, do you think the trickery lies in his argument? Try to formulate an objection to it.

What other things could you prove the existence of, using an argument like St Anselm's? Try the following format to prove the existence of whatever you like:

1 So-and-so is the greatest possible such-and-such.
2 It is greater to exist in reality and in the understanding.
3 Therefore so-and-so, if it is to be genuinely the greatest such-and-such, must exist.

Issues: Gaunilo's 'perfect island' objection

One of Anselm's contemporaries, the monk Gaunilo of Marmoutier (c.994–1083), suspected that something was amiss with Anselm's argument and rejected it in his work entitled 'On Behalf of the Fool'. Gaunilo believed in God, but objected to Anselm's move from 'understanding God to be the greatest possible being' to the conclusion that 'God must exist in reality'. Gaunilo argued that we can use this method to define anything we like into existence, so long as we claim it has the property of being the 'greatest' or 'most excellent'.[8] But clearly the real existence of such things is doubtful without further evidence. And if the logic of Anselm's argument is the same as with these other examples, then it too must be unsound.

anthology 1.5

> *For example: it is said somewhere in the ocean is an island ... And they say that this island has an inestimable wealth ... it is more excellent than all other countries ... Now if someone should tell me that there is such an island, I should easily understand his words ... But suppose that he went on to say ... 'since it is more excellent not to be in the understanding alone, but to exist both in the understanding and in reality, for this reason [the island] must exist'.*
> Gaunilo, 'On Behalf of the Fool', Section 6

Gaunilo uses his counter example of the perfect island to undermine Anselm's proof, and we can summarise it as follows:

1 We can imagine an island which is the most excellent island.
2 It is greater to exist in reality than merely in the understanding.
3 Therefore the most excellent island must exist in reality.

We can see Gaunilo structures his argument in the same way as Anselm's, but it leads to a questionable conclusion: there may be no such island. For Gaunilo, using an ontological argument to prove that a perfect island exists does not actually work, as the existence of the island is always going to be in doubt until we find real evidence for it. The fact that we can imagine such an island (and, as Anselm would say, it then exists in my understanding) has no bearing on whether the island does in fact exist. Instead, according to Gaunilo, we must demonstrate as a 'real and indubitable fact' the excellence and greatness of the island. The same doubts can be raised over Anselm's argument for the existence of God. The fact that we can conceive of the greatest possible being does not imply that it actually exists, and the fool is right to say he can conceive God as not existing. Gaunilo goes on to say that the fool would be right to demand that we must prove that God is in fact (and not just by definition) the greatest possible being.

Gaunilo attempted to undermine Anselm's ontological argument by using it to show that all manner of perfect things, including God, could exist, but they could easily be imagined not to exist. However, we shall see below that a twentieth-century philosopher, Norman Malcolm (1911–90), identifies a second version of Anselm's ontological argument, which if successful shows that Gaunilo's criticism fails. According to Malcolm, Anselm's second ontological proof aims to show that God is a necessary being, and so is different from perfect islands, perfect friends, perfect chocolate cake and so on. Because God is a necessary being, God (and only God) cannot be conceived of as not existing. So Norman Malcolm believes that Anselm has shown that the very nature and meaning of God entails that God must exist (see page 53 for Malcolm's analysis of this version of Anselm's proof).

ACTIVITY

Consider the proposition 'God exists'. (You may want to refer back to page 39.)

1. What is the subject of this proposition?
2. What is the predicate?
3. From Anselm's perspective, in what sense might you say the subject contains the predicate?

Because we do not know the essence of God, the proposition ['God exists'] is not self-evident to us.
Aquinas, *Summa Theologica* 1:2:1

Criticism

The theological genius of the Middle Ages, St Thomas Aquinas, rejected Anselm's proof in favour of his own five ways of proving of God's existence (see page 97).

Aquinas agreed that some things were self-evident, and could be known to be true *a priori*: for example, that 'man is an animal'. But in order to know these things we must be able to define both the subject (man) and the predicate (being an animal). However, humans have a limited intellect, and it is impossible for them to understand or define the nature of God. According to Aquinas, Anselm is overstepping the mark when he claims to know that God is the greatest possible being. Our minds cannot truly grasp what it means to call God this. Now, if the concept of God is not one that we can genuinely understand, then Anselm's argument cannot get off the ground. For if we cannot really grasp the idea of God in the first place, then we are hardly in a position to know what must or must not follow from that idea, so Anselm's ontological argument fails.[9]

Descartes' ontological argument

Perhaps because of the apparent success of Aquinas' cosmological proofs of God's existence, ontological arguments lay abandoned for several centuries. They were eventually revived by René Descartes (1596–1650). As you may remember, in his *Meditations on First Philosophy* Descartes sought certain and indubitable knowledge, and he began by subjecting all his beliefs about the world to extreme doubt (see pages 163–9 in our *Philosophy for A-level Year 1 and AS* textbook). He famously discovered that he could not doubt his own existence, but he wanted to go further than this in his search for knowledge. He believed that if he could prove the existence of God then this should provide the secure foundations for his beliefs about the world. However, because he did not trust his own senses, he would have to prove God's existence to be true *a priori*, and this meant using an ontological argument.

You will be familiar with Descartes' ontological proof from your study of his *Meditations* in your first year of the A-level. But we shall repeat our explanation of the proof here, in this new context, so that you can see how Descartes' proof compares to the ontological arguments put forward by other philosophers.

By *Meditation 5*, Descartes has argued that, with careful attention, his intellect can take any intelligible object and work out which features are essential to it – for example, a triangle having three sides and straight lines. He cannot conceive of a triangle without three sides, so it must be the case that having three sides is an essential feature of a triangle. Descartes claims that he is aware of such things clearly and distinctly, so they must be true. Once we are aware of the essential features of the triangle, he claims we are then able to deduce other features that also must be the case – such as Pythagoras' theorem. Descartes then takes this approach to the idea of God. It follows that any properties of God that he clearly and distinctly perceives to be part of his idea of God must really be part of God's essence.

ACTIVITY

Go back to pages 4–6 above and remind yourself of the attributes that the God of the philosophers was said to possess. Would you say that 'existence' should be included as one of his attributes?

So what is Descartes' idea of God? Well, it is the idea of a supremely perfect being. Now, one property that he perceives as belonging to God's nature is *existence*, and therefore God must exist. In general, understanding the essential feature of an object (say a triangle) does not tell you whether that object exists or not, and Descartes accepts this principle. However, Descartes claims that in the case of God things are different. Unlike the case of a triangle, God's existence cannot be distinguished from his essence. For if we try to subtract the property of existence from the idea of God, we take away something essential, much as to subtract the property of three sidedness from the idea of a triangle is to subtract something essential from it. Thus Descartes claims that he cannot think of God as not existing, just as he cannot think of highlands in a world with no lowlands. Descartes claims that the idea of a non-existent God would not be an idea of God at all, as a perfect being must have all perfections. Descartes elaborates why he believes that the very concept of God entails his existence. We do not know whether Descartes was familiar with Anselm's proof, but the one he constructed took a very similar form. As with Anselm's argument, Descartes' argument relies upon a particular definition of God, in this case that he is 'a supremely perfect being'.

The idea is that God is the supremely perfect being and a perfect being must be perfect in every way. This means he must be omnipotent (all-powerful), omniscient (all-knowing), all-good, all-loving, and so on. In other words, he must have all perfections. Now, Descartes claims, existence is itself a perfection. That is to say, as Anselm had argued centuries before, it is more perfect for something to exist than not to exist. And this means we must include it in the list of perfections possessed by God. And so it follows that God must exist. Put more formally, Descartes' argument would resemble something like this:

- **P1:** I have an idea of God, that is to say, an idea of a perfect being.
- **P2:** A perfect being must have all perfections.
- **P3:** Existence is a perfection.
- **C** (from P2 and P3): Therefore God exists.[10]

In his proof Descartes brings out what Anselm presupposes, namely that an ontological argument assumes that 'existence' is a predicate (or a property) that belongs to the concept of 'God'. By making this assumption both Descartes and Anselm are able to conclude that 'God exists' is true by definition, because the subject ('God', who contains all perfections) already contains the predicate ('exists', which is a perfection).

From the fact that I cannot conceive of God without existence, it follows that existence is inseparable from him, and hence that he really exists.
Descartes, *Meditation 5*

Descartes also agrees with Anselm (see page 53) on the type of existence God must have: God is a necessary being. Descartes argued that it is impossible to imagine God as not existing, just as he argues that it is impossible to imagine an uphill slope existing without a downhill slope, or imagine a triangle without its internal angles adding up to the sum of two right angles. God's existence is a part of his essence as the supremely perfect being. Because God is perfect his non-existence is impossible; in other words, God necessarily exists.

We shall now look at some of the criticisms that have been made of ontological arguments like Descartes' proof, most significantly those made by empiricists such as David Hume, and by Immanuel Kant (page 49 below).

In order to remind yourself of the empiricist approach to knowledge (in contrast with a rationalist approach), revisit the activity below, which you may have done in Year 1.

ACTIVITY

Consider the following list of ideas or concepts or beliefs, and answer the questions below.

1. The belief that two plus two makes four
2. The idea of the colour red
3. Your belief that parallel lines never meet
4. Your concept of beauty

5. Your belief that every event has a cause
6. Your idea of God
7. Your moral belief that killing innocent people is wrong

Where do you think that you, personally, got these ideas and beliefs from?

Where would a rationalist say you got the ideas/beliefs from? (Give specific examples for each one.)

Where would an empiricist say you got the ideas/beliefs from? (Give specific examples for each one.)

Issues: Empiricist objections to *a priori* arguments for God's existence

As you might guess, the ontological argument is the sort of metaphysical proof beloved by rationalists, but loathed by empiricists: it is based on *a priori* premises (empiricists smell a rat straight away), it proceeds by deduction (meaning that there is nothing new in the conclusion that wasn't already in the premises, so what's the point?) and it concludes with a firm and certain conclusion that God exists (except without offering up one single iota of evidence to an empiricist that God exists). At no point in the ontological argument are you required to leave your room, to look at the stars, or the starlings – but how on earth are you going to prove anything about the universe without going and investigating it?

As an empiricist David Hume (1711–76) was temperamentally opposed to the idea that we could acquire knowledge concerning what exists by the use of reason alone. If we are to establish whether there is a beast living on Bodmin Moor (see page 38 above) then we will have to make empirical enquires; in the same way, if we are to establish that there is a God, we can only do so by reference to our experience. Arguments that try to show that God's existence can be established *a priori*, therefore, must fail. To show this, Hume has a simple argument which he regards as 'entirely decisive':

There is an evident absurdity in pretending to demonstrate a matter of fact, or to prove it by any arguments a priori. Nothing is demonstrable, unless the contrary implies a contradiction. Nothing, that is distinctly conceivable, implies a contradiction. Whatever we conceive as existent, we can also conceive as non-existent. There is no being, therefore, whose non-existence implies a contradiction. Consequently there is no being, whose existence is demonstrable.[11]
Hume

There are echoes of Hume's argument in A.J. Ayer's criticism of the ontological argument written one hundred and fifty years later:

It is only a priori *propositions that are logically certain. But we cannot deduce the existence of a god from an* a priori *proposition. For we know that the reason why* a priori *propositions are certain is that they are tautologies. And from a set of tautologies nothing but a further tautology can be validly deduced. It follows that there is no possibility of demonstrating the existence of a god.*[12]
A.J. Ayer

Both Hume and Ayer (1910–89), who was strongly influenced by Hume, are empiricists who take issue with the ontological argument on similar grounds. Lying in the background behind their objections to the ontological argument is a distinction that is known as 'Hume's fork'. You may remember that according to Hume, all claims we can make must be of two kinds: either they are 'relations of ideas', or they are 'matters of fact'. You encountered Hume's fork at various points in your first year of the A-level, and may remember the key differences between the two 'prongs' of the fork.

- On the first prong of Hume's fork are 'matters of fact', which can only be determined from our experience of the world. These 'synthetic' statements are known to be true *a posteriori* and they can never be certain but are instead measured by how probable they are, or how much confidence we have in their truth (which is dependent on the evidence we have). Hume's example is that 'the Sun may rise tomorrow', which we can be pretty confident of; so although we can go to sleep free from anxiety about sunrise, it's a (remote) possibility that the Earth may stop spinning and you may wake up tomorrow in permanent darkness. One of the advantages of building arguments by using matters of fact is that our conclusions should tell us new information about the world – information that goes beyond what is already contained in the building blocks (the premises).
- On the second prong are 'relations of ideas' which are determined to be true, or false, simply through the analysis of the meanings of the terms involved. For most philosophers this means they can be known *a priori* – without any further reference to experience. Take Hume's example that 'three times five is equal to half of thirty'. This can be shown to be true without pouring out bags of Skittles and carefully counting these out (and then doing the same thing with Smarties and so on). Hume calls these types of truths 'demonstrable', meaning they can be shown to be certainly true. There is a test we can apply to statements to assess whether they are *a priori*, and hence whether they are certainly true. Hume's test is this: deny the statement and see whether you've ended up with a contradiction. We can apply this 'denial implies a contradiction' test to Hume's example above. If we say 'three times five is *not* equal to half of thirty' then we are saying '15 is not equal to 15' which is a contradiction, which means that the original proposition is *a priori*, and necessarily true (for more on this test see the section on the cosmological argument, page 125, and the corresponding activity on page 126). So, drawing on Hume, one of the indicators of a demonstrable truth is that its denial implies a contradiction.

Ayer's quote emphasises his own version of empiricism, and his own interpretation of Hume's fork. You may remember, from studying ethical language, how Ayer devised a verification principle, which divides meaningful statements into two: those that are tautologies (relations of ideas) and those that are empirically verifiable/falsifiable (matters of fact). An example of a tautology is the one given by Hume, that 'three times five is equal to half of thirty'. The truth of this statement is known *a priori*, and deductive arguments can be built up on the foundations of these *a priori* premises. The conclusions of valid deductive argument can be known with certainty. But Ayer points out that an argument based on *a priori* foundations – on tautologies – will only be able to draw a conclusion that is a further tautology.

So, drawing on Ayer, one of the shortcomings of an *a priori* argument is that it can't tell us anything new about the world, and it can't prove the existence of anything, God included.

How then do these ideas apply to the ontological argument? Well, an empiricist might say that the argument has been well and truly skewered by Hume's fork on one of these grounds:

- Following Ayer's train of thought, *if* the ontological argument is actually a demonstrable (*a priori*, deductively valid) argument then its conclusion tells us nothing new about the world, it only tells us about the definitions, and relations, of the ideas already contained within its premises. In which case the argument hasn't, and cannot, prove that God actually exists.
- Following Hume's train of thought, if the ontological argument is demonstrable (deductively valid) then its conclusion should have all the certainty of an *a priori* statement. But for Hume the conclusion 'God exists' fails the 'denial implies a contradiction' test. When you apply the test, the denial of the statement results in the statement 'God does not exist' and this statement isn't a contradiction. Which means that 'God exists' is not an *a priori* statement – yet it should be if it is the conclusion of a genuinely valid, deductive argument. In which case, once again, we have shown that the argument has not proved that God actually exists (as it is possible to conceive of a non-existent God without contradiction).

We shall see when we look at religious language that Ayer, who thinks he has shown that God's existence cannot be proved using an *a priori* argument, goes on to argue that God's existence cannot be proved using any empirical *a posteriori* argument either. This is because Ayer argues that 'God' is a metaphysical term and as such is meaningless (see below, page 163).

Issues: Kant's objections based on existence not being a predicate

In the eighteenth century Immanuel Kant (1724–1804) claimed to have conclusively refuted the type of argument put forward by Anselm and Descartes.[13] In his *Critique of Pure Reason* Kant coined the term 'ontological argument' to refer to this kind of proof and he offers two main objections to the argument.

Kant's first criticism is based on this claim: that it is possible to accept a proposition as true by definition (in other words to accept that the subject and predicate are inseparable) and yet to deny that there is anything in the world to which the subject refers.[14] For example, we might agree that the proposition that 'a unicorn has a horn' is true by definition; but, as Hume would have pointed out, it does not follow from this that there are any actual unicorns. Similarly, for Kant, Descartes' claim that 'God necessarily exists' may be a proposition that is true by definition, but it does not follow from this that there is an actual God. The most Descartes can claim is that 'if there is a God, then God necessarily exists'.

Descartes is free to define God however he likes, and it may well be that the proposition 'God exists' is true by definition. But that tells us only about the definition of the word 'God' and nothing about the existence of God in the world. Nothing in the definition can ever bridge the gap to tell us what must exist in reality.[15]

Kant, however, was not satisfied with this criticism and sought to destroy the most important assumption made by ontological arguments: namely the claim that existence can be a part of our definition of God. To do this he puts forward a second criticism to show that existence cannot be a property of God, because it is not a *property* at all.

'Existence' is obviously not a real predicate.[16]
Kant

Experimenting with ideas

To begin to see what Kant means by this, try the following exercise:
1 Imagine a piece of paper.
2 Picture it in detail in your head: what does it look like, where is it, what is it made of, how big is it? Write down a description of the paper, starting with the phrase 'The piece of paper I'm imagining is …'
3 Now add the following features to your image or picture of the paper:
   - It is splattered with chip grease and batter.
   - It is made of eye-catching lime green paper.
   - It says the words 'Congratulations, you've won a trip of a lifetime' at the top.
   - It is scrunched up in a gutter.
   - It exists.
4 Which of these further features changed your image of the paper?

In the activity above your initial description of the paper contained a number of predicates, to which we invited you to add some more. These additional predicates should have enriched your original idea of the paper: in other words, they have added to the concept by giving it new properties. However, what happens when you add the last feature and imagine the scrunched-up, greasy paper existing? Does this make any real difference to your idea?

Kant thinks not. He proposes that a genuine predicate is one that really does describe the thing we're talking about and so adds a descriptive property to it and enriches our concept of it. However, 'existence' does not do this. If I think of something as existing, the idea is the same as if I think of it as not existing. The properties it has are the same in both cases. This means that existence is not a property that a thing can either have or not have.

Kant makes his point by asking us to imagine 100 Thalers (or dollars), coins used as the currency of his day; we might think of them as gold, heavy, round, musty and old. According to Kant's rule, these are all genuine predicates as they all change our concept of the '100 Thalers'. However, if we now add 'existence' to our description then nothing changes: there is no difference between our idea of '100 coins' and of '100 coins that exist'. In contrast, if we add the words 'covered in pink anti-theft paint' to the description then our concept definitely changes.

The conclusion of Kant's second criticism is that 'existence' (unlike 'covered in pink anti-theft paint') is not a genuine predicate. If he is right, then ontological arguments must fail. They fail because it is essential to the ontological arguments of both Anselm and Descartes that 'existence' is a part of what we mean by 'God'. But, if 'existence' is not a predicate, then existence cannot belong to our definition of anything including 'God'.[17]

Russell's objection based on existence not being a predicate

The second criticism proposed by Kant anticipates a problem raised by philosophers of language in the first part of the twentieth century. Philosophers such as Gottlob Frege (1848–1925) and Bertrand Russell (1872–1970) thought that there was a real difference between the surface structure of language and the true logical structure that underlies it, and that we must be careful not to confuse the two. For example, on the grammatical surface a statement like 'Nothing matters' seems to have a straightforward subject–predicate structure. However, on closer inspection we find that the term 'nothing' doesn't name or refer to anything, and so is not a genuine subject. So sometimes what appears on the surface to be a subject (or a predicate), can be shown by further analysis not to be a genuine, logical subject (or predicate).

> *Existence quite definitely is not a predicate.*[18]
> Russell

The suggestion is that there is a similar deceit when it comes to the word 'exists'. 'Exists' seems to function as a normal predicate, appearing as a verb after a subject; so just as we can say that 'Bill laughs', 'Jesus saves' and 'the lion sleeps', we can also say 'God exists'. However, Frege and Russell would agree with Kant that 'exists' is not a genuine predicate, as it does not refer to any real property. Frege argued that 'exists' is really just a shorthand way of saying 'there is some object in the world that this concept refers to'; in other words to say that lions exist is to say that there are things in the world to which the concept of 'lion' corresponds. It is not to say that lions have a very special property known as existence.

Take another example. When we say 'A moon-jumping cow exists', we are not adding something new to our description of 'cow'. We are not saying 'A cow is a four-stomached ruminant which jumps over moons *and exists.*' All we are saying is that the description 'four-stomached ruminant which jumps over moons' identifies some object in the real world. Figure 1.13 represents how Russell might analyse the claim that 'The cow that jumped over the moon actually exists.'

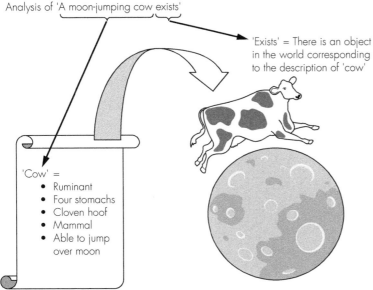

Figure 1.13 How Russell might illustrate the meaning of 'exists' in the statement 'A moon-jumping cow exists.'

Another way to see the point is to contrast propositions like 'All cows eat grass' with 'All cows exist'. While the predicate 'eat grass' tells us something meaningful about the habits of cows, the apparent predicate 'exist' seems oddly tautological. For obviously all the cows that there are must exist, otherwise they wouldn't be all the cows. Similarly, while 'Some cows are mad' makes perfect sense, 'Some cows exist' is odd. By using 'exists' as a real predicate this sentence implicitly contrasts cows which happen to exist, with those that do not. But we cannot properly describe some cows as existing, as though there were others that do not, because, of course, there are not any others. There just aren't any non-existent cows. These observations suggest that to say that something exists is not to describe it or to ascribe a special kind of property to it, but rather to say simply that there is such a thing in the world.

If Russell is correct then 'existence' is not a predicate, but simply a term that informs us that there is something in the world corresponding to a particular description. When we say 'God exists' we are simply saying 'There exists a being to which the word "God" refers' (see Figure 1.14).

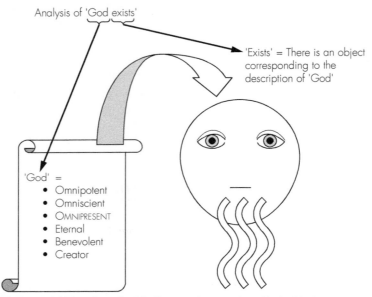

Figure 1.14 How Russell might illustrate the meaning of 'exists' in the statement 'God exists.'

Like Kant's, Russell's analysis of existence profoundly damages the ontological arguments of Descartes and Anselm. These sought to show that 'God exists' is true by definition because existence is a property and so part of the meaning of 'God'. But if existence cannot be a property of God, in order to show that the statement 'God exists' is true, we need to find something in the world corresponding to our description of 'God', and this means producing empirical evidence for such a being.

Norman Malcolm's ontological argument

In his 1960 article 'Anselm's Ontological Argument' the philosopher Norman Malcolm accepts that St Anselm's initial proof of God's existence in *Proslogion* 2 (page 40) is guilty of fallacious reasoning because it relies on the false premise that existence is a predicate. However, Malcolm argues that Anselm puts forward a second, stronger proof of God's existence which can be found in *Proslogion* 3, although he admits that there is no evidence that Anselm thought of these as two separate proofs.[19] Malcolm opens the article with the claim that:

> *I believe that in Anselm's* Proslogion *and* Responsio *editoris there are two different pieces of reasoning which he did not distinguish from one another, and that a good deal of light may be shed on the philosophical problem of 'the ontological argument' if we do distinguish them.*
> Malcolm

Malcolm argues that Anselm's second proof revolves around an extension to his definition of God, namely that he cannot be thought of as non-existent.

> *God cannot be conceived not to exist … That which can be conceived not to exist is not God.*
> St Anselm, *Proslogion* 3

To help us understand why Anselm makes this claim, let us once again compare two conceptions of God and ask which is the greater being: 1) a God who can be conceived of as not existing, or 2) a God who cannot be conceived of as not existing? To Anselm it is pretty clear that the second conception of God is greater: because God is the greatest possible being, it must be impossible to conceive of his non-existence. In fact the idea of a non-existent greatest possible being is a contradiction in terms, claims Anselm, and so only a fool could think that God existed only in his or her mind.

If successful, this second proof goes some way to defeating Gaunilo's 'perfect island' counter example. Gaunilo is right to say an island, or any other physical thing, can be imagined not to exist: for example, we can imagine the sea level rising, or volcanic activity making the island disappear. However, it is impossible to imagine the greatest possible being, God, as not existing: for if you could you would not be imagining the greatest being. The implication here is that there are two types of existences, or beings: those things that we can conceive of as not existing, and those things that we cannot conceive of as not existing.

In his analysis of Anselm's argument Malcolm employs two technical terms to distinguish between these two types of existence, although Anselm himself did not use these terms. Physical things, like islands, have a CONTINGENT existence; in other words they depend upon other physical things for their existence. This means that for any physical thing certain changes in the state of other physical things could mean it would no longer exist. Your existence depends, among other things, on the existence of your parents, and so it is conceivable, if they had not met, that you would never have been born. The existence of any island depends on the sea level of the water around it, and the tectonic plates supporting it. If these were to change then the island might cease to exist. In fact it is logically possible for any physical thing not to exist. Gaunilo's criticism makes the mistake of assuming that God's existence is like that of an island, that God is a being with a contingent existence.

However, for Malcolm the account of God given by Anselm reveals that God's existence is NECESSARY (we return to this in the section on the cosmological argument, pages 124–6). Because God is the greatest possible being he 'cannot be thought of as being brought into existence by anything or as depending for His continued existence on anything'.[20] This means that he would have to exist no matter what the world happened to be like and so no changes in the state of other things will have any impact on his existence.

Malcolm's account of Anselm's ontological proof adds a further layer of subtlety (or complexity) by introducing a 'modal' element to the argument. In the twentieth century philosophers and logicians used the term 'modal' to describe those statements which are *possibly* the case, those that are an *impossibility* and those that are *necessarily* the case. It is possible to imagine all sorts of ways in which the world could be different: you could have been born with different coloured hair, or slightly taller, or in a different town; you might have gone to a different school, or fallen in love with someone else, or chosen a different subject to do at A-level (I bet you're wishing you had) – these things are all logical possibilities. But there are other things that could not be different, no matter how we imagine the world: a bachelor can't be married, two plus two can't equal five, a square cannot be round (except in the world of Willy Wonka where the square sweets literally look round[21]) – these things are all logical impossibilities. Related to this are things which have to be the same, no matter how we imagine the world: a bachelor is unmarried, two plus two equals four, a square has right angled corners. Philosophers use the idea of possible worlds (see below, page 143) to convey the differences between these types of modal statements:

- A statement which is necessarily false, is false in all possible worlds.
- A statement which is contingently false, is false in some possible worlds.
- A statement which is contingently true, is true in some possible worlds.
- A statement which is necessarily true, is true in all possible worlds.

Malcolm reconstructs Anselm's second ontological proof, using these modal concepts above, by asking us to consider which category God's existence falls into (see Anthology extract 1.7). We can think about Malcolm's summary of the proof in the following way:

Consider four possibilities concerning God's existence:

1. God's existence is necessarily false – it is logically impossible for any being that has God's properties to exist.
2. God's existence is contingently false – it is possible that a being with the properties of God could exist, but it just so happens that there isn't such a being.
3. God's existence is contingently true – it is possible that a being with the properties of God could exist, and it just so happens that there is such a being.
4. God's existence is necessarily true – it is logically necessary that any being with the properties of God exists.

Malcolm argues that possibilities 2 and 3 simply cannot apply to a being like God. This is because God is the greatest possible being, and as such he must be unlimited, independent and eternal. However, 2 and 3 suggest that his existence is contingent; that is, limited by and dependent upon other factors. For Malcolm there is a crucial difference between an eternal being, and a being who just happens (contingently) to exist for ever: eternity is a quality of God whereas eternal duration is not. Malcolm argues that, because God is the greatest possible being, God's existence cannot be contingent, and thus the claim that 'God exists' cannot be contingently true (or contingently false).

This leaves either 1 or 4 as the remaining possibilities. Statements that fall under 1 are logically contradictory propositions, such as 'This square is round' or 'That bachelor is on his fifth marriage'. Malcolm argues that there is nothing logically contradictory about the claim that 'God exists'. This leaves 4 as the only remaining possibility: God's existence is necessarily true. For Malcolm this doesn't mean that 'existence' is a predicate of 'God'; instead it means that 'necessary existence' is a predicate of 'God'. Malcolm believes he has shown that because God is the greatest possible being he must be a necessary being, and therefore he must exist. If we wanted to offer a brief summary of Malcolm's argument it might look something like this:

- **P1:** God cannot come into existence.
- **P2:** So if God does not exist then his existence is logically impossible.
- **P3:** If God does exist then his existence is logically necessary.
- **P4:** Either God's existence is logically impossible or it is logically necessary.
- **P5:** God's existence is not logically impossible (because the concept of God is not self-contradictory).
- **P6:** Therefore God's existence is logically necessary.
- **C:** Therefore God exists.

ACTIVITY

Revisit Kant's second criticism of the ontological argument above (page 50).

Why would Malcolm claim that his modal version of the ontological argument avoids Kant's second criticism?

Criticism

John Hick (1922–2012) criticises modal ontological proofs like Malcolm's on the grounds that they confuse two different kinds of logical necessity.[22] Hick argues that we need to draw a distinction between logical necessity, and factual (or ontological) necessity. The first type – logical necessity – is a property that statements have of being true because of the meanings of the words which make up that statement. We have seen above, when looking at Hume and Ayer (page 47) that logical necessity applies to statements which are tautologies and true by definition, and which cannot be denied without contradiction. Hick argues that existential statements (such as 'unicorns exist' and 'God exists') cannot have this type of necessity because existence is not a property but instead, as Russell highlighted, the term 'exists' simply tells us whether a certain concept is instantiated in the world (whether there is an actual example of it in the world). The second type of necessity, which Hick calls ontological or factual necessity, is completely different from logical necessity. A being has the property of 'ontological necessity' if it exists independently and eternally, without being contingent on anything for its own existence. Hick argues that Malcolm and others have confused the ontological necessity of God (which Hick agrees is a valid insight) with the idea of logical necessity. This is how Malcolm's argument is flawed:

1. God's existence is either logically impossible or it is logically necessary.
2. God's existence is not logically impossible (because its denial is not a self-contradiction).
3. Therefore God exists as an *ontologically* necessary being.

But for Hick 3 does not follow, it is a leap to a completely different type of necessity. So while it is perfectly reasonable to accept that the concept of God is not logically impossible, it does not follow from this that a God exists which is ontologically necessary. For Hick the claim that there is a God which is ontologically necessary is a 'hypothesis'.[23] As Russell has already pointed out, if you define God as an ontologically necessary being you still have to go out into the world and find evidence that such a being exists.

Summary: Ontological arguments

Ontological proofs attempt to establish the existence of God in a purely *a priori* manner. They claim that it is possible to discover God by reasoned reflection on premises that make no reference to observation of the world around us. It's hard to overestimate quite how remarkable such a feat would be, if it could be pulled off. To establish that God exists with the same degree of certainty as we can establish the solution to a mathematical proof would surely be the greatest accomplishment of human reason. Atheism could be finally dismissed as an irrational and confused hypothesis that only a fool could sincerely entertain. However, we have also seen that there are serious objections to the various attempts to prove God's existence in this way, so that it is far from obvious that any is successful and the atheist, even if he or she cannot confidently identify the error, is likely to remain unconvinced. While detecting where precisely the sleight of hand lies is not easy, we still may have the impression that some trick has been played on us.

However, there is a different way of interpreting what ontological arguments are attempting to do. Rather than trying to establish the existence of God, they may be seen as an expression and exploration of what God means to the believer. To the reflective believer the argument reveals what God means, or who God is. Once you begin to understand God then you see that God's existence is of a different order from the existence of the rest of the universe. For the believer, God is a being unlike anything else because his existence stems from his own nature, and not from any external cause. God's existence, as Descartes has it, is part of his essence and is therefore 'necessary', which suggests it is unlimited, independent, without a cause, without a beginning and without an end.

In the end perhaps the twentieth-century philosopher, Karl Barth, has got it right when arguing that St Anselm's ontological argument should be read more as an exploration of faith than a proof of God's existence. Barth points out that Anselm's argument is framed at the beginning and the end as a prayer. As St Anselm says at the beginning of the *Proslogion*:

I do not seek to understand so that I may believe, but I believe in order to understand.
St Anselm, *Proslogion* 1

This seems to suggest that for Anselm philosophical analysis (in the form of his ontological argument) takes a back seat to faith. He does not use philosophy in order to prove to himself that God exists; instead he uses philosophy to help him explore and understand his own faith.

1.2.2 Teleological/design arguments

What could be more clear or obvious when we look up to the sky and contemplate the heavens, than that there is some divinity of superior intelligence?[24]
Cicero

I cannot see as plainly as others do, and as I should wish to do, evidence of design and beneficence on all sides of us. There seems to me too much misery in the world.[25]
Darwin

People with faith in God see the world very differently from the way atheists see the world. Believers might experience the beauty of a sunset as filled with the love and light of God; they look at the stars and see evidence of a divine intelligence; they see the hand of a designer at work in the stunning precision of the eye. But, for non-believers, stars, sunsets and eyeballs are not indications of a superior, supernatural intelligence; moreover their observations about the world point to the very opposite conclusion: that there is no God. Charles Darwin, in his letter to Asa Gray quoted above, gives as an example of 'misery in the world' the stomach-churning nesting instincts of the Ichneumon wasp. Rather than create a snug and cosy nursery for their babies, perhaps decorated with a few tasteful mobiles floating above the cot, these wasps inject their eggs directly into the living larvae of other insects, such as caterpillars; when the wasp larva hatches inside its host, it then eats its way out of the caterpillar.[26] Darwin writes, 'I cannot persuade myself that a beneficent and omnipotent God would have designedly created Ichneumonidae with the express intention of their feeding within the living bodies of caterpillars.'

ACTIVITY

Read through the following observations made about the world and answer the questions that follow.

1 The discovery by Mary Anning in 1811 of the fossilised skeleton of a dinosaur in the cliffs of Charmouth.
2 The massacres of thousands of men, women and children in churches throughout Rwanda between April and July 1994.
3 The overwhelming sensations of sublime beauty that eighteenth-century travellers experienced as they passed through the Alps from France to Italy.
4 The observation (made by Charles Darwin in Chapter 7 of *The Descent of Man*) that the brains of humans and of apes resemble one another in their fundamental character.
5 The invisible hand that wrote a terrible warning on the walls to King Belshazzar as he was feasting with all his nobles, wives and concubines in the sixth century BCE.
6 The measurement of 'redshift' in the light from distant galaxies by Edwin Hubble in 1929, which supported the conclusion that the universe was expanding from an original Big Bang.
7 The evidence published by William Ryan and Walter Pitman in 1998 that there had been a 'great flood' from the Mediterranean into the Black Sea circa 5600BCE – with water pouring across the landscape at 200 times the rate of the Niagara Falls.
8 The testimony by Professor Michael Behe under oath to a court of law in the United States that certain features of the world, such as the eye, are irreducibly complex and could not be the product of evolution.
9 The lifelong charity work of Mother Teresa throughout the last century, which helped thousands of the poorest people of the world to stay alive and die in relative peace.
10 The fact that the universe exists at all.

For each observation:
a) Does it support the claim that God exists?
b) If it does, how might an atheist account for this observation?
c) Does it support the claim that God doesn't exist?
d) If it does, how might a believer account for this observation?

Can we look to the world for proof of God's existence, or will our observations point towards the opposite conclusion, that there is no God? Later in the book, on pages 129–51, we examine claims that belief in God is incompatible with our experiences of the world: the horror, cruelty and suffering that are a daily occurrence among humans and every other creature. This PROBLEM OF EVIL (as it is called) suggests that there is no God (or that if there is, God is certainly not a being of supreme goodness and power). But in this section we look at the claim that the world does provide positive evidence for God's existence, on the grounds that the universe and everything in it seems to have been designed by a supernatural designer. This type of argument is known as the design argument.

Features of teleological arguments

Thou dost cause the grass to grow for the cattle, and plants for man to cultivate ... Thou hast made the moon to mark the seasons, the sun knows its time for setting.
Psalms 104: 14, 19

All things bright and beautiful, all creatures great and small. All things wise and wonderful, the Lord God made them all.[27]
Anglican hymn

To the writer of Psalm 104, and to millions of others throughout history who have looked up at their surroundings and marvelled at its wonder, the universe looks as if it has been deliberately made. From the features of earthly creatures, great and small, to the order and regularity of planetary motion, there seems to be every sign of a supernatural craftsman or artist at work – a designer, in fact, who 'made them all'. These types of arguments are known as design arguments or teleological arguments. They are probably the most commonly cited type of argument, as anyone who has ever talked to a door-to-door evangelist will know. In the words of Immanuel Kant:

This proof always deserves to be mentioned with respect. It is the oldest, the clearest, and the most accordant with the common reason of mankind.[28]
Immanuel Kant

Sometimes teleological arguments are referred to simply as 'arguments from design'. However, as Antony Flew and others have pointed out, the label 'argument from design' is an unhappy one.[29] The term 'from design' suggests that the conclusion (that the world has been designed) is already assumed in the premises, and hence there is hardly much argument that needs to be done. Flew proposes 'argument to design' as a better label for this cluster of arguments, and this phrase is certainly less of a mouthful than Kant's suggestion, which was to call these the PHYSICO-THEOLOGICAL ARGUMENTS (page 85 below). We will use the terms 'design arguments' and 'teleological arguments' interchangeably.

Design arguments are concerned with the specific details of the universe: why does the universe possess the particular qualities that it does and how can we best explain them?[30] These qualities include many puzzling features that scientists, philosophers and theologians have noted, including:

- the way that the parts of the world fit together and function as if, just like a machine, they have been designed in that way
- the way that living things appear constructed so as to suit their environment
- the regularity and order of the universe and its physical laws
- the fact that life developed in the world at all

Before we look at the different types of design arguments which account for these features, we should again revisit some of the technical terms that we examined at the start of section 1.2.

- 'Teleology' has its origins in ancient Greek thought. The word 'teleological' comes from the Greek *telos*, which means 'end' or 'goal', and *logos*, which means 'an account of' or 'study of'. Hence 'teleology' literally means 'the study of final ends' (something you may recall from your study of Aristotle). The term 'teleological' has also come to refer to the view that everything has a purpose and is aimed at some goal. So teleological arguments or design arguments draw on evidence that the world has been designed and has a purpose in order to conclude that there exists a being with the intelligence and skill capable of designing the world.
- Design arguments are *a posteriori*. Because teleological arguments are based on our experience of the universe they can be categorised as *a posteriori* proofs, in contrast to ontological arguments which are *a priori* (see page 339). The observations that form the basis of design arguments include specific observations about the way animals have been put together, the way they fit into their environments, as well as more general observations about how the Earth is so suitable for life, and how law-like the physical universe is.
- Design arguments come in a variety of formal structures: deductive, inductive and abductive. Some design arguments move from particular observations to general features about design, and then infer the existence of a designer whenever those features are observed; some use an analogy to conclude that there is a designer, others conclude that a designer is the best explanation for certain features of the world. For those design arguments which are not deductive they cannot conclusively prove the existence of God even if they are based on true premises. At best a non-deductive teleological argument can only show that God's existence is probable.
- In contrast to cosmological arguments (see page 92 below) design arguments offer more detail about the nature of the God they are attempting to prove. A being who designed the world must have certain attributes that are reflected in the sophistication and complexity of the world. So the attributes of a divine designer might include thought, wisdom, intelligence (mentioned by Hume), intention, artistry, skill, workmanship (mentioned by Paley), and power, rationality, incorporeality

and agency (mentioned by Swinburne). However, we shall see that for some philosophers, Hume included, other characteristics can be attributed to God on the basis of observations of the world, if those observations include the enormity of the pain and suffering of creatures in the world. For these philosophers our observations imply that any being who designed the world could not be all-powerful, nor all-knowing nor supremely good (we return to this problem of evil on page 129).

This section on teleological arguments is broadly divided into two halves. In the first half we examine three of the main design arguments:

- Design arguments from analogy (as put forward by Aquinas and Hume)
- William Paley's argument from spatial order and purpose
- Richard Swinburne's more modern argument from temporal order/regularlity

In the second half we look at general criticisms of design arguments, many of which originate with David Hume:

- Hume's objections to design arguments from analogy
- The problem of spatial order
- The problem of arguing from a unique case
- Whether God is the best or only explanation

We then finish the section off by revisiting some of Swinburne's responses to Hume's objections.

The design argument from analogy

The design argument as presented by Aquinas

Like many philosophical ideas we can trace the teleological argument back to Plato, who argues in the *Timaeus* that the world was created by a divine craftsman, or demiurge. But we start our investigation into the design argument fifteen hundred years after Plato, with the medieval theologian and philosopher St Thomas Aquinas. In his book, the *Summa Theologica*, Aquinas offers five ways in which God's existence can be demonstrated. The first three ways are all forms of cosmological argument (which we examine on pages 97–108);[31] the fourth way is an argument from morality, and in his fifth Aquinas offers a version of a design argument. It is an argument by analogy, in that it compares the natural world (the fact that it appears to have a purpose and goal) with human activity (which does have a purpose and a goal). The example Aquinas uses in his argument by analogy is that of an archer:

1. Things that lack intelligence, such as living organisms, have an end (a purpose).
2. Things that lack intelligence cannot move towards their end unless they are directed by someone with knowledge and intelligence.
3. For example, an arrow does not direct itself towards its target, but needs an archer to direct it.
4. Conclusion: Therefore (by analogy) there must be some intelligent being which directs all unintelligent natural things towards their end. This being we call God.

The key premise in Aquinas' argument is the claim that 'things that lack intelligence cannot move towards their end unless they are directed by someone with knowledge and intelligence'. However, this is a controversial premise in so far as it very nearly assumes what the argument is setting out to prove, namely that there is an intelligent being who created the universe. Yet we observe that most ducklings, acorns, embryos and so on grow and develop very successfully without any interference from an intelligent being. And so the claim that some intelligent hand must directly shape the natural world simply is not supported by our observations of it.

In the five hundred years after Aquinas the success of science changed the way people saw the universe. The traditional Aristotelian view of the universe, which placed the Earth at the centre surrounded by unchanging heavenly bodies, was undermined by the work of Copernicus (1473–1543) and Galileo (1564–1642). The new discoveries showed that the Earth was just one planet among many revolving around the Sun. Isaac Newton (1642–1727) claimed to have discovered the laws of motion that governed the movement of all objects, and the universe came to be viewed as a complex machine. Indeed European craftsmen started to build complex mechanical models of the universe (or orreries, page 82 below) for rich patrons throughout the eighteenth century. Some thinkers saw these breakthroughs as a threat to Christianity – indeed the new discoveries did undermine much traditional Church teaching – but other thinkers used the new science as evidence that the universe was a glorious work of divine craftsmanship. As well as breakthroughs in physics, new advances in biology were also taken as further evidence of God's handiwork. William Harvey (1578–1657) gave the first systematic description of the circulation and properties of the blood; Robert Hooke (1635–1703) used technological developments in lenses to see and describe a fly's eye and plant cells in his work *Micrographia*; Carl Linnaeus (1707–78) studied and analysed thousands of specimens of plants and animals, drawing connections between them, and attempting the first comprehensive taxonomy of the natural world.

So by the 1700s scientific descriptions at both a large-scale (the structures of the whole universe) and a small scale (the structures of human and plant life) pointed towards a world that was machine-like.

If the universe is machine-like then it needs a designer, just as an ordinary machine needs a designer. This analogy between the universe and a machine was the basis for a design argument put forward by David Hume. Before reading Hume's argument, try the next activity to get used to how arguments from analogy work.

Experimenting with ideas

Read through the following arguments from analogy and answer the questions below.

a) In many ways a dog is like a cat, for example they both are warm-blooded mammals. Dogs give birth to live young, therefore cats do too.

b) A dog is like a duck-billed platypus, in that they are both warm-blooded mammals. Dogs give birth to live young, therefore duck-billed platypuses do too.
c) Just as a curry is a more stimulating dish if it contains a variety of flavours, so a nation will be more stimulating if it contains a variety of cultures.
d) Just as a garden is more interesting if it contains a variety of flowers, so a public park will be more interesting if it contains a variety of plants and trees.
e) I have a mind, and a variety of mental states which cause my body to move and behave in certain ways (cry, laugh, kick footballs, write philosophy). I notice that Jeremy cries, laughs, kicks footballs, writes philosophy and so on, just like me. So, just like me, Jeremy's behaviours must be caused by mental states, and he must have a mind too.
f) I have a car which contained a defective airbag that exploded, nearly killing me. The model of my car is the UW Filosofi 2005. I notice that Jeremy has a UW Filosofi 2005 just like me. So, just like me, his car contains a defective airbag that might explode – and he needs to return it to UW, the manufacturer, immediately.
g) If you suddenly found yourself being used, against your will, as a life-support device for a famous violinist and knew it would last nine months, you would not have a moral obligation to keep the violinist alive. Similarly, if you suddenly found that you were pregnant, against your will, you would not have a moral obligation to see the pregnancy through to birth.
h) If you suddenly found yourself attached to a stranger who was acting as your life-support machine for nine months, and they are the only person who can keep you alive, then you have a right to be kept alive by that stranger. Similarly a foetus, while in the womb, has a right to be kept alive until birth by its mother.
i) A machine consists of parts that are finely adjusted in order to work together with complete accuracy, which is because a designer has deliberately made them that way. The world resembles a machine in that it too consists of parts that are finely adjusted to work together with complete accuracy. This suggests that (like a machine) a designer has deliberately made the world that way.

1 What words or phrases indicate that an argument uses an analogy?
2 Which of the above did you think were strong analogies, and which were weak?
3 What do you think makes an analogy a strong or successful one?

The design argument as presented by Hume

In David Hume's *Dialogues Concerning Natural Religion* published in 1779 we listen in on three fictional philosophers discussing the nature of God. The arguments are engaging, Hume's writing is free flowing, and (writing at a time when it was still dangerous to deny the existence of God) the dialogue format gives Hume an opportunity to explore his own scepticism about God by putting forward arguments (using the mouthpiece of another character) that undermine a belief in God. The three fictional characters created by Hume (see Figure 1.15) are:

- Philo (characterised by his 'careless scepticism')
- Cleanthes (characterised by his 'accurate philosophical turn')
- Demea (characterised by his 'inflexible orthodoxy').

Figure 1.15 Hume created three characters in his Dialogues – Demea, Philo and Cleanthes – which he used as a device to explore and critique a range of philosophical arguments about God.

Early on in the *Dialogues* Cleanthes puts forward an argument that is clearly recognisable as a design argument from analogy.

> Look round the world: contemplate the whole and every part of it: You will find it to be nothing but one great machine, subdivided into an infinite number of lesser machines, which again admit of subdivisions to a degree beyond what human senses and faculties can trace and explain. All these various machines, and even their most minute parts, are adjusted to each other with an accuracy which ravishes into admiration all men who have ever contemplated them. The curious adapting of means to ends, throughout all nature, resembles exactly, though it much exceeds, the productions of human contrivance; of human designs, thought, wisdom, and intelligence. Since, therefore, the effects resemble each other, we are led to infer, by all the rules of analogy, that the causes also resemble; and that the Author of Nature is somewhat similar to the mind of man, though possessed of much larger faculties, proportioned to the grandeur of the work which he has executed. By this argument a posteriori, and by this argument alone, do we prove at once the existence of a Deity, and his similarity to human mind and intelligence.
>
> Hume, *Dialogues Concerning Natural Religion Part II*

▶ ACTIVITY

Read the passage above and then refer to the framework for analysing arguments outlined on page 36 above.

1. Highlight the key argument indicator words in the passage.
2. Write down the main premises as a list, and then outline what type of premise it is (an observation, an assumption, a fact, an intermediate conclusion, etc.).
3. Look at the structure of the argument – is it deductive, inductive or abductive? How can you tell?
4. How do the premises 'add up' to the conclusion? Are there any hidden premises that need inserting to strengthen the argument?
5. Are the premises true, are they probable, are they evidence-based?
6. Finally, assess the strength of the conclusion. Is it valid (if it's a deductive argument)? Is it strong or reliable or probable (if it's not a deductive argument)?

Cleanthes is arguing that we can see the same effects in the world as we see in all manner of machines, namely that the parts are finely adjusted to fit each other and work towards some definite end or purpose. Moving through the analogy, Cleanthes' conclusion is that the cause of these effects must also be similar: just as the design of a machine is caused by human intelligence, so the design of the world is caused by divine intelligence – the existence of a deity. We can see that this argument is based on an analogy (between a machine and the world), and it moves backwards from observation of the effect (the machine/the world) to a conclusion about the cause (the designer/God). See Figure 1.16.

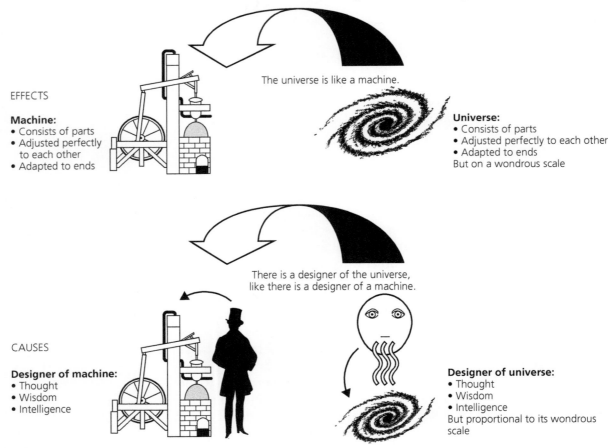

Figure 1.16 The analogy between a machine and the universe: we observe that the effects resemble each other, so the causes must resemble each other too

The conclusion of Cleanthes' argument goes beyond merely saying there is a deity; it also gives some details as to the nature or attributes that God (as designer of the universe) might have. The being who designed the universe is similar to the mind of humans (consisting of thought, wisdom and intelligence) but 'of much larger faculties, proportional to the grandeur of the work'.

As we mentioned when introducing Hume's argument from analogy, the format and structure of the *Dialogues* gave him the opportunity to explore both the argument (as put forward by Cleanthes) but also the many and various problems with this argument, as put forward by Demea and Philo. Hume was not convinced of the success of the design argument from analogy, and we look at criticisms of this type of argument below (pages 72–5) as well as at other general criticisms that Hume made of the design argument (on page 77, page 79 and page 84) which also apply to this argument from analogy.

Paley's argument from spatial order and purpose

Experimenting with ideas

In Figure 1.17 there are five boxes, each containing an object. Boxes 1–4 contain a wrist watch, a pebble, a honeycomb, a coin; box 5 contains an unknown object.

1 Which of the objects in boxes 1–4 would you say have been designed?
2 What do the designed objects have in common?
3 List all the things you would be looking for (some criteria for design) in the fifth object, in order to determine whether it had been designed.

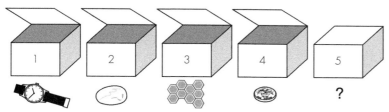

Figure 1.17 What's in the mystery box? How could we tell if it had been designed?

The Archdeacon of Carlisle, William Paley (1743–1805), put forward the most well-known design argument in his book *Natural Theology* (1802). Paley imagines himself walking across a heath and first coming across a stone, which he strikes with his foot, then finding a watch on the ground. The same question occurs to him on both occasions: 'How did that object come to be here?' In the case of the stone, for all Paley knows it may have lain there for ever. However, in the case of the watch such an answer is unsatisfactory: there is something about the presence of the watch on the heath that demands further explanation.

So, what is the difference between a watch and a stone in this case? Paley undertakes an examination of the watch which yields a very popular version of the teleological argument. What Paley actually notices at this examination of the watch is a variety of features indicating spatial order and purpose:

- It has several parts.
- The parts are framed and work together for a purpose.
- The parts have been made with specific material, appropriate to their action.

anthology 1.8

- Together the parts produce regulated motion.
- If the parts had been different in any way, such motion would not be produced.

In the activity above you might have found further features that indicate some sort of design in a watch, for example its aesthetic appearance, or its complexity. We might think of this list as Paley's criteria for (or indicators of) design, and if an object meets these criteria then Paley will take it as evidence that the object has been designed. For Paley the watch on the heath has all the evidence of what he terms 'contrivance'; that is, design, and where there is design or contrivance there must be a designer or 'contriver'.[32] He concludes that the watch must have had a maker.

▶ **ACTIVITY**

Draw a table like the one below.

1. Along the top row, write in your criteria for design, referring to either:
   a) the list you established in part 3 of the activity above, or
   b) the criteria Paley proposes.
2. For all the natural features listed, decide which criteria they meet.
3. Are there any natural features you can think of that do not meet any of the criteria?

	Criteria				
Natural features	1	2	3	4	5
A snake's eye					
A peacock's tail					
The changing of the seasons					
The 'flu virus					
The solar system					

Every indication of contrivance, every manifestation of design, which existed in the watch, exists in the works of nature.[33]
Paley

So Paley spends time at the start of *Natural Theology* examining this watch and going to great lengths to establish some criteria which can be used to determine whether something has been designed. It is only once Paley has established these foundations that he turns his attention to the natural world. He finds that all the indicators of design that we observed in the watch we can also observe in nature, except that the works of nature actually surpass any human design. This leads him to infer that nature must have a designer wondrous enough to have designed such a universe.

We can summarise Paley's argument in the following way:

1. A watch has certain complex features of spatial order and purpose (for example, it consists of parts, each of which has a function, and they work together for a specific purpose).

2 Anything which exhibits these features of spatial order and purpose must have been designed.
3 From 1 and 2: Therefore the watch has been designed by a designer.
4 The universe possesses features of spatial order and purpose, except on a far more wondrous scale.
5 From 4 and 2: Therefore the universe has been designed, except the designer of the universe must be a wondrous designer.
6 Therefore God exists.

William Paley takes great care in his *Natural Theology* (1809) to anticipate and respond to some of the criticisms that people might make of his design argument. It is not known for certain whether Paley had read Hume's *Dialogues Concerning Natural Religion* (which was published after Hume's death in 1779), but several of the criticisms that Paley anticipates do seem to address challenges that Hume raises. We turn to examine the main criticisms in the second half of this section, but let us deal here with Paley's response to the claim, made by Hume (page 84) that there are other explanations of spatial order and purpose in the universe.

Paley considers a cluster of criticisms that question whether the features of design that we find in the watch could be explained without reference to a designer. He considers, and dismisses, the claim that the watch might arise merely out of a 'possible combination of material forms', or out of a 'principle of order', or even a 'law of metallic nature'. Paley is here rejecting the possibility that the structure of the watch may have come together out of purely random processes, a hypothesis that Hume considers as the Epicurean hypothesis (see below, page 84). Paley is also rejecting the claim that the watch could have come together out of purely natural processes, and the reference to a 'law of metallic nature' seems to be a dig at people who invent spurious laws of nature which have no explanatory power (or perhaps a dig at Hume and his vegetative account of the universe, page 74). However, when we come to look at Darwin (see below, page 87) we shall see that, even if a law of nature cannot account for the coming together of the parts of a watch, it may be able to account for the coming together of the parts of an eye.

The possibility that the watch might not have been made by a watchmaker leads into Paley's second examination of the watch. Paley supposes that, upon this further investigation, it turns out that the watch is also some kind of watchmaking machine, capable of making other watches with all the same fine features that it has. This gives rise to the possibility that this watchmaking machine was itself made by a watchmaking machine, which in turn was made previously by a watchmaking machine, and so on. The issue for Paley is whether this possibility undermines his design argument, by showing that the watch did not need to be designed by a watchmaker, and similarly the universe (if it arose from previous iterations of the universe) did not need to be designed by God. But for Paley this simply defers the problem, because the watchmaking machine which made our watch on the heath still has the same features of contrivance; that is, ordered and regulated parts, framed for a purpose. For Paley, however far we go back in terms of watchmaking machines we still need to account for these features, which still indicates that there is a designer (Figure 1.18 on page 68).

Our going back ever so far, brings us no nearer to the least degree of satisfaction on the subject. Contrivance is still unaccounted for. We still want a contriver.[34]
Paley

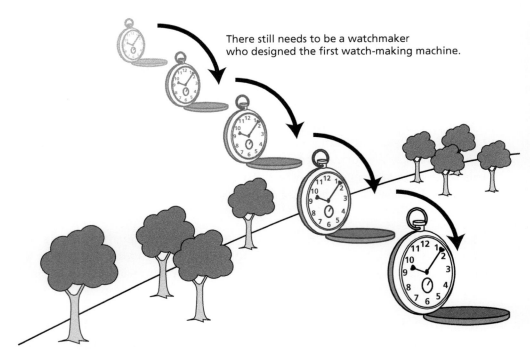

There still needs to be a watchmaker who designed the first watch-making machine.

Figure 1.18 The watch on the heath could have been made by a watchmaking machine. But this cannot go back for ever – there still needs to be a watchmaker who designed the first watch-making machine

Paley is here borrowing one of the features from the cosmological argument (below, page 116), namely the rejection of the possibility of an INFINITE REGRESS. We do not escape the need for a watchmaker just because we find that the watch could have been made by a watchmaking machine, which itself could have been made by a watchmaking machine. Paley is not rejecting the possibility of an infinite regress for the reasons that Aquinas' three ways (see page 97) or the Kalām arguments (see page 96) reject it (that is, because they consider it to be self-contradictory). Instead, Paley is rejecting it on practical grounds as it simply defers the question of 'Yes, but who designed *this*?' As Paley says, 'a chain, composed of an infinite number of links, can no more support itself than a chain composed of a finite number of links'.[35] Where there is contrivance there must eventually be found a contriver; where there is design there must be a designer.

Paley does consider the possibility that the question 'Who designed this?' could be done away with 'if nothing had been before us but an unorganised, unmechanised substance, without mark or indication of contrivance'. But for Paley this clearly isn't the case, as if it were then it would make no difference whether we found a stone or a watch. But it does make a difference, and the implication is that watches (and eyes and universes), unlike rocks, could not have come from unorganised, un-mechanised substances. The conclusion from the first examination of the watch is that there must be a designer of this watch. But the conclusion from the second examination of the watch, raising the possibility that it was made by a watchmaking machine, also yields the same conclusion: that there is a skilled designer. Paley thinks that the alternative (that there is no designer) is absurd, and this is the position of the atheist.

> **Criticism**
>
> We can amend Paley's analogy of the watchmaking machine being built by a watchmaking machine, to introduce the idea that each generation of watchmaking machines is able to produce a new generation which, through mechanical processes alone, is a slight improvement on the previous generation. Or, to put it another way, each preceding generation of watchmaking machines is slightly more primitive than the current generation. In this case we can imagine the possibility that this could go far enough back until there was a watch-generating mechanism that was so primitive that it perhaps could create the first proto-watchmaking machine through a 'metallic law of nature' alone. This rather far-fetched scenario (but perhaps no more outlandish than Paley's watchmaking machines) is analogous to how we now think eyes, and so on, have evolved.36 So Paley is vulnerable here to the discoveries and theories of modern science which believe they can trace the origin of sophisticated living creatures (which Paley thinks are designed) back to 'unorganised mechanised substances'. And in this case, as Paley himself acknowledges, the question of design does not arise.
>
> For more on how evolutionary theory undermines the design argument see the challenges raised by Darwin, below on page 87.

What is the logical form of Paley's argument?

Learn More

One traditional view (held for example by religious philosophers such as John Hick and Brian Davies) of Paley's watchmaker argument is that it is an argument from analogy. There is some merit in this view: we saw in the quotation above that Paley moves from a discussion about the watch on the heath to a discussion about the natural world. Paley believes that the indicators of design which he found in the watch are also in the works of nature, which calls to mind the very simple analogical argument given by Hume's character of Cleanthes.

> *I know no better method of introducing so large a subject, than that of comparing a single thing with a single thing; an eye, for example, with a telescope ... To some it may appear a difference sufficient to destroy all similitude between the eye and the telescope, that the one is a perceiving organ, the other an unperceiving instrument. The fact is that they are both instruments. And, as to the mechanism, at least as to mechanism being employed, and even as to the kind of it, this circumstance varies not the analogy at all.*
> Paley

However, recent readings of Paley suggest that his design argument is not an argument from analogy after all. Some philosophers, for example, Kenneth Himma (in his 2005 article on 'The application-conditions for design inferences') have suggested that Paley's argument is best read as a precursor to modern arguments to the best explanation, which have recently cited INTELLIGENT DESIGN, of the type Paley identifies, as evidence that God exists. Another contemporary religious scientist and philosopher, Del Ratzch (in his book *Nature, Design and Science*), has revived Paley's efforts to bring the supernatural (that is, God) back into our scientific understanding of design in the world. In this book, as well as his article on design arguments in the *Stanford Encyclopaedia of Philosophy* (an excellent free resource for students), Ratzch also claims that Paley's watchmaker argument is not an argument from analogy. For Ratzch, Paley's argument is to show that we all make the inference from seeing the watch to understanding that the watch has a designer, and this inference is based on particular features of design. Paley then goes on to show that we make the same inference when looking at the world, identifying those features, and realising that the world has been designed. The advantage of this reading, Ratzch points out, is that it avoids Hume's criticisms of arguments from analogy (see below, page 72).

The inference that Ratzch identifies is one that occurs at the start of the book. Paley, however, does go on to refer to specific analogies between nature and human 'tools of art' and 'instruments' throughout the rest of *Natural Theology*, as he examines all aspects of the natural world to demonstrate God's hand in its making. He may have had one (designed, not evolved!) eye on avoiding Hume's criticisms of the simplistic analogy between a watch and nature. But with his other eye he saw analogies between the human and natural world everywhere he looked. One of the pleasures, and frustrations, of reading philosophy before it became 'professionalised' (that is, before academics were paid by universities to research and write philosophy) is that our neat categories of arguments ('inductive', 'deductive', 'abductive', and so on) do not quite fit over the poetic, lyrical, rambling, sarcastic (in Hume's case) and literary arguments written by non-professional philosophers such as Paley.

Paley may have successfully avoided the problems (including problems of analogies) raised by Hume, and we shall look at these in the second half of this section when we turn to examine criticisms of the design argument. But the issue that is most damaging to Paley's argument is Darwin's theory of evolution, which accounts for all the marvellous natural phenomena that Paley observed, and yet also has more explanatory power than Paley's divine watchmaker. We return to this criticism below on page 87.

Swinburne's argument from temporal order/regularity

Richard Swinburne (1934–) revived the teleological project towards the end of the last century and put forward a design argument that he believed avoided the formal objections made by Hume in the *Dialogues* (pages 89–90 below). At the beginning of his paper, Swinburne outlines some clear parameters within which he thinks his argument succeeds.

First, he acknowledges that the design argument cannot prove the existence of an omnipotent, omniscient and wholly good being, nor can it prove the existence of the God of Abraham, Isaac and Jacob. Swinburne thinks instead that the design argument shows the existence of 'a very powerful, free, non-embodied rational agent' who is responsible for the order or regularity of the universe.[37] By moderating his conclusion in this way, Swinburne also hopes to have side-stepped Kant's criticism (below, page 86), namely that design arguments claim to show too much in their conclusion – they claim to have proved the existence of God (as understood by theologians).

Second, Swinburne concedes that his argument is an argument from analogy, and as such it is vulnerable to the criticism that the analogy between (order found in) human productions and (order found in) the universe may be considered by some people to be too weak to support the conclusion. As Swinburne's argument proceeds towards its conclusion he draws on elements of abductive arguments to show that the explanation he offers (that God is responsible for the order in the universe) is better than other explanations because it is a simple, unifying explanation.

Third, Swinburne thinks we need to make a distinction between two types of regularity or order. The first type of order is 'spatial order' (or regularities of *co-presence*), which is the arrangement of objects in space; the parts of Paley's watch are an example of this, as are the different parts of a human eye, or the arrangement of books in a library. The second type of order is 'temporal order' (or regularities of *succession*), which is the pattern of the way objects behave in time; a billiard ball being moved when it is hit, or a stone falling to the ground, or a friend arriving at your house because you have asked them round. This is an important distinction for Swinburne because he thinks that most well-known design arguments, Paley's in particular, rely on the first type of order (regularities of co-presence) to prove that God exists. This has made them vulnerable not only to Hume's criticisms, but also to Darwin's theory of evolution (below page 87), which Swinburne acknowledges had a devastating effect on the traditional design arguments. The theory of evolution explains natural 'regularities of co-presence' without any reference to God; for example, it explains how the parts of an eye evolved to work together with such efficiency and success.[38] So arguments like Paley's, which could not account for regularities of *co-presence* without reference to God, no longer succeed as evolution can now account for such regularities. Swinburne thinks that his revised argument, which is based on regularities of *succession* like Aquinas' proof (above, page 60), can avoid these criticisms.

Within these parameters Swinburne then proceeds with his argument:

anthology 1.9

1. Regularities of succession occur both as natural phenomena (as a result of natural laws) and as a result of free human action (for example, billiard balls moving and stones falling can be explained by natural laws; friends actually turning up to your house on time for once can be explained by the free action of humans).
2. Regularities of succession in the human world can be properly and fully explained by the rational choices of a free agent (for example, 'I said to my friend to turn up at seven, and she didn't want to be late, so she got her act together and rushed over on time').
3. This (point 2) is because free agents have the intelligence, power and freedom to bring about regularities of succession.
4. Regularities of succession that are the result of natural laws (for example, gravity) cannot be *explained* by reference to other natural laws.
5. However, by analogy with point 2, regularities of succession in the natural world can be fully explained by the rational choices of a free agent.
6. The universe, and its natural laws, is immense and complex.
7. Therefore (from points 5 and 3) regularities of succession in the natural world are best explained by a free agent who has the immense intelligence, power and freedom needed to bring about such order in the universe.

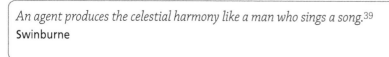

An agent produces the celestial harmony like a man who sings a song.[39]
Swinburne

There is one final supposition we should consider, which leads Swinburne to conclude that the powerful, rational agent who shapes the universe has a different physical status from us. We humans are free rational agents who control our own bodies, and it is through our bodies that we are able to act on the universe. Swinburne argues that an agent who could directly control the whole universe cannot have a body. So we should amend the conclusion (point 7) to acknowledge that the being who shapes the universe is disembodied; the amended conclusion reads thus:

7a Therefore (from points 5 and 3) regularities of succession in the natural world are best explained by a free agent who is disembodied and has the immense intelligence, power and freedom needed to bring about such order in the universe.

If Swinburne's conclusion is correct then this is a game-changing conclusion: even though his argument doesn't prove the existence of God (the God of the philosophers, or the God of Abraham), it demonstrates the existence of a being which even the most hardened atheist would have to admit comes pretty close to a description of a divine being, and if true this would leave atheism in tatters.

Having looked at three significant design arguments (from Hume, Paley and Swinburne), we shall now turn to look at the main issues raised against design arguments like these, many of them made by Hume in his *Dialogues Concerning Natural Religion*. These issues are:

- Hume's objections to the design argument from analogy
- the problem of spatial disorder (as posed by Hume and Paley)
- the failure of the design argument because it is an argument from a unique case
- whether God is the best or only explanation.

We return to look at Swinburne's response to these criticisms at the end of this section, on pages 89–90 below.

Issues: Hume's objections to design arguments from analogy

Hume was an empiricist, and believed that all our justifiable beliefs come from observation and experience: 'a wise man proportions his belief to the evidence' was his guiding principle.[40] Such a starting point is very close to the critical scepticism of Philo, and many commentators assume that Philo's position is also Hume's.[41] Cleanthes' argument relies heavily on the analogy between machines and the world, and Philo responds to Cleanthes' argument with a barrage of objections. In this section we focus only on those criticisms that Hume makes (through the voices of Demea and Philo, Figure 1.15 on page 63 above) of arguments from analogies – but these can be applied to Aquinas' and Swinburne's arguments as well as the one put forward by Cleanthes.

An argument from analogy claims that, because X is like Y in one (observed) respect, they are therefore probably alike in some other (hidden) respect. However, arguments like this are only reliable when the two things being compared have lots of relevant similarities. A reliable example of an argument from analogy (taken from the problem of other minds, see page 234 below) might be this: I notice that you and I behave in similar ways when we miss the nails we are hammering and hit our thumb; from this I infer that you and I have similar sensations following thumb-hammering incidents.

I conclude, by analogy with my own case, that when you smash your thumb with a hammer you feel pain. This conclusion seems justified even though it is impossible for me to feel your pain. It is justified because you and I are similar in at least one important way: we both share a similar human physiology.

Experimenting with ideas

The arguments in the activity above (pages 61–2) all relied on analogies. However, although two things might be similar in some respects, they might be very dissimilar in other respects.

1   Examine the table below. List the similarities and dissimilarities between each pair of things listed.
2   How might the dissimilarities you have listed damage the arguments on pages 61–2?

	Similarities	Dissimilarities
a) A dog and a cat		
b) A dog and a duck-billed platypus		
c) A curry and a nation		
d) A garden and a public park		
e) My behaviour caused by my mental states and your behaviour		
f) My car and your car		
g) Acting as a life-support machine for a violinist and carrying an unborn child		
h) Your right to be kept alive by using another person as a life-support machine and a foetus's right to be kept alive by its mother		
i) A machine and the universe		

You might have concluded from the activity above, that analogies work best (or only work at all) if the two things being compared really are alike, and the closer in likeness they are, the stronger the analogy. Moreover the two sides of the analogy must be alike in relevant ways – relevant to the conclusion being drawn. Take example b) from the activity above; it is true that a dog and a duck-billed platypus have many similarities: they can both be found in Australia, they are both mammals, they both have hair, they are both carnivores, they both like swimming and so on. But in one critical, relevant, way they are completely unalike – their reproductive system is different. If the conclusion of the analogy being drawn in b) aims to show that they both give birth to live young, then the argument has failed to give due attention to the relevant differences (in this case the reproductive system), as duck-billed platypuses lay eggs!

Returning to Hume, one of the main assumptions on which Cleanthes' teleological argument rests is that 'like effects have like causes';[42] that is, two things that are similar in their effects have similar causes. Cleanthes must make this assumption, and show genuine likeness, if he is successfully to conclude that the universe has a designer:

1   Machines and the universe exhibit similar features of design ('like effects').
2   Therefore they have both been designed by some intelligent being ('like causes').

Yet Cleanthes does not examine in detail how far the likeness of causes can extend, being happy to move swiftly to the conclusion that the designer of the universe is God. The question is: does a machine have enough relevant similarities with the universe to support the conclusion that they were both designed?

Hume (through the character of Philo) suggests that the universe is not like a machine, not even a vast and complex one. Hume argues that the universe resembles something more organic than mechanical; it is far more like an animal or vegetable than 'a watch or a knitting-loom'.[43] If so, the appearance of function and purpose among the parts of the universe is due more to 'generation or vegetation than to reason or design'. And since a vegetable does not have any designer; since its organisation appears to develop by some blind natural process, we have no reason to suppose that the universe is designed. Perhaps it simply grew! Now, it may seem rather absurd to compare the universe to a giant vegetable, but this is partly Hume's point: it is only as absurd as comparing the universe to a machine. For Hume there is nothing to choose between the world–machine analogy and the world–vegetable analogy: both are equally flawed comparisons. Flawed because, as we have noted, for an argument from analogy to be reliable the two things being compared need to be alike in all the relevant ways. Unfortunately in Cleanthes' teleological argument the two things being compared (a man-made object and the universe) are hardly like each other at all. Therefore Cleanthes cannot conclude, on the basis of the analogy with a machine, that the universe has a designer.

Experimenting with ideas

In the examples below, you know what the effects are, but you don't know what caused them. Think about how you might reason backwards from the effect to the cause.

Effect	Cause
a) A stylish and ergonomic wooden shelving unit	a) A five-year-old girl
b) Concentration camps	b) An unshaven and smelly carpenter
c) A simple metal ruler	c) A murderer and common thief
d) A classic racing car	d) An engineer working from his London garage
e) A miniature cottage made from small plastic building blocks	e) A power-hungry megalomaniac
f) A shoddy, badly made, wooden table	f) A team of world-class designers
g) One small piece of a quilt	g) A vegetarian who hates the sight of blood
h) A stunning sixteenth-century painting of Jesus being entombed	h) A 90-year-old woman
i) An efficient legal system	i) A smart and trendy carpenter

1 For each effect try to work out who created (or caused) it. We have connected one as an example.
2 What reasons can you give for each decision you've made?
3 What problems are there with reasoning backwards from effects to causes in this way? (Hint: G is a possible description of Adolf Hitler.)

Hume's criticism of the design argument from analogy continues with Philo seizing the idea of 'like causes' and gleefully running with it, bringing out some potential absurdities in comparing the universe with machines. He finds that by staying true to the analogy he arrives at possible causes of the universe that are nothing like a perfect, unique God. He makes the following points:

1. In most cases complex machines are the product of many years of trial and error, with each new generation of machine an improvement on its predecessors. If the universe is to be considered analogous with the way machines have been developed then 'many worlds might have been botched and bungled' (as Philo says) before this one was created. In other words this universe may be the product of trial and error, one in a long line of 'draft' universes, and may well be superseded by a better one in the future. This line of argument is fully in keeping with the analogy and suggests that the designer of the universe would be far from the perfect being that the argument is supposed to prove.
2. Complex machines are not usually the product of a single brilliant designer. Instead teams of people are involved in their design and construction. So, by the 'like causes' principle, the universe may also have been designed and created by many gods, not by a single deity.
3. Finally we can take the analogy to its extreme by fully 'anthropomorphising' the designers of the universe; that is, making them very similar to humans. For example, the designers and constructors of complex machines can be foolish and morally weak people. In the same way the gods who built the universe may well be foolish and morally weak. Humans involved in manufacture are both male and female, and reproduce in the usual fashion; so perhaps the deities are gendered and also engage in reproduction (like the gods of ancient Greece and Rome).

anthology 1.10

Issues: The problem of spatial disorder (as posed by Hume and Paley)

ACTIVITY
Read through the experiences of life on Earth and answer the questions below:
a) The unpredictable movement of the Earth's crust, causing earthquakes, volcanoes and destruction across the planet
b) The existence of certain wasps that lay their eggs inside living caterpillars
c) The way that sometimes your Wi-Fi doesn't work on a train
d) Quantum uncertainty, meaning that the more accurately we know the position of a sub-atomic particle, the less accurately do we know its momentum
e) The existence of meteors that randomly hit the Earth, including the one that wiped out the dinosaurs
f) The apparently unstoppable growth of certain abnormal cells in our bodies which invade other cells and lead to cancer
g) The complex, unpredictable, fluctuations in the temperature of the Pacific Ocean, leading to the El Niño weather system that can cause chaos and destruction around the globe
h) The fact that there's always one question in a Philosophy exam that no one was expecting[44]
i) The Ebola virus that kills 90 per cent of humans infected by it

j) The high probability that in a billion years' time the Earth will be inhospitable, and that in five billion years' time it will be wiped out as the Sun becomes a red giant and absorbs Earth, destroying everything on it
k) The free will of humans

Questions:

1 For each example, decide whether it is an indication of disorder or a fault in the workings of the universe.
2 What further examples of imperfections/disorder/faults in the universe can you think of? In what way are your examples signs of disorder?
3 Overall do you think the universe is a disordered or an ordered one? Why?
4 Can you imagine a more ordered universe with fewer flaws and faults? If 'yes' then go to 5. If 'no' then go to 6.
5 If there is a God why didn't he create that more ordered universe?
6 How might you persuade someone who held the opposite point of view that they were wrong? (See Flew's Invisible Gardener parable on page 168.)

The issue of disorder as raised by Hume

One of the many criticisms noted by Hume (through the character of Philo, in his *Dialogues*) concerns the issue of spatial disorder in the universe, in contrast to the spatial order that Cleanthes and Paley claim to observe. Philo says that for all we know this universe is full of faults and imperfections, compared to other more superior universes, and we have to admit the reality of the amount of 'evil and disorder' that there is in the world. Where there are design faults in a machine we usually infer that the designer lacked resources or skills, or simply did not care. The list of imperfections you compiled in the exercise may lend support to Philo's belief that the universe appears to contain too much disorder and too many design faults. It might be helpful to classify these possible faults and imperfections into two types. First there may be faults you identified in the smooth running of the mechanisms of the universe. Richard Swinburne, who we return to below, notes that:

anthology 1.11

Although the universe contains many striking regularities ... it also contains many examples of spatial disorder. The uniform distribution of the galactic clusters is a marvellous example of spatial order, but the arrangement of trees in an African jungle is a marvellous example of spatial disorder.[45]

Swinburne

We return to the issue of whether jungles are actually examples of order or disorder when we look at Antony Flew's parable of the invisible gardener below (page 168). Some less ambiguous examples of spatial disorder might include the erratic and uncertain behaviour of quantum particles, the instability of the Earth and of its solar system, and the unpredictability of beings, including examiners, in the universe (due to human free will!). But you may also have identified a second, more troubling, type of fault or imperfection in the universe, namely those that result in the extraordinary suffering of those creatures that live in the universe. In Book X (Ten) of the *Dialogues* both Demea and Philo respond to Cleanthes' overly optimistic view of the order and purpose in the universe. Demea lists in detail the pain and torments of the natural world.

> *The whole earth is cursed and polluted. A perpetual war is kindled amongst all living creatures. Necessity, hunger, want stimulate the strong and courageous; fear, anxiety, terror agitate the weak and infirm.*[46]
> Hume

Demea sets human beings aside from this suffering, while Philo firmly places human suffering alongside animal suffering as a permanent part of the universe. Philo addresses Cleanthes' optimism head-on: if there is purpose and intention in the natural world then what is the purpose and intention behind the misery of animals (including humans) struggling to survive and reproduce? Whatever positive experiences there are in nature are 'overbalanced by the opposite phenomena of still greater importance.'[47] Do these faults exist because the universe was created by a God who lacked the power, skill or love to create something better – or perhaps, Philo muses, it was created by an infant or a senile God (Figure 1.19).

Figure 1.19 Flaws and faults in the design indicate flaws and faults in the designer. The watch on the left is faulty … it was built by an infant human. The universe, according to Philo, is faulty … so was it built by an infant deity?

Taking into consideration these flaws and disorder, Philo says that the most reasonable conclusion of this argument is that the designer of the universe 'is entirely indifferent … and has no more regard to good above ill than to heat above cold or drought above moisture'.[48] This is a far cry from the all-loving God envisaged by Cleanthes and Paley, and Hume makes the same point in his *Enquiry Concerning Human Understanding*. Here Hume frames his religious scepticism inside a discussion about the Greek gods (to Hume this was a safe intellectual space for an analysis of religious ideas in general, within which he could avoid scandal and prosecution). He argues, again by the 'like causes' principle, that theologians are simply not justified in concluding that God is a perfect being because of the existence of such pain and suffering in the world. Hume thinks that instead of acknowledging this, theologians busy themselves in trying to 'save the honour' of their gods by showing why a perfect being would allow such unhappiness to exist.

The issue of disorder as raised by Paley

Paley anticipates the issues that critics (such as Hume) might raise about the apparent spatial disorder of the universe, namely that people might observe problems in the functioning of the watch; for example, an irregularity of movement, or simply a failure for it to work (after all the watch may have been lying on that particular heath for weeks before you discovered it). However, we would still be able to observe the details of the machinery, the cogs and gears, and all the qualities Paley outlined in his first examination of the watch.

For Paley it is not necessary that a machine be perfect in order to be designed; all that is important is that the machine exhibits some sort of purpose.

Paley argues that, whether or not the mechanism actually works, these qualities in themselves still lead us to the conclusion that the watch was designed. How might this apply by analogy to the universe? Many theologians and philosophers have wondered whether the universe may be considered flawed in its workings if there is an all-powerful, all-loving, good God who created it. The flaw that is highlighted most frequently is the pain and suffering that are endured by creatures in this world. So is this problem of 'evil' (as it is called) one of the ways in which the world has gone wrong? For Paley, following his line of reasoning above, even if it could be shown that the existence of pain and suffering were a flaw in the workings of the universe, it would not therefore follow that God did not exist.

The objections raised about the world's spatial disorder and faults, and which draw on the problem of evil, may not be fatal for a teleological argument. We shall see when we examine the problem of evil (pages 129–51 below) that the existence of God isn't necessarily incompatible with the presence of apparent design flaws (like unnecessary pain and suffering) in the universe. In that section we shall look at the many defences proposed by theologians which account for why such an apparent 'flaw' exists in a universe created by an omnipotent and benevolent God.

Issues: The failure of the design argument because it is an argument from a unique case

As an empiricist, Hume argues that the most reliable foundations for any of our beliefs are those based on observation and experience, and moreover those based on multiple observations and experiences. On the principle that 'like causes have like effects' we need to build up a large data bank of experiences so that we can recognise which effects/causes are alike and which causes/effects are not alike. By the time a child is ten she has seen in real life, on television and in films, numerous examples of glass things shattering when struck by hard objects (often stuntmen) – she has built up a rule of thumb that like causes (stuntmen hitting windows, glasses dropped on floors) have like effects (windows and glass shattering). But if a one-year-old has only seen a glass break once, then she won't know (and she might not even guess) that dropping a drinking glass on the floor might shatter it. She doesn't yet have enough information to work out that dropping the glass onto a hard floor will break it.

How does this relate to the design argument? Hume argues in his *Dialogues* that we don't have a large collection of experiences of universes (or things like universes) being made – in fact we don't have any experience at all of universes being made. So we have no experience of universe-like causes. And worse than that we only have *one* experience of the effect of universes being made – this universe – and worst still we only have experience of one tiny fraction of the universe, 'this narrow corner' as Hume puts it. In the final paragraphs of part II of Hume's *Dialogues*, Philo directly raises the issue that the universe is a unique and difficult case (see anthology extract 1.12 for the full passage):

anthology 1.12

> *When two species of objects have always been observed to be conjoined together, I can infer, by custom, the existence of one whenever I see the existence of the other. ... But how this argument can have place, where the objects are single, individual, without parallel, or specific resemblance, may be difficult to explain. [...] Have worlds been formed under your eye? And have you the leisure to observe the whole phenomenon [of world-making] from the first appearance of order to its final consummation?*[49]
> **Hume**

In order to understand Hume's criticism more fully it would be helpful to understand his theory of causation (a theory you will also need to be familiar with when looking at Hume's criticisms of the cosmological argument on page 120) and his idea of the 'constant conjunction' which underpins our beliefs.

Hume on causation and constant conjunction

Learn More

We are all aware of causes and effects. A cat's tail knocks a glass on a desk; the glass falls over. The cat has caused the water to spill. The water in turn causes the ink on the essay to run, and so on. Every minute we can witness multiple examples of causation all around us, but where does the concept come from? What would an empiricist say? At first sight it seems obvious. We can see that the cat has caused the water to spill. We can see the effect of the water on the ink. We observe the one thing causing the other and, like anything else, the concept of causation derives from sensation.

However, Hume points out that things are not as simple as we might suppose. Using his own example, let us consider observing one billiard ball approaching another, striking the second and the second moving off (we return to this example in the cosmological argument, below on page 121). Here it seems we have a clear case of observing one ball causing the other to move. So surely this must be the origin of our concept of causation? However, when we look more closely at this experience, it becomes clear that all we ever saw was one ball approach and come into contact with another; we heard a sound and saw the second move off; we never actually witnessed any sense datum corresponding to the cause. Imagine that all the time there were elaborate magnets under the table and that these moved the first ball up to the second, and then a separate magnet moved the second ball away, such that the first ball did not cause the second to move at all. Would this look any different? The answer must be no; but if there is no difference between the first and the second case, then we must conclude that indeed a cause is not something we actually experience in the sense impressions themselves, as the sense impressions may be the same with a completely different cause or even if there were no cause at all.

So it seems that the concept of cause is not drawn from the senses. So where does it come from? Hume claims that we tend to use the word 'cause' to link together experiences that frequently occur together. In other words, we notice patterns that repeat themselves and come to regard them as governed by causal laws. This is something that our minds do automatically for us. Imagine you clap your hands and a split second later you hear thunder in the distance. You would probably think nothing of it. Imagine the same thing happens again a minute later. Again, you would put it down to coincidence. But imagine the same thing happens a third, fourth, fifth and sixth time. Eventually you would begin to suppose that your clapping was causing the thunder. But this supposition cannot be based simply on the sense impressions involved for there is nothing different about the first clap compared with the sixth. The only difference is in the repetition, the constant joining together (what Hume calls 'conjunction'), of the two events. By the sixth clap your experience of the event feels very different; it now starts to feel like a causal event.

Thus Hume suggests that what we mean and experience as cause and effect is really just the *constant conjunction* of events. The feeling of one event inevitably following the other is the result of repetition, and is little more than custom or habit. For Hume, our idea of 'causation' stems from this feeling of anticipation that arises in our minds when we come to expect one event to follow another, because it has done in the past. In this way he is able, true to his empiricist convictions, to trace the source of our concept of cause back to experience: in this case, not an experience of something external to us, but the internal feeling of expectation we develop that one event will follow another.

Figure 1.20 If every time you clapped your hands you heard a thunder clap, it wouldn't be long before you developed the conviction that the one was the cause of the other. According to Hume, the feeling of anticipation you would have of an imminent thunder clap whenever you clapped your hands is the source of our ordinary idea of causation

▶ ACTIVITY

Read through the following situations (with their causes and effects) and answer the questions below:

A	**Part 1** Two people are carrying a very large sheet of glass across a road at the bottom of a steep hill. A car, escaping from the police, travels at great speed down the hill towards the glass (**cause**) and the glass explodes and shatters on the road (**effect**).
	Part 2 Several years later you find, by the side of a completely different road, a large amount of shattered glass. *The glass by the side of the road was shattered because ....*

B	**Part 1** 'Hurricane' Higgins is playing snooker against Ronnie 'The Rocket' Sullivan and a white ball hits a red ball (**cause**) and the red ball rolls gently into the corner pocket (**effect**).
	Part 2 Several years later, in a bar on the other side of the world, you want to play snooker with a friend and search for the white ball and find it at the bottom of the corner pocket. *The ball was at the bottom of the corner pocket because* ….
C	**Part 1** After the First World War, Raymond Unwin argued that Londoners living in its Victorian slums needed to be re-housed, and he designed homes for them (**cause**), thousands of which were built (**effect**) on an estate in Downham, and all around the outskirts of London.
	Part 2 One hundred years later you are with your dad driving through Dagenham, on the outskirts of East London, looking for the birth place of two of the greatest England football managers ever (Sir Alf Ramsey and Terry Venables). You see a number of houses, which are about a hundred years old, on Valence Street. *The houses on Valence Street were built because* ….
D	**Part 1** You once went to a factory on a school trip to see how cars were designed and manufactured. You watched the car designers at work (**cause**) and then went to the factory floor to see the cars being assembled (**effect**), which was an amazing feat of engineering.
	Part 2 You look around you at the universe, at the trees and plants, at the eyes of your cat, at the tiny fingers of your little baby cousin, and at the stars and planets. *The universe is like this because* ….

a) For each example would you say that you have had a large enough number of experiences to believe that the effect was directly brought about by the cause (what Hume would call 'constant conjunction')?
b) Is your experience of the effects enough for you to be able to infer what the cause is? If so, you should be able to complete the part 2 sentences.
c) For each situation above how many more, and what, examples of constant conjunction would you need to experience to be more confident (confident enough even to say 'This is what caused it') when inferring the cause of part 2?

Let us return now to see how Hume's analysis applies to the teleological argument. The claim made by Cleanthes (among others) is that the features of order, regularity and purpose in the universe lead us to infer that the universe has been designed. The effect is regularity and order in the universe, and the cause is the designer of the universe. The question raised by Hume's analysis of causation, is this: 'Have we built up enough experience to be able to infer securely from our experience that the universe has been designed?' In the cases above we have built up enough examples to infer, in future, that a ball is moving because it was hit, or a glass has shattered because it has been struck – these effects and causes are constantly conjoined in our minds. We might be wrong of course (perhaps the ball is being moved by a magnet, perhaps the glass was shattered by an opera singer), but without multiple experiences of a particular cause and effect no inference is even possible.

The same is true for objects that appear to have been designed. We can only recognise that certain sorts of things, such as houses, have an intelligent designer because we have had direct or indirect experience of houses being designed and manufactured. So it is by observation of the way in which houses, for example, come into being in our world that we learn that they require a designer. But if we had never had any experience of manufacture, engineering or design, then we could never infer that an object such as a house had been designed (just as the one-year-old might never infer that dropping a glass onto a concrete floor might break it).

For Hume the inference that two things are causally connected (e.g. inferring from the regularity and order in an object that the object has a designer) must be based on experience. But more than this, the experience must be both relevant and multiple – an irrelevant experience, or just a single experience, will not suffice. As Philo says, experiencing cities being designed is not relevant enough to make any inference about whether the universe is designed; any inference about the design of the universe must be based on experiences of other universes being designed. Worse still for supporters of the design argument, if this universe is unique, without parallel, then multiple experiences of universe-design are not even possible. So if our universe is unique we cannot make any inference about what, if anything, caused it to have regularity and order.[50]

Defence by Paley

anthology 1.13

Paley, anticipating criticisms such as this one, thinks that it does not matter if we have never seen a watch being made, and have no understanding of how it is manufactured. Paley asks 'Does one man in a million know how oval frames are turned?'[51] Since the answer is doubtless 'no', then how is it we nonetheless are certain that they have been designed? His answer is that there are certain intrinsic features possessed by certain objects which show that they are designed.

For example, in 1902 divers recovered a piece of bronze from the bottom of the Mediterranean Sea near the Greek island of Antikythera. This was no ordinary piece of bronze though, as it carried with it gears, dials, inscriptions and cogs. The so-called Antikythera mechanism puzzled scientists and historians alike, but, in the manner of Paley's abandoned watch, the assumption made of this mysterious piece of ancient craftsmanship was that it was designed for a purpose. Through a process of reverse engineering, scientists have come up with several competing models accounting for the gears and cogs, the most plausible being that the mechanism was an orrery: a working model of the solar system (Figure 1.21) based on the highly sophisticated computational methods used in Babylonian astronomy.

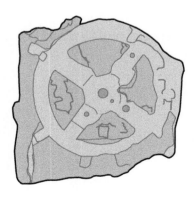

Existing fragment of the Antikythera

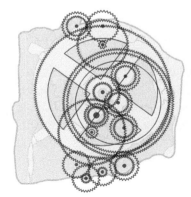

Reverse engineered orrery built from the Antikythera fragment

Figure 1.21 Reverse engineering to determine the function of the Antikythera mechanism

So, even though no one had witnessed the Antikythera mechanism being constructed – it is sort of a 'unique case' – the people who analysed it concluded that it had been designed and built. In the anthology extract 1.13 Paley may be attempting to deflect Hume's criticism that we have no experience of worlds and hence cannot draw any conclusions from the basis of a world to how that world may have come about. For Paley, even though we are ignorant of the design process, it is still legitimate to infer the existence of a designer from mysterious objects that exhibit all the characteristics of design.[52]

▶ **ACTIVITY**

Read carefully through Anthology extract 1.13. Imagine we say to Paley: 'you can't conclude that the watch on the heath has a maker if you've never seen a watch being made'. What other reasons does Paley think we might give to undermine his conclusion? Why does Paley think these reasons don't weaken his conclusion at all?

Hume's point cuts deeper than this though. It is indeed possible, as Paley says, for us successfully to infer that some unfamiliar object has been designed. But this is only because we can compare it to other manufactured objects that we have previously encountered, so the Antikythera mechanism, and other one-off objects like it, aren't really 'unique cases'. If we had absolutely no experience, direct or indirect, of the manufacturing process, then the object would remain a mystery to us. Yet we have no experience at all of the process that causes universes to come into being, as the universe is unique and there is nothing we can compare it to. The only experiences we have of the universe are of its separate parts, and these parts on their own cannot tell us about the origin of the whole. As Philo says, 'from observing the growth of a hair, can we learn anything concerning the generation of a man?'.[53] On grounds of Hume's empiricism, because we have no experience of this universe being designed, and because we cannot compare it to other universes that have been designed, then we have insufficient reason for concluding that God or anyone else has designed it, and the design argument fails.

Issues: Whether God is the best or only explanation

Design arguments proceed from observations of the natural universe (which may or may not be like a machine, or may or may not have certain features of design) to a conclusion that the best explanation for these phenomena is the existence of God. But over the past three hundred years philosophers and scientists have given alternative (non-supernatural) accounts and explanations of these phenomena which may be better explanations than the God hypothesis. Below we look at a number of these alternative explanations (which account for natural, spatial and temporal order, without reference to God) as suggested by Hume, Kant and Darwin. But first you should think about what makes one explanation *better* than another explanation.

Experimenting with ideas

1 For each of the following observations, decide whether a), b) or c) is the best explanation for what was seen:
   1.1 Ilham has been all around the world, studying thousands of birds, but he has never seen a white raven. This is because:
      a) All ravens are in fact black.

b) All ravens are in fact black up until the year 2025, after which they might become any colour of the rainbow.
   c) All ravens that Ilham is about to see quickly change their colour, like chameleons, so that they appear black to him.
1.2 People in Cadiz harbour see the masts of ships disappear as they move away from port towards the horizon. This is because:
   a) The human eye is limited in its range: it can only see up to 29 miles in the distance.
   b) The Earth is round.
   c) The masts don't actually disappear. It's the heavy mists in the air above the Atlantic Ocean around the coast of Spain that makes them seem to disappear.
1.3 Hayley found a rock on a heath, and brought it home as an ornament. But she found it interfered with the smartphone that it was placed next to. This is because:
   a) The rock is a magical stone, out to take vengeance on humanity for its destruction of Mother Earth.
   b) The rock is a lodestone, and has strong electro-magnetic fields that interfere with other magnetic fields such as those in smartphones.
   c) It was sheer coincidence that the smartphone broke soon after the rock was put next to it: there is no connection between the two events.
1.4 Blaine needs to throw six 6s in a dice game in order to win. He picks up the dice and rolls exactly six 6s. This is because:
   a) Blaine is a cheat and switched the ordinary dice for loaded dice when it came to his turn.
   b) It is entirely possible to roll six 6s purely by chance, and that's just what happened here.
   c) Blaine is naturally lucky: good fortune has shone on him throughout his life, and this is just another example of his good luck.
1.5 Hudson watches a cuckoo lay an egg in the nest of a robin. The cuckoo chick hatches and shifts itself around until all the robin eggs have fallen out of the nest. Eventually only the cuckoo is left, and the robin spends all day foraging for food to feed this parasitic bird. This is because:
   a) The cuckoo egg was laid in the robin's nest by accident, and when it hatched it moved around too vigorously, which unfortunately knocked the robin eggs out of the nest.
   b) God designed cuckoos as parasitic birds in order to destroy the eggs and chicks of unsuspecting robins.
   c) Cuckoos have evolved behaviour over millions of years which exploits the maternal instincts in other bird species like robins.

2 Explain why you have made your choices.
3 Make a list of all the things that make an explanation strong.

The appearance of design may be explained by random processes (Hume)

We have already seen above (page 74) that Hume suggests that there is no need to posit the existence of God to explain the fabric of the world, and that a better explanation is 'generation or vegetation'. David Hume, again through the character of Philo, suggests another alternative to the claim that the universe, with its appearance of purpose and order, must have had a designer. Hume argues that it is at least possible that the universe is ordered and life-supporting as a result of chance and not intelligence.[54] This theory is often referred to as the Epicurean hypothesis, after the ancient

Greek philosopher Epicurus (341–270BCE) who proposed that the universe exists in the way it does as a result of the random movements of a finite number of atoms. Over an infinite period of time these atoms will take every possible position, some of them ordered, some of them chaotic. It just so happens that the physical universe is currently in a state of order, and that, by chance, conscious beings have evolved that are capable of reflecting on the universe and why it is here. Philo argues that, although this may be a remote possibility, it cannot be disregarded as a plausible explanation for the so-called design in the universe.

anthology 1.14

Hume himself might take issue with Philo's proposal – we do not have enough experience to conclude that God is the best explanation for this universe, and the same is true of the Epicurean hypothesis. As a fairly radical empiricist Hume would be sceptical about any abductive argument that attempts to explain this universe.

Experimenting with ideas

A long time ago in a universe far away there lived the Yahoos, a species of self-conscious, carbon-based alien life forms. At a certain point in their intellectual evolution the Yahoos began to ponder the mysteries of the universe, where it came from and why they were here. Some of them argued that the universe was purposeful, with each part contriving to enable the evolution of the Yahoos themselves. The Yahoos believed that such a finely adjusted universe, which had resulted in the existence of Yahoos, clearly required an explanation.

1. Which explanation best accounts for the existence of the Yahoos:
   a) a teleological explanation, relying on the guiding intelligence of God; or
   b) an 'Epicurean' explanation, relying on blind chance?
2. Are there any other explanations that might account for the existence of the Yahoos?
3. Are the Yahoos justified in their belief that the universe has been perfectly adjusted so that they might come into existence? Why/why not?

The appearance of design may be explained by a 'worldly architect' rather than by God (Kant)

Immanuel Kant, in his *Critique of Pure Reason*, examines and names three of the most important arguments for the existence of God. The names of two of these proofs are now familiar to students of the philosophy of religion – the 'ontological' and the 'cosmological' arguments – while the name he gave to the third argument didn't really take off: the 'physico-theological' argument, or the design argument. Kant is extremely sympathetic to design arguments, stating that they should be treated with respect (in contrast, perhaps, to Hume's treatment of them). We owe these arguments respect, says Kant, because they are the oldest and clearest proofs, and are the ones that most strike a chord with the way we think about the world.

For Kant the physico-teleological argument works as an *a posteriori* argument, based on clear evidence of order in the world; order that could not have just come about by itself, but which must be the product of a sublime and wise cause beyond the world.

Kant's criticism 1

There are several issues with this design argument that Kant briefly considers, then passes over, possibly because he thinks that he has found a decisive flaw that renders the argument inadequate as a proof of God's existence. Kant does not think we need to criticise too strictly the analogy between the natural world and the world of human artefacts. Nor does he think that we need to question whether the design argument actually shows that the designer of the world really does have an understanding and a will (a conclusion that its defenders wish to draw, but which Kant thinks they may not be entitled to draw). The real issue that Kant finds within the design argument is that its conclusion is not enough to prove the existence of God in the way that its supporters want.

If we are to be careful in our use of the argument from analogy then Kant thinks we are only justified in actually specifying a cause which the argument merits. Yet the design argument does not do this, but instead it draws a conclusion which it is not justified in making. When we look closely at the world of human artefacts (such as houses, ships and watches) then we are entitled to conclude that those artefacts have properties which indicate that they were designed by architects, shipbuilders and watchmakers. However, the architects and builders did not create these houses and ships from nothing; they used materials that already existed.

What Kant seems to be saying here is that in the first part of the design argument ('evidence of design in the watch implies a watchmaker') we only conclude that the maker designed and put together the *form* or structure of the watch; we do not actually conclude that they also created the material (the metal, glass and leather strap) that the product was made from. When we transfer this argument, by analogy, to the universe, we are only entitled to conclude that there is a worldly architect. We are not entitled to draw from the analogy the conclusion that the designer of the universe also created the materials with which they built the world. In other words the fact that there is order and harmony in the universe does not lead to the conclusion that there is a creator of the universe, but can lead only to the 'existence of a cause proportioned to' this evidence, namely to the existence of a worldly architect.[55]

▲ **Figure 1.22** William Blake, *The Ancient of Days*, 1794. For Kant, the design argument can only demonstrate the existence of a designer (not a creator) of the universe

Kant's criticism 2

The 'lofty purpose', as Kant puts it, of the design argument is to prove two things: that there is a being who created the universe and that being contains all perfections. We have just seen that Kant thinks the argument shows at most that there is an architect of the universe, not a creator. But does the argument show anything about this architect's qualities (that they are omnipotent, omniscient, wholly good and so on)? Again, for Kant, the argument cannot stretch that far. The argument works by our imagining the qualities needed for a human watchmaker to construct a watch, then amplifying them until they are of sufficient magnitude to account for the design of the universe. Which means that the worldly architect must have great power, great skills, great knowledge and so on …? But, Kant says, we cannot conclude from the argument that the worldly architect has the perfect, infinite qualities normally ascribed to God: omnipotence, omniscience, supreme goodness. This is the problem, Kant thinks, as you cannot move from evidence in the world (for example, that the world has uncanny regularity, order and so on) to the conclusion that God is perfect. This last step to perfection, which is the most crucial step, cannot be taken purely on the basis of observation:

To advance to absolute totality by the empirical road is utterly impossible.[56]
Kant, Critique of Pure Reason, page 522

Although Kant was a devout Christian, he was also a rigorous and disciplined philosophical thinker, and he believed that God was a being who lay beyond the limits of our intellect and our experience. Kant thought it was not, then, possible to prove God's existence through *theoretical* arguments such as the ones explored here. However, Kant did think it was possible to show that there were strong *practical* reasons for believing in God, even if these reasons did not amount to a formal proof or demonstration. The practical reasons that Kant gave are that only God can give meaning to our moral actions. (We explore this 'moral' argument in another of our books.[57])

The appearance of design may be explained by the natural processes of evolution (Darwin and Dawkins)

Design arguments such as Paley's, based on the 'spatial order' of organisms in the natural world, were faced with a potentially fatal blow when the biologist Charles Darwin's work on natural selection was published.

Darwin (1809–82) had first proposed the theory of evolution by natural selection in his book *On the Origin of Species* (1859). He argued that there is 'natural selection' for characteristics that enable an organism to survive. In turn this means more offspring that share these advantageous characteristics, which themselves have more offspring, and therefore the characteristics, over a number of generations, become more common throughout the species. Hence a species becomes more adapted to its environment (followers of Darwin are often referred to as adaptationists).

For example, in Victorian London, light-coloured peppered moths were replaced by dark-coloured peppered moths as pollution got worse. This was because lighter moths were easier for predators to see and catch (see Figure 1.23). However, as London became less polluted in the early twentieth century, darker moths became easier for predators to catch, and the moth population eventually became predominantly lighter-coloured once again. This on-going natural selection means a species is continually adapted to its environment, and gives rise to the appearance of design.

Figure 1.23 As the environment changes so does the frequency of light/dark-coloured moths

Much of the persuasive power of an argument like Paley's lay in examples of design taken from the natural world: it seemed obvious that the intricacy of a human eye and the beauty of a peacock's tail could not have come about by chance; they must have been designed. However, Darwin's research and publications provided an account of how such perfectly adapted features could and did come about, not by intelligent design, but by the struggle of every generation of species to compete, survive and reproduce.

The old argument from design in nature, as given by Paley ... fails now that the law of natural selection has been discovered. We can no longer argue that, for instance, the beautiful hinge of a bivalve shell must have been made by an intelligent being, like the hinge of a door by man. There seems to be no more design in the variability of organic beings ... than in the course which the wind blows.[58]
Darwin

Darwin's revolutionary account of the evolutionary origins of apparent design in the natural world has been advanced in recent years by the work of the evolutionary biologist Richard Dawkins (1941–). His contribution to the debate began with his most important work, *The Selfish Gene* (1976). In this book Dawkins argued that the central unit of evolutionary selection is the gene.

Dawkins argued that natural selection works at a genetic level (not at the level of groups of organisms, or the physical traits of individual organisms) by showing how genes 'out-replicate' each other. So, in the case of the peppered moths, above, the gene (or rather the allele) for light-coloured wings was widespread in the population until the industrial revolution caused the trees on which the moths rested to become darkened with soot. Moths carrying the light-coloured-wing gene (allele) were eaten before they had a chance to reproduce, while moths carrying the dark-coloured-wing gene survived and replicated this gene in the next generation, and so on until the majority of peppered moths had the gene for dark wings.

So, a crucial task for an adaptationist is to examine the features that organisms have, and through 'reverse engineering' try to work out what benefit they must have been to the species. Reverse engineering is a term used to refer to the practice of working backwards from an unknown object, such as one that's been found on an archaeological site (page 82 above), to try to establish the origins and purpose of the object. So the critical question that an adaptationist has to ask herself when looking at an organism is: How does this feature (for example, dark-coloured wings) benefit the gene(s) which gave rise to it? Or to put it shortly: 'What is its survival value?'[59]

There is a complication, in that an organism not only needs to survive but it also needs to have offspring for its genes to be replicated: so the choice of sexual partner that individuals make works as part of natural selection, determining the number of offspring an organism has, and hence how widespread a feature becomes in a population. Features such as a peacock's tail, which appear to be a severe hindrance to a peacock fleeing from a swift-moving predator, spread through the population because they are advertisements of the peacock's strengths: 'I'm tough enough to survive even though I have this ridiculous and cumbersome tail, so mate with me.' Features that promote success in reproduction, as well as ones that promote survival, eventually appear throughout a population. Every feature of the universe cited by Paley as evidence of design can be explained by evolutionary theory. Moreover, evolutionary theory can explain why, on islands, there are unique adaptations which don't appear anywhere else in the world: because evolutionary pressures continued on those isolated species, in their new environment, until completely different features emerged – as Darwin observed first-hand on the Galapagos islands.

Nonetheless, teleological arguments have proved to be extraordinarily robust in the face of other challenges from NATURALISM (theories such as evolution that claim the universe can be explained in a fully naturalistic, non-supernatural, way); this is despite the success of modern physics and biology in explaining the apparent order and purpose of the universe.

Swinburne's responses to Hume's criticisms

We have now looked at some of the main criticisms, made by Hume and others, of the teleological arguments. You may recall that Swinburne proposed his own version of the design argument while avoiding the criticisms that Hume had made. To do this, Swinburne based his argument on regularities of succession (rather than on co-presence such as the parts of an eye); and by being careful in how far his conclusion extends (he doesn't claim it proves the existence of a perfect being); and by acknowledging that his argument is an argument from analogy and so is vulnerable to criticisms made of analogies.

> **Criticisms and Swinburne's response**
>
> Let us briefly go through some of the criticisms, which have already been outlined above and look at Swinburne's responses.
>
> 1 **The design argument fails as it is an argument from a unique case.** Swinburne argues that Hume is wrong to criticise the design argument on this count; after all, science proceeds by proposing and testing theories both for things they have not observed and for things which are unique. Most obviously, theoretical physicists and cosmologists propose respectable theories about the universe, which is unique. For Swinburne this suggests that Hume has an inadequate understanding of how science and scientists work.
> 2 **Is God the best or the only explanation?** Hume proposes the Epicurean hypothesis as an explanation for the order of the universe. For Swinburne this criticism made by Hume is aimed against design arguments that are based on 'regularities of co-presence', such as the parts of an eye. So Hume is suggesting that the current ordered state of the physical universe may be, as Epicurus suggests, the result of random processes that bring about occasional spatial order. But, for Swinburne, the Epicurean hypothesis does not apply to the more fundamental laws of physics that underpin the structure of the universe, and so this hypothesis does not apply to his version of the design argument.
> However, we have seen that Swinburne is prepared to concede that the argument does not demonstrate the existence of a perfect being, and he accepts that his argument may only prove the existence of an immensely powerful, immensely intelligent, free and rational agent who is disembodied and who shapes the universe. It is unlikely that atheists will consider this to be a significant concession, as if Swinburne has successfully proved

the existence of such a being then the case for atheism has been severely damaged.
3. **Hume's objections to design arguments from analogy.** Finally, we know that Swinburne is prepared to concede that his argument is vulnerable to criticism from people who are not convinced by the analogy, and who are prepared to hunt out and find disanalogies.

▶ **ACTIVITY**
1. Read through Swinburne's argument above, and in Anthology extract 1.9 on page 323.
2. Identify the points at which Swinburne is using an analogy.
3. What problems do you think there are with this analogy?
4. How might Hume, if he were writing philosophy today, respond to Swinburne?

Summary: Teleological/design arguments

Design or teleological arguments aim to prove the existence of God on the basis of evidence drawn from our observations of the universe. These include the observation that living beings, the components they are made up of and the environment they live in appear to be purposeful, as well as the observation that the universe has a regularity of motion and an order of events, particularly in its physical laws. These two types of worldly observation – of purpose/spatial order and regularity/temporal order – are indicators for many people that the world has been designed, because these features are ones we expect to find in objects that we have designed. Some design arguments proceed by what philosophers call an argument from analogy: the universe is analogous to a human artefact, and when we find that these both have general features in common (including purpose and regularity) then this suggests that they also have their origins in common, namely that they have both been designed.

Of all the proofs of God's existence, design arguments are the most reliant on empirical observation and scientific theories. For this reason we might think that they would be the most vulnerable to scientific criticism; and yet they have consistently proved to be resilient and adaptive. Design arguments have managed to incorporate developments like the mechanical universe of Galileo and Newton, and Darwin's theory of evolution. As they have responded to scientific developments, so teleological arguments have shifted their focus from one special feature of the universe to another: from wondering at the place of the Earth at the centre of the universe, to puzzling over the perfect spiral of a snail's shell.

An atheist might find this unacceptable. After all, a theory that shifts and adjusts according to the prevailing intellectual wind seems to be unfalsifiable; that is to say, there would appear to be no way of demonstrating that it is false. Theories that cannot be falsified are regarded by some thinkers as meaningless, and this is an idea we will be examining more closely when we look at Flew below (page 172). However, the popularity of teleological arguments with ordinary believers and religious philosophers is undiminished. We are still struck by the beauty and orderliness of the universe, whether in the equations of theoretical physics, or in watching a thunderstorm above a city. To the atheist, it is a wonder that chance has led to such things and to our being here to appreciate them. But the atheist also looks at other features of the world and asks, 'How can you believe in God when this is the world we live in?' It is not the order and regularity of the natural world that strikes many atheists, but the disorder and disharmony that creates so much pain, suffering and misery. We will return to this issue when we look at the problem of evil in detail in section 1.2.4 (see page 129).

1.2.3 Cosmological arguments

Features of cosmological arguments

> *What was it then that determined something to exist rather than nothing?*[60]
> **Hume**

COSMOLOGICAL ARGUMENTS appeal to our intuition that the existence of the universe (along with everything else) needs an explanation. In its most basic form, a cosmological argument attempts to understand and answer the question 'Why is there a universe rather than nothing at all?' Humans thirst for answers to 'why' questions, and looking up at the stars at night it is easy to move from asking 'Why are we here?' to asking 'Why is any of this here?' Many people feel that the existence of the universe demands an explanation; that there must be some reason why it is here. The cosmological arguments propose that an explanation for the existence of the universe cannot be found within the universe, but must be located in some external source or cause. This external cause, the arguments claim, must be God. Moreover, the arguments conclude that God doesn't need an explanation, and doesn't have an external cause, because God is his own cause: his existence is necessary.

- The term 'cosmological' is a portmanteau phrase drawn from two ancient Greek words *cosmos*, meaning 'universe', and *logos*, meaning 'the study of', or 'a rational account of'. Like the ontological proof, the cosmological argument was a term coined by Kant (as part of his general attacks on metaphysical proofs of the existence of God) to describe arguments which aim to demonstrate that there is a cause of the universe, and that this cause is God.[61]
- Like ontological proofs many cosmological arguments claim that God has a necessary existence (in contrast to the universe, which is dependent upon God for its existence). However, unlike ontological proofs, cosmological arguments base their conclusion that God exists on our experience of the universe. So the premises of cosmological arguments are usually said to be *a posteriori* premises. However, there is some disagreement between Kant and Hume over this. Hume refers to cosmological arguments as *a priori* because they hinge on *a priori* premises.[62] However, Kant categorises them firmly as *a posteriori* because the premises depend upon our experience.[63]
- In general cosmological arguments take the logical form of deductive arguments, although they might be based on inductive generalisations about the universe (and what we observe in the universe). The arguments proceed from premises drawn from what we know of the universe through experience and they infer from these the existence of God. So, unlike the ontological proofs, cosmological arguments like the Kalām proceed deductively on the basis of *a posteriori* premises. Because they have a deductive form, if the premises are true, and the argument is valid, then the conclusion carries a weight of certainty that the conclusions of teleological arguments simply don't have. However, to philosophers who are atheists the conclusion 'there is a God' is always going to sound suspicious (false) which means the arguments are scrutinised for false premises or unsound reasoning.

- Compared with teleological arguments, cosmological arguments yield fewer details about the nature of the God they aim to prove. Cosmological arguments aim to show that the universe requires an ultimate cause, or ultimate explanation, but they do not conclude that this ultimate cause is a loving or good or wise being. Indeed Aquinas has to give separate, supplementary analyses to show that the God he claims to have demonstrated the existence of (in his cosmological proofs) is God in the Christian sense of the term.[64] However, despite the fairly abstract nature of cosmological proofs, there are some attributes of God that may be inferred from these arguments, for example that God is a necessary being (see page 107 below), or that God exists outside of space and time (is eternal or everlasting, see page 10 above).

There are various ways of categorising cosmological arguments. One traditional way is to cluster them as arguments based on causation (including motion or change) or as arguments from contingency. Cosmological arguments based on causation, or a causal principle, tend to move from the claim that things in the universe all have a cause to the claim that the universe itself must have a cause (and theologians would argue this 'first' cause is God). 'Contingency' in this metaphysical context roughly means the dependency upon something else, but we shall examine this concept in more detail below. The cosmological arguments based on contingency are built around the claim that the universe is contingent and it depends upon something outside of itself for its existence and creation (again for theologians that 'something' is God).

There is another way of thinking about different types of cosmological arguments that you might find helpful, and that is to distinguish between 'horizontal' and 'vertical' cosmological arguments, a distinction that F.C. Copleston (1907–94) makes when analysing Aquinas' cosmological proofs.[65] A horizontal cosmological argument traces events or causation back in time until a first cause is arrived at which started the universe: the Kalām argument is the main example of this. A vertical cosmological argument traces causation or contingency (see below page 105) upwards in terms of a hierarchy of dependency, the existence of one thing dependent on the existence of another thing higher up the chain. This goes on until a first cause is arrived at which sustains the existence of the whole universe and keeps it going even now: Aquinas' three ways are examples of this. The differences between horizontal and vertical types of cosmological argument are illustrated in Figure 1.24.

In this section we briefly sketch the origins of cosmological arguments in the work of Plato and Aristotle before focusing on the different types of these arguments (causation/motion and contingency) put forward by a number of religious philosophers. The formulations of the cosmological argument we look at are:

- The Kalām argument – an argument from temporal causation
- Aquinas' three ways:
    - first way – an argument from motion
    - second way – an argument from atemporal causation
    - third way – an argument from contingency
- Descartes' cosmological argument – an argument from causation
- Leibniz's argument from sufficient reason – an argument from contingency.

We then move on to examine some of the key criticisms made of these arguments by philosophers such as Hume, Kant and Russell. These criticisms include:

- the possibility of an infinite series
- objections to the 'causal principle'
- the fallacy of composition
- the impossibility of a necessary being.

Horizontal arguments trace events backwards in time to a first cause which started the whole chain.

Vertical arguments trace causes and effects 'upwards' to a first cause, or unmoved mover, sustaining the whole chain even now.

Figure 1.24 The differences between horizontal and vertical types of cosmological argument: the chain of events can be traced either backwards (horizontally) to a first cause; or upwards (vertically) to a first cause.

Experimenting with ideas

Why are you doing this?

1 On the right-hand side of a piece of paper write down the following event: 'This book lands on the floor.'
2 Now just to the left of it write down another event that caused the book to land on the floor. (Perhaps you were told to drop it by a teacher, or perhaps you were bored with it.)
3 Now to the left of this event write down another event that caused the event in 2 to happen.
4 Keep going as long as you can, writing down a cause for each event.

Your sheet of paper should look something like Figure 1.25.

Figure 1.25 A chain of causes and effects

You probably found that the chain of cause and effect appears to have no end and could go on for ever. You might have found that you were creating a chain that was horizontal (the explanations went backwards in time), or you might have found it was vertical (the explanations became more general or universal). Whichever type of chain you created you may have wondered how, in that case, the whole chain got started in the first place. Proponents of cosmological arguments reckon that chains like this just have to be started by something and that this something must be God.

To see how these arguments work in detail we must begin in the ancient world where they were first articulated.

Shall we say then that it is the soul which controls heaven and earth.
Plato, *Laws* (Book X, 897c)

The contributions of Plato and Aristotle

You won't be surprised to learn that the origins of various forms of cosmological argument lie in the works of two ancient Greek philosophers, Plato (428–348 BCE) and Aristotle (390–323 BCE). In the *Laws* Plato categorised different kinds of motion or change.[66] His most important distinction was between things that had the power to move or change both themselves and others (which he termed 'primary movers') and things that could only move or change others once they had been moved (called 'secondary movers'). For Plato, primary movers were the ultimate source of change, as they alone possessed the power spontaneously to cause motion.

Plato argued in the *Laws* that only souls could be primary movers, and that whatever causes the whole universe to change and move must also be a soul. So Plato's contribution to cosmological arguments is the suggestion that the universe is dependent on some ultimate, intelligent primary mover.

The series must start with something, since nothing can come from nothing.
Aristotle, *Metaphysics*, Book 3 (999b)

Aristotle also believed that all changes in the universe must come from some ultimate source. In the *Metaphysics* he put forward an argument to prove that there must be an 'unmoved mover' who is the ultimate cause of the universe. His argument asks us to consider two competing claims: that the universe has an ultimate mover, and that the universe has no ultimate mover. By showing that the second claim is not possible, he leaves us with only one option, namely that there is an ultimate mover (itself unmoved). We can represent his attack on the second claim as follows in Figure 1.26.

The argument we have presented here, on the basis of Aristotle's argument, is known as a REDUCTIO AD ABSURDUM. This means taking a point of view and reducing it to absurdity in order to show that it is false. The absurdity here is in step 3, as clearly there is a chain of movers and moved: after all, the universe undoubtedly exists. But as step 3 follows on from step 2, and step 2 follows from step 1, Aristotle feels entitled to reject these claims as well. Having shown that step 1 – that the chain of movers has no beginning – is false, he has proved that there must be an ultimate mover, which itself is not moved. However, for technical reasons that go beyond the scope of this book, Aristotle argues that the chain of movers and moved does go back in time for eternity, and the 'unmoved mover' that sustains this chain of movers and moved must itself be an eternal unmoved mover. This claim that the universe is eternal is challenged by the first cosmological argument that we look at, the Kalām argument.

1. The chain of movers and moved has no beginning; there is no ultimate mover:

2. (From 1.) In which case nothing is causing the first thing to move:

3. But if nothing caused the chain there would be no chain at all (one of Aristotle's metaphysical assumptions is that 'nothing comes from nothing').

4. However, there clearly is a chain of movers and moved, as the universe around us does actually exist. So the original assumption (that there is no ultimate mover) must be false. The only other possibility is that there is an ultimate mover, one that lies behind the chain of movers and moved, and which itself is unmoved: this is the Unmoved Mover.

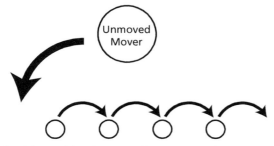

Figure 1.26 Aristotle's proof that there must be an unmoved mover

The Kalām argument (an argument from temporal causation)

Every being which begins has a cause for its beginning. Now the world is a being which begins. Therefore, it possesses a cause for its beginning.[67]

al-Ghazali

Parallel to the development of philosophy in Western Europe in the Middle Ages, there was a strong philosophical tradition developing among Muslim philosophers in the Middle East who had access to the works of Plato and Aristotle. This tradition, like the Christian tradition in the West, aimed to assimilate the intellectual insights and tools of Greek philosophy. One of the most significant Islamic philosophers was al-Ghazali (1058–1111), who proposed an argument for the existence of God which has the form of causal cosmological argument, and which became known as the Kalām argument. *Kalām* is the Arabic for 'speech' and refers to the theological claims made by Islamic philosophers and the arguments put forward to support these, together with any defences or criticisms of the position. In the Christian tradition of the Middle Ages this kind of theological writing and debate was known as scholasticism, but in the Islamic world it was known as *kalām* and studied by the *mutakallimin*.

Al-Ghazali's argument has been revived recently by the theologian William Lane Craig (1949–), (who can be seen debating this in numerous clips online). His argument in its simplest form is presented as having the structure of a deductive argument or a SYLLOGISM. As you will remember, a syllogism is a particular type of deductive argument consisting of three parts: a major premise (All 'B's are 'A'); a minor premise (This is a 'B') and a conclusion (Therefore this is an 'A'). You have already met an example of a syllogism (above, page 32) that is much repeated by philosophers (possibly because of the poignant way in which Socrates died):

1. All men are mortal.
2. Socrates is a man.
3. Therefore Socrates is mortal.

The foundations of cosmological arguments are based on *a posteriori* claims (Craig sometimes refers to these as 'inductive evidence'), and they differ from cosmological argument to cosmological argument. For example, they could be based on a general claim about motion or causation or contingency; but with the Kalām argument it is about *time* (hence the reference in the AQA A-level specification to the Kalām argument as 'an argument from temporal causation'), and it is a horizontal argument (see Figure 1.24 above) tracing causes back in time to an original cause. This is how that structure appears in Craig's summary of the Kalām argument:

P1 Everything with a beginning must have a cause.
P2 The universe has a beginning.
C3 Therefore the universe must have a cause.[68]

As you can see, this presentation of Craig's argument has the straightforward form of a syllogism, but Craig does, however, move beyond this simple syllogism to make a further claim which gives more detail about the nature of this first cause:

C4 Moreover, this cause of the universe must be a personal cause, as scientific explanations cannot provide a causal, or mechanical, account of a first cause. This personal cause is God.

One of the assumptions underpinning the Kalām argument, and the claim being put forward in premise 2, is that the universe cannot have existed for an infinite period of time. The Islamic philosophers who had read Aristotle disputed his argument (Figure 1.26 above on page 95) that the universe has always existed; after all, it would be hard to reconcile any of the monotheistic religions – Islam, Christianity or Judaism – with the claim that the universe had no beginning. Philosophers like al-Ghazali sought a number of different ways to show that past time could not be infinite, and hence that it must be finite and the universe must have had a beginning.

The sciences and astronomy flowered as disciplines in medieval Islam and one of the arguments put forward by al-Ghazali relied on the latest understanding of the movements of the planets in order to generate a mathematical paradox. (We must bear in mind here that medieval astronomers believed the planets orbited the Earth, not the Sun.) It only takes twelve years for Jupiter to orbit the Earth, while it takes Saturn thirty years to complete its orbit. If, says al-Ghazali, past time is infinite then Jupiter and Saturn must have orbited the Earth the same number of times; but this is impossible as we know that Jupiter must have orbited the Earth at least twice as many times. Al-Ghazali concludes from this paradox (which you can try out for yourself in the activity on page 118 below) that 'infinity' is not a coherent concept, and the universe cannot have existed for an infinite past. In which case the universe must have a beginning and therefore it must have a cause, as everything with a beginning has a cause. We have seen that Craig there is a further step needed to show that the cause of the universe (the first cause, or the unmoved mover) cannot be a naturalistic scientific cause, but instead must be a supernatural cause of immense power. For Craig, as for his predecessors, this cause is God.

On page 117 below we return to the criticism made of the Kalām argument (and other cosmological arguments) that an infinite series is possible which, if true, would seriously damage this Kalām argument. A further issue, which we look at below (page 104) is whether the Kalām argument and other forms of the cosmological argument, really do demonstrate that the cause of the universe is God (either the God of Abraham or the God of the philosophers) or whether the cause is a more 'impersonal' first cause.

Aquinas' three ways

Among the medieval Christian philosophers known as the Scholastics, St Anselm put forward a very succinct cosmological argument,[69] but it was St Thomas Aquinas who explored these types of proofs in most detail. Aquinas made it his life's work to assimilate into Christian theology the rediscovered philosophy of Aristotle,[70] and he drew on Aristotle's ideas in his own cosmological arguments for God's existence.

In his book the *Summa Theologica* Aquinas offers five ways in which God's existence can be demonstrated, and the first three ways are all forms of cosmological arguments:[71]

- first way – the argument from motion
- second way – the argument from (atemporal) causation
- third way – the argument from contingency
- fourth way – a type of moral argument
- fifth way – a type of teleological argument (see pages 60–1 above).

The first way and the second way are both forms of causal cosmological argument, and they seek to show that certain general features of the world (causation and motion) must be dependent upon a higher source, which is uncaused or unmoved, namely God. The third way is a cosmological argument based on the contingency of the universe, and it aims to show that the universe is dependent on a necessary being: God. Aquinas' three ways are all examples of 'vertical' cosmological arguments (see Figure 1.24 above) as Aquinas is not tracing events or causes backwards in time, but he is seeking explanations for what is sustaining the universe even as we speak.

Aquinas' first and second ways of proving the existence of God have a similar structure. Both ways begin by noting there are features of the world that we all experience: in the first way it is the existence of motion (in the Aristotelian sense of 'change'); in the second way it is the existence of causation. One possible explanation of such features of the universe is that they have existed for ever. However, Aquinas argues that this explanation must be false, by showing that there cannot be an infinite regress of movers or causers. He does this primarily by using a type of *reductio ad absurdum* similar to the one outlined in Figure 1.26 above. Aquinas then goes on to *show* that these features need an explanation that lies beyond the ordinary chain of motion or causation. Because an infinite regress is not possible, the only other explanation is a cause or a mover that does not fall under the ordinary rules governing causation or motion. Such a being would need no further explanation; it would be the source of all causation without itself having a cause and would be, as Aristotle said, the unmoved mover. Aquinas says that we call such a being 'God'.

Let us look at each of those two ways in more detail.

Aquinas' first way (argument from motion)

The first way is the argument from motion, which for Aquinas included any type of change. A simple formal summary of the first way might look like this:

1. There are some things in motion or a state of change, for example wood burning in a fire.
2. Nothing can move or change itself (in Plato's terms everything is a secondary mover).
3. Imagine everything was a secondary mover – then there would be an infinite regress of movers.
4. **Reductio ad absurdum**: If 3 were true then there would be no prime mover and hence no subsequent movers, but this is false.
5. **Conclusion:** There must be an unmoved prime mover (the source of all motion/change) whom we call God.

This short summary, which uses Plato's simple idea of a 'secondary mover' actually disguises the complexity of the Aristotelian metaphysics that underpins much of Aquinas' philosophy. As we mentioned above, the works and ideas of Aristotle were gradually finding their way back into western thought having been lost, or forgotten, for a thousand years. Aristotle's ideas had been discussed and kept alive by Islamic scholars, but in Europe he was primarily known for his logical work. The full extent of his writings only became apparent in the twelfth and thirteenth centuries, as his writings on ethics, physics, metaphysics, aesthetics and so forth were translated into Latin from Arabic.

Among Aristotle's metaphysical concepts were those of 'actuality' and 'potentiality' which emerge from his analysis of what is called 'motion' (but which we would understand as 'change'). You may remember from your study of Aristotle's ethics that there were different parts of our soul (rational and non-rational) and each part had the *potential* to become excellent (a virtue) if we worked hard, practised, trained and reflected. For those people who did develop virtues Aristotle would say that they had 'actualised' (or fulfilled) their potential; they have moved from one state (for example, being cowardly) to another state that they had the potential to achieve (being courageous). If your nature doesn't include the potential for something, then it cannot be actualised. In the *Ethics* Aristotle gives the memorable example of someone trying to 'train' a stone to move upwards by constantly throwing it up in the air, efforts which are doomed to failure (stones can't be trained to move upwards) … stones, unlike sparrows, don't have the potential to fly.

Aquinas draws on Aristotle's theory of change (motion) in the first way when he argues at the central point of his proof that 'it is not possible that the same thing should be at once in actuality and potentiality in the same respect, but only in different respects' and then goes on to draw an intermediate conclusion 'therefore whatever is in motion must be put in motion by another.' Change (motion) is about moving from a state that a thing is currently in to a new state that the thing is not yet in. A cold radiator has the potential to become a hot radiator, and *change* takes place in the process of that potential becoming actualised.

So far, so good. Aquinas then goes on to argue that something else (something other than the radiator) must be bringing about that change, or movement in states – and more critically than that, the thing bringing about the change must be in the state that the thing is moving towards. So a cold radiator can't make itself hot; it must be made hot by something else (a boiler) and that other thing (the boiler) must itself be hot (Figure 1.27). Moreover, Aquinas argues that a thing cannot be both potentially in one state (for example, hot) and actually in that state (for example, hot) at the same time. There must be some other thing that is already in that state (of hotness) and which brings about the change. This enables Aquinas to draw the intermediate conclusion that whatever is in motion (in the process of change) must be put in motion by another. With this in place, Aquinas can then move on to the next phase of the argument (already outlined in the simple version of the argument above, page 94) showing that an infinite regress of movers is not possible, and he concludes that the chain of movers must have as its source an unmoved mover (which everyone calls God).

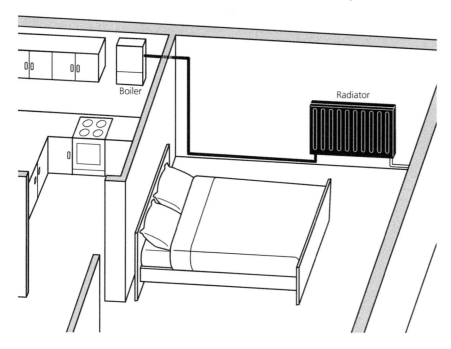

Figure 1.27 According to Aquinas nothing can be reduced from potentiality to actuality, except by something already in a state of actuality. So a radiator cannot become hot by itself, it must become hot by something that is already hot (the boiler, so long as it works)

We can expand the simpler summary of Aquinas' argument into a proof which more closely captures the original:

1. There are some things in motion or a state of change.
2. Motion is the reduction of something potential to something actual (for example, something cold to something hot).
3. A thing can only be reduced from potentiality to actuality by something already in that state of actuality (for example, a thing that is cold becomes hot through something else that is already hot).
4. A thing can't be actually and potentially in the same state at the same time (for example, a thing can't be potentially hot and actually hot at the same time).
5. Therefore nothing can move or change itself – it must be moved or changed by something else.
6. Imagine everything was moved or changed by something else – then there would be an infinite regress of movers.
7. *Reductio ad absurdum*: If 6 were true then there would be no prime mover and hence no subsequent movers, but this is false.
8. **Conclusion**: There must be an unmoved prime mover (the source of all motion/change) whom we call God.

▶ ACTIVITY

This is your opportunity to test Aquinas' claim in premise 3 that everything being actualised is being actualised by something already in that state.

Read through the following examples and for each **thing (X)** in bold:

a) Identify the state X has the potential to be in (and is moving towards actually being in).
b) Identify the 'something else' (external to X) that is bringing about that state.
c) Assess whether the 'something else' (that you identified in b) is already in the state (that you identified in a).

We have completed the first example for you:

1. The tub of melted **ice-cream** that you have just put back into the freezer (wondering whether it would have been more sensible if you'd eaten it all in one go)
    a) *The melted ice-cream in the freezer has the potential to be frozen, and is moving towards the state of being actually frozen.*
    b) *The thing that is bringing about this change of state (the ice-cream actually freezing) is the freezer itself.*
    c) *Yes, the freezer is itself already freezing.*
2. A **Dutch Elm tree** in a forest clearing is dying.
3. A **lake** in a desert oasis is gradually filling up during the spring.
4. A **friend** of yours is starting to fall in love with someone famous.
5. **You** are getting better and better marks (moving towards the top grade) from your philosophy teacher.

Criticism

One immediate problem that arises is with Aquinas' claim (which is a factual premise and so can be challenged on factual grounds, using counter-examples) that if something causes another thing to change towards a particular state, then that first thing must already be in that state. This works well with cold radiators, and burning wood: the wood can't make itself hot, although it has the potential to become hot; it must be made hot by something else, which itself must be hot (for example, a match or a fire). But there are other processes which don't seem to match this pattern. William Rowe (1931–2015) gives the example of a plant that is dying and asks whether the thing bringing about that death is itself dead.72 It may be that the soil is dead, completely lacking in nutrients, or that the atmosphere is dead, lacking water or full of fumes. But it may be that a fungus (like Dutch Elm disease), or insects, or small children, have attacked the plant, causing it to die, but the fungi/insects/children are very much thriving and living, exactly while the plant is dying. If Aquinas' claim is true he would have to show that it is dying creatures that have brought about the dying of the tree. But it is the very life of these creatures that has brought about the death of the plant. So Rowe's example can be used to undermine premise 3 of the more complex summary of the first way.

▶ **ACTIVITY**
1 Read Anthology extract 1.15 on page 326.
2 Identify in this original text where you think the premises outlined above (page 98) are.

Aquinas' second way (argument from causation)

Let us now turn to Aquinas' second way. You can begin the investigation by doing the activity below.

▶ **ACTIVITY**
1 Carefully read through Aquinas' second way below.
2 Flick to Section 4 and familiarise yourself with the five lenses on page 320.
3 Use the lenses to help you write Aquinas' second way as a formal, numbered argument (as we did with the first way on page 98 and page 100).

> *The second way is from the nature of the efficient cause. In the world of sense we find there is an order of efficient causes. There is no case known (neither is it, indeed, possible) in which a thing is found to be the efficient cause of itself; for so it would be prior to itself, which is impossible. Now in efficient causes it is not possible to go on to infinity, because in all efficient causes following in order, the first is the cause of the intermediate cause, and the intermediate is the cause of the ultimate cause, whether the intermediate cause be several, or only one. Now to take away the cause is to take away the effect. Therefore, if there be no first cause among efficient causes, there will be no ultimate, nor any intermediate cause. But if in efficient causes it is possible to go on to infinity, there will be no first efficient cause, neither will there be an ultimate effect, nor any intermediate efficient causes; all of which is plainly false. Therefore it is necessary to admit a first efficient cause, to which everyone gives the name of God.*
> Aquinas

Aquinas' second way is very similar to his first way in its essential structure, but there are some critical differences. First, it is much shorter than the first way, and has not been embellished with examples (Aquinas' first way included two examples to clarify the argument). Secondly, its focus is different: it is not looking at change/motion but at causes and effects. It may seem odd that Aquinas gives a second proof which is so closely connected to the first (especially as his third, fourth and fifth ways are all so different from one another). In the first way, Aquinas argues that the move from a potential state (potentially being frozen) to an actual state (actually being frozen) requires an external cause – something else brings the change about (in this case, a working freezer). So how is the second way, which is also about causes, different? Copleston suggests that the first way is about things being acted upon and being changed (as passive recipients), whereas the second way is about things acting and bringing about change (as active agents).73 So the first and second way explore a change in perspective: from things changing (the first way) to things doing the changing – efficient causes (the second way).

In order to understand the second way more fully we need to introduce another bit of Aristotelian metaphysics, namely the concept of 'efficient cause' and the different types of other causes he identified. Aristotle's categorisation of the concept of cause can be helpful, as it will help us to understand all the different types of answers we might give to the question 'well, why did it happen?' Aristotle proposes that there are four different types of answers (four different categories of causes) to the question 'why?' and we can use his example of a bronze statue to illustrate each type of cause.74

- The *material* cause – the stuff out of which something comes to be. In the case of the bronze statue the material cause would be the molten bronze.
- The *formal* cause – the form (structure, blueprint). In the case of the bronze statue this would be the mould that the artist had designed, and into which the molten bronze could be poured. (You encountered the Aristotelian concept of 'form' when looking at the soul in Book 1 of the *Ethics*).
- The *efficient* cause – the principle that brings about the change. In the case of the bronze statue this would be the art of bronze casting (as evidenced in the skill and knowledge of the sculptor).
- The *final* cause – the end, goal or purpose. In the case of the bronze statue, this would be to stand at the entrance of a palace or grand house, and impress visitors to the house. (You encountered Aristotle's concept of a 'final cause' when considering happiness and the ultimate goal in life in Book 1 of the *Ethics*, pages 298–301 of our Year 1 textbook.)

Figure 1.28 illustrates these different types of causes.

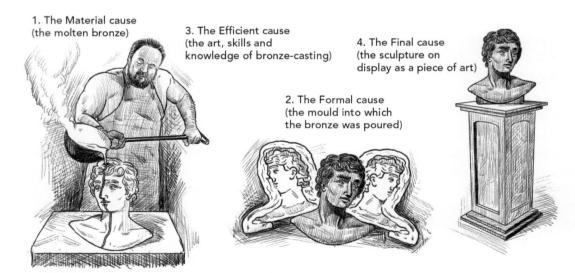

Figure 1.28 Aristotle's four types of causes

In his second way, Aquinas is interested in the 'why?' of efficient causes – what is it that immediately brings something about (and hence explains that thing)? Let us explore an example from his first way, that of a stick being moved and the efficient cause of the stick is the person moving the stick. But there is a question 'why is the person moving the stick?' Now, we can see straight away that this question might have four different types of answers, depending on which aspect (material, formal, efficient or final) we were interested in. For Aquinas, it is the efficient cause that demands an explanation – why, or what caused the hand to move the stick? The efficient cause might be the capacity of humans to make decisions like 'move this stick'. But the question then arises 'why, or what caused humans to have the capacity to make free decisions?' So although it might be tempting to read Aquinas' second way as a 'horizontal' cosmological proof (going back in time, like the Kalām argument) it is better read as a 'vertical' chain of causes, with each explanation given requiring a higher-order explanation.

Aquinas argues that as soon as you take away one of the efficient causes (for example, the capacity of humans to make decisions) then the chain falls apart – the effect of the stick moving would be absence if humans didn't have brains (but were empty-headed zombies – see page 214 for more on zombies). For Aquinas the chain of causes and effects (that led to the stick being moved) requires an ultimate explanation – what he calls a first efficient cause – and if it doesn't have one then the whole chain falls apart. But given that he can now see the stick being moved then there must be a first efficient cause. Note that he doesn't conclude that he's proved the existence of God, he just says that most people call 'the first efficient cause' by the name of God.

Here is a short, formal version of the second way:

1 There is an order of efficient causes (sometimes rephrased as every event has a cause).
2 Nothing can be the efficient cause of itself.
3 Imagine this order of efficient causes goes on infinitely – then there would be no first cause among efficient causes.
4 **Reductio ad absurdum**: If point 3 were true then there would be no subsequent efficient causes, but this is false.
5 **Conclusion**: There must be a first efficient cause (the source of all efficient causes) and this we call God.

Some issues raised against Aquinas' first and second ways

Towards the end of this section we shall look at some of the sustained criticisms made of the cosmological argument by David Hume and Bertrand Russell among others (pages 124–127), and many of these criticisms apply to Aquinas' first and second ways. For example, why does there need to be an explanation for everything – why can't some things just be 'brute facts' that require no explanation at all (see page 126 below)? But other issues have also been raised, which we shall briefly look at here.

What is the nature of God that is being concluded by Aquinas?
When we consider the chain of causation or of motion, it is easy to think of it temporally (or 'horizontally'), with each event preceding and causing the next event. On this interpretation, a cause refers to the factor that brought about

the effect. The chain of causation is thus one that goes backwards in time, with God, the first cause, at the beginning starting the whole thing off, rather like a finger knocking over the first of a chain of dominos, or winding up a clockwork machine (see Figure 1.29).

Figure 1.29 God as the (temporal) first cause

If we take the 'temporal', or horizontal, interpretation of causation then the cosmological argument seems to show that a first cause, God, once existed and once created the universe. However, it is crucial to believers that God is still present to act upon the world and still cares about the world; this after all is the God of Abraham, the God described in the Bible. So even if Aquinas' arguments are sound we might criticise them for failing to prove the existence of a being who is worthy of worship, either the God of the philosophers or the God of the Bible. After all, it is possible to imagine a first cause which does not have some of the essential properties of God, and which may not be personal or benevolent or omniscient.

In the eighteenth century, during the Enlightenment, a branch of religious belief known as deism became popular among some thinkers who rejected revealed theology, while embracing natural theology. Deists held that the universe had an original cause that lay outside it, but that this first cause was not the personal God of Abraham, and was not the supremely good and loving God of the philosophers. So the 'domino-flicking' first cause may satisfy deists, but such a view is not one that a Christian philosopher such as Aquinas could subscribe to.

However, there is another interpretation of the chain of causation that lends itself better to the belief that God, as the first cause, is acting on the world here and now. This interpretation sees 'causation' in terms of the factors that sustain an event, or keep it going once it has begun. For example, a farmer may plant a seed, and so cause the seed to grow in that patch of land, but it is the particular qualities of the seed, together with a fertile environment, that sustains its growth into a mature plant. The chain, or order, of causation can be thus seen as a hierarchical, or vertical, one with God as the ongoing and ultimate sustaining cause of the universe.[75]

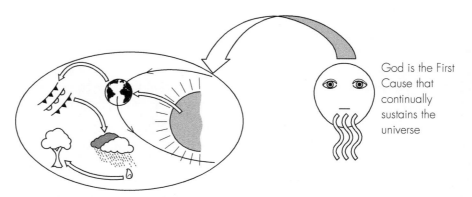

Figure 1.30 God as the (sustaining) first cause

In Figure 1.30 we can imagine tracing the cause of a tree back to its seed, then to the weather conditions that enabled the seed to grow, then to the movement of the Earth round the Sun that created the weather conditions. Aquinas' arguments aim to show that ultimately there is an on-going explanation of all these things (not just a deistic first cause).

Perhaps when looking at the conclusions of Aquinas' arguments we should remember that he believed that there were limits to human understanding, and that his proofs had to remain within those limits. Aquinas' three ways were never intended to reveal the nature of God, only to demonstrate that there was some ultimate explanation for the existence of the universe.

Do Aquinas' arguments rest on a contradiction?

At first sight the first and second ways appear to rest on a contradiction. On the one hand Aquinas says that everything must have a cause and nothing can cause itself, but he then concludes that something must exist that can be the cause of itself, namely God. So the original assumption is contradicted by the conclusion.

A defender of a cosmological argument might say that this is precisely what the *reductio ad absurdum* is supposed to prove: that there has to be at least one exception to the rule 'nothing can be the cause of itself'. If there were not such an exception, then the universe would have no cause and would never come to exist. But if there is an exception, let us call it the first cause, then it must be something without a cause, in Aristotle's terms an 'unmoved mover'. This defence has similarities to Anselm's defence against Gaunilo; namely that when we are talking about God we are dealing with a being unlike anything else, a being who has a special form of existence.

However, a critic might come back with the response that if we are going to allow for exceptions to the rule 'nothing can be the cause of itself' then why make God the exception? Could we not just as well make the universe itself the exception? In other words we would be saying that nothing that occurs in the universe is its own cause, but the universe itself *can* be its own cause. The existence of the universe requires no further explanation: it simply is (see Russell's criticism on page 126 below). This would rule out the need to posit God.

Alternatively, a critic might ask of the cosmological argument: why must God be the ultimate cause and why is God the point at which our search for an explanation for the existence of things must end? Why, in other words, does the existence of God not require any further explanation? David Hume offers a version of this criticism, which we look at below (page 119 and Figure 1.33).

Aquinas' third way (argument from contingency)

Aquinas' third way is from a different tradition of cosmological arguments – ones that are based on the contingency of the universe and of everything in it. We have noted already that contingency has a close connection with the idea of dependency. So, for example, the existence of a forest is contingent upon the existence of the availability of water to the trees' roots; or the existence of our democratic system of government is dependent upon our having the freedom to vote for different parties. Contingency is also bound up with the idea of mortality or 'shelf life': contingent events occur and then stop, and contingent objects come into being then cease to be. So, once all the rivers are dammed, the forest disappears; take away our freedom to vote for different parties and our democracy will disappear. Finally contingency implies that things are not fixed: they could have been different if the past had been different. If the climate had been hotter, then the forest would never have existed; if Plato's experimental system of 'philosopher kings' had been proven to work, then there may never have been any need for democracy.

Experimenting with ideas

What, if anything, is the existence of the following contingent upon?

1. Life on planet Earth
2. Your own existence
3. The continuing good health of your neighbour's cat
4. A successful marriage
5. Public trust in politicians
6. An acrobat balancing on top of a human pyramid
7. The whole universe

Cosmological arguments based on contingency claim that everything in the universe is contingent, and thus dependent upon something else.[76] They go on to argue that it is impossible for everything to be contingent; there must be a non-contingent being; that is, a necessary being, upon which the contingent universe is dependent. This necessary being is God. Aquinas' third way is a slightly different version of the argument from contingency. In this argument he emphasises the 'shelf-life' aspect of contingent beings; that is, the fact that they have an expiry date, they come and go, live and die, are generated and destroyed. In other words they are impermanent. Aquinas seems to argue that if everything has an 'expiry date' then at some point everything will expire and cease to exist. Since this has not happened he concludes there must be a permanent being which has no expiry date, and which all impermanent beings depend on for their existence. Let us look at how he reaches this conclusion.

We find in nature things that are possible to be and not to be, since they are found to be generated and then corrupted.
Aquinas, *Summa Theologica* 1:2:3

Aquinas' third way can be divided into two parts as follows.[77]

Part one

1. Things in the world are contingent (they come into existence and pass out of existence).
2. Imagine everything was contingent; then there was once a time when everything had passed out of existence – that is, there was nothing.
3. **Reductio ad absurdum**: If 2 were true then there would be nothing now (as nothing can come from nothing), but this is false.
4. **Conclusion of part one:** Therefore not everything can be contingent – there must be at least one thing that is necessary.

Part two

5. Every thing that is necessary either has the cause of its necessity in itself or outside of itself.

6 Imagine every necessary thing has the cause of its necessity outside of itself.
7 **Reductio ad absurdum:** If point 6 were true then (as with the causal argument outlined above) there would be no ultimate cause of necessity.
8 **Conclusion of part two:** There must exist a necessary being which causes and sustains all other necessary and contingent beings – this being we all call God.

In the first part of his argument Aquinas is saying that contingent and impermanent things cannot continually furnish the universe throughout its infinite existence. There must come a point in time when impermanent things all cease to exist: their expiry dates all coincide. In which case, Aquinas says, we would expect there to be nothing now. But that is plainly false: the world is still stocked full of contingent beings. Therefore there must exist a permanent (NECESSARY) being that guarantees the continuing existence of impermanent beings, even if they all expire at once. Figure 1.31 shows how we might try to picture this: we can see there is a point at which contingent beings all expire, but a necessary being sustains the existence of the universe over this 'gap' and generates fresh contingent beings.

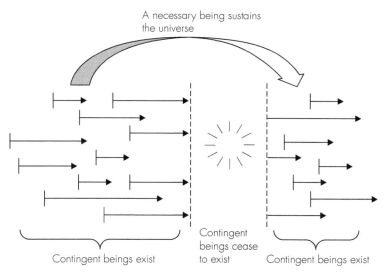

Figure 1.31 God as a necessary being sustaining the universe

So Aquinas has established that there must exist a permanent, necessary being, which the universe (and the impermanent parts of the universe) depend on for their existence. In the second part of Aquinas' argument he considers whether such a necessary being is itself dependent on another necessary being, which in turn would be dependent upon another necessary being, and so on. Aquinas denies the possibility of an infinite regress of necessary beings. There must, ultimately, be a necessary being who needs no other cause, but who is the cause of itself. So Aquinas concludes that there must exist a necessary being who needs no further explanation or cause, namely God.

Aquinas' conclusion: God is a necessary being

We saw above that if something is contingent then:

- its existence is dependent on other things
- it has a 'shelf life'; it came into existence and will one day cease to exist
- it might have been different (or might never have existed) if the past had been different.

What Aquinas', and other philosophers', cosmological arguments seek to prove is the existence of a non-contingent, necessary being. In contrast to contingent beings, a necessary being:

- has an existence that is independent of everything else
- is eternal; it has always existed and will never cease to exist
- has to exist; and it is impossible that it could be different, no matter how past, present or future circumstances might vary.

It is the existence of such a necessary being, one we call God, which Aquinas believes he has proved through his third way.

> ### Criticism
> Later in this section we look in detail at several criticisms of Aquinas' proofs, but let us mention one issue immediately. Aquinas seems to be saying that, over an infinite time period, all contingent things must come to an end, because they are impermanent, and that this would leave nothing left in existence. He concludes that there must be a necessary being that 'keeps things going' even when all contingent beings have ceased to exist. However, Mackie argues that Aquinas is committing a fallacy if he thinks that he can jump from 'every thing at some time does not exist' to 'at some time everything does not exist'.[78] Thus it might be the case that there is an infinite series of overlapping, yet contingent, things in the universe. If this were a possibility, claims Mackie, then there would be no need to hypothesise the existence of a necessary being.

Descartes' cosmological argument based on his continuing existence (argument from causation)

> *Wherein are demonstrated the Existence of God and the Distinction of Soul from Body.*
> **Descartes**

The subtitle of Descartes' *Meditations* boldly asserts that inside its pages God's existence will be proved, as will the distinction between the soul and the body (the theory that became known as DUALISM). We have already seen above (page 45) that Descartes put forward an ontological argument to prove the existence of God, and this can be found in *Meditation 5*. However, in *Meditation 3* Descartes offers two further proofs of God's existence:

- The trademark argument
- The cosmological argument

The first of these proofs you will have looked at in some detail when studying epistemology in Year 1 of your A-level. The central claim of the trademark argument is that Descartes has an idea of God, a perfect being, and this idea of a perfect being must have been caused by something. Descartes believed there must be 'at least as much reality in the cause as in the effect', which is known as his causal principle. Descartes' causal principle is a cousin of a family of philosophical principles, which stipulate that everything has a reason or a cause. Aristotle's claim that 'nothing can come from nothing' is a part of this family, and these principles are also referred to as the 'Principle of Sufficient Reason' which is the term coined by Gottfried Leibniz (1646–1716) and which Leibniz used to underpin his own version of the cosmological argument (see below, page 113). Descartes uses the causal principle to show that the cause of his idea of a perfect being must itself be a perfect being. In other words, God must have planted the idea of God in Descartes' mind (imprinted on it like a trademark), and therefore God must exist. Descartes' trademark argument is an *a priori* argument, reliant only on understanding God as a perfect being, and on an understanding of the causal principle (that any cause must have sufficient power to bring about the effect).

▶ ACTIVITY

Read through the following situations and decide which one of the possible causes below them – a), b) or c) – would count as having 'at least as much reality in the cause as in the effect', that is, which cause would have sufficient power to bring about that effect:

Effect 1: A teenage girl has just won a multi-million dollar contract to advertise cosmetics for a well-known fashion brand.

a) She has been doing video blogs for a few months on her haul, the stuff she buys in shops, and now has thousands of followers.
b) Her unique look was spotted at an airport, in a fairy-tale manner, by a director of a modelling agency as she flew back to Croydon.
c) Her parents are ridiculously good-looking, rich and famous – as is she.

Effect 2: An astrology student got the highest grade for the A-level in this subject.

a) He was naturally good at astrology and as a result he knew in advance what the questions were going to be.
b) There was a mistake in the marking of his exam paper which had not been spotted by the exam board.
c) He had developed a systematic approach to all his subjects, working hard, redrafting each of his essays, taking mock exams and following his revision plan.

Effect 3: A window shatters in your classroom.

a) A butterfly had flapped its wings earlier in the week, causing a complex chain of meteorological events that eventually resulted in the shattering of the glass.
b) A politics student had thrown a stone from outside your class, as part of the 'People In Glass Houses Shouldn't …' campaign against government cuts, but had misjudged her own strength.
c) It was an example of SGB (Spontaneous Glass Breakage).

Effect 4: A skier on holiday says to a man at the top of a mountain 'You're my hero'.

a) He had just saved her life by pulling her from an avalanche.
b) She had just discovered that he was the author of a textbook that she found quite helpful when teaching her A-level classes.
c) He had lent her some factor 50 sun-block for her nose, which he kept with him at all times (just in case).

Effect 5: You have an idea that God is defined as a perfect being.

a) This was something you read about in detail when you studied the ontological argument.
b) You understand what Power is, what Love is, what Knowledge is; you also know what *omni* means; and you understand how to create new words using prefixes.
c) This idea must come from a perfect being in order for you to have it.

Now put Descartes' causal principle into your own words.

Descartes' version: 'The cause of something must contain at least as much reality as the effect.'
Your version:

Putting the trademark argument to one side, we find embedded in the final stage of the trademark argument in *Meditation 3* a second argument, which is an *a posteriori* argument for God's existence and which you may recognise as having the form of a cosmological argument. It is prompted, as cosmological arguments are often prompted, by the search for an explanation for existence: the Kalām argument and Aquinas' arguments sought to explain why the universe existed, and what causes it to continue to exist; but Descartes has a much narrower line of enquiry, asking himself what caused him, Descartes, to exist and what causes him to continue existing.

This may strike us a rather self-absorbed question, and it would help to remember here the personal philosophical journey that Descartes has taken in the *Meditations* and which led him to this juncture. He began his reflections by questioning whether he knows anything for certain, and reached the troubling position where he now doubts everything that he sees and senses around him. However, he finds he cannot doubt that he is currently doubting or that he is thinking; and he arrives at the conclusion that so long as he is doubting, and thinking, then he *knows* he exists ('I think, therefore I am'). Having reached this narrow foundation of knowledge, Descartes wished to build up for himself other beliefs that he could be certain of, beliefs that were also as clear and distinct as his belief that he himself existed. When reading the *Meditations* you get a sense of the intense focus that Descartes is bringing to his task; it's almost as if we are inside his head travelling on the journey with him, which in a sense we are, as we go through the same processes he goes through in order to fully understand what he is saying. So this lonely but compelling philosophical journey inside one man's mind leads us to the point where Descartes has found another clear and distinct idea: God. But what is the cause of this idea of a perfect being? This stage of the trademark argument was explored in the first year of your A-level, and it is just at this point that Descartes wonders:

Whether I myself, who have the idea, could exist, if no such being existed. Now from what source could I have my being?[79]
Descartes

So Descartes is now looking for the explanations that underpin *two* of the facts that he has established:

- The fact that he has in his mind the idea of a perfect being (God), and
- The fact that he has a continuous existence as a conscious being.

So what power is it that both causes him to exist, and also causes him to have the idea of a perfect being? We see time and again in the cosmological argument that there is a need to find an explanation, a rationale or a cause, that lies behind the very existence of the world. But Descartes (who has not at this point established any proof of an external world) is less ambitious and he simply wants to know what is the cause of his existence. What is it that sustains his continued existence from one moment to the next?

He first considers the possibility that he could be his own cause; that the power from which his own existence derives comes from within himself. Presumably then in this case all the ideas he holds (including that of a perfect being) would also have their source in himself. Descartes applies the causal principle to this; in other words, the principle that the cause must be sufficiently powerful to create the effect. So, in order to bring about the idea of a perfect being, the cause must itself be a perfect being. As Descartes is considering the possibility here that he is the cause, then it follows that he must be a perfect being. As he clearly is not God, Descartes can reject the claim that he is his own cause.

A second possibility examined by Descartes is that he has always existed as a conscious being, in which case there is no need to look for the cause or seek any further explanation. But he rejects this idea on the grounds that we can divide our life into countless small parts, each independent of one another, and for each of these moments we can ask, 'What is causing me to exist as a conscious being?' So saying, 'I have always existed in this way' does not answer the issue at stake here, which is: 'What causes me to exist as a conscious being now and at the next moment, and the next?' For Descartes, the continuation of us, as conscious beings, from one moment to the next requires explanation: there must be something that sustains our existence. He briefly considers the possibility that he might have the power within himself necessary to bring about his continuous existence from one moment to the next. Descartes rejects this possibility on the grounds that if he had such a power then he would be aware of having it, but he is not aware of having any such power.

So Descartes cannot be the cause of his own being, nor can he avoid the issue by saying that he has always been a conscious being and that there is no need to look for a cause. The cause of Descartes' idea of God, and of his existence as a conscious being, must come from something outside of himself. Could this cause be something imperfect, something like his parents for example? After all it is plausible to argue that the explanation for why we exist is that we were born to our parents. Descartes is pretty quick to reject this, as they do not sustain me as a conscious being (and did they really have the power to actually make me a conscious being?). It is at this point that we see Descartes' cosmological argument in its clearest form:

1. The existence of the idea of God in my mind needs explaining; the continuing existence of me as a conscious being also needs explaining.
2. I cannot be the cause of my idea of God (a perfect being) because I am not God (a perfect being). I cannot bring about my continuing existence as a conscious being because I do not have the power.
3. Therefore the cause of me as a conscious being, and the cause of my idea of God, must lie outside of myself.
4. Either a) this external cause is itself caused by something else, or b) it is its own cause.
5. If a) is true then either c) this other cause must be caused by a further thing, or b) it is its own cause.
6. This sequence of causes cannot run back to infinity, and eventually we will reach an ultimate cause – b).
7. The ultimate cause; that is, the thing that is its own cause, is God.
8. Therefore it is God who ultimately causes my idea of God, and it is God who ultimately sustains my existence as a conscious being.
9. Because I do have an idea of God, and because I know that I am sustained as a conscious being, therefore God must exist as the cause of both these things.

▶ **ACTIVITY**
Write the paragraph above in the form of an argument with numbered premises, an intermediate conclusion and a conclusion (that Descartes is not the cause of his own existence).

anthology 1.16

The cosmological part of Descartes' trademark argument ends here, but Descartes goes on to draw to an end his overall trademark argument with the conclusion that God, when he created Descartes, implanted the idea of God in him, in the same way that a craftsman stamps his work with a trademark (see Figure 1.34 of the *Philosophy for A-Level Year 1 and AS*[80]).

> **Criticisms of Descartes' cosmological argument**
>
> Is Descartes' argument here a circular argument? There are specific criticisms that we can make of Descartes' argument which arise from the particular philosophical project that he is engaged with. This project is the attempt made by Descartes to establish solid foundations of knowledge, and to build his beliefs up from that point, knowing he has secure foundations. One of the most damaging criticisms is known as the Cartesian circle, and it suggests that steps which Descartes takes to establish the existence of God are not permitted at this point in his project, and that he is pulling his argument up by his own boot-straps. You may remember looking at this criticism in your first year of philosophy (*AQA A-level Philosophy Year 1 and AS: Epistemology and Moral Philosophy*, Hodder Education 2017, page 141), but essentially it is this: Descartes has established that he exists as a thinking thing, and even an evil demon cannot deceive him about his own existence. From that point Descartes uses an array of 'clear and distinct' ideas (including the causal principle, the rules of logic and his idea of God as a perfect being) to prove the existence of God. Once he has proved the existence of God, Descartes argues that God, being benevolent, would not deceive him about his clear and distinct ideas. The circularity is that he relies on clear and distinct ideas to prove the existence of God, but then uses the existence of God to show that he can genuinely rely on clear and distinct ideas. If Descartes were as strict in *Meditation 3* as he had been in *Meditation 1* then he would not have been able to use the causal principle to prove the existence of God.

In addition to the specific criticism of circularity made against Descartes' cosmological argument, some of the general issues we raise in the second half of this section also apply to Descartes:

- the possibility of an infinite series
- objections to the causal principle (raised by Hume and others).

Leibniz's argument from the Principle of Sufficient Reason (an argument from contingency)

The philosopher and mathematical genius Leibniz produced a variant on the cosmological argument, based his Principle of Sufficient Reason (for more on Leibniz, refer to our *Philosophy for A-level Year 1 and AS* textbook, pages 99–102). We have explored versions of the cosmological argument based around the idea of one event being caused by another, and that this sequence cannot go on for ever. Leibniz's argument has a similar theme, but is not limited solely to a discussion of causation.

anthology 1.17

Leibniz claims that every fact/event in the world is (theoretically) susceptible to a full explanation. (This is known as the Principle of Sufficient Reason.) In other words, a sufficient reason can be given as to why any object exists or why any event occurs. He contends that all the (contingent) facts in the world can never be fully explained by reference to other (contingent) facts alone, but only by reference to a necessary being (God).

▶ **ACTIVITY**

Read Anthology extract 1.17 on page 327. Try to construct a shorter version of Leibniz's argument.

Put formally, his argument would look something like this:

- **P1:** No fact can ever be true or existent unless there is a sufficient reason why things are as they are and not otherwise (Principle of Sufficient Reason).
- **P2:** Contingent facts exist (hidden premise, not given in the Anthology extract).
- **P3:** Contingent facts can only be partially explained in terms of other contingent facts.
- **C1:** The whole series of contingent facts cannot be sufficiently explained by any contingent fact within that series (from P1–P3).
- **C2:** The sufficient reason for all contingent facts and for the series of facts, must lie outside of the series of contingent facts (from P1–P3).
- **C3:** The ultimate reason for facts/things must be in a necessary substance which we call 'God' (from C2).

To consider Leibniz's argument in more detail, we first need to immerse ourselves in some more metaphysical concepts, and consider both his Principle of Sufficient Reason as well as his distinction between necessary and contingent facts.

Principle of Sufficient Reason

Here are some truths:

A $8 + 4 = 6 \times 2$.
B All bachelors are unmarried men.
C A tree in Nunhead Cemetery fell over at 9:06 p.m. on Sunday 1/6/2018.
D Chelsea Ladies vs Arsenal Ladies football match kicked off at 7:36 on 17/5/2017.

Consider example C. Presumably, if a tree fell over then there must have been a reason for this. Moreover, a reason as to why it fell then and not a moment later or sooner. This much seems obvious. Trees can't fall over for *no* reason. Underpinning this feeling of obviousness, Leibniz claims, is what he termed the Principle of Sufficient Reason. (Although the idea existed before, Leibniz was the first to use this name and give a systematic account.)

> *No fact can ever be true or existent, no statement correct, unless there is a sufficient reason why things are as they are and not otherwise – even if in most cases we can't know what the reason is.*
> Leibniz

Leibniz's claim is that any fact or object's existence has a sufficient reason for occurring/existing (even if that reason is not known).

Leibniz's Principle of Sufficient Reason (PSR) is a claim about human reasoning (an epistemic claim). This is the claim that humans seek reasons for events in the world. It is also a claim about the world itself (a metaphysical claim) and that is that every event in the world occurs for a reason. Events cannot occur for no reason. Further, that any event's occurrence has a reason sufficient to fully explain its occurrence (even though humans may not be able to give the full reason). The PSR has great intuitive appeal and underpins much human intellectual endeavour. For example, science tries to discover the reasons for events precisely because we believe that events occur for a reason – although quite how full or sufficient a reason a fact needs to 'have' can be disputed (see below).

Necessary truths

In the Anthology extract 1.17 Leibniz makes the distinction between necessary and contingent truths. These terms will be familiar to you from your study of the ontological arguments.

Leibniz claims that, for some truths, the opposite is impossible/inconceivable: these are termed necessary truths. As the opposite is impossible, such truths could *not* have been otherwise, so they are necessarily true.

Consider example A: $8 + 4 = 6 \times 2$. By using reason alone, we can simplify this equation to the following $12 = 12$. This is obviously true. But why is this true? Leibniz claims that the obviousness of the truth lies in other basic principles of thought/the world: the principle of contradiction (a proposition cannot be true and false at the same time) and the principle of identity (an object is identical to itself). Both our thoughts and the world are bound by these principles. To think that '12 = not 12' would be a violation of these principles, which makes it both inconceivable (in the mind) and impossible (in the world). Leibniz thought that these principles are so basic or self-evident that they, in turn, do not need further explanation (he also thought we are innately aware of these principles). All necessary truths can be fully shown to be true in this way, in that they are all reducible to an identity statement of a similar form, $A = A$. So, for necessary truths we can provide a full and sufficient explanation as to why they are true – nothing more can be added.

Contingent truths and the crux of the argument

However, this is not so easy for contingent truths, even though the Principle of Sufficient Reason states that a full and sufficient reason exists for each truth (though we may not know it). Consider the example D. Although it is true that Chelsea Ladies vs Arsenal Ladies kicked off at 7:36 on 17/5/2017, this truth is not necessary, it is merely contingent. This means that it could have been otherwise and that the opposite is conceivable. Also, unlike necessary truths, we cannot show the truth of this event using the principle of contradiction. However, there is still a reason that the match kicked off at that moment. After all, it did not happen for *no* reason. The contingent truth of the kick-off time has a sufficient reason, even though we might not be able to explain it all.

In fact, as soon as we start to explain the event, we run into some difficulties. Firstly, there are a myriad of reasons that lead to the kick-off at that moment: the scheduling of the football season; each footballer arriving and getting ready; the referee blowing her whistle; the minute's silence for the death of a former player; the invention of football; the standardisation of Greenwich mean time and so on. We could not explain *all* the reasons for the event. But even if we tried to articulate more and more reasons, we would run into another, more fundamental, difficulty. We are attempting to explain this contingent fact –

the start of the football game at 7:36 – by reference to more contingent facts, such as the invention of football. But these contingent facts, in turn, have to be explained by yet more contingent facts and so on. We can go on for ever with this process: the end result is that nothing is fully explained. Just as saying 'I was born because I was conceived by my parents' still leaves the question hanging of how my parents were conceived, so explaining any contingent event in terms of another contingent event never provides a sufficient reason (which the PSR says it *must* have). Unexplained events are still being used in the explanation. Leibniz's argument is that a sufficient and full explanation of any contingent fact can only end with a necessary being – a being that *must* exist, and so no further explanation is needed.

Another way of reaching the same point is to consider all the contingent facts in the whole universe – that is everything that has ever happened – as a single series. The reason/explanation for this entire series cannot be found in any particular fact of the series itself. This would make the series self-explanatory and therefore not contingent, but necessary. The sufficient explanation can only be found outside the series of facts. That is in a necessary being, a being who self-explains.

Using a loose analogy, consider a particular game of football as a series of particular events. The reason for the game of football itself can never be explained by reference to the particular throw-ins, goal kicks and so on, which occur within the game. To fully explain the game, concepts such as sport and leisure need to be introduced from outside of the game. Likewise, with all of the contingent events in the universe. This series of events cannot be explained by particular events within the series.

In summary Leibniz's argument is an *a posteriori* deductive argument. It is a deduction from the premises that contingent facts exist (this in only known *a posteriori*) and from the Principle of Sufficient Reason which states that no contingent fact can ever be true or existent unless there is a sufficient reason why things are as they are. The crux of the argument is that one contingent fact (or series of facts) cannot provide a sufficient reason for any other contingent fact. A sufficient reason must involve a necessary being/fact at some point. And this is God.

Criticism

Equating laws of thought with laws of the world

There is some philosophical dispute about whether laws of thoughts should be equated with laws of reality. In other words, just because something is not conceivable, does that automatically mean that it is not possible? (For more on this, see page 215 and the zombie argument.) Likewise with the Principle of Sufficient Reason: just because we mentally conceive that every fact has a sufficient reason for being that way, maybe it isn't the case in reality.

Indeed, as we discuss later (page 122), ideas from quantum mechanics can be used to suggest that on the very smallest levels events are not caused in the way our minds like to think. For sub atomic events, sufficient reasons may not exist to explain their occurrence.

How detailed does a 'sufficient' reason need to be?

What might count as a 'sufficient' reason for an event is open to some dispute. Consider an experiment in a lab where chemicals X and Y are mixed to make chemical Z. For the purposes of science, if I can explain the initial starting conditions of the experiment and articulate the scientific laws in question then I have given a full reason for the creation of chemical Z. Nothing more is needed. If this seems sufficient to you, then perhaps we can explain one contingent state of affairs in terms of other states of affairs. However, defenders of Leibniz might question whether this account is complete. Surely a complete account of the chemical reaction would also require me to give a reason for why the laws of science are exactly as they are and also why matter exists.

Could the existence of matter be necessary?

Leibniz argues that the contingency of objects/events can never fully explain the existence of other contingent objects/events. They can only be fully explained by reference to a necessary being. However, does this have to be God? Perhaps the necessary object (or objects) is matter/energy. This, it is claimed, can be neither created nor destroyed, so, in a sense, necessarily exists. The events in the universe can be explained fully (perhaps not completely) in these terms. Events are explained in terms of movements/arrangements of matter and the question of why there is matter is answered by the assertion that matter necessarily exists – it just is and this needs no more explanation. (Critics might say that this explanation for why matter exists is still lacking.) We examine the question of whether or not the concept of a necessary being is a coherent concept on page 124.

We have now looked at half a dozen examples of cosmological arguments (the Kalām argument, three ways from Aquinas, Descartes' causal principle and Leibniz's Principle of Sufficient Reason) and some specific criticisms associated with them. Let us turn to some general criticisms made of different forms of cosmological argument:

- The possibility of an infinite series
- Hume's objection to the causal principle
- The fallacy of composition
- The impossibility of a necessary being

Issues: The possibility of an infinite series

If the material world rests upon a similar ideal world, this ideal world must rest upon some other; and so on, without end. It were better, therefore, never to look beyond the present material world.[81]

Hume

'Turtles all the way down'

The quotation from Hume above suggests that if we genuinely wish to avoid an infinite regress of causes, then we should not search for an explanation beyond the natural universe, as if we move to a supernatural cause then we may be in the same situation as the apocryphal old lady at the philosophy lecture.

This story (told by Stephen Hawking, citing an incident possibly recounted by Bertrand Russell, or William James, and with a history tracing back to Hume and John Locke) is the equivalent of a philosophical urban myth. At the end of a lecture on modern cosmology the philosopher asks the audience if they have any questions, and a lady at the back of the audience puts up her hand. 'Your theory', she says, 'that the Earth and all the planets are little balls rotating around the Sun … it's completely wrong.' This particular philosopher is a patient chap, and asks her, 'What, in your view, is the right theory?' 'Well,' the lady is quick to respond, 'the Earth is a flat disc resting on the back of an elephant.' The philosopher, spotting the opportunity for the whole audience to learn about regresses, asks the lady, 'And what, exactly, is the elephant resting on?' 'A turtle,' the lady says. 'And what exactly,' the philosopher asks, 'is the turtle resting on?' 'Oh that's easy,' she says, 'it's turtles all the way down.'

So the search for an explanation for the universe seems to have hit a problem, for both believers and non-believers alike: is the universe 'turtles all the way down'? There seem to be three possible responses to her assertion:

- The woman in the cosmology lecture is wrong. The chain of explanations, or causes, comes to an end with a 'first cause' or 'prime mover' – which, as Aquinas reminds us, is what everyone calls 'God'. This claim, that an infinite regress isn't possible, is a claim that is central to most cosmological arguments. (We have already looked at this in the various cosmological arguments above.)
- The woman in the cosmology lecture is wrong, but so are supporters of the cosmological argument. We don't need to look for an explanation of the universe – whether it is an infinite series, or a very, very long series, we could just accept it exists as a brute fact, without further need of an explanation. (We look at this on page 126 below.)
- The woman in the cosmology lecture is sort of correct: it is turtles all the way down (but without any need to talk about turtles). In other words, we might be happy to accept that an infinite series (or infinite regress of explanations) is a coherent possibility. Many philosophers have criticised the cosmological argument because it fails to recognise the possibility of an infinite series, and in this section we look at this criticism in more detail.

The possibility of an infinite series and the Kalām argument

Mathematicians at least since the time of Newton and Leibniz (who separately invented the branch of mathematics called calculus) were able to work comfortably with the idea of infinitely small numbers. However, it wasn't until the work of the mathematician George Cantor (1845–1918) that maths was able to accommodate infinite numbers, and solve some of the paradoxes described by al-Ghazali (above, page 97, and in the activity below) which arise from infinite numbers. Cantor created a new form of mathematics, known as Set Theory, which was able to accommodate both finite and infinite sets. Set Theory is now a well-established branch of maths, and because 'real' infinity is now no longer thought of as a self-contradictory idea, the paradoxes of al-Ghazali do not show that the universe must be finite.

▶ **ACTIVITY**

Re-read the Jupiter/Saturn orbit paradox above on page 97, then complete the activity below to see how al-Ghazali arrived at the orbit paradox.

1. On a blank sheet of paper write out a long sequence of whole numbers starting with 1 and adding 1 each time:
   1 2 3 4 etc.
2. Underneath each number write down the list of even numbers, starting with 2.
   1 2 3 4 etc.
   2 4 6 8 etc.
3. Draw a line between the two sets of numbers:
   1 2 3 4 etc.
   | | | |
   2 4 6 8 etc.
4. If both sequences continue for infinity, will each list of numbers have the same number of numbers in it? Why? Why not? What puzzles do you think this raises?

Our whole universe was in a hot dense state,

Then nearly 14 billion years ago expansion started. Wait ...[82]

Over the last 90 years another route has opened up to support the claim of the Kalām argument that the universe has a beginning. Since Einstein first proposed his theory of general relativity and Edwin Hubble first discovered cosmological redshift, there has been an increasing scientific consensus that the universe had a finite past. The theory of the Big Bang, as we all know it, proposes that the universe began with a burst of cosmic inflation 13.7 billion years ago (Figure 1.32), and, even as recently as 2014, evidence in the form of gravitational waves was found to support this theory. In this case al-Ghazali seems to be vindicated in his claim that the universe had a finite past, independently of whether his attacks on the alternative proposition (that the universe had an infinite past) succeed.

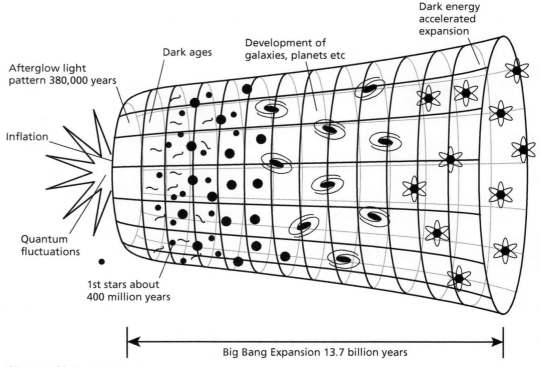

Figure 1.32 The Big Bang theory

Even if we concede, as most people now would, that the universe had a beginning, there are a number of other problems that face the Kalām argument. For example, do we need to concede that everything that has a beginning has a cause (premise 1 of the Kalām argument)? We shall see below (on page 122) that Russell uses another branch of modern science, quantum physics, for evidence that there are things which have a beginning but which do not have a cause. Another challenge can be made in the assumption that even if the universe has a cause (let us call it a first cause) then this first cause does not itself have a cause. David Hume asks why believers do not ask for an explanation for why God exists, and look for a cause of God; and if people are happy to accept that at least some things (first causes) don't have an explanation, or a cause, then could we not be happy to accept the universe without a cause or explanation?

The possibility of an infinite series and Aquinas' first and second ways

The idea of an infinite series also raises problems for Aquinas' first and second ways. Aquinas seems to be confusing a (very long) finite chain of causes, for which there would indeed have to be a first cause to begin the chain, with an infinite chain of causes. In the first instance, it is true, if you take away the first cause, then everything else disappears. But in the second instance there is no first cause to take away; the series of causes is infinite. J.L. Mackie gives the example of a series of hooks, all hanging from each other.[83] With a finite series of hooks, each one hangs on the one above it, until we reach the last (or first) hook, which must be attached to something. Take away the wall attachment and the hooks fall – that seems to be how Aquinas is imagining the chain of causes and effects. But with an infinite series of hooks, each is attached to the one above, and so on for ever: there is no first hook attached to a wall.

So philosophical critics of both the Kalām argument and Aquinas' arguments seem prepared to admit that an infinite regress is after all possible, and that there is no need to postulate a 'first cause'. However, by admitting this possibility such critics might be undermining a key weapon in the armoury of philosophy, what we might call the 'infinite regress fallacy'. Philosophers often aim to show a position is flawed precisely because it results in an infinite regress. However, we've just seen that some critics of cosmological arguments are proposing an infinite regress of causes as a coherent and valid alternative to a first cause. Such critics cannot have it both ways: either they hold on to the infinite regress fallacy, which is a useful tool against many a suspect idea, or they discard the fallacy in order to undermine such cosmological arguments. The contemporary theologian James Sadowsky (1923–2012) argued that philosophers stand to lose more by jettisoning the infinite regress fallacy, than by abandoning this line of attack on cosmological arguments.[84]

Hume's criticism – why stop at God?

Both types of cosmological arguments outlined above, those from contingency and those of causation, try to avoid an infinite regress of explanation by giving a privileged status within the chain of causes and effects to the 'first cause', or the being that is purported to be sustaining the universe. This privileged status, which the arguments hope that they have demonstrated, is caused by the first cause itself not being subject to the same rule as the things that it has caused (the universe): unlike everything else it is uncaused, unmoved, necessary. The first cause is its own explanation. But Hume questioned this assumption, asking why believers are happy to stop at God in their search for an explanation; instead they could continue their search and ask, 'Why God?' Alternatively, if we accept that there are some things that exist without explanation (like God) then is it possible that the universe could be one of those things, or as Hume says:

Why may not the material universe be the necessarily existent Being, according to this pretended explication of necessity?[85]
Hume

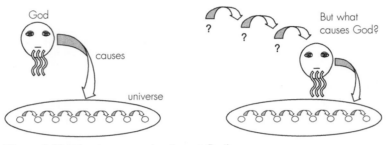

Figure 1.33 Why stop our explanations at God?

Hume suggests that seeking explanations beyond the physical universe will also lead to an infinite regress of explanations. So perhaps we would do better to stop our search for explanation with the universe: either accept it has no explanation, or find an explanation for the universe that lies within the universe.

Issues: Hume's objection to the causal principle

In a word, then, every effect is a distinct event from its cause.[86]
Hume

▶ **ACTIVITY**

Re-read the section on Hume in the teleological argument (above page 80) and consider how Hume's accounts of causation and constant conjunction might undermine the cosmological argument.

Several cosmological arguments rely on the everyday assumption that there is a series of causes such that 'every event has a cause', and we can identify this phrase as a causal principle. There is also a more technical causal principle, employed by Descartes in his version of the cosmological argument, namely that 'you cannot get more out of the effect than was already in the cause'. Both types of causal principle are vulnerable to Hume's scepticism about causation, which you may remember from his criticisms of the teleological argument. Hume's analysis of cause and effect, if correct, seriously undermines the foundations of those cosmological arguments that rely on causation or the causal principle to prove the existence of God.

Hume believed that we never actually experience causation; it is something our minds impose upon our perception of the world as a result of past experience. As you know, Hume gives a psychological account of causation, arguing that we develop our idea of causation by watching numerous instances of one thing happening (for example, a glass falling towards the floor) and another thing happening soon afterwards (the glass shattering). We have learnt from experience to associate one kind of event with another kind of event, and we start to think of these events as joined together by something we call 'causation'. Although we think we see one snooker ball cause another to move when it strikes it, all we in fact see is one ball move toward another until they touch, then the second ball move away (see Figure 1.34). We add the concept of 'cause' to this experience, once we have seen these two events happen together frequently enough (which Hume refers to as a 'constant conjunction'), but we can easily think of a particular event as not having this cause.[87] Causation, for Hume, is something that our minds add to our observations of the world, rather than something we observe in the world itself.

How does this apply to Descartes' causal principle? Remember that Descartes' cosmological argument is prompted by his thought that something must have caused his idea of God as a perfect being. Descartes' technical definition of the causal principle tells us that you cannot get more out of the effect than was already in the cause; the cause must be sufficiently powerful to bring about the effect. Descartes' conclusion that a perfect being must have caused his idea of a perfect being is built on this causal principle.

Well, for Hume, we cannot know *a priori* what is the cause of something – we cannot work backwards from the effect to determine the cause of it – and this is particularly true if we are seeing the effects for the first time. For example, if we have never seen ice before we wouldn't be able to work out how the ice was caused: I only learn that cold weather causes water to freeze by observing water freezing in cold weather. On this account the causal principle does not even get off the ground, as we would have no idea (for those events or effects that we had not observed before, or had not observed on many different occasions) what would even count as a sufficient cause.

If Hume's scepticism about causation is correct then it seriously damages Descartes' technical causal principle as well as the other 'causal principle' that every event has a cause. Hume is claiming that we don't know, for certain, if even simple events that we see with our very eyes are caused. We *believe* that they are caused, but only as a result of their constant conjunction (if we see them enough times) – we don't *know* they are caused. If we don't even know a single event is caused then how can we make claims (as Descartes and Aquinas make) that 'every event has a cause' or that 'you can't get more out of the effect than there was in the cause'? And if we don't even know if every event has a cause, then how can we know that the universe has a cause – that claim is so hopelessly removed from our experience as to be fantastical speculation. For Hume we cannot make such claims, and any proofs of God based on such a premise must fail.

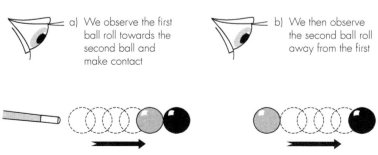

Figure 1.34 According to Hume we do not observe 'causation'

However, Hume's sceptical account of causation is a controversial one that many philosophers have taken objection to. A defender of cosmological arguments such as Elizabeth Anscombe (1919–2001) would say that Hume's concept of causation is a strange one, stemming from an unreasonably sceptical view of the world. Anscombe agrees that it may well be possible for us to imagine an event without having one cause or other.[88] For example, in Figure 1.34 we can imagine that the first snooker ball did not cause the second ball to move; perhaps it is a trick snooker table where the balls are moved by hidden magnets or wires. But even if it is possible to imagine an event without the cause we think it has, it is impossible for us to imagine an event as genuinely having no cause at all. And, so long as every event has some cause or other, then Aquinas' argument can indeed get off the ground.

Modern objections to the causal principle

Bertrand Russell offered a number of criticisms of the cosmological during his debate (in 1948, broadcast by the BBC) with the theologian F.C. Copleston (often referred to by his title, Father Copleston). In this debate Russell raises further questions about causation with Father Copleston. Copleston argues that something that is caused must either have another cause or be the cause of itself; that is, it must be a contingent being or a necessary being. So if there is an event which is caused by nothing else, nothing outside of itself, then it must be the cause of itself, which for Copleston is a necessary being: God. Russell pursues this angle of attack by questioning the idea that every particular thing in the world must have a cause (so crucial to cosmological argument).[89] Russell suggests that he is able to conceive of events that do not have a cause, and which clearly are not necessary beings. He illustrates this by drawing on the example of quantum physics, which at the time of the Copleston–Russell debate was cutting edge theoretical science, but which is now used in standard technology, embedded in all of our electronic devices, such as flash memory in USBs and smartphones. Since the 1920s, theoretical physics has raised the question of whether there are indeterminate events taking place at a sub-atomic, quantum level that have no cause at all (this has become known as the Copenhagen Interpretation, although there is not a complete consensus among physicists about this). Quantum fluctuations are often cited as an example of such uncaused events. Russell uses this theory to show that not all events have a cause, and that these particles that appear (for example, quantum tunnelling) are not 'necessary beings'. This invites the possibility that other events have no cause, including the appearance of the universe itself. If this is a genuine possibility then it again undermines one of the key premises of causal cosmological arguments: the assumption that everything must have a cause.

Issues: Cosmological arguments commit the fallacy of composition

But the WHOLE, you say, wants a cause.[90]
Hume

Even if it can be shown that Hume is wrong about causation, and every event does have a cause, then theologians have to defend the cosmological argument against a further criticism made by Hume. He attacks the move that cosmological arguments make from 'every event has a cause' to 'the whole series of events has a cause'.[91] Hume argues that if we have explained the cause of each event in the series, then it is unreasonable to ask what caused the whole series.

To illustrate the fallacy of composition Paul Edwards (1923–2004) gives the memorable example of the separate appearance of five Canadians in New York City.[92] Upon investigation we find that each of the Canadians is there for a different reason – one is moving there permanently, one is there to audition for an advert, one is there as a detective who is following the person going to the audition and so on. On a case-by-case basis we are able fully to explain their presence in New York (Figure 1.35). According to Hume it would be unreasonable for an investigator then to say 'I agree you have explained why each Canadian is here, but I want an explanation for the group as a whole – why is *it* in New York?' There is nothing more to say: an explanation of why each individual is there is enough; to demand an explanation of the whole group is unreasonable.

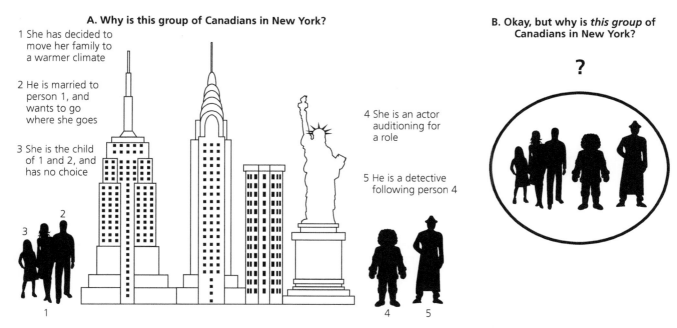

Figure 1.35 An example of the fallacy of composition. Each individual Canadian has a reason for being in New York, but it is an error to ask what reason the group *as a whole* has for being in New York

This has become known as the fallacy of composition: it is the fallacy of thinking that because there is some property common to each part of a group, this property must apply to the group as a whole. So just because a group of events all share the property of 'being caused' it would be a fallacy then to conclude from this that the group as a whole has the same property of 'being caused'.

Bertrand Russell, in the radio debate with Father Copleston, gives his own example of the fallacy of composition. It is true, says Russell, that every member of the human species has a mother, but it would be a fallacy then to conclude from this that our species as a whole must have a mother.[93] Similarly, every event within a series may indeed have a cause, but it is a fallacy to conclude that the whole series must have a cause. So 'cause and effect' is taken to be a concept which applies to particular events occurring in the universe, but it is a mistake then to try to apply the concept to the universe as a whole.

If Hume and Russell are right, then Aquinas is mistaken in thinking that there must be a first cause that started the chain of cause and effects, and this type of cosmological argument fails.

▶ACTIVITY

Read through the following claims:

1. Every nice girl loves a sailor; therefore there is one sailor that all nice girls love. (*This is part of a song from the Second World War.*)
2. Every journey has a destination; therefore there is one destination for all journeys.
3. All activities are aimed towards some goal; therefore there is one goal that all activities ultimately aim at. (*This is the opening section of Aristotle's* Ethics.)
4. Everyone in Tunbridge Wells voted Tory in the last election; therefore Tunbridge Wells is a Tory constituency.
5. Every proof of God's existence is flawed; therefore trying to prove God's existence is a flawed activity.
6. Each person's happiness is a good to that person; therefore the general happiness is the good to the general aggregate of all persons. (*This is part of Mill's proof of utilitarianism.*)
7. Every atom is colourless; therefore a collection of atoms (for example, in the form of a postbox) is colourless.
8. You can get much better video footage if you stand and hold up your phone at a concert; therefore everyone can get much better footage if everyone stands and holds up their phone at that concert.
9. It is good for each individual's bank balance to save as much money as possible; therefore it is good for the economy as a whole for each individual to save as much money as possible. (*In economics this is known as the 'paradox of thrift'.*)
10. As a philosophy student you will become a better philosopher if you practise and take your homework seriously; therefore everyone studying philosophy will become a better philosopher if they practise and take their homework seriously.

Which of the claims are guilty of the fallacy of composition? Explain why.

Which of the claims are not guilty of the fallacy of composition? Explain why not.

The Austrian–American moral philosopher Paul Edwards acknowledges that perhaps the fallacy of composition is misplaced, and that what the defender of the cosmological argument is searching for is not a *cause* (one above and beyond all the contingent causes) but an *explanation*.[94] A series of contingent events, even an infinite series of contingent events, is best explained by something non-contingent, a necessary being. We explore the concept of a necessary being immediately below, and we return to the question of whether the universe really does need an explanation on page 126.

Issues: The impossibility of a necessary being

Towards the start of his debate with Russell, Copleston puts forward a version of the cosmological argument which we have referred to as the argument from contingency, drawn from Aquinas' third way. The world, Copleston maintains, consists of beings and events which are not dependent on themselves for their own existence, but *are* dependent upon a preceding, or higher-order, being or event. If we are to explain this then we cannot go back infinitely, but must come to a being that contains within itself the reason for its own existence. In other words, contingent beings are ultimately dependent on a *necessary being*. Both David Hume and Bertrand Russell would take issue with this kind of claim (made, as we have seen, by Aquinas and by Leibniz). You have already encountered Hume's angle of attack when studying his criticism of the ontological argument but it is worth revisiting his words, and seeing how these are echoed in Russell's:

> *I shall begin with observing, that there is an evident absurdity in pretending to demonstrate a matter of fact, or to prove it by any arguments* a priori. *Nothing is demonstrable, unless the contrary implies a contradiction. Nothing, that is distinctly conceivable, implies a contradiction. Whatever we conceive as existent, we can also conceive as non-existent. There is no being, therefore, whose non-existence implies a contradiction. Consequently there is no being, whose existence is demonstrable. I propose this argument as entirely decisive, and am willing to rest the whole controversy upon it.*[95]
> Hume

> *The word 'necessary', it seems to me, is a useless word except as applied to analytic propositions, not to things.*[96]
> Russell

Hume and Russell separately argue that we can talk about necessary propositions or statements, but we cannot talk about necessary beings and to do so is a misuse of the term 'necessary'. The concept of necessity only applies to statements, not to things that exist. In the light of this account of necessity, the meaning of the statement 'God is a necessary being' is that 'the proposition "God exists" is necessarily true' – in which case, we should investigate whether or not the statement 'God exists' is a necessary truth.[97]

Hume and Russell are adhering to the general understanding that a proposition which is a necessary truth is one that it is self-contradictory to deny; it is analytic and it is true by definition. For example: it is not possible to deny that 'all bachelors are unmarried men'; denying it would yield 'it is not true that all bachelors are unmarried men', which is equivalent (because of the meanings of the terms) to 'it is not true that all unmarried men are unmarried men', which is self-contradictory.[98]

▶ **ACTIVITY**

Which of the following statements (1–9) are necessary truths? (You may recall some of these from your study of the ontological arguments.) In order to work out whether they are necessary truths or not you should:

a) Identify the predicate in the proposition.
b) Change the predicate so that it is the opposite, or converse or is just very different.
c) Rewrite the proposition, including the new predicate (determined in b).
d) Ask yourself 'Is this proposition now self-contradictory?'
e) If it is self-contradictory then the original proposition was a necessary proposition.

The first example has been completed for you.

1   A bachelor is an unmarried man.
   a) The predicate is 'unmarried man'.
   b) The converse of this predicate is 'married man'.
   c) 'A bachelor is a married man.'
   d) This is a contradiction. It is now asserting that an unmarried man is a married man.
   e) Therefore the original proposition 1 is a necessary truth.

2 A brother is a male sibling.
3 Your teacher's brother is a bachelor.
4 A triangle has three sides.
5 Ghosts exist.
6 A unicorn is a horse with a horn.
7 Unicorns exist.
8 Theresa May is the Prime Minister of Great Britain.
9 There are nine examples of propositions in this activity.

For both Hume and for Russell there is no *being* for which it would be self-contradictory to deny. For any being, X, we can assert 'X does not exist' without contradiction. Take the existential propositions, such as 'Ghosts exist' or 'Socrates once existed', or even 'God exists' – these can all be denied without self-contradiction. As Hume points out, anything we can conceive of as existing, we can also conceive of as non-existing. Russell, during his debate with Copleston, links the cosmological argument to the ontological argument, which as you know is an argument that tries to prove the necessity of God's existence. But for Russell (see page 52, in his criticism of the ontological argument) any claim about existence cannot be analytic, but must be synthetic. It is not possible to list all the attributes of a being (its essence), and then add a further characteristic – namely 'existence' – to this list, because existence is not a predicate (it is not a characteristic).

Russell and Hume agree that we cannot ascribe the property of 'necessity' to anything which exists, and even Aquinas accepted that 'God exists' was not self-evident and could be meaningfully denied.[99] If the existence of an alleged 'necessary being' can be denied without contradiction, then it turns out that the being did not have the quality of being necessary after all. As Hume puts it, 'The words "necessary existence" have no meaning, or, which is the same thing, none that is consistent.'[100] Not all philosophers agree with this analysis of necessity, but if it is correct then the conclusion (made as part of Aquinas' third way or Leibniz's Principle of Sufficient Reason) that God is a necessary being is seriously undermined.

One final issue – does the universe really need an explanation?

A final criticism is put very well by Bertrand Russell in his radio debate with Father Copleston. Earlier we mentioned that cosmological arguments sprung from a very real need many of us have to answer the questions 'Why are we here?' and 'Why does the universe exist?' Cosmological arguments can be seen as complex and arduous expressions of this need for an answer. To some it may seem obvious that the universe is crying out for an explanation: it must have come from somewhere, there must be a reason that it exists. However, to others it is not so obvious. The Copleston–Russell debate does eventually settle on the crucial issue of whether or not the universe is in need of an explanation. For Copleston he needs to be able to answer the question 'Why is all this here?' And his answer is God. But for Russell:

I should say the universe is just there, and that's all.[101]
Russell

In the context of the debate, Russell is arguing that it is meaningless even to ask the question 'What caused the universe?' We have already seen above Russell's reasons for saying this; namely that it is a fallacy to argue that, because the parts of the universe have a cause, therefore the whole must have a cause. But in his dismissal of Copleston's religious position, Russell is expressing something much more primitive than this: he simply does not feel a need for any ultimate answers; he does not think the universe is crying out for an explanation. For Russell the universe *just is*, period.

▶ACTIVITY

1. Read through each of the five main cosmological arguments above.
2. Create a table (like the one below) and complete it by taking steps 3 and 4.
3. Now go through each criticism, identifying for each argument which criticism applies to it.
4. Where a criticism does apply, write in the table the specific premise (or hidden premise, or assumption or conclusion) that the criticism applies to: for example, identify the specific premise it undermines, or the invalidity of a particular step.

Type of cosmological argument	Possibility of an infinite regress	Objections to the causal principle	The fallacy of composition	Impossibility of a necessary being
Kalām's argument				
Aquinas' first way				
Aquinas' second way				
Aquinas' third way				
Descartes' argument from his continuing existence				
Leibniz's argument from the Principle of Sufficient Reason				

Summary: Cosmological arguments

Cosmological arguments are attractive to people who feel that the universe is lacking something, and needs explaining. This feeling makes the conclusion that God is the ultimate explanation for why the universe exists more palatable. However, for people who do not see the universe in this way, a cosmological argument remains puzzling: if someone is seeking an explanation, then stopping at God seems arbitrary. Why not stop looking for explanations before you get to God? Or why not search for an explanation of why God exists? It may simply be that, as with other arguments for God's existence, they only make sense if you already have some faith. And if you do believe in God, then cosmological arguments help to reveal another facet of God: that he must be the unmoved mover, the uncaused cause and a necessary being.

You have now studied three of the most important types of arguments put forward by religious philosophers and thinkers in order to demonstrate God's existence. Of these three proofs only one type, the ontological argument, is an *a priori* argument through-and-through, in other words it is constructed on the basis of reason alone, without reference to experience. It appears to work as an argument because it carefully analyses the concept of 'God' and in particular it highlights the special nature of God as a 'necessary' being – one whose non-existence we cannot conceive. So apparently part of the very essence of God is that he must exist.

The other two types of arguments are both built from our experience of the world. Cosmological arguments draw on very general facts about the universe (for example, the fact that it exists at all, or that everything must have a cause) but are generally constructed as deductive arguments. Design arguments draw on very specific features of the universe (for example, that living things appear to be made of parts, each of which has a purpose in helping that living thing to survive) and many use inductive or abductive reasoning to draw the conclusion that the universe must have been designed.

By exploring and unpacking key metaphysical concepts like causation, existence and necessity you will have begun to manipulate and analyse the key building blocks on which metaphysical claims and arguments are made. By studying these arguments for God's existence and the issues raised against them, you will have improved your critical and logical thinking skills, whether or not you agree with their conclusions. By understanding how an argument is built up, what its component parts are and how it 'adds up', you will strengthen the construction of your own arguments. By finding systematic errors that can occur in our argument construction (for example, the fallacy of composition or weaknesses in analogical reasoning) then you will find it easier to identify them when they occur in other proofs. By reading about counter examples or coming up with your own counter evidence, you will be better equipped to make your own arguments more robust and to find flaws in the arguments other people propose. So reading about and analysing the arguments for the existence of God has, we hope, made you a better philosopher.

1.2.4 The problem of evil

I didn't want to harm the man. I thought he was a very nice gentleman. Soft-spoken. I thought so right up to the moment I cut his throat.[102]
The killer, Perry Smith

I form light and create darkness, I make peace and create evil, I the Lord, do all these things.
Isaiah 45:7

Experimenting with ideas

1 Write down a list of ten things that have happened in the world in the last fifteen years that you regard as evil. Try to be as specific as you can.
2 What do these things have in common – what makes them evil?
3 Can you categorise your examples into different types of evil?

Whether God's attributes can be reconciled with the problem of evil

The problem of evil remains one of the most contentious and unsettling areas in the philosophy of religion. We have encountered it, in a nutshell, on page 27 when looking at the possible incoherence of the concept of God. The issue is whether the attributes ascribed to God (either the God of the philosophers or the God of Abraham), such as God's supreme goodness, omnipotence and omniscience are compatible with the continuous, ongoing and unavoidable 'evil' that exists in the world God has purportedly created.

The problem of evil is important to believers and non-believers alike: believers because they have to reconcile their belief in a loving God with their knowledge of the terrible suffering that exists in the world; non-believers because they often claim that the existence of evil is the reason that they don't believe in the existence of God. Unlike some of the other metaphysical issues that we have encountered (What are the attributes of God? Can his existence be proved? Is he a necessary being?), the problem of evil is encountered directly in our experience of life, and not simply through intellectual investigation. Before we outline the problem of evil in more detail we should first examine what is meant by 'evil' in the context of the philosophy of religion.

At a very general level, 'evil' is taken to refer to those unpleasant, destructive, painful and negative experiences that sentient beings have. These negative experiences can be grouped into the physical (including hunger, cold, pain) and the mental (including misery, anguish, terror), and we can summarise these two types of experience as pain and suffering.[103] Pain and suffering are commonplace in the lives of creatures on this planet, and so evil confronts us on a daily basis.

Theologians have offered other, more technical, definitions of evil. For example, St Augustine defines evil as that 'which we fear, or the act of fearing itself'.[104] The idea of fear as an evil in itself is echoed in Truman Capote's *In Cold Blood*, in an account of a horrific multiple murder (by two drifters, Perry Smith and Dick Hickock) and its aftermath in a sleepy mid-west American town in 1959. In the townspeople's panic following the murders there is a rush to buy locks and bolts to protect their homes:

> *Folks ain't particular what brand they buy; they just want them to hold. Imagination of course can open any door – turn the key and let terror walk right in.*[105]

If we apply Augustine's account of evil to the situation that these townsfolk find themselves in, then we can identify both the cold-blooded murderers and the terror they leave behind as evil. But Augustine and Aquinas are careful to argue that evil is not a 'thing' (a mysterious substance or presence, for example) but is the absence of goodness. Their account of goodness was strongly influenced by Plato and Aristotle's understanding of 'good', which contained the idea of goal or purpose. For Aristotle, 'good' refers to the complete fulfilment of a thing's natural potential. So a good can-opener is one that is excellent at opening cans – it possesses all the relevant features (the Greeks would call them 'virtues') necessary for opening cans safely and efficiently. Similarly a good oak tree is one that has all the virtues of an oak tree – it has strong roots, is disease free, efficiently photosynthesises and produces numerous acorns.

> *[Evil is] nothing but the corruption of natural measure, form or order. What is called an evil nature is a corrupt nature ... It is bad only so far as it has been corrupted.*[106]
> **Augustine**

For Augustine, and for Aquinas, evil is not a concrete presence or substance, it is simply the 'privation of good';[107] that is, a lack of goodness, a failure to flourish or fulfil a natural purpose. We shall see later that this account of evil is fundamental to Augustine's explanation of why it exists. Augustine sees the world, as created by God, in terms of goodness; evil is introduced only later as some disorder within the goodness of God's creation.

The nature of moral evil and natural evil

In the activity above you might well have found that your examples of evil fell easily into two types: 'pain and suffering caused by humans' and 'pain and suffering caused by nature'. Philosophers of religion have traditionally identified two sources of evil: physical (or natural) and moral.[108] Physical or 'natural' evil refers to the pain and suffering of sentient beings that occurs independently of human actions. On the morning of All Saints' Day (1 November) 1755, the city of Lisbon in Portugal was hit by an earthquake that wrenched streets apart by 5 metre fissures and turned the city into ruins. Soon afterwards a massive tsunami swept into the remains of the city, as a result of the earthquake, and in the areas not destroyed by earth or water, a fire broke out that lasted for days. Around a third of all the inhabitants of Lisbon were burned, drowned or crushed – possibly 90,000 people. When the French philosopher Voltaire heard the news he wrote his 'Poem on the Disaster of Lisbon' (see the extract below) that had a huge impact on European intellectuals of the day.

> *Mistaken philosophers who cry: 'All is well',*
>
> *Approach, look upon these frightful ruins ...*
>
> *These scattered limbs beneath these broken marbles;*
>
> *A hundred thousand wretches swallowed by the earth[.]*

For Voltaire, the immense and pointless suffering of innocent people caused by the Lisbon earthquake was a troubling sign that this was not, after all, the 'best possible world'. The Boxing Day tsunami in 2004 that killed 230,000 people around the Indian Ocean is another instance of a disaster that would fall under the heading 'natural evil'. There are countless other examples of pain and suffering that could be given: the 'cloaking' device of cancerous cells that enables them to stay hidden from our immune systems and multiply their cancer unchecked; the habits of certain types of wasps to lay their eggs in caterpillars which are then eaten alive from the inside out; the mass extinction of dinosaurs 65 million years ago; the human and non-human victims of viruses, bacteria and other microscopic killers. Nature is red with blood and pain.

'Moral evil' refers to those acts of cruelty, viciousness and injustice carried out by humans upon fellow humans and other creatures, and which, for theologians, includes the concept of 'sin'. According to the American scientist and writer Jared Diamond, since the murderous genocides of Hitler and Stalin in the 1930s and 1940s, in which tens of millions of people were killed, there have been a further 17 known genocides across the world. The soul-searching and hand-wringing after the Second World War, the creation of the United Nations, the pursuit of democracy and global capitalism have been accompanied by an increase, rather than a decrease, in the number of politicised mass murders around the world. For Jared Diamond these genocides have a close connection with tensions arising in society for geopolitical reasons: there are not enough resources to go round an increasing population and the situation is set to get worse.[109] But it was humans, not nature, who in 1994 executed around 800,000 people of Rwanda in a few weeks. As with natural evil, the suffering on this headline scale is more than matched by the daily torture and abuse of individuals around the world that goes unnoticed, unpublicised and unpunished.

The relationship between moral evil and natural evil

What is the relationship between natural and moral evil? For some, natural evil might be seen as a consequence of human action or inaction, and hence as a subset, of moral evil. For example, crop failure, drought and starvation are often brought about by overpopulation, over-farming, the destruction of the environment, and so on. So these 'natural evils' might be read as 'moral evils', but there are other, more controversial examples of this reading. The human immunodeficiency virus (HIV), which has killed over 25 million people in the last 35 years, has controversially been seen by some as a punishment for human sinfulness. St Augustine argued that the once perfect world of the Garden of Eden has been made imperfect by the 'original sin' of Adam (pages 141–2, the Free Will defence) and that the suffering caused by natural disasters and disease is God's punishment for this original moral evil.

It is also possible to regard moral evil as a form of natural evil, although this involves a philosophical view of human nature and freedom that is far removed from the teachings of western religious traditions: namely the view that humans do not hold a privileged position within the natural world. If humans are on a continuum with the rest of nature, then 'moral evil' is not distinct from the 'natural' pain and suffering caused by earthquakes, rabid dogs and malaria-carrying mosquitoes. If our species is governed by the same principles as all other forms of life, then moral evil is just one specific type of the pain and suffering that all animals inevitably endure. John Stuart Mill (1806–73, in *Three Essays on Religion*, 1874) argues that natural evil arises from the malfunctioning of the universe, which was originally intended for the preservation, not destruction, of life. If we assume, as Mill and Darwin did, that humans do not have a divine purpose or privileged place in the hierarchy of animals, then it is easier to see moral evil as a form of natural evil. Humans are jealous, live in close social groups, compete with one another for food, resources and mates, and have trouble controlling their violent and sometimes murderous impulses. Without any theological scaffolding, such as that of original sin, it is possible to view human actions that cause pain and suffering ('moral evil') as simply an extreme case of the 'natural' pain and suffering inflicted in the rest of the animal kingdom.

The logical and evidential forms of the problem of evil

Experimenting with ideas

Refer to the examples of evil you gave in the activity on page 129.

1 Which of these evils would you prevent if you were:
    a) a billionaire
    b) Superman
    c) even more powerful than Superman?
2 In the case of c) are there any evils you would allow to persist? Why/why not?

The problem of evil affects all the theistic religions, which have as their object of worship a God who is the all-powerful creator of the world, and who cares deeply for his creation. We find the problem clearly stated in the works of both St Augustine and Aquinas,[110] but we can also find earlier versions dating back to the ancient Greek philosopher Epicurus. This is how Epicurus frames the problem:

> *God either wishes to take away evils, and is unable; or he is able, and is unwilling; or he is neither willing nor able; or he is both willing and able. If he is willing and is unable, he is feeble, which is not in accordance with the character of God; if he is able and unwilling, he is envious, which is equally at variance with God; if he is neither willing nor able, he is both envious and feeble, and therefore not God; if he is both willing and able ... from what source then are evils? Or why does he not remove them?*[111]
>
> Epicurus

As John Hick puts it: 'Can the presence of evil in the world be reconciled with the existence of a God who is unlimited both in goodness and in power?'[112] More recently, philosophers have identified at least two different formulations of the problem of evil: the logical problem and the evidential problem. The first formulation, the logical problem of evil, is an *a priori* argument put forward by atheists to show that belief in God is false because it involves holding a set of contradictory beliefs. The second formulation, the evidential problem of evil, is an *a posteriori* argument proposed by atheists to show that the existence of evil makes it less likely that God exists.

The logical problem of evil

> *In its simplest form the problem is this: God is omnipotent; God is wholly good; and yet evil exists. There seems to be some contradiction between these three propositions, so that if any two of them were true the third would be false. But at the same time all three are essential parts of most theological positions: the theologian, it seems, at once* must *adhere and* cannot *consistently adhere to all three.*[113]
> J.L. Mackie

We can find one of the clearest statements of the logical problem of evil in J.L. Mackie's paper 'Evil and Omnipotence'.[114] Put simply, for Mackie the logical problem of evil asserts that believers are committed to holding three inconsistent beliefs:

1 God is omnipotent.
2 God is wholly good.
3 Evil exists.

There is a contradiction that needs resolving here, and Mackie argues that for any two of these propositions to be true then the third one would be false. Moreover, believing in the truth of all three propositions is an essential part of what it is to be a theist, so, as Mackie points out, the believer must hold all three to be true, and at the same time cannot hold all three to be true (because there is a contradiction).

ACTIVITY

a) Using these three propositions do you think it is possible for an atheist to construct an argument to prove that God cannot exist?
b) Write down any additional premises that you think would be needed to make the argument watertight.
c) How might believers criticise such an argument? (Which premises or steps would they deny?)

Mackie states the problem more clearly by adding two further propositions that really bring out the contradiction:

4 A good being eliminates evil as far as it can.
5 There are no limits to what an omnipotent being can do.

We shall see later that Alvin Plantinga (1932–) disagrees with Mackie, but it is Plantinga who wants to make Mackie's argument as clear as possible before attacking it. He thinks that Mackie needs to add an amendment to 4, to avoid the charge that God might be all-loving and all-powerful, but might not actually know about the pain and suffering in his creation. Plantinga amends proposition 4 to:

4a Every good thing always eliminates every evil that *it knows about* and can eliminate.[115]

With these crucial additions in place, Mackie believes he is able to show that all believers agree with propositions 1–5, and yet these propositions cannot be held to be true simultaneously. In which case believers must give up their

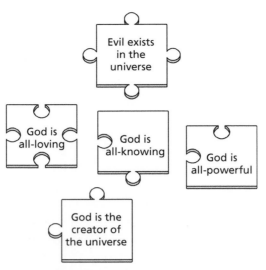

Figure 1.36 It appears that not all of these beliefs can be true at once. Yet evil certainly seems to be real, so, does God not know about it? Does he not care about it? Is he unable to stop it? If we opt for any of these it seems that the God of the philosophers does not exist

belief in at least one of these statements, or they must admit that they have a 'positively irrational' and contradictory belief in God.

If Mackie is right, then which statement should the believer surrender? It seems undeniable that there is pain and suffering in the universe; after all, a central tenet of Christianity is that Jesus himself suffered when he was crucified, and thus believers will agree that 3 is true.[116] Proposition 5 appears to be just a simple clarification of what is meant by 'omnipotent', so believers may be happy to accept 5 as true. What about propositions 1 or 2? The contradiction would disappear if believers jettisoned some, or all, of the qualities of God, as in that case either God would not be able to do anything about evil, or he would not know that it is happening, or he would not care. But as Epicurus points out, if God does not have the will to eradicate evil (he is not all-loving) or if he does not have the power to do so (he is not omnipotent) then he would no longer be God at all. In which case the believer, in order to remain a theist, cannot give up their belief in God's power or goodness. So has the believer been revealed by Mackie to hold a set of inconsistent and contradictory beliefs?

Plantinga thinks not, and the significant disagreement with Mackie is over proposition 4. This is the crux of the argument: Mackie thinks he is able to formulate a statement that all believers will accept is true, which runs along the lines of 'good and loving creatures aim to get rid of evil'. But Plantinga argues that believers do not accept this, and that there is far more subtlety to belief in God than Mackie gives credit for. We shall see below that many proposed solutions to the problem of evil argue that evil is in some way good, or contributes to something good. In which case, believers do not accept proposition 4, even in its revised versions, because they hold that getting rid of evil will in some way damage an even greater good that God intends for his creation. What these greater goods are we shall explore in detail later. But first let us turn to the other formulation, the evidential problem of evil, which accepts that 'believing in God' and 'knowing that evil exists' are not logically contradictory, but which tries to show that evil still seriously undermines the truth of theism.

The evidential problem of evil

> *God who could create the universe, is to our finite minds omnipotent and omniscient, and it revolts our understanding to suppose that his benevolence is not unbounded, for what advantage can there be in the sufferings of millions of the lower animals throughout almost endless time?*[117]
> Darwin

Darwin's experiences as a biologist brought him face to face with the daily pain and suffering of animals. For many thinkers, including Darwin, David Hume and the contemporary philosopher William Rowe, the sheer amount of evil in the world weighs against there being a God who is omnipotent and wholly good. After all, would an almighty, all-knowing, all-loving God allow such extraordinary pain and suffering to exist? Why does he not intervene to prevent earthquakes that kill tens of thousands, or viruses that kill millions? Why does he allow psychopaths and serial killers to unleash their cruelty on innocent people? Why has he permitted genocide after genocide in the last hundred years?

This is not a logical argument, as it does not aim to show that the theist holds a set of inconsistent beliefs. Instead it is posing a question: 'Given the existence of evil, which of the following is the more reasonable hypothesis?'

- **H1:** There is an infinitely powerful, wholly good God who created the world.

  or

- **H2:** There is no such God.

For Hume and Rowe, the existence of evil is clear evidence in favour of the second hypothesis. As Hume says:

> *We must forever find it impossible to reconcile any mixture of evil in the universe with infinite attributes ... But supposing the Author of nature to be finitely perfect, though far exceeding mankind, a satisfactory account may then be given of natural and moral evil.*[118]
> Hume

William Rowe cites gratuitous and pointless evil as evidence that a theistic God does not exist at all.[119] As an example of gratuitous evil, Rowe describes the suffering of a deer, trapped and horribly burned by a forest fire, which lies in agony for several days before dying. The agony endured by the deer seems to be pointless, and preventable, but Rowe accepts that such an example does not prove that God does not exist. However, he does maintain that such gratuitous evil makes it reasonable to believe in H2 and reject H1.

ACTIVITY

Refer to the examples of evil you gave in the activity on page 129.

Think of as many reasons as you can why God might permit such evils to exist. (Write down every reason, no matter how absurd, or whether or not you believe it to be true.) It may help if you consider the analogy of why loving, or generous, or thoughtful people (doctors, parents, teachers, charity workers and so on) might sometimes allow someone to suffer, and what they hope to achieve by allowing this.

Responses to the problem of evil, and issues arising from these responses

The response of atheists – there is no God

We have already encountered one way of resolving the problem of evil, which is the solution that Mackie was arguing for, namely the atheist's solution:

- God *does not* exist. There is no such omnipotent, omniscient, benevolent being, and we should realise that humans just have to cope alone with the enormity of pain and suffering in the world.

Clearly this is not an acceptable solution to the problem of evil for people who believe in God. However, nor is it an easy or comforting solution to those people who have properly embraced a considered form of atheism.

Sartre's response

> *When we speak of abandonment ... we only mean to say that God does not exist, and that it is necessary to draw the consequences of his absence right to the end.*[120]
>
> **Sartre**

The French philosopher and author Jean-Paul Sartre (1905–80) claimed that the realisation that there is no God, no support, no help available to us in this cruel world, gives rise to deep feelings of 'abandonment'. When we are growing up we often believe, or are told, that there is a purpose to life or some kind of meaning to existence and some reason for the suffering in the world. It is very comforting to believe that an external authority exists, someone who is there to look after to us, to support us, to give purpose to our lives and to dish out justice when we die. But for Sartre we are simply deceiving ourselves and once we realise that there is no God then the residue of our past belief (that is, our belief that there was a being who was on our side, and looking out for us) lingers and we feel abandoned, even though for Sartre there never was a God. We still deeply feel the loss of the security which we had when we believed in God. Sartre's philosophy of EXISTENTIALISM urges us to shed ourselves of our deceptions and to embrace our freedom and live more authentic lives, which means truly confronting the consequences of atheism.

For Sartre this feeling of abandonment must spur us forward philosophically: if there is no God then what else follows from this? Well, at least one of the consequences is that we must face the horror of human and animal suffering alone and without explanation, without meaning, and without any hope that people will get their just deserts in the end. Without God, Sartre claims, there is also no real possibility of any external set of moral beliefs. For Sartre there is no human nature and without God we are free to invent our own moral systems, or behave in whatever way we want to – an unsettling prospect for many of us. Sartre writes that 'man is nothing else but that which he makes of himself',[121] which within Sartre's theory could mean that we each individually forge our own paths and in doing so create the kind of individual we are, or it could mean that we as human beings are free to create an image of humanity that we want others to aspire to.[122] So perhaps the solution to the problem of evil arrived at by the authentic atheist – namely that God does not exist and we are free to create our own moral paths bearing all the responsibility this brings – is one of the most difficult solutions to live with in the end.

Mary Midgley's response

The moral philosopher Mary Midgley (1919–) wrote *Wickedness: A Philosophical Essay* in order to understand why it is that human beings treat each other so abominably and cause avoidable suffering. This problem of evil (or 'wickedness' as she refers to it) is our problem not God's, says Midgley, and she steers away from the 'God on trial' approach taken by some philosophers. Like Sartre, Midgley is an atheist, but she disagrees with Sartre's extreme view of human freedom noting Sartre's arrogance in claiming that we are nothing else but that what we make of ourselves.[123] Midgley argues that we need properly to explore human nature and our natural motivations, and she draws on psychology, evolutionary biology, psychoanalysis and philosophy to achieve her goal of understanding the natural tendency humans have towards wickedness.

Midgley uses a definition of evil which resonates with that of Augustine's (above, page 130), namely that evil is the absence of good.[124] Midgley's definition emphasises her point that we are mistaken if we think that wicked acts are caused by wicked people. She quotes the psychologist Erich Fromm, who wrote that 'as long as one believes that the evil man wears horns, one will not discover an evil man.'[125] For Midgley, all of us are capable of wickedness through caring about ourselves more than others, through thoughtlessness, through weakness of the will, and through allowing one motive to dominate all others. Instead of looking at evil primarily as a tendency to behave in a particular way, Midgley thinks we should see wickedness as a kind of failure, which we are all vulnerable to, of not living the kind of positive life that we are all capable of living.

Midgley identifies two types of failure which lead to wickedness; the first type is that which she locates in 'the followers'. These are people are just like us and allow themselves to be passively drawn into wickedness through their inaction, or through turning a blind eye to their ideals and principles – something that Socrates noted over two thousand years ago.

anthology 1.18

For an example of a follower, Midgley draws on the writings of Hannah Arendt who reported on the trial in Israel of the senior SS officer Adolf Eichmann in 1961. Eichmann was responsible for co-ordinating the deportation of millions of Jews to death camps and concentration camp during the Second World War. He was found guilty of war crimes and was hanged in 1962. What struck Arendt was the 'banality of evil' she saw in Eichmann: he was a bureaucrat, eager to be promoted, lacking imagination. Arendt noted how 'he was not stupid. It was sheer thoughtlessness … that predisposed him to become one of the greatest criminals of that period'[126]. Individual moral responsibility may be obscured by being part of an organisation (a business or government or society) which is acting wickedly – but the 'followers' must still bear individual responsibility for their own actions as cogs in the machinery of that organisation.

The second type of failure is that of 'the instigators', those people who actively initiate wicked acts. Their actions are driven by an obsessive motive, such as pride, ambition, envy or desire, which is not wicked in itself but which the 'instigator' fails to control and which is allowed to swallow up all other motives to destructive effect.

Midgley argues that searching for something, or someone, to blame for the existence of wickedness will not help us in solving this problem. We should not blame God, or criminals (in or out of government!) or society, if we genuinely want to understand how human conduct goes wrong. Nor should we blame our biology, even though it is true that wickedness can be understood as emerging from a set of innate motivations which humans possess (aggression, territoriality, possessiveness, competitiveness, dominance). Midgley argues that we should not be fatalistic about the consequences of these natural motives; the fact that we have these motivations does not mean that they inevitably lead to wickedness. For Midgley we are not forced to act by our fate or by our biology: even though we are determined by natural laws, we still have free will (page 140 below) that enables us to operate within these laws and so are each responsible for our own actions. If we have powerful natural motivations, then we must learn to direct these motivations properly, for example in the moral outrage and anger we feel at witnessing evil, and we must create societies in which these natural motivations are given proper boundaries.

The response of believers: theodicies and defences

Since the problem of evil was first posed, theists have sought to resolve it without abandoning their belief in an all-powerful, all-knowing and all-loving God. There have been many theistic solutions to (or defences against) the problem of evil, but we can group the main responses into four types:

1 God *does* exist, and the enormity of pain and suffering in the world is real, but we should realise that God is *not* in fact omnipotent, omniscient and benevolent. (There are several alternative theologies to mainstream, traditional, belief in God.)
2 God *does* exist, and is omnipotent, omniscient and benevolent, but we should realise that the enormity of pain and suffering in this world is *balanced by* even greater good – namely justice in the next life. (We can term this the 'Afterlife defence'.)
3 God *does* exist, and is omnipotent, omniscient and benevolent, but we should realise that the enormity of pain and suffering is the *consequence of* an even greater good – namely humans having free will. (This is known as the 'Free Will defence'.)
4 God *does* exist, and is omnipotent, omniscient and benevolent, but we should realise that the enormity of pain and suffering actually *leads to* an even greater good – namely humans fulfilling their potential. (This has become known as the 'soul-making defence'.)

Of these, the last three preserve theism as a religious system, and solutions of this type have come to be termed THEODICIES.[127] John Hick, in his book *Evil and the God of Love*, identifies two major theodicies in western philosophy of religion: the Augustinian theodicy, which we examine below in the exploration of the Free Will defence, and the Irenaean theodicy, which we look at when we assess Hick's own soul-making defence. We might further categorise such solutions as either 'strong' or 'weak' theodicies. A strong theodicy provides an explanation or justification of why God permits the existence of evil within his creation. A weak theodicy (or 'defence') may not venture to explain *why* evil exists, but it does offer a defence of theism and shows that the existence of God is not incompatible with the existence of evil as the atheist claims.

Response 1: Alternative theologies

- God *does* exist, and the enormity of pain and suffering in the world is real, but we should realise that God is *not* in fact omnipotent, omniscient and benevolent.

In the last hundred years theologians have proposed alternative interpretations of what it is to believe in God. Examples of such theologies are: theological anti-realism (see page 177), in which God is not understood as a real being existing independently of our minds; and process theology, where God is 'the fellow sufferer who understands', who can affect his creation through infinite persuasive powers, but cannot eradicate evil or prevent it from happening.[128] Dualist perspectives, in which God is not the only powerful deity, also offer a solution to the problem of evil, as with the Manicheans who saw a benevolent God vying with an evil deity.

> **Criticism**
>
> It is clear that these types of solutions lead in a direction often far away from Christian teachings, and so they are unacceptable to many believers. However, for those who have spiritual leanings, and are attempting to make sense of the universe and of evil from a position outside traditional theism, such solutions may be reasonable and plausible.

Response 2: The Afterlife defence

- God *does* exist, and is omnipotent, omniscient and benevolent, but we should realise that the enormity of pain and suffering in this world is *balanced* by even greater good – namely justice in the next life.

The belief in life after death is one of the fundamental tenets of Christianity; it recurs throughout the New Testament, and finds support from the traditional view of God, the 'God of the philosophers' (see page 4). As Hick argues, an omnipotent, personal creator would not allow his human creations to cease to exist while his aspirations and purpose for them had not been met.[129] So how does belief in life after death resolve the problem of evil? Or to put it another way: is the existence of a benevolent God compatible with a world in which there is a finite amount of suffering in this life, but an infinite amount of happiness in the next life?

> *If there is any eventual resolution of the interplay between good and evil, any decisive bringing of good out of evil, it must lie beyond this world and beyond the enigma of death.*[130]
> John Hick

It might be true that, from the perspective of life in this world, the cruelties and horrors seem very difficult, if not impossible, to reconcile with the existence of a loving, caring God. However, from the perspective of eternity, a limited amount of suffering in this life becomes infinitesimal compared with the potential for unlimited happiness in the next life. And belief in hell as well as heaven means that the people who inflict injustice and suffering on us in this life will be punished in the next life. The possibility of justice in the future goes part way to resolving the moral problem of evil for some people: vicious people will get their comeuppance; virtuous people will be rewarded.

> **Criticism**
>
> However, it seems as if the existence of hell simply defers the problem of evil to the next life, and amplifies it. If we found it difficult to reconcile the existence of a benevolent God with the existence of (limited) suffering in this life, how much more difficult are we going to find it reconciling such a God with the unlimited suffering of hell in the next life?

We will return to the idea of life after death, and examine some further philosophical problems with it, when we come to examine John Hick's parable of the Celestial City (page 166).

Response 3: The Free Will defence: St Augustine and Alvin Plantinga

Learn More

Free will and determinism

Metaphysical freedom or free will is, in general terms, the capacity of a being to make choices. In the activity below, the number of actual choices available to the man diminishes in each case; however, the ability to make choices remains the same. A man confined to a prison cell can still choose to sit down, stand up, walk to the window or close his eyes. Even the man chained to the wall, although he has fewer choices available, can still choose whether to open or close his eyes and is free to choose what to think about. The ability to make free choices remains and has not been removed; it is the availability of actual options to choose from that has diminished.

ACTIVITY

Consider a man in each of the following situations, and then answer the questions below.

1. He is living in England with no criminal convictions.
2. He is living in England but has a driving ban and his passport withheld.
3. He is living in an open prison.
4. He is in prison, but is confined to his cell.
5. He is in prison, confined to his cell and chained to a wall.

For each situation:

a) Consider what the man can do, and what he can't do.
b) Do you think the man is free, or not free?
c) What is it that determines whether the man is free?

In contrast to free will is the concept of DETERMINISM. When one billiard ball hits another, the laws of physics that govern material objects (including motion, density, friction, speed, vectors) determine the movement of the second ball. There are many different forms of determinism but they all hold in common that the future is somehow determined, and this can even be applied to humans, who are also material objects like billiard balls. Determinism could either mean that the future is already pre-determined or that at every moment the future is created as an inevitable consequence of the past, in other words that the past determines the future. Either way, the future is inevitable and this would seem to imply that humans have no free will. It may appear as if we have lots of choices at any given moment, but if the future is inevitable then it would seem to be the case that we are determined to pick one particular option. The inevitability of the future could be caused by a number of different things: fate, God or the laws of nature.

Many philosophers believe that physical determinism is compatible with the claim that humans have free will. This approach, known as COMPATIBILISM, can be found in the philosophy of David Hume, who believes that humans both have free will and are determined. He believes in determinism – which he claims simply means that particular human actions are constantly conjoined with particular effects (page 80 above). He also believes that free will can only mean freedom to act on your desires free from coercion and restraint, which is perfectly compatible with determinism.

Theologians and philosophers of religion have frequently drawn on the metaphysical concept of free will in order to provide an explanation, and justification, of the existence of evil in the world. We have already seen how the atheist philosopher Mary Midgley (who holds a compatibilist position) draws on a nuanced account of free will to argue that we must reject fatalism, and take responsibility for our actions, wicked or good. We now turn to an early medieval philosopher, St Augustine, and a contemporary philosopher, Alvin Plantinga, to see how they use the concept of free will to resolve the problem of evil.

St Augustine's Free Will defence

- God *does* exist, and is omnipotent, omniscient and benevolent, but we should realise that the enormity of pain and suffering is the *consequence of* an even greater good – namely humans having free will.

In many of the most influential explanations of the existence of evil, human free will is an essential element. St Augustine provides one of the earliest and best-known defences that takes this approach, arguing that God is good and powerful, and created a perfect world with humans to whom he gave free will. Evil was then introduced into the world because some of his creatures chose to turn away from God. Augustine places particular blame on the fall of the angel Satan from heaven and on the failure of Adam and Eve to resist temptation in the Garden of Eden. This, for Augustine, constitutes the 'original sin' of humans and resulted in Adam and Eve's subsequent expulsion from paradise by God, and the introduction of pain and suffering into their lives and the lives of all their offspring.[131] Through these sins God's creation was corrupted, and the natural goodness of the world disappeared: there was a 'privation' of the good. Augustine's defence thus places the blame for moral and natural evil on the freely chosen acts of God's creatures (humans and angels). So Augustine maintains that, although God created a perfect world, evil was introduced by the choices humans made, and thus it is the responsibility of humans not of God. Alvin Plantinga highlights the following line from St Augustine:

> *As a runaway horse is better than a stone which does not run away because it lacks self-movement and sense perception, so the creature is more excellent which sins by free will than that which does not sin only because it has no free will.*[132]
> **St Augustine, quoted in Alvin Plantinga,** *God, Freedom and Evil*

So for Augustine it is clear that God has made a better world by giving some of his creatures the freedom to choose between good and evil, even if a consequence of this is that some of his creatures choose to sin and perform evil acts. A world which consisted of stones, or robots who were not able to sin because they lacked free will, is a world that is less perfect than a world which contains both free will and evil. Plantinga calls this Augustine's 'Free Will Theodicy', because it explains precisely why God permits evil. (This precision makes it different from Plantinga's own 'Free Will *defence*' which we look at below.)

As other philosophers (including both Hick and Swinburne below) point out, God does not wish to create a snug cage for his human 'pets' to live in.[133] So it is a mistake to look at the world and wonder why it is not more pleasant for humans. A much greater good than pleasure is the relationship humans can have with God, and this can only be a genuine relationship if we have free will. And, as we have seen, freely chosen evil is a terrible side effect of free will, but one that on this view is worth it.

Before we look at Plantinga's revival of the Free Will defence it is worth considering some of the criticisms that have been made of the classic, Augustinian, Free Will defence.

Criticism – Augustine's Free Will defence only explains moral evil

The Free Will defence provides a possible reason for why pain and suffering exists in a world created by a supremely good and omnipotent God. But it only seems to account for moral evil; in other words, the pain and suffering caused by humans themselves. What of physical or natural evil? After all, humans are not responsible for the behaviour of Ichneumonidae, those wasps which, as in the *Alien* films, lay their eggs inside the body of a host so that when the larvae hatch they can eat the host from the inside out. There was horrific pain and suffering in the animal kingdom before humans evolved, and at first sight the Free Will defence does not explain why natural evils exist.

St Augustine's version of the Free Will defence, in his account of original sin, does explain why natural evil exists – it was because creatures who had been given Free Will (angels and humans) rebelled against God. First Satan, and then Adam and Eve, disobeyed God, bringing about The Fall, and Adam and Eve's expulsion from the Garden of Eden. This in turn caused God's creation to go askew, bringing pain and suffering into the whole world. For Augustine then, natural evil is actually just a consequence of moral evil.

Apart from the unfairness of this account (why should other animals suffer because of the decision of Eve to eat from the Tree of Knowledge?), there is also the issue that this part of the Free Will defence depends upon a literal interpretation of the first book of the Bible. For Augustine, the succumbing to temptation by Eve and then Adam in the Garden of Eden is the real origin of sin and evil. Many believers do not now read the account of what happened in the Garden of Eden as literally true, preferring to read it symbolically. Nor do many modern believers subscribe to the view that the angel Satan turned away from God, and that this too introduced evil into the world. So the Free Will defence is primarily a defence against the existence of moral evil, not natural evil.

Experimenting with ideas

You have a summer job as a shop assistant in Worlds 'R' Us – the Ultimate in Universe Shopping. One day God walks in and says he wants to buy a universe. More specifically he wants to buy the best possible universe (which he can easily do, given he is God). He browses through the billions of shelves, which contain every possible universe, and then asks you for more details of their specifications: the quantity of pain and suffering, the extent of free will, the level of determinism, the degree of order and regularity, the balance and beauty in each universe. Eventually, after examining all the billions of universes in the shop, God comes up to the counter and says 'I'll take this one'; and that is the universe we now live in.

1 What 'health warnings' or 'unique selling points' would you have told God about when selling him this universe?
2 Do you think God made a good choice? Why/why not?
3 Was there a better universe on offer? In what way would it have been better?
4 What do you think God was looking for in a universe (what 'specifications')?

Leibniz and possible worlds

Gottfried Leibniz asks us to consider the situation of God as one of an all-powerful and good being whose task it is to select, from among all the possible universes that he could create, the one he will actually create. Now, given that God knows the whole histories of all the possible universes, and is wholly good, then the one he selected to create must be the very best one possible. Therefore the pain and suffering of this world are just some of the many essential ingredients which go into the construction of the best possible world. This means that all the evil which exists in this universe must, in some way, contribute to making it a better place than every other possible universe.

Learn More

Criticism

Leibniz's position has had many critics, and the French philosopher and writer Voltaire (1694–1778) was one of the first to attack Leibniz's theodicy. In Voltaire's novel *Candide*, the character Dr Pangloss regularly announces that this is the best of all possible worlds. As the eponymous hero is tortured by religious fanatics, and as he watches his mentor Dr Pangloss hanged, Candide wonders to himself: 'if this is the best of all possible worlds, what can the others be like?'[134] What Voltaire does is to confront the cool intellectual approach that Leibniz takes to the problem of evil with the pain and suffering of the world. In so doing, Voltaire does not really refute Leibniz's theodicy; but it is certainly not easy to support Leibniz's position when faced with the concrete reality of pain and suffering.

> **Criticism – there are better possible worlds than this one**
>
> Antony Flew criticises the Free Will defence on the basis of the very meaning of 'free will'.[135] For Flew, freely chosen actions are ones that have their causes within the persons themselves, rather than externally (Flew holds a compatibilist position). For example, when you have the chance to marry the person you love, your decision to do so will ultimately stem from the type of person you are: whether you find them funny, whether you fancy them, whether you 'click' with them, whether you trust them, and so on. As long as your choice to marry is internal to you, that is to say, powered by your own character and desires, then it is freely chosen. We have just seen that Leibniz argued that God's omnipotence entailed that he could create any possible world and would therefore create the best possible world, which must be this world as God is not just supremely powerful but also supremely loving. Drawing on this modal notion (see also above, page 54), Flew then goes on to say that God could have created a possible world in which all humans had a nature that was good, and yet in which they were free in Flew's sense. In such a world, humans would always freely choose to do the right thing, and such a world would surely be a better one than this. But God didn't create that better world, which means for Flew that the problem of evil remains, despite the Free Will defence.

However, Flew's attack on the Free Will defence may be objected to on the following grounds. What would be the difference between Flew's 'naturally good' people, and automata or mere puppets who had been created always to act in a good way? It is important to theistic belief that God gave humans the freedom to choose to worship and love him, or the freedom to turn away from him. But, in Flew's world, God seems to have manipulated the key parts of his creation (humans) in order to bring about his desired results. Imagine a hypnotist persuading someone they were in love: what would be the worth of this love? Just as we would question the value of the feelings manipulated in someone by a hypnotist, so we might question the value of the love felt for God by the 'naturally good' humans in Flew's world. Moreover, is a God who manipulates the end results, in the way Flew describes, a God who is worthy of worship?

J.L. Mackie offers another version of Flew's modal approach, arguing that a world in which we all freely chose to do good is a logical possibility, and that creating such a world is perfectly within God's omnipotent powers.[136] Mackie's argument is as follows:

1. It is logically possible for me to choose to do good on any one occasion.
2. It is logically possible for me to choose to do good on every occasion.
3. It is logically possible for any individual to choose to do good throughout their life.
4. God is omnipotent and can create any logically possible world.
5. Therefore God could have created a world in which we were all genuinely free, yet we all chose to do good.
6. God did not create such a world.
7. Therefore either God is not omnipotent, or he is not wholly good.

So Mackie's attack on the Free Will defence leads to a restatement of the logical problem of evil (above page 133).

Alvin Plantinga's Free Will defence

Alvin Plantinga puts forward a version of the Free Will defence, which does not claim to state *precisely* what God's reason for the existence of evil might be (that would be a theodicy), but only that to show what God's reason might *possibly* be. So the Free Will defence is part of Plantinga's efforts to defeat atheists like Mackie by demonstrating that there is no inconsistency in believing in an omnipotent, omniscient, benevolent God, and believing that God created a world with immense pain and suffering in it. Plantinga begins his Free Will defence by clarifying what he means when he says people are 'free'. The freedom that is relevant to his argument is the freedom to act: either to carry out an action, or to refrain from carrying out an action (see the activity above, on page 140). Plantinga rejects determinism regarding human actions, in so far as there are no prior conditions and no causal laws which determine whether or not someone will perform an act.

With that in mind Plantinga reminds us that the task of the Free Will defender is to find some way of marrying the claim that God is omniscient, omnipotent and wholly good, with the acknowledgement that there is evil. According to Plantinga the Free Will defender will succeed in their defence if they can show that it is *not* within God's power to create a universe with moral good without that universe also containing moral evil.

Plantinga mounts his defence by rejecting the idea prompted by Leibniz (page 143 above), and which is crucial to the attacks by both Flew and Mackie, that God can create any possible world. Plantinga refers to this as Leibniz's Lapse,[137] implying that Leibniz (although an incredibly clever philosopher and thinker – for example he invented mathematical calculus at the same time as Isaac Newton) didn't take proper care when analysing what God's omnipotence entailed, and Plantinga questions whether God really could create any possible world. For example, God cannot create a world in which humans are not created by God. And even within the possible worlds that God could create there are limitations. Plantinga asks us to imagine some person (Plantinga names him Curly Smith) who has a corrupt nature such that, in every possible world that God could create, he will always choose to do at least one evil action. In this case, it is not possible for God (even an infinitely powerful and loving one) to create a world in which Curly is free yet always does good actions. Plantinga believes he succeeds in his goal of showing that an omnipotent, omniscient and wholly good God does not have the power of creating a world with moral good in it without that world also containing moral evil.

We might summarise Plantinga's Free Will defence as follows:

1. A world with creatures who are free is more valuable than a world containing no free creatures at all.
2. God can create free creatures, but he cannot (without removing their freedom) *cause* them to do what is morally right.
3. Therefore God created a world with free creatures capable of doing both what is morally right and what is morally evil.

anthology 1.19

Furthermore, Plantinga goes on to argue, this defence does not count against the belief that God is all-powerful and wholly good. God's goodness is what led him to create a world with creatures who had freedom (rather than creatures who were robots), and God's omnipotence gave him the power to actually create such a world. The fact that God does not prevent evil does not mean he lacks omnipotence or benevolence, as he could only prevent evil by removing our capacity for free choice, and hence removing the possibility of moral good.

So Plantinga would maintain that despite the criticisms of Flew and Mackie he has mounted a successful defence (what we called above a 'weak' theodicy) of evil, showing that the existence of evil is compatible with a wholly good and all-powerful God.

Response 4: The soul-making theodicy: St Irenaeus and John Hick

■ God *does* exist, and is omnipotent, omniscient and benevolent, but we should realise that the enormity of pain and suffering actually *leads to* an even greater good – namely humans fulfilling their potential.

The Free Will defence aims to provide a solution to the problem of evil by showing that an omnipotent, benevolent God may not want to eliminate evil (at least moral evil) because there is a higher value at stake here, namely free will and the opportunity for moral goodness that stems from it. In his book *Evil and the God of Love*, Hick identified an alternative tradition which gives a different account of why God allows evil to exist. In this tradition evil exists, not simply because it is caused by human free will (although for moral evil that is true), but also because a world in which there is evil enables humans to grow and develop, and provides an environment in which our souls can be forged and strengthened. This soul-making tradition is one that Hick traces back to another early Church father, St Irenaeus (130–202CE), and he termed this the 'Irenaean theodicy'.

Experimenting with ideas
For each of the evils outlined below, think about what good could come of them.
1 Children starve in drought-ridden central Africa.
2 Homeless people, who are sleeping rough, freeze on the winter streets of New York.
3 Forest fires sweep round the outskirts of an Australian town, burning livestock and choking people.
4 A tidal wave destroys all the coastal villages of Indonesia.
5 The bubonic plague wipes out half the population of Europe in the fifteenth century.
6 A ruthless dictator sends his enemies to die in labour camps.

It was possible for God himself to have made man perfect from the first, but man could not receive this [perfection], being as yet an infant.
Irenaeus, *Against Heresies*, 4.39.1

There are some important similarities between the two theodicies that John Hick identified, the Augustinian and the Irenaean theodicy.

- Both traditions agree that human free will is central to any explanation of why evil exists.
- Both traditions agree that God bears ultimate responsibility for the existence of evil, which is why a theodicy (an explanation of God's reasons for allowing evil) is needed.
- Both theodicies agree that a greater good emerges as a result of evil happening – greater than if God interfered to ensure no evil happened.
- Both traditions agree that there are limits to God's omnipotence, most importantly that God cannot create beings with genuine free will who are 'ready-made' to do good (this is closely related to the discussion of freedom and omniscience above, page 26).

However, there are fundamental differences between the two types of theodicy. We have seen that the Augustinian tradition places a high value on our freedom itself. So God permits evil to exist because it is better that we have free will than that we are robots, even if that means we choose to act immorally. Within the Augustinian theodicy God's creation was originally perfect, including the perfect humans that God created, but as time passed, evil was introduced into the world through the free actions of humans. So the immediate responsibility for the existence of evil lies with humans, although God does bear ultimate responsibility by having created beings with free will. On Augustine's account goodness lies at some point in the past, and evil was introduced into the world through our free will (Figure 1.37a).

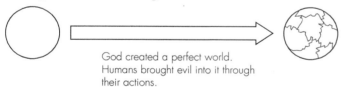

Figure 1.37a The Augustinian theodicy

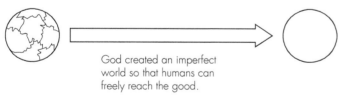

Figure 1.37b The Irenaean theodicy

St Irenaeus takes a different approach to St Augustine, seeing humans as developing in two stages. In the first stage they were created by God as intelligent animals, originally imperfect and immature, but with the capacity for spiritual and moral development. In the second stage, which is the stage we are now in, humans use their free will to gradually transform themselves and become 'children of God'. On Irenaeus' account goodness lies at some point in the future, and our free will enables us to grow towards that point of goodness. We can visually represent the main differences between the two traditions as follows:

By probing deeper into the Irenaean theodicy Hick believes that a more sophisticated explanation can be given as to why God allows evil to exist. Hick asks why would humans have been created by God as imperfect and immature,

rather than the perfect creatures that Augustine imagined? One consideration is that the human goodness as envisaged by Irenaeus is *better* than the human goodness as envisaged by Augustine. For Hick there is more value in human goodness that has come about through the freely chosen actions of toil, effort, like children learning to make the right moral choices, than there is in human goodness which has been 'ready-made', and which required no free will to achieve it. A further consideration is a Christian one, with Hick arguing that it is *better* for humans to work towards being in the presence of God (through the efforts of free will) than for humans to be created in the direct presence of God. The Irenaean theodicy recognises the journey that humans have to go on, overcoming their natural selfishness and using their free will to make the right spiritual and moral decisions that bring them closer to God.

For Hick, God's aim in creating the world is to enable humans to freely understand and reach him, and that aim will determine the kind of world that God creates. Hick is dismissive of the claims of atheists such as Mackie, that God could have created a world without suffering, and believes it is utterly wrong-headed of atheists to argue that God, by not creating a 'hedonistic paradise', is somehow therefore not powerful, or knowledgeable or loving enough. Hick says such atheists:

> ... *think of God's relation to the earth on the model of a human being building a cage for a pet animal to dwell in ... he will make his pet's quarters as pleasant and healthful as he can.*[138]
> Hick

What then does Hick have to say about the existence of pain and suffering? Vast amounts of pain and suffering can be traced back to the freely chosen actions of human beings – often the result of a misuse of our freedom. So our free will explains the existence of moral evil. But the existence of moral evil is justifiable within Hick's Irenaean theodicy, as it is a by-product of our free will; and we have seen that it is essential that God created humans with free will in order to work towards moral and spiritual understanding, striving to develop in this life and eventually achieving perfection in the next life.

But there are other causes of pain and suffering that do not have their source in human behaviour: viruses, tsunamis, plagues, cancers, droughts, meteor strikes, floods. How does Hick's theodicy explain the existence of these natural evils? The answer can be found in the quote above: God did not create the world in the way that someone creates a wonderful cage for their pet hamster, or (against Hume) in the way that an architect builds a beautiful house. Hick says we should see the world as a place where our souls are forged, where we encounter pain and suffering but we learn from it, build on it, develop virtues as a result of it, and grow spiritually and morally. The young Romantic poet John Keats (1795–1821) wrote in a letter to his brother that we should not think of this world as a 'vale of tears' (from Psalm 84:6) but instead as a 'vale of soul-making'.[139] By this Keats meant the world is a place in which spiritual creation and development is possible, and John Hick uses this exact phrase to describe his own theodicy (outlined in Chapter 13, section 3 of *Evil and the God of Love*). All the pain and suffering of the world has value insofar as it enables us to progress towards the ultimate good, which is understanding and being in the presence of God.

Hick also invites us to consider the opposite view, namely a world in which God ensures there is no pain and no suffering. A glass might fall from a building and break on the ground, but a human wouldn't; a knife would cut bread, but it couldn't cut a human; there would be no need to work as no harm could be done to us from not working; banks could be robbed but no one would suffer from a loss of money. Does this world sound tempting? Such a world would be one in which we would never grasp any physical laws, there could be no scientific progress, and no understanding of how the world works. Moreover, according to Hick, there would be no moral development, or any form of morality at all: no courage, no kindness, no generosity – characteristics that humans wouldn't need to develop because there would be no need of them. Our lives would be aimless; we would be like fat pigs sitting in the Garden of Eden. We would not reach the second stage of spiritual and moral development without our current environment, one which is harsh but which offers us the potential for change, for understanding, for improvement, and for moving, according to Hick, closer to God.

To summarise: Hick agrees with the approach of Irenaeus, that is to say, he also argues that the imperfections and suffering of this world will eventually lead to a better state. For Hick the world is a 'vale of soul-making'[140] in which our souls are strengthened and matured by the struggle and suffering of this life, with the possibility of infinite rewards in the next life. (We shall see later, page 165, that the possibility of heaven, which Hick refers to as ESCHATOLOGICAL, in which humans are able to meet God, also plays an important role in his philosophy of language.) Hick acknowledges that there is some mystery in this process, as God maintains an 'epistemic distance' from us (that is to say, he does not provide us with the knowledge of what our destiny or purpose in this life is) so that we do not know what our purpose is and must exercise our genuine free will in order to approach the good (a state of holiness).[141]

Criticism

The claim that evil exists as a means to some other good (such as spiritual maturity or noble virtues) has been bitterly contested. Hick himself acknowledges that the distribution of misery in the world seems to be random and meaningless, so that it may be heaped upon those who seem least deserving.[142]

In such cases it is hard to see what good can come of such evil. Dostoyevsky put forward a series of particularly painful examples of evil in his novel *The Brothers Karamazov*. The character Ivan Karamazov cites three cases of appalling and pointless cruelty to Russian children (to which could be added the holocaust in Belarus in 1942,[143] or the Beslan school massacre of 2004), which in his view clearly give reason to reject God and the world he has created. Ivan does not deny the existence of God, but instead, disgusted at the universe God has created, he rejects God as a being who is worthy of worship.[144]

Experimenting with ideas

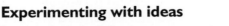

Read through the following two examples given by Ivan Karamazov in Dostoyevsky's *The Brothers Karamazorv* and answer the questions below.

1 A young girl, abused by her parents, wets her bed and is forced by her mother to eat her own excrement, before she is made to sleep in a freezing cold shed.
2 A boy throws a stone and injures a general's dog. The boy is stripped and sent out as quarry for a hunt. He is eventually caught and torn to pieces by dogs in front of his mother.

a) How might these examples of evil be explained within Hick's soul-making theodicy and Plantinga's Free Will defence?
b) Do you think these explanations are satisfactory?

Criticism

The problem Dostoyevsky poses is a question about whether the outcome justifies the method. For any theodicy that views the existence of evil as a means to an end we can ask, 'Is the end worth it?' In other words, is God justified in creating a world that contains so much pointless and gratuitous evil in order to attain certain goals? For Ivan Karamazov the answer is no – there can be no goal so worth having that young children are allowed to be tortured in order that this goal might one day be reached.

Summary: The problem of evil

Once we have got over the use of the term 'evil' (which conjures up badly made, or even terrifying, Hollywood films full of swirling smoke, dark cellars and scuttling hands) the problem of evil becomes a compelling and genuine issue for all of us, atheists and believers alike. The enormity of the pain and suffering of humans and animals is too much for most of us to bear thinking about, so we don't. But the problem of evil, even though it stems from an issue in the philosophy of religion, forces us all to turn our attention to suffering and ask ourselves 'Why?' Perhaps for atheists there is no answer to this question: there is no reason why creatures suffer; it is pointless, senseless even, but that is life. Believers fare no better in their search for a solution because the problem of evil, clearly framed, genuinely calls into question whether a God who is powerful and loving would allow such suffering to go on, and whether such a God really does exist. Perhaps human freedom partly explains evil, at least the parts that we are responsible for (but what about the rest?). Or perhaps suffering really is good in the long term, as Irenaeus and Hick argue; or at least it is better than the alternative in which there is no suffering at all. Though neither solution rings fully true to neutral ears.

Philosophers love a knotty problem, and the problem of evil certainly is that. The ability to clearly explain, explore and resolve problems is another philosophical skill that you will need to develop. The problem of evil cannot be easily avoided, as you have seen. Once you have defined your terms (What do we mean by 'evil'? What are the different types of evil? What do different examples of evil have in common?) you can go on to formulate the issue and explain exactly why it is a problem. Most importantly it is a problem for believers because of their particular definition of another concept, namely 'God'.

The clash between these two concepts demands a solution, and you have explored a variety of different solutions and a variety of criticisms laid against these solutions. But the problem of evil does not disappear once you close this book and you will have to weigh up which of these solutions (or others you may have thought of yourself, or read elsewhere) is the most compelling.

Ultimately our position on the problem of evil may come down to our prior metaphysical beliefs about the universe, and what we think does or doesn't exist in it. If we are committed atheists, then we may use the existence of evil to justify our atheism. However, it does not seem as if evil proves the non-existence of God. The most evil does is to show that belief in the non-existence of God is rational. From the believer's point of view the existence of evil is an agonising and lived problem. The Book of Job in the Bible underpins this, as God proves to the devil that Job will love him whatever his circumstances. The devil destroys Job's life, family, livestock, leaving him with nothing. Job's friends argue that he must have done something wrong. But throughout his trials, Job maintains his faith in God's righteousness, despite being in ignorance about why he is suffering so much. This story of faith in God, in the face of pain and suffering, is an inspiration to many believers. But the story of Job does not solve the problem of evil, it merely tells us how it is possible to live with evil and yet still believe in God. The story reassures believers, but frustrates atheists who will continue to ask how such a juggling act is possible.

1.3 Religious language

The French monk and writer François Rabelais once described how two fictional scholars conducted a philosophical argument using only grotesque signs and obscene gestures to convey their meaning. As one of the scholars explained: 'these matters are so difficult that human words would not be adequate to expound them to my satisfaction'.[1]

But, for most of us, words and language are indispensable to communicating complex ideas; indeed, it would be very hard to imagine how the ideas discussed in this book could be effectively communicated by any other means, such as through images, dance or mime. Language is essential for, and some would say identical with, complex thinking, and as philosophers tend to indulge in complex thought they naturally use language to do so. However, over the last hundred years or so philosophers have become ever more interested in the nature of language so that now the philosophy of language has become one of the most important areas of philosophical inquiry. The philosophy of language addresses such questions as:

- What do words or concepts mean?
- How do propositions refer to the world?
- What is the relationship between language and thought?

Some philosophers have argued that such questions are the most important of all on the grounds that we need first to have answers to these before we can pursue any further philosophical questions. Until we understand how the medium through which we engage in philosophy works, how can we hope to do philosophy properly? Some philosophers of language also claim that many, if not all, philosophical problems arise simply because of the way in which we misuse, and so become confused by, language. At the more radical end of this view is the claim that metaphysical problems aren't genuine problems about the universe, or reality, at all, but instead arise from a misunderstanding of language. We have already seen how this approach can be applied to the metaphysics of God. For example, Bertrand Russell argued that a proper examination of the meanings of the words involved can reveal what is wrong with the ontological argument: this trick of proving God exists is foiled once we see how the proof misuses the term 'existence' by treating it as a predicate (see above, pages 49–52).

You will be familiar from your study of ethical language with some of the issues that we investigate in this section. The questions we address are broadly:

- What is the distinction between cognitivism and non-cognitivism when applied to religious language?
- What challenges does empiricism raise for the status of metaphysical (in this case religious) language?
- How do debates about verification and falsification throw light onto our understanding of religious language?

To begin addressing these questions we should first look at some of the distinct features of religious language and revisit some of the different theories of meaning that philosophers have put forward.

Features of religious language

The philosophy of religious language looks at the meaning of both religious concepts (such as *God, omnipotence, evil*) and at religious propositions. A proposition is an assertion or statement about the world, what in an English lesson might be called an 'indicative' sentence. We all express our beliefs in the form of propositions; here are some examples:

- The world is round.
- I am a student.
- The grass is always greener on the other side.
- We should treat others as we would like to be treated.

Now, on the surface, religious propositions appear very much like other kinds of proposition. They appear to be giving us information about the world, telling us what the world is like or what is true of it. In other words, they appear to be FACTUALLY SIGNIFICANT. However, compare the following religious propositions with some ordinary propositions:

God is the Father, the Son and the Holy Ghost.	Jeremy Jones is a father, a son and a teacher.
God is all-powerful.	Jeremy Jones is always around.
The Lord spake unto Moses about the liberation of the Israelites.	Jeremy Jones spoke to Mischa about the incident in the school lunch hall.
Our Father, who art in Heaven, hallowed be thy name.	Jeremy Jones, who lives in Downham, has an unusual middle name.

On the face of it, both sets of propositions are very similar. However, on closer inspection, it becomes evident that propositions like those on the left – religious propositions – reveal themselves to have features that make them rather different from those of ordinary language. For example:

- Religious propositions are often contradictory or paradoxical. To say that 'God is the Father and the Son and the Holy Ghost' is to say that he is at once one and three: a claim that is rather puzzling. We can understand how Jeremy Jones might be a father and a son, because there exist separate persons, Jeremy's son and Jeremy's father, who explain these relations. It is hard to understand how God could be a father and son to himself. The claim that 'God is all-powerful' appears to be contradictory, as we saw above (page 19), because an omnipotent being both can and cannot give itself a task which it could not perform. Does this mean that such claims are incoherent or meaningless?
- The word that is most central to religious language, 'God', refers to a being that lies beyond human experience. Many theologians have held that 'God' is a concept beyond our understanding, and that our language is woefully inadequate when it comes to talking of God. For example, the early Christian mystic Pseudo-Dionysius said this of our attempts to talk about God: 'the inscrutable One is out of reach of every rational process. Nor can any words come up to the inexpressible Good ... Mind beyond mind, word beyond speech, it is gathered up by no discourse, by no intuition, by no name.'[2] Do all our attempts to talk meaningfully about God fail, because of his transcendent nature?

- Religious language is also peculiar in that it often describes God in human terms. In Genesis, for example, we are told that God walked in the Garden of Eden. Does this mean that God has legs? God also spoke to Moses on Mount Sinai. Does this mean he has a tongue and lips? How are we to make sense of such talk if God is a being who is outside of space and time?
- Finally, there are peculiarities in the uses made of religious language, for example during religious ceremony or prayer. Are we supposed to interpret prayer as a literal request for help, like dialling 999 for the fire brigade? Or are we supposed to find in it another layer of meaning, perhaps a form of worship, an expression of faith or an act of devotion?

One task, then, is to determine whether and how religious language can be meaningful. To do this we will examine cognitivist and non-cognitivist approaches to understanding the meaning of religious language.

Learn More

The idea of 'meaning'

Before turning to cognitivist and non-cognitivist approaches to meaning, it may be instructive to think a little about what meaning is or what we mean by 'meaning'.

Experimenting with ideas

How many different meanings does 'mean' have? What do the following examples of 'mean' mean?

1. I mean to send you a get well card.
2. Dark clouds mean rain.
3. He had a mean look on his face.
4. When your boy/girlfriend says 'I think we need a break' what they really mean is 'I've fallen in love with someone else.'
5. I mean the world to Julia.
6. Do you know what I mean?
7. The mean rainfall in Morecombe is 10 centimetres.
8. I'll report you to the police next time you slash my tyres – I mean it!

In each of these propositions the word 'mean' is used in a different way, and there are other ways too. Ogden and Richards in *The Meaning of Meaning*[3] identified sixteen different meanings of the word 'meaning', which shows how ambiguous the meaning of the word can be. But superficial ambiguity is not the only problem with 'meaning'. It seems that, although we may be able to use words happily enough, and can even explain what most words mean, it is much harder to say what it is for a word to have a meaning in the first place.

A useful starting point in giving a theory of meaning is to try to establish which sentences are meaningful and which are not. If we can establish whatever it is that all meaningful sentences have in common and meaningless sentences lack, then we should have a good idea of what makes them meaningful and so we will be well on the road to building a theory of meaning. Now obviously sentences with made-up or crazy words will not be meaningful. For example:

'Twas brillig, and the slithy toves did gyre and gimble in the wabe[4] clearly makes no sense. For even though some of the words are English, and even though it seems to make sense (some slithy animals are doing something like gyring in some place called a wabe), and these carefully chosen 'words' allow us to recognise the grammatical structure of the sentence, we do not really know what toves are or what it is to gimble, and so cannot make proper sense of what is being said. This suggests that the constituent parts of any sentence must be recognisable words for the sentence to be meaningful.

However, any old collection of English words is not necessarily going to make a meaningful sentence. Consider the following, for example:

With happily six the and swim.

This is clearly not meaningful because the words used are not put together in a meaningful way. This suggests that meaningfulness requires at least two conditions: that the words used are themselves meaningful, and also that they are combined in ways that follow certain rules. But what rules are these? The example we have just looked at suggests one answer: the words must be combined in ways that follow the rules of grammar. For one obvious thing that is wrong with the sentence above is that it is not grammatical.

However, to be meaningful a sentence needs more than to be composed of proper words arranged grammatically. To see this, consider the following (originally composed by Noam Chomsky):

Colourless green ideas sleep furiously.[5]

Can ideas sleep? Can something be colourless and green? Probably not. So, although this sentence is grammatical, and uses real English words that you would find in any dictionary, it is still empty of significance, because nothing clear is being communicated in this sentence.

So it seems we have identified three features that meaningful sentences possess: they use real words, they are arranged grammatically and they are trying to communicate something. So we have here the beginnings of a theory of meaning, that is to say, we have begun to consider what the criteria are by which we can determine whether a sentence or use of language is meaningful or not. However, our theory remains rather vague at this stage. In particular our third condition would need to be unpacked and examined in a good deal more detail before it became at all interesting. What exactly does it mean to 'try to communicate something'? How can we decide whether or not a sentence does this effectively?

Experimenting with ideas

Each of the following sentences uses proper words and is grammatically correct. However, it may still be that not all of them are meaningful. Read through each sentence in turn and for each decide whether it is:

a) meaningful
b) apparently meaningful (but actually meaningless) or
c) obviously meaningless.

  1 It is morally wrong to believe in something without sufficient evidence.
  2 It is possible to doubt everything; it is even possible to doubt whether you are doubting.
  3 Two-thirds of the universe is made up of dark matter.

4 Birth is one of the miracles of nature.
5 I love you.
6 One, two, three, jump!
7 What came before time?
8 God loves the world like a father loves his children.
9 Respect!
10 The universe and everything in it doubled in size last night while we were asleep.
11 There are invisible pixies that live in my fridge who disappear without trace as soon as I open the door.
12 Jesus is the Way, the Truth and the Light.
13 It is possible for an infinitely powerful being to create a stone so large that they cannot move it.
14 There is a German aeroplane overhead.
15 Bondi Beach contains more than one billion particles of sand.
16 The history of all hitherto existing societies is the history of class struggle.
17 There are two mistakes in the the sentence written here.
18 It is possible to know the unknowable.
19 The sunset over Waterloo Bridge (not Victoria Falls) is the most beautiful sight on Earth.
20 I am who I am.

Now make a note of all the sentences that you thought were meaningful. You may find it helpful to draw up a table as follows and list some of the features that meaningful and meaningless sentences appear to have.

A sentence is meaningful if:	A sentence is meaningless if:

What do the meaningful sentences have in common? What is it about them that makes them meaningful? Write down some criteria for what makes a sentence meaningful.

In completing this exercise it is hoped you will have come up with your own criteria for a meaningful sentence. You may have decided that all the sentences were meaningful, in which case you probably reckon that a) being grammatical and b) using genuine words are sufficient conditions for meaningfulness. Perhaps you added additional criteria to these, such as c) not being paradoxical or contradictory. Alternatively you may have thought that only the sentences that you could do something with, that you could see a practical use for in your daily life, were meaningful.

1.3.1 The distinction between cognitivism and non-cognitivism about religious language

You have already studied in some detail, in Year 1 of the Philosophy A-level, two types of theories that explain what makes a sentence meaningful: cognitivist and non-cognitivist theories. This section covers some of the same ground, as the concepts of COGNITIVISM AND NON-COGNITIVISM apply to religious language in the same way as they apply to ethical statements.

But let us go over the essentials again, hopefully building on your understanding of the philosophy of language and developing this understanding still further.

First it is helpful if you think of language not as one homogeneous whole, but as innumerable instances of things we write and say, which could be divided in a multitude of ways into lots of different clusters. For example, we might divide up 'language' into the different types spoken throughout the world – are there logical structures underpinning language that are shared across all 7000 human languages? Or we could divide 'language' up by its subject matter: historical language, scientific language, literature and poetry, artistic language, legal language, philosophical language, religious language, ethical language and so on. Or we might divide up language by the different uses we put it to: to query (interrogative sentences), to command (imperative sentences), to ponder (subjunctive or conditional sentences – 'what if …?'), to express or swear (exclamatory sentences) or to inform (indicative sentences – propositions or statements). We return to these different forms and uses of language when we look at Wittgenstein below (page 178).

Secondly it is worth recalling what a statement or a proposition is. Often when we express our beliefs (for example, about chairs, books or electrons) we are making claims about the world. These claims take the form of propositions or statements – we write them down or say them out loud. Now these propositions are capable of being either true or false, depending on whether they describe the world truly or falsely (in technical terms, propositions have a 'truth value' or are 'truth apt'). For example, if you sincerely state that:

The philosophy teacher is a brilliant woman who surfs

then this statement tells us that what you believe is that the philosophy teacher is a brilliant woman who surfs. Now this statement may well be false (the teacher might be a brilliant woman who hates surfing), but false statements still make claims about the world (except they happen to be false claims). Philosophers are deeply interested in statements because these are the building blocks of arguments and theories, and because philosophers really do think they are saying something about the world, or at least (within the philosophy of language) they are saying something about saying something about the world.

So there are two important features of propositions or statements:

- They make claims about the world and therefore we should be able to state the conditions under which they might be shown to be true or false.
- They express a type of mental state which we call a 'belief'.

Thirdly, some philosophers of language have developed a theory of meaning that is centred on 'belief-based', or *cognitive*-based, sentences. This kind of belief-based theory of meaning is called *cognitivism*, and it is characterised by the two features of statements that we have just encountered:

- Cognitivists argue that a sentence is meaningful insofar as it is making a claim about the world and so the truth conditions (stating when it might be true, and when it might be false) for that sentence can be clearly stated.
- Related to this, cognitivists argue that a meaningful sentence is an expression of a belief about the world (hence the name of the theory, *cognitivism*). Figure 1.38 illustrates a cognitive approach to language.

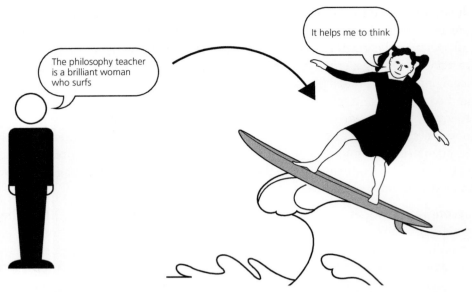

Figure 1.38 Within cognitivism a meaningful sentence expresses our beliefs about the world (truly or falsely)

Fourthly it is important to also recall that a philosopher can be a cognitivist about some areas of language (for example, about scientific language, or historical language) while putting aside cognitivism when it comes to other areas of language (such as talk about God, or ethical language, or aesthetic language). When you studied A.J. Ayer you would have noted that he strictly applied cognitivism to what he called 'factually significant' statements – those statements that could be shown to be true or false – but he took a non-cognitivist view of ethical language, which he argued were not statements at all, but were expressions of our feelings about a particular action or moral situation. This is a very important point, and it is why we took time above to think about the different clusters into which language can be divided. You can be a cognitivist about one cluster (scientific language) but a non-cognitivist about another cluster (for example, religious language).

Fifth, and finally, you will remember that non-cognitivism is a theory of meaning that rejects cognitivism, at least with regard to some clusters of language. Non-cognitivist approaches may reject cognitivism on various grounds. For example, a non-cognitivist might argue that there are many kinds of things that we say and write which are not statements (go back to the 'uses of language' list above, on page 157) and so they are not true or false but are still meaningful. Or a non-cognitivist might argue that there are many kinds of statements that include objects or properties which are not natural (they might be metaphysical) and so don't straightforwardly refer to the world and so cannot be shown to be true or false. Or a non-cognitivist might argue that some sentences don't express beliefs, even though they appear to (see Wittgenstein's point below, page 180), but they express a different type of mental state (an emotion, or a 'way of seeing' or a 'BLIK' – see page 175) and still serve a valuable purpose or function. So there is a wide variety of different forms of non-cognitivism, which have in common only their rejection of cognitivism within a particular cluster of language.

Taking the example above ('The philosophy teacher is a brilliant woman who surfs'), a non-cognitivist might say that the term 'brilliant' doesn't refer to any property in the lecturer, but may simply be an expression of approval – that this teacher is hitting all the right spots in you as a learner.

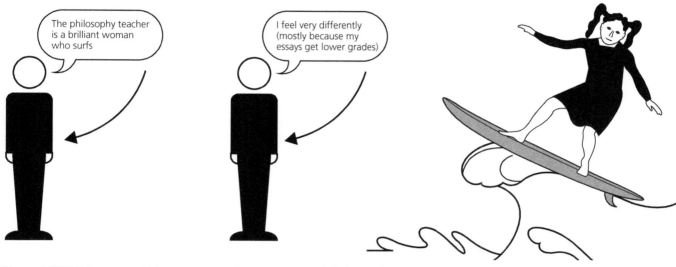

Figure 1.39 Within non-cognitivism, a statement does not express a belief about the world and is neither true nor false

Experimenting with ideas

Read through the following judgements and answer the questions below:

1. That new ring tone on your mobile is bad.
2. The morning BBC newsreader looks very fit.
3. Lying to the police is never wrong.
4. Atoms are made up of protons, neutrons and electrons.
5. The chair is bright red.
6. Your philosophy lecturer is tall.
7. It's good to fulfil your potential.
8. Everyone has a soul.
9. It was sad that her mum and dad split up.
10. The creator of the universe is all-loving.

For each judgement:

a) Do you think it is true/false (you are taking a cognitivist position on this statement)?
b) Do you think it is neither true nor false but still expresses something (you are taking a non-cognitivist position on this statement)?

In the rest of this section we look in some detail at examples of cognitivist and non-cognitivist accounts of meaning, how they apply to religious language and the issues arising from these accounts. First we examine some cognitive theories of meaning, including VERIFICATIONISM in A.J. Ayer and John Hick and the debate around FALSIFICATIONISM in Antony Flew, R.M. Hare and Basil Mitchell; we then go on to look at two non-cognitive accounts of religious language, that of Richard Hare and far more importantly, that of Ludwig Wittgenstein.

1.3.2 The empiricist/logical positivist challenges to the status of metaphysical language

You have already studied Ayer when looking at meta-ethics and ethical language in the first year of your A-level, and much of what is written here is taken from our *Philosophy for A-level Year 1 and AS* textbook. A.J. Ayer (1910–89) was a philosopher, within the British empiricist tradition, who as a young man fell under the influence of a radical group of Austrian philosophers who held regular gatherings in Vienna between the First and Second World Wars. This group of philosophers (who were referred to as the 'Vienna Circle') were unified in their rejection of the metaphysical nonsense that (for example) Central European philosophers had been writing about in the nineteenth century, and as a group they wanted to develop a rigorous and coherent response that set a new direction for philosophy in Europe. One of the principles that the Vienna Circle established was that language was only meaningful if it confined itself to discussing what fell within human experience. Once our language steps beyond the realms of what we can experience then it easily ventures into nonsense. This group of philosophers (including Moritz Schlick and Rudolf Carnap) became known as the logical empiricists or logical positivists, which highlighted their association with the scientific movement of the nineteenth century called 'positivism'. This positivist movement argued that knowledge should be based on verifiable facts rather than on metaphysics or theology, and so positivism looked to the empirical research methods of science for the foundations of authentic knowledge. The logical positivists extended this idea beyond science, applying it to the way we use language, and arguing that we must take a rigorous, logical approach to the meaning of statements.

A.J. Ayer and the verification principle

You may recall that Ayer, as well as being a logical positivist, also saw his views as descending from the Scottish Enlightenment philosopher David Hume, whose empiricist, sceptical and common-sense approach to philosophy we encountered when looking at the arguments for the existence of God.

Like Hume, I divide all genuine propositions into two classes: those which, in his terminology, concern relations of ideas, and those which concern matters of fact.[6]
Ayer

As you know, the division between these two types of statements became known as Hume's fork (see above, page 48), and was a springboard for Ayer's philosophy of language. When he was in his mid-twenties Ayer wrote a book called *Language, Truth and Logic* that popularised the ideas of the logical positivists in Britain and America. In this book he used the ideas of the Vienna Circle, along with Hume's fork, and rigorously applied them to all aspects of philosophy. He defended what is known as the VERIFICATION PRINCIPLE, which as you may remember can be seen as a test that a sentence must pass if it is to count as genuinely meaningful. Ayer's verification principle proposes that:

- A sentence is meaningful if and only if:
  a) it is a tautology; that is, true by definition, or
  b) it can – in principle – be proved to be true or false; that is, it is verifiable. As an empiricist Ayer argued that sentences could only be verified by observation-statements – a report by someone that they have experienced something that demonstrates the truth or falsity of the sentence.

- If a sentence isn't either a) or b) then it isn't meaningful.

So Ayer's verification principle claims that in order to say something that is meaningful we must know what would make our statement true or false. One way in which we can know a statement to be true is if it is true by definition, because of the meanings of the words it contains (prong 1 of Hume's fork in Figure 1.33 of *Philosophy for A-level Year 1 and AS*).[7] The other way in which we can know a statement to be true is if we can check it by looking at the world and seeing if the claims it makes about the world can be proved to be true or false (prong 2 of Hume's fork). Ayer refers to these second types of meaningful statements as 'factually significant'. You may remember from your studies last year (page 127 of *Philosophy for A-level Year 1 and AS*), that the first type of knowledge is referred to as *a priori*, and statements of the first type are termed *analytic*; in contrast, the second type of knowledge is referred to as *a posteriori* and statements of the second type are termed *synthetic*. Let us apply the verification principle to the following statement:

Today it rained in London.

and ask whether this statement is meaningful and why. We have seen that for Ayer there are two possible answers to this question:

1. *It is true by definition*. It does not fall into this category (although some joker may claim that part of what 'London' means is 'the city in which it always rains'; in which case the claim becomes 'today it rained in the city in which it always rains', and this is a tautology).
2. *It can be shown to be true or false as a matter of fact*. It does fall into this category, as it can be verified or falsified by images of wet pavements, grumpy commuters holding wet, battered umbrellas, and piles of today's free newspapers piled up and sodden outside Tube stations.

But what are we to make of other sorts of statements, like 'Today it rained in my heart'? With regards to these, Ayer, like the other logical positivists, is fairly ruthless in his application of the verification principle: it is meaningless. We should not be surprised by this as the whole purpose of the principle is to sift what is meaningful from what is not. If a proposition is not a tautology, and there is no empirical way of discovering its truth, then it is meaningless; it is a 'pseudo-proposition'. Ayer accepts that such statements may have emotional or literary significance, they may strike a chord in us or sound beautifully poetic, but they are not *factually* significant. Ayer's point is that meaningful propositions must make claims about the world; they must say that the world is this way or that way. So, if upon reading a proposition we are unsure what the world would be like if the statement were true as opposed to false (that is, if we did not know what would count as verifying it) then the proposition is not making a claim about the world after all. It is factually insignificant and meaningless.

▶ **ACTIVITY**

Refer to the list of propositions in the previous activity on page 156.

1. Re-categorise each proposition (as meaningless, etc.) according to Ayer's verification principle.
2. Are there any propositions that Ayer would say were meaningless, but which to you are obviously meaningful?
3. What implications does this have for Ayer's theory?

anthology 1.21

The verification principle can be used to identify statements which look as if they are meaningful but are in fact word games, grammatical errors or simply incoherent. John Hick gives two useful examples of sentences that appear at first sight to be meaningful and about the world but which cannot be verified, and so must be nonsense according to the verificationist.[8]

The universe and everything in it doubled in size last night.

There is an invisible, intangible, odourless, tasteless and silent rabbit in this room.

According to Ayer's verification principle both these sentences would be meaningless because neither of them can be verified or falsified. They appear to be making claims about the world, but when you look at them closely you see that whether they are true or false (that is, whether the world is the way they say it is) makes no difference to our experience. There is no possible experiment we could perform which could establish their truth or falsehood and so they are not factually significant.

Strong and weak versions of the verification principle

The bravado of the young A.J. Ayer was gradually watered down throughout the rest of his life as he defended and moderated his verification principle according to the criticisms that his theory faced. One of the first issues raised was about scientific statements: what of generalisations such as 'At sea level water boils at 100 degrees centigrade'? The problem with the truth of general claims like this is that they can never be conclusively proved, not even in principle, since we cannot boil all the water in the world to confirm that it always boils at 100 degrees. This category of propositions looks as though it could represent a serious difficulty for the verification principle, as most scientific claims are of this general sort, and yet Ayer regarded science as the paradigm case of a body of meaningful claims. Note also that much of science deals with entities which are not directly observable, for example, sub-atomic particles such as protons and quarks – how can we verify their existence, and the truth of propositions which refer to them?

So how can there be (scientific) claims which are meaningful according to the verification principle, even though we cannot verify them in practice? For example, it is meaningful to say that there is life on the planet Neptune, even though at present we have no means of verifying this claim. Ayer gets round this problem by differentiating between a strong and a weak version of verification, with scientific theories fulfilling the weaker conditions:

- The strong version states that a statement is meaningful if we can directly verify it by observation-statements – and therefore establish its truth/falsity for certain.
- The weak version states that a statement is meaningful if there are some observations relevant to determining the truth/falsity of the statement.

anthology 1.22

Ayer's weaker version of the verification principle is saying that a proposition counts as meaningful just if we can articulate what observations would count towards or against the likelihood of its being true or false. For Ayer, such claims are meaningful because we could in principle verify them. Going back to the claim that there is life on Neptune, we know the kinds of things we would need to do – send a sophisticated space probe to Neptune, for example – to determine whether they are true. So the modified verification principle is not saying that we can as a matter of fact verify all meaningful propositions, just that we could do so in principle.

The verification principle and the metaphysics of God

An important implication of logical positivism and Ayer's verification principle, if correct, is that large swathes of what philosophers have written and talked about over the last two thousand years are ruled out as meaningless. One branch of philosophy which is rendered meaningless by the principle is metaphysics: the account of ultimate reality and of what substances and beings might lie beyond our ordinary perception. For the Vienna Circle the (empirically verifiable) writing was on the wall for this branch of philosophy. Rudolf Carnap (1891–1970), in an article entitled 'The Elimination of Metaphysics Through Logical Analysis of Language' (1932), argued that metaphysical statements are pseudo-statements: they appear to be making claims about the world but in fact they are not. Almost by definition metaphysics attempts to describe the world beyond observation (see Figure 0.5 in the introduction to this book, page viii) and so cannot be verified through any observation statement. No empirical truth conditions can be specified for metaphysical statements and Carnap concludes that they are devoid of meaning. Given that the entirety of this book is about metaphysics the logical positivists might argue that almost everything in this book is entirely unverifiable and unfalsifiable, and is therefore meaningless (hey, no sniggering at the back).

This part of the A-level exam is rightly entitled the 'metaphysics of God', rather than the usual 'philosophy of religion' because, as we saw in the introduction to the book, discussions about God are metaphysical discussions about what 'really' exists beyond sense experience. So, one of the most significant consequences of Ayer's logical positivism is that it appears to make all claims about religion and about God meaningless.[9] This is because many theological claims are about something transcendent; that is to say, about objects which lie beyond human experience – such as God, heaven or life after death. But all talk about what lies outside experience is, according to the verification principle, meaningless. After all, how might you verify Aquinas' claim that the universe is dependent upon God for its existence; or Plantinga's claim that there are a very large number of logically possible worlds; or Hick's belief that there really is life after death; or St Augustine's claim that we have free will? Statements such as 'God loves the world' or 'God is the Father, the Son and the Holy Ghost' *appear* to be telling us something about someone. But when we look at such statements from the point of view of verificationism it becomes clear that there are no possible ways of checking whether they are true or false. There are no experiments we could carry out, or observation-statements we could report, to verify them, and so such statements are not factually significant.

What about all the arguments for the existence of God that you have been studying – what does Ayer have to say about them? Here it is useful to recall again Hume's fork, and how this was re-forged in Ayer's hands into the verification principle. On one side of the fork are tautologies, analytic and true by definition, while on the other side are observation statements, synthetic and empirically verifiable. When exploring the ontological proof (page 48 above), you encountered Ayer's attacks on *a priori* attempts to prove the existence of

God. For Ayer these *a priori* proofs fail because tautologies, even when combined into an argument, yield only further tautologies and cannot prove the existence of anything. So, according to Ayer, the existence of God cannot be demonstrated *a priori* – it cannot be proved with certainty. But can God's existence be shown to be at least probable, drawing on the *a posteriori* arguments for God's existence, such as the design arguments? Ayer thinks not:

> *In talking about God [the theologian is] talking about a transcendent being who might be known through certain empirical manifestations, but certainly could not be defined in terms of those manifestations. But in that case the term 'god' is a metaphysical term. And if 'god' is a metaphysical term then it cannot be even probable that a god exists. For to say that 'God exists' is to make a metaphysical utterance which cannot be either true or false.*[10]
>
> Ayer

Within Ayer's logical positivism the *a posteriori* arguments for God's existence fail because they rely on premises that contain metaphysical terms, which are pseudo-statements, and which cannot be verified or falsified. So, Hume's fork and Ayer's verification principle skewer both *a priori* and *a posteriori* arguments for God's existence. It is important to remember that Ayer does not regard the claim that 'God exists' as false, but instead as meaningless. Equally the claims of the atheist that 'God does not exist' are also meaningless, as they too fail the verification principle's test. For Ayer we simply cannot meaningfully talk about God.

You will remember from your Year 1 studies that another area of philosophy that falls foul of Ayer's verification principle is ethics. Ethical statements which make judgements of what is right/wrong are not true by definition nor, says Ayer, can they be verified as matters of fact. In which case much of what is written in moral philosophy is meaningless, and for Ayer we should start to realise that moral judgements are simply expressions of what we feel (this theory became known as emotivism). But is Ayer right in dismissing religious, ethical and metaphysical language as meaningless?

▶ ACTIVITY

Revisit the list of key metaphysical concepts in the introduction on page xi.

1. According to Ayer's verification principle which of these key concepts are meaningful and which are meaningless?
2. Once again ask yourself: Do you disagree with Ayer – are there any propositions that Ayer would say were meaningless, but which to you are obviously meaningful?
3. What implications does this have for Ayer's theory?

Criticism 1

There are some serious difficulties facing Ayer's verification principle. The first criticism is that the principle seems far too strong since it not only outlaws religious language from the realm of the meaningful, but it also makes much of what humans speak and write about meaningless as well, including art, beauty and our inner feelings and sensations. After all, how can we prove that the *Mona Lisa* is beautiful? The verification principle also makes poetic and metaphorical language meaningless: for example, I cannot verify that my love is a rose. Moreover, it makes all ethical judgements simply a matter of personal feeling and it makes most philosophical speculation nonsense. This all suggests that Ayer's notion of meaning is very different from the one we operate with in everyday life.

But perhaps Ayer's prescriptive account of meaning in general should trouble us. The philosopher Stewart Sutherland (1941–) described Ayer's theory as 'conceptually restrictive and intellectually imperialistic in its character'.[11] Sutherland goes on to compare the prescriptions of Ayer (on what we can and cannot talk about) with George Orwell's invented language 'Newspeak' described in his novel *1984*. Newspeak is an artificial language that is developed by a totalitarian government with the specific intention of limiting what can be said by people. The ultimate goal of Newspeak is to enable people to speak about practical matters, and things that are permitted by the government, but to prevent people from talking about, or even thinking about, anything that might encourage heretical behaviour. This is a terrifying thought, as all human creativity, philosophy, religion, literature, theorising would be impossible within Newspeak. Rather like, Sutherland says, the effects of Ayer's verification principle, which would also rule out as 'non-sense' these areas of human activity, and eventually diminish human thought. We explore later (pages 178–81) Wittgenstein's attempts to give a different, i.e. non-cognitivist, account of meaning which captures the full complexity of human language and meaning.

Criticism 2

A second criticism is that the principle of verification is itself meaningless according to its own criterion. The principle claims that 'for any proposition to be meaningful it must either be verifiable or true by definition'. So if this claim is itself meaningful it must either be verifiable or true by definition. However, it is clearly not true by definition. We cannot recognise its truth simply by examining the meanings of the terms it uses. But neither does it appear to be verifiable, as it is hard to see in what way the world (if the principle were true) would differ from the world if it were false. So, if the verification principle is neither verifiable, nor true by definition, then it must be meaningless!

1.3.3 John Hick's response to Ayer (eschatological verification)

A further significant criticism of Ayer comes from the Christian philosopher John Hick, who argued that religious statements can in fact be verified and therefore that they are factually significant and so meaningful, even according to the verification principle. There are three main aspects to Hick's approach: first, his definition of 'verification', which is different from Ayer's; second, his parable of the Celestial City, showing that verification of religious statements is possible and reasonably straightforward; third, his account of personal identity after death, showing that resurrection is possible. Let us deal with each aspect in turn.

Hick agrees with Ayer that only statements that are factually significant are meaningful, and that FACTUAL SIGNIFICANCE is judged by whether the truth or falsity of an assertion makes a difference to our experience of the world. For example, whether the statement 'There is an invisible, odourless, intangible rabbit in this room' is true or false makes no difference to our experience. Hence it is not factually significant; it tells us nothing about the world and is not meaningful. Like Ayer, Hick proposes that the factual significance of an assertion is best assessed by whether it can be verified. Unlike Ayer, Hick argues that verifiability should be judged by whether it is possible to remove the grounds for rational doubt about the truth of the claim in question. For example, claiming that there is a family of foxes living at the bottom of the garden can be verified if you keep finding mutilated bin bags on the path, if you have seen a red furry tail sticking out from a hole under the shed and if your night-vision goggles reveal frolicking fox cubs. Such evidence would effectively remove any serious doubts about the matter.

Now, Hick accepts that religious propositions cannot be falsified. They cannot be falsified because, if there is no God and the atheists are right, then after they die they will just be dead and they will not be able to say 'Ah-ha – there is no God, those theists got it wrong!' But Hick's argument is that although religious statements may never be falsified they can be verified, in the sense that rational doubt about their truth can be removed. For Hick it is the potential verifiability of religious statements that makes them meaningful. To illustrate how such verification is possible he offers his celebrated parable of the Celestial City:

Two men are travelling together along a road. One of them believes that it leads to the Celestial City, the other that it leads nowhere; but since this is the only road there is, both must travel it ... During the journey they meet with moments of refreshment and delight, and with moments of hardship and danger. All the time one of them thinks of his journey as a pilgrimage to the Celestial City. He interprets the pleasant parts of the journey as encouragements and the obstacles as trials of his purpose ... The other, however, believes none of this ... Since he has no choice in the matter he enjoys the good and endures the bad ... When they do turn the last corner it will be apparent that one of them has been right all the time and the other wrong.[12]

John Hick, 'Theology and Verification'

Remember that Hick believes that the journey of our lives through this world, and its hardships and pains, are part of the process of soul-making (see above, page 148). You may also recall that, as part of Hick's theodicy, the rewards of life after death are sufficient to compensate for the suffering people experience in their lives on Earth. But in this passage it is the destination (heaven), not the journey (life), that Hick is exploring.

This parable points to the possibility of what Hick calls 'eschatological verification', that is to say, verification after our death in the next life. (ESCHATOLOGY concerns what happens at the end of things, for instance at the Last Judgement.) Hick is arguing that many religious statements, particularly in Christianity, rest on the claim that there is an afterlife, and they are meaningful because they can be verified in the afterlife. I can verify whether there is a heaven or not if, after I die, I find myself in heaven. For Hick such experience would remove grounds for rational doubt about the existence of heaven.

Issues arising from eschatological verification

Hick recognises that the possibility of eschatological verification relies on the metaphysical concept of personal identity, and on me retaining my identity through the processes of death; but there are certain difficulties with this idea. One important difficulty is that we all know that when people die their bodies quickly decompose. How, if the body of which you are made has dissipated, can you possibly be thought to have survived? If someone subsequently appears in heaven, in what sense can it be said to be the same person? If I am resurrected how can this new body be thought of as still me?

To answer such questions, Hick presents three separate 'thought experiments' which try to show that a person appearing in an afterlife can meaningfully be considered as the same person as someone who had lived and died in this life.

1. First Hick asks us to imagine a person, X, disappearing in America, while at the very same moment someone else, who is the exact double of X (same physical features, the same memory, and so on), appears in Australia. If this happened would you consider the person appearing in Australia to be the same as X? Hick thinks that we would.
2. Now imagine that person X, instead of disappearing, dies in America, and at the very same moment their double appears in Australia. Would we not still say they were the same person? Hick thinks that if we accept that it is the same person in the first scenario, we would have to accept that it is the same in this scenario.
3. Finally, imagine that person X dies in America, and their double now appears, not in Australia, but in heaven. Again Hick thinks that if we accept that it is the same person in scenarios 1 and 2, then we must accept it is the same in this scenario too. And if we accept that it is the same person, then we are accepting that it makes sense to talk about surviving one's death and preserving one's personal identity.

What these thought experiments are supposed to show is that resurrection is at least logically possible. And if we are resurrected in heaven, we (or at least some of us) will be in no doubt that it is heaven that we are in. For Hick there are two factors that will remove all rational doubt that we are in heaven: first, our final understanding of the purpose and destiny given to us by God; and, second, our encountering our saviour Jesus Christ. Note that Hick says that only some people may be able to verify this, namely those who reach heaven. But, nonetheless, if it is logically possible that at least someone will be able to verify (remove rational doubt from) the claim that 'God exists', then this claim is meaningful.

Experimenting with ideas

Scenario 1: You are a guest on the Starship Enterprise and Captain Kirk invites you to take a trip to a local planet in their matter transporter. The machine will decompose your body into its constituent atoms, channel them along a laser beam across space and recompose you on the planet's surface.

- If you stepped into the matter transporter do you think you would arrive safely on the planet's surface as the same person?

Scenario 2: Suppose that the matter transporter does not operate over great distances, but that luckily the ingenious technicians on the Enterprise have invented a tele-transporter. The tele-transporter works by first decomposing your body and recording the precise pattern of the constituent atoms. It then transmits the pattern to the distant planet where another machine recomposes you out of local materials. Keen to cross the galaxy you agree to step into the machine. The person appearing on the other planet believes they are you.

- Do you think you would arrive safely on the planet's surface as the same person?
- Is your answer the same for the matter transporter? What differences are there between the two cases?

Scenario 3: What if the tele-transporter does not destroy your original body, but simply creates a copy out of local materials on the planet so that now there are two of 'you' in the universe. Which one would be the real you and why?

- Do your answers to the three scenarios in this activity cast doubt on, or confirm, Hick's claim that it is possible for you to survive your death? Why?

Criticism 1

One line of criticism against Hick is to question the conclusions he draws from his thought experiments. Each scenario, it may be urged, really produces a duplicate person in a new location, and so is not really the self-same person who disappeared or died. To see this, consider altering the scenarios slightly, such that in each case the original person remains alongside the double appearing in Australia or heaven. In such cases we would be inclined to think the double a different person from the original. However, this alteration to the scenario has not changed the status of the double itself, and so the double cannot be the same as the original. God could certainly create a duplicate of me in heaven on my death, but a duplicate of me is not me. Our intuitions appear to suggest that, for my personal identity to survive the process of death, there would have to be some form of bodily continuity. Simply rebuilding a perfect copy is not resurrecting the self-same person.

Criticism 2

A second difficulty concerns whether we truly can verify through our post-mortem experience the various religious claims in question. Consider the most obvious claims that God and heaven exist. In order to verify that we are now in heaven, or are now experiencing God, we need first to recognise that this vision in front of us is heaven (or God). But it may not be possible to recognise something we have never seen before and that lies beyond our understanding. So if, as some philosophers say, God is beyond our comprehension, then perhaps it will not be possible to recognise, and hence verify, that this is God or heaven we see before us.

1.3.4 The *University* debate: Flew, Hare and Mitchell

Antony Flew on falsification (and Wisdom's gardener)

In the early 1950s, as part of a symposium in the journal *University*, three philosophers debated whether or not religious statements could be falsified, and whether this helped throw light onto the meaningfulness (or meaninglessness) of religious propositions. Two of the philosophers, Richard Hare (1919–2002) and Basil Mitchell (1917–2011), were believers and the third, Antony Flew (1923–2010), was an atheist, but all three used memorable parables to make their points. It was Flew who opened the symposium with an attack on the meaning of religious propositions. Like Ayer and Hick, Flew believed that propositions are only meaningful if they are factually significant, in other words if they make a genuine assertion about the world. However, unlike Ayer or Hick, he argues that it is not the possibility of verification, but more particularly the possibility of falsification, that shows whether a statement is meaningful.

Flew borrows a parable from John Wisdom's article 'Gods', written in 1944, and amends it to make his case. In the original parable Wisdom (1904–93) asks us to imagine two people arriving at a run-down garden (Figure 1.39). One person notices the flowers and the organisation of the plants and takes this as evidence that someone has been caring for the garden. The other person notices the weeds and the disorder and concludes that no one has been tending the garden. Wisdom's point is that although two people can be presented with exactly the same empirical evidence – it is the same garden that both are experiencing – their responses need not be the same.

This shows that empirical observation or evidence does not, by itself, determine the very different conclusions that people draw about the world. How we interpret the evidence presented to us is, at least in part, influenced by our attitudes towards it. The atheist may focus on the disorder of the universe and interpret this as evidence of the absence of any divine plan. Meanwhile, the theist attends to the order and beauty of things and sees this as evidence of the work of a divine intelligence.

Figure 1.40 Is there a gardener or not?

Experimenting with ideas

Why do you think some people see the world as a divine creation and others as a meaningless lump of rock?

1 Read through Paley's design argument (anthology extract 1.8). Think about the way that William Paley sees the world as he walks across the hills with a friend looking at the landscape, the sun setting, the birds of prey hunting. Describe how each of the following affects what he sees:
   a) His existing set of beliefs (What do you think he believes?)
   b) His expectations as to what he might observe
   c) The suggestions that might have been made to him
   d) His emotional states
   e) The culture he has grown up in
2 Read through the points Charles Darwin raised against the argument from design (see above, page 88). Think about a modern scientist walking through the same hills, observing the same features as Paley had done a hundred years before. Describe how a)–e) (above) affect what the scientist sees.

In Flew's reworking of Wisdom's gardener parable, the two people find a clearing in a jungle, containing many flowers, but also many weeds. Since they do not observe any gardener visiting to tend the plants, the sceptic reckons there must be no gardener. However, her companion, rather than give up the belief that there is a gardener, concludes that the gardener must come at night. So the two of them stay up all night keeping vigil, hoping to spot the mysterious gardener, but none appears. Again the sceptic takes this as evidence that there is no gardener, but the believer stubbornly responds that the gardener must be

> **ACTIVITY**
>
> In Flew's and Wisdom's parables what might the following represent:
>
> a) The garden?
> b) The flowers?
> c) The weeds?
> d) The differences in belief between the two people in the garden?

invisible. So they put up an electric fence around the garden and guard it with sniffer-dogs, but still they find no evidence of a gardener sneaking in to tend the land. Despite this the believer continues to maintain that there is a gardener, but now claims he is not only invisible, but also odourless and intangible, which accounts for why they have so far been unable to find direct evidence of his activity. So the believer continues to assert that there is a gardener, despite the complete lack of evidence, and each time their effort to find the gardener fails the believer simply modifies her assertion. Eventually the sceptic despairs and asks the believer, 'How does your claim that there is an invisible, odourless, intangible gardener differ from the claim that there's no gardener at all?'[13]

Flew is using the parable to show how a statement can start out as an assertion about the world: 'There is a gardener', but is then modified bit by bit so that it ends up not being an assertion at all. And for Flew this has significant implications for religious assertions and whether or not they are meaningful.

Flew does not use the following example, but this is a well-documented case of a religious assertion that has been modified over time, namely the assertion found in the Bible (Genesis 1.20ff) that God created humans and animals, fully formed, and that they flourished in a fully formed world that he had also recently created. According to the Christian tradition God created the universe and everything in it in six days, rested on the seventh, and also created the first human out of earth, and this event happened in around 5500BCE (counting generations backwards to Adam). Modern cosmology and evolutionary theory have cast serious doubts on such an assertion: in Victorian times the discovery and analysis of fossils, the work of Darwin on evolution and the work of geologists on the age of the Earth all undermined the assertions that were made in Genesis. These discoveries could have been accepted by believers as showing that the assertions made in Genesis are false, but modern theists have instead modified and qualified their claims that God created humans and animals in order to accommodate these scientific advances. God, it is now urged, created humans and animals through a process of evolution over hundreds of millions of years, and the text of Genesis is to be understood metaphorically. Another example, which theologians have themselves grappled with, is the claim that God is omnipotent, which can be modified in the light of counter examples (see above, page 8).

But such manoeuvrings worry Flew. If we repeatedly qualify our original assertion in the light of the new evidence to avoid having to give it up, then our assertion suffers what Flew calls 'death by a thousand qualifications'. In other words the assertion has been watered down and qualified so much that the assertion no longer says anything at all.

Let us look at our own example of how an assertion can be continuously qualified. Imagine you have a friend who is convinced that the *La La Land* actor Emma Stone has romantic feelings for him. More than this, he claims that Emma Stone actually *loves* him. So his claim appears to be straightforward, namely that:

Emma Stone loves me.

In querying this statement you remind him that he used to say that he loved Scarlett Johansson, and prior to that Jennifer Lopez, with equal fervour – in fact you point out that the whole 'Hollywood A-List' thing is getting a bit creepy. He replies that he doesn't even remember J-Lo, that the whole

Scarlett Johansson affair was just a youthful crush anyway, and he's moved on with his life even if Johansson hasn't. You then explain patiently that Ms Stone doesn't even know him; that she has never even seen him; and that it is all over social media that she is in love with a good-looking, rich and famous person. You also explain that times have moved on, and that it's far easier to prosecute possible stalkers like him these days. However, your friend insists that Emma has to keep her love for him a deep secret in order to avoid a scandal on social media. His original claim is now qualified as follows:

Emma Stone loves me (but it is a deeply secret love, just like her love for Ryan Gosling's character at the end of La La Land).

After a while your friend admits to you that Ms Stone's agent has recently called him, and told him to stop sending flowers, love poems and personal effects. The agent made it very clear that Ms Stone was not interested. But your friend explains to you that the agent was merely protecting his client from the damaging effects of her passion. Eventually Ms Stone herself contacts him online to tell your friend that if his pestering doesn't stop she will call her lawyers. Your friend tells you that he knows she is just playing hard-to-get; it's all part of the dating game. You realise that he's made a further adjustment to his claim:

Emma Stone loves me (but it is a deeply secret love and she is playing hard-to-get).

Even when the court order arrives forcing your friend to keep at least two miles away from Ms Stone, your friend explains to you that her entourage and entire legal team don't want her to become romantically involved with someone so young and so poor. He is now claiming that:

Emma Stone loves me (but it is a deeply secret love, she is playing hard-to-get and her entourage and legal team are conspiring to prevent us from getting together).

Eventually you ask him if there is anything that anyone could say or do, anything that could happen, that would demonstrate to him that Emma Stone doesn't love him. He confesses that nothing could come between him and Emma, that he knows her love for him is for ever, and even if she doesn't yet realise it, deep down she will always be in love with him.

Ian McEwan's novel *Enduring Love* ends on a similar, and sinister, one-sided declaration of 'love'. A stalker, who has finally been imprisoned, continues to write passionate letters to his victim, finding in his prison cell all sorts of signs that his victim returns this love. His thousandth letter ends as follows: 'Thank you for loving me, thank you for accepting me, thank you for recognising what I am doing for our love. Send me a new message soon.' The 'message' that the deluded man is referring to is simply the sun rising over the prison.[14]

Let us now return to Flew's argument. Flew is particularly interested in how believers surrender or adapt their assertions in the face of evidence that goes against these assertions. He uses the example of the assertion that God loves us like a father loves his children. If we point out to the theist that no father would let his children suffer what humans suffer, they typically respond by qualifying their statement and saying that God's love is a mysterious love. We saw above when examining the problem of evil how believers such as Hick and Plantinga have argued that God's love is compatible with the existence of horrific pain and suffering. So, Flew asks, how much suffering and evil must there be before the

anthology 1.23

theist will admit that God does not love us, or even that he does not exist? Flew's answer to this question is that *nothing* will count against the believer's assertion that God loves us; in other words, that no amount of evidence that God does not in fact love us will ever lead believers to give up the assertion that God does love us. After all, in one of the most important books of the Old Testament, Job, who has lost everything (his family, livelihood, friends, health) and who is sitting on a dungheap wondering what on earth he has done to deserve this (nothing, actually), still asserts that 'I know my redeemer liveth.'[15]

According to Flew, it looks as if religious assertions are not really assertions at all. Flew, like Ayer, thinks that an assertion is a genuine, meaningful assertion when it is factually significant; that is when it is making a claim about the world, saying that 'such-and-such is the case'. If you assert that your philosophy teacher can surf, then you are saying that 'my philosophy teacher is a surfer' is true, but you are also saying 'my philosophy teacher cannot surf' is false. In other words your assertion is a genuine assertion because you know what the world needs to look like in order to make your assertion true *and* you know what the world needs to look like in order to make your assertion false. For Flew, then, to know the meaning of an assertion you also need to know the meaning of its opposite. But if there is no 'opposite'; that is, if you cannot imagine any circumstances in which your statement could be false, then it is not an assertion at all. And if it is not an assertion (that is, it has no factual significance) then it is not meaningful.

For Flew there are very strong indicators, based on how religious people actually respond to facts, which seem to falsify their claims that religious assertions are not falsifiable. Flew argues that religious people, rather than accept that their assertions may be false, change and qualify their assertions and keep doing this rather than give them up. We saw this in the case of the believer in the invisible gardener, who refused to give up their assertion that a gardener looked after the clearing in the jungle (summarised in the Figure 1.41).

Figure 1.41 The believer's assertion that 'there is a gardener' cannot be falsified, but is instead modified and qualified

Believer	Sceptic
	1.0 There is no gardener.
2.0 There is a gardener.	
	Look, there are many weeds among the flowers.
2.1 There is a gardener (… but he has let weeds grow).	
	We've sat here and watched and watched but we've never seen a gardener.
2.1.1 There is a gardener (… but he's let weeds grow and he is invisible).	
	We've got guard dogs, but the dogs never bark.
2.1.1.1 There is a gardener (… but he's let weeds grow and he's invisible and he is odourless).	
	We've set up an electric, barbed wire fence, but the fence never moves and we've never heard any shrieks.
2.1.1.1.1 There is a gardener (… but he's let weeds grow, and he's invisible, and he's odourless, and he is intangible).	
	Really – how does 2.1.1.1.1 differ from 1.0?

Flew concludes that if believers cannot articulate what will make their assertion that 'God loves the world' or 'God exists' false, or if believers continue to qualify these assertions despite being given falsifying evidence, then they are not making any assertions at all. For Flew there are already strong indicators (for example, explanations of why a loving God allows so much horrific suffering) that religious statements cannot be falsified, and therefore are not meaningful. The challenge then, laid down by Flew to his fellow debaters, is this:

What would have to occur or to have occurred to constitute for you a disproof of the love of, or the existence of, God?[16]

Experimenting with ideas

Imagine the following people are having a conversation (similar to the one in the table above), and construct a dialogue that might take place between them:

Person A has an unshakeable belief that they will never give up no matter what the evidence.	Person B wishes to provide evidence that shows person A they are wrong.
1 The Prime Minister believes that a certain country in the Middle East has weapons of mass destruction.	1 The United Nations chief weapons inspector is carrying out thorough inspections and finds nothing.
2 Someone from the Flat-Earth Society sincerely believes that the Earth is flat and there is a conspiracy to 'prove' it is round.	2 A specialist in astronomy and geography is out to disband the Flat-Earth Society.
3 A child believes that there are monsters under his bed.	3 A mother is trying to reassure her child to help him get to sleep.
4 A fanatical England football supporter believes that the England team play the best football in the world.	4 A football historian wants to show this fan that all the evidence of past tournaments shows the England team are simply average.
5 A student is convinced that all her lecturers are out to ruin her life, no matter how helpful they might appear.	5 A counselling tutor is trying to help this student, so that she might rejoin her classes.
6 A believer is convinced that God loves the world.	6 An atheist is convinced that a loving God does not exist, because of the amount of suffering in the world.

Basil Mitchell's response to Flew (the Partisan)

Following directly on from Flew's contribution to the 'Theology and Falsification' debate, two other philosophers, Basil Mitchell and Richard Hare, responded to Flew's claim that religious statements cannot be falsified.

Flew's frustration with believers is related to how they accommodate and deal with evidence that apparently falsifies their assertions. We have seen that Flew concluded that this was because believers were not making any assertions at all; he based this conclusion on the fact that believers and atheists see the world very differently, and that believers have a blind spot when it comes to accepting evidence against their claims. His examples, and the parable of the Invisible Gardener, may have been selected to make the atheists' perspective appear fair and reasonable, while the believers' perspective appears to be unreasonable and defensive.

Both Mitchell and Hare (page 175 below) try to show that the believer's position is more nuanced than this, and they both argue against Flew: it is not the case (as Flew suggests) that the believer is simply being stubborn in the face of some pretty obvious facts. Mitchell and Hare reject Flew's position, and both offer their own parables which also hinge on the world being seen from two different perspectives, just as Hick did through his parable of the Celestial City and Flew did in his Invisible Gardener parable. Emerging from these parables is a new understanding of how religious statements can be meaningful even though they are not straightforwardly falsifiable. Let us look at Mitchell's response to Flew first.

Mitchell disagrees with the view that religious beliefs are unfalsifiable and he tells another parable to make his point, this time about a stranger who may, or may not, be on the side of the Partisans.[17]

Imagine your country has been invaded and you become a Partisan, a member of the resistance movement hoping to overthrow the occupiers. One night you meet a man claiming to be a resistance leader, and he convinces you to put your trust in him and the movement. Over the months you sometimes see the man act for the resistance, but sometimes you also see him act against the movement. This troubles you: you worry that he might be a traitor, but your trust in him eventually overcomes your concerns and you continue to believe in him. Your belief that 'the stranger is on your side' is one that you do not give up, even though you see many things that suggest you are wrong.[18]

Mitchell argues that your belief in the resistance leader is meaningful, even though you refuse to give it up. Unlike Hare (below), Mitchell does not think that it is a blik because there are many occasions when you do doubt your own belief (the concept of a 'blik' is explained more fully on page 175). This doubt shows that your belief is falsifiable; that is, that you can quickly imagine circumstances under which you would give up your belief.

Mitchell's parable reflects the doubts that religious believers sometimes have when they encounter great suffering in their lives (see the problem of evil, pages 129–51). These 'trials of faith' show that Flew is wrong to think that believers simply shrug off evidence that goes against their beliefs. Some believers, after all, do lose their faith in the face of painful and apparently senseless episodes in their lives.

We could take Mitchell's parable further, and develop it along the lines of John Hick's eschatological verification (see above, page 166), suggesting that one day the truth will be revealed and verified. In the parable this happens when the war is over; in real life this would happen after we die. So, by extending Mitchell's parable, we may show that a belief that 'God exists' is both falsifiable (there are trials of faith) and verifiable (after we die), and therefore religious statements are meaningful assertions about the world.

Mitchell, a Christian like Hare, does not take Hare's non-cognitivist approach to religious statements. Mitchell thinks that statements like 'God loves the world' are genuine statements, and factually significant. So, like Flew, Mitchell adopts a cognitivist approach; however, unlike Flew, Mitchell thinks that the statements are capable of being falsified (see the table at the end of this section on page 182).

Hare's response to Flew (bliks and the lunatic)

Let us now turn to the third and final philosopher who took part in the symposium for the journal *University*. Richard Hare also offers a critical response to Flew, but from a different angle to that of Mitchell. Hare gives his own parable to help us to understand the strange nature of religious statements, centred around a lunatic at university.

> *A certain lunatic is convinced that all dons* [i.e. tutors] *want to murder him. His friends introduce him to all the mildest and most respectable dons that they can find, and after each of them has retired, they say, 'You see, he doesn't really want to murder you; he spoke to you in a most cordial manner; surely you are convinced now?' But the lunatic replies 'Yes, but that was only his diabolical cunning; he's really plotting against me the whole time, like the rest of them; I know it I tell you.' However many kindly dons are produced, the reaction is still the same.*[19]
> R.M. Hare

We can term this the parable of the Paranoid Student: like the person who believes in the Invisible Gardener, the paranoid student cannot imagine being wrong, and his claim that 'my tutors are out to murder me' is unfalsifiable. Hare concedes to Flew that the student's claim fails the test of falsifiability, and therefore it cannot count as a genuine assertion. Instead Hare proposes that we view the student's claim as something more like an expression of the student's way of seeing the world or scaffolding that underpins his other beliefs.

Hare invented the word 'blik' to refer to such foundational interpretations (possibly based on the German/Dutch words 'blick/blik' meaning 'view'), attitudes and ways of seeing and he argued that we all have bliks. The paranoid student has a deluded, and wrong, blik; the tutors (who can see that he is deluded as they all know they do not want to murder him) all have a correct blik. But the tutors still have a blik, and when they say, 'The other tutors really don't want to kill the student' they are expressing their own bliks. The differences between what Hare and Flew would have to say about the paranoid student are something like this:

- **Flew:** When the paranoid student says, 'the tutors are trying to kill me' he appears to be making an assertion, but we know this claim cannot be falsified, therefore it is not an assertion at all. The people who tell the student, 'the tutors aren't trying to kill you' are making an assertion and it is a true one.
- **Hare:** When the paranoid student says, 'the tutors are trying to kill me' he is not making an assertion. He is expressing a fundamental interpretation and attitude that underpin his beliefs. The people who tell the student, 'the tutors aren't trying to kill you' are not making assertions either; they are also expressing their own fundamental interpretations and attitudes that underpin their beliefs.

Hare's point is that we are all in some ways like the student in his parable; we all have bliks. We all have, and express, fundamental interpretations and foundational beliefs, that we would not let go of easily and which are, to all intents and purposes, unfalsifiable. These thoughts and principles often form the very basis for our other beliefs about the world, just as the student's paranoid blik does. In support of his concept of 'blik', Hare refers to the work of David Hume, who led the way in investigating the assumptions that we all make about the world. In particular Hume argued that we believe that all events have a cause (page 80), and we base our lives on this assumption without questioning whether it is true. Moreover, this assumption that 'every event has a cause' cannot actually be falsified, and so in Hare's terminology it is a blik.

Imagine that someone tried to falsify this belief. They might point to events for which no cause could be observed, such as the unexpected disappearance of your cat, or the sudden appearance of a puncture in your bicycle tyre. We can suppose that you spent months trying to find out how or why your cat disappeared, or hours looking for the offending object that had pierced your tyre's inner tube, but had found nothing. Would you accept such failure as evidence that these events just happened without any reason or cause? Probably not. For what you would try to do instead is hold on to your belief that 'everything has a cause', and explain away your failure to find any cause in these cases by thinking that you had not searched long or hard enough. You would probably think to yourself that given enough time and the right resources you would have found the cause. And no matter how many events the sceptic might describe that appear to lack a cause, you may well respond in the same way: refusing to give up your belief that all events have causes despite the mounting number of events cited where no cause is forthcoming. 'Cause and effect' is how we interpret our experience, and we rely on it when moving through the world, when conducting experiments, when planning for the future – we cannot get rid of it: in Hare's terms, it is a blik.

Hare and non-cognitivism

For Hare many religious statements fall into the category of 'blik'. Religious statements do not just state facts about the world, but they go beyond that to express our attitude to those facts, and the value we put on those facts. So, for Hare, when believers say that 'God exists', they are expressing a blik: it is a belief that informs their perspective on the world, and in terms of which they interpret their whole lives. They may never be prepared to give it up, but the fundamental nature of the belief ensures that it remains important to them, and distinctly meaningful.

The mistake of the position which Flew selects for attack is to regard this kind of talk as some sort of explanation, as scientists are accustomed to use the word.[20]
R.M. Hare

So if bliks have meaning then it is a mistake to presume, as Flew does, that all the statements we make are assertions or propositions that can be falsified. Hare's argument represents a significant move away from a cognitivist approach and towards a non-cognitivist approach to religious language (see above, page 158). If Hare is correct then many religious statements are actually expressions of bliks, and are not assertions, yet they are still meaningful. A non-cognitivist approach to religious statements may help to prise 'meaningfulness' away from the logical positivists, and away from those who argue that a statement has to be factually significant in order to be meaningful. We explore this rejection of simplistic cognitivism more fully when we look at Wittgenstein, below (pages 178–81).

▶ ACTIVITY

Read through the following statements and answer the questions below.

1. Every event that you have experienced, or will experience in your lifetime, has a cause.
2. God loves the world that he created.
3. As you walk or run down any street (avoiding potholes, men-at-work, wobbly paving stones, sudden crevasses and so on) the ground in front of you is basically going to be solid.
4. Someone, somewhere, loves you.
5. The cars that you sit in when you drive are not going to suddenly fall apart as you turn a corner.
6. There is life after death.
7. It always rains in London.
8. The sun will rise tomorrow (even if we may not see it because of the cloud cover).
9. Your teachers are not out to murder you.
10. The world outside this room continues to exist when the door is shut.
11. Physical objects don't just disappear into thin air.

a) Which of the statements above do you hold to be true? (We will call these your convictions.)
b) How might someone get you to change your mind about these convictions (and would they be able to shake up your convictions without giving ridiculous or unlikely scenarios?)
c) So, which of your convictions would Hare say are your 'bliks'?

Criticism

Flew gives short shrift to Hare's efforts to analyse religious statements as bliks, claiming that such an analysis is fundamentally misguided. Flew argues that religious people, when they make statements about God, about God's love and God's creation are in fact trying to refer to the world, to make assertions. As Flew says:

> *If Hare's religion really is a blik, involving no cosmological assertions about the nature and activities of a supposed personal creator, then surely he is not a Christian at all?*[21]

Flew isn't quite on the mark here, as there is a recent (controversial) movement, led by Don Cupitt (1934–) which takes an anti-realist approach to Christianity and which does not see religious statements as assertions about the world, but as expressions of value. Hare's concept of bliks would fit quite comfortably into this tradition (see also our discussion of alternative theologies on page 139 above). However, Flew is right to think that this is not an orthodox interpretation of religious statements, and that in general when believers do make statements involving religious terms or ideas (such as 'God loves his creation') then they are actually trying to make assertions about the world.

> Learn More

Wittgenstein and non-cognitivism

We noted above (page 158) that, while there is only one way to hold a cognitivist position, there are many ways to reject cognitivism, and so there are many different varieties or flavours of non-cognitivism. We have just encountered one position that rejects cognitivism: Hare's notion of 'bliks', which captures the idea that we do state convictions about the world which we are not really prepared to surrender (they are not easily falsified) but that these statements are meaningful. We now turn to a more wide-ranging, philosophically important, theory of meaning which also rejects cognitivism – that of Wittgenstein.

Wittgenstein's rejection of cognitivism

Ludwig Wittgenstein (1889–1951) was one of the most significant philosophers of the last century. He was primarily a philosopher of language, and it was his reflections on the nature of meaning that led him to the conclusion that religious claims are not claims about the world in the same way that scientific claims are. Wittgenstein believes that to treat religious claims as akin to scientific hypotheses is to seriously misunderstand the meaning of religious language. But before we come to look at what Wittgenstein had to say about expressions of religious conviction, we should first sketch the philosophy of language that lies behind his thoughts on religion.

Wittgenstein put forward two distinct theories of meaning, one when he was young and the other towards the end of his career. Wittgenstein in both his early and later phases believed that the heart of philosophy lay in the study of language and that by studying language we could clear up many of the disputes of philosophers and perhaps even make philosophy no longer necessary. The early Wittgenstein adopted a 'picture theory' of meaning, arguing that language is a way of representing facts. So a sentence like 'The cat is on the mat' is meaningful because it represents or pictures some state of affairs in the world. Wittgenstein argued that when we attempt to use language to do anything other than to say things about the world, we stray into the realm of nonsense. This picture theory of meaning had a significant influence on the logical positivists of the Vienna Circle (see above, page 160) and on A.J. Ayer.

However, later in his life Wittgenstein became one of the foremost critics of this simplistic view of meaning. He attacked his own early work and the logical positivists, arguing that it utterly failed to capture the complexity of language. We have seen that for the logical positivists the only meaningful statements were ones about science or about the world we see, or ones that were true by definition. But Wittgenstein realised that our language was so much richer and more varied than this, and it was a great error for philosophers to rule out as meaningless the rest of language because it could not be true or false. For example, when we talk about beauty, or love, or poetry, or religion, or art, or the meaning of life, we seem to understand one another – yet Ayer tells us that we are talking nonsense. So Wittgenstein rejected cognitivism and searched for a new understanding of the nature of meaning.

▶ **ACTIVITY**

1 Construct as many different sentences as you can that contain the word 'down'.
2 How many different meanings of the word 'down' have you used?

From this simple exercise you can immediately see that words do not have a single meaning. There are many, many different meanings of the word 'down'; over twenty if you include slang and colloquial uses. The later Wittgenstein argued that there was no such thing as 'the' meaning of a word or sentence, since there are many different ways in which language can be meaningful. He rejected the idea that a single theory of meaning was possible. Presuming that words must have some specific meaning, he argued, is the source of many philosophical difficulties. What we need to do is to be alive to the vagueness of words, to the great variety of different meanings they can have, and to the many ways they can be used.

Go back to the ways in which the word 'down' can be used. In the context of rambling (the South Downs Way); of upholstery (down as in duck feathers); of giving directions (you go down the road); of dog training (a command for a dog to grovel); of crosswords (down clues); of emotions (feeling down); of dancing (get on down); of drinking (down in one) and there are many, many more. And the nature of meaning itself is as variegated as the meanings or uses of words. Understanding the meaning of a word is not a matter of catching hold of some abstract idea which is the meaning, but is a practical matter of being able to use the word appropriately in a variety of contexts. So you know the meaning of the word 'down' just because you can use it, but this does not mean that there is one thing, the word's meaning, which you have in your head.

> *The meaning of a word is its use in the language.*[22]
>
> **Wittgenstein**

So Wittgenstein's later theory of meaning denied that the meaning of language could be reduced to how it pictured the world. This may be one function of language, but it is certainly not the only one. We saw in the introduction to this section above (page 157) that language can be used to do so many more things than this, and Wittgenstein cites the following as some examples of the multiplicity of language use: to give orders, to describe an object, to report an event, to make up a story, to tell a joke, to ask, thank, curse, greet, pray, and so on.[23] All these uses are legitimate. So if we wish to know the meaning of a word we should look for how it is used, according to Wittgenstein, and this view is sometimes condensed into the phrase 'meaning is use'.

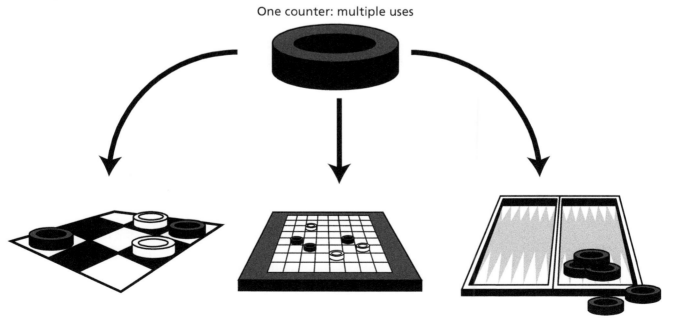

Figure 1.42 Just as a counter can have a different use in many different games (Draughts, Othello, Backgammon) so a word can be used with a different meaning in different language games

The term 'LANGUAGE GAME' is meant to highlight the fact that the speaking of language is part of an activity.[24] The different uses of language are activities that take place in different social contexts, which Wittgenstein famously termed 'language games'. He did not mean 'game' in a flippant or competitive sense, but in the sense that language use is an activity governed by certain rules, and these rules vary from context to context. For example, the rules governing the use of the word 'experience' in science are very different from those governing this word in a religious context. But Wittgenstein argued that it was a mistake to think that one use of a word was better or more fundamental than another.

> ▶ **ACTIVITY**
>
> 1 How many different types of language games can you think of?
> 2 Can you describe how some of the rules of these language games differ?

Remember what Ayer and Flew claimed: for a statement to be meaningful it must refer to the world. But Wittgenstein is now suggesting that statements are meaningful so long as they are understood by other language users in a specific context. He therefore thinks (unlike Ayer) that morality, art, poetry and so on, are all meaningful; they are all language games. Now, when it comes to religious statements and concepts, according to Wittgenstein's approach, they are meaningful because they form part of a religious language game. Believers are users of this language; they are immersed in the practice of following its rules and, if we consider meaning to be equated with use, then such a language is meaningful to whoever is able to use the language appropriately, that is to say, to 'players' of the game.

So, to understand religious statements we need to be a part of the religious language game; as Wittgenstein said, we need to be immersed in the religious 'Form of Life'. If we are not immersed in that particular way of living, if we don't share those beliefs, or use those concepts in a familiar and regular way, then we cannot properly understand religious statements. This is the problem with cognitivist philosophers like Ayer and Flew. They think that there is only one way language can be meaningful, namely if it is factually significant; so when religious language fails to be factually significant they accuse it of being meaningless. But the error is to think that meaning lies in factual significance; that is, in statements that describe the world. The fundamental mistake made by Ayer and Flew is to treat statements from one language game (expressions of religious faith) as if they came from another (descriptions of the world): in other words, to treat religious talk as if it were scientific talk and as if it involves making a hypothesis.

> *Suppose someone were a believer and said: 'I believe in a Last Judgement', and I said: 'Well, I'm not so sure. Possibly.' You would say that there is an enormous gulf between us. If he said 'There is a German aeroplane overhead', and I said 'Possibly, I'm not so sure' you'd say we were fairly near.*[25]
> **Wittgenstein**

For Wittgenstein, science and religion are two different language games; they are not in competition with one another, and neither can help solve the problems of the other. According to Wittgenstein, it might be appropriate for us to take a hard-nosed approach to the meaning of scientific statements, in the way Ayer and Flew suggest: scientific claims are hypotheses that need to be verified or falsified. However, religious claims about God and the Creation or Last Judgement are not hypotheses and are not subject to the same rules as scientific claims.

When a believer says 'The Creator exists' they are not using 'exists' in the same way as when a scientist says 'Duck-billed platypuses exist'. For when a believer is talking about the Creator they are also being reverential; they are expressing their faith and their understanding of the purpose of life. Although 'The Creator exists' looks very similar to a statement like 'The chairs exist', it is a much richer and resonant phrase, and is an expression of faith, of belief in the grace of God and of salvation. Atheists just do not get it, and they cannot get it unless they become involved in a religious way of life.

Criticism

However, there are problems with Wittgenstein's theory. The most fundamental problem arises because a meaningful statement (within a religious language game) no longer has to be connected to the world; it no longer has to be true or false. So we can imagine a group of religious language users who can talk meaningfully about the existence of Jedi, the Force and the Dark Side so long as they have a consistent set of rules governing their concepts. The fact that the Jedi are fictional is irrelevant to the meaningfulness of the language game. This view about the nature of language, that it does not refer to the world, is termed ANTI-REALISM and is closely related to non-cognitivism (see page 158). However, being anti-realist about religious language does not sit well with what most believers think they are doing when they talk, for example, of God or the afterlife. Making religious statements does appear to involve making claims about what does and does not exist in reality. So there is a problem in supposing, as Wittgenstein does, that religion is nothing other than a game played in words and deeds by a community of people. The religious language game includes a set of substantive metaphysical claims, regarding the existence of God, heaven, Jesus, the afterlife, the creation and so on. So, many believers would disagree with Wittgenstein's point that religion is different from science. For believers, the Creator is real, and not simply another piece in a complicated language game.

Summary: Religious language

Here we have looked at two broad approaches to understanding religious language. The first approach, cognitivism, is characterised by the logical positivists and it holds that statements are meaningful insofar as they are factually significant: they express a belief about the world, and make claims that can be verified or falsified. The challenge that cognitivism poses to religious believers is to question whether religious statements are genuine assertions – do they make claims that are verifiable or falsifiable?

A.J. Ayer argues that religious statements cannot be verified because they are metaphysical pseudo-statements, and metaphysical claims are about things that cannot be observed or verified (concepts like God and heaven). John Hick, however, argues that religious statements can be verified (i.e. rational doubt can potentially be removed), after we die; in that case then religious statements are genuine assertions and are meaningful because they are verifiable, at least in Hick's sense.

Antony Flew argues that religious statements cannot be falsified, because whenever we try to point out to a believer some falsifying piece of evidence, they simply modify their original claim. In the end, Flew says, we just have to accept that religious assertions may appear to be assertions, but they are not really. However, Basil Mitchell disagrees. He proposes that believers are subject to crises of faith, in which their belief in God really is challenged, and they really do consider that their assertions may have been falsified. For Mitchell, then, religious statements are genuine assertions because they are falsifiable.

After Mitchell we turned to a second approach which rejected cognitivism as being too simplistic, and not capturing the complexities and nuances of language and how we use it. This approach was hugely influential on the philosophy of language in the second half of the twentieth century and was pioneered by Wittgenstein (1889–1951).

R.M. Hare, in debate with Flew and Mitchell about whether religious statements were falsifiable, suggested that we think of them as 'bliks'. These are meaningful and significant (but unfalsifiable) expressions of the way in which we see the world: our convictions, our interpretations, our attitudes, our values.

Ludwig Wittgenstein was primarily interested in language and meaning in general, and only tangentially applied his approach to religious statements. He rejected cognitivism because it fails to capture the many different ways in which statements and words can have meaning. Wittgenstein's own theory can be summarised by the phrase that 'meaning is use', and that where a statement has a part to play in a specific language game – such as religious language games – then it has meaning.

Summary of this section

Name of philosopher	Are meaningful statements factually significant?	Is verification or falsification the most important feature of factual significance?	Are religious statements factually significant?	Are religious statements meaningful?	Does the philosopher believe in God?
Ayer	Yes – cognitivist	Verification and falsification	No	No: because they are not verifiable or falsifiable	No
Hick	Yes – cognitivist	Verification	Yes	Yes: because they are verifiable (in the afterlife)	Yes
Flew	Yes – cognitivist	Falsification	No	No: because they are not falsifiable	No
Mitchell	Yes – cognitivist	Falsification	Yes	Yes: because they are falsifiable	Yes
Hare	No – non-cognitivist	N/A	No	Yes: because they are expressions of 'bliks'	Yes
Wittgenstein	No – non-cognitivist	N/A	No	Yes: because they are part of a coherent language game.	Probably

Metaphysics of God revisited

Throughout this section you may have felt the tension between three groups of people with an interest in religious belief: philosophers who are atheists, such as David Hume, J. L. Mackie and A.J. Ayer; philosophers who are believers, such as St Thomas Aquinas and Alvin Plantinga; and non-philosophers who are believers – those ordinary folk who happen to believe in God.

From the point of view of religious philosophers, it might seem as if the criticisms and alleged 'insights' of atheistic philosophers are beside the point. The atheists make demands that have no real bearing on the metaphysical belief in God. These demands include: water-tight proofs of God's existence; evidence for every religious belief; a complete justification for why there is suffering in the world; an account of how we can talk meaningfully about a metaphysical being who is beyond experience. When Pascal left behind that accusatory note after his death, telling us that his God was the God of Isaac, Jacob and Abraham, not the God of the philosophers, he was echoing the thoughts of many religious philosophers before and since. Atheistic philosophers just do not get it: they do not understand what it is really to believe in God. Wittgenstein made a remark along the same lines: to be able really to understand what someone is saying you have to immerse yourself in their way of life. And this is something that few atheist philosophers appear to have an interest in, or the capability of, doing.

From the point of view of some atheist and agnostic philosophers, the metaphysics of God is an obstinately evasive subject: it's like eating jelly with a fork (although not Hume's fork). Religious philosophers use all the tools and methodologies of western philosophy (construction of arguments, conceptual analysis, clarification of questions, and so on) but only up to a point. To the atheist philosopher it seems as if the moment the beliefs of the religious philosopher are under threat they resort to some non-philosophical, non-rational trick which preserves their belief in God. For example, they offer various proofs of God's existence, and then when it is shown that these do not work, they claim that actually these are not like other sorts of proofs, because they are not supposed to persuade non-believers of the truth of the conclusion. Other tricks include: redefining and qualifying their beliefs in response to any piece of evidence that could knock down their old beliefs; or playing around with the idea of meaning, even to the extent that some 'anti-realist' theologians claim that when they assert 'God exists' what they really mean is not that there is a thing, God, who exists, but something else entirely! In other words it seems to the atheists that religious philosophers are breaking Plato's cardinal rule of philosophy, which is to follow the argument wherever it leads.[26] Religious philosophers follow the argument where it leads, so long as it leads to the place where they want it to go. As soon as it does not go there, rational argument is thrown out of the window and it is all 'mystery and faith'.

Finally from the point of view of the ordinary believer, the approaches of both types of philosopher (atheist and believer) are simply wrong-headed. Philosophy has little bearing on the thoughts, actions and lives of most believers around the world. When ordinary believers do come across philosophical questions (Can God make a stone so large that he cannot move it? What caused God? What does 'God' mean?) they may well shake their heads, and wonder in bewilderment why anyone would want to waste their time thinking about such ridiculous and obscure questions. For the ordinary believer, God is someone who is woven into every part of their lives, like breathing or thinking or feeling, and there is no more to it than that.

Perhaps we must finish with two more sobering remarks, one from a believer (Blaise Pascal) and one from an atheist (Steven Pinker (1954–)), about our capacity to discover and understand metaphysical and religious truths.

Reason's last step is the recognition that there are an infinite number of things which are beyond it. It is merely feeble if it does not go as far as to realize that. If natural things are beyond it, what are we to say about supernatural things?[27]
Pascal

Maybe philosophical problems are hard not because they are divine or irreducible or meaningless ... but because the mind of Homo Sapiens lacks the cognitive equipment to solve them. We are organisms, not angels, and our minds are organs, not pipelines to the truth. [28]
Pinker

Section 2 The metaphysics of mind

2.1 What do we mean by 'mind'?

In this chapter we will be exploring a range of interconnected metaphysical questions concerning the nature of the mind, and how it relates to the body. So that we can begin to clarify what we are asking, it will be helpful to have at least a rough idea of what we mean by 'mind' and by 'body'. Now, the idea of the body is fairly straightforward. It is the living physical form that all humans have, that is, our legs, arms, torso, head and so on, including all our bodily organs and, importantly, the brain. In common with other physical things, like toasters or turnips, my body is composed of matter, occupies space, and can be seen and touched. It is the part of us that medical science is primarily concerned with. My body is, at the very least, a very important part of what I am. Certainly we all have a special interest in our own bodies and make efforts to keep them in reasonable condition, for example, by avoiding damaging them and providing them with what they need (food, warmth and so on) to keep them from malfunctioning or dying.

Trying to define conscious experience in terms of more primitive notions is fruitless.[1]
Chalmers

However, I appear to be more than just a physical thing like a toaster or a turnip. For I have CONSCIOUSNESS; I have a mind and am aware (in a way that toasters and turnips are not) of myself and of the things around me. What exactly this conscious awareness is, though, is a far trickier question than asking what the body is, and a key piece of the mind–body puzzle is directly concerned with trying to understand its true nature. Before we can get properly to grips with this question, we need to get a clearer idea of what philosophers are talking about when they use the terms 'mind', 'mental state' and 'consciousness'. So, to this end, have a go at the activity below.

▶ **ACTIVITY**

What is the mind?

If you are reading this book then you probably have a mind. So a good way for you to begin to see what is meant by the 'mind' is to reflect on what it is like to have one, what it is like, in other words, to be *conscious*. Make a list of things that you are aware of right now; that is, a list of the contents of your mind. To do this you will need to 'introspect' or look into your own mind. ('INTROSPECTION' is a word we will be using a good deal in this chapter. It means literally 'looking inwards' and is used in philosophy of mind to refer to our ability to examine the contents of our own conscious experience.) This obviously doesn't need to be a complete list, but try to include a good range of different sorts of things. Then try to group the things you're aware of into different categories. Here is a possible list of categories for you to compare with your own list:

- *Sensations produced by objects around you*, such as the hardness you feel from the chair you are sitting on, the smell of stale coffee, the sound of the rustling paper as you turn the pages of a book.

- *Sensations in your body*, such as a sore throat or itchy nose.
- *Inner feelings*, such as emotions and moods such as anger or joy.
- *Desires*, such as the thirst for a fresh cup of coffee, the urge to scratch your nose or to go on holiday to Sri Lanka.
- *The sense of self.* Most people claim to have a sense of themselves as a particular personality which endures through time and which is the owner or subject of all their experiences.
- *Imagination*, for example, conjuring images of things in your mind such as of a winged horse or of what it feels like to stroke a cat.
- *Ideas or concepts*. You can think of all kinds of ideas, such as the ideas of a triangle, snow or fairness. Empiricists argue (as you may know from studying epistemology in the first year of your Philosophy A-level) that such concepts ultimately derive from sense experience.
- *Beliefs*, such as the thought that philosophy is hard, or that too much sugar is bad for your health.
- *Memories*, such as the memory of a day trip to Margate or of your first day at school.[2]

2.1.1 Features of mental states

When I talk about consciousness, I am talking about the subjective quality of experience: what it is like to be a cognitive agent.
Chalmers, *The Conscious Mind*, p.6

One traditional way of understanding the mind, and a way that Descartes employs, is to see it as composed of everything I am conscious of. So it is equivalent in meaning to subjective awareness or experience. And, as we have seen, we are able to access the contents of our own minds via introspection. This inner experience isn't something we can define in terms of anything else. But if you are conscious then you are directly aware of what it is like, in all its variety. Chapter 1 of Chalmers' *The Conscious Mind* is one of the Anthology extracts and you may want to read through this chapter before continuing. In it Chalmers (1966–) gives a florid description of what consciousness is like.

Some mental states have intentional properties

One feature of mental states which introspection appears to reveal is termed 'INTENTIONALITY'. If I believe it is raining or hope that it will stop, the mental states which are my belief and my hope are about something: the fact that it is raining. It is an integral part of such mental states that they represent states of affairs out there in the world. This means that they have a particular 'content' which they 'point to', as it were. This capacity to be about things is known as intentionality, and states of mind which possess this capacity are called 'intentional'. What an intentional mental state is about can be expressed in a proposition. So this content is often called 'propositional content'. My belief that it is raining has a certain propositional content which can be expressed in a 'that' clause, for example, 'I believe *that it is raining*.' Similarly with a hope, a regret, a desire and so on: I can hope *that it rains*, regret *that it is raining*, desire *that it rain*, and so forth.

*[W]e can say that a mental state is conscious if it has a **qualitative feel** – an associated quality of experience. These qualitative feels are also known as phenomenal qualities, or **qualia** for short.*[3]

Chalmers

Some mental states have phenomenal properties (qualia)

What appears in the mind may be termed 'phenomena' (from the Greek for what 'appears') to make clear that they are mere appearances, existing only within and for consciousness and so only accessible subjectively via introspection. Thus philosophers often speak of the PHENOMENOLOGY OF THE MENTAL when talking of the conscious aspects of mentality which appear subjectively to each of us. Another important aspect of this subjective awareness are what philosophers term QUALIA. Qualia are the qualitative natures of certain phenomenal experiences, the 'what it is like' to experience something, for example, a headache, the colour red, or the smell of petrol. These subjective experiences or phenomenal properties seem to have a very specific nature which makes them what they are. There is, in other words, an intrinsic quality to my experience of red which seems impossible to define. If asked *what it is like* to see red, or smell petrol, we may be inclined to say 'It's like this!' as we try introspectively to point at the inner experience. Beyond this, it is hard to see what we could say to explain what it is like. Certainly we can't draw it out of our own minds and bring it into public view. It is as though you have to have experienced the quale (singular of 'qualia') to know what it is like. Philosophers who are interested in qualia normally suppose them to be also non-intentional. My experience of red isn't about anything: it just is what it is. It has no propositional content and doesn't point beyond itself to the world.

So, we can define:

- intentionality as the 'aboutness' of certain mental states which have a propositional content
- qualia as the non-intentional phenomenal properties of certain mental states.

Well, then, what am I? A thing that thinks. What is that? A thing that doubts, understands, affirms, denies, wants, refuses, and also imagines and senses.[4]

Descartes

The conscious mind is also often thought to be that which makes me *me*. In other words, it is what constitutes my personal identity; it is the essence of what I am. And it is this view that René Descartes (1596–1650) expresses in the quotation above from the *Meditations* (1641). Descartes held that all mental states are conscious and so accessible to introspection. For him the very idea of an unconscious mental state would have been an oxymoron, a contradiction in terms. Today, however, it is generally accepted that there are mental processes that occur of which we are not consciously aware. In Chalmers' *The Conscious*

Mind (which is in the AQA Anthology) he discusses the reasons we have for believing in unconscious mental states and processes and briefly traces the history of this idea, beginning with Sigmund Freud[5]. What Freud recognised is that we can explain certain behaviours by reference to mental states, such as desires, of which the person need not be aware. More recent research in neuroscience showing the existence of unconscious mental states is discussed by Patricia Churchland (1943–) in *Brain-wise*[6]. One example she uses is of the language processing which goes on as we speak but of which we are unaware: in conversation, you produce complex grammatically accurate sentences but while you are aware of what you want to say (the meaning of your speech) you are not aware of how you selected the words and phrases, or of the way you applied grammatical rules in the construction of sentences. It seems a good proportion of our cognitive processes happens beneath the surface, as it were, of conscious awareness.

The investigation into the nature of the mind and consciousness amounts to asking: What medium do thoughts, feelings, emotions and ideas take place in? How are mental states produced? Is the mind really just the same thing as the brain? Or is it some sort of product of the brain? And if so just 'how and why', as the contemporary philosopher David Chalmers poses the question 'do physical processes give rise to experience? Why do not these processes take place "in the dark," without any accompanying states of experience? This is the central mystery of consciousness.'[7]

Chalmers calls this 'mystery' the 'hard problem' of consciousness. The problem may also be expressed by pointing out that there seems to be an 'explanatory gap' between understanding the nature of brain processes, which many believe underlie conscious experience, and the nature of that experience itself.[8] For example, we may know what happens physiologically when someone experiences pain, that is, we may be able to point to certain neurons firing in the brain. But this doesn't seem to answer the question of why pain feels the way it does: it doesn't explain the quale. We can understand the brain's processes without this appearing to give us any explanation of how these give rise to certain sorts of experience. Because of this explanatory gap, some philosophers deny that the mind is produced by the physical at all, arguing that it is a special spiritual thing, different in kind from our physical self, but somehow attached to it.

This gives rise to a basic division of views on these issues. On the one hand, DUALISM is the view that there are *two* basic sorts of thing that make up a human being: one is *spiritual* or *mental* (the mind) and the other *physical* (the body). Dualists argue that the mind cannot be *reduced* to the physical, which is to say that we cannot ever explain the mind in terms of the body, or any part of the body such as the brain. Dualism is the view that mental states and processes are not states and processes of a purely physical animal, but constitute a distinct kind of phenomenon that is essentially non-physical in nature. According to dualism, as it is often put, no REDUCTION of the mental to the physical is possible.

By contrast, MONISM is the view that there is just *one* kind of SUBSTANCE. In this context, 'substance' means a kind of *stuff*; something that can exist on its own. Substances are contrasted with properties, which are qualities of substances and which depend for their existence on substances.

For example, water may be regarded as a substance as it can exist on its own. But wetness is a PROPERTY of water and depends on water to exist. In other words, wetness cannot exist on its own. Now, what monists argue is that fundamentally there is just one kind of substance. Some monists claim this substance is spiritual, a view known as IDEALISM (a version of which you may be familiar with from studying George Berkeley (1685–1753) in the first year of the A-level). Others claim that it is physical: the view known as PHYSICALISM or materialism[9]. What most physicalists believe is that what we think of as mental can ultimately be explained in terms of, or reduced to, the physical. For example, some physicalists argue that what we call mental events and processes are really nothing more than events and processes of a physical organ, namely the brain. What this means is that the mind can successfully be *reduced* to the brain and its operations.

Some historical background

Examples of *physicalist* theories: Epicurus and La Mettrie

Physicalist theories of mind are generally allied to a more general physicalist worldview which regards the whole universe as composed of matter. Such physicalism has a long history. One well-known physicalist from the ancient world is Epicurus (341–270BCE). Following the teachings of Democritus (460–370BCE), Epicurus argued that the universe consists exclusively of indestructible physical atoms moving in empty space. Out of these atoms, their combinations and their movements, all the things and all the events in the universe are to be explained. Everything, including human minds, is ultimately nothing more than matter in motion. For Epicurus, the mind or soul is not made of any special spiritual stuff, but rather of particularly fine material atoms like breath or air, which animate the body and make us alive but disperse at death. Death involves the decomposition of both the body and the mind and so there is no afterlife. Moreover, there is no transcendent or spiritual dimension to the universe: in other words, no God.

These two denials of an immortal soul and of a transcendent God clearly go against Christian teaching, and so physicalism has long been regarded in the West as a threat to religious authority. However, during the Enlightenment – around the seventeenth and eighteenth centuries – a new optimism in scientific explanations emerged in Europe. To some, it began to seem that everything could be explained in terms of physical laws, and so any distinct 'spiritual' realm would become superfluous in a complete account of humankind and of the universe. Descartes argued that animals were purely physical beings, the behaviours of which could, in principle, be explained in terms of physical laws. Some influenced by this approach came to believe the same might also be possible for humans. It was La Mettrie (1709–51) who most famously defended a physicalist vision of humans in his *L'homme machine* (*The Human Machine*) of 1748, and went as far as to say that it might be possible to build a talking, sensing and feeling machine.

Learn More

Example of an *idealist* theory: Berkeley

As you may remember if you have studied epistemology, Berkeley argued that everything that we can possibly think or experience – all our *ideas*, to use his terminology – must be our *own* thoughts and experiences. We cannot think what is not our own thought, or experience what is not our own experience. Since ideas are clearly *mental* entities, it follows that everything we can ever be acquainted with must be mental. Consequently it is in vain to suppose that there might be something other than the mental since we can never have access to it. Matter, therefore, can be discarded from our account of what there is in the universe. What we think of as physical objects are no more than collections of our perceptions of them. His conclusion was that all that there can be in the universe are minds and their various *ideas*, hence 'idealism'. However, we won't be looking at idealism in any detail in this chapter, but rather will focus on dualism and physicalism.

Example of a *dualist* theory: Plato

While the term 'dualism' covers several quite different theories of mind, as we have seen they are all agreed in regarding the essential nature of consciousness as residing in something *non-physical* and so beyond the understanding of the physical sciences. According to this view, mind and matter are so fundamentally different that, no matter how much we know about one, certain aspects of the other will remain unexplained.

One influential dualist theory is that of Plato (428–348BCE). Plato believed that the virtuous soul would be rewarded by living a better life after bodily death. In Book X of *The Republic* (c.380–360BCE), in the discussion of 'the Myth of Er', Plato talks of the soul's surviving bodily death and facing the crossroads of judgement. As Er – a man who has miraculously come back from the dead – explains, the scales of justice are presented to individuals after their death and the decision is taken whether to reward or punish them for their earthly existence. This takes the form not of heavenly salvation, or hellish damnation, but of rebirth in a suitable body. The choice of new life made will depend on the character of one's soul. In the *Phaedo* (c.380–360BCE) Plato argues that the philosophical life essentially involves a preparation for death through the soul's efforts to escape imprisonment in the body. The acquisition of knowledge, and with it of virtue, involves purifying the soul of its contamination with the body. For this reason, Plato argues, death is not something the philosopher should fear.

anthology 2.3

Plato's arguments for dualism are not ones we will be examining here. Instead we will begin with those from the modern period that Descartes puts forward in his *Meditations*, which have had a profound influence on modern philosophy of mind. Indeed his version of dualism was so influential in the centuries that followed that Gilbert Ryle (1900–76) was able to call it the 'official doctrine' in his 1949 work *The Concept of Mind*, which is one of the Anthology texts. It would be best to read the Anthology extract for Ryle's outline of the main ideas of the Cartesian view of mind and body before reading the next section.

Summary: What do we mean by 'mind'?

In this section we have tried to bring to life the puzzle lying at the heart of the phenomenon of consciousness. One reason why trying to understand the nature of mind is so tricky is that it doesn't behave like other things in our experience. It has some very strange properties, such as qualia and intentionality, which seem so very unlike anything else in the universe. And it doesn't seem to follow the rules that govern other things, in particular the physical things we observe around us. Even putting a finger on what exactly we are talking about when we use the word 'mind' is not straightforward. But there is another reason consciousness is so difficult to understand. Usually when scientists try to understand some phenomenon they are able to approach it from the third person perspective. They can compare their observations with the observations of other scientists in the field and so check their findings against each other's. But if we want to study the mind, it seems we are unable to follow this strategy. I cannot compare my mental life with yours since we are each stuck within our own private realm. We can, of course, compare our researches into the structures and functions of the brain. We may even be able to correlate these observations with first person reports of what people experience. But, as Chalmers points out, this doesn't get us anywhere near solving the 'hard problem' of just how what we are able publicly to observe could account for the subjective point of view and for what it is actually like to have a mind and to be conscious.

Philosophy often begins with a puzzle, and, the more effort we expend trying to resolve it, the more complex and perplexing it becomes. What appears at first as a relatively clear-cut problem, under investigation can quickly sprout an array of new and intractable difficulties. In the sections that follow we will be looking at a range of attempts to unravel the problem of consciousness and in the process we will be exploring alternative theories of the mind, each of which raises a further set of puzzles peculiar to it. By the end, it is likely that you will not have reached a definitive conclusion about how to resolve all the issues raised. But at least you should have a clearer understanding of why the problem is so thorny and of which avenues towards a solution are most promising.

2.2 Dualist theories

Experimenting with ideas

Suppose one member of your class were to relate an experience of leaving her body. Last night while lying in bed before going to sleep, she found she was able to float upwards, look down upon her motionless body, and rise up through the ceiling, through the attic and out above the roofs and chimney pots. From there she could fly anywhere she pleased and look around the town, seeing all the people going about their business, and could listen in on their conversations. After a while she flew back into her bedroom, returned to her body and went to sleep.

Experiences of leaving one's body – out-of-body experiences – are not uncommon. But do they provide us with good evidence for the view that mind and body are distinct things (dualism)? Why, or why not?

Now try to imagine yourself without a body, as a disembodied consciousness or pure soul. To do this, you might imagine opening your eyes one morning to find you cannot see your body. Thinking you may be invisible, you try to touch yourself, but find you have no hands to move. Is this possible to imagine? What difficulties do you encounter? Take note of your thoughts.

Minds exist, and are not identical to bodies or to parts of bodies

Part of the attraction of dualism is the sense that 'I' cannot be identified with my physical form: if I lose parts of my body, it seems I don't cease to be the person that I am. I am still completely me, even if my body is diminished. As Descartes has it: 'The whole mind seems to be united to the whole body, but not by a uniting of parts to parts, because: If a foot or arm or any other part of the body is cut off, nothing is thereby taken away from the mind.'[1] You can even imagine being consumed by a boa constrictor from the feet up, and as the snake gradually swallows your torso and neck, the person contemplating your fate would still be you. For as long as you remain conscious you would be entirely the self-same person, despite having lost almost all of your body. But what about when the snake consumes your head? Can you imagine remaining conscious without any body at all?

Figure 2.1 As long as you remain conscious, it would still be you whose body had been eaten. This seems to suggest that you are not the same thing as your body

Descartes certainly thinks so as we can see from a comparable thought experiment he conducts in *Meditation 1* (one which you may be familiar with from studying epistemology in the first year of your Philosophy A-level). Descartes supposes that an extremely powerful evil spirit or demon would be capable of feeding his mind with perceptions which appear to represent a physical world to him. He even imagines that his own body could be part of the illusion produced by the demon. But although it is possible that he has no body, he would still remain the self-same consciousness or person that he now is. He would still be able to philosophise, do mathematics and to imagine. He concludes that his true self can be identified with his consciousness or mind; that his essential nature is thought. I, as he says, am a 'thinking thing' and it is conceivable that this thing might exist without a physical body.

At last I have discovered it – thought! This is the one thing that can't be separated from me.[2]
Descartes

The idea that 'I' might exist without my body is given some EMPIRICAL support from reports people give of out-of-body experiences (the experience of leaving one's body and very often being able to look down upon it). Such experiences sometimes occur when a person is near to death (near-death experiences), or quite commonly when near to sleep and can be induced by meditative techniques. If it could be established that such experiences genuinely involve the mind leaving the body, then this would present us with some powerful evidence for dualism, since they would show that consciousness can exist outside of the body. However, there are serious difficulties with such evidence, some of which we will be examining in this chapter (see particularly the *Mind without body is not conceivable* section, page 208). You will doubtless have begun to explore some of these in discussion, using the question in Experimenting with ideas on page 192 as a starting point, but perhaps the main problem is how to establish that such experiences are not simply hallucinatory. If we cannot prove that such experiences genuinely involve leaving the body, then their force as evidence for dualism is limited.

Direct empirical evidence for dualism seems at best inconclusive (the view that it is meaningless or confused even to talk about immaterial minds is one we will return to below when discussing PHILOSOPHICAL BEHAVIOURISM – see page 262). But let's now turn to the philosophical arguments that Descartes uses in *Meditation* 6. The first of these draws on a consideration we've already begun to explore, namely the fact that the body can be divided into parts – and so separated from 'me' without this seeming to impact on the wholeness of my consciousness or mind.

2.2.1 Substance dualism

> *For we are not able to conceive of the half of a mind as we can do of the smallest of all bodies; so that we see that not only are their natures different but even in some respects contrary to one another.*[3]
> Descartes

In this short comment from the synopsis of the *Meditations*, and again in the longer extract from *Meditation* 6 (see Anthology extract 2.4), Descartes is drawing our attention to the fact that my awareness of myself is of something unitary or indivisible: whether I am experiencing a pain in my foot, smelling coffee, imagining a sunny day, or considering a philosophical problem, it is all the time the same self or mind which is enjoying these conscious experiences. So different aspects of my consciousness, such as willing, understanding, imagining or perceiving something, are not like *parts* that could be removed from me, since it is the same mind that wills, understands, perceives or imagines. In other words, my self is *indivisible*: I am a single centre of consciousness and my consciousness cannot be divided into parts. To see this, try to imagine your consciousness dividing into two separate streams. In doing so, you are capable only of imagining it from the point of view of just one stream so that it appears to be impossible to be conscious in two places at once. It seems to follow that there can only be one me; my consciousness cannot be divided in two. If I am aware of an experience, it is to me and me alone that the experience is happening.

 Experimenting with ideas

Imagine aliens have captured you. They want to better understand humanity and have decided to experiment on you. This involves dividing your mind into two by opening your skull, removing half your brain and transplanting it into another human body. Try to imagine what it would be like when you wake up. Is it possible to imagine having two distinct consciousnesses occupying different bodies? Why is this so hard to imagine?

Contrast this now with the body. Any physical thing, because it is by nature extended in space (it necessarily has three-dimensions), can always be divided up into parts, at least in principle. So you can take an axe to anyone's body, cleave it in two, then into quarters, and continue in this fashion indefinitely (or at least until the police arrive and cart you away). Bodies, in other words, are by their nature *divisible*. Descartes concludes that since minds and bodies differ in this important way, they must be different substances. This is the central claim of the first type of dualism we will be examining, namely SUBSTANCE DUALISM (also called CARTESIAN DUALISM, after Descartes). It says that human beings are composed of two distinct types of substance. A substance in Descartes' understanding is a thing that can exist on its own and doesn't depend on anything else (except God) for its existence (see the line about water and wetness, page 189). Substance dualism is saying that both mind and body can exist independently of the other: What this means is that while mind and body are linked together in this life, when the body dies and decomposes, this will not extinguish the mind. In this way, Descartes' argument can 'give men the hope of another life after death'.[4]

2.2.1.1 The indivisibility argument

It's worth noting that Descartes' argument makes use of a principle known as LEIBNIZ'S LAW (named after Gottfried Leibniz, 1646–1716). This law says that if two things share all the same properties, they must actually be one thing; but that if one has any property that the other lacks, they must be distinct things. Since divisibility is a property of bodies which minds lack, minds must be different from bodies.

Although this sounds complex, the principle is intuitively easy to grasp. Consider the following example: At the time of writing, 'Theresa May' and 'the present Prime Minister' are different names for the same person. So anything that is true of Theresa May will also be true of the present Prime Minister and vice versa. For example, if it is true that Theresa May is married to Philip, then it must also be true that the present Prime Minister is married to Philip. But if there is one thing true of Theresa May that is not true of the Prime Minister, then we would be able to prove that they are different people. If Theresa May's party won 318 seats in the June 2017 election, but the Prime Minister's party won just 262, then Theresa May would not be the Prime Minister.

This same principle is used in courts of law every day. Imagine a murder case in which the accused is called Finbar Good. What the prosecution are trying to prove is that 'the murderer' and 'Finbar Good' refer to the same person. They do this by showing that lots of things that are true of the murderer are also true of Finbar Good. For example:

- The murderer was left handed.
- Finbar Good is left handed.
- The murderer was in Peckham on Friday the 13th.
- Finbar Good was in Peckham on Friday the 13th.

This could even go right down to:

- The murderer has fingerprint xyz.
- Finbar Good has fingerprint xyz.

The defence, on the other hand, are trying to show that they are not the same person, by trying to prove that what is true of the murderer is not true of Finbar Good. For example:

- The murderer was over 6 ft tall.
- But Finbar Good is 5' 6".

If these last two claims are both true, then it follows that Finbar cannot be the murderer. So, this application of Leibniz's Law is clearly valid.

We can summarise the indivisibility argument thus:

- **Premise 1:** My mind is indivisible.
- **Premise 2:** My body is divisible.
- **Conclusion:** My mind is not my body.

This argument is clearly valid – the conclusion must follow from the premises. In other words, it is impossible for anything to be divisible and indivisible at the same time, so if mind is indeed indivisible and body is indeed divisible, then, by

Leibniz's Law, they cannot be the same thing and dualism would be established. So, in order to establish whether the argument is sound, we need to determine whether these premises are actually true.

Premise 2, 'my body is divisible', is hard to question. Our bodies and all the organs that compose them, including our brains, are physical objects and can be divided. But what about the first premise? Is the mind truly indivisible? Well, there certainly does seem to be something important about the nature of consciousness that Descartes has hit upon. Our minds do seem to have a unified nature. I am a single conscious entity and all my conscious experiences belong to the one thing that I am. So while we know from NEUROSCIENCE that our brains are composed of millions of individual cells and that our brains are divisible, we do not experience the mind as anything but a singular consciousness. Surely, this must mean that the mind cannot be the brain.

Another way of making this point about the mind is to consider that mental things, like beliefs, desires and thoughts, cannot be thought of as having any size or shape. In other words, they do not seem to be the kinds of things we can think of as being extended in space. For example, if I believe that it is raining, I cannot say:

- My belief that it is raining is five centimetres long.
- My belief that it is raining is triangular.
- My belief that it is raining is to the right of my desire for a beer.

It also means that it makes no sense to talk about dividing a belief into parts. If the contents of my mental life don't seem to be extended in space, then they must be indivisible.

Response 1: The mental is divisible

However, the apparent unity of consciousness has been questioned by modern neuroscience. The sense I have of being a singular consciousness may be an illusion, meaning that what we perceive when we look into our own minds – when we introspect – need not be an accurate representation of our selves. If, as physicalists argue, the brain is responsible for consciousness and for our sense of self, then cutting the brain up might well literally involve dividing the mind. Experimental evidence that seems to support this idea concerns what happens to people who have the corpus callosum – the main link between the left and right hemispheres of the brain – severed; an operation which has occasionally been performed on patients suffering from severe epilepsy. Patients whose brains had been divided in this way often reported unsettling experiences. While shopping, one such patient described her efforts to pick what she wanted from the shelves. No sooner had her right hand collected the item, and placed it in the basket, than her left hand set about returning it to the shelf, as though part of her had a different idea about what she should be shopping for. Such experiences are most naturally interpreted as showing a divided mind, or two distinct consciousnesses occupying the same skull.

It is known that the two hemispheres of the brain play different roles: the left is responsible for processing visual information from the right side of the visual field, and the right hemisphere from the left. The left hemisphere is also responsible for motor control and tactile information from the right side of the body, while the right hemisphere deals with the left side of the body. If split-brain patients have the two sides of the visual field artificially separated, for example by wearing special contact lenses, then information available to one hemisphere appears not to be available to the other. In one experiment, a patient was asked to press a button when he saw an image flashed on a screen. When the left hemisphere was presented with an image, his right hand pressed the button and he was able also to name what he saw. This is what we would expect, since the left hemisphere has the main responsibility for speech. But whenever the right hemisphere was shown an image, the patient would report verbally that he could see nothing, and yet his left hand would still press the button, suggesting that the right hemisphere was aware of the image but the left was not. Similar experiments have also shown that the right hemisphere is able to report what it has seen by producing accurate drawings of the image, at the same time as the patient denies verbally that he sees anything.[5]

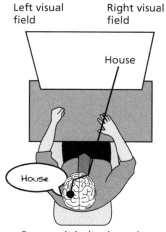

Because it is dominant in language, when the left hemisphere reads the word 'house' it verbally reports what it sees.

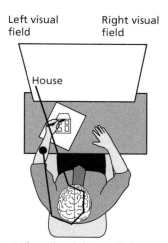

When the right hemisphere reads the word, the patient denies seeing anything, but the right hemisphere is nonetheless able to draw a house.

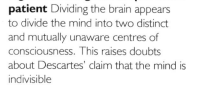

Figure 2.2 Diagram of split-brain patient Dividing the brain appears to divide the mind into two distinct and mutually unaware centres of consciousness. This raises doubts about Descartes' claim that the mind is indivisible

Another important line of attack on Descartes' claim about the unity of consciousness comes from the eighteenth-century Scottish philosopher David Hume (1711–76). As you may recall from studying epistemology in the first year of your Philosophy A-level, Hume was an empiricist philosopher and so believed that all our concepts come from experience. This means that if I have a concept or idea of my self or mind then I should be able to trace this idea back to some sort of conscious experience. Introspection is the method by which Descartes claims to arrive at the experience of his mind as a unity. In Hume's words, Descartes' claim is that 'we are every moment intimately conscious of what we call our self; that we feel its existence and its continuance in existence'.[6] But Hume claims that when he introspects he finds he is conscious of no such thing.

Experimenting with ideas

Close your eyes and look into your own mind to see if you can find your self, or what the word 'I' refers to. Can you find it? Is there an actual experience you can identify which is where you get the idea of 'me' from?

Now read the opening four paragraphs of 'The Self' in Ryle's *The Concept of Mind* (Chapter 6, Section 6). See if you can explain why the concept of my self, or what the word 'I' refers to, appears so elusive.

> *For my part, when I enter most intimately into what I call myself I always stumble on some particular perception or other, heat or cold, light or shade, love or hatred, pain or pleasure. I never can catch myself at any time without a perception, and never can observe anything but the perception.*[7]
> Hume

According to Hume, all I am ever aware of when introspecting is a series of conscious experiences, but never of any single thing which is having these experiences. In this respect, he agrees with what the Buddha said over two thousand years earlier. According to Buddhists, the self is an illusion. There is no thing that is the singular owner of your experiences; there is just the stream of conscious experiences itself. If Hume is right, then Descartes is misdescribing the way the mind appears to us. We have no immediate consciousness of an indivisible self. There's no denying the awareness of the many and varied experiences that make up mental life, but *I* am nothing over and above these experiences; rather, I simply am the collection or bundle of experiences themselves. If this is right, then the mind is not a singular entity at all, but a multiplicity of experiences. And since these many experiences are distinct from each other, the mind appears to be divisible.

But then what of the fact that I cannot imagine my consciousness dividing and remain aware from two perspectives at once? One response is just to say that what our imaginations find impossible to frame need not be a good indication of what is actually possible. Split-brain patients do indeed seem to have two streams of consciousness operating in the same skull. And the fact that I cannot imagine myself as having a divided consciousness doesn't show that two streams of consciousness cannot simultaneously exist. After all, I cannot imagine seeing the world from your point of view and from mine at the same time, but it doesn't follow from this that you and I cannot both have minds.

Response 2: Not everything thought of as physical is divisible

A second criticism focuses on the inference from the fact that it is difficult to make sense of the idea of dividing the mind or mental states to concluding that they cannot ultimately be physical. For there would appear to be states humans can be in which it is senseless to talk about dividing, but which are clearly physical, such as being too hot, being soaking wet or running. Perhaps mental states need to be understood as being like such bodily states. Running, like thinking, is not divisible, yet we don't on that account need to suppose that running must be the activity of an indivisible thing. No one would want to argue that because it makes no sense to imagine my temperature divided into two or to say that being wet is triangular, that these must be non-physical states. To take a different example, the solubility of sugar is not something that it makes sense to divide, but it wouldn't follow that solubility is an indivisible non-physical substance somehow connected to the sugar. So, the fact that it makes no sense to talk about splitting the mind doesn't in itself show that it is a special kind of indivisible stuff. It may simply be that the concept of divisibility doesn't apply to the self. We can't talk about dividing beauty or music either, but this doesn't mean they are indestructible substances.

This sort of objection to Descartes' dualism is one we will return to when examining the work of Gilbert Ryle. Ryle argues that Descartes' mistake is to presuppose that the mind is a kind of *thing*, and when he sees that it lacks the properties normal physical things have, such as divisibility, to conclude that it must be a strange non-physical thing. Actually, thinks Ryle, the mind only seems strange because Descartes doesn't recognise that it isn't a sort of *thing* or *substance* at all. To escape from the confusion, what we need to do is to pay careful attention to how we use words such as 'mind'. Ryle's own analysis of its use leads him to claim that the word doesn't refer to any mysterious substance, but is really a way of talking about our behaviour. This means there is nothing surprising in the fact that it is senseless to talk of dividing the mind, since we cannot divide other terms which describe our actions and capacities, such as running or being swift. We will explore this idea further below (under 2.3.1 Philosophical behaviourism, see page 262).

2.2.1.2 The conceivability argument

Strictly speaking, then, I am simply a thing that thinks – a mind, or soul, or intellect, or reason.[8]
Descartes

▶ **ACTIVITY**
What is conceivable?

Some things that you've never experienced in real life are pretty easy to imagine. For example, you can probably imagine winning the lottery jackpot or going to the Moon. Other things never actually happen, but we can still imagine them. For example, you can probably imagine a log fire that gives off no heat or bears that can talk. These things, we might say, are *conceivable*. Then there are other things that are much harder, perhaps impossible to imagine or conceive. Can you imagine a ball that is blue and red all over at the same time? Or a cube with just five sides? Can you conceive of its being Tuesday *and* Sunday today? Or of a married bachelor?

So what makes these inconceivable? One plausible answer is that they involve a contradiction or inconsistency of some kind. A specific patch of an object's surface can only be one colour, never two at once; the essential nature of a cube includes having exactly six sides, and so it cannot have fewer; each day of the week excludes all the others, so none could be two at once; and it is part of the meaning of 'bachelor' to be unmarried, so a married bachelor is contradictory. These ideas are said to be logically impossible.

Try to categorise the following into those that are inconceivable because logically impossible, and those that are conceivable.

1. Round pyramids
2. Alcohol-free whisky
3. A flying horse
4. Jeremy Corbyn becoming the Prime Minister of the UK
5. A wooden horse made exclusively from glass
6. Gold that floats on water
7. You choosing not to study philosophy
8. Vegetarian haggis
9. A snowfall on Christmas Day 2027 in Brighton
10. Water that boils at 50 degrees Celsius at sea level
11. 5 being less than 4
12. Life on Mars
13. J.K. Rowling being the same person as Banksy
14. A cold-blooded cow
15. The Earth having two moons

You probably thought that some of these were logically impossible. Round pyramids are inconceivable in the same way as five-sided cubes. The same goes for 5 being less than 4. And a wooden horse cannot also be made purely of glass. We might say that no matter how the world happened to go, these could never be in it. At the other end you probably felt that it was certainly conceivable for Jeremy Corbyn to be the Prime Minister. If Labour had won the election in May 2017, then presumably he would have been; and for all we can tell at the time of writing, he may be by the time you read this. Similarly a snowfall on Christmas Day in Brighton is certainly conceivable and whether or not it happens, we would certainly want to say that it was a possibility. And while, if you are reading this, it is very likely that you chose to study philosophy, it is easy to imagine a scenario in which you chose otherwise, so this too looks like it was possible. The conceivability of these eventualities, then, seems to give us some indication as to whether they should be considered possible regardless of whether they actually happen or not. Such situations could occur without breaking any laws of nature, so we might say that they are *physically* possible. However, you may have been unsure how to categorise some others that seem to lie between these two sets. These are the ones that seem to be conceivable but which we wouldn't want to say could ever actually happen. Water that boils at 50 degrees Celsius would fall into this category, as must gold that is light enough to float. These may be conceivable in the sense that they don't appear to involve any contradiction, and yet given what we know of the laws of chemistry and physics, they are surely not genuine possibilities in our universe. Such things may be said to be *logically* possible, but not *physically* or naturally possible. They break the laws of nature rather than the laws of thought.

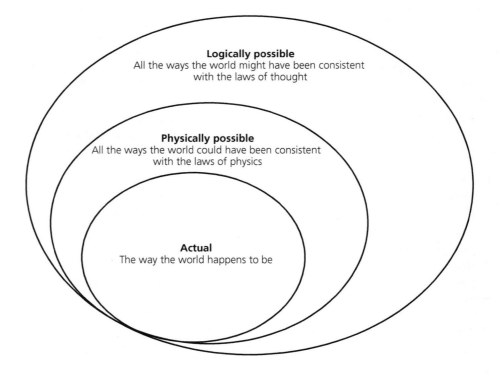

Figure 2.3 The relationship between logical possibility, physical possibility and what is actual. What is actual, that is, what actually happens to occur in our universe, is a subset of what is physically possible, such as Napoleon losing the Battle of Waterloo. For what actually happens or exists must conform to the laws of physics. But there are also other possibilities which, while physically possible, are never actualised, such as Napoleon winning the Battle of Waterloo. Physical possibilities must be logically possible: it is logically impossible, and so physically impossible too, for Napoleon to have both won and lost the Battle of Waterloo. But what is logically possible, may not be physically possible in our universe, for example, Napoleon ordering the earth to swallow up the English army

Logical possibility, physical possibility and metaphysical possibility

The activity above gets you to think about the distinction often drawn by philosophers between what is logically possible and what is physically possible. As we have seen, things that cannot be conceived without contradiction are logically impossible. So, into this category we would place things which contradict the rules of mathematics or logic or which go against some definition. It seems we can work out such logical possibilities *a priori*, simply by analysing the meanings of the terms involved. If something is logically impossible it could never happen – not just in the entire world, but in any *possible* world. 'World' here is to be understood as a whole universe, and a possible world is all the ways a universe might be. So what we are saying is that, if we imagine all the different ways a universe could be, then none of them would contain logically impossible objects or states of affairs, such as round pyramids or wooden horses made exclusively from glass. By contrast, if something is conceivable, then this suggests there is nothing contradictory in the idea and so it must be logically possible. Although they may never have actually happen, we would want to say that such states of affairs *could have* happened, or, as philosophers sometimes have it, there are possible worlds in which they do. So while there is no possible world in which the Egyptians built round pyramids, there are possible worlds in which it snows in Brighton on Christmas day 2027, or you never studied philosophy. Now, the scenarios in which it snows at Christmas or you do not study philosophy break no physical laws and so we could say that they are both *physically possible*; in other words, there are possible worlds with the same physical laws as ours where they do happen. But what of flying horses? It certainly seems that they are conceivable, and that they involve no inherent contradiction. It is not part of the definition of a horse that it be unable to fly, as seems to be shown by the appearance of flying horses in mythology. But are they physically possible in this world? Well, given the laws of nature that hold here and given the weight and aerodynamic properties of horses, (not to mention their lack of wings), we might say that they are *physically impossible*. But because they are conceivable, then we can say that there are possible worlds in which horses *do* fly, and one way of making this claim is to say that such beasts are *metaphysically possible*.

This gives us three categories: logical possibility, physical possibility and metaphysical possibility. The set of logical possibilities is the broadest and physical possibilities are a subset of logical possibilities. Whether or not a logical possibility is also physically possible is something we can only determine by empirical investigation. But what of metaphysical possibilities? Well, standardly it has been assumed that if something is logically possible then it must be metaphysically possible, but that if it is logically impossible, then it is metaphysically impossible too. In other words, all the logical possible ways the world would map onto what is metaphysically possible. If this is right, then it suggests we should be able to work out what is metaphysically possible purely *a priori*, by reflecting on whether we can discern any contradiction in an idea or state of affairs. If not, this means it is logically possible and hence metaphysically possible too. Whether this is a correct assumption is something we will be examining again below. But first we need to turn to Descartes' second argument for dualism and see how we can employ some of the conceptual distinctions we have drawn here in its evaluation. Have a read through Anthology extract 2.5 before continuing and see if you can work out how Descartes argues.

Descartes' argument

In the passage quoted in Anthology extract 2.5, Descartes begins by arguing that if he is able 'clearly and distinctly' to conceive of two things separately, then it must be possible, at least in principle, for them to be separated. Descartes makes the point by saying that if they can be conceived of separately, then it would be possible for God, since he is omnipotent, to separate them. Note that Descartes' argument doesn't rely on the existence of God here. Rather, he is using the idea of God as a way of talking about what is logically possible. Since God is all-powerful, he can do anything that it is logically possible to do. However, he cannot do what is not logically possible. Even God can't make round squares. This claim relies on the general principle we introduced above that whatever is clearly conceivable, in other words, anything that we can think which is not logically contradictory, is metaphysically possible. For example, there is nothing contradictory in the idea of a horse without a mane. So, according to this principle, it follows that it is metaphysically possible for a horse to lack a mane. Conversely, anything that is not conceivable would be impossible. For example, a square without four sides is not conceivable (the idea is self-contradictory) and this shows that a three-sided square is not possible.

Recall that the principle doesn't imply that what is conceivable is *physically* possible in the real world. After all, I can conceive of myself as being able to fly by jumping out of the window and flapping my arms. However, this clearly doesn't mean that this is a real physical possibility and I would be reckless to think it did. But while conceivability doesn't entail that something is physically possible, it is often thought to entail that something is *metaphysically* possible. As we have seen, to say that something is metaphysically possible is to say that there is a possible world in which that state of affairs obtains. So while there is no possible world in which squares have three sides (because this is logically impossible), there is a possible world in which the laws of physics are different from this one and in which flapping one's arms will allow one to fly. Descartes might say that it would be possible for God to have created a world in which humans could fly, since God is omnipotent.

Next he returns to a point he began to explore in *Meditation 2*, the idea that introspection reveals the true nature of the self or mind to be thought or 'thinking'. As we have seen, in *Meditation 2* he argued that he can conceive of himself without a body, but that he cannot conceive of himself as not thinking. In other words, thought or consciousness is the only attribute which cannot be taken away from me, without my ceasing to be what I am, and so I must in essence be a 'thinking thing'.

Then he claims to have a clear conception of the essence of his own body and of bodies in general as extended things – that is to say, things which necessarily have three spatial dimensions. Since this conception of body is not part of the idea he has of his self or mind, he can conclude that his mind is really distinct from his body and could exist apart from it. And if they could exist separately, then they must ultimately be distinct things or *substances*. In other words, since his ideas of his mind and of his body reveal the true natures or essences of these things, and because the essences of the two are clearly different, they have to be distinct things even though they may be mixed together in some way in this life. Note that Descartes doesn't appear to be claiming that his mind and body are ever separated from each other, but just that they could be separated if God chose to separate them. It is, in other words, a metaphysical possibility that they be separated. And it is this possibility which he claims implies that they are distinct substances.

We can summarise the conceivability argument like this:

- **Premise 1:** If I can clearly and distinctly conceive of the essential natures of two things separately, it must be metaphysically possible to separate them.
- **Premise 2:** I clearly and distinctly perceive myself (my mind) to be essentially a thinking and unextended thing.
- **Premise 2:** I clearly and distinctly perceive my body to be essentially an extended and unthinking thing.
- **Conclusion:** It must be metaphysically possible for mind and body to be separated, meaning that they are distinct substances.

But so far as I can see, all that follows from this is that I can obtain some knowledge of myself without knowledge of the body. But it isn't transparently clear to me that this knowledge is complete and adequate, enabling me to be certain that I'm not mistaken in excluding body from my essence.[9]
Antoine Arnauld

Response 1: What is conceivable may not be metaphysically possible

Descartes invited comments from the scholars of the day on his *Meditations* and an important objection to his conceivability argument was made by Antoine Arnauld (1612–94). The objection focuses on the credibility of Descartes' appeal in the first premise to the principle that whatever is conceivable is metaphysically possible. Arnauld offers a parallel argument to Descartes' which is clearly fallacious which makes use of Pythagoras' theorem that the square of the hypotenuse of a right-angled triangle is equal to the square of the other two sides (Figure 2.4). He points out that someone ignorant of the proof of this theorem might well suppose that they could conceive of a right-angled triangle that lacked this property. But it wouldn't follow from this that it is possible for a right-angled triangle to lack the property. Indeed, this would be logically impossible. Not even God could make a right-angled triangle with the square on its hypotenuse not equal to the squares on the other two sides, so this property is not separable from a right-angled triangle, even in principle, despite it being conceivable that it could be. So, in the same way, the fact that Descartes may conceive of the essence of his mind as distinct from his body doesn't guarantee that it is actually possible to separate them. Arnauld concludes that while I may clearly and distinctly recognise my nature as something which thinks, I may be wrong in thinking that nothing else belongs to this nature and it may be that being extended is indeed a part of what I am.[10]

This objection only works if Descartes' conceptions of mind and body are in some way incomplete or confused, like the idea of the triangle possessed by the person in Arnauld's example. So Descartes defends his argument by emphasising that it depends on his thought of the natures of mind and body being, as he has it,

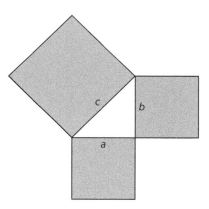

$a^2 + b^2 = c^2$

Figure 2.4 Pythagoras' theorem
Pythagoras' theorem shows that the square on the hypotenuse of a right-angled triangle is always equal in area to the sum of the squares on the other two sides. But if you didn't know this, you could think it possible for a right-angled triangle to lack this property

'vivid and clear'[11]. For if indeed he has an accurate and complete understanding of the essential natures of both, then he can conclude with confidence that they really are different things. The case of the person contemplating attributes of the triangle is different since their ignorance of the true nature of the triangle means their conception of it isn't really possible. However, Descartes' conception of a mind is supposed to be complete, nothing is hidden from his view, as it were, and so he can clearly see that extension is not a part of its nature. As he puts it 'I know [...] that nothing else belongs to my nature or essence except that I am a thinking thing; from this it follows that my essence consists solely in my being a thinking thing.'[12]

And yet this response is not altogether convincing. Descartes' efforts to discover what an object's essential nature is, are based purely on what he can and cannot conceive, in other words on how those things appear to him. But, the problem is that appearances may be deceptive or incomplete and it remains the case that there could be aspects to himself of which he is not directly aware. In other words, while it is reasonable to say that consciousness is essential to me, it is a big step to say that consciousness *alone* is essential and that, therefore, I might exist without a body or brain. Thought might still be the product of some material processes in the brain of which we are not directly aware via introspection. So just because there *appear* to be two things here, wouldn't necessarily mean that there really *are* two things.

To see the flaw, consider a parallel argument. I have a vivid and clear perception of heat. My idea here is simple, readily recognisable and I don't perceive anything else to be part of this idea. I also have a vivid and clear idea of motion. Again, I can recognise movement and appear to understand everything which is a part of this idea. Yet, can I conclude from this that heat and motion are totally different? Certainly they appear very different and so, from the subjective point of view, I would have to say that they have different essences. And yet, if science is to be believed, heat turns out to be no more or less than the vibration of molecules and atoms. Heat, in other words, is REDUCIBLE to motion. Despite a vivid and clear appearance to the contrary, they are not in reality different. So even though two things can be conceived of separately, it does not follow that they must be separate in reality. Descartes' error is to suppose that by contemplating the natures of mind and body he is determining their objective or true essences, whereas he is really only describing the way they appear to him.

The masked man fallacy

In trying to distinguish objects on the basis of what can or cannot be conceived, Descartes may be accused of committing what is often termed the *masked man* fallacy. To understand this fallacy we need to examine Descartes' use of Leibniz's Law (see page 195).

Descartes puts forward two differences between his self or mind, and his body; namely that he is aware of one as being conscious and unextended, and the other as being extended but not conscious. So we can distinguish two separate arguments:

- **Premise 1:** I have an idea of my mind as a thinking thing.
- **Premise 2:** I have an idea of my body as a non-thinking thing.

- **Conclusion:** Therefore my mind and body are different.

- **Premise 1:** I have an idea of my body as an extended thing.
- **Premise 2:** I have an idea of myself as unextended thing.
- **Conclusion:** Therefore my mind and body are different.

By applying Leibniz's Law here it seems Descartes can prove that the mind and the body are distinct entities and that they do not depend on each other for their existence. However, there is an important exception to Leibniz's Law. In 'intentional' contexts, it does not hold. Intentional contexts are those that involve the mind's thinking *about*, or being aware *of* something, such as when it has a belief, a hope or a desire. Beliefs, hopes and desires are said to be intentional states, in that they are directed at something in the world, or are about something. Now, since here Descartes' argument involves the intentional states of being aware of his body and mind, and having an idea of their properties, he cannot apply Leibniz's Law. This is because Descartes' awareness of his body and mind need not reveal the true nature of either. In other words, while Descartes may have an *idea* of his body as extended and unthinking, and an *idea* of his mind as unextended and thinking, this doesn't guarantee that the two really do possess these properties in themselves.

To understand the point, consider the following argument:

- **Premise 1:** My idea of Batman is of a masked crusader.
- **Premise 2:** My idea of Bruce Wayne is not of a masked crusader.
- **Conclusion:** Therefore Batman is not Bruce Wayne.

This argument is clearly fallacious since Bruce Wayne could well be Batman if, on occasions and unbeknownst to me, he dresses up in a cape and mask to perform heroic deeds. And in the same way, my mind could well be my body, if, unbeknownst to me, the activities of some part of it, say my brain, are able to produce conscious experiences. The fact that I am unaware of my brain doing this doesn't show that it doesn't, so while my mind and body may appear very different, in reality they could still be the same.

Note, however, that we may have distorted Descartes' intended argument somewhat in making this criticism. While he does state the argument in intentional terms, he is careful to say 'I have a vivid and clear idea of myself as something that thinks and isn't extended, and one of body as something that is extended and does not think'.[13] As we saw above the fact that his awareness of his body and mind are said to be 'vivid and clear' clearly involves the claim that his awareness reveals the true nature of each. As you may remember from studying the earlier *Meditations*, Descartes' strategy involves arguing that anything he understands 'vividly and clearly' must be true, so he is not simply distinguishing the way mind and body appear to him, but rather talking about their real properties. So perhaps a fairer interpretation of his arguments would be:

- **Premise 1:** The true nature of my mind is a thinking thing.
- **Premise 2:** The true nature of my body is a non-thinking thing.
- **Conclusion:** Therefore my mind and body are different.

- **Premise 1:** The true nature of my body is an extended thing.
- **Premise 2:** The true nature of my mind is an unextended thing.
- **Conclusion:** Therefore my mind and body are different.

In this version, the criticism above does not hold, as the key differences identified are not intentional states but real properties of the objects in question. So if the premises of these arguments are true we must accept the conclusion. However, the problem now is whether we should accept these premises. In other words, can we be sure that Descartes' ideas of his mind and body are accurate? For while it may well be true that Descartes believes himself to have a clear and distinct idea of himself as an unextended thing, this is not quite the same thing as saying he really *is* an unextended thing. Physicalist philosophers will deny the second premises of both arguments and claim that the mind is indeed extended (for example, they may claim it occupies the same space as the brain) and that the body is indeed capable of thought (for example, consciousness may be produced by the electrochemical activity of the brain). So does Descartes really have a clear and distinct idea of his mind as unextended and of his body as non-thinking?

One reason to think not is that it is difficult to see how he could ever be clearly and distinctly aware that his mind and body *lack* any property at all. While he may not be aware of his body being able to think or of his mind being extended, this is not the same as being able positively to say that they couldn't be. In other words, it is not that he is aware that his body and mind lack these qualities, rather it is that he is not aware that they have them. All that Descartes can clearly and distinctly know is that when he examines his idea of his body, he is unaware of its being able to think, and when he examines his mind, he is unaware of its being extended. So his arguments should really be of the following form:

- **Premise 1:** I am aware of myself as a thinking thing.
- **Premise 2:** I am not aware of my body as a thinking thing.
- **Conclusion:** Therefore my mind and body are different.

- **Premise 1:** I am aware of my body as an extended thing.
- **Premise 2:** I am not aware of myself as an extended thing.
- **Conclusion:** Therefore my mind and body are different.

However, these arguments are fallacious since the fact that he is not aware of his mind and body in either of these ways is not the same as saying that they cannot be such. Not being aware of an aspect of something is not the same as being aware of the absence of that aspect. To see the point, consider the following example:

Imagine you are at a masked ball, where the identity of all the guests is disguised. Someone enters the room wearing an elaborate mask and you try to reason as to the identity of this person along the following lines:

- **Premise 1:** I am aware that my best friend has blue eyes.
- **Premise 2:** I am not aware that the woman in the mask has blue eyes.
- **Conclusion:** Therefore the woman in the mask is not my best friend.

Here something is true of your friend – you are aware she has blue eyes – that is not true of the woman in the mask. Both premises are true, and so it would seem that, according to Leibniz's Law, the two terms 'best friend' and 'woman in the mask' cannot refer to the same person. There must be two people involved. However, this is plainly wrong. The woman in the mask could be your best friend, but with a mask on. Leibniz's Law fails in this instance because the two premises of the argument tell us more about your state of mind than about the colour of the woman's eyes. So the fact that you are unaware of the colour of her eyes doesn't tell us anything for sure about whether or not she actually has blue eyes in reality. In other words, not being aware that she has blue eyes, is not the same as being aware that she doesn't have blue eyes, yet it is this premise that is needed for Leibniz's Law to apply.

In the same way, imagine if someone, Kevin, did not follow politics very closely and doesn't know who the Prime Minster is at the moment. After asking Kevin several questions we might be able to put the following argument together.

- **Premise 1:** Kevin is aware that the Prime Minister works in the Houses of Parliament.
- **Premise 2:** Kevin is not aware that Theresa May works in the Houses of Parliament.
- **Conclusion:** Therefore Theresa May is not the Prime Minister.

Again the conclusion may be false, even though the premises may be true since they do not reveal any real differences in the objects themselves (the Prime Minister and Theresa May), but merely in the way she is conceived by Kevin. Not knowing that Theresa May works in the Houses of Parliament is not the same as knowing that she doesn't, and this is what would be needed for Leibniz's Law to work here; and likewise with Descartes' argument. Not being aware that his mind is extended is not the same as being aware that it is not. And not being aware of his body as a thinking thing is not the same as being aware that it is not. Putting forward differences between the mind and body on the basis of what he is or is not aware of does not really tell us that minds and bodies are in fact different. Minds may well be extended. And bodies may well be thinking.

▶ **ACTIVITY**

The masked man fallacy

Which of the following arguments commit the masked man fallacy? Why?

- **Premise 1:** I am aware that I have a cold.
- **Premise 2:** I am not aware that germs exist.
- **Conclusion:** Therefore my cold cannot depend upon the existence of germs and might exist without them.

- **Premise 1:** Harry believes Severus Snape is out to get him.
- **Premise 2:** Harry does not believe the Half-Blood Prince is out to get him.
- **Conclusion:** So Severus Snape is not the Half-Blood Prince.

- **Premise 1:** Derren knows that the Morning Star is the planet Venus.
- **Premise 2:** Derren does not know that the Evening Star is the planet Venus.
- **Conclusion:** Therefore the Morning Star is not the Evening Star.

- **Premise 1:** Abi wants to become famous.
- **Premise 2:** Abi does not want to be hounded by the press and general public.
- **Conclusion:** Therefore becoming famous does not involve being hounded by the press and general public.

- **Premise 1:** I am aware of looking out for my own safety when crossing roads.
- **Premise 2:** I am not aware of a having a guardian angel who looks out for my safety when crossing roads.
- **Conclusion:** Therefore my safety depends only on myself and not on a guardian angel.

Response 2: What is metaphysically possible tells us nothing about the actual world

If we accept that dualism is metaphysically possible, and that God could have created human beings composed of two substances, what can we legitimately infer from this about the actual situation in this world? We've seen that Descartes argues that conceivability entails metaphysical possibility and therefore that there are possible worlds where minds are distinct from bodies. However, such metaphysical possibility doesn't show that it is physically possible in our world. The natural laws governing the behaviour of everything in the universe may prohibit consciousness from appearing without a properly functioning brain to produce it. For, as we have seen, metaphysical possibility doesn't entail physical possibility. We may not now understand just how the brain produces consciousness, but this is a limitation in what we know. And limitations in what we know about the natural world do not tell us anything about how things actually work in nature.

At the same time, we could point out that just as dualism is conceivable, so too is physicalism. There is nothing obviously contradictory in the idea of consciousness being a product of the physical brain. So this would appear to be a metaphysical possibility which stands on a par with dualism; some possible worlds contain minds which are ontologically distinct from bodies, and others contain minds which are not. But this gets us no nearer to determining which of these possible worlds we happen to live in.

What this objection shows is that we cannot use *a priori* reasoning – that is reasoning without any reference to experience – to analyse our concepts of mind and body and thereby to make substantive empirical claims. We may be able to work out what the metaphysical possibilities are, but not the physical ones which actually matter to us in our universe. So, on this view of the situation, it may be a CONTINGENT fact about consciousness that it can only be produced by brains, and whether or not it is, is something that can only be determined by empirical investigation.

Response 3: Mind without body is not conceivable

Descartes' and Plato's claim that the true nature of my self is not physical also seems to go against our common sense understanding of what it is to be a person. In everyday life we recognise people as being the same by their bodies. Your friends and family members are flesh and blood beings, not disembodied souls. And if they were to lose their bodies you would be unable to recognise them. So, for example, you recognise your teacher as the same person who taught you last week because they have the same face. If next week someone turned up to teach you with a different face and different body, doubtless you would conclude that it was a different person. I doubt that you would be persuaded that it was really the same person, no matter what they said. This suggests that wherever someone's body goes, they go, and that their body is an essential component of who they are. Certainly in the ordinary course of things we are unable to detach ourselves from our bodies and take off as disembodied spirits to roam another plane, or to hitch up with a new body. But if dualism were true, there would seem to be no principled reason why we shouldn't do this kind of thing regularly.

Experimenting with ideas
- How can you tell that a student is absent from a particular class?
- If a student claimed they were present even though their body was not, should their name be put on the register?

What do your answers suggest about the relationship between someone's body and their self?

The Experimenting with ideas activity on page 192 asked you to try to imagine losing your body. Is this actually conceivable? It may appear so on the face of it. You seem to be able to imagine looking down on your body and floating upwards. But on reflection it seems that such accounts must make implicit reference to embodiment. For example, to talk of *looking down* on your body implies you have eyes to see. Looking in different directions must involve turning one's head or body around. Moreover, how could someone float upwards and through the roof without having some physical body to move through space? Indeed, the very idea of moving around in space implies having some physical position, and yet it seems that without any physical form not only could you not perceive anything, you couldn't actually *be* in any place either.

Another difficulty for out-of-body experiences is the apparent impossibility of verifying them. Because the experiences are essentially private, there can be no independent checks by others that what is experienced genuinely involves leaving one's body. Contrast such experiences with the evidence a scientist uses when conducting experiments. The claims they make must be subject to independent test. They must be repeatable. Logical positivists such as A.J. Ayer (1910–89) argue that for an apparently empirical claim to be meaningful, it must be verifiable. But the possibility of establishing the existence of anything non-physical, such as a mind, lies beyond any possible empirical test, and so such entities cannot be considered scientifically respectable. In this case, according to VERIFICATIONISM, it is literally nonsense to talk about a non-physical substance or of being outside of one's body.

We can arrive at the same conclusion by following David Hume's argument that we can have no idea of the mind or self. For Hume, genuine concepts have to originate in sense experience. So, if I have the concept of hand or pear, it's because I have seen and felt these things at some point. However, if we reflect on our sense experience we find, claims Hume, that there is no impression of the mind. We are aware of the various experiences we enjoy, such as sensations, emotions, beliefs and so forth, which are the contents of consciousness. But we are never aware of any *thing* which is the owner of these conscious experiences. Moreover, if the mind is, as dualists claim, immaterial and lacking extension, then it could not be a possible object of sense experience. Sense experience, after all, is necessarily of physical things which are extended in space. For this reason, the idea of an immaterial mind as a thing which is not a possible object of experience, must lack any meaning for Hume.

Immanuel Kant (1724–1804) argues similarly that for a concept such as 'mind' to be meaningful it must apply to some possible experience. But if we cannot conceive of an experiential situation in which the concept could be used then we don't really have any proper idea what we are talking about. Here a word may seem meaningful, but without any application it would just be an empty sound. And if the concept of immaterial minds has an application to experience there must be criteria we could apply to identify and so distinguish them. But what if each morning I awoke with a

Learn More

new mind? How could we tell that this is not the situation? There are no criteria available to establish this either way, because minds are not the kinds of things that can be individuated. Physical bodies can be precisely because they occupy specific positions in space. But since minds do not, it seems we have no basis for identifying them. And if we cannot identify them, we have no basis for making claims about their existence.

A related problem with identifying minds concerns how we distinguish one person from another. Recall that dualism is saying that it is my mind, rather than my body, that is to be identified with the person that I am. This means that the distinction between me and anyone else must be to do with the nature of differences between our minds. However, it is possible to imagine that someone else might have exactly the same thoughts, feelings and so forth as me and yet still be a distinct consciousness. We might imagine such a person as being a kind of mental twin, with their mind having exactly the same content as mine. But now let's ask, in this case: What is it that distinguishes my mind from my twin's? How do we know there are two minds here, rather than just one? The dualist is not able to appeal to anything physical to distinguish the two (such as our bodies), and cannot appeal to anything mental either, since they are, in this respect, identical. So it seems there can be no way for them to draw the distinction. And so it seems to follow that I must have a body in order to be differentiated in such a case and therefore that a body must be essential to who I am.

Note also that without a body it would seem to be impossible to communicate with other people, for communication involves the use of the sense organs: the eyes, mouth and ears. So if disembodied consciousness is possible, it would appear to be a rather lonely prospect, perhaps a form of torturous solitary confinement; unless we could commune with others through some form of telepathy. And yet there are good reasons to doubt that telepathy is possible. Ordinary experience, for one, suggests we cannot peer into other people's minds to see what they are feeling or thinking. If you want to know someone's secret thoughts, after all, you need to wait for them to tell them to you.

Powerful reasons for doubting substance dualism accumulate with the increasingly detailed observations of the dependencies between brain structure and mental phenomena. The degeneration of cognitive function in various dementias such as Alzheimer's disease is closely tied to the degeneration of neurons. The loss of specific functions such as the capacity to feel fear or see visual motion are closely tied to defects in highly specific brain structures in both animals and humans. The shift from being awake to being asleep is characterised by highly specific changes in patterns of neuronal activity in interconnected regions. The adaptation of eye movements when reversing spectacles are worn is explained by highly predictable modifications in very specific and coordinated regions of the cerebellum and brainstem. And example can be piled upon example.[14]

Patricia Churchland

The dependence of mind on brain

Finally it is worth mentioning here a crucial argument we will be returning to and which has had a profound influence on the direction the philosophy of mind has taken since Descartes' day. The argument draws on the evidence provided by modern neuroscience (science of the brain) to suggest that our mental life depends on our brains. Memories are stored in the brain, for example, and stimulation of specific points in the brain can cause a person to recall events from their past. Brain damage can cause memory loss and this suggests that when the brain decomposes, our memories must disappear (if not before). So how can we retain a sense of self without our memories? Sensations also appear to be produced by the activation of specific areas of the brain. Most fundamentally, the evidence is that consciousness itself is the product of a living, functioning brain. Disrupt the operations of the brain with drugs or trauma and consciousness can be radically affected. This dependence of mind on brain suggests that the destruction of the brain must destroy consciousness, so that the person cannot survive independently of the body and that substance dualism must be false.[15]

Although the soul is united to the whole body, its principal functions are, nevertheless, performed in the brain; it is here that it not only understands and imagines, but also feels; and this is effected by the intermediation of the nerves, which extend in the form of delicate threads from the brain to all parts of the body.[16]
Descartes

Note, however, that Descartes was not unaware of the importance of the brain to the proper functioning of the mind, as this quotation shows. Indeed, he was one of the first to recognise that the brain is the true location for much of our conscious experience. He based his conclusions on his own researches into anatomy and physiology which showed that the system of nerves by which sensations are communicated from the body to consciousness and by which motor movement is controlled in our limbs, have their ultimate centre in the brain, and he rejected the common opinion of the day that it is in the heart that our feelings of emotion, our 'passions', are located.[17] So while in the *Meditations* he maintains that the mind is a distinct substance, he was nonetheless alive to the fact that consciousness of the body in sensation, our capacity to imagine and perhaps even some of our higher cognitive functions such as memory and even some reasoning are a product of the union of mind and body, and so his dualist view can arguably accommodate some, if not all, of the evidence of modern neuroscience. Nonetheless, if Descartes is right, then the destruction of your brain will not ultimately destroy your consciousness and you will be able to continue to think without it and it is this which many find hard to accept in the face of the neuroscientific evidence.

Evolutionary history

Charles Darwin's (1809–82) theory of evolution is a well-established account of the origins of all living things including human beings.[18] According to the theory, all species derive from a common ancestor and differences between them are the product of random variations between parents and offspring and the pressures of 'natural selection', which mean that those best adapted to their environments are most likely to pass on their genes and survival strategies to their offspring. We need not go into the theory in detail, but assuming it is correct, it implies both that humans are related to all other animals and that our appearance on the planet can be explained in purely physical terms. From the perspective of evolutionary theory, the appearance of a non-physical mind cannot be explained. If humans are the only creatures with minds, as Descartes claimed, then their appearance is a complete anomaly, something that would stand out as unexplained and inexplicable within the theory of evolution. Where did minds come from? Why did they appear? How did they become attached to our brains? And when in our evolution did this miraculous event take place? Such questions cannot be answered by evolutionary theory and this suggests they are misguided questions. So how would evolution explain the appearance of consciousness?

Like many other species we have a nervous system and ours is distinguished from those of other species only in its degree of complexity and power, not in kind. The theory of evolution suggests that the mind evolved in the same way as the capacities and organs of all living things, as a survival strategy emerging from the physical processes of genetic variation. Consciousness is certainly a remarkable evolutionary development and its usefulness is not hard to see. Being aware of one's environment and one's body via sensations will clearly help an organism to find sustenance, avoid being eaten and so on. Advanced cognitive capacities also have an obvious benefit in helping us to solve the problems of survival in hostile environments. Observation of other animals suggests strongly that they too are conscious and that the nature of their mental capacities is related to the structure of their brains. All this points to the conclusion that our minds evolved gradually over millions of years and that mentality is the product of the increasing complexity of our brains, and not something else entirely. We can reach the same conclusion by observation of the development of the individual person from birth, or even before, and through to adulthood. Consciousness is not something which appears all at once and fully formed. Rather it emerges gradually as the baby and its brain grows. When you wake up in the morning too, it seems your consciousness gradually surfaces, suggesting it is a complex phenomenon, not a simple and unitary substance.[19]

2.2.2 Property dualism

The evidence of neuroscience and evolutionary theory is pretty compelling against substance dualism and has led many philosophers to embrace physicalism. But there is an alternative form of dualism, known as PROPERTY DUALISM, which appears better able to accommodate the scientific evidence. We have seen that a property is a quality of a substance which depends for its existence on the substance. And what property dualism claims is that the brain has a special set of non-physical properties alongside its ordinary physical properties; properties possessed by no other kind of physical object. The properties in question are the ones you would expect, namely mental phenomena such as experiencing sensations, thinking, desiring and so forth. So consciousness is a real phenomenon, but is not *substantial*, that is, it cannot exist alone without a living brain to produce it. In one account conscious experiences are thought to appear or emerge when the developing brain reaches a certain level of complexity. In other words, mental properties are *emergent*, that is, they do not appear until ordinary biological matter has managed to organise itself into a sufficiently complex system (by evolution, for example). Other examples of properties that are emergent would be that of being coloured or living. All these require matter to be suitably organised before they appear. But the property dualist is arguing that *mental* properties are a special sort of emergent property in the sense that they are *irreducible* to matter, meaning that they cannot be explained in terms of the physical properties of the body or, more specifically, of the brain. So all the physical facts about a human being do not account for everything that is going on; there are, in addition, certain non-physical facts concerning consciousness. Because property dualists believe in the irreducibility of mental phenomena they remain dualists even though they claim there is just one kind of substance.

2.2.2.1 The 'philosophical zombies' argument for property dualism

Experimenting with ideas

In the eighteenth century Leibniz criticised the view that the mind might be reducible to matter with this argument:

> One is obliged to admit that perception and what depends upon it is inexplicable on mechanical principles, that is, by figures and motions. In imagining that there is a machine whose construction would enable it to think, to sense, and to have perception, one could conceive it enlarged while retaining the same proportions, so that one could enter into it, just like into a windmill. Supposing this, one should, when visiting within it, find only parts pushing one another, and never anything by which to explain a perception. Thus it is in the simple substance, and not in the composite or in the machine, that one must look for perception.[20]
>
> Leibniz

In this quotation Leibniz invites us to imagine going inside a thinking, perceiving machine. If physicalists are right we are machines of this sort. So let's turn the thought experiment around and imagine ourselves reduced in size so that we could walk around inside someone's brain. We can imagine being able to watch neurons sending electrical signals across synapses, neurotransmitters sluicing around and so forth. But the question is, would we be able to find inside this brain the person's thoughts, feelings and perceptions?

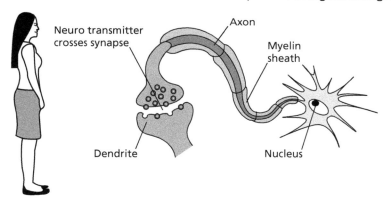

Figure 2.5 If you were shrunk to the size of a cell and could wander around inside someone's brain, would you be able to find their thoughts, sensations or emotions?

A variety of mental phenomena may appear impossible to account for in purely physical terms. Descartes pointed to our ability to use language and to reason, especially about mathematics, as beyond the capacity of any physical system. In the quotation above, Leibniz focuses on thinking, sensing and perceiving, and his argument is that we could know everything that there is to know about a physical mechanism that thinks, senses and perceives, and yet this knowledge would not provide us with an explanation of these conscious states. Physicalism must therefore be an incomplete account of what there is in the world and we need to posit a non-physical mind, what he calls here a 'simple substance', to locate consciousness.

Arguments of a similar nature have been put forward by contemporary philosophers, notably David Chalmers in an article given in the Anthology, 'Consciousness and its place in nature'. The problem Chalmers is wrestling with is how to explain subjective experience, or what it is like to be a conscious human being. (See Anthology extract 2.6 for Chalmers' outline of what he means by 'consciousness'.) He has a similar list of what consciousness involves to Leibniz – 'perceptual experience, bodily sensation, mental imagery, emotional experience, occurrent thought, and more.'[21] And he illustrates these: 'There is something it is like to see a vivid green, to feel a sharp pain, to visualize the Eiffel tower, to feel a deep regret, and to think that one is late.'[22] What Chalmers is keen to emphasise here is what he calls the 'PHENOMENAL character' of these conscious states, that is, what it is like to be in such a state or how they appear in my mind: the qualia (see page 187).

Now Chalmers asks us to imagine a human that lacks qualia and other mental states; a human with no conscious experiences at all. He calls such a being a ZOMBIE. But Chalmers' zombie bears little resemblance to the walking dead of horror movies and so is normally called a PHILOSOPHICAL ZOMBIE to mark this distinction. The difference is that it exactly resembles a normally functioning person. It is physically identical to a normal human; even its internal constitution, in particular the functioning of its brain, is indistinguishable from that of the rest of us, and it behaves just like you and me. The only difference is that it has no subjective awareness. When it hears the chink of a spoon on china, sees the colour brown and sips its cup of tea, it enjoys no qualia. And while it will scream when you step on its foot, there is no actual pain going on. There is nothing that it is like to be the zombie.

Figure 2.6 A philosophical zombie is an exact physical duplicate of a human being but is not conscious. Although it displays the outward signs we associate with beings with consciousness, in the zombie's case there is nothing going on inside

A normal human being   A zombie

▶ **ACTIVITY**

Is a philosophical zombie conceivable? Is it possible?

If you are in a class, work in pairs and consider whether your partner might be a philosophical zombie. Consider the evidence or reasons you have for thinking they have a mind. Is this evidence conclusive? If not, does this mean it is conceivable that they have no consciousness? If it is conceivable, is it physically possible? Is it metaphysically possible?

Now imagine you are God and you create a world which is exactly like this one right down to the positions and movements of all the elementary particles and the laws which govern their behaviour and including, of course, humans and their complex brains. Having completed this work, you sit back and ask yourself whether there are any finishing touches to be made to your creation. Suppose you would like conscious beings in your universe. Is there anything more that needs to be done to bring them into being?

You may have thought the easiest way to find out whether your partner was a zombie would be simply to ask: 'Are you a zombie?' However, obviously the zombie is going to deny it – its behaviour is, after all, indistinguishable from ours. If you ask it to explain its thoughts or describe its qualia, it will be able to do as convincing a job as you or I, even though it has neither conscious thoughts nor qualia. But if your partner was a zombie, what could it have been talking about when it told you it was conscious, that it was enjoying its cup of tea and wondering whether you could enjoy the same mental states as it? Clearly it couldn't have been telling the truth since it has no mental states. So was it lying about its mental states? No. A zombie couldn't lie either since lying presupposes having mental states. But if the zombie's utterances are neither true nor lies, then what is their status? It seems hard to make sense of what is going on when a zombie talks about its consciousness. Considerations such as this might make you wonder whether the zombie idea is really conceivable after all.

We cannot tell, no matter how closely we inspect someone, whether or not they are a zombie. This is because zombies are, by definition, identical to us in every possible physical test we can make. They only differ in a way we cannot physically test. But in this case you can never know that someone else is not a zombie and worse, you cannot even know that everyone else is not a zombie. Perhaps the whole world, apart from you, is made up of mindless machines which merely appear to you to be conscious.

Chalmers accepts this line of thought. He thinks it is conceivable that there exist philosophical zombies – after all, there seems to be nothing contradictory in the idea since we seem to have no difficulty imagining zombies and so they are logically possible. But he doesn't think they actually exist. Indeed, he thinks it is very likely that they are physically impossible given the psychophysical laws (the natural laws that determine certain mental states to be produced by brain states) which operate in this universe. But the fact that we can conceive of such beings shows, he argues, that there are other possible universes – other ways things could have been – in which such beings could exist. So there is a possible world which is physically identical to this world, except that in this parallel universe all the human beings are zombies. Zombies are, in other words, metaphysically possible. It follows that consciousness cannot be identical to physical properties and there is more to being conscious than can be captured in a complete physical description of you.

Chalmers' argument can be outlined as follows:

1 Physicalism claims that consciousness is ultimately physical in nature.
2 It follows that any world which is physically identical to this world must contain consciousness.
3 But we can conceive of a world which is physically identical to this one but in which there is no conscious experience (a zombie world).
4 Therefore a zombie world is metaphysically possible.
5 Therefore physicalism is false.

Property dualism and supervenience

Property dualists like Chalmers agree with the physicalist that mental states depend upon brain states in our universe. There is, what philosophers call, a relation of SUPERVENIENCE between mental and the physical properties. Supervenience is an important concept in the philosophy of mind, and is to do with the way two sets of facts relate to each other. One set of facts (A) is said to supervene on another set (B) if you cannot change the A facts without changing the B facts. For example, if the mind supervenes on the brain, this means that mental states cannot change without there being a corresponding change in the brain. Or, to put things the other way around, the workings of the brain determine what happens in the mind. So, whenever certain neurons are firing, we can be assured that a person will be experiencing a particular mental state. (Note that this doesn't mean that those neurons have to fire for this mental state to occur. The same mental state could occur with different brain states.)

However, while Chalmers accepts that the natural laws in this universe mean that the mind supervenes on the brain, he argues that this is not the case in other possible worlds. So zombies are impossible in this world: a full physical duplicate of a human being here would have to be conscious. But the conceivability of zombies shows, he claims, that there are possible worlds where the psychophysical laws that happen to obtain here don't hold, and so where physical duplicates of human beings may not be conscious.

Response 1: A zombie world is not conceivable

But just try to keep hold of this idea in the midst of your ordinary intercourse with others, in the street, say! Say to yourself, for example: 'The children over there are mere AUTOMATA; all their liveliness is mere automatism.' And you will either find these words becoming quite meaningless; or you will produce in yourself some kind of uncanny feeling, or something of the sort.[23]
Wittgenstein

To evaluate this argument let's start at the beginning. The premise at step 1 (page 215) is a fair statement of physicalism and the inference drawn at 2 is a valid one. So it is the second premise (step 3) which we need to examine. Now Chalmers defends the conceivability of zombies by pointing out that there is no obvious contradiction involved. But care is needed here because contradictions don't have to be obvious. The American philosopher Daniel Dennett (1942–) has argued that Chalmers' zombies are not actually conceivable,[24] that we may think we can conceive of such a being, but if we examine the idea more carefully we will discover that it contains hidden contradictions. He claims that consciousness is necessarily linked to our various capacities to act, but in ways we may not immediately recognise. We fool ourselves into thinking we can strip consciousness away from a person's ability to converse or react appropriately to perceptual stimuli, but, Dennett urges, having a mind is integral to being able to perform such tasks and he encourages us to appreciate the way such abilities are inextricably linked to such mental states. Is it really conceivable that a zombie would be able to respond intelligibly to you in conversation without having any understanding of what it was talking about? Can we make proper sense of the idea of a human describing their experience of qualia which they don't have? Certainly to many it seems practically impossible to imagine that the person you are talking to has no consciousness – try pricking them with a pin and telling yourself they may be experiencing no pain. In the quotation on page 216, Wittgenstein suggests that reflection on the zombie possibility involves using words in ways that make them lose their meaning. We take words which make good sense in everyday contexts, and begin to use them in ways which stretch their applicability to breaking point. The 'uncanny feeling' should make us realise that we have lost any clear grip on what we are talking about.

Dennett uses an analogy with health to help make a similar point:

> *Supposing that by an act of stipulative imagination you can remove consciousness while leaving all cognitive systems intact ... is like supposing that by an act of stipulative imagination, you can remove health while leaving all bodily functions and powers intact. ... Health isn't that sort of thing, and neither is consciousness.*[25]
> Dennett

When he speaks of 'an act of stipulative imagination', Dennett is saying that we are quite capable of randomly making up or imagining things, such as a human with all the physical signs of mindedness but with no mind, or with all the physical signs of health but unhealthy. But in the second case, it's obvious that good health is constituted in some complex way by the good functioning of the body. So long as your various organs and biological processes are operating effectively, or, as we might say, as they should, then you will be healthy. It follows that any body that functions in the appropriate way must enjoy good health and that it would be nonsensical to suppose it possible for a body to function in every way like a healthy body, and yet not to be healthy. In sum, health supervenes on the state of my body and so if I am healthy, an exact physical duplicate of me must be healthy too. Now, for Dennett, consciousness is like health: it is constituted by the proper functioning of the body and brain of a living human being. And so, just as with health, as long as a human being is functioning appropriately physically, then, necessarily, they will be conscious. The fact that we cannot currently explain exactly how this physical functioning constitutes consciousness, means we seem to be able to imagine the proper functioning without the consciousness (a zombie). But, for Dennett, we appear to be able to conceive of this possibility only because we have an incomplete grasp of the details. So all this act of imagination shows is just how impoverished is our current understanding of how consciousness is produced.

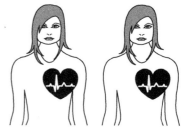

Figure 2.7 Imagine an exact physical duplicate of a healthy human being. Is it conceivable that the duplicate not be healthy too?

Let's consider again what exactly Chalmers is asking us to conceive. What is clearly not possible is to bring to mind what it is like to be a philosophical zombie, since there is nothing it is like. He sometimes speaks metaphorically of the life of the zombie as empty or dark to suggest the absence of consciousness. But while we can imagine experiencing darkness or emptiness, this is not a literal description of the zombie's inner life since it doesn't just lack light or objects of awareness but any awareness at all. In fact, the zombie's real inner life is non-existent and so is literally unimaginable.

If we cannot imagine life as a zombie, however, then we surely can imagine meeting one, that is, imagine how the zombie appears to me, from the outside, as it were. But according to the hypothesis, from this perspective the zombie is the same as any other person; and it would appear we are being asked simply to imagine a normally functioning human being. So, in sum, it seems that we are being asked either to imagine something that can't be imagined, or something which is very easy to imagine but which doesn't differ from everyday experience. Perhaps, then, the puzzling nature of this thought experiment stems from us mistakenly thinking we can hold these two conceits together: imagining being mindless, a being with a dark or empty mind, crossed with imagining an encounter with an ordinary person.

Considerations such as these may lead us to claim that because the zombie hypothesis cannot be distinguished from the world we live in by any empirical test, that it is actually a hypothesis empty of meaning. For if utterances get their meaning from what they tell us about the world, then any which cannot be shown to be true or false by reference to experience would appear not to be telling us anything. So if we are genuinely to make sense of a situation we are being asked to conceive, we have to be able to point to some experience which would differentiate it from the normal situation. Yet in the zombie case, according to the hypothesis, this is not possible; zombies cannot be distinguished from ordinary people. But in this case we may be led to the conclusion that the zombie hypothesis merely seems to be conceivable, but is actually a nonsensical idea. This is the line verificationists take. Wittgenstein argues in a way that has affinities with verificationism in his 'private language' argument (see page 238). And BEHAVIOURISM is a school of thought in the philosophy of mind which also rejects the zombie hypothesis for similar reasons. We will be exploring these approaches when examining the problem of other minds below (see page 231).

Response 2: What is metaphysically possible tells us nothing about the actual world

Activity

Does conceivability imply metaphysical possibility?
- Try to imagine or conceive of the possible worlds below.
- Divide the worlds into those you can conceive of and those that you cannot.

1 A world where Napoleon won the battle of Waterloo
2 A world where it's possible to travel back in time
3 A world where events can happen without being caused
4 A world where water is not H_2O
5 A world where some trees are made of chocolate
6 A world where sisters are male
7 A world where people can be shrunk to the size of an atom
8 A world where murder is good
9 A world where honey is made by rabbits
10 A world where squares are sometimes round
11 A world where cows give birth to kittens
12 A world where you can travel from London to Canterbury without covering any distance

Having divided up the possible worlds, consider these questions:
- Is there a clear distinction between what you can conceive of and what you cannot?
- If the distinction is reasonably clear, does it indicate what is and what is not logically possible?
- Are the logically possible worlds the same as the metaphysically possible ones?

Time travel is a good example of something which appears straightforwardly conceivable. After all, you are probably familiar with stories of people going back in time and these stories seem perfectly comprehensible. However, closer inspection may make us question this appearance. It is surely contradictory to go to a time before I was born, since I didn't exist before my birth. So we are imagining a situation where I both do and don't exist at the same time. If I go back to a point after my birth I could meet my younger self, but then the self-same person that I am would be two persons not one, which is also incoherent. And what if I then kill my younger self? Then I would not have been alive to travel back in time. In which case I wouldn't have killed myself and so would be alive after all. But in that case I could have travelled back and killed myself, and we are caught in a paradox. Many of the stories told of time travel exploit paradoxes like these as a plot device. What this shows is that we are very capable of imagining (perhaps conceiving of) scenarios which are not logically coherent and the lesson to draw is that we need at the very least to be careful before assuming that what we can conceive of is logically possible.

Another issue to consider is whether the conceivability or otherwise of these worlds is an indication of whether they are metaphysically possible. For instance, we may be able to conceive of chocolate trees, but the precise sense in which they are therefore possible is not immediately clear. Clearly they are not physically possible – they wouldn't be able to photosynthesise, grow or reproduce. And they would melt in the summer. But beyond this we might also question whether a chocolate tree is really a tree at all. Real trees are made of wood after all, so we might wonder whether chocolate trees can still be trees. The chocolate things in a parallel world might be called 'trees' by its inhabitants, but they would have to be sufficiently different from trees in this world as to be different sorts of things altogether.

Response 3: What is conceivable need not be metaphysically possible

A related response is to accept that a zombie world is conceivable, but to deny that this allows us to draw safe conclusions about what is possible. A zombie world may not be logically contradictory, yet zombies may nonetheless not be genuine metaphysical possibilities. Consider whether it is conceivable that water not be H_2O. It certainly seems it is. It's possible to imagine that the water in your glass has a very different molecular structure. We can even imagine an entire possible world almost exactly like ours with a transparent liquid which behaves just like water, but with an alternative chemical composition. However, what are we really imagining in such a scenario? Given that water actually is H_2O, any liquid with a different composition, no matter how similarly it might behave to real water, is not actually water. So it seems that it is not possible in any world for water not to be H_2O and it can only seem possible if we have an insufficient grasp of the detailed facts about the chemical nature of water. If this is right, it means that the statement 'water is H_2O' is metaphysically necessary even though we cannot discover this by conceptual analysis and so isn't logically necessary. We cannot discover that water is H_2O *a priori*; we need to do some scientific investigation. So this looks like an example of a necessary truth which is only discoverable *a posteriori*. In the same way, it can be argued that philosophical zombies may be conceivable, but are nonetheless not metaphysically possible. In any physical duplicate of this world the humans would have to be conscious. And if they were to lose consciousness, they could not possibly continue to behave in all the complex ways that we do.

2.2.2.2 The knowledge/Mary argument for property dualism

anthology 2.7

> *I am what is sometimes known as a 'qualia freak'. I think that there are certain features of the bodily sensations especially, but also of certain perceptual experiences, which no amount of purely physical information includes.*[26]
> Jackson

Another contemporary philosopher, Frank Jackson (1943–), introduced a now famous thought experiment into the literature to question the physicalists' claim that phenomenal consciousness can be explained in terms of the physical. The paper appeared in 1982 and was called 'Epiphenomenal Qualia'. (The meaning of the title of the paper will become clearer below when we explore a form of property dualism known as 'EPIPHENOMENALISM'.) Like Chalmers, Jackson argues that the intrinsic nature of certain mental states – qualia – is irreducible. This is an argument for a kind of dualism. However, Jackson, like Chalmers and most contemporary philosophers, accepts that the brain must have some role to play in the production of consciousness. The evidence of neuroscience is in this regard pretty overwhelming, making Cartesian or substance dualism seem untenable. So Jackson supports a version of property dualism whereby the mental is irreducible, but nonetheless a product of the physical brain, a view introduced above.

Jackson introduces his paper by confessing to being what he calls a 'qualia freak'; that is someone for whom it appears obvious that no amount of physical information can capture what it is like to experience qualia. He gives a very simple argument to this effect: 'Nothing you could tell of a physical sort captures the smell of a rose, for instance. Therefore, Physicalism is false.'[27] However, while this argument may be very appealing to other qualia freaks, Jackson thinks he needs to develop the basic intuition behind its premise to persuade the more stubborn physicalist. And so he develops his 'Knowledge Argument'.[28]

The knowledge argument begins with a thought experiment about a brilliant neuroscientist named Mary. Mary, we are asked to suppose, has been confined her whole life to a black and white room and has access to the rest of the world only via a black and white television screen. The point of this is that we must suppose that she has never seen any colours herself. Despite this handicap, she has studied the science of vision and come to know everything there is to know about what happens physically when someone sees and talks about colours. So she knows all about which wavelengths of light produce which effects on the retina, and how this information is translated into certain excitations in the brain's visual system and how this in turn leads people to announce they have had certain colour sensations of red, blue or whatever. Next suppose that one day Mary leaves the confines of the black and white room and is able for the first time to look directly at the sky, the grass and a rose, and so to experience colours.

Does she learn something she didn't know already? Jackson thinks it is clear that she does – she learns what it is like to experience colours. It follows that her knowledge before she left the room must have been incomplete. Since this prior knowledge included everything there is to know physically about colour vision, physicalism leaves something out; specifically it cannot explain qualia. Hence physicalism is not a complete account of reality.

The knowledge argument can be summarised like this:

1 Mary knows everything about the physical processes involved in colour vision.
2 But she learns something new when she experiences colour vision herself.
3 Therefore there is more to know about colour vision than what is given in a complete physical account of it.
4 So physicalism is false.

Response 1: Mary gains no new propositional knowledge, only acquantaince knowledge

An initial defence of physicalism against this argument makes use of a distinction you may be familiar with from studying the epistemology unit in the first year of your Philosophy A-level, namely the distinction between PROPOSITIONAL KNOWLEDGE and ACQUAINTANCE KNOWLEDGE. Propositional knowledge is knowledge of facts and can be expressed in propositions; it is knowledge *that* such and such is the case. This kind of knowledge includes Mary's knowledge of the facts of colour vision. For instance, she would know that the wavelength of red light is between 620 and 750 nanometres on the electromagnetic spectrum. Acquaintance knowledge is the kind you get from encountering something, as when we speak of knowing a person or a place or a type of object. For example, we might say that Mary knows her father, London or spaghetti bolognese, in that she has encountered them and is familiar with them.

Now, to say that Mary knows everything there is to know about colour vision is to say that she knows every physical fact about it. So it concerns her propositional knowledge. Then, when she leaves the room she does indeed learn something new, but it is not new propositional knowledge and so she learns no new facts. Rather, she becomes acquainted with the phenomenal character of colours, that is, with certain qualia.

To see the point, suppose you are a big fan of some celebrity; you follow their career avidly and know all there is to know about their professional and private life. Now suppose that you are introduced to them for the first time. As your eyes meet and you shake hands, do you learn anything new about them? In one sense you need not. You already knew what colour eyes they have, and might even have known what clothes they would be wearing and that they would be meeting you. So you have acquired no new factual knowledge. However, having met the person, you are now *acquainted* with them and so have acquired a different type of knowledge.

So, according to this objection, the plausibility of the knowledge argument rests on an equivocation on the word 'know' (that is, it uses the word in two different senses) and if we use it just in the sense of propositional or factual knowledge, the argument fails.

Jackson's response is to deny that what Mary learns on her release is confined to acquaintance knowledge. Certainly she does become acquainted with colours for the first time, but she also acquires some propositional knowledge in the process. For now she is able to know facts about what it is like for human beings to see colours. Before, she knew everything physical about human colour vision; on her release she knows something more about it, so her new knowledge isn't confined to mere acquaintance with colours herself.

Let's suppose she has a companion who shared her black and white prison all her life and she returns to the room after her foray into the outside world. Like Mary, her companion, let's call him Marvin, also knows all the facts about human colour vision, yet we can imagine him being eager to hear about her experiences and we can imagine him questioning her concerning what she has learnt. Doubtless Mary would make efforts to communicate what it was like to see a red rose or the blue of the sky. But Marvin would remain in the dark about what these experiences are like, and so he would appear to lack important factual knowledge that Mary has recently acquired. Marvin may know the physical facts about Mary but still not know about her qualia.[29]

Mary gains no new propositional knowledge, only 'ability knowledge'

Others[30] have also argued that Mary doesn't acquire any new propositional knowledge, but rather than confining what she does know to acquaintance knowledge, claim that she gains ability or practical knowledge. Practical knowledge is the knowledge of how to do something, such as tie shoelaces or ride a bike. On this account, it is also accepted that Mary learns something new on her release, but it is not any fact she didn't already know. Rather, what she acquires are new abilities or skills. By becoming acquainted with colours she acquires the capacity to remember and to imagine the colour of ripe tomatoes, to recognise objects of similar colours by sight, to group objects together according to their common hues, and so on, which she didn't possess before. These new abilities are important in their way, but, the objection runs, they are not knowledge of new facts about what is the case. So the fact that she learns something new doesn't undermine physicalism since it is perfectly possible for her to acquire new abilities without this meaning she didn't have complete factual knowledge of what happens when people view colours.

It shouldn't surprise us that we cannot learn how to do things just from learning all the relevant facts. After all, it's not possible to teach someone how to ride a bike just by teaching them all the facts about the dynamics of cycling. We can imagine Mary also having learnt all there is know about what happens physically when someone rides a bike – the mass distribution and balance, the gyroscopic effects and so on – but not being able to ride herself. If she then learnt to ride, would she learn something new about what happens physically? Surely not. She has simply acquired a new skill. In the same way it may be that Mary learns no new facts about colour vision.

Jackson's response to this objection is to accept that Mary does acquire new abilities, but that she also acquires factual beliefs about the mental life of others. She now knows what others have been experiencing all along when they see ripe tomatoes. To force this point home he asks us to imagine Mary debating with herself over whether other people really do have the same sorts of experiences as she does when they see red tomatoes. The sceptical question here is whether, since I cannot directly access anyone else's subjective experiences, I can truly know that their experiences resemble mine. This is an aspect of the problem of other minds which we will be considering in detail below (see page 231). Jackson's concern here is not with resolving the problem, but merely with pointing out that the problem could worry Mary. But in order to worry about the problem, she has to be asking herself a factual question: 'Is it the case that others have the same experiences as me?' Whatever the answer, her question concerns whether she has sufficient evidence to accept a factual claim, whether, in other words, a belief she only acquires after her release can count as knowledge. If she decides she can know what others' experiences are like, she may be wrong, but this doesn't matter to Jackson's argument for it is still propositional beliefs she is trying to justify in overcoming scepticism. All he needs to show is that she lacks knowledge of others' experiences – what they are like – before her escape, despite having all the physical information, and so some information about other people's experiences escapes a complete physical account.

Response 2: All physical knowledge would include knowledge of qualia

> *How can I assess what Mary will know and understand if she knows everything there is to know about the brain? Everything is a lot, and it means, in all likelihood, that Mary has a radically different and deeper understanding of the brain than anything barely conceivable in our wildest flights of fancy.*[31]
> Patricia Churchland

Some have resisted the knowledge argument by insisting that if Mary did indeed know all the physical facts about colour vision, then she would be able to work out what colours would look like, and so, even in the black and white room, could imagine what it is like to look at the sky or at a red rose. To persuade us of this, Dennett urges us to recognise just how hard it really is to imagine Mary knowing *absolutely everything* about colour vision. We currently know really very little about how it works, so are not in a position to get a proper imaginative handle on what it would mean to know it all. So, faced with the invitation to imagine Mary's body of knowledge, we must conjure a very vague and general sense of what she would know. But this vague idea is not, says Dennett, a safe basis upon which to make judgements concerning what it would or would not be possible for Mary to understand. We may well be unable to imagine how she could come to know qualia, but this just shows that our imaginations here may be limited. Here we may be guilty of what Dennett calls 'Philosophers' Syndrome: mistaking a failure of imagination for an insight into necessity'.[32]

Jackson himself changed his mind about the knowledge argument and came to endorse this objection.[33] He argues that it may seem to us that Mary would have to learn something new on first seeing red, but this may just be because we have only a very confused idea of what knowing all the physical information would involve. We acquire information via the senses, which seems to have an intrinsic and unanalysable nature and it is as well that we do, as this allows us to

Figure 2.8 The blue banana trick Suppose to test Mary upon her release we present her with a trick banana – a banana we have surreptitiously coloured blue. Would she be able to recognise that it was the wrong colour? If Jackson's original argument in 'Epiphenomenal qualia' is right, then she would not. However, Dennett, whose example this is, argues this conclusion is based purely on intuitions generated by a bad thought experiment and asks us to imagine Mary's complete knowledge of colour vision enabling her to spot the trick

recognise salient features of our environment, such as tastes and colours, very efficiently. But this doesn't mean these experiences really are unanalysable. In reality, qualia may represent complex internal states, so that if Mary genuinely knew everything about such states, she might well be able to work out what colours would look like before seeing them herself. Despite this, in practice, knowing 'everything' physical about colour vision is likely to be beyond us, so that nobody could ever actually have a complete neuroscientific understanding of how colour vision works. So we are likely never to be able to work out what it's like to see red without actually seeing it. But this just shows the limitations of our understanding of neuroscience and so it remains true that *if* Mary knew everything then she wouldn't learn anything new when she first sees red.

Response 3: Mary gains new propositional knowledge (the 'new knowledge/old fact' response)

One defensive strategy used by physicalists begins by accepting that there is a sense in which Mary acquires new factual knowledge but denies that this implies that there are non-physical facts. The facts she learns, namely what it is like to see colours, are really the same facts that she knew before, but now presented in a new way or under a different description. This is because after her release she acquires a new set of concepts based on her experience of colours. And it is possession of these 'phenomenal concepts' that now enables her to describe the same facts in a new way. Before her release Mary knew all about the physical facts from the third person point of view; after her release she comes to know them from the subjective, first person, perspective. This subjective access is simply a different way of presenting the same neurophysiological states that Mary already knew under the third person description, and so is not knowledge of a new set of facts.

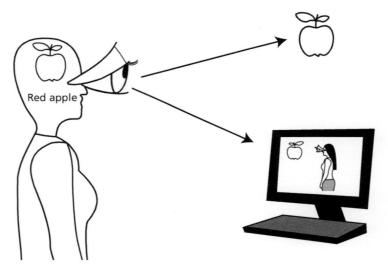

Figure 2.9 Mary looking at a red apple Upon her release Mary acquires the phenomenal concept of red and learns what it is like to see red. Her knowledge is new in the sense that it employs phenomenal concepts that she didn't have before. But because what she knows remain the same neurophysiological facts about colour vision, she hasn't learnt of any new non-physical facts

The point may be made clearer through an example. Suppose that Mary goes to a party and meets Bruce Wayne and learns that he is a billionaire. Never having heard of Batman, she could not claim to know that Batman is a billionaire. But suppose that later that night she meets Batman and learns that he is a billionaire. Would she be gaining new knowledge? In a sense, yes. She has learnt something about Batman that she didn't know before. But is she learning a new fact about reality? Presumably not, for the fact that Batman is a billionaire and the fact that Bruce Wayne is a billionaire are not two facts, but one. So while we may say that the knowledge is new, the fact that it concerns is one she knew before, but under a different description. So when she meets Batman she acquires a new concept with which to pick out the same individual, but doesn't learn any new facts.

In the same way, prior to her release Mary may know all the physical facts concerning what goes on in the brain when we see red things. And when she sees red for herself she learns that the experience of seeing red things involves a certain 'red-like' qualitative feel and she acquires a phenomenal concept from this experience. So now she is able to represent the same physical facts going on in her brain under two different descriptions, one involving physical, the other phenomenal terms. But these are just two ways of describing the same fact about seeing red and so the knowledge argument fails to show that she becomes aware of new non-physical facts about the world.

Response 4: Qualia do not exist and so Mary gains no new propositional knowledge

> *Nothing, it seems, could you know more intimately than your own qualia; let the entire universe be some vast illusion, some mere figment of Descartes' evil demon, and yet what the figment is made of (for you) will be the qualia of your hallucinatory experiences. Descartes claimed to doubt everything that could be doubted, but he never doubted that his conscious experiences had qualia, the properties by which he knew or apprehended them.*[34]
> **Dennett**

We've seen that qualia present physicalism with a problem; for there appears to be an explanatory gap between the physical facts about our neurophysiology and the subjective feel of our phenomenal experiences. But if qualia could be shown not to exist, this would provide the physicalist with a powerful counter to the knowledge argument. For if there are no such things as qualia, then we no longer need to suppose that Mary learns anything new on leaving her black and white room. However, on the face of it, this strategy doesn't look particularly promising. After all, there seems nothing more real than qualia. And, as Dennett points out in the quotation above, we may follow Descartes in doubting the existence of the entire universe beyond our minds, but the qualitative feel of our sense experiences appears an indubitable fact about consciousness. Surely we cannot be mistaken about qualia since we are directly aware of them in our experience!

But despite the initially counter-intuitive nature of the claim that qualia don't exist, both Patricia and Paul Churchland (see Anthology extract 2.8[35]) have been attracted by this route to a defence of physicalism. The central claim they advance is that the whole range of mental-state terms which are part of our common sense picture of the nature of our minds, such as qualia, but also beliefs, desires, emotions and so on, should be *eliminated* from a proper

anthology 2.8

understanding of human mentality. This is because there is nothing in reality that corresponds to terms such as 'qualia', 'beliefs' or 'desires'. So in the future when neuroscience is sufficiently advanced, we will be able to abandon talk of such mental states and speak instead of brain processes. This view is known as ELIMINATIVISM, and we will be examining this theory in more detail below. For now, though, it will be worth examining just how eliminativists think we can eliminate qualia.

The eliminativists' argument begins with the claim that our common sense understanding of the mind is really a kind of pre-scientific theory about human behaviour. This theory is called FOLK PSYCHOLOGY, meaning that it is the theory of mind (psychology) of ordinary people (folk). This theory employs entities such as beliefs, sensations and desires to explain and predict human behaviour and it does so tolerably well. I can, for example, predict that someone will exhibit certain pain behaviours (holding their foot and screaming) if I drop an anvil on their foot; and I can explain why they might subsequently hobble off to A&E on the basis that perceiving the anvil land on their foot and the accompanying sensation of pain has caused them to form the belief that their foot may be broken, and this, coupled with the desire to have the foot restored to working order, along with various other beliefs (about modern medicine, the location of the hospital and so on), will cause this behaviour.

If folk psychology is indeed an empirical theory of this kind, then it follows that it is open to refutation. If a better theory comes along, one which explains and predicts human behaviour more effectively, then we should abandon folk psychology in favour of the new theory. Now, modern neuroscience is making dramatic advances in its ability to unravel the complex relationships between the brain and behaviour. This research looks much more fruitful than folk psychology as a way to a better, more complete understanding of our behaviour. And as it advances it will eventually, perhaps quite soon, show that folk psychological concepts are redundant. In defence of this prediction, eliminativists point to the weaknesses of folk psychology: the things it singularly fails to explain. These include the nature and purposes of sleep, the causes of mental illnesses, how learning works, how we remember, and so on. In fact, folk psychology hasn't made any significant advances in the last few thousand years and so is, they urge, in need of overhauling. Once we adopt the new science of the mind, we will see that there is no place within it for qualia.

Experimenting with ideas

The language which ordinary folk use to talk about our minds has not remained completely static over the years. Since Sigmund Freud (1856–1939), for example, people have become inclined to accept the idea of unconscious motives, defence mechanisms, projecting their fantasies or of people being 'anal'. Nowadays you may also hear people speak about having a 'caffeine spike', rather than feeling edgy; an endorphin rush as opposed to feeling elated; a serotonin imbalance rather than feeling low and tired; or an adrenaline overload rather than feeling excited. Does this mean that folk psychology is on the way out?

Imagine a world, in the future, where no folk-psychological terms are used, only medical/scientific terms. Would this change the way we think about ourselves? Would the idea of qualia still have a role?

Paul Churchland (1942–), in the anthology paper 'Eliminative materialism and the propositional attitudes' offers many examples of entities which were once thought to exist and which were abandoned when a new and superior theory emerged which could explain the phenomena better. One such example comes from cosmology. The ancient Greek astronomer Ptolemy claimed that there were rigid crystal spheres which surrounded the Earth like the layers of an onion and these kept the various heavenly bodies, such as the Moon and planets, from crashing down to Earth. These spheres played an important function in Ptolemaic cosmology, but with the advance of modern physics, the crystal spheres became obsolete and we came to see that they just don't exist. Patricia Churchland also discusses this example in Chapter 4 of *Brain-wise*, another of the Anthology readings. The Ancient Greek physics distinguished between the earthly realm with its own set of physical laws and the realm above the moon where a different set of rules were thought to prevail. In the realm of the spheres, objects naturally move in circular orbits around the Earth. But in the earthly realm, objects were thought to fall because they have a 'natural place' at the centre of the universe. Isaac Newton's revolution in physics in the sixteenth century involved recognising that the law governing both the movement of the heavenly bodies and those of objects on earth was ultimately the same – the law of gravity – and in so doing he got rid of the idea of objects having a 'natural place'. This theoretical notion, in other words, was *eliminated* from physics.[36]

anthology 2.9

But, we might ask, surely qualia cannot be compared to theoretical entities like 'natural place' or 'crystal spheres'. No one could actually see the spheres, and so they could easily be abandoned once we developed a better way of explaining the movements of the heavenly bodies. But things are not the same with qualia; we are directly aware of them and so it seems implausible to suggest we could ever jettison them completely from our theory of the mind.

However, this response can be resisted. Take a different example from the history of science. 'Caloric' was a theoretical substance thought to be responsible for making things hot. According to the theory, caloric was a very fine gaseous substance that was suffused through objects rather like liquid in a sponge, and which flowed from where it was dense to less dense and so moved from hotter to colder objects. Modern thermodynamics has abandoned caloric and we now no longer suppose there is any substance corresponding to the term. Heat is not a substance, but is produced by the mean kinetic energy of the particles which compose objects.[37] Now suppose that someone were to defend the existence of caloric by pointing out that it must exist because we can directly feel it when we touch hot objects. This proof of the reality of caloric should not convince. The reason this fails is that caloric's reality is being presupposed in the concepts they use to interpret the experience of heat. In the same way, it may be that we are so in thrall to the theoretical framework of folk psychology that we have to interpret the data of introspection in terms of its theoretical entities, such as qualia. When we adopt the new neuroscience of the future, we will have a more sophisticated set of theoretical concepts to operate with and so will no longer need to think in terms of qualia. So what we think we directly perceive is not something which is free of any theoretical framework. If qualia are part of a theory, then when we change the theory we may have no need for the concept of qualia either.

[Learn More] We will be examining eliminativism in more detail below (see page 285) and much of the discussion there will be relevant to whether you think this solution to the knowledge argument is successful. But for now let us return to another contemporary philosopher who denies qualia exist, Daniel Dennett. He does not go so far as to deny that consciousness has certain properties, but rather his point is that qualia cannot have the properties standardly given to them. For example, the standard view says they have an *intrinsic nature* that cannot be broken down into parts. A particular quale, for example the taste of beer, is that it is completely independent of any other qualia. Similarly, pain is thought to be inherently horrible and this horribleness is inextricably bound up with the experience so that it is not something that could be subtracted from the pain. Qualia are also said to be *directly accessible* via introspection so that we cannot be mistaken about what they are like or confuse them with other qualia. So, for example, it is not possible to think you have a headache, when in fact you are experiencing an itchy foot. And they are also supposed to be *private*, meaning that my qualia are only accessible to me. If I am experiencing the pain of child birth, for example, then you cannot peer into my mind to see what this experience is like. Finally, they are *ineffable*, meaning that their essential nature cannot be put into words and so they are impossible to communicate to someone not acquainted with them already. So while it is possible to compare our reactions to our qualia, it is not possible to compare qualia themselves. For example, we may be able to discuss our different reactions to the taste of beer, perhaps you like it while I hate it. But it is not possible to compare the taste of beer to me with the taste as it is to you. And it would be impossible adequately to explain to a person who has never drunk it, what beer is like.

Dennett tries to show that these features of qualia are ultimately incoherent and therefore the concept is hopelessly confused. There is nothing that could have the properties given to qualia, so while their existence may seem intuitively obvious, we are actually subject to a philosophical confusion. He concludes that the judgements we make about our conscious experience are comprehensible in terms of what is publicly observable to anyone and thus are ultimately explicable on physicalist terms.

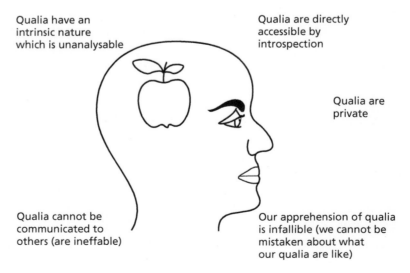

Figure 2.10 The standard picture of qualia according to Dennett

To help us out of our confusion, Dennett offers a series of thought experiments and arguments, some of which we will briefly look at here.

One argument focuses on the phenomenon known as 'reactive dissassociation', which can be brought on by the use of morphine to control pain. Some patients report being in pain, but not finding the pain unpleasant. How are we to understand such reports by the lights of the standard picture of qualia? Two options are possible. Either the patient is mistaken about being in pain so that they think they are in pain, but are not. Or we have to say that it is possible to subtract the horribleness from the pain experience. Either way, we violate the standard picture since we are either saying someone can make a mistake about what qualia they are experiencing, which means introspection is not infallible, or we have to say that qualia are not, despite appearances, unanalysable, but may be broken down into parts so that what seemed to be intrinsic to the experience turns out not to be.

Experimenting with ideas

1 Suppose you hate cauliflower. One day you see me tucking into a plate of cauliflower and get to wondering how it could be that I can enjoy that horrible taste. But, you then consider, perhaps it tastes different to me than it does to you.
   Questions for reflection: Does cauliflower taste the same to someone who likes it as it does to someone who doesn't? Suppose you hated cauliflower as a child and then grew to like it as you got older. Did the taste change? Or did you come to change your mind about the same taste?
2 Imagine someone whose colour vision is inverted so that when they look at the sky they see what you call yellow, and when they look at a banana they see what you call blue. Since this has been their situation since birth, they have learnt to call bananas 'yellow' and the sky 'blue', and as their colour vision is systematically inverted by comparison to yours for all the colours of the rainbow, there seems to be no way they could ever have noticed that their experience of colours is different from anyone else's and they would behave in their use of colour words exactly like me or you.
   Questions for reflection: Would there be any way of detecting the fact that someone has inverted spectrum colour vision? If there is no way of telling, is it still conceivable that their vision is different from yours?[38]

A matter of taste

A thought experiment Dennett employs uses the example of acquiring a taste for beer in order to argue that we appear not to be able clearly to identify the supposedly intrinsic nature of qualia. So what happens when you acquire a taste? There are two possible ways of describing the situation. One is to say that the taste itself gradually changes from an unpleasant one, to a pleasant one and this implies that the way beer tastes can change. In this case it seems not to have an intrinsic nature, but one at least partly constituted by one's past experiences of tasting beer. But if one's changing reaction to it has altered the taste itself then its nature cannot be what it is only in virtue of itself alone. And so, this goes against one of the defining characteristics of qualia. On the other hand, we might then suppose that the taste doesn't change, but that it is just your reaction that has changed; in other words, that prolonged exposure teaches you to enjoy a taste you previously thought was horrible. But this way of viewing the situation is also problematic for the traditional view of qualia, since it becomes puzzling how you could come to enjoy a taste if its horribleness is an intrinsic part of the taste. Surely, if tastes have an intrinsic nature, then we cannot experience them differently from how they are. So either way we look at the situation we seem to be saying that the way we experience a taste and the taste itself are not identical which contradicts the idea of qualia having an intrinsic nature.

In fact, Dennett argues that we cannot tell which of the two situations has occurred when we acquire a taste. That is, by introspection, we are unable to determine whether the taste itself has changed, or whether our liking for it has. For while we might try to retrieve the original quale from memory in order to compare it with the taste now, we could never be certain that the memory was accurate or that our current attitude towards the quale wasn't colouring how we now recall it. But if it is not possible neatly to distinguish the part of the quale of beer that has remained the same and the bit that has changed, then this problematises the idea of qualia as intrinsic and directly and indubitably known. If we can't tell whether we have the same qualia or not, then Dennett argues, we should abandon talking about qualia altogether. For if qualia are indeterminate then we cannot claim that they have intrinsic properties and if we cannot unambiguously identify qualia, then we cannot claim that such entities exist.

The inverted spectrum

Consider finally the inverted spectrum case from the Experimenting with ideas activity on page 229. If two people behave in exactly the same way when it comes to their use of colour terms, and there is no way of checking whether their qualia are inverted or not because they are private and ineffable, it seems we could never know whether or not this were the case. This has led some philosophers to argue that we imagine such a case is a real possibility, but that if there were genuinely no way of detecting the difference between you and the person with inverted spectrum vision, then there is no real difference between us. Since the hypothesis cannot be refuted or confirmed, it is not a situation we can make genuine sense of, despite appearances. As we have seen, Wittgenstein famously likened this way of viewing the matter to each of us having a beetle in a box that no one else could see.[39] In such a situation, the intrinsic nature of our respective beetles cannot be compared, and without such INTERSUBJECTIVE comparison, their natures cannot meaningfully be spoken about. Perhaps, then, we are talking nonsense when we speak of the intrinsic nature of qualia, precisely because linguistic meaning must be connected to what is publicly verifiable.

Dennett is clearly influenced by this way of considering the issue. But he goes further in trying to persuade us that there is something incoherent about the very idea of spectrum inversion. Other versions of the spectrum inversion idea have tried to get around the problem that qualia cannot be intersubjectively compared by supposing that you wake up one morning to find your qualia of the colour spectrum have been inverted (perhaps some evil scientist has switched the neural pathways from the colour receptors in your retina to your visual cortex). You wake up to see the sky as yellow and bananas as blue and because you can compare your current qualia with your qualia from the day before and so recognise what has happened, this shows such inversion is a genuine possibility.

However, in this case, we cannot eliminate the possibility that you would notice the switch because of a change in the way you are disposed to react to different colours. That is, you notice your red–green qualia have been switched because you now have a tendency to pull away from traffic lights when the top light comes on and to stop at the bottom light. Or you are put off your spaghetti bolognese sauce because it now has a peculiar rotten-looking hue. So the experiment must be modified so that these extrinsic clues as to the switch are eliminated so that we can establish for sure that it is just the intrinsic natures of the qualia that we are able to recognise have changed. But if we somehow were to switch these as well, claims Dennett, it is far from clear that we would indeed be able to tell that the switch had happened. With the full switch, you would regard your qualia of the top light on the traffic signal as exciting and vibrant and it would cause you to apply the brakes. The bottom light would now be calm and cool and would incline you to accelerate away. And if all your reactive dispositions to these different colour experiences were systematically switched, surely you would be none the wiser. In this way, Dennett urges us to accept that we cannot really isolate the intrinsic properties of qualia from our reactions to them and so that the idea that we have an intrinsic awareness of them independently of these reactions is a mistake. In other words, with the complete switch you could never detect it had happened. And if we cannot detect qualia changes, then we should abandon the notion that we have direct and infallible access to their intrinsic natures.

2.2.3 The issues facing dualism

2.2.3.1 The problem of other minds

anthology 2.10

Descartes put in place a conceptual framework which can be understood to give rise to a radical scepticism about the mind of another. Once the mind is radically divorced from the body, then even if we can show that there can be knowledge of body there remains the further question, how do we know whether there is a mind connected with any given body that we may encounter?[40]
Anita Avramides

Earlier we examined how non-reductivists like Chalmers argue that it is conceivable that others may not enjoy mental states at all. This was the zombie world hypothesis (see page 215). If, as dualists hold, the mind is irreducible to the physical, then knowing everything there is to know physically about someone needn't involve knowing the content of their consciousness and so it seems that it is conceivable that others don't have minds at all. In this section we are going to focus on the sceptical worry touched on in these discussions: the sceptical worry known as the *problem of other minds*.

Experimenting with ideas

To get a handle on the issue, consider the following argument. Then discuss how the sceptical conclusion might be avoided.

I have many beliefs about other people's moods and emotions, for example whether they are sad or angry. I also have many beliefs about their thoughts and desires, for example that they believe it is raining or fancy a beer. More fundamentally, and underlying this, I believe that each person has their own mind with their own experiences, and that much of what they do is because of what they believe and desire. In other words, I believe that people have minds.

Now consider what evidence I have for these beliefs. In all my dealings with other people, all I ever observe are the movements of their bodies, the expressions on their faces and the words that they utter. What I cannot observe, however, are the feelings they experience nor the thoughts they are thinking. All I have to go on in supposing them to be in pain or entertaining a certain thought is their behaviour. So when I see someone stand on a nail, scream out loud and hop around holding their foot, I infer that they are experiencing pain. But we can question whether this inference is sound. I have no way of checking that other people have experiences that are anything like what I experience when I step on a nail. Their 'pain' might be very different from mine. Moreover, not only is it conceivable that other people don't really experience my kind of pain, but, worse, it may be that they don't experience anything at all! All that I can be sure of is that when they stand on nails this causes them to hop around and produce a horrible noise. All that I can be sure of is what they do, not what they think or feel. So, for all I know, I am the only person with a mind. Everyone else could be zombies.

Do you agree with the conclusion that you cannot know that anyone else has a mind? If so, will this change the way you deal with them? How?

If not, why not? What could justify the inference from their behaviour to the existence of their minds?

According to dualism, my own mind is perceived *directly* by introspection, while the external world is perceived only *indirectly* via the senses. It follows from this picture, one inherited from Descartes, that we can only know about the minds of *other* people indirectly. This inevitably raises the question of precisely *how* I can judge what state of mind some other person is in. An initial answer would have to be that I must come to such knowledge on the basis of their behaviour. If, for example, someone is writhing on the floor screaming, the obvious inference would seem to be that they are in pain. But this just leads us to the more fundamental question, namely how this inference is made and whether or not it is justified. All the evidence about other people consists of what they do or is done to them, yet we think we know things about what they think and feel. If, for the dualist, pain is a sensation felt in my own mind, how can I infer the existence of a pain that is not mine and not felt by me? The evidence would seem only to be sufficient for us to make the generalisation that when people sit on drawing pins they jump up sharply and emit strange noises from their mouths, not that they are in pain, for their pain is not perceived. More radically, the dualist picture raises the possibility that we lack any firm basis for positing the very existence of other minds. This version of the problem is known as the epistemological problem of other minds because it is concerned with how we acquire *knowledge* of other minds. Another version, the conceptual problem, will be discussed below.[41]

> *Suppose everyone had a box with something in it: we call it a 'beetle'. No one can look in anyone else's box, and everyone says he knows what a beetle is only by looking at his beetle. – Here it would be quite possible for everyone to have something different in his box. One might even imagine such a thing constantly changing. – But suppose the word 'beetle' had a use in these people's language? – If so, it would not be used as the name of a thing. The thing in the box has no place in the language-game at all; not even as a something: for the box might even be empty.*[42]
> Wittgenstein

Wittgenstein likens the dualist picture to a situation in which each of us has his or her own box into which only he or she can look. I can see directly what I have, but no one else can; they have to rely on my report about what I have. Wittgenstein asks us to imagine that each of us calls what we have in our box a 'beetle'; and while we may suppose that everyone's beetle is the same, it is possible that we all have something different in our boxes. Because we can never compare what is in our boxes, we can never be sure. It is even possible that some people have nothing in their box at all! What this picture suggests is that when I talk about my beetle, no one else can truly understand what I mean by the term, since it refers to a wholly private object. It could be that we are all talking at cross-purposes, and using words to refer to private objects which are very different from each other's.

In the same way, it would seem that we can never know what anyone else means by sensation words such as 'pain'. Your pain could be radically different from mine, or you might not experience it at all, and I would be none the wiser. Wittgenstein thinks this consequence is enough to raise serious doubts about the way dualism sets up the situation in the first place, as we will see below (see page 236ff). And Gilbert Ryle is another philosopher who agrees that the problem arises because of a mistaken view of how we acquire knowledge of other minds in the first place. According to Ryle, dualism would entail that 'each of us lives the life of a ghostly Robinson Crusoe'.[43] If, as dualists suppose, our language of the mind refers only to private mental states, we could never be sure that they are being correctly applied to others, a situation which suggests that 'absolute solitude is ... the ineluctable destiny of the soul'.[44] For Ryle, this consequence of dualism was one reason (of many reasons) to reject it.

However, dualists have tried various strategies to try to avoid this sceptical conclusion. To do this, they need to argue that the inference to the conclusion that others have minds and that we can know about their mental states is justified, and two major defences of its legitimacy are traditionally offered: namely the *argument from analogy*, and the *argument to the best hypothesis*. (Ryle's own solution, rather than answer the problem directly, tries to defuse it and we'll be looking at that below when discussing philosophical behaviourism.)

Responses: The argument from analogy with my own case

The argument from analogy contends that we learn the connection between behaviour and mental states by observing it in our own case. Subsequently we suppose that there is an analogous connection between the behaviour of other people and internal states. John Stuart Mill (1806–73), who appears to be the first philosopher to articulate the argument, wrote:

> I conclude that other human beings have feelings like me, because, first, they have bodies like me, which I know, in my own case, to be the antecedent conditions of feelings; and because, secondly, they exhibit the acts, and other outward signs, which in my own case, I know by experience to be caused by feelings.[45]
>
> Mill

Here Mill is arguing that I learn there are law-like connections between occurrences in my body and in my mind. My foot steps on a nail and I feel a pain in my mind. The pain in my mind is typically followed by shouts and screams, efforts to remove the source of the pain and so on. So when I observe someone else behaving in similar ways in response to similar occurrences in their bodies, I infer that they have similar conscious experiences. This inference is based on an analogy. That is, it begins by drawing a parallel between observable similarities between my case and others (similar bodies, similar behaviours), and it then infers that others are also similar to me in certain unobserved (and unobservable) ways (other minds).

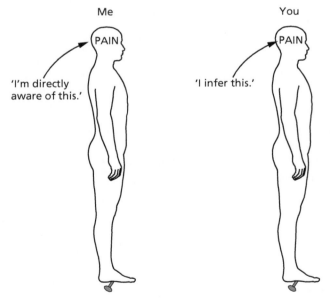

Figure 2.14 The argument from analogy with my own case When I step on a nail it causes a pain. The pain in turn causes pain behaviour. When others step on nails they also exhibit pain behaviour. So, by using my own case as an analogy, I am able to infer that they, like me, experience pain

Problems with the argument from analogy

Criticism 1

What is the justification for the assumption that other people are analogous to my own case? Is the evidence of my own case sufficient to generalise to all other people? In general, to argue by analogy with a single case is not a very strong procedure. For example, suppose you were travelling in a strange land and you came across a red fruit hanging from a tree. You pick the fruit, open it up, and find blue flesh inside. Would you be justified in inferring that all red fruit must have blue flesh? Inductive generalisations surely require rather greater evidence than that. After all, this fruit could be a freak of nature, the only one of its kind. Or there could be many types of red fruit, each with different interiors. So to have a good basis for making the claim that all red fruit have blue flesh, you would need to inspect a good number and range of red fruits. In the same way, to find good support for the claim that others in general have minds, I would need to inspect more cases than just my own.

The argument from analogy may be defended against this objection by pointing out that the idea that others are similar to me has rather more going for it than a simple inductive generalisation based on one observation. There is a great range of ways in which my body and behaviours are similar to others' bodies and behaviours. Other people are very like me not just in the way they react to standing on nails. Their bodies are composed of the same kind of stuff, they have the same limbs, and sense organs. And their behaviour is like mine in a whole range of complex ways. Language use is just one striking example of complex behaviour which is causally connected in my own case in a systematic way to thought processes. This complexity and the regularity of the connections between the inside of my mind and the outside of my behaviour may give us greater reason to suppose that others also have similar internal processes when they exhibit similar behaviour.

Moreover, we are members of the same species. And we know that members of the same species tend to be very similar in respect of a whole range of characteristics, including things we tend not directly to observe, such as the structure of their internal organs. It would be rather odd, we might think, if others were different from me when it comes to having a mind. After all, my mind is a very important part of what I am. So important, in fact, that it is reasonable to suppose that it is an essential component of what it is to be a typical human. Surely, then, we have very strong reasons for supposing that all humans have a mind, not just me.

Criticism 2

However, the inference from my own case may still appear problematic. For what makes an analogical inference reasonably secure is that there is some possibility of making independent checks. Thus, if I reason from the similarities between the external appearance of two human bodies that they both have similar internal organs it is possible for me directly to check whether the analogy holds. So suppose I listen to someone's chest and hear beating and infer on the basis of other similar beatings that they have a heart. In this case, it is always possible, at least in principle, to cut them open to check. But in the case of other minds there is no possible means of checking, and so no possible way of ever verifying the claim that others do indeed have minds.

It's not just that we cannot check as a matter of contingent fact. It is impossible to check whether others have minds *in principle*. 'Since ... one person cannot in principle visit another person's mind ... there could be no way of establishing the necessary correlation' between their external behaviour and internal mental states.[46] And it is this, Gilbert Ryle argued, that makes the analogical inference in this case ungrounded.

However, it is not obvious that the inability to make independent checks completely undermines the inference. If, as dualists hold, minds are by their nature private, then it is going to be impossible to check, and certainly this makes it impossible to guarantee the soundness of the reasoning. Nonetheless, the inference still has some basis and so some force even if it cannot be conclusive.

Learn More

So the argument from analogy leaves the existence of other minds probable at best, and this has struck many philosophers as unsatisfactory, in part because it doesn't sit well with our everyday conviction that they do exist. Those, such as Wittgenstein, who reject this attempt to explain our belief in the reality of other minds often claim that the whole problem derives from the dualist approach which begins with the idea that knowledge of my own mind is secure, while that of others is problematic. As normally conceived, the problem is a direct consequence of Cartesian dualism – a consequence of regarding *mind* as something inner and private, which is accessible only through introspection, while other people's bodies form part of the public world, and propositions about them can be shown to be true or false in the same way as any physical object statement. A theory of mind which allows that you know that you have a mind while leaving the possibility of other minds in doubt cannot really be a satisfactory theory of mind. And if we do not, as Descartes did, insist upon this sharp distinction between mind and body, or at least do not make a distinction between them in quite the way that he did, we need not, it is claimed, inherit the problem in the same way at all.

We need an understanding of how it is that we so much as think that there are other minds, given that my knowledge of mind comes from reflection on my own case.[47]
Avramides

If one has to imagine someone else's pain on the model of one's own, this is none too easy a thing to do: for I have to imagine pain which **I do not feel** *on the model of pain which* **I do feel**.[48]
Wittgenstein

The conceptual problem of other minds

Wittgenstein develops his attack on dualism and the argument from analogy by exploring what is sometimes called the 'conceptual problem of other minds' (as distinct from the 'epistemological problem of other minds' – the problem of how I can *know* that others have minds). This version of the problem concerns how I can even form the concept of other minds, let alone how I can know that others have them. The worry here is that if I gain the concept of mind exclusively from direct access to my own mind, then the process whereby I generalise in order to frame the concept of another person's mind, or other minds in general, looks problematic. After all, if my idea of mind is originally of 'my mind' then the idea of a mind which is *not* mine, a consciousness I am not conscious of, looks on the face of it like a stretch we would be unable to make. Wittgenstein argues that if the Cartesian picture were correct, I would find it impossible even to form a coherent concept of someone else's experiences on the basis of acquaintance only with my own. If I learn the meaning of the word 'pain' from my own case, how can I make sense of the idea of someone else's pain? For if 'pain' means *pain that I feel*, then someone else's pain would be a pain that I don't feel and so wouldn't be something I could understand. A pain that is not felt by me would surely be a contradiction in terms if the only basis for understanding the word was my own experience of it.

Further, according to Wittgenstein, in order for me to be able to judge that this particular sensation is a pain that *I*'m feeling I need first to have something to contrast it with, namely pains that *others* feel. The idea of a pain that *I* feel only makes sense in the context of pains in general which are felt by others. If this is right, then the argument from analogy with my own case can't get off the ground, since I cannot judge myself to be having particular experiences, such as pains, if I've not *already* made judgements about other minds with pains. Knowledge of my own mind without prior knowledge of others is impossible, and so it cannot be the basis for knowledge of other minds.[49] In other words, to have a concept of myself as a SUBJECT OF EXPERIENCE I must have the concept of subjects of experience other than myself.

Wittgenstein also tries to show that the idea of ascribing mental states to others by analogy with my own case is far more problematic than the dualist recognises. This is because, according to the Cartesian picture, there is no conceptually necessary connection between having a certain sort of physical form and having a mind, or between certain events occurring in your body, and your mind experiencing certain sensations. That is, on the dualist picture it is a purely contingent matter that my behaviour happens to be caused by my mental states and that sensory information conveyed to my brain happens to cause me to have certain types of sense experience. This is why, according to dualism, the ideas of spectrum inversion and philosophical zombies are conceivable. But if there is no conceptual connection, then surely any behaviour and any physical form could be secretly attached to a mind. I would therefore have no good reason for singling out other human beings from among all the physical things around me, as those to consider minded. Why not suppose that my toaster or my teapot has a mind? If Descartes were right, this should be quite easy to do. And it should also be easy to imagine that someone writhing on the floor with a nail in their foot is not really in pain. But can you actually do this in real life? Wittgenstein asks us whether we can make proper sense of the idea of attributing thoughts to a teapot or denying pain to a person in obvious distress. The fact that both of these are impossible for us seriously to imagine suggests a closer connection between the behaviour and physical form of human beings and the workings of their minds.

According to Wittgenstein, the connection may be understood in terms of the conditions under which we ascribe mental states to others. In other words, there are certain criteria or rules which we apply which specify when someone is in a particular mental state. Take for example being in pain. The criteria for ascribing a toothache to someone might be that they are groaning, holding their jaw, searching for aspirin and so on. And if someone is exhibiting all these symptoms then one is justified in concluding that they have a toothache. Wittgenstein argues that there must be criteria such as these which are publicly observable since otherwise we would be unable to learn the language of mental states. If dualism were true, we would be unable to ascribe mental states to others, since we could never know whether we were correctly ascribing the terms or not. Since we do, for everyday purposes, have little trouble using mental-state terms when talking about other people ('Greta has toothache'; 'Adam loves chips and curry sauce'), we must have a good command of the rules for correct and incorrect ascription. And these must be conceptually connected to behaviour – behaviour which is publicly observable. How else could a child ever learn to ascribe pain to others unless they did so on the basis of what they can observe? It is for this reason that we cannot meaningfully ascribe mental states to teapots – they just lack the requisite behaviours. And it is why it is not practically possible to doubt that someone is in pain when obviously injured and screaming: these just are the kinds of behaviour which entail that they are in pain. This way of seeing the issue had a great influence on Hempel's hard behaviourism which we will be examining below.

Wittgenstein's 'private language' argument

Wittgenstein's so-called 'private language' argument is found in his *Philosophical Investigations* (1953)[50] and represents an attempt to undermine the Cartesian approach to epistemology. Wittgenstein's arguments try to show that no coherent sense can be made of the SOLIPSISTIC position that Descartes entertains, that is the possibility that only his own mind exists, since it implicitly relies on what it claims to doubt. In other words, his argument questions the assumption of the primacy of knowledge of our own minds over those of others, by trying to show that the identification of private mental states is only possible if one presupposes a world of publicly observable objects, and the reality of other minds.

Wittgenstein's argument begins by pointing out that the ability to identify specific elements within one's own experience, such as qualia, requires some kind of classification system, in other words, something akin to a *language*. The Cartesian approach must presuppose such a language since only by the use of one could I classify and re-identify my experiences, and on that basis hope to build up knowledge about the external world and of other minds. The sort of world Descartes inhabits in *Meditation 2* in which he can identify his own private experiences but is not certain of the existence of the external world is just the sort of world that would be inhabited by a 'private language' user.

Note that the private language I would have to use will only be comprehensible to me, since its terms refer to my own immediate and private mental states, and such mental states cannot be properly known to anyone else because such things are private. In other words, their meanings are given by *me*, and not by any public agreement.

The next step is to point out that any system of classification, including a private language, must allow for a distinction between correct and incorrect use of its terms. For if there were no distinction, then whatever is being classified could no more be said to be one thing than another. Any language must be able to distinguish between correct and incorrect usage, since otherwise we couldn't determine whether a term meant one thing rather than another.

Now, our ordinary *public* language clearly has criteria for distinguishing between the correct and incorrect use of terms. When someone misuses a word this can be pointed out to them. We have dictionaries and grammar books and so on, which tell us how to use words properly. It is the existence of such publicly available rules that allows language to operate as, among other things, a system of classification. So now the question becomes whether a *private* language could satisfy these conditions. Could the Cartesian solipsist devise a language in which to classify his or her own experiences?

Wittgenstein claims that he or she could not, and does so through the following thought experiment. Suppose, in the world of Cartesian solipsism, we experience a quale and identify it with a name 'S'. Here we appear to have instituted a private name for a private sensation. But have we? A necessary condition for having successfully named something is that we could recognise a second instance of the same thing. But if we experience a second sensation, how are we to decide if it is an 'S' or not? In other words, how are we to tell whether this second sensation is similar to the original one in the relevant respect? How are we to be sure that we are not making a mistake?

The solipsist's answer is that so long as the new sensation *appears* to be 'S' then it *is* 'S'. For when it comes my own qualia, appearance and reality are one. In a private language, the rules would be just those which it seems right to apply on this or that occasion. And this is what is meant by saying that here I cannot make an error. I can be absolutely certain of the way things appear to me. But, complains Wittgenstein, if there is no chance of going wrong here, there is no legitimate sense in which we can be said to go right either. If the 'private language' user does not risk the possibility of going wrong in his or her re-identification of a sensation then he or she is not actually re-identifying the sensation at all. For if there are no objective criteria for determining correct identification, then we haven't succeeded in instituting a legitimate rule for classification.

Considerations such as these led Wittgenstein to suppose that the public world is primary, and is a necessary condition for the possibility of talking about our mental life. He suggests that the terms that describe our minds, emotions, sensations and so on are acquired in the same way as any other term in our language, by our being shown how such terms are used. It follows that the attempt of traditional dualism to begin with the immediate data of consciousness is misguided because it cannot make the first move. That is, I cannot even identify those immediate data. The mistake is to think that I can know what terms such as 'red' or 'pain' mean by direct acquaintance with the private objects they supposedly stand for. Whereas the only reason we are able to use such terms properly is because there is a public world in which correct and incorrect usage is determined.

Responses: The existence of other minds is the best hypothesis

If we return now to the epistemological problem of other minds we can examine an alternative solution to the argument from analogy. The argument that the existence of other minds is the best hypothesis is an abductive argument. That is to say, it takes the evidence of other human beings' behaviour and asks what the best explanation of it is that we can give. This strategy involves accepting the dualist picture according to which it is at least conceivable that the objects I call persons are zombies, but insists that I have sufficient reasons for thinking that they are not. These reasons are similar to those that lead scientists to believe in the existence of unobservable entities such as atoms. No one has directly seen such entities and yet atomic theory is the best explanation of the phenomena we can and do observe. For example, it predicts that heated copper will gain weight because oxygen atoms from the atmosphere will combine with copper atoms to create a film of copper oxide. Similarly the supposition of the existence of other minds with their own thoughts and feelings, that is to say, the hypothesis of our everyday folk psychology, is the best explanation of the elaborate behaviour we observe in other human beings. The supposition that someone is in *pain* when they are writhing on the floor and screaming with a nail in their foot, or that they are having thoughts about philosophy when discussing the problem of other minds with you, is the best hypothesis available to account for their behaviour. And it is not just that folk psychology *explains* human behaviour. It is because I suppose others have beliefs, desires and sensations of different kinds that I can also *predict* their behaviour in a range of circumstances. Standing on a nail causes pain. Pain is undesirable. If it is extreme enough it causes people to scream and to make efforts to remove the cause of the pain. So folk psychology predicts that someone who stands on a nail is likely to scream and attempt to remove the nail from their foot.

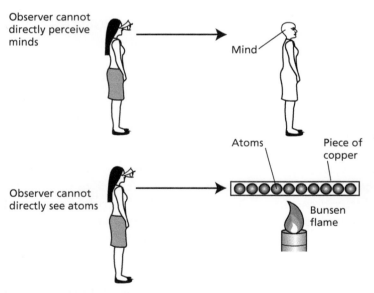

Figure 2.15 Atoms within a piece of metal being heated Atomic theory explains and predicts the behaviour of matter in a range of circumstances. Because it does this better than any rival theory it is the best hypothesis. So it is reasonable to believe in atoms, even though we cannot directly observe them. In the same way, it is reasonable to believe in beliefs and desires even though we can't observe them directly, since they successfully explain and predict human behaviour

Note that those persuaded by the best-hypothesis argument may also appeal to the inconceivability of the idea that other human beings could act in the complex ways that they do if they did not have minds. Why would they talk if they did not have thoughts? What possible explanation for this complex behaviour could there be, other than that they are trying to communicate their inner ideas? Also, if others don't have minds, why do they act as if they do? Why do they *say* that they do when asked? And why are they able to describe an inner life so similar to mine, if they possess no such thing? No other answer to these questions comes near to being as plausible as the hypothesis that they do indeed have minds.

Nonetheless, no matter how plausible a hypothesis folk psychology might be, it may well turn out to be false. That is, the unobserved entities that it posits may not actually exist. Just as concepts used in the past to explain behaviour such as possession by demons, fate or curses are not now thought to correspond to anything in reality, so our concepts of beliefs, desires, intentions and so on may turn out to be inadequate in a more complete explanation of human behaviour. Compare this possibility with advances in science where theories are superseded by new theories which explain the phenomena more adequately. As we have seen, eliminativists argue that the neuroscience of the future will supersede folk psychology. But supporters of the best-hypothesis argument emphasise that folk psychology is by far the best theory available and that we are, therefore, justified in accepting it.

> *According to Descartes 'a real man' uses language and is able to adapt his actions to suit the circumstances. It is by reference to language and adaptability that men are to be distinguished from mere automata.*[51]
> **Avramides**

In his *Discourse on Method* (1637) Descartes offers a version of this argument to show that others must have immaterial minds. He argues that there are two ways to test whether 'machines bearing the image of our bodies, and capable of imitating our actions' are genuinely minded, namely their use of language and of reason. For language and reason cannot be explained mechanically. What he has in mind here is that competent language use involves the ability to construct completely novel sentences that no one has ever uttered before. It also allows us to understand such sentences. But, thinks Descartes, something purely physical could never create or comprehend novelty since it would be bound to behave and respond in a preprogrammed or reflex manner. Understanding is also required for genuinely intelligent behaviour which can respond appropriately to new situations. Any purely physical device, no matter how complex, would, therefore, not be able to cope with unexpected situations or solve the most basic of practical problems since it would be bound to repeat reflex behaviours. Read the quotation below for Descartes' own account of this argument.

> *for we may easily conceive a machine to be so constructed that it emits vocables, and even that it emits some correspondent to the action upon it of external objects which cause a change in its organs; for example, if touched in a particular place it may demand what we wish to say to it; if in another it may cry out that it is hurt, and such like; but not that it should arrange them variously so as appositely to reply to what is said in its presence, as men of the lowest grade of intellect can do. The second test is, that although such machines might execute many things with equal or perhaps greater perfection than any of us, they would, without doubt, fail in certain others from which it could be discovered that they did not act from knowledge, but solely from the disposition of their organs: for while reason is an universal instrument that is alike available on every occasion, these organs, on the contrary, need a particular arrangement for each particular action; whence it must be morally impossible that there should exist in any machine a diversity of organs sufficient to enable it to act in all the occurrences of life, in the way in which our reason enables us to act.*[52]
> **Descartes**

Dualism makes a category mistake (Ryle)

My destructive purpose is to show that a family of radical category-mistakes is the source of the double-life theory. The representation of a person as a ghost mysteriously ensconced in a machine derives from this argument.[53]
Ryle

We have mentioned that Ryle believes that the problem of other minds only arises because of a confused dualist picture of the nature of mind and body which has bewitched our imaginations. This picture is pretty all pervasive, but he singles out Descartes as its main defender and calls it the 'dogma of the Ghost in the Machine'.[54] The main tenets of this dogma are familiar by now. The governing image is of humans leading a 'double-life': on the one hand we each possess a private 'inner' realm of our own conscious minds; on the other a publicly observable body which inhabits the 'outer' world of material objects. But the key claims we need to focus on here are that each of us can directly perceive only the bodies and behaviour of other human beings, which represents just one half of their dual existence. The other aspect, their inner 'ghost', is for ever hidden within the bodily 'machine', and for this reason we are condemned to make questionable inferences when trying to determine the nature of their mental states. While these claims about minds may seem self-evident, according to Ryle both betray a fundamental confusion. This confusion arises because we misconstrue how our ordinary talk about the mind works. So if we can get clear about what is really going on when we talk about our own and others' mental states we will come to see that there really was no problem of other minds at all.

anthology 2.12

The confusion into which the Cartesian philosopher has fallen is of a special kind that Ryle labels a 'category mistake'. In Ryle's words 'It represents the facts of mental life as if they belonged to one logical type or category, [...] when they actually belong to another.'[55] To help explain what he means by a category mistake Ryle gives some illustrations. One concerns a foreigner in England who watches a cricket match for the first time and who is taught to recognise who is responsible for the batting, the bowling, the wicket-keeping and so on, but then asks who is responsible for the team spirit. The point is that the team spirit is not another cricketing task executed by one of the players; rather it refers to the players' tendency to play well together. It is a way of talking about how the team performs.[56] So the foreigner's mistake is to misunderstand how the term 'team spirit' functions. For its function is not to refer to a specific operation accomplished in the game, but to how well all of them are accomplished. This involves a 'category mistake' because the foreigner has muddled one logical category (specific cricketing tasks) with another (the way the tasks are performed). Ryle points out that playing well is not doing two things, but doing one in a certain way. 'Certainly, exhibiting team-spirit is not the same thing as bowling or catching, but nor is it a third thing such that we can say that the bowler first bowls and *then* exhibits team-spirit.'[57]

The mind is not a 'thing'

Now, Ryle thinks the same sort of mistake is being made when we ask how we can be sure that others have minds. For this question only makes sense if we accept the Cartesian 'dual-life theory' according to which minds are a weird kind of thing: ghostly substances somehow hidden within the bodies of other people. But, he argues, the mind is not a kind of *thing* at all. For, according to Ryle, when we ascribe mental states to other people we aren't making reference to private mental events hidden from view within an arena called the 'mind'. Instead we are ultimately talking about the way in which they behave. If this is right, when we talk about the mental states of other people we must really be talking about what is publicly observable. And if that is right, then there is no problem about how we can have knowledge of other minds since we can directly observe them. So when I observe someone writhing on the floor and screaming, I don't need to infer that there is a hidden process going on within that cannot be directly known. Rather to say that the person is in pain is just a shorthand for saying that they exhibit these types of behaviour. Since this means there is no gap between the behavioural evidence and the existence of the pain, there is no longer any way for the sceptic to challenge my claim to know that others are in pain.

We might question the plausibility of this sort of account of other minds by asking how it could be that we might become so taken with a picture of other minds as private if really they were on display all along. Surely it is just obvious that I have privileged access to my own mental states through introspection and that, by contrast, others' mental states can never be directly observed. But, points out Ryle, if this were true we would be in a continual state of uncertainty, not just about the nature of others' mental lives, but about the very existence of their minds. The problem of other minds would, in other words, plague our everyday lives. Yet, in the ordinary course of things we have absolutely no problem ascribing mental states to others. I never doubt that someone writhing on the floor is in pain or that the person I'm talking to has thoughts. It is only once we start doing philosophy that doubts arise and this suggests it is the acceptance of the dualist picture which is the cause of our conceptual tangles. The everyday pre-theoretical ability to use mental-state terms in ways that everyone can understand strongly suggests that our language of the mind isn't about something unobservable.

Ryle offers a diagnosis of Descartes' error in Chapter 1 of *The Concept of Mind*.[58] Descartes' problem begins with his recognition that the complex intelligent behaviour of human beings seems inexplicable in mechanical terms. Recall that Descartes thought that the fact that human beings use language is itself sufficient evidence of the existence of other minds precisely because he thought it impossible for a purely physical mechanism to replicate such behaviour. But if human mentality is not something that could be replicated by a machine, then how are we to explain it? Descartes' solution is to suppose that there is a special non-physical, non-mechanical *thing* hidden within the body which produces this behaviour. In order for us to be able to perform these special activities, he thought that we must be doing something which is not observable, and so must be doing it in some invisible ghostly realm. In other words, when Descartes wondered what the mind could be, noting that it couldn't be seen or touched, didn't seem to exist in space, and didn't follow physical mechanical laws, the conclusion he drew is that it had to be a *very special kind of thing*: one that has none of the characteristics of normal (physical) things – no spatial dimensions, no capacity for being divided, not subject to physical laws, and so on. But the mistake here is that Descartes held on to the idea that the mind is a kind of *thing*. But, says Ryle, the mind is not a weird type of substance; it is not a substance at all. Rather it is just a way of talking about the capacities of human beings to perform a whole range of actions. When we talk of other minds 'we are not referring to occult episodes of which their overt acts and utterances are effects; we are referring to those overt acts and utterances themselves'.[60] Like 'team spirit', 'mind' must not be categorised as a type of thing, but a manner of doing.

By understanding just how our talk about the mind can be made sense of in terms of human behaviour we will be freed from the spell cast on our thinking by 'Descartes' Myth'.[61] Now, the precise way in which publicly observable behaviour relates to our talk of the mind is complex, and Ryle sets himself the task of unravelling this complexity in *The Concept of Mind* and, in so doing, of breaking the spell that dualism has over us. A more detailed discussion of the positive account that Ryle gives of the nature of our language of the mind will have to await our examination of philosophical behaviourism below.

Heidegger and 'being with others'

[Learn More]

The influential twentieth-century thinker Martin Heidegger (1889–1976) also argues that the appeal of the problem of other minds lies in a mistaken picture of how we acquire knowledge of other minds in the first place. Like Wittgenstein and Ryle, he thinks it is a mistake to suppose that we must infer the existence of their minds from others' behaviour. But, he argues, I don't need to discover the minds of others by making such an inference, because I am already aware of their consciousnesses *within* the structure of my own experience. A proper analysis of the lived experience reveals that it involves the recognition of other consciousnesses from the very beginning. We inhabit a world which was always intersubjective and so we cannot uncover the solipsistic starting point from which intersubjectivity would be derived. In other words, for Heidegger, Descartes is mistaken when he thinks he could be conscious of his self through the cogito argument. A self completely isolated from others is an illusion since our primary mode of experience is already what he calls 'being with others'. So the problem is not how to reach out to others, but to account for how we come to separate ourselves off from other minds in order to come to see ourselves as a distinct individuals.

If we do have an innate sense of 'being with others', a primordial sense of their consciousness, then this may well be something which is hardwired into our biology (although such empirical evidence is not something Heidegger explores). A social animal such as ourselves is arguably one which has an innate capacity for its sense of 'being with' members of its own species. Babies will imitate facial expressions, showing that there exist hardwired mechanisms whereby they can recognise the same action or expression performed by another. Such hardwiring allows for the development of our consciousness and our sense of self within a social context. Contemporary attachment theory in psychology also supports the idea that our sense of self and our ability to read and interact successfully with other minds is based on the nature of our relationships with our caregivers in our earliest years. Such empirical evidence also suggests that by the time we develop self-consciousness we are already enmeshed within an intersubjective world.

Sartre on other minds and self-consciousness

Similar conclusions have been reached by Jean-Paul Sartre (1905–80) in his analysis of self-consciousness. Under the influence of Heidegger, Sartre came to the view that I am *directly* aware of the existence of other minds when I encounter other people. This immediate awareness is not something inferred, but an integral part of my experience of being in the world. Consequently, the issue of whether I am justified in believing in other minds doesn't arise. I can be as sure of the existence of other minds as I am of the existence of any object of my awareness.

He argues that to be aware of one's self takes more than some isolated act of Cartesian introspection. We must encounter other consciousnesses before we become self-aware. Sartre draws our attention to the *phenomenology* of the experience of 'the other', the way it feels to me, to encourage us to recognise this primordial truth about ourselves. Without others I can go about my business with no sense of self at all. My conscious life is completely absorbed by what I am doing. It is directed away from myself into the world. We might imagine a Robinson Crusoe, who never met another soul from birth, never focusing attention inwards on himself. No conscious distinction would be drawn by such an individual between self and world. But as soon as I encounter someone else who is looking at me, for example, I become aware of myself as an object of their consciousness. And with this experience I become for the first time self-conscious. So self-consciousness actually presupposes awareness of other minds, rather than the other way round.

Reid on other minds

Thomas Reid (1710–96) tried to defeat scepticism about other minds in a related vein over two hundred years earlier. He argued that the problem only arises if we allow a certain sceptical approach to gain a foothold in our imaginations.[62] And this happens when we allow ourselves to ask the question of *how we know* of the reality of other minds. The mistake here is that it was never a matter of amassing evidence or developing an argument in the first place. We do not 'know' that others have minds in the sense of having compelling reasons in favour of this belief. For this would imply the possibility of doubt, and yet here there is none. Reid draws our attention to the way a baby when first brought into the world is immediately drawn into a relationship with its nurse as another consciousness. This is the starting point for human reality, and so not something that can or needs to be proved or justified. We don't learn the connection between facial expressions and others' emotions, for example; rather this recognition is instinctive, a consequence of the 'constitution of our natures'.[63]

2.2.3.2 Issues facing interactionist dualism

The idea that mind and body interact is an article of common sense. After all, if I decide to reach out for my cup of tea then (under normal circumstances) my arm will move and my hand will grasp the handle. Here a mental act of VOLITION (my willing my hand to grasp the cup) seems to have caused a physical action to occur in my body (my hand reaching for the cup). And this causal relationship also works in the other direction. If I sip my tea, the contact between the warm liquid and the inside of my mouth causes various tea-like sensations to appear in my consciousness. These sensations may in turn cause me to form various beliefs, such as that this is a nice cup of tea or that it needs another spoon of sugar. Here, physical changes in my body seem directly or indirectly to have caused mental events such as sensations and beliefs. And my beliefs and thinking in turn often lead to speech, such as asking my friend to pass the sugar.

So how does this interaction work? Descartes' dualism gives us one influential account which we need first to examine.

> *The mind isn't immediately affected by all parts of the body but only by the brain – or perhaps just by the small part of it which is said to contain the 'common sense'. [Descartes is referring to the pineal gland. The 'common sense' was a supposed faculty, postulated by Aristotle, whose role was to integrate the data from the five specialized senses.] The signals that reach the mind depend upon what state this part of the brain is in, irrespective of the condition of the other parts of the body.*[64]
> Descartes

You will recall that according to Descartes' *substance* dualism (see page 194ff), the non-physical mind is a distinct substance from the body but, in this life at least, they are linked together. Part of the relationship involves the kind of causal interaction outlined above: physical changes in the sense organs cause various sensory experiences in the mind. And, conversely, the desires and decisions of the mind cause the body to behave in purposeful ways. Descartes identified the brain as the organ most directly connected to the mind so that it is changes in the brain that cause sensations. Descartes suggested that body and mind communicate with each other via a small organ in the centre of the brain called the pineal gland. This is one of the brain's 'smallest parts' that Descartes conjectures in the quotation above is the seat of the 'common sense' – the point where all the sense experiences we enjoy come together in one unified consciousness. This 'common sense' is what enables me to be aware that my foot aches, that I am hungry and that I can see the pie shop, all within the one mind. From the pineal gland, information is communicated via the nervous system to and from all parts of the body by means of what he terms 'animal spirits', a kind of fine air or fluid. Although distinct substances, the mind and body are in an intimate union so that the mind feels itself projected throughout the body. I do not feel myself to be a distinct substance, but rather experience life as an embodied being. So, for example, when the animal spirits communicate information about the state of the body to my brain I experience the sensations of pain, thirst or cold as located in the body rather than in the mind. It is through these sensations that the mind is made aware of the needs of the body and it is via the sensations of colours, sounds, smells and so on, communicated via the sense organs, that my mind becomes aware of my physical surroundings.

The conceptual interaction problem

> *Given that the soul of a human being is only a thinking substance, how can it affect the bodily spirits, in order to bring about voluntary actions?*[65]
> Princess Elisabeth of Bohemia

Experimenting with ideas

Look around you and identify an object, a cup or book, say, which is out of reach. Now try to lift the object up into the air just by the power of thought and wiggle it around.
- How did you do? Did you manage it? If not, why do you think you failed?

Now focus on your own body and try to wiggle your ears.
- Can you do it?

Repeat the experiment with your hand or your foot.
- Can you wiggle them? Can you lift them into the air?

How did you do? Did you have similar success with all these objects? If not, why exactly is it easier to move some things by the power of thought than others?

One problem for Descartes' INTERACTIONISM is its apparent inability to explain how causal interaction between the mind and body is possible. For, let us recall, the mind, in Descartes' view, is unextended in space, it is immaterial and has no solidity or mass. And it makes no sense to ascribe physical properties (such as size or shape) to minds. By contrast, the body is extended, and it makes no sense to ascribe mental properties (such as thoughts or sensations) to bodies. But, it is plausible to suppose that for two things to causally interact they need to have properties in common. There must be some common medium in which transactions between one and the other can take place. We accept that we cannot move objects just by the power of thought, no matter how hard we try, and yet we are able to move our bodies and this power may appear as miraculous as if we were able to move the objects at a distance, since in both cases it is the immaterial and ghostly mind which is impacting on gross matter.

Princess Elisabeth of Bohemia in her correspondence with Descartes expresses the problem in terms of the inconceivability of substances interacting without there being some *contact* between them. Since the mind has no extended surface, it is unable to touch the body and so cannot causally interact with it.

anthology 2.13

We can summarise this objection to interactionism thus:

1 It is inconceivable for two things to causally interact, unless their surfaces come into contact with each.
2 The mind has no surface.
3 So, it is inconceivable for the mind to interact with the body.
4 If such interaction is inconceivable, it is impossible.
5 Therefore, mind–body interaction is impossible.

We can formulate the problem of interaction as a challenge to Descartes' claim to have a clear and distinct idea of the different natures of the mind and body, and so to substance dualism. For if causal interaction requires two substances to come into contact with their surfaces, and mind does interact with body, then mind must have a surface and must be extended. This suggests that the mind must have more in common with physical things than dualism allows; it might even be taken to show that the mind must be physical and therefore that substance dualism is false.

Another way of approaching the problem of interaction is to consider how a particular mind can be linked to a particular body. For since minds have no spatial characteristics, they can have no location in space. But, in this case, there would seem to be no particular *place* where the mind might come into contact with the body. So the idea of its connecting at the pineal gland is hard to make sense of. And although we may talk of the mind being 'inside' the body, this is only a metaphor since non-spatial minds can't really be anywhere. Yet without being located within the body it's hard to see how the mind could be connected to your physical being. Just how does your mind attach itself to your body as opposed to someone else's?

Note that this argument works by conceptual analysis alone. Elisabeth has simply reflected on our concept of causation, claimed that an essential element of this concept is the contact between surfaces in space, and so concluded that mental causation is not possible.

In his response to Elisabeth, Descartes argues that mind–body union is a basic notion and 'thus can be understood only through itself'.66 By this he means that we shouldn't try to make sense of it in terms of anything else. Elisabeth's mistake is to think of mind–body causation on the model of the way physical things causally interact. He writes: 'The principle cause of our errors lies in our commonplace attempts to use these notions to explain things that they aren't right for. For example, … when we try to conceive how the soul moves the body in terms of how a body moves a body.'67 For while it may be true (and Descartes believed that it was) that physical things can only causally affect each other through contact, it is not the case that we can make no sense of the idea of causation which doesn't involve such contact. After all, he points out, it makes sense to think of a physical object being caused to fall to Earth because of its weight. Here, weight impels the object downward, but we don't need to suppose the weight must come into contact with the object, like a hand pushing it down. In the same way, we are able clearly to conceive of mind–body interaction, claims Descartes, involving no surface-to-surface contact. So it may be that we need to rid ourselves of a naive view of the nature of causation which sees it in terms of the impact of two objects. Certainly there doesn't appear to be anything contradictory in the idea that two things could act upon each other at a distance, such as when the Earth's gravitational field holds the Moon in its orbit. (Note that Descartes doesn't actually think that weight causes the object to fall in the way described. The point is rather that we have a primitive notion of such causation, one which in fact should only be applied to the mind–body relation.)

*If the unlikeness of draughts and colds in the head does not prevent one from admitting a causal connexion between the two, why should the unlikeness of volitions and voluntary movements prevent one from holding that they are causally connected?*68
Broad

We could also question the assumption that for two things to interact they must have common properties or be similar in some way. C.D. Broad (1887–1971) writing in the 1920s makes the point well, arguing that the dissimilarity between mind and body doesn't warrant us claiming that they cannot be causally related and he uses the example of draughts and colds in the head which we are happy to regard as causally related and yet which are not at all alike.

*The mind can never possibly find the effect in the supposed cause by the most accurate scrutiny and examination. For the effect is totally different from the cause and can never be discovered in it.*69
Hume

We can elaborate on this defence of interactionism by following Hume in arguing that we cannot make any *a priori* judgements about what can or cannot be causally related. Causal relations, according to Hume, can only be discovered by empirical investigation. To show this, Hume points out that if we encounter an object for the first time we would not be able to work out by reasoning alone what its causal powers are: 'No object ever discovers, by the qualities which appear to the senses, either the cause which produced it, or the effects which will arise from it'.[70] So, if I were to encounter a loaf of bread for the first time, having never observed anything like it before, I would be unable to deduce how it was made or that it could nourish me. In order to know how bread is made, we need experience of the various complex processes from harvesting the wheat to baking the dough which bring it about, and to discover that it is nourishing I would have to experience myself or others actually eating it and note the effects. In other words, the idea of one event has no necessary relation to the idea of its effect and the relation between cause and effect is arbitrary or contingent.[71] But so long as experience provides us with repeated occasions where two events are connected, then we may infer that the two are causally related. Repeated experiences of gaining nourishment from eating bread persuade us that there is a natural connection between the two. So there can be nothing in principle to prevent us from supposing that mental events cause physical events; so long as we experience a constant conjunction between acts of will and actions, this is the only basis we can have of establishing a causal connection. Indeed, presumably it is by experience that we learn which parts of our body we can cause to move by acts of volition, that is, which we are able to move by *intending* or *willing* them to move. If you try to move your ears you may find you can or you may find you can't, but it doesn't seem to be something you could know was possible without making the experiment. In the same way we learn that we have the power to move our arms by experience of acts of will apparently doing just this – I intend my arm to move, and immediately it moves. So since the empirical evidence supports causal interaction, this is all we need and no *a priori* reasoning to the contrary can carry any weight.

> *An interaction whereby a nonphysical mental event causes some physical effects, such as a change in the behaviour of neurons, would violate the law of the conservation of mass-energy. So far, no such violations are seen in nervous systems.*[72]
> Patricia Churchland

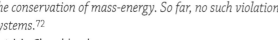

The empirical interaction problem

Causal closure of the physical and the law of the conservation of energy

If the *a priori* argument against mind–body interaction fails, what of empirical arguments? Well, it is often pointed out by critics of dualist interactionism that physical science tells us that everything that happens within the universe is caused to happen by something else within it. All physical occurrences, in other words, are to be explained by reference to some other physical occurrence, meaning that the physical universe is *causally closed*. Now, if it is true that objects are only affected by physical forces then our own bodies cannot act because of the intervention of some force beyond the physical such as the mind. In other words, if we accept the principle that we can give a 'complete' account of the causes of any event without appealing to anything non-physical, then bodily actions, since they are a part of the physical universe, must be explicable without reference to the non-physical and so there is no place for mental to physical causation.

We can give further support to this conclusion by appeal to a fundamental law of physics known as the principle of the conservation of energy. The principle states that within a closed system such as the whole universe, the overall amount of energy remains constant; it cannot be created or destroyed. It is because of this principle that perpetual motion machines are impossible – any mechanism in motion will lose some energy to friction and since no energy can be added to it, it will tend to run out of energy. To keep any mechanism moving we need to give it some injection of energy from outside, and this includes ourselves via food. However, if substance dualism is correct, then minds would add energy to the physical universe by acting on our bodies. Every time I choose to raise my arm or run for a bus, my mind exerts some force on my body to impel it this way or that and in so doing the net amount of energy in the physical world would go up, so breaking this law of physics. So if interactionist dualism is at odds with well-established physical laws about the conservation of energy then perhaps we need to reject it.

To see the point, imagine you are driving and you run out of petrol. How are you going to move the car forwards? If there is no force acting on the car, either gravity (because you are on the flat) or by pushing it, then it will not move. Simply sitting in the car and willing it to move will not work. It needs an injection of energy from within the physical universe. But now consider your own body. Suppose you are running a marathon and your body runs out of glycogen, the main fuel your body uses for aerobic exercise. This is known as hitting the wall and involves dizziness, confusion and an inability even to stand unaided. Without an intake of energy you are unlikely to be able to continue. But unlike cars our bodies are able to draw on another source of energy, our fat reserves, and so if these can be accessed, you may be able to continue for a while. However, once all possible sources of energy are depleted, the result is inevitable: total collapse. You will not be able to will your body forward unless there are some physical reserves of energy to deploy. But if interactionist dualism were true, we might expect marathon runners to be able to continue on will power alone, running, as it were, purely on the energy produced by the mind.

This objection can be framed as an argument for physicalism:

1. The physical universe is a closed system.
2. And in any closed system, energy must be conserved.
3. Mind and body causally interact.
4. But causation involves the transfer of energy.
5. Therefore, the mind must be physical.

This argument is empirical as it is based on physical laws that are established by investigation of how the world behaves. For this reason, it could be refuted if we could find empirical evidence of the mind's influence on the body. If we could detect an increase of energy within the nervous system as a result of an act of will, we would have reason to reject the claim that the physical universe is a closed system. However, neuroscience has not detected any such increase, and until such time as it does, we are rationally justified in continuing to accept this well established empirical law, and so reject dualism.

In defence of interaction

Interactionism could be defended by arguing that the overall amount of energy can remain constant since the effects of mind on body and of body on mind cancel each other out. Perhaps whenever I inject energy into my body by getting up to make a cup of tea, energy also escapes from it by some other wormhole, thus keeping the overall energy levels constant. However, to be convincing, such a solution would need some explanation as to why imports and exports of energy should exactly balance each other out. Otherwise, to suppose there is such a mysterious mechanism at play looks like an article of faith simply brought in to save interactionism, but with nothing else to recommend it. It appears, in other words, as an *ad hoc* manoeuvre to save interactionism.

Another strategy is to question the fourth step in the objection argument outlined above: that causation must involve a transfer of energy. Perhaps this is an overly restrictive idea of how causation must work and it may be that it is possible to interact with the physical without actually adding energy to it. On this picture, the mind wouldn't inject new energy into the body via the brain, but could 'steer' the body by redistributing the energy which already exists within the physical world. It would not be possible to move a body depleted of energy by will power alone on this model, but if there were some energy left in my body to use, it would be possible to choose whether to walk a few more steps or sit down and wait for assistance.

However, if the principle of the conservation of energy is properly understood, this redistribution idea seems less plausible. For the principle is saying that any change of trajectory can only be brought about by some expenditure of energy. When driving a car, the petrol is providing the energy for the forward motion, but in order to steer the car left or right, I also need to expend some energy, albeit comparatively little. In the same way, if the mind steers the body in different directions using the physical energy reserves the body contains to perform various actions, this steering process must at the least change the direction of movement of neurons in the brain, and this will take some energy, even if it is very little. So once again, it seems that mind–body interaction breaks this law of physics.

2.2.3.3 Epiphenomenalist dualism

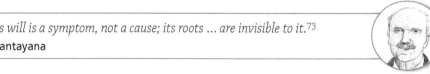

Conscious will is a symptom, not a cause; its roots ... are invisible to it.[73]
George Santayana

As we have seen, property dualists accept that the mind depends upon the brain. As a property of it, it is unsurprising that damage to the brain can affect your mind, or that alcohol consumption can affect your ability to do mental arithmetic, for example. Moreover, property dualism fits rather better with the theory of evolution than does substance dualism. Minds don't mysteriously appear fully formed at some arbitrary point in our evolutionary past, but emerge gradually over millions of years as the brain has become increasingly complex. Similarly your own mind wasn't transplanted whole into your body, transforming you from a mindless baby into a fully conscious person, but developed gradually, beginning in the womb and throughout your early life as your brain grew. However, if mental properties are irreducible, but at the same time physical causes alone are needed to explain behaviour, then we are led to the view that the mind is a product of the brain, but one which can have no causal influence on the body and its actions. In other words, if property dualists accept the causal closure of the physical, then mental states may be produced by physical brains, but they cannot have any reciprocal influence on bodies. This is the view known as epiphenomenalism, meaning that mental phenomena sit 'above' the brain but do not causally affect it.

T.H. Huxley (1825–95) was an early advocate of Darwin's theory of evolution and so of a naturalistic account of the nature of human beings which saw them as closely related to the rest of the animal kingdom. In his well-known paper 'On the Hypothesis that Animals are Automata' of 1874[74], Huxley develops a mechanistic account of the body and its actions, inspired by Descartes. Focusing first on animals, he defends Descartes' thesis that we can explain their behaviour in purely physical terms; that is to say, the actions of animals are determined completely by their complex physiologies, in particular their nervous systems, interacting with the environment. Animals, in other words, are in reality complex machines. Descartes had already observed that reflex actions show that we can react to certain stimuli without the intervention of the conscious mind or will. Huxley quotes Descartes' example of when someone 'moves his hand rapidly towards our eyes, as if he were going to strike us'[75] leading us to blink involuntarily even if we know he isn't actually going to hit us. This, according to Descartes, is explained by the nervous system and brain reacting automatically without the mind having to be consulted, and there is no reason to suppose the same sort of process isn't going on when a sheep receives the visual impression of a wolf and reacts by bolting. Further observations concerning how the body can continue to act despite consciousness being absent are explored, such as how victims of spinal injury who may have no feeling in their legs and feet will nonetheless react to being tickled by curling their toes. Experiments with frogs in which the spinal column has been severed but whose legs continue to react to stimuli are also used to argue that the nervous system can produce complex behaviours without the presence of conscious experience. Huxley also discusses the case of a brain-damaged soldier who would perform complex tasks such as singing, or loading a rifle, while appearing to be unconscious, as evidenced by his failure to react to loud noises, having pins stuck into him, or drinking vinegar. The soldier appeared to be acting on 'auto-pilot', so supporting the claim that complex behaviours don't require conscious experiences as their cause.

Now, despite all this evidence, Huxley doesn't follow Descartes in the claim that animals are not conscious. Automata they may be – they may act automatically and without the intervention of conscious experiences – but we nonetheless have good reason to suppose that they have experiences like us. One reason for this is that, with the benefit of evolutionary theory, we now know that we are related to all other animals and so it would be peculiar were we to be very different from them in respect of having conscious experiences correlated with certain types of physiological reactions. But we have no reason to suppose, argues Huxley, that these conscious experiences are involved in the causal process. So while a frog may feel discomfort when acetic acid is placed on its foot, the discomfort doesn't cause it to move its foot; this happens automatically.

> *The consciousness of brutes would appear to be related to the mechanism of their body simply as a collateral product of its working, and to be as completely without any power of modifying that working as the steam-whistle which accompanies the work of a locomotive engine is without influence upon its machinery. Their volition, if they have any, is an emotion indicative of physical changes, not a cause of such changes.*[76]
> Huxley

Finally he argues that we have no reason to suppose that humans are any different from other animals in this respect, so that mental states, such as our sensations, beliefs and desires are caused by the various activities of the brain, but they do not have any causal effects in turn on the physical world. This means that mental phenomena are merely incidental, and that the universal conviction that our actions are determined by our beliefs, desires and decisions is false. Our actions are completely causally determined by processes in the brain and body, and while these processes produce conscious experiences of sensations and volitions, these have no causal role to play in our behaviour. So volitions and actions are closely correlated. I have the urge to move my arm and my arm reaches for the cup of tea. But the causal process goes in one direction only. Neither my thirst nor the desire for tea cause me to reach for the cup. And the sensation of heat doesn't cause me to drop the cup. Both are automatic. Both are caused by unconscious physiological processes like reflex actions. We are, as Huxley puts it, 'conscious automata',[77] machines whose actions are physically determined and in whom conscious experiences are a mere by-product. 'Volition' concludes Huxley, 'is an emotion indicative of physical changes, not a cause of such changes'.[78]

Figure 2.12 Epiphenomenalism
Huxley likens conscious experiences to the whistle on a steam train, and the body and brain to the train itself. The steam that drives the whistle is produced by the engine which drives the train forward, but the whistle doesn't affect the forward motion, it is just a by-product and the train would move as well without it. The whistle, like consciousness, is a 'collateral product' or 'epiphenomenon', meaning it is produced by underlying processes but has no causal impact on those processes

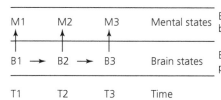

M1	M2	M3	Mental states	Each mental state is a by-product of a brain state
B1 →	B2 →	B3	Brain states	Each brain state is caused by previous physical cause
T1	T2	T3	Time	

Figure 2.13 The relation of mental states to brain states according to epiphenomenalism
If the body requires liquid, signals are sent to the brain and, after some complex neurological processing, these will lead me to reach out and take a sip from my cup of tea. Accompanying this physical process will be a sensation of thirst and a feeling of willing my arm to reach for the tea. But neither of these has any causal role to play in the process

Such a view avoids the Cartesian problem of accounting for how a non-material substance can intervene in the normal course of nature. This means that we may be able to produce an account of human behaviour exclusively in terms of physical mechanisms. In this sense, epiphenomenalism is able to respect the desire for a scientific explanation for human behaviour. As a form of property dualism it is also able to accommodate the dependence of conscious life on the brain and the apparent fact that consciousness emerges with the evolutionary development of the brain. It is also consistent with experience. Mental states are caused by changes in the brain and so accompany the impact of physical things on our bodies, as when, for example, damage to your foot causes pain.

Experimenting with ideas

Despite the advantages of epiphenomenalism outlined above, many philosophers have been very hostile to it, and you may also find it rather implausible. Reflect on the following questions and see if you can turn your answers into possible objections to epiphenomenalism.

- Do you have any good reasons for supposing that your volitions (your acts of will or intentions whereby you choose to do something) really cause your actions?
- Do you have any good reasons for supposing that your sense experiences cause behaviour, such as a pain causing you to flinch?
- What of conscious perception? Is there good reason to suppose that your visual awareness of a cup of tea is causally involved in you reaching for it?
- Consider other mental states such as beliefs. In what ways do they seem to be causally related to the physical world? Do you have good reasons to suppose they really are so related?

Issues facing epiphenomenalist dualism
The challenge posed by introspective self-knowledge

Our mental conditions are simply the symbols in consciousness of the changes which takes place automatically in the organism; and that, to take an extreme illustration, the feeling we call volition is not the cause of a voluntary act, but the symbol of that state of the brain which is the immediate cause of that act. We are conscious automata.[79]

Huxley

Perhaps the most significant objection to epiphenomenalism is that it seems to be an affront against common sense and against what appears to be revealed to us through INTROSPECTION. To start with, epiphenomenalism goes against the common sense opinion that our volition causes our actions. Surely, we may object, when I decide to reach out for a cup of tea, the conscious decision must be what causes me to reach out. To deny this seems to fly in the face of everyday experience. Moreover, introspection seems to show that different mental states are causally related to each other. For example, the smell of melted butter on toast may transport my mind back to reminiscences of my grandmother's kitchen. The belief that it is raining and the desire to stay dry cause me to deliberate over where I might find an umbrella. So our introspective awareness of our minds strongly suggests that they represent a stream of causally linked events.

Huxley is unconcerned about this consequence of the theory and reminds us that the causal closure of the physical requires that we explain all actions in terms of physical causes and so the idea of mental states being causally involved must be given up. And while we may think we have conscious control over our actions there is actually nothing in experience that can establish that we do – after all, if volitions are indeed a 'collateral product' and epiphenomenalism is right, our experience would be no different than if they were causally involved. For all experience reveals is that volitions tend to be conjoined with certain actions, and this is consistent both with them being the cause and with them being a side effect.

Some have seen support for the idea that the sense of volition is a side effect of action in the experiments of Benjamin Libet.[80] Libet (1915–2007) asked subjects to watch a clock for a period of time and at a point of their choosing to perform a voluntary action such as raising their hand. They were also asked to identify the time when they became conscious of the urge or intention to raise their hand. While they performed this task, Libet monitored their brain activity and found that he could identify the beginnings of the neural process that led to the voluntary action occurring *before* the subjects identified becoming aware of deciding to act. The brain, it appears, is already preparing to perform an action before the person is conscious of any volition. This suggests that at least some conscious decisions are not the initiating causes of actions and therefore that – at least in some cases – it is an illusion to suppose that our feelings of volition cause actions. This at least shows that our common sense assumption that experience demonstrates that decisions or intentions cause our actions can be mistaken and therefore that it is possible that this is the case for all our actions.

Nonetheless, there remains a difficulty with squaring epiphenomenalism with the evidence of introspection. For an uncomfortable consequence of epiphenomenalism is that it appears to be incompatible with being able to form beliefs about, or meaningfully to talk about, our own mental states. For if mental states cannot cause anything physical then they cannot cause me to talk about them. So when I say 'I am in pain' this cannot have been caused by my introspective awareness of the mental state of pain, for the pain causes nothing. But if the pain doesn't cause me to say that I'm in pain, what am I talking about when making a complaint about a headache? Surely, the meaning of the term 'headache' must come from the experience itself, and if it doesn't, then the term would appear to have no meaning. Similarly, the possibility of having knowledge of my own mind requires that mental states are causally related to these beliefs. If the introspective awareness of my headache is unconnected with the belief that I have a headache, then the belief seems unjustified. If epiphenomenalism were true, then we wouldn't be able even to talk about our mental states, since to do so, those mental states would have to be causally connected to our utterances about them. So the very act of talking or writing about mental states such as intentions, and qualia, and then denying that they have a causal role to play in human behaviour, is self-refuting. For if qualia and intentions don't affect the physical, then they cannot have anything to do with the appearance of these words on the page.

In response, the epiphenomenalist may argue that the brain could evolve a capacity to employ sensation words without these having any causal connection with sensations themselves. Zombies, after all, may be imagined who can speak our language. All that's needed is that they be caused to speak of certain colours when in the presence of certain objects. The zombie's eyes pick up on certain wavelengths of light and its unconscious brain has been trained to connect the subsequent neural activity with certain vocalisations. And the same process may be going on in us. Our qualia words need not get their meaning from our experience of qualia. All that's needed is for these words to be causally connected to the neural correlates of qualia.

The challenge posed by the phenomenology of mental life

Introspection suggests sensations cause our actions

But what of our reactions to the way sensations feel within the mind, to the phenomenology of qualia? Surely, we may be inclined to say, it is the pain I feel when I touch something hot which causes me to withdraw my hand. And surely the intrinsic horribleness of pain must have something to do with why we make efforts to avoid it. After all, it seems that when I hit my thumb with a hammer, it is the pain that causes me to scream out, and if, for some reason, it doesn't hurt, I would not scream. Moreover, if it never hurt when I hit my thumb, I would doubtless take far less care to avoid doing so when hammering nails. These observations seem such obvious articles of common sense as to render the epiphenomenalist position absurd.

However, once again we can point out that pains may occur whenever I exhibit pain behaviour without this proving that they must be the cause of it. The two may be distinct effects of another underlying cause, namely the activation of the brain's pain centres. In Anthology extract 2.14 from Jackson's 'Epiphenomenal Qualia', he likens the situation to watching a punch fly in a cowboy film. The appearance is clearly one of the punch causing the person punched to collapse. But we know in this case that this appearance is an illusion. The conjunction of the two events is produced by the film projector and there is no direct causal link between one frame and the next. So, once again, we cannot conclude from the fact that two events are regularly conjoined that there is a direct causal link. There may be a third factor causing both. In the case of pain and pain behaviour, the third factor is the brain, which, like the projector, causes the pain and the pain behaviour to occur together.

Reflex actions also show that the conscious experience is not always necessary for a reaction to occur. It can happen that you touch a hot stove and react by withdrawing your hand before any pain is felt. This at least shows that pain doesn't have to be present for someone to react to damage to the body and so that it is possible that the pain is merely epiphenomenal in ordinary situations too.

Introspection suggests the will causes our actions

But epiphenomenalism also seems to be in conflict with another central aspect of the phenomenology of everyday experience, namely the sense that our actions are free. When I deliberate over whether to go to bed early with a book, or go out to the cinema, I seem to be exercising my free will. If I choose to go out, this decision was reached freely, meaning that I was not forced to go out and I could have chosen to stay in. However, if my actions are determined exclusively by physical processes, and the intention or decision is causally impotent, then it seems I have no choice over my actions. If human actions are determined by physical laws, then the choices I make in any given instant are the result of these laws, meaning that I could not have chosen otherwise than I did. And yet if I could not have chosen otherwise, then it seems I am not free.

Epiphenomenalists may again be unconcerned by this consequence. Free will and the feeling we have that we could have chosen otherwise may be another illusion. This illusion may be the consequence of not having access in our consciousness to the workings of our brains. The human brain is, after all, one of the most complex objects in the known universe: it is said that there are more potential connections between the 100 billion or so neurons in the brain, than there are atoms in the entire universe. And at the neurological level, decision-making must be a very complex process. The urges we are aware of may reflect some of the brain processes going on, but the true complexity is clearly beyond our conscious reach. Since we are in the dark about the processes underlying our decisions, it may appear to us that we are making the decision freely. However, being unaware of the causes of an action is not the same as being aware that there is no determining cause. Our mistake may be to suppose that because we cannot observe how an action comes about that it must have come about by some mysterious indeterminate cause.

However, the denial that our decisions are free faces another difficulty. For freedom of the will seems to be critical to our understanding of moral responsibility. For example, if, for whatever reason, I decide to murder Jones, then we would normally suppose that my action was not inevitable. This is because I could have chosen not to do it. And it is precisely because I did choose to, having freely weighed up the options, that I can be held responsible and punished for my actions. Let's suppose that I argue in court that I didn't intend to kill him; that the gun went off in my hand while I was cleaning it. This would represent a legitimate defence against the murder charge. In this case, it was a mechanism outside of my control which caused his death, not me. Murder must involve a guilty intention.

But if epiphenomenalism is true, then the intention to kill Jones is not what made me kill him; and if my decision to pull the trigger has no causal role to play in my pulling the trigger, then it seems that I am not responsible for his death. Indeed, I could legitimately defend myself in court by saying, as I did with the gun above, that it wasn't me that did it, but my brain. Could I not reasonably claim that I could have done nothing about it, that the action was caused by processes beyond my conscious control?

This is a hard conclusion to draw. The implications for the criminal justice system would be devastating. So, rather than accept this consequence, it may be urged, we should reject epiphenomenalism.

Proponents of this line of argument may defend interactionist dualism as the only theory which can make sense of the lived experience of free will and our common sense conviction that people are responsible for their actions. Because the mind is non-physical, it is not bound by physical laws and so it is possible to locate the will within it. After all, if you allow your mind to wander it doesn't appear to be bound by any laws. You can imagine or think what you please, suggesting that the mind is by its nature free and unbounded. And when it intervenes in the physical world through acts of will, according to the dualist, it changes the course of nature, meaning that our actions are not determined by causal laws.

However, even if the mind escapes from physical causation this may not provide the interactionist with a full explanation of free will. For suppose I am deliberating over whether to kill Jones. I may weigh up the various slights I have suffered at this hand over the years against my concerns about being caught and spending a lifetime in gaol. And let's suppose I decide to go ahead with my evil plan. Wasn't the decision necessitated by the various considerations I weighed up? In other words, were we able to rewind time and replay the process of deliberation, is there any reason to suppose I would choose anything different? After all, my mind would have exactly the same set of considerations to weigh up, and if it was tipped one way the last time, then surely it would tip the same way every time. If my choices are done for reasons, and the reasons are the same, the choice would be the same. This suggests that the idea that an immaterial mind could act in different ways in the same circumstances is not true and therefore that our actions are determined after all.

But let's suppose it could have acted differently. Would this actually involve my being free? Arguably not, for if my decision not to kill Jones is based on exactly the same reasons as my decision to kill him, then the decision appears to be completely random. But if it is random, a matter of pure chance, then it doesn't seem as though I am responsible for it either. It would be as though the mind made its choices based on the throw of a die. This might mean I could have done otherwise, but it doesn't seem to mean that I chose to do the action freely. So it may be that the interactionist's claim that dualism is needed to make sense of free will fails.

Must we then accept that our common sense notion that our actions are free and the associated concepts of moral responsibility are fundamentally confused? Not necessarily. What is needed, perhaps, is a better analysis of what we are after when we require that human actions be free. We've seen that we don't mean that they are random. And many philosophers have argued that a proper analysis of free actions will show that they are indeed causally determined, but what makes them free is the manner in which they are determined. Huxley was well aware of the free will objection to epiphenomenalism but argued that it is quite possible to allow that our brains determine all our decisions and yet, at the same time, to consider ourselves free. Huxley, in other words, is a COMPATIBILIST about free will. This means that he believes that actions can be free in the sense that matters for moral responsibility, *and* that they can be determined by physical processes. In this, his view has affinities with Hume's analysis of free will where he argues that an action cannot be completely random if it is to be considered free. Rather what makes it free is that it is appropriately caused. So long as the action is in accordance with your motivations and desires, then it is a free action. In Huxley's hands, my desires may not cause my actions, but so long as the action I perform is one which fulfils the desire, then it can be considered free. 'An agent', he writes, 'is free when there is nothing to prevent him from doing that which he desires to do'.[81]

So the feeling of acting freely – in accordance with our intentions and desires – is distinguishable from being coerced. If, holding a gun to Jones, I order him to hand over his cash, then Jones may rightly say that giving up his money was not a free act. Conversely, if I desire to kill Jones, and there is nothing that prevents me from performing this action, then the action is free. But if an action occurs which is not in accordance with my intentions, then it is not free. So we can distinguish free actions from constrained ones in terms of whether they are accompanied by the epiphenomenal intention or not. This means that free and constrained actions are both equally determined by physical causes. Neither could have happened otherwise than as they did. But it doesn't follow, according to Huxley, that we cannot identify free actions and so attribute moral praise and blame. A consequence of this revision of our concept of free will may well be that we cannot justify punishing people as retribution for the crimes they couldn't help committing. But we may still be able to justify punishment as a way of reforming their behaviour and possibly as a deterrent.

The challenge posed by natural selection/evolution

If conscious experiences have no causal role to play in our behaviour, then we may find ourselves puzzled about why we have them at all. The universe and all human behaviour would, it seems, be exactly the same as it is now if there were no mental phenomena at all. In other words, a zombie world would be possible. But if a zombie world is possible, what explains the fact that brains in this world happen to produce minds which are completely causally redundant? This concern can be given additional force if we consider human evolution. If we accept that the process of evolution is driven by natural selection then we are committed to the idea that evolved traits must benefit the species in some way. In other words, evolved characteristics should help us to survive and pass on our genes. But, if mental states have no causal role to play, then they cannot have any survival value and, therefore, we would expect them not to have evolved. If we can operate successfully without minds, why would evolution have favoured beings with them?

Jackson considers this objection and rejects it. His argument begins by drawing an analogy with a polar bear's thick coat, which we can say with some confidence evolved to enable the bear to survive in cold conditions. However, the polar bear's coat is also very heavy, and this heaviness is not conducive to the bear's survival. But the fact that a heavy coat is not a survival advantage is not inconsistent with evolutionary theory. This is because evolving a heavy coat is an inevitable by-product of evolving a warm coat. And so long as the benefits of a warm coat outweigh the drawbacks of a heavy one, it will still be an advantage to have one. In the same way, it could be that mental states are a by-product of the complex brain process which our ancestors evolved in order to help them to survive. The abilities to identify ripe fruit may inevitably produce the qualia of red as a collateral product, for reasons we don't understand. Pain may be the epiphenomenal product of a nervous system which guides us to avoid damage to the body. If so, mental states could have evolved even though they have no causal role to play in our behaviour.

anthology 2.15

The 'other minds' objection

We have already examined the problem of other minds, but it is often felt that epiphenomenalism has a particular difficulty in answering it. The standard answers, the argument from analogy and the best hypothesis argument, begin by pointing out that we can directly observe other people's behaviour and that we must therefore infer that they have conscious experiences which we cannot directly observe, based on their behaviour. So, for example, if someone steps on a nail and hops around the room holding their foot and screaming, I use this behaviour to infer that they are in pain. The fact that animals behave in similar ways to us is presumably one important reason why we suppose they have conscious experiences like us, while the fact that plants and stones do not is the reason we tend not to ascribe mentality to them. However, if, as epiphenomenalism asserts, someone's behaviour is not the product of their conscious mental states, then on what basis can I make the inference from their behaviour to their mental state? If hopping around the room screaming is not caused by the person's pain, then surely the inference that the person is in pain is not justified.

Jackson's response is to point out that we may infer a correlation between behaviour and mental state even though there may be no direct causal link. I know in my case that there is an association between certain mental states and certain behaviours, and so there is an indirect causal inference that can be made. I know in my case that stepping on nails causes pain, and hopping and screaming behaviour. So, I can infer from the behaviour of others back to its cause; the nail in the foot is the likely cause, not just of the pain-behaviour, but also of the experience of pain. As Jackson has it:

> [T]he epiphenomenalist allows that qualia are effects of what goes on in the brain. Qualia cause nothing physical but are caused by something physical. Hence the epiphenomenalist can argue from the behaviour of others to the qualia of others by arguing from the behaviour of others back to its causes in the brains of others and out again to their qualia.[82]
> Jackson

Summary: Dualist theories

The mind strikes us as very different from other phenomena. Dualists have noted that it appears not simply *unlike* physical things, but often completely *contrasting*. Rather than having a particular size and shape, it doesn't even seem to make sense to think of it as being extended in space. Rather than being a part of the common world of publicly observable objects, each mind must remain the concealed preserve of its owner. Rather than following the strict laws science tells us the physical universe must obey, from the planets in the heavens to the mundane objects of everyday experience, it seems to be able freely to follow its own train of thought, create original ideas and solve completely unfamiliar problems. The general intelligence of human beings and their ability to use language seem possible only through genuine conscious understanding, the kind of understanding which appears beyond any purely physical device.

And yet, despite all these oddities, it is in many ways the central phenomenon of our condition, the starting point for our sense of self and of our place in the world, and so one that cries out for some explanation. One way of trying to explain some phenomenon is to reduce it to something else of which we have a better grasp. The physicalists hope this can be done for consciousness by explaining it in terms of the material world and its operations. But dualists maintain that consciousness must for ever escape such reduction. Descartes insists that the mind is so unlike the physical that we are forced to posit the existence of an alternative substance to account for it. Property dualists too figure that there necessarily exists an explanatory gap between a complete understanding of the physical and an account of mental phenomena. But to many the dualist approach looks like an admission of defeat. As our scientific understanding of the universe improves, we have been able to account for a greater and greater array of phenomena in terms of the physical. Many contemporary philosophers, therefore, hold out the hope that we can also provide an account of the phenomenon of consciousness which need not make reference to anything beyond the physical universe. This is the ambition of physicalism which is the approach to our topic to which we now must turn.

2.3 Physicalist theories

Having examined various types of dualist theory it is time to turn our attention to physicalism. Physicalist theories generally take their cue from the idea that everything in the universe must ultimately be physical and so a proper explanation of consciousness will have to show how it can arise within this purely physical universe. So conscious mental states and processes cannot take place within non-physical substance, and nor can they be a set of non-physical properties. For all substances and properties are, in the final analysis, physical. The first physicalist theory which we will examine is known as philosophical behaviourism.

2.3.1 Philosophical behaviourism

The distinction between a conscious man and an unconscious machine resolves itself into a distinction between different types of perceptible behaviour … When I assert that an object is conscious, I am asserting no more than that it would, in response to any conceivable test, exhibit the empirical manifestations of consciousness. I am not making a metaphysical postulate concerning the occurrence of events which I could not, even in principle, observe.[1]
A.J. Ayer

In our discussion of the problem of other minds above we introduced Ryle's view that there is nothing beyond the behaviour of others the existence of which needs to be inferred (see pages 242–4). The solution is that what you directly observe, namely others' bodies and their behaviour, is all there is. A key consideration in favour of this approach concerns the strangeness of the dualist claim that minds are ghostly substances which are for ever hidden 'within' other people's bodies. Many philosophers have wondered whether we can make good sense of such a claim. The problem is that it implies that there can be no empirical test to establish the existence of minds. But if something cannot be detected, not by any conceivable test, then, arguably, it is not something we can meaningfully regard as real.

So philosophical behaviourism[2] claims that minds are just what people say and do. All statements concerning mental states or processes are not really, as dualists claim, concerned with a private world which each of us is directly aware of through introspection. Rather, talk about minds is completely *reducible* without remainder to talk about people's *behaviour*. This theory is often termed 'analytical' behaviourism, because *analysis* of the meanings of the language of mind will reveal that it all boils down in the end to statements about behaviour. This is termed an 'ANALYTIC REDUCTION', meaning that statements about minds mean the same as statements about behaviour in the same way that 'mother' means the same as 'female parent'. What this means is that statements about emotions, sensations, beliefs and desires are not about hidden processes going on 'inside' people, but are rather a shorthand way of talking about publicly observable actual and potential patterns of behaviour; so, they are concerned with what we can all directly see. If this is right, then there is no longer a problem of whether belief in the existence of other minds is justified. If you can observe what another person says and does, since saying and doing *is* mind, you are amply warranted in believing that the person is minded.

Arguments for philosophical behaviourism

The motivation for such a view is firstly that, as a matter of fact, as the dualist admits, we do only have access to the behaviour of others, and consequently that that behaviour must be the basis for all our language about other people. Thinkers such as Ayer, whose verificationist theory of meaning we examined when looking at religious language, consider that meaningful propositions must be to do with what can enter into our experience, and so reject as confused the idea that other minds could be isolated from any possibility of detection. Talk of things the existence of which cannot be verified is meaningless. It is the failure to recognise this that allows dualists to become embroiled in the pseudo-problem of other minds. Behaviourism, by equating mind with what is observable, eliminates the problem.

Secondly, the behaviourist position overcomes the problem of interaction that, as we have seen, plagues all forms of dualism. For if the mind is not a distinct SUBSTANCE or PROPERTY mysteriously linked to the body, then there is no causal interaction to account for.

Thirdly, if words acquire their meaning from the public context in which they are used, then there must be rules governing their use. This means it must be possible to determine whether they are being used correctly by reference to what is publicly observable. But if mental-state terms get their meaning by reference to private experiences within each of our minds, it would be impossible to tell whether the words were being used correctly or not. Communication with others about our minds would not just be subject to occasional misunderstanding, it would be literally impossible to talk about our own or others' mental states (see Wittgenstein on the argument from analogy, page 236ff.). So, given that we can talk about minds, and generally have little difficulty ascribing mental states to people, we must be talking about what is publicly observable, namely behaviour.

Hard behaviourism

All psychological statements which are meaningful, that is to say, which are in principle verifiable, are translatable into statements which do not involve psychological concepts, but only the concepts of physics. The statements of psychology are consequently physicalistic statements. Psychology is an integral part of physics.[3]
Hempel

There are different versions of behaviourism, often known as 'hard' and 'soft'. We will begin by focusing on the so-called 'hard' behaviourism of Carl Hempel (1905–97).

Hempel was a member of the Vienna Circle, a group of philosophers active in the 1920s and 1930s in the promotion of LOGICAL POSITIVISM. Logical positivism is a form of empiricism which insists that meaningful propositions must have empirical content and so make positive claims about our experience. So Hempel, like Ayer, adhered to the verificationist account of meaning, according to which all meaningful propositions are either ANALYTIC and so trivial or they must be provable by reference to observation statements. Since other minds cannot be observed, talk about them is either meaningless or reducible to what can be observed. Ultimately, for Hempel, this means that if we are to talk meaningfully about human beings' minds, we have to be able to show just how our claims about them can be reduced to behavioural descriptions. Hempel saw this approach as allowing for a properly scientific approach to psychology, one that would eschew reference to supposedly private mental states which are not directly available to objective empirical investigation such as, to quote Hempel, '"feeling", "lived experience", "idea", "will", "intention", "goal", "disposition", "repression"'. Because such terms cannot be rendered in terms of behaviour, they are to be 'proscribed as non-scientific'.[4] And because bodily behaviour is publicly observable it is ultimately this, and this alone, which we must use in our efforts to understand human mentality. So his project was to replace the language of mental states with descriptions in terms of physical movements which could ultimately be rendered in the language of physics.

So how exactly would such a translation from the language of mind to that of behaviour work? An initial example may be useful here so that we can get the idea. Suppose your friend Dolores has trodden on a nail. She is swearing at the top of her lungs and jumping around on one leg, making efforts to remove the nail from the sole of her foot. According to Hempel, this observable behaviour must constitute what it means to say that she is in pain. The pain is not a private experience causing Dolores' behaviour, it just is the behaviour. And what it means to say 'Dolores is in pain' is established by how the statement can be verified. To assert that someone is in pain is the same as to assert that certain 'test sentences' about her behaviour, can be empirically established – that she is swearing, jumping, removing the nail and so forth. Hempel gives his own example, the statement 'Paul has a toothache' and he asks:

> *What is the specific content of this statement, that is to say, what are the circumstances in which it would be verified? It will be sufficient to indicate some test sentences which describe these circumstances.*
>
> a *Paul weeps and makes gestures of such and such kinds.*
>
> b *At the question 'What is the matter?' Paul utters the words 'I have a toothache.'*
>
> c *Closer examination reveals a decayed tooth with exposed pulp.*
>
> d *Paul's blood pressure, digestive processes, the speed of his reactions, show such and such changes.*
>
> e *Such and such processes occur in Paul's central nervous system.*
>
> *This list could be expanded considerably, but it is already sufficient to bring out the fundamental and essential point, namely that all the circumstances which verify this psychological statement are expressed by physical test sentences.*[5]

Experimenting with ideas

Before we examine some of the objections that have been levelled against Hempel's hard behaviourism, take a moment to reflect on how persuasive you find his claims.

1 Using the examples of Dolores and Paul above, can you think of any problems with reducing talk of their pain to purely physical descriptions of their behaviour?
2 Then try translating these statements about other minds into behavioural language.
   a) Rowena is hungry.
   b) Eli has an itch on his knee.
   c) Candice loves football.
   d) Beatrice is happy.
   e) Solomon has an inferiority complex.
   f) Konstantin day-dreams of being rich.

How did you do, making your behavioural translations? One test of their success is whether you were able completely to eliminate all reference to mental states. For if the reduction is going to work, we must translate into the language of what is observable without making any reference, implicit or otherwise, to minds. Mental states need to be completely analysed away since otherwise the analysis would be circular – it would be reintroducing the mind instead of making reference exclusively to behaviour. So have another look at your translations. Do they refer only to bodily movements?

Issues facing philosophical behaviourism

Issue with defining mental states adequately: circularity and multiple realisability

One important issue with Hempel's version of behaviourism is that in order to complete his reduction to the language of behaviour, he cannot be satisfied with expressions like 'Rowena orders some food', 'Eli scratches his knee' or 'Candice kicks a ball'. This is because such expressions make implicit reference to human agency, that is, to the notion that the person acted deliberately, with a specific intention, or with some goal in mind. In other words, to say that someone kicked a ball involves the idea that this bodily movement wasn't just a reflex, it was performed wittingly. But, to say that someone acted with intent is to make implicit reference to a mental state, the intention to produce that action and not some other action. So in order to completely replace the language of mind, it seems we would need to translate such expressions into those of pure bodily movements. Thus, 'Candice kicked a ball' would need to be rendered as something like 'Candice's foot lifted from the ground, the knee flexed and her leg swung forward causing the foot to impact with a ball.' In this way, all reference to supposedly hidden mental-state terms can be eliminated and we have a scientifically respectable and verifiable description of what has happened.

However, a problem is that there doesn't appear to be a way of translating particular types of action defined partly in terms of mental states, into particular types of bodily movement. This is because the same bodily movement may, on different occasions, manifest itself in any number of different actions. For example, impacting your foot on a ball may be an attempt to score a goal, returning the ball to its owner, a gesture of contempt for a refereeing decision, a demonstration of how to kick a ball, testing to see if the ball is pumped up, tripping over a ball, squashing a mosquito that's alighted on the ball, trying to relieve an itch on your toe, and so on.

▶ **ACTIVITY**

Below are five bodily movements. (Note that arguably some still make some implicit reference to human agency, but they will do as shorthand versions of pure bodily movements.) Examine them and list how many different actions each could be.

1. Your knees bend and your bottom rests on a rock.
2. You raise a finger in the air.
3. Your hand grips a glass and lifts it from a table.
4. Your grip loosens on a pen so that it falls to the floor.
5. Air blows out of your mouth.

Hopefully you have seen from the activity on the left that a given bodily movement can represent different actions. But this presents a problem for philosophical behaviourism since in order to reduce actions to bodily movements, it would need to be able to identify some differences in the bodily movements that would account for them being different actions. Otherwise the reduction cannot adequately account for the range of mental states we attribute to people.

At the same time, the same action may be manifested by very different bodily movements. The action of greeting someone may be achieved by raising a hand, uttering certain words, punching the air, kicking a ball to them, raising your eyebrows and so on, so that, again, no one-to-one correspondence seems to obtain between actions and bodily movements. The fact that the same action may be manifested in a great variety of bodily movements may be expressed by saying the action is 'MULTIPLY REALISABLE' in behaviour. And if actions are multiply realisable, it means it will be impossible to smoothly translate particular actions into purely behavioural descriptions.

It also seems clear that being in a particular mental state need not always lead to a specific type of action. Suppose I am feeling thirsty. This might lead me to exclaim 'I'm thirsty!', or (if I am in a library for example), I might keep quiet. I might go to a cafe for a cup of tea, a pub for a beer, or home for a glass of water. Or I might do none of these and wait for the feeling to go away on its own. All of these and an infinite number of others are possible behaviours that the mental state could be associated with so that a full analysis of it couldn't be completed. When it comes to my holding certain abstract beliefs, such as that philosophy is hard or that Britain should not leave the European Union, the range of ways such mental states might manifest themselves is bewildering. But if the analysis cannot be completed, not even in principle, then the project of reducing mental states to pure behaviour must fail.

The failure to complete the reduction occurs not just because it would be infinitely long, but also because it necessarily would reintroduce agency and mental-state terminology into it. Consider that a mental state, such as a desire to drink beer, would only lead one to drink a beer if you didn't also have the belief that you had to drive later or that the beer was poisoned or that this pub doesn't keep its beer properly, and so forth. But if our analysis of 'desires a beer' needs to take account of this, then it needs to translate these mental states into behavioural language as well. But the attempt to analyse 'believes she must drive later' or 'believes the beer is poisoned' in terms of its behavioural manifestations will *in turn* have to reintroduce mental-state terminology. This means that the reduction cannot be completed without circularity; that is, without reintroducing at each level of the analysis, precisely what the analysis is supposed to be reducing: the mind.

Experimenting with ideas

Imagine watching a game of football with a Martian. The Martian is interested to know what is going on, but, because Martians know nothing of minds, doesn't understand mental-state terms or references to the intentions of human agents. Can the game be reduced to a purely physical explanation, one that refers only to the laws of motion and attraction of physical objects such as balls, and human bodies? Even if a complete description of the game could be given, would the Martian understand what was going on?

This suggests that the reduction to purely physical descriptions which make no mention of human agency is not going to work and that the language by which we describe human behaviour necessarily involves reference to actions.

> *The further objection will perhaps be raised that men can feign. Thus, though a criminal at the bar may show physical symptoms of mental disorder, one would nevertheless be justified in wondering whether his mental confusion was 'real' or only simulated.*[6]
> Hempel

Another obvious difficulty, which you may well have already considered when doing the activity on hard behaviourism on page 265, is that observable pieces of behaviour are not sufficient to determine someone's mental state. They could be pretending. In such a case it seems a person could exhibit pain behaviour, for example, without being in pain. Hempel considers this objection in the Anthology reading 'The logical analysis of psychology'. We wouldn't simply accept the behavioural evidence of someone on trial if they acted as though they were mad, since we know they might feign mental illness to avoid criminal charges. This suggests that actual behaviour cannot be sufficient for the ascription of mental states to people and the analysis will need to be a little more sophisticated.

anthology 2.16

Another example might be the analysis of a desire. To say that Myrtle wants a beer need not be reducible to any actual piece of behaviour. For it may be the case that Myrtle has a strong desire to drink a warming pint of her favourite stout, but that she does nothing to satisfy her desire. We can imagine her spending a few hours in the pub with friends, harbouring this desire, but that she repeatedly turns down each offer of a drink. Because she shows no overt signs of wanting a drink, can we safely conclude that she has no such desire? The answer is surely not – she may be turning down the drinks because she has to drive. So the fact that her behaviour gives no immediate indication of a desire doesn't warrant us in concluding that she doesn't have it. And this shows that any simplistic reduction of mental states to behaviour is not going to work.

Figure 2.16 Myrtle sits in the pub for hours, nursing one glass of orange juice. She turns down several offers of a pint. So her behaviour gives no indication of any desire for a stout. Despite this, there is nothing she would enjoy more than a pint of Winter Wobbler, and it is only because she knows she must drive that she chooses not to satisfy her desire. So how can her mental states be reduced to her behaviour?

Hempel's response is to say that while there may be no directly observable basis for telling whether someone is feigning, a 'more penetrating examination – which should in principle take into account events occurring in the central nervous system – would give a decisive answer; and this answer would in turn clearly rest on a physicalistic basis'[7]. So if we examine the criminal's nervous system we should be able to tell that he is merely feigning the mental illness. In the same way we should be able to examine Myrtle more closely, and so reveal that she is suffering from the physiological effects of alcohol withdrawal.

But what if we push the objection further and insist that it remains conceivable that someone could fail to display the overt behaviour and the physiological 'symptoms' of a mental state while nonetheless being in it? After all, it certainly seems that we can conceive of Hempel's criminal being a 'perfect actor' who can also simulate the physiological condition of someone with a mental disorder. Can a person show all the outward signs of having a particular mental state, while not actually having it?

Hempel argues that this is not, in fact, a coherent idea. If literally all the possible empirically observable signs of mental illness are on display, then we would have no basis for supposing he wasn't really mentally ill. The point of contention here hangs on whether we think it is conceivable for someone to show all the symptoms but not actually have the condition, as it were; whether we can draw a conceptual distinction between the full set of overt physical signs and mental state, and this is an issue we will pick up again below when discussing Putnam's super-spartans example (page 272). But first let us turn to how Ryle tries to address this difficulty.

Soft behaviourism

Ryle's version of behaviourism is less ambitious in the sense that he doesn't think a reduction of the language of the mind to pure bodily movements is possible, and for this reason it is often called 'soft' behaviourism. Recall that Ryle's intention in *The Concept of Mind* (1949)[8] is to 'explode the myth' of Cartesian dualism, a picture of mind and body which he thinks fuddles our thinking and which generates the various problems we've been grappling with – including the problem of other minds (as we have seen) and the problem of interaction. Once we have clarified the proper ways in which the language of the mind is used in everyday discourse, these problems should dissolve. Ryle's task therefore is to analyse our ordinary talk about the mental and the physical and show that while it may invite the idea that there is substantial distinction between an observable body and an unobservable mind, a proper understanding of its logic shows the distinction to be explicable in terms of differences in observable *behaviour*.

Ryle's dispositional analysis

anthology 2.17

How then does Ryle go about making the reduction more plausible? The answer is that his analysis of mental terms is not conducted in terms of *current* behaviour but in terms of *dispositions* to behave. It is in Chapter 5 of *The Concept of Mind* (1949) that Ryle gives his analysis of dispositional properties. A dispositional property of something is its liability, or proneness to act or react in a certain way. For example, the property of being soluble is a liability or proneness to dissolve if placed in water. To say of sugar that it is soluble is not to say that it is *currently* being dissolved, or indeed that it is *doing* anything, but only that it is *disposed* to dissolve under certain conditions. And this in turn is equivalent to saying that *if* the sugar were put in water *then* it would dissolve. Thus the sentence 'sugar is water soluble' is logically equivalent (or translatable into) 'if sugar were put in water then it would dissolve'. Dispositions are to be contrasted with occurrences, that is processes and events which are identified as actually happening. So to say that a sugar cube is soluble is not to say that the sugar cube enjoys some *current* but ghostly inner state of solubility, but that certain HYPOTHETICAL PROPOSITIONS (*if ... then ...* propositions) about its non-actual behaviour are true of it.

According to Ryle, a similar analysis holds for mental states. Thus, to say that someone wants a pint of stout is simply to say things like: (1) 'If asked whether stout is what she wants, she would answer yes'; (2) 'If given a choice of stout or lager, she would choose the stout'; (3) 'If she is in the pub and she isn't driving, she will drink stout', and so forth. A similar analysis holds for beliefs. A belief is not a state of mind hidden from view, causing various behaviours, but signifies someone's tendency to do certain things. Mental states, in other words, are ultimately *dispositions* to behave in certain ways and sentences expressing dispositional properties are always, in the final analysis, hypothetical in form. They sum up past behaviour in a law-like way and are used to make predictions about future behaviour. Because dispositions are behaviour patterns, people do not possess them as a state of themselves but rather display them through what they do in various situations and so we need not think of mental terms as signifying 'ghostly processes',[9] as Ryle disparagingly refers to the dualist conception of mental states, but simply dispositions. So 'to explain an action as done from a certain motive is not to correlate it with an occult cause, but to subsume it under a propensity or behaviour-trend'.[10] And so, 'to explain an act as done from a certain motive is not analogous to saying that the glass broke, because a stone hit it, but to the quite different type of statement that the glass broke, when the stone hit it, because the glass was brittle'.[11] This being the case, mental concepts behave differently from the way the dualist model supposes – they are not 'occult causes and effects'[12] but what Ryle calls 'inference tickets',[13] ways of inferring future behaviour or of forming hypotheses about persons' likely behaviour based on their past behaviour.

Figure 2.17 To say that a sugar cube is soluble is not to say that anything is currently happening hidden within the cube. Rather it is to say that if it were placed in liquid, then it would dissolve. It means, in other words, that the sugar is disposed to dissolve. In the same way, to say that someone is thirsty is not to say that they have a ghostly invisible thing within them which causes them to drink. Rather it is to say that if the circumstances were right, *then* they would drink. In other words, to be thirsty is to be disposed to drink

▶ **ACTIVITY**

Now that you have an idea of how Ryle's dispositional analysis of beliefs and desires is supposed to work, try to translate the following propositions about people's mental states into behavioural language.

1. Kev loves to discuss philosophy with his friends.
2. Angela is afraid of spiders.
3. Olly is in pain because of an infected appendix.
4. Liz believes that giraffes don't wear ties.
5. Craig hopes one day to become a long-distance runner, but is embarrassed to admit this to anyone.
6. Emma has secret doubts about whether God exists.
7. Steph is pretending to understand philosophical behaviourism.
8. Giles is day-dreaming about his childhood in Zanzibar.
9. Lucy hates her mother's brussel sprouts, but will never let on.
10. John has an odd twinge in his earlobe which he immediately forgets about.

What difficulties did you encounter? See if you can use any difficulties as the basis for an objection to philosophical behaviourism. Is there any reason to think it may be impossible to translate any and all claims about our minds into behavioural terms?

Further issues facing philosophical behaviourism

It is customary to raise the following fundamental objection against the above conception. The physical test sentences of which you speak are absolutely incapable of formulating the intrinsic nature of mental process; they merely describe the physical symptoms from which one infers, by purely psychological methods [...] the presence of certain mental processes.[14]
Hempel

Dualists defend the evidence of introspection

Perhaps the most intuitively obvious objection to behaviourism, and one favoured by dualists, is that it involves denying what appears evident in my own case, namely the reality of the 'inner' aspect of my mental states – the reality of qualia. To have a pain, for example, seems not to be (or at least not merely to be) a matter of being inclined to moan, to wince, to take an aspirin, and so on. Pains also have an intrinsic qualitative nature (a horrible one) that is revealed in introspection, and any theory of mind that ignores or denies qualia fails to do justice to our knowledge of our own mental life. So while behaviourism might make sense of how we learn to ascribe mental states to others, it doesn't appear to do justice to the subjective point of view and the direct awareness I enjoy of my own mental states. We might say that the behaviourist is effectively claiming not simply that everyone else is a zombie, but that *I* am too. And yet all I have to do is look inwards to plainly see that there is more to my mind than outward behaviour.

Hempel considers this objection in the Anthology paper 'The logical analysis of psychology' and responds by repeating the point that we can only appeal to the 'observable physical data' in order to make any meaningful claims about someone's psychology or mental life. Even the dualist has to admit that they must look to another person's outward behaviour since it is accepted that we cannot peer directly into another person's mind.[15] In response to this one can still insist that there remains a meaningful distinction between a *symptom* of a mental process and the mental process itself. And the claim that what is meaningful must reduce to what is directly publicly observable is not unproblematic as you will have recognised from studying the use of the verification principle in the Metaphysics of God section above. One major difficulty concerns how the verification principle itself can be meaningful according to its own strict criteria (see page 161). We don't need to rehearse these problems again here, but instead the critic of Hempel need merely insist that the evidence of my own case, the immediate awareness of the phenomenology of my own mental processes, is far more compelling than Hempel's problematic appeal to the verificationist criteria of meaning.

The asymmetry between self knowledge and knowledge of other people's mental states

In defence of the view that we are directly aware of our mental states via introspection, we may also point out that the subject of experience has no need of behavioural evidence in their own case in order to discover the contents of their mind. I can know I'm in pain without having to check by examining my behaviour. So while I may observe you groaning, holding your jaw and searching in the medicine cabinet and then infer that you have a toothache, it would be absurd to suppose that I learn that I have a toothache by observation of similar behaviour in myself. So while it is doubtless true that I have to observe the behaviour of others in order to know what they are thinking or feeling, I can know similar things about myself without taking any notice of my behaviour. So my knowledge of others is inferred, but it seems that of my own mind is not. And while I can have doubts and make mistakes about others' mental states, knowledge of my own seems to be incorrigible. Indeed, one absurd consequence of behaviourism would seem to be that others would have a better idea than I do of what I am thinking and feeling, because they have a better view of my behaviour. And if behaviourism were true, it would surely be common to find myself asking my friends how I am feeling or to confirm what I am thinking. And yet this just doesn't happen. I don't need to ask because knowledge of my own conscious states is immediate and infallible. What this shows is that there is an 'asymmetry' between my knowledge of my own mind and my knowledge of other people's minds. We do not gain such knowledge in the same way and Ryle's account glosses over this crucial difference.

Dualists defend interaction

We have seen during our discussion of epiphenomenalism that the dualist interactionist thesis appears to have powerful support from common experience and the evidence of introspection. By denying that beliefs, desires and sensations causally interact with our behaviour, Ryle seems to fly in the face of common sense. Surely it is because I want a cup of tea that I make one. And it is because of the pain in my foot that I jump about screaming. And I don't remove the nail from my foot simply to change my behaviour, but because it hurts!

Circularity

But it is not just that interactionism sits well with our common sense understanding. It also gives us an effective *explanation* for people's behaviour. If we suppose pains cause pain behaviour, and desires cause people to seek out the objects of their desires and so on, then we have a causal explanation for their actions. But if these mental states just are these actions, then there is nothing to explain them. If the desire and the sensation are translated into behaviour, then they cannot explain behaviour without circularity. We would be trying to explain behaviour in terms of behaviour.

The distinctness of mental states from behaviour

Imagine a community of 'SUPER-SPARTANS' or 'superstoics' – a community in which the adults have the ability to successfully suppress all involuntary pain behavior. They may, on occasion, admit that they feel pain, but always in pleasant, well-modulated voices – even if they are undergoing the agonies of the damned. They do not wince, scream, flinch, sob, grit their teeth, clench their fists, exhibit beads of sweat, or otherwise act like people in pain or people suppressing the unconditioned responses associated with pain. However, they do feel pain, and they dislike it (just as we do). They even admit that it takes a great effort of will to behave as they do. It is only that they have what they regard as important ideological reasons for behaving as they do, and they have, through years of training, learned to live up to their own exacting standards.[16]

Putnam

anthology 2.18

The American philosopher Hilary Putnam (1926–2016) defends a functionalist account of mental states in 'The nature of mental states', one of the Anthology extracts which we will be examining later. Putnam is also a critic of philosophical behaviourism and argues that we can conceive of cases where someone may be in a particular mental state but without there being any behavioural manifestation. He asks us to imagine a community of 'super-spartans', who have trained themselves to suppress any outward signs of the pains they endure. If philosophical behaviourism were correct, then it would seem to follow that super-spartans don't experience pain, but of course they do. So behaviourism cannot be correct.

Now, as we have already seen, Ryle has a response to this sort of objection. The super-spartans may not display any *actual* pain behaviour, but they remain *disposed* to display the behaviour were it not for the fact that they have Putnam's 'important ideological reasons' for not doing so. So, *if* the super-spartan were placed in a situation where these reasons didn't apply – perhaps she stands on a nail while perfectly alone, secure in the knowledge that no one will observe her – *then* she would wince, scream and so on.

To deal with this response, Putnam introduces the idea of *super*-super-spartans:

These have been super-spartans for so long, that they have even begun to suppress talk of pain ... [they] do not even admit to having pains. They pretend not to know either the word or the phenomenon to which it refers ...[17]

Putnam

If such a fantasy is not self-contradictory in some way, then it shows, says Putnam, that a reduction of pain to behaviour cannot work. For here we have a race who, according to the scenario we are imagining, are not even disposed to pain behaviour.

Putnam concludes that behaviourism confuses the evidence we use to ascribe mental states with the mental states themselves. He uses the analogy of a disease, such as polio. Before people knew what caused polio they would identify the disease by its symptoms. But later when they discovered the virus that causes it, they came to see that having the virus is necessary and sufficient for having the disease, irrespective of whether the patient exhibits the symptoms. Someone may have the virus without displaying any symptoms; or, they may display the symptoms without having the virus. So while the symptoms are evidence of having the disease, they do not constitute having it.

In the same way, we may identify people's pains by the symptoms – the pain behaviour. But this doesn't mean that the symptoms exhaust the meaning of the word 'pain'; or that pain just is the behaviour. Pains are not equivalent in meaning to pain behaviour, but are the cause of pain behaviour, and this is why it is possible to be in pain without exhibiting the behaviour, and possible to exhibit the behaviour without being in pain.

Hempel responds to the 'perfect actor' objection

anthology 2.16

Hempel also uses the idea of a 'symptom' when formulating this sort of objection to his own version of behaviourism. As we saw above regarding 'perfect actors' (see page 268), he rejects the complaint by insisting that displaying literally *all* the symptoms does indeed exhaust the meaning of the mental state. If someone were really in pain, but showed absolutely no symptoms, not just in terms of behaviour, but also physiologically, then Hempel urges, it would indeed be senseless to insist that they could still be in pain. Indeed, using the example of someone displaying the symptoms of a mental illness, he argues that it would literally be *logically contradictory* to claim that someone could have all the symptoms but not actually have the illness since, in this sort of a case, the symptoms are what constitute having the illness. In the same way, Hempel would argue, if there were really no observable differences, not even physiological differences, between Putnam's super-super-spartans and people who don't experience pain, then it would be absurd to insist that they do experience pain. In fact, though, Putnam does not want to push his argument this far. He is a physicalist and so thinks there must be some physical difference between someone who is in pain and someone who is not, even if they exhibit no behavioural manifestations. The physical basis, according to Putnam, is the state of their brains. For if the super-super-spartans are like normal human beings and we can correlate pain with certain spikes in the activity of specific regions of our brains, then if the super-super-spartans also exhibit those same brain activities, we can infer that they experience pain. The idea that it is to the brain that we need to look to understand mentality is one we can now turn to.

2.3.2 The mind–brain type identity theory

The central claim of the identity theory is that the mind is the brain, and so each mental state or process is literally one and the same thing as a state or process within the brain. What this means is that facts about the mind are *reducible* to physical facts about the brain, so that pains, beliefs, desires and so forth, are nothing more and nothing less than neurological (brain) states. Now, clearly, at present we do not know enough about the intricate workings of the brain to be able to say exactly what all mental states are in neurological terms, but the identity theory is committed to the idea that research can (and hopefully will) eventually identify what each thought, feeling or desire is in the brain.

Numerical and qualitative identity

In order to be clear about what the identity theory is saying, we need to be clear about what is meant by 'identity' in this context. Philosophers traditionally oppose NUMERICAL IDENTITY and QUALITATIVE IDENTITY. Identical twins, for example, may have identical *qualities*, they look the same, talk the same, dress the same and so on, while they nonetheless count as two people. So they may be said to be qualitatively identical but not numerically identical. Note that according to Leibniz's Law, which we encountered in our discussion of Descartes' arguments for dualism (see page 195), if we come across what appear to be two things, but discover that they literally share *all* their qualities, then they must in fact be *one* thing.

So if you meet someone on the bus who looks just like your dentist, to determine whether it is indeed your dentist rather than her twin sister, you would need to determine whether what is true of your dentist is also true of the person on the bus. And if the person on the bus is not your dentist, then there must be at least one thing by which they might be distinguished. For example, the person on the bus might have a different first name from your dentist. Identical twins, after all, do not share *all* their qualities, if only because they do not occupy the same portion of space. On the other hand, if it turns out that everything that's true of the person on the bus is also true of your dentist (including where she is at any given moment), then the person on the bus must *be* your dentist rather than her twin. Now, what the identity theory claims is that everything that is true of the brain, all of its qualities, are identical with the qualities of the mind and therefore that the terms 'brain' and 'mind' – like 'your dentist' and 'person on the bus' – refer to the same thing.

Note that the type of reduction involved here is importantly different from the one the reduction philosophical or analytical behaviourists try to perform. The identity theorist is not saying that our talk of the mind *means* the same as our talk about the brain. It clearly does not. For when I say I am experiencing a certain sensation or that I hold a specific belief, I do not mean the same as when I say that certain neurons are firing in my brain. So to say 'the mind is the brain' is not to claim that the terms 'mind' and 'brain' are synonymous and so it is not something that can be demonstrated *a priori* by the analysis of our talk about minds. Rather, what is being claimed is that the mind and the brain happen, as a matter of empirical fact, to be the same. It is, in other words, a scientific hypothesis that these terms refer to the same object and so the truth of the identity theory is to be established by empirical investigation, not by philosophical analysis.

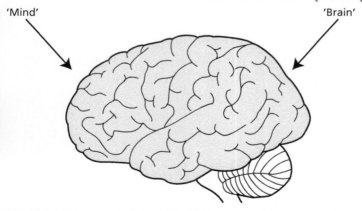

Figure 2.18 The terms 'mind' and 'brain' do not have the same meaning so analysis of our talk about the mind will not demonstrate that it is really talk about the brain. Rather, the identity theorist is saying that the two terms refer to the same object. This claim is a hypothesis to be proved by scientific investigation into the brain and its operations

Other ontological reductions in science

The kind of reduction proposed by the identity theory is very different from that proposed by philosophical behaviourism. Rather than an analytic reduction of the mind to behaviour and behavioural dispositions, the identity theory hopes to perform an 'ONTOLOGICAL REDUCTION'. ONTOLOGY concerns the nature of being or existence, and ontological reductions involve showing that beings or entities of one kind are in reality the same as entities of another kind. The successful reduction of the mental to the neural predicted by identity theorists has parallels in the history of science. For example, it has been shown that sound is identical with a train of compression waves travelling through the air; that water is identical with H_2O; and that lightning is identical with an electrical discharge. In the same way, the identity theorist claims that what we call 'mental states' will turn out to be identical with brain states, and that neuroscience will eventually be able to reduce our folk-psychological concepts to neurological phenomena.

anthology 2.19

Experimenting with ideas

Think back to the arguments for dualism that we explored in Section 2.1. Which could be used to criticise the identity theory?

Try to turn one argument for dualism into an attack on the identity theory.

Arguments for the identity theory

> [S]cience is increasingly giving us a viewpoint whereby organisms are able to be seen as physiochemical mechanisms: it seems that even the behaviour of man himself will one day be explicable in mechanistic terms. There does seem to be, so far as science is concerned, nothing in the world but increasingly complex arrangements of physical constituents .... That everything should be explicable in terms of physics ... except the occurrence of sensations seems to me to be frankly unbelievable. Such sensations would be 'nomological danglers'.[18]
>
> J.J.C. Smart

Identity theorists defend their position by pointing to the physical processes which we know have been responsible for the development of human beings, both as individuals and as a species. As we have seen in the discussion of Descartes' conceivability argument (see page 199), it is hard to make sense of the idea that an immaterial substance should become attached to our brains at some point in our evolutionary history or in our development from conception. A physicalist account of our origins, therefore, fits far better with our current scientific understanding.

What is more, modern neuroscientific exploration into the structure and workings of the brain and nervous system is making great advances in its understanding of the mechanisms underlying human behaviour and our various mental capacities. The physicalist argues that we know the brain exists; what it is made of; something about its internal structure; how it is connected to the muscles and sense organs and so forth. The neuroscientist can tell us a great deal about the brain, about its constitution and the processes that occur within it; and can explain much of our behaviour in terms of its physical, chemical and electrical properties. This knowledge is unfavourably compared with the lack of detailed or precise information the dualist can provide about the nature and workings of spiritual substance.

Not only does the idea that the mind is the brain hold out the promise that we should be able to understand our minds better by investigation of the brain, but it is increasingly evident that there is a precise and systematic correspondence between different types of mental process and processes in the brain. The evidence of real-time imaging techniques shows that subjects engaged in specific mental activities, such as mental arithmetic, imagining performing some activity, recalling events in the past, and so on, are correlated with specific areas of the brain becoming active. If the identity theory is correct, this is exactly what we would expect to see.

Now, as we have seen, property dualism also recognises the dependence of the mind on the brain, and so is also consistent with this evidence. But the identity theorist argues that a thoroughgoing PHYSICALISM is to be preferred on the grounds of simplicity. To allow immaterial properties just looks untidy, given that everything else appears to be explicable in terms of physics. Smart (1920–2012) says that if states of consciousness cannot be accommodated within the physicalist picture, they would be 'NOMOLOGICAL DANGLERS', meaning they would not fit into the system of laws which govern everything else in the universe[19] and this offends against OCKHAM'S RAZOR – the methodological principle that, given two competing hypotheses, if their explanatory power is equal, then the simpler should be preferred. (The principle is named after the medieval philosopher William of Ockham (c.1287–1347).) So if we can explain mental phenomena in terms of the physical brain, and dualism has no explanatory advantage, then a physicalist account should be preferred.

Another important consideration concerns the problem of interaction, that is the difficulty dualist theories have explaining our common sense conviction that my decisions or volitions can cause my actions and, conversely, that events in my body can cause sensations in my mind. The difficulty for a substance dualist like Descartes is that if mind and body are distinct substances with no properties in common, it's hard to see how they can come into contact with each other. Moreover, as we have seen, the idea that mind can influence body appears to contradict the principle of the conservation of energy. Property dualism may also appear less than satisfactory as an account of the relationship, since it too has difficulty explaining how mind can influence behaviour. However, if the identity theory is correct and the mental *is* the physical then clearly the difficulty disappears.

The identity theory may also be regarded as preferable to philosophical behaviourism because it can allow a causal role for our mental states. As we saw above, one of the main problems for behaviourism is the fact that it cannot explain behaviour; if mental states are nothing more than behaviour, then there is nothing to account for why we act as we do. But if the identity theory is right, then behaviour is caused and so can be explained by mental states and processes – just as our common sense suggests they are.

These considerations support some form of physicalism, but not the precise claim that there is a one-to-one correspondence between types of mental state and types of brain state. However, the identity theorist argues that no conclusive *philosophical* arguments are to be expected. As far as philosophy is concerned, the mind could be any bodily organ, the liver, the heart or whatever. But there are good scientific reasons for thinking the brain is responsible for consciousness. And if scientists eventually discover that there is indeed a one-to-one correspondence between all mental phenomena and structures and events in the brain, then the identity theory will be well established. Ultimately we need to wait to find out whether this will turn out to be the case.

Issues with the mind–brain type identity theory

> Many philosophers believe that the statement 'pain is a brain state' violates some rules or norms of English.[20]
> Putnam

Criticism 1: Talk about the brain doesn't mean the same as talk about the mind

In the Anthology extract 2.18, Putnam considers a common objection to the identity theory, namely that it is initially implausible since the words we use to talk about our mental states and processes do not *mean* the same as our vocabulary of physical states and processes occurring in the brain. When I say that I fancy a drink I do not *mean* that my brain is in a certain state. Similarly, if instead of saying that I have a headache I say that a certain neural pathway is being activated, don't I lose something in the translation? If I complain that my C-fibres[21] are firing, even if we know that this always happens when someone has a headache, surely this is not to say the same thing as when I complain of a headache.

Smart also considers this objection and observes that someone who has no knowledge of the brain can still speak meaningfully about his or her mental states. The 'illiterate peasant' in the quotation in Anthology extract 2.20, is fully conversant with the vocabulary of folk psychology; he knows what he means by 'after image', 'ache' and 'pain', and so knowing the meanings of mental vocabulary doesn't involve knowing anything about the brain. It follows, according to this objection, that we are talking about different things when we talk about our mental states from what we are talking about when talking about our brains. So any reduction of folk-psychological talk to talk about brain states will change the meaning of the terms.

Meaning and reference

To deal with this difficulty, the identity theorist can draw on a philosophical distinction between 'MEANING' and 'REFERENCE'.[22] The *meaning* of a term or phrase is the way the thing it identifies is presented to the mind; it is the way an object is conceived. On the other hand, the *reference* is the actual thing in the world to which the term refers. If we draw this distinction, what is clear is that it is quite possible for two terms which have different meanings to have the same reference.

This distinction will be clearer if we illustrate it through an example (see the discussion of Anthology extract 2.20 above). The terms 'Morning Star' and 'Evening Star' clearly have different meanings. The idea of a star which appears in the morning is different from that of a star appearing in the evening. However, as it happens, they both refer to the same object, namely the planet Venus. So the two terms have the same reference. Importantly, the fact that these terms refer to the same heavenly body cannot be worked out *a priori* by reflection on the meaning of the terms involved. Instead it was an empirical discovery made by astronomers in ancient Greece.

Now, according to identity theorists, the same thing is going on with our talk of minds and of brains. They accept that our vocabularies of mental and physical states have different *meanings*. However, their claim is that they nonetheless *refer* to the same things.

This means that when we say 'Pain is a C-fibre firing in the brain' the identity in question is not an identity of meanings. To say that C-fibres are firing does not *mean* the same as to say that pain is occurring. If the two meant the same then this proposition would be *analytic* (true by definition). But, says the identity theorist, it is not an analytical or necessary identity of *meanings* which is being claimed, but rather, an empirical identity of *things*. In other words, it is an ontological reduction rather than an analytical reduction. The point is not that the words we use to describe our minds *mean* the same as those we use to describe our brains, but rather that both vocabularies *refer* to the same things.

It is important to realise that this means that the identity theorist wants to claim that there is a CONTINGENT IDENTITY (not a necessary one) between mental states and brain states. As Smart puts it, the claim is that to report that you have a mental state such as a pain is to report a process that *happens* to be a brain process, as a matter of empirical fact, and so it is not a claim about the meanings of our mental-state terminology. Sensation statements don't *mean* the same as statements about brain states and the one cannot be translated into the other. It is for this reason that the identity theory can only be established empirically, by advances in our understanding of neurophysiology, just as the discovery that the Morning Star is the Evening Star had to be made by astronomical investigation. As has already been pointed out, science in many other fields has been successful in achieving a reduction of complex phenomena to a material basis, such as lightning to an electrical discharge, or clouds to droplets of water.

Criticism 2: The spatial location problem

Leibniz's Law states that if one thing is identical with another then everything that is true of one must be true of the other. Thus if we can identify a property of mental states that brain states don't have, the identity theory would be refuted.

Now, spatial properties have often been cited to this end. The argument runs that since brain states must have some spatial location, a specific size and shape, the identity theorist is committed to saying that mental states have the very same location, size and shape. But, it is nonsensical to say that my belief that rabbits have long ears is two centimetres to the right of my desire for spaghetti bolognese; that it is pear-shaped or four nanometres wide. Mental states are just not the sorts of things that have spatial location, size or shape.

Response to this issue

The identity theorists can defend themselves against this objection by saying that the fact that it sounds strange to ascribe spatial properties to mental states is just because ordinary language lags behind the neuroscientific advances we are now making. Once our understanding of the brain has developed sufficiently, and once we become well versed in its terminology, we may all find ourselves complaining that our C-fibres are firing, rather than talk about pains, and will no longer find it odd to talk about a belief being two nanometres long, and located in the cerebellum.

Moreover, it can be pointed out that just because it makes no sense to ascribe certain spatial properties to states of mind, doesn't establish that they are not physical states. Take examples of obviously physical states, such as being wet, or running. It makes no sense to say that being wet is square, or running is three metres long, but this doesn't mean that they are not physical states. Such states are conditions of physical beings, not physical objects in their own right, which explains why we cannot ascribe shapes and sizes to them. In the same way, a belief or a desire may be a condition realised in someone's brain. And just as we can say meaningfully that Rodney is running in the park and that Winny is wet in the bathroom, surely we can also say that Anna's musing that her cat is very wise is also taking place in the park where she is taking her stroll, and that Gemma's desire for hot chocolate is also happening in the bath where she is daydreaming. These mental states cannot be given precise shapes and sizes, but they do take place where the person having them is, and so do have spatial characteristics on a par with other types of physical state.

Putnam on the spatial location problem

Putnam considers a slightly different version of this objection in 'The nature of mental states'.[23] He points out that it does seem reasonable to suppose that for one phenomenon to be reduced to another, they have to occupy the same spatial location. If lightning is an electrical discharge, then the lightning flash and the electrical discharge occur in the same physical location. And, if temperature is reducible to the mean kinetic energy of molecules in an object, then the temperature and the vibrating molecules must be in the same physical place. But, a pain in the arm and a brain state are in different spatial locations – one is in the arm, the other in the brain. And so the one cannot be reduced to the other.

anthology 2.22

Putnam himself dismisses this objection on the grounds that the principle that a reduction requires that the two phenomena occupy the same space is not sound. To show this he uses the example of a mirror image which is located behind the surface of the mirror but which can be explained in terms of the way light reflects from an object and then from the surface of the mirror before entering the eye. The reduction and the phenomenon being reduced are in different spatial locations, but this doesn't mean the reduction fails. In the same way, the apparent location of pains in parts of the body doesn't mean that they are not in fact brain states.

> ### Criticism 3: Dualist arguments: appeal to the evidence of introspection
>
> Introspection reveals to me a world of thoughts, sensations, emotions and so on, not a domain of electrochemical impulses in an organ in my head. Mental states and properties are radically unlike neurophysiological states and properties, and therefore they cannot be the very same things. Another way of making the point is by reference to the supposed irreducibility of subjectivity. In other words, the claim is that the subjective experience of pain (what it feels like) is an essential part of our concept of pain. Any attempt to reduce this experience to purely objectively observable neurological processes inevitably leaves something out. For while brain processes are (in principle at least) publicly observable, my pain is a private event. No matter how much we may know about the neurological basis of pain, there remains some aspect of the conscious experience of suffering pain which must escape scientific explanation. And if this is so, by Leibniz's Law, brains and minds cannot be identical.
>
> We have encountered considerations of this kind when exploring dualism above. Descartes' conceivability argument (2.2.1.2, page 199) and Chalmers' 'philosophical zombies' argument (2.2.2.1, page 213) both appeal to the apparent irreducibility of the way consciousness appears to the subject of experience and to qualia.

One way the identity theorist can respond to these sorts of complaint is to point out that it is quite possible for the same thing to appear in different ways. So the way my brain appears to itself via introspection may be as a realm of conscious experiences. But when we examine the brain via our outer senses, it appears as a physical organ pulsating with impossibly complex electrochemical activity. Just as we saw when discussing the masked man fallacy as a response to Descartes (page 204ff.), the fact that the mind appears radically unlike the brain doesn't show that it isn't in fact the brain. It may simply be that the nature of the access that introspection provides to the goings on of our brains is very different from the access provided by our eyes.

Consider the fact that when our external senses discriminate between colours or sounds, they are actually making distinctions between subtle physical differences in objects of which we are not directly aware. Colour differences are produced by differences in the ways the surfaces of objects absorb and emit different wavelengths of electromagnetic radiation. But when I see red, I am not aware of the wavelength of the light which produces this sensation in me. In the same way, it shouldn't be any real surprise that our introspective sense should not be particularly penetrating in the way it discriminates the physical states and properties of the brain. Introspection may reveal to us the goings on in our brains, but only in a rather confused way. And we may well be able to discriminate between a great variety of neural states by introspection, without being aware of the detailed nature of those states.

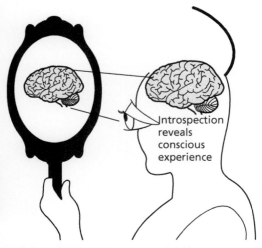

Figure 2.19 The brain may appear in two different ways By introspection my brain and its processes appear as a realm of conscious experiences. But when I examine my brain using my eyes, it appears to be a physical organ. These radically different appearances, though, need not indicate that I am dealing with two actually distinct things

But notice that in the preceding discussion we talked about the brain's appearance to us through introspection. But who or what is this 'us', the subject of experience to whom the brain appears? Are we not making implicit reference to a Cartesian soul, the subject of experience, before which the phenomena of consciousness appear? And, if so, then it would seem that the reduction of the self hasn't been completed. The problem here is that we can suppose that the brain might represent aspects of its own working to itself, but still fail to explain how these workings actually become conscious. Where in the brain do all the various brain processes come together so that I can become aware of them?

The way of thinking about consciousness that this objection involves is the idea that there has to be a kind of mental screen within us onto which our various conscious experiences are projected so that the inner *me* can observe them. The intuition that this is how consciousness must work is one reason dualism can seem attractive since it suggests that I who introspect cannot be identical with what I introspect into. However, as an explanation of how consciousness works, this picture is problematic. For in positing a self which observes my conscious experiences, we have merely displaced the problem of how consciousness arises. How, in other words, do the experiences presented to this inner self *themselves* become conscious? The inner me would have to have inner eyes gazing upon a second mental screen in order for it, in its turn, to become aware. But then how does this inner self become aware? What is clear is that positing an inner self merely leads us into an infinite regress and so explains nothing. But if the dualist intuition that there must be some place where conscious experiences are presented to the self is incoherent, then it cannot be the basis for an objection to the physicalist's efforts to explain consciousness in terms of the workings of the brain. The hard problem of exactly how the brain performs the trick remains perhaps, but as far as identity theorists are concerned, it will be through further empirical investigation that we may hope to solve it.

Criticism 4: The irreducibility of intentionality

Sceptics about the possibility of reducing consciousness to the brain may appeal to another feature of mental states that we outlined earlier, namely INTENTIONALITY. Intentionality is the property of certain conscious states, such as beliefs, desires, hopes and fears, that makes them represent or point to states of affairs which lie beyond them. So, I cannot simply believe, or desire, or hope; I must believe *something*, desire *something* or hope for *something*. So these states of mind are necessarily *about* something, and 'intentionality' denotes the quality these mental states have that enables them to be *about*. Now, it is often claimed that no purely physical system can represent, or be *about* something in this sense. For it is hard to see how an arrangement of material particles could come to represent anything. Surely physical material can only ever be what it is and cannot point beyond itself to something else. If this is right, then brain states cannot be intentional, and so mental states cannot be reduced to the brain.

To see why it may be thought impossible for intentionality to be explained physically consider just how remarkable this feature of our mentality is. My mind is able to wander freely around the universe. I can wonder where I put my keys, think about the weather in Moscow and the next moment speculate about objects on the far side of the solar system, and beyond. One reason the mind's capacity to do these things seems difficult to explain physically is that there would appear to be no physical connection between me and what I'm thinking about. If there were a physical connection, then surely it would take longer to think about things the further away they are, and yet I can think about the Moon or the Crab Nebula as quickly as I can think about the objects close to hand on my desk. My mind can also go back into the distant past and latch onto long-dead figures such as Cleopatra, or even extinct species from millions of years ago. Again, this cannot be a physical process since no physical thing can go back in time. I am also able to think about the future, as when I plan a holiday in Broadstairs, in which case I'm thinking about something that hasn't even happened and may never happen. A future event surely cannot be physically connected to a current one precisely because the future is not physically with us. Even more extraordinary, I can think about things that never have and never will exist. I can be afraid of monsters under the bed or wish I had my own unicorn. Such mental states have intentionality; they are directed beyond themselves and represent something, even though there is no actual thing out in the world that they are directed at. Again, we can wonder how it could be possible for such mental states to be physical since I cannot be physically influenced by the things they are about.

One way of explaining how intentionality might be a feature of physical states is to explain it in terms of resemblance. Perhaps my brain is able to represent the Moon because its inner workings are able to picture the Moon in some way. The difficulty here is that even if we can make sense of the idea that a brain state could resemble something, it still doesn't seem enough to explain intentionality. We might imagine that something within the microstructure of our brains is systematically arranged in a way as to resemble an object in the world, but we still wouldn't seem to have explained why this resemblance should make the brain state *about* the world. After all, my brain resembles a walnut, but this doesn't mean it is *about* a walnut.

Another account suggests that brain states can be about a feature of the world if they are caused in the right way by that feature. If my brain is in a particular state because of the Moon – perhaps the Moon has impacted on my sense organs and so been causally involved in producing it – then that brain state might be about the Moon. We might think here of animal tracks indicating that an animal has passed that way. Aren't the tracks, in a sense, about the animal? Those who oppose such efforts to give a physical explanation of intentionality will insist that they are not. There is a causal connection, but the ability to see the tracks as an indication that an animal has passed requires a mind. If there were no one to interpret them, they would represent nothing.

Criticism 5: The chauvinism of the type identity theory

> [P]hysicalism is a CHAUVINIST theory: it withholds mental properties from systems that in fact have them. In saying mental states are brain states, for example, physicalists unfairly exclude those poor brainless creatures who nonetheless have minds.[24]
>
> Ned Block (1942–)

The version of the identity theory we have been considering is known as the type identity theory. To understand why it is called this we need to draw a technical distinction between 'TYPES' and 'TOKENS'.

A type is a general class and a token is a particular instance of that class. For example, the word 'oak', as it is printed here, is a particular instance or 'token' of the word and instances like this can be repeated. But these instances are all members of a general class or 'type'. In the same way, a specific oak tree is a token of the type or species of tree that it is a member of. Turning to the mind, if I wish it were Friday on Thursday this week and wish it were Friday on Thursday last week, then these mental states would be different tokens of the same type of mental state. The type of mental state called 'wishing it were Friday' can be instantiated in the same person at different times and each occasion would represent a different token of that same type. At the same time, tokens of this type can (and do) occur in different people. So both you and I might now wish it were Friday, in which case we would both be enjoying a different token of the same type of mental state.

Now, what the type theory says is that every type of mental state, for example, seeing red, or wishing it were Friday, is identical with a particular type of brain state; let's call these brain states 'R-fibre firing' and an 'F-fibre firing' respectively. This means that seeing red occurs if and only if the R-fibre fires in the visual cortex; and wishing it were Friday occurs if and only if the F-fibre is firing (presumably in some other part of the brain).

This version can seem plausible for mental events like seeing colours and experiencing pains which might be expected to have a relatively straightforward neurophysiological basis. After all, it seems likely that similar things go on in all human brains when our nervous systems are similarly stimulated. The type theory implies that if my brain were damaged and the R-fibres in my visual cortex were destroyed, then I would cease to be able to see red. Or if the part of the brain responsible for receiving sensory information from my arm were damaged, for example through a stroke, I might lose all sensation in my arm, including the ability to feel pain. And this is what we do see happen. However, the type theory is less plausible for other states of mind, such as beliefs or desires.

Consider someone driving home wishing it were Friday, who meets with a terrible accident and damages the F-fibres in their brain. In the process we can suppose that the wish that it were Friday is destroyed. If the person then recovers to live a normal life, are we going to want to say that this person could never have this wish again? Surely not. And yet this is what is implied by the type theory. The recovery of stroke victims also suggests that the brain can regain all kinds of functions by using different parts of itself to do the work, so it seems unlikely that a particular type of wish or belief could be numerically identical with a particular type of brain state. In other words, the evidence suggests that, at least for certain mental states, we cannot expect precisely the same type of brain state to be responsible, either between different individuals or even in the same individual at different times.

The mental life of other species

Another unhappy consequence of the type theory concerns the status of the mental life of other species. For consider that other animals have different types of brain from human beings. So when an animal exhibits pain behaviour, the brain events causing this will be different from the brain events that go on in humans when we judge them to be in pain. But if pain *is* a human brain process, then it seems to follow that animals without human brains cannot be in pain. A further consequence is that any aliens we might one day encounter with very different types of brain from us would also be incapable of experiencing mental life. A Martian with spaghetti in its head rather than human grey matter could never be in pain, even though it might act very much as though it were in response to damage to its body. What these considerations are taken to suggest is that the type theory is overly *chauvinistic*, meaning it singles out human beings as the only proper possessors of mental states, and unfairly denies them to all other species. This not only goes against our intuition about animal mentality, but also against our sense that a creature that behaves as though it is in pain should be judged to be in pain regardless of what kind of a brain it has, or perhaps even if it has no brain at all. (See section 3 of Putnam's 'The nature of mental states', one of the Anthology readings, which discusses this objection to the identity theory.)

The multiple realisability of mental states

To deal with this objection the identity theorist may adopt the token approach. This amounts to saying that different types of brain state can be the same type of mental state at different times in one brain or in different individual brains. So while each token mental state is identical with a particular token brain event, there is no type-to-type identity. What this would mean is that mental states are multiply realisable. Each type of mental state, such as the belief that it is Friday, can be identical with a different type of brain state. Moreover, different creatures can have different types of brain and brain states, which nonetheless are identical with the same mental states that we enjoy, such as pain. So we no longer need to deny that dogs and Martians can suffer.

The idea that the mind is multiply realisable is closely linked to the concept of SUPERVENIENCE which we encountered earlier. Mental states are said to 'supervene' on brain states if there can be no changes in mental states without corresponding changes in brain states. At the same time, though, there can be changes in brain states without changes in mental state. The relationship of supervenience holds, for example, between an object and its shadow. The shadow depends for its existence on the object and so no changes can occur in a shadow without changes occurring in the object. However, it is possible for changes to occur in the object without there being any change in the shadow. If the mind supervenes on the brain this means that the patterns in the brain determine certain mental states so that having those brains states is enough to guarantee having certain mental states. Any brain having those patterns will have those mental states. But those who believe that the mental is supervenient on the brain reckon that different things can be going on in the brain to produce the same mental event – in other words, mental states are multiply realisable.

There is a difficulty for this move, however. For although it seems to allow for different species to experience pain despite their possession of different types of brain, we now have as many different types of pain as there are creatures with brains. There is dog pain, hedgehog pain, Martian pain and so on. But if each type of brain has its own type of pain, we have no way of specifying what it is about these different brain states that makes them all pains. What is it that these various pain states have in common in virtue of which they are painful? If the only answer is that creatures in these states act as though they are in pain we seem to have retreated to a behaviourist definition of pain and abandoned the effort to identify it neuro-physiologically.

> Learn More

In the previous section we entertained the possibility of a Martian with a very different type of brain from humans experiencing the same type of mental states as us. If this possibility is conceivable, then it seems we are committed to saying that it is metaphysically possible for brain states not to be identical with mental states and therefore for someone to be in pain without having the appropriate brain activity. But, in this case, we might wonder, how can there be said to be a numerical identity between brain and mind? For if the mind is the brain, and pain is C-fibres firing, it must be impossible to be in pain without one's C-fibres firing.

The response to this is to remind us that the identity theorist accepts the metaphysical possibility that someone could be in pain without their C-fibres firing, but insists that, *as a matter of empirical fact*, it never happens. If it did, of course, this would disprove the theory. So if we had good reasons to believe that an alien were in pain, even though its brain were made of spaghetti, this would disprove the numerical identity of pain with certain brain states. In other words, the identity being argued for, as we have seen, is said to be a *contingent* one.

However, we may counter by asking whether it makes sense to speak of a 'contingent' identity, that is, of two apparently distinct entities just happening to turn out to be the same thing. If we look at the example of the Morning Star and the Evening Star once again, it is clear that since, as has been established, both terms refer to the same object, then there plainly is only one object out there to which they refer. Given this, it is impossible for the terms to refer to different things. To take a different example, if it is the case that water is H_2O, then it is not possible, and never was possible, for water not be H_2O. In other words, there is no possible world in which water turns out to have a different molecular structure, for if what the people there call 'water' did have a different composition, then it wouldn't really be water. So if two apparently distinct things turn out to be numerically identical there is no sense in which they *could* be distinct and this means that the very idea of a contingent identity is incoherent. We may have been unsure of whether the Morning Star really was the Evening Star, but this is not to say that the Morning Star might not have been the Evening Star. It follows, the argument runs, that the identity between mind and brain which the identity theory claims holds can only be a *necessary* identity even though it is only discoverable through empirical means. But if this is right then it would be logically impossible for the mind not to be the brain, and so impossible for there to be minded aliens with spaghetti for brains, which, it is argued, is plainly absurd.[25]

2.3.3 Eliminative materialism

Eliminative materialism is the thesis that our common sense conception of psychological phenomena constitutes a radically false theory, a theory so fundamentally defective that both the principles and the ontology of that theory will eventually be displaced, rather than smoothly reduced, by completed neuroscience.[26]

Paul Churchland

Reduction or elimination?

In the past, people were well acquainted with water, but they didn't know what it was made of. The ancient Greeks supposed it was a basic element, that is, something that couldn't be broken down into anything simpler. Indeed, the thinker credited with being the first philosopher, Thales (c.624–546BCE), believed that it was *the* basic element out of which everything else was made. With the development of modern chemistry, however, it has been shown that water is composed of molecules of hydrogen and oxygen. In other words, water has been ontologically *reduced* to more basic elements. This reduction, however, leaves the existence of water intact. We wouldn't want to say that water doesn't exist because it is *really* just hydrogen and oxygen. Water is still a real thing, it's just that we now have a fuller grasp of what it is. In the same way, as we have seen above, the identity theory claims that mental states will be ontologically reduced to brain states, and that when we have discovered the various identities, our vocabulary of mental states will remain intact and we will still be able truthfully to talk about our possession of beliefs, desires and sensations.

Eliminative materialism (or simply eliminativism), however, is sceptical about the chances of the neuroscience of the future being able to account for all our folk-psychological concepts in terms of the brain. There will, in other words, be no 'smooth reduction' of mental states to the physical. The reason for their scepticism, however, is not that eliminativists believe the mind is ultimately non-physical. Rather they consider that (at least some) mental states as they are currently understood *do not exist*.

To understand what this claim amounts to, consider a parallel story to the one about water. When a plague ravaged Europe between 1346 and 1353, people became all too familiar with the disease. They called it the Black Death and they could accurately identify victims by their symptoms, which many believed were brought on by exposure to 'bad air'. With the advance of germ theory, we are now pretty confident the disease was caused by a pathogen, most probably a bacterium called *Yersinia pestis*, and was spread by fleas carried by rats.[27] Germ theory has shown that 'bad air' has nothing to do with the spread of disease, indeed, we would probably want to say that 'bad air' doesn't really exist. The concept of 'bad air' is part of a way of seeing the world which misrepresents the phenomena of disease so seriously that we have decided it can have no place in a proper account of the Black Death. By explaining the disease in terms of a bacterium we have been able to *eliminate* bad air from our vocabulary and from our picture of what exists (from our *ontology*). In the same way, the eliminativist argues that our vocabulary of mental states will be eliminated once we have a more advanced understanding of what makes us tick. Like 'bad air' our folk-psychological concepts present an inaccurate conception of what there is and need to be eliminated.

What the parallel with the Black Death brings out is the idea that our common sense talk about the mind makes use of a *theory*. We've come across this idea before when discussing the problem of other minds where we saw that folk psychology may be considered a theoretical framework by which we interpret and predict human behaviour (see page 226). Now, what eliminativism is claiming is that this theory – folk psychology – is literally *false*. In other words, our talk about beliefs, sensations, memories and so on, is fundamentally flawed and misleading as an account of the causes of human beings' behaviour and cognition and the nature of their internal states. What is needed therefore is a neuroscience which can explain what is really going on with human beings, and which makes no reference to the terminology we currently use to talk about the mind.

anthology 2.8

Paul Churchland begins his defence of eliminativism in the Anthology paper, 'Eliminative materialism and the propositional attitudes'[28] by defending the claim just outlined that folk psychology is indeed a theory. To this end he draws attention to many common sense or 'folk' ways of viewing different phenomena, which we now recognise to be theories which turned out to be false. For example, it used to be thought that the sky was a great sphere that turns daily, allowing the Sun and other heavenly bodies to rise and set.[29] We now know that it is the rotation of the Earth that produces the appearance of a sun which 'rises' at dawn and 'sets' at dusk, and so this 'folk' understanding has had to be abandoned. In the same way, we should be prepared to allow our folk psychology to be superseded by a fuller scientific account.

It is very natural to think of heat as a kind of stuff that moves from hot things to cold things. As natural philosophers investigated the nature of changes in temperature, they gave the name 'caloric' to the stuff that presumably made hot things hot. [...] The caloric-fluid theory of heat was eventually rejected because its fit with other parts of science slowly became worse rather than better, and because, in the explanatory realm, it was vastly outclassed in explanatory and predictive power by the theory that heat is a matter of molecular motion.[30]
Patricia Churchland

The eliminativist can look to the history of science for further parallels in which the development of a new theory leads to the junking of an old ontology. To return to the example we discussed earlier (page 227) which is discussed by Patricia Churchland,[31] it was once thought that heat was a very subtle fluid called caloric which was suffused through material bodies. With the development of modern atomic theory it was established that heat is in fact the mean kinetic energy of the molecules making up physical bodies, and caloric was dispensed with. Note that this process is different from a *reduction* of talk of a caloric fluid to talk of mean kinetic energy. Rather, talk of caloric has been *eliminated* because it posits the existence of an entity which does not in fact exist. Another example of entities that have been eliminated from our current ontology are sound particles. It was once thought that sound particles of different sorts occupied different substances and were dispersed into the air when these substances were hit. So, for example, a table might contain woody sound particles and so when struck with a hammer it emits these particles into the air which we detect with our ears. Nowadays it is thought that sound is actually produced by compression waves in the air. And, according to eliminativism, once neuroscience has advanced sufficiently, all our folk-psychological concepts can be dispensed with, just as caloric and sound particles have been. Hopes, fears, sensations and so on will be shown not really to exist; all there are are different states and processes of the brain.

In defence of what is, at first glance, a somewhat implausible thesis, the eliminativist points to the failure of folk psychology accurately to explain much of how we function. We don't understand, for example, how we learn things, nor how memory works, why we sleep, or what happiness is. The concepts used even in modern psychiatry, grounded as they are in our ordinary folk-psychological concepts, are deeply inadequate as an account of what goes on in mental illness. So, just as we no longer explain people's behaviour by reference to their being possessed by devils, so too we will someday dispense with talk of paranoid delusions and stress.

Figure 2.21 For most of their time on the planet, human beings have explained a range of natural phenomena in intentional terms. 'The wind could know anger, the Moon jealousy, the river generosity, the sea fury, and so forth.'[32] With the advance of naturalistic explanations, we have come to recognise this way of thinking as mere superstition. So too, the eliminative argues, we will come to see human behaviour as better understood without reference to intentional terms

Moreover, folk psychology is a theory which hasn't developed for thousands of years. Its basic elements and the theoretical rules governing how they operate which are current today haven't changed much since the time of the ancient Greeks (at least). This, says Paul Churchland, 'is a very long period of stagnation and infertility for any theory to display'.[33] His point here is that successful scientific theories are able to develop and expand, and so provide us with a deeper and richer understanding of some phenomenon. Those that fail to do so should be regarded with suspicion and as in need of overhaul. Moreover, folk psychology harmonises poorly with the rest of our scientific understanding of human beings, for example, in the areas of biology, evolutionary theory and neuroscience. We seem to be as far as we have ever been from being able to explain intentionality in physicalist terms. And if intentional states cannot be accommodated within the rest of science then this gives us good reason to jettison them. Paul Churchland likens the current position of folk psychology to that of alchemy when modern chemistry was developing as we begin to see that its categories are fundamentally muddled.

In a passage from the Anthology readings, Patricia Churchland discusses the way in which science develops and matures as it struggles to make sense of some aspect of reality.[34] In the prescientific stage we typically employ the concepts of common sense to categorise some group of phenomena. These folk systems of classification are often based less on real differences in nature, and more on what happens to be important to us. 'Plants may be classified as edible or poisonous [...] Likewise, animals that are docile or dangerous are more likely to be grouped with others that are docile or dangerous, respectively.'[35] But as our understanding of the domain of plants and animals develops, we no longer classify them in terms of the way they superficially appear to us, but increasingly in terms of genuine differences in their true natures. This process need not mean that we abandon completely terms such as 'edible' or 'dangerous'; after all, presumably human beings are always going to be interested in what they can and cannot eat, and in avoiding being eaten themselves. But whether or not a plant is edible, or whether an animal is dangerous to humans, is not important to the classification system that develops as the scientific understanding of the plant and animal worlds matures.

As new discoveries are made, Churchland continues, the boundaries of certain categories can shift. In the past the term 'fire' was used to refer to anything that produces heat or light. So, the Sun was thought to be composed of fire, and so too lightning and fire-flies, as well as burning wood. As we developed a proper scientific account of combustion we came to see that the process of wood burning, involving as it does oxidation, is very different from what goes on in the Sun, in lightning and in the bodies of fireflies. These have turned out not to be types of fire at all. At the same time we can say that the process of rusting is actually the same basic process of oxidation that goes on when wood burns. So the application of our concept of 'fire' has had to be redrawn. If a similar process happens with some of our folk-psychological concepts, we will too come to see either that they are obsolete, or, if we continue to use them in everyday speech, that they need to be redrawn in order to account for the reality of our mental life. Just as there is no real feature of the world which corresponds to our folk concept of fire, so too, it may turn out that there are no real features of our brains which neatly correspond to our folk-psychological concepts.

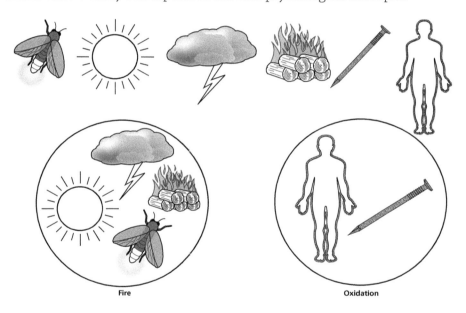

Figure 2.22 Our pre-scientific or 'folk' concept of 'fire' included anything that glowed and emitted heat. The word seemed to pick out an essential feature of reality. But with the development of our scientific understanding, we now recognise that the process involved when wood burns, when iron rusts and when a living body produces heat are all oxidation. At the same time, the processes involved in producing light in the Sun, in lightning and the fire fly are very different. So the new scientific categorisation of reality makes no use of the folk concept of 'fire'[36]

▶ **ACTIVITY**

Elimination or reduction?
a) Which of the following terms do you think pick out real features of the world?
b) Which exist but can be *reduced* to some more basic entities?
c) Which should be eliminated from a complete scientific picture of what exists?

1. Hydrogen
2. Student loans
3. Chairs
4. Monsters
5. Dyslexia
6. Metal
7. Time
8. Average income
9. Hurricanes
10. Mondays
11. Gravity
12. Medicine
13. Grandmothers
14. Great Britain
15. Music
16. Evil
17. Freedom
18. Life
19. Green
20. Austerity

anthology 2.23

An advantage of eliminativism is that its approach provides a solution to the problem of other minds. For, if folk psychology is indeed a theory, then we are justified in supposing others have minds on the basis that it is the best theory we have for explaining and predicting others' behaviour. To the extent that it is successful, it is a reasonable hypothesis that others are minded (see page 239 'The existence of other minds is the best hypothesis'). But, of course, the eliminativist is also saying that once we have a *better* theory we will be able to give up on the claim that others have minds, and within the new theoretical framework of a future neuroscience, the problem will not arise.

Issues facing eliminativism

The certainty about the reality of mental states

Perhaps the most obvious objection is to appeal to the deliverances of introspection, that is to my own experience of my interior mental life. Surely, you might say, I am directly aware of the existence of desires, thoughts and pains, and therefore any theory that denies their existence has to be false. My conviction that I experience such mental states trumps any other consideration. It is something I am more sure of than I could be of any philosophical argument to show the contrary. We may recall Descartes' sceptical arguments from *Meditations 1* and *2*, which lead him to conclude that I cannot reasonably doubt that I am aware of the contents of my own mind, such as that I am doubting that I am awake or that I am experiencing a headache.

This objection, however, need not be fatal. Consider an analogous argument that might have been made by a believer in caloric against modern theories of heat. How, they might ask, can you doubt the existence of caloric when I can feel it with my own hands as I place them by the fire? Similarly, a believer in bad air might insist that it is real on the grounds that they can directly see people dying of its effects! Those who doubted Galileo's claim that the Earth spun on its axis and orbited the Sun pointed out that they could directly feel that the Earth wasn't moving. And how can anyone deny that the Sun rises when we can see it doing so daily with our own eyes!

Clearly we would not today be particularly impressed by such arguments. The problem with them is that they assume that observation of a phenomenon can occur independently of a conceptual framework; that experience delivers to us the nature of what we observe with no mediation from our theoretical expectations. But what these observations actually do is interpret the experience in terms of the conceptual framework the people making them already possess. What this shows is that we cannot assume that entities are identifiable in isolation from the concepts we use when identifying them. So in the same way, we may be in thrall to our folk-psychological concepts when we think we are directly aware of our states of mind. We are allowing our concepts of belief and pain to determine how we interpret the phenomena. What the eliminativist is saying is that we need to rethink the background assumptions within which we identify beliefs, pains and so forth. Once we have a more sophisticated way of theorising our selves, our internal states and behaviour, the phenomena will be conceived in different ways and we will no longer feel the force of the intuition that we are directly aware of the existence of entities corresponding to our folk-psychological concepts.

Paul Churchland makes the point by saying that judgements about your own mind don't have any privileged status, rather it is an acquired habit which depends upon the conceptual framework with which one is operating: 'Accordingly, one's *introspective* certainty that one's mind is the seat of beliefs and desires may be as badly misplaced as was the classical man's *visual* certainty that the star-flecked sphere of the heavens turns daily.'[37]

Folk psychology has good predictive and explanatory power

Paul Churchland admits that folk psychology 'does enjoy a substantial amount of explanatory and predictive success'[38] while nonetheless arguing that its shortcomings are so serious that we need to reject it. However, are these failings really as terrible as he suggests? Churchland complains that it fails to explain mental illness, the mechanisms underlying memory, how we learn, or why we sleep. To say we need sleep because we need to rest is not satisfactory since no matter how much rest we get, we still need to sleep. And to say that we need sleep because we become tired explains nothing, since tiredness is simply a desire for sleep. Still, to focus on areas where folk psychology has little useful to say, may be unfair. If we consider it to be first and foremost a theory of human behaviour used to predict our actions, it performs quite well. Armed with this theory we can predict and explain a good deal of what we observe in our own and others' behaviour in a range of circumstances, from why you are sitting staring at this book (you are reading it, to try to understand about philosophy of mind), to what happens when someone shouts 'Fire!' in a crowded theatre (we can predict everyone will suddenly stand and make for the exits). We can also use the concept of tiredness and the fact that it tends to increase in intensity the longer you're awake, to predict that someone will go to bed by a certain hour. Does neuroscience come anywhere near giving us an alternative? Certainly it hasn't yet, and so at the very least we may defend folk psychology as the only game in town, putting the onus on the eliminativist to show us a better one. Until that happens, we have a right to be sceptical that elimination is a genuine possibility.

Defenders of folk psychology may also ask just how and why folk psychology has managed to endure so well if its failings are really as significant as Paul Churchland suggests. Moreover, folk psychology is a human universal; every culture employs the same basic concepts. Again, what explains this if it provides so misleading an account of our inner life and actions? Certainly it would appear that the adoption of this theory has had a good deal to do with our success as a species. Can we imagine the great civilisations being built if the people involved did not employ folk-psychological concepts to communicate and predict each other's behaviour? Surely a theory of such remarkable antiquity and ubiquity must have something going for it.

Even supposing, for the sake of argument, that we do develop an alternative, neuroscientifically respectable theory of human behaviour and mentality. Would we ever actually give up talking with each other about our thoughts, feelings and desires? If we take examples from the history of science, examples which Churchland himself uses of successful elimination, we note that it is quite common for the 'folk' ways of talking to persist. We still talk about the Sun rising and setting even though we know that in reality the Earth is turning.

In the same way, we may continue to use folk psychology for everyday human social exchange no matter what the neuroscience of the future teaches.

In support of this response to eliminativism, we may also argue that the examples where theoretical entities have been eliminated, don't actually suggest that we are likely to give up on folk psychology. The Black Death may have turned out to be caused by a bacterium rather than bad air, and yet we still talk about the disease. Heat may be the mean kinetic energy of molecules instead of caloric; sound may be compression waves of air, not sound particles, but heat and sound are as real as ever. Surely, the argument here is over how to reduce these phenomena and what is being rejected is the ontology of a failed theory, not the ontology of the original phenomena requiring explanation. So just as we still talk about the Black Death, sound and heat, so too we will surely still talk about beliefs and desires, whatever it is that these turn out to be.

This last point, though, need not be one that the eliminativist needs to resist. It may well turn out that we will continue to use at least some of our folk-psychological concepts once the new neuroscience has developed. But the point the eliminativist must insist upon is that at least some of these concepts will no longer be employed within the conceptual framework of neuroscience. The persistence of folk ways of speaking doesn't undermine the key claim of the eliminativist that these prescientific ways of making sense of human mentality do not cleave to real features of the phenomena in question.

A degenerating research programme

However, there is another way we might defend folk psychology. Paul Churchland makes the claim that it represents a 'degenerating research programme',[39] that is, a stagnating theory which is not keeping pace with developments elsewhere in our understanding of the world and human nature. However, we might point to contemporary theoretical work in the area of clinical psychology directed at helping people with mental ill-health which continues to employ the basic framework of folk psychology. Cognitive Behavioural Therapy, for example, is one of the most successful treatments for conditions such as anxiety and depression; far more successful than drug treatments which concern themselves directly with neurological mechanisms. And yet it is grounded in folk-psychological notions such as that thoughts, feelings and sensations are causally interconnected. It encourages patients to *reflect* on their *inner mental life* in order to *learn* new *patterns of thought*. It tells us *we can change our emotional landscape* by *consciously changing our behaviour*. All this buys into the folk-psychological picture of a conscious realm of desires, emotions and so on, all causally interrelated and linked to behaviour, and the prospects for us improving our understanding of ourselves by developing rather than junking this basic framework currently look pretty good.

We may also argue that folk psychology may not be like scientific theories that can be learnt and replaced. It may be that our folk-psychological concepts are part of our evolutionary heritage such that we would be incapable of social intercourse without them. Experiments on young children suggest that we gradually develop proficiency in employing folk-psychological concepts, but that this process is a consequence of our hardwiring rather than like learning an artificial skill such as swimming or riding a bike. People on the autistic spectrum find it hard to become proficient in utilising folk psychology and as a consequence find it hard to make sense of other people's behaviour and may have difficulty forming relationships. This syndrome appears to have a neurological basis, suggesting that interpreting others as possessors of minds with a subjective point of view and a private world of desires, beliefs, emotions and sensations is an integral part of the normal social development of individuals of our species.

Again, though, the eliminativist may retort that at best this shows that we cannot escape our folk-psychological framework for the purposes of everyday social intercourse. It doesn't show that this framework is the correct or even the best account of human behaviour and cognition. So if this objection is correct, it may turn out that we are condemned to continue to employ folk psychology even once we have come to see that it is false. Our sense of self and the unity of conscious experience, for example, are thought by many neuroscientists to be an illusion created by the brain. There is no agent which is the single origin of our decision-making processes, and there is no little person, no homunculus, sitting within, which is the central point of awareness of all my conscious experiences. And yet this sense of self may well be a natural creation of the human brain, and one that we cannot escape. Nonetheless, an illusion it may be.

Eliminative materialism as a theory is self-refuting

> [T]he statement of eliminative materialism is just a meaningless string of marks or noises, unless that string is the expression of a certain belief, and a certain intention to communicate, and a knowledge of the grammar of the language, and so forth. But if the statement of eliminative materialism is true, then there are no such states to express. The statement at issue would then be a meaningless string of marks or noises. It would therefore not be true.[40]
> Paul Churchland

A final objection to eliminative materialism that Churchland considers in the quotation above is that it is self-refuting. For if it is true, then there are no such things as beliefs. But if there are no beliefs, then the proponent of eliminativism cannot really *believe* the theory to be true, but in this case why should we take seriously what they are saying? In other words, the belief expressed by the eliminativist can have no sense if it is true. On the other hand, if it is meaningful it must express a genuine belief. But, in this case, since it denies there are such things as beliefs, it must be false. So, either way, we don't need to take it seriously.

Paul Churchland responds by pointing out that this objection presupposes the truth of folk psychology in order to claim that the proponent of eliminativism cannot be making sense. And he gives an analogous argument to show the circularity in the reasoning. In the eighteenth century people believed in a substance called 'vital spirit' which was supposed to animate living things and so distinguish them from inanimate objects like stones or clocks. Suppose someone who denied the existence of vital spirit were challenged by the following argument:

> *The antivitalist says that there is no such thing as vital spirit. But this claim is self-refuting. ... For if the claim is true, then the speaker does not have vital spirit and must be dead. But if he is dead, then his statement is a meaningless string of noises, devoid of meaning and truth.*[41]
> Paul Churchland

This defence of vitalism presupposes the existence of vital spirit in order to say that someone who denies its existence must be dead. But those who reject vital spirit are giving an alternative account of what it is to be alive. In the same way, the denial that beliefs are real would involve an alternative account of humans' internal life and behaviour.

However, we may not be impressed by this analogy since what eliminativism denies is the very idea of meaning and of the notion that a belief could be true or false, well or poorly supported by reasoning. So the status of the eliminativist's claims looks precarious – it seems we can make no sense of supposing them to be true or well evidenced. What would be needed for the analogy with vitalism to work would be some account of an alternative to intentional states, such as beliefs, in which to frame the theory, but without this we can't even make sense of the claim that folk psychology is false since making sense of the claim involves presupposing that it is true.

2.3.4 Functionalism

> *I shall, in short, argue that pain is not a brain state, in the sense of a physical-chemical state of the brain ... but another kind of state entirely. I propose the hypothesis that pain, or the state of being in pain, is a functional state of a whole organism.*[42]
> Putnam

We have seen that common sense is on the side of the interactionist thesis that our mental states cause some of our actions. The epiphenomenalist's denial of this apparent aspect of our everyday experience strikes many as reason enough for us to reject it. Similarly, philosophical behaviourism seems to get things the wrong way round when it claims that having a pain is simply to be disposed to behave in certain ways, such as to pronounce the words 'I am in pain'. Surely, we might think, it is the pain which disposes us to pronounce these words, rather than the pain simply *being* our disposition to pronounce them. The problem with behaviourism is the strangeness of its insistence that my desire for a drink, for example – an apparently private state – is no more than a disposition to drink under certain circumstances, while normally we are inclined to assume that it is the *cause* of my drinking. Eliminativism, by disputing the very existence of entities such as beliefs and desires, denies them a causal role, and so it too opposes this article of common sense. So if we are dissatisfied with epiphenomenalism, behaviourism and eliminativism, we may be inclined to look for a theory which allows mental states to play some causal role in human behaviour, and if dualism and the identity theory are considered unsatisfactory, we may turn to *functionalism*. The American philosopher Hilary Putnam, who we have already encountered in our discussions of behaviourism and the identity theory, urges us to do just this in his Anthology paper 'The nature of mental states' (see Anthology extract 2.24).

Reducing mental states to functional roles

The functionalist identifies mental states with FUNCTIONAL STATES. To understand what is meant by a functional state, consider first that many everyday objects are defined less by what they are made of, or how they are designed, than by what task they are intended to perform. If you open the kitchen drawer you will find an array of devices created for specific functions: the can-opener, corkscrew, knife sharpener, garlic crusher and so on. Each of these comes in a range of different designs and is made from different sorts of material. Your can-opener could be the sort you get on pen knives which you have to lever into the can lid and use to make a series of incisions; or it may be the kind which pierces and clips onto the lid and you then turn the handle; or perhaps you have a modern battery-operated contraption that latches onto the lid with magnets and automatically rotates, cutting into the side as you look on in wonder. These different types of can-opener look very different, they are made out of different materials, but this doesn't prevent them from all being can-openers. This is because what makes something a can-opener is the fact that it opens cans. It is defined by its *function*, that is, by what it does or is used for, rather than in terms of the stuff of which it is made or the details of its design.

Think also of a bodily organ such as the heart. What makes something a heart is not what it is composed of or precisely how it is put together, but what it does. Anything that pumps blood around the body counts as a heart and different animals have hearts of different designs and materials. We now have artificial hearts composed of metal and plastic, but for all that, they are still hearts. What makes them hearts is the task they perform.

▶ ACTIVITY

Which of the following is best defined functionally? Which is best defined in some other way, such as in terms of what it is composed of, or the processes that brought it into being?

1. A wheel
2. The Moon
3. A screwdriver
4. A mobile phone
5. A rabbit
6. A pound coin
7. An ear
8. Salt
9. The prime minister
10. A carburettor

Come up with your own example of something that is best defined functionally.

Now, functionalists believe that mental states are best understood as being functional entities like hearts, or can-openers. On this view, the essential or defining feature of any type of mental state is the set of causal relations it bears to (1) environmental effects on the body, (2) other types of mental states, and (3) bodily behaviour. Put another way, functionalism explains mental phenomena in terms of the *causal* (or *functional*) role it plays within a sequence of events. To be a particular sort of mental state is to have a particular sort of functional role. A pain in the foot or the belief that it is raining should be defined in terms of the role that it plays in mediating between sensory inputs, other mental states and behavioural outputs. So a functional definition of pain would treat it as that mental state which is produced by damage to the body and whose role is to trigger other mental states such as wanting to avoid the source of the pain as well as pain behaviour such as inspecting the damage, wincing or hopping on one leg. And *any* state that plays exactly that functional role *is* a pain. Similarly, my belief that it is going to rain is the mental state caused by the perception of an overcast sky which, when coupled with my desire to keep dry, causes me to wear a raincoat and take an umbrella when I go out.

Now, just as can-openers and corkscrews can be made of very different substances, so the belief that it is raining need not be instantiated by any particular type of stuff. For if being minded is a matter of being organised in the right way, a great range of substances could realise minds. Indeed, it is possible for a functionalist to be a dualist and claim that it is mind-stuff or spirit, arranged in a particular way, that happens to instantiate human minds.[43] In practice, functionalists are generally physicalists and view the brain as the material basis for consciousness. This means that functionalism holds that mental states depend upon physical states and their causal powers, and so mental properties *supervene* on states of the brain. Thus there can be no change in mental states without some change in the physical organisation of the brain. But because the precise material is not what defines a mental state, I can hold the same type of belief as you without precisely the same type of brain process taking place. So functionalism allows for the multiple realisability of mental states which we saw in our discussion of the identity theory and is preferable to a type-to-type reduction of mental to neural. For this reason, functionalism is fairly liberal about what kinds of entity might be minded. Aliens might have very different types of stuff in their skulls, but so long as it is organised in the right way, then aliens can be minded.

Functionalists were originally inspired by the analogy between computational systems and the operations of the mind. Computers receive inputs, react by following a series of rules, and produce an output, and living organisms similarly process sensory inputs and convert them into behavioural outputs. These parallels suggest that a further analogy can be drawn between, on the one hand, the computer *hardware* and our physiological make-up (the brain), and between, on the other, the *software* and the mental functioning or thinking of the mind. This analogy provides an unmysterious account of the relation of mind to body. For hardware and software are not different entities, still less different substances, but nor are they identical with one another. Rather, it is the way the brain is organised and the manner of its operations that enables it to be minded. Even if computers are not yet sufficiently complex to count as minded, the claim is that for them to be so all that is necessary is to run a sophisticated enough software program on a sufficiently powerful hardware platform for it to instantiate the relevant functional economy. Organic brains, in other words, are not necessary.

'MACHINE STATE FUNCTIONALISM' is the term given to the view that minded human beings are to be understood as a complex system of inputs and outputs, the inputs being sensory and the outputs behavioural. A very simple input/output device is a vending machine – it receives coins as inputs and follows a set of instructions in its program to deliver various products as the outputs. We can capture the operations of such a machine in a diagram termed a MACHINE TABLE. A machine table specifies which inputs will produce which outputs and the changes in internal states that mediate between them.

	S_1	S_2
50p input	Emit no output Go to S_2	Emit a coke Go to S_1
£1 input	Emit a coke Stay in S_1	Emit a coke + 50p Go to S_1

Figure 2.20 The machine table for a simple drinks vending machine. Adapted from Ned Block's example given in 'Troubles with functionalism' (page 267)

Ned Block gives an example of a simple machine table which captures the functioning of a drinks dispensing machine (see Figure 2.20). What the table shows is how the machine reacts to two different inputs: pound coins and 50p pieces. The machine has two internal states, S_1 and S_2. S_1 is its original state as it waits for a customer. If you input £1, the machine will deliver a coke and stay in S_1. However, if you input 50p the machine will not deliver a drink, but will move from S_1 to S_2. If you now insert another 50p it will emit a drink and return to S_1. And if you input a £1 while it is in S_2 it will have too much money and so will emit a drink and 50p change.

One point to note is that the internal states of the machine could be realised by a range of different hardwares. The internal mechanism could be one of weights, springs and pulleys; it could be electronic; or there could even be a trained monkey inside following the rules specified in the machine table. In other words, the machine table is multiply realisable, and similarly, it is held, mental states may be realised in a variety of different ways.

Now, functionalists do not generally claim that simple machines of this sort have mental states, but the internal states specified by the machine table are regarded as analogous to mental states in human beings so that, in principle at least, a machine table could be written specifying the functional economy of a human being in response to the great range of possible inputs it might encounter. The machine table for a human being would be bewilderingly complex with countless serially nested subsystems. And Putnam and others don't consider humans to be deterministic automatons like the vending machine, but *probabilistic*. That is, our programming doesn't specify a determined reaction to a specific input, but instead the probability that we will change into certain states or produce certain outputs. Still, the basic idea is that the difference between the vending machine and a human being is one of degree rather than of kind.

Advantages over behaviourism

There are some obvious similarities with behaviourism, but also one fundamental difference. Where the behaviourist hoped to define each type of mental state solely in terms of environmental input and behavioural output, the functionalist denies that this is possible. An adequate characterisation of a mental state cannot be confined to what is observable on the outside, but must involve reference to a variety of other mental states with which it is causally connected. Thus, there is a cluster of events that form around the state of any person and it is how they combine that determines his or her mental state. In sum, functionalists recognise the role mental states have in causing behaviour and other mental states and this accords far better with our common understanding of the nature of the mind.[44] What this means is that the functionalist doesn't face the difficulty, often considered fatal for behaviourism, that we can conceive of people being in mental states but without them displaying the associated behaviour – the perfect actors and super-super-spartans we discussed earlier. This is because it is quite possible for someone to be in a state which typically produces certain behavioural outputs, but which, because of some countervailing consideration, doesn't on this occasion. Putnam's super-super-spartan doesn't show pain behaviour because she possesses other mental states, the desire to suppress the behaviour, which prevent the typical causal sequence from occurring. Because functionalism is clear that mental states are defined in terms of their causal role in this complex network of other mental states, we shouldn't expect the same mental state always to produce the same behaviour.

Advantages over the identity theory

We have seen that the functionalist agrees with the identity theorist in regarding a mental state such as a pain as the cause of pain behaviour. The important difference in their positions, however, emerges out of a consequence of the type identity theory, namely that no being whose brain is not made out of the same basic stuff as ours has a mind. And yet to claim that a Martian displaying characteristic pain behaviour when its body is injured would not be in pain simply because its brain were made of spaghetti seems implausible. In response, the identity theorist claims that we can conceive a spaghetti-brained Martian with a mind because the identity between mind and brain is not a conceptual one. It is a contingent identity of things rather than an identity of meanings. So, on this view, evidence of a Martian in pain would count against the identity theory, were it ever to be an empirical reality. But, their bet is that we never will encounter such creatures. However, as we have seen, the coherence of the idea of a contingent identity can be questioned. For the claim that there is a contingent identity can only mean that there *might have been* two distinct things to which the words 'mind' and 'brain' refer, but that, as a matter of (contingent) fact, they refer to one and the same thing. So it would mean that there are possible worlds in which Martians have minds. But if they are simply two terms for the same thing, then there is (necessarily) only one thing, and things could not have been otherwise. If 'mind' and 'brain' refer to the same thing then there could not possibly be any other thing for the terms to refer to and so there can be no possible world in which a creature with spaghetti rather than brains can be minded, just as there is no possible world in which water is something other than H_2O. What this suggests is that if the identity theory is right then it is empirically necessary, and so logically speaking our Martian could not have a mind. Yet since it seems it is logically possible for such a being to have a mind, the identity theory must be false.

Functionalists are able to deal with this problem by allowing that an alien with a physiology very different from ours might nonetheless be functionally equivalent to the extent that they instantiate a similar set of internal states. In other words, the machine table which describes the functionings of the Martian is the same as that which describes us, even though it has spaghetti for brains. If when the Martian damages its body it attends to the affected area, avoids the source of the pain and so on, then it would appear that, from a functional point of view, its internal state is a parallel of a human pain state, and since mental states *are* functional states we can confidently assert that the alien feels pain. In the same way the brains of reptiles, or molluscs, such as octopuses, can also feel pain, even though their brains are composed of rather different physical-chemical states than mammalian brains like ours.

Experimenting with ideas

Suppose for some reason you need to go to hospital for a brain scan. After a while, you notice a group of hospital staff have gathered around the monitor scratching their heads in disbelief. When you make inquiries, it turns out that you don't have a brain! Instead, inside your head is a swarm of flea-like creatures, apparently organised into a bafflingly complex arrangement and functioning to control your behaviour in response to sensory stimuli entering your skull via your sense organs and spinal column.

Is this conceivable? If it is, does it show that brains are not necessary for consciousness? If it is not conceivable, does this mean functionalism must be false?[45]

Issues facing functionalism

The possibility of a functional duplicate with inverted qualia

A standard objection to physicalist theories is also one levelled at functionalism, namely that it fails to account for the intrinsic qualitative nature of our mental states. Dualists will claim that any theory of mind must explain qualia and that reductive approaches such as functionalism necessarily leave the first person perspective out of the picture. The first argument we will examine that tries to expose this difficulty employs the inverted spectrum thought experiment, which we considered earlier (see 'Qualia do not exist and so Mary gains no new propositional knowledge', page 225). The basic idea is that the spectrum of private colour qualia that I experience might be systematically inverted by comparison to yours. So the quale I experience when looking at a banana is like the quale you experience when you look at the sky and vice versa. Because this has been our situation since birth, we use the vocabulary of colour terms in the same way and so never notice the difference.

If this were the case, from a functional point of view we would be identical to each other. I react in the same way as you to the same sensory stimulations. We both call bananas 'yellow' and describe the sky as a beautiful, unfathomable blue. And internally, the mental states caused by bananas and the sky play the same role in relation to other mental states. Bananas remind us both of cornfields and the Sun. The sky makes us both feel calm and wistful. So a machine table describing our internal states would be identical. But if we are functionally equivalent, then, according to the functionalist definition of mental states, we must be experiencing the same visual sensations. Thus the possibility of spectrum inversion is ruled out by definition. And yet, the objection runs, it remains quite conceivable, and so functionalism must be false. It is conceivable because qualia appear to have intrinsic qualities which are what they are regardless of how they relate to other mental states or to sensory inputs and behavioural outputs. To repeat, because qualia are not defined in terms of their relationship to anything else, and functionalism says all mental states are defined in terms of their relations to sensory inputs, behavioural outputs and other mental states, functionalism cannot account for qualia.

In defence of functionalism we may ask whether the inverted spectrum thought experiment is really conceivable. If the hypothesis is both irrefutable and unconfirmable we may be inclined to conclude that the idea of inverted qualia is nonsensical. We cannot make coherent sense of the supposed difference between you and me if we cannot point to anything in the world that would establish the difference. Those of a verificationist bent might say that a difference that makes no difference is no difference at all. And, as we have seen, physicalists in general may reject the objection on these grounds (see the discussion of Dennett, page 230). Yet, if we modify the thought experiment slightly we can generate a problem which is specific to functionalism rather than physicalism generally. Suppose I was born with normal vision, but that an operation was performed on me at birth to switch the neural pathways travelling from the optic nerve to the visual cortex. If this were to happen, it seems we would have good empirical reasons to suppose that my qualia were now inverted relative to yours. And yet, although my visual system is no longer physically identical with yours, we could imagine me learning the vocabulary of colour words to become fully functionally equivalent to you and everyone else. This scenario is conceivable and because it involves empirical evidence of inverted qualia can't be dismissed as unverifiable and meaningless. So this revised version may provide a stronger argument to the conclusion that there is more to qualia than can be captured by a functionalist account.

In response to this, functionalists can deny that in such circumstances I could learn to use colour words in a functionally equivalent way to you. The switching of the neural pathways would involve a functional change too. Perhaps I would be unable to associate the colour of the sky with calm, for example, so that we would have good functionalist reasons for thinking that my mental state when seeing the sky is different from yours. And if I really did become functionally equivalent to you then the functionalist may want to insist that this is all we need to be sure that we are in the same mental state. For if the range of qualia really were to play the same complex role in relation to other mental states and behaviour right down to our tendency to find blue calming, red exciting, green peaceful and so on, it certainly becomes harder to hold on to the intuition that they could nonetheless have distinct intrinsic natures. In spite of this, some functionalists concede that in the version of the thought experiment just considered, the intrinsic physical differences would produce a different qualitative feel, and so concede that qualia cannot be given a complete functional definition. In conceding this, however, functionalists need not give up on the theory as an account of the rest of our mental states such as beliefs and desires.

The knowledge/Mary argument can be applied to functional facts

We have discussed Jackson's knowledge argument and the attempt to show that no reduction of mentality to the physical is possible. The same argument can be employed against functionalism. For if Mary were to know all the physical facts, including all the functional facts, about what happens when humans experience colours, and yet learn something new when she herself sees colour for the first time, then there is more to experiencing qualia than is captured in a complete functionalist account (for a fuller discussion of this objection, see Section 2.2.2.2, page 220).

Functionalism can be defended, however, and Jackson himself came to reject his own anti-reductivist argument and accept that a functionalist account of qualia could be correct. On this view, qualia provide us with a short-cut by which we represent complex functional and relational information. It is clearly going to be useful to an organism that needs to survive in a hostile environment to recognise when its body is damaged, but having an explicit and detailed grasp of the nature of the damage and of one's physiological reactions to it is not needed or practically possible to attain. A complete functional analysis of pain would involve bringing together a great range of information about the physiological reactions undergone in the nervous system and the brain. And similarly with colour experiences. A complete functionalist account would be fiendishly complex. When we experience colour we get access to this information more quickly than would be possible if we came to an explicit understanding of all that is really going on. Because we acquire it in this way, it appears as though we are aware of something different from a set of functional and relational properties – but this is, nonetheless, what they are. So if qualia are really confused representations of functional states, then there is no reason why Mary wouldn't be able to deduce their nature from her complete knowledge of the physical facts.

The possibility of a functional duplicate with no qualia

anthology 2.25

In 'Troubles with functionalism' Block accuses functionalism of 'LIBERALISM', that is, the tendency to ascribe minds to things that do not have them. He outlines two systems which could be functionally equivalent to a human being but which we would be reluctant to ascribe mentality to. Imagine a body like yours on the outside but with the head hollowed out and replaced with a set of tiny people whose job is to realise the same machine table as you. Clearly, the overall task would be immensely complex but we can suppose that each individual's job would be fairly simple. Now, according to the functionalist account of mentality, this 'homunculi-head' (head full of people, *homunculus* being Latin for 'little man') would have a mind just like you do, including experiences of pain, colours and also intentional states such as beliefs and desires. However, Block argues, we have a strong intuition that such a system would not be minded – there is nothing it is like to be the homunculi-head.

Block then modifies the thought experiment so that the billion or so citizens of China are engaged in realising the same machine table, this time with radios connecting them with each other and the body. Suppose that the body now stands on a nail. The people of China would have a busy time of it reacting to the input signals and would – we must imagine – successfully cause the body to hop on one leg, yelp and make efforts to remove the nail. But would anyone feel any pain? If we think not, the system can be in a state which is functionally equivalent to feeling pain in you, but not actually be in pain. So once again we are saying that functionalism is too liberal and so not an adequate account of mentality.

In response functionalists may search for differences between the human brain and the homunculi-head or population of China. Putnam argues that we should exclude systems the elements of which are themselves minded. He writes in 'The nature of mental states' that 'No organism capable of feeling pain possesses a decomposition into parts which separately possess' the functional organisation appropriate for feeling pain.⁴⁶ But just why this should be isn't clear and so this appears to be an ad hoc move designed purely to dispose of Block's type of example. Putnam says as much in admitting that this caveat is there 'to rule out such "organisms" (if they can be called such) as swarms of bees as single pain-feelers.'⁴⁷ Another move is to argue that the population of China would operate far too slowly to be a genuine equivalent of the human brain. And yet, the speed at which it operates doesn't seem to be relevant to whether it can replicate the functional economy of the brain.

So an alternative line of defence for functionalists is to question the intuition that such systems would not experience qualia. After all, it may be mere prejudice that makes us suspicious of genuine mentality being found in things so very different from the kinds of bearers of minds our experience typically encounters. And if the system really were complex enough to succeed in realising an equivalent machine table to a human being, then perhaps conscious states would indeed emerge. We may note also that it remains mysterious just how qualia emerge from the complex arrangement and actions of neurons in the brain, but, unless we are substance dualists, we must suppose that somehow they do it. As Block himself admits:

*No physical mechanism seems very intuitively plausible as a seat of qualia, least of all a brain. Is a hunk of quivering gray stuff more intuitively appropriate as a seat of qualia than a covey of little men? If so, perhaps there is a prima facie doubt about the qualia of brain-headed systems too.*⁴⁸

(Block, though, goes on to give arguments for supposing that the doubt about homunculi-heads is reasonable after all in his 'Troubles with functionalism'.)

Could computers have minds?

If, as functionalist accounts of the nature of mind claim, there is nothing mysterious about being conscious over and above the functional arrangement of particular organisms, the way would seem to be left open to the possibility of our constructing a conscious machine. For, as we have seen, a purely functional description of the operations of a given 'system', such as a human being, Martian or robot, makes no *ontological* commitment to the kind of stuff of which it is made, and so if functionalism is the correct account of the nature of mentality, then a sufficiently powerful computer could one day be minded.

Experimenting with ideas

Consider whether you think it is conceivable that a mechanical device could have a mind. For example, do you believe a vending machine has desires and beliefs? Can it want more money, or believe it must deliver change? What about the various computer programs you can access via the internet for information, such as to plan a train journey. Does it understand that you will be travelling during the busy period when it apologises that it can't make a seat reservation? Is it genuinely sorry? Think of why you answer these questions as you do.

Next think of some of the artificial minds appearing in science fiction films, such as HAL from *2001: A Space Odyssey*, or the robots in *I, Robot* or C3PO or R2D2 from *Star Wars*. Do you think it is possible that we could build such machines? If you encountered a machine that behaved in this way, would you be persuaded it had a mind, or would you think it was just an unconscious machine?

The Turing test

The mathematician and cryptanalyst Alan Turing (1912–54) was instrumental in the early development of computers and played a key role in helping to break the German 'enigma' code during the Second World War.[49] In philosophical circles he tends to be better known for his proposal for a test of whether a computer could be said to be intelligent. If a computer could communicate with a human being via a keyboard in such a way that the human being could not tell the difference between conversing with the computer and conversing with another human being, then to all intents and purposes, Turing suggested, the computer should be considered minded. According to the TURING TEST, then, competence in linguistic conversation is the criterion for the possession of beliefs and other intentional states by an artificial intelligence.

In support of the view that computers *already* have minds (as proponents of Artificial Intelligence – AI – sometimes are) we may point to our ordinary understanding of their basic operations. We say that a computer has so much 'memory', that it processes information, uses language, calculates, obeys commands, follows rules and so forth. On the face of it, it may seem as though computers carry out the same functions carried out by human beings with minds. And if we think back to the vending machine from earlier (page 296), perhaps it is not too much of a stretch to characterise S_1 as a simplified version of what goes on in us when we want £1.

The American philosopher John Searle (1932–) is well known for his opposition to the machine functionalist's claim that organic brains are not required for consciousness. Searle insists that mental states are essentially natural phenomena. They are the product of human evolution and in this respect no different to all other biological functions such as digestion and respiration. This means that it is essential to being minded that one have a certain neurophysiology, a living brain, and so Searle insists that no artificial intelligence could be conscious. His attack on functionalism tries to show that a computer which was functionally equivalent to a human being with respect to linguistic behaviour, and so could pass the Turing test, still wouldn't be conscious. To show this he constructs his well-known thought experiment, the Chinese room.

The Chinese room argument

Searle's focus in this argument is on intentionality, the feature of our mental states which enables them to be *about* things. He distinguishes different sorts of intentionality. There is what he calls *as-if* intentionality, which is possessed by things like rivers as they flow towards the sea, or plants as they grow towards the light. Here there is the appearance that the water 'wants' to flow downhill, or that it is 'trying' to reach the sea, but in such cases most people would not say that the river truly has desires and intentions and it is not able to think about the sea. Rather we should say that this is a short-hand manner of speaking, or that it is merely a way we might choose to represent the river, but not something really possessed by the river itself. Similarly, we might, in certain moods, speak of the beliefs or desires of flowers to attract insects, or of a swarm of bees to protect the queen, while strictly we would be disinclined to ascribe intentional states to them. *Intrinsic* intentionality, by contrast, is the real thing: the sort that is supposedly only possessed by *minds*.

Searle's thought experiment goes roughly as follows:

> *Suppose a man who speaks only English is locked inside a room with only a slot through which to communicate with people in the outside world. Outside is a Chinese speaker who is eager to discover whether the person inside speaks Chinese and who passes messages into the room written in Chinese. The English speaker has several baskets containing Chinese symbols and a rule book written in English which he consults to determine how to respond to the messages. The Chinese characters are completely meaningless to the English speaker, but nonetheless, because of the sophistication of the rule book, he is able to respond in ways which are meaningful to the Chinese speaker outside the room. In other words, we must imagine that the person in the room passes the Turing test and fools the Chinese person into thinking he is a fluent speaker of Chinese.*

Searle contends that the Chinese room undermines the notion that computers have intrinsic intentionality. For the set-up contains everything relevant to a computer. The person in the room functions like the central processor of a computer. He manipulates physical symbols and uses an instruction book which can represent the computer program. The baskets full of symbols would be the database; the messages that are handed in are the input and the replies handed out are the output.

While it is unapparent to outside observers, it is clear to us that the person in the room does not understand Chinese. Also clear, contends Searle, is that the entire system of the room plus the person and its contents is ignorant of Chinese as well. None of the responses made has any intrinsic *intentionality* or *means* anything, except as it is viewed by outside observers. And it follows, according to Searle, that computers also cannot have intrinsic intentionality. For if the person in the room does not possess intrinsic intentionality (does not understand Chinese) solely on the basis of following a set of instructions or program, then neither could any computer. Like the man in the room, or an ants' nest, a computer only has as-if intentionality.

Searle's thought experiment tries to undermine the functionalist thesis that the mind is in the same relation to the brain as computer software is to computer hardware. For what a functionalist in essence claims is that it is not the physical instantiation which is of importance to having a thinking thing, so long as it is compatible, as it were, with the *software*. Searle, along with linguists, calls rule following or grammar in language, 'SYNTAX', and the meaning we construct from those rules, 'SEMANTICS'. The idea, in other words, is that a computer does not deal with *meanings* (semantics) but simply follows *rules* of syntax. It cannot understand what the Chinese figures mean, since it merely follows rules for manipulating symbols. Thus, Searle concludes, a computer can only ever simulate consciousness, but never duplicate it.[50]

Criticism 1

One response that Searle considers is what he calls the systems reply. This basically says that while the person in the room may not understand Chinese, the entire system – baskets of symbols, rule book, and so on – does. The English speaker is just one part of a complex system responding in Chinese, including a huge database and complex set of rules. As a whole, if such a system could genuinely pass the Turing test then it would demonstrate genuine understanding.

Searle's response to this is that we can imagine the person in the room internalising the database and the rule book. He could then leave the room and even convince Chinese speakers that he can speak Chinese. However, he would still only have learnt a set of instructions and memorised a huge number of meaningless squiggles and so still wouldn't possess intrinsic intentionality.

Criticism 2

Another response is to accept that neither the person in the room, nor the system as a whole would be able to understand Chinese, but insist that this does not show that more sophisticated kinds of machines could not. Searle's thought experiment evokes an overly simplistic mechanism which, while it could not understand Chinese, surely would not fool anyone in a conversation either. In fact, it may not be as obvious as Searle supposes that we would be reluctant to grant intrinsic intentionality to a system that actually *can* hold its own in a complex conversation. In the end, Searle's argument rests on our intuition that machines could not be conscious and yet intuitions are not necessarily reliable. In the future, when we are used to talking machines, we may find our intuitions change. In making this point, Steven Pinker (1954–) asks us to imagine a race of intelligent aliens with very different physiology from ours, who cannot believe that we humans are conscious because our brains are made of meat. If their experience to date is exclusively of minds in silicon-brains, then they might well find it inconceivable that our sort of brain could produce consciousness.[51]

Criticism 3

Critics of Searle may point out that we are in the same position with respect to others as we are to the Chinese room in deciding whether to ascribe genuine understanding. The only basis we have for ascribing minds to others is that they behave appropriately, for example, in conversation; so if we are happy to ascribe mentality to other humans we should be happy to do so to a machine capable of behaving in the same way. Any other attitude would be chauvinistic – denying mentality to the machine, simply because it is a machine. We would be behaving like Pinker's aliens. Moreover, aren't we in search of some wholly mysterious property if we insist the machine must possess supposedly *intrinsic* intentionality? After all, it's not obvious that any theory of mind is able to explain this feature of consciousness. If the dualist insists that a purely material mechanism could not be intentional, he or she still needs to account for how an *immaterial* mind-substance *is* able to be intentional. Simply to assert that it is essential to thinking substance that it be capable of intrinsic intentionality, is to present a non-solution to the general problem of how things represent, much as to explain why it is that opium puts people to sleep by saying it possesses 'dormitive power'.

Criticism 4

This may lead us to consider whether we can deny that *anything* – computer, Chinese room or human being – possesses *intrinsic* intentionality. After all, as we have seen in our discussion of the identity theory, it is not easy to see how intentionality is to be incorporated into a physicalist picture of mind. Since the very notion of intrinsic intentionality is highly elusive, perhaps the only kind of intentionality is of the as-if kind. On this way of viewing the situation, we are subject to a kind of illusion in supposing that we have beliefs and desires that genuinely point to the world. In reality, this is just a way of interpreting and predicting human behaviour that is ultimately reducible to a set of causal relations. Complex mechanisms like us can be usefully understood as having internal states which are directed outwards to their environments, and any system the behaviour of which can be reliably predicted in this way can be considered to have intentionality. In reality, though, the only difference between our desires and the internal states of a vending machine concerns the level of organisational complexity.[52]

Criticism 5

A final response we will consider is called the robot reply. What Searle's scenario seems to show is that a computer might well be able to manipulate symbols and respond appropriately to verbal stimuli, but for it to understand what is being spoken *about* it would need to be able to recognise what things in the world the words refer to. Otherwise, as Searle rightly says, it will be manipulating symbols but with no understanding of what they mean. But if it were to be given access to its environment and so to the world that gives the Chinese symbols their meaning, couldn't it then develop genuine understanding? Suppose we equip the Chinese room with sensors of various sorts and provide it with a robotic body that can move around and interact with the environment. In this scenario, the robot would be more in the position of an organic being, in that it would be able to learn about the objects around it and so attach meanings to the symbols it manipulates. Since this is how we learn the meanings of words, surely such a robot might be able to do the same.

Searle's response is that even in this scenario, it is still only data inputs that the person in the room would receive via the sensors and so he would still be in the same position as before. For if the room were now mounted on a robot, the information about the robot's movements and what its sensors detect would have to be fed into the room as syntactical information, and so the person in the room would simply have more meaningless squiggles to deal with and still no way of making the leap to genuine understanding.

Summary: Physicalist theories

What physicalists have in common is the conviction that a scientifically respectable account of consciousness must not make reference to what they regard as occult supernatural substances or properties. If we are to make sense of the mind we cannot posit the existence of things of an extraordinary kind lying beyond the ordinary world yet mysteriously joined to it. Instead, the solution to the mind–body problem must ultimately lie in this world, the world of physical objects. But under the heading of physicalism there is a great range of very different kinds of approach to the resolution of the mind–body problem.

The neuroscientific evidence of the dependence of mental phenomena on the brain has led many to see mentality as identical to the brain and its complex operations. If mental states and processes cannot literally be brain states and processes, nonetheless the conviction is that the explanation must show how the functioning of the brain must underpin and constitute mentality. Other approaches have questioned whether the problem really lies in a misconstrual of the way our language of the mind operates. Perhaps our mistake lies in the assumption that mental-state terminology accurately picks out real entities or processes; if not, a proper account of human mentality may look very different from what our ordinary language of the mind seems to suggest to us it will.

Opposed to these efforts, dualists hold on to the conviction that the first person experience of what it is like to be conscious necessarily escapes any physicalist reduction or elimination. For these philosophers, no amount of scientific research into the brain, nor clever conceptual analysis, is ever going to fully explain the first person awareness of my thoughts, emotions and sensations.

It is likely that having read this far you are still unsure which of the various approaches we've examined comes closest to the truth. It may appear that the problems that beset each theory remain intractable. Some have argued that this intractability is of a different order to the difficulties we encounter in other areas of philosophy such as ethics, epistemology or the metaphysics of God. For the metaphysical problems involved in understanding the mind concern understanding the very thing with which we must understand in the first place. And the concepts available to us via introspection of our own minds and from our perception of physical objects, such as brains, may never be adequate to the requirements of a working naturalistic explanation of consciousness. If we accept an evolutionary account of our origins, this may give us further reason to be sceptical about the possibility of a solution to the mind–body problem. For if our capacities to make sense of things have been fashioned by the processes of natural selection, then they should not be seen, as Descartes thought they were, as a God-given ability to discover the truth by careful and painstaking enquiry. Rather our cognitive faculties are a hodge-podge of strategies which have been selected for their usefulness to a certain form of life. The conceptual apparatus available to us is, therefore, designed to help us to understand phenomena that have helped us to survive. Given this, there is no reason to suppose that we have the wherewithal to be able to explain all phenomena in the universe. Just as a rat will never be able to do long division, so we may be for ever incapable of forging the conceptual framework with which to understand just how natural processes in the brain produce consciousness.[53]

Section 3 How to prepare for the exam

These pages should be read alongside the equivalent section in the *Philosophy for A-level Year 1 and AS* textbook (which additionally contains advice on how to read philosophy).

The Assessment Objectives

The AQA A-level Philosophy specification has two Assessment Objectives (AO). These tell the examiners what they should look for in your answers when awarding marks. So, if you are to succeed in the exam, it is important that you are clear both about what the different skills are that they will assess, and also which questions will assess which skills:

- **Assessment Objective 1** (AO1) concerns how well you are able to show your *understanding* of the topic, ideas, methods and arguments and your ability to analyse and explain them by identifying the key ideas and showing how they fit together.
- **Assessment Objective 2** (AO2) builds on your understanding and tests your capacity to *analyse* philosophical positions, theories and arguments in order that you may *evaluate* how strong they are by exploring the quality of the reasoning, considering their implications and exploring objections and counter arguments.

For the A-level examination, 60 per cent of the marks are awarded for AO1 (Knowledge and Understanding) and 40 per cent is awarded for AO2 (Analysis and Evaluation).

The exam

The A-level exam consists of two, three-hour papers. Paper 1 examines sections 1 and 2 of the A-level specification (epistemology and moral philosophy) and Paper 2, sections 3 and 4 (the metaphysics of God and the metaphysics of mind).

Both exam papers will contain five questions on each section, so a total of ten questions in each paper. The breakdown of the questions on each of the sections is as follows:

- 1 × 3-mark question (all 3 marks awarded for AO1)
- 2 × 5-mark questions (all 5 marks awarded for AO1)
- 1 × 12-mark question (all 12 marks awarded for AO1)
- 1 × 25-mark question (5 marks awarded for AO1, 20 marks for AO2)

This gives a total of 50 marks for each section (30 for AO1 and 20 for AO2).

Linking this breakdown to the Assessment Objectives, you need to be aware that the *only* time you can gain marks for showing your ability to analyse and evaluate (AO2) is in answering the 25-mark question. The other questions only enable you to show your knowledge and understanding (AO1). The format of the question usually reflects this difference. In general, the 3-, 5- and 12-mark questions will ask you to outline or explain a philosophical idea or argument.

This tests your knowledge and understanding. For all these questions you should select the relevant information and explain it with clarity and precision. Stay focused on the question so as to avoid redundancy – you may lose marks if you go off topic. The amount of detail you need to put in will depend on the time available, but the better the relevant detail, the more marks you will collect. Importantly in these answers, because marks are awarded for AO1 only, you will not be credited for evaluating the arguments and positions you discuss. In answering these questions, you should *not* offer an evaluation of the idea/argument – so avoid suggesting problems, exploring counter arguments or explaining why you disagree. In contrast, the 25-mark question will ask, in some form of words, for an evaluation of an idea/position/argument. (See page 313 for more on this.)

Timings

In the exam it is important that you divide your time evenly between the sections: spend one and a half hours on each. You should practise answering questions under timed conditions as only then will you get a feel for the amount you can write in the time, and how much depth and detail can reasonably be expected of you. The exam is written in an answer booklet which leaves a certain amount of space for each question. This provides another indication of the approximate upper limit of the amount you are expected to write. But do not feel that you ought to fill up the space allocated for each answer. It is not the quantity of writing that will determine your grade and there is a danger, when the adrenalin is pumping, that you might write far more than you should and might lose focus and ramble. You need to stay in control of your material; keep a clear eye on the question and avoid including material which does not advance your answer. It is important that you take the time to think carefully through what you want to say before you begin to write. Perhaps even plan a thought-map, or a skeletal essay structure beforehand. (This can be crossed out after completing the question.)

Here are the approximate timings for each question. (These suggested timings do not correspond precisely to the division of marks.) If you are able to do the shorter answer questions quickly this will leave you more time for the last question, where you can access the AO2 marks. However, you may find that you need more time to answer the shorter questions properly, in which case it may be best for you to work more slowly through them. Remember, precision is the key to gaining marks, so care needs to be taken over framing your response and this will take time. Whatever pace you work at, be sure to leave yourself at least 40 minutes for the last question.

- 3-mark question: 3–5 minutes
- 5-mark questions: 5–10 minutes (× 2)
- 12-mark question: 15–25 minutes
- 25-mark question: 40–50 minutes

The questions

Exams are not really the time for *new* or *experimental* thinking. You need to do this during the year as you learn the material and reflect on the arguments in class and in your own writing. Rather exams are about drawing selectively on what you have learnt and framing it in a way that communicates effectively in response to the precise question. So read a question carefully and make sure you are clear about its focus – that is, what precisely it is asking – before you begin to write. Make efforts to organise your material clearly and coherently so that examiners can definitely see what you are saying. In the longer questions, this means briefly planning the order in which you will present the ideas and including a conclusion and an introduction (see below). In the shorter answer questions, this means answering the questions concisely but precisely.

Three-mark questions

These questions will test your grasp of essential concepts that you have covered on the course and your ability to encapsulate them with precision. They may ask you to provide a definition, or briefly outline an idea or theory.

Practice questions

Write answers to the following 3-mark questions. Give yourself about 3–5 minutes for each – if you know the material, it should not take long to give a short definition. Briefly outlining a theory may take a little longer. As a rough rule, you should try to answer in just one or two sentences. Think carefully about the wording so that you are as economical and precise as possible. Illustrations or examples are usually not needed, and if used should be kept brief.

Epistemology (3 marks)	**Moral philosophy** (3 marks)
1 What is a false lemma?	1 What is a consequentialist ethical theory?
2 What is *a posteriori* knowledge?	2 What is preference utilitarianism?
3 What is idealism?	3 What is moral cognitivism?
4 What is direct realism?	4 What does the humanity formula of the categorical imperative claim?
5 What is innatism?	5 What, according to Aristotle, is a virtue?
Metaphysics of God (3 marks)	**Metaphysics of mind** (3 marks)
1 What is the verification principle?	1 What do mind–brain identity theorists claim about mental states?
2 What is natural evil?	2 What is a 'philosophical zombie'?
3 What is the paradox of the stone?	3 What are qualia?
4 Briefly outline the problem of evil.	4 What is folk psychology?
5 How does Descartes define God?	5 What does property dualism claim?

Answers need to be accurate and to the point but do not need to be developed. Here are some examples.

A lemma is a premise taken for granted in an argument. A false lemma is one that is not true.

A consequentialist ethical theory claims that the moral value of any action is determined only by the consequences of that action.

The verification principle is the claim that a proposition is meaningful if and only if it is true by definition or can be verified empirically.

A mind–brain identity theorist claims that any mental state is identical to a brain state, so pains and beliefs and so on are nothing more than brain states. This means that facts about the mind are (in theory) reducible to facts about the brain.

(You may want to come up with your own versions of such questions. The glossary on page 339 will help.)

Five-mark questions

The 3-mark questions risk giving the impression that you can explain a difficult idea or argument in a sentence. Philosophical ideas are rarely so simple. The 5-mark questions require you to go further than just giving a pat definition. Rather you need to give a full explanation of a philosophical issue, and this means you must try to show that you have a detailed understanding of the complexity involved. This means doing more than simply describing. A description may fail to show an understanding of *why* someone would believe the theory or position. You must therefore try to make sense of it in order to show how it hangs together and what considerations support it. You need also to demonstrate that you understand and can use accurately the technical vocabulary you have learnt. This means you cannot merely gesture at an idea with a few words, but will need to take it apart and show how it fits together. As with the 3-mark questions, you will be awarded marks here for the precision with which you can explain the ideas.

These questions may ask you to explain particular arguments for or against a theory, or to make distinctions between particular concepts or ideas. If focusing on arguments, then your answer will not gain full marks if it does not show awareness of the way the argument might be structured. So you should be clear about the distinction between the premises and conclusion of an argument or the logical interrelations between the elements of a theory.

You may include illustrative examples to support your account, which could be drawn from the texts, but only if these help to illuminate the ideas. Quotation, however, is not necessary.

Practice questions

Write answers to the following questions, giving yourself 10 minutes for each. Be sure to reflect carefully on the wording so that your response is as clear and precise as possible.

You should try to explain the different elements of the idea and how they are connected. Examples may help to illustrate the points.

Epistemology (5 marks)	Ethics (5 marks)
1 Outline Descartes' three waves of doubt.	1 Explain the distinction that Kant draws between acting in accordance with duty and acting out of duty.
2 Explain the time lag argument against direct realism.	2 Explain Mill's distinction between higher and lower pleasures.
3 Explain the idea of the tabula rasa.	3 Outline what Aristotle means by Eudaimonia.
4 Outline Hume's fork.	4 Explain the theory of prescriptivism.
5 Outline the theory of infallibilism.	5 Explain Hume's view that moral judgements are not beliefs.

Metaphysics of God (5 marks)	Metaphysics of mind (5 marks)
1 Explain Gaunilo's objection to the ontological argument.	1 Outline the knowledge/Mary argument for property dualism.
2 Explain Paley's version of the argument from design for the existence of God.	2 Explain how the argument from analogy can be used to solve the problem of other minds.
3 Explain how a religious claim might be verified eschatologically (Hick).	3 Explain the 'super-spartan' objection to behaviourism.
4 Outline Leibniz's cosmological argument (based on the Principle of Sufficient Reason).	4 Outline Descartes' conceivability argument for substance dualism.
5 Outline the evidential form of the problem of evil.	5 Explain the difference between an ontological reduction and an analytic reduction.

Twelve-mark questions (AO1)

Like the 5-mark questions, these will ask you to explain an aspect of the syllabus, although it is likely to be a more substantial element. You might be asked to explain a theory *and* an objection, to explain and contrast two related ideas or to show how a theory may be applied.

The nature of the question should enable you to provide a greater level of detail and to develop your explanation in more depth. As the answers to these questions will be longer you will need to pay attention to the way you organise the material so that it is not just accurate, but is structured into a coherent whole.

Begin by identifying the key elements of the theory or argument and then, when giving your account of it, make sure you avoid merely describing, but show how it fits together into a logical structure which makes sense. It may be helpful to illustrate your answers with examples either drawn from the texts or some of your own. Examples can help to show examiners that you understand an idea because you can apply it, but take care to ensure your illustrations support your answer, as, once again, if you include superfluous material you will lose marks. Although these questions require longer answers remember that no marks are available for AO2 (analysis and evaluation). Your answer needs to explain how the argument/theory works as clearly as possible; you should not evaluate the argument/theory.

Practice questions

Have a go at writing answers to these 12-mark questions. Each response should take you around 20 minutes. In that time you will need to go into a reasonable level of detail, so if after 5 minutes you find you are running out of things to say, then it is likely that you need to know the topic in more depth and so will need to revise further.

Make sure you avoid merely describing; you need to explain. Be sure to pay attention to how you organise your material so that it reads as a coherent whole.

Epistemology (12 marks)	Moral philosophy (12 marks)
1 Outline and explain why Locke opposes innate ideas. 2 Outline one of Gettier's counter-examples and explain why it is considered a problem for the JTB account of knowledge. 3 Explain Russell's coherence argument for the primary-secondary quality distinction. 4 Explain how reliabilism could be used as a response to scepticism. 5 Outline Descartes' trademark argument for the existence of God and explain how this is an attempt at an *a priori* deduction.	1 Explain how a preference utilitarian might morally judge the eating of meat. 2 Explain Aristotle's function argument. 3 Compare and contrast the universal law and the humanity formulations of Kant's categorical imperative. 4 Explain the criticism that utilitarianism ignores the moral integrity and intentions of the individual. 5 Outline the meta-ethical theory of moral realism and explain how Mackie rejects the theory with his arguments from 'queerness'.
Metaphysics of God (12 marks)	**Metaphysics of mind (12 marks)**
1 Compare and contrast the versions of the cosmological arguments put forward by Descartes and Leibniz. 2 Explain why Kant objects to the design argument. 3 Explain one of Hume's objections to the cosmological argument. 4 Explain Hick's response to the problem of evil (soul-making). 5 Explain why, according to logical positivism, religious claims are meaningless.	1 Explain Ryle's view that dualism makes a 'category mistake'. 2 Compare and contrast substance and property dualism. 3 Explain the criticism of eliminative materialism that says it is self-refuting. 4 Outline functionalism and explain how the knowledge/Mary argument can be used as a criticism of the theory. 5 Explain how the possible asymmetry between self-knowledge and knowledge of other people's mental states might challenge philosophical behaviourism.

Twenty-five-mark questions (5 AO1 + 20 AO2)

All the questions we have discussed thus far involve giving accounts of historical arguments and theories. However, philosophy is much more than this. It is also about engaging meaningfully with the arguments for yourself and trying to argue for a point of view. This is exactly what the 25-mark questions involve. However, is not an easy skill to learn.

While it is important to show proper respect for the great philosophers' arguments, you must not suppose that you should not question their conclusions. Be prepared to think for yourself about how plausible you find their arguments. And when you come to the exam, make sure that you are aware of some of the main difficulties that they face; you will need to explore these to access the AO2 marks.

These are the only questions that test your capacity to develop an argument in defence of your own judgement. So to answer them you will need to consider arguments for and against a position and then reach a conclusion which follows from what you have argued. These, therefore, are the most philosophically demanding questions. If you can leave yourself around 45 or 50 minutes, this is likely to be time well spent, although not if this is at the expense of precision and clarity in your other responses.

1. **Unpack the issues raised in the question**
   Make sure you introduce your answer by briefly outlining what the question is asking. A helpful way to approach this can be to define the key terms, to identify and briefly explain the position identified in the question and/or outline the main alternative views relevant to the issue. It can also be helpful briefly to state what you intend to conclude. This helps make it clear to the examiner where you are trying to get to, but more importantly, it makes it clear to you, and this will help you to maintain focus and avoid tangential material.

2. **Analyse the relevant arguments and concepts**
   Then work through a series of arguments. When selecting points for discussion, make sure they are directly relevant to the question and also explain why they are relevant. When exploring the arguments, try to avoid merely juxtaposing different philosophers' views on the topic. Rather you should examine the cogency of each view by looking at the reasons that support it and making a judgement about how strong the support is. Before moving on, say something about whether you are rejecting a position. If you are able to make each point follow from the previous point, you will help to give the essay a sense of overall development, which is something examiners will be looking for when awarding AO2 marks.

3. **Develop a coherent overall argument in support of a judgement**
   Having explored arguments for and against a view, avoid a conclusion which simply summarises what you have said (for example, 'I have looked at Descartes' arguments and then at Kant's objections', and so on). A conclusion is not a summary; it should be a *judgement* which responds to the question. So you will need to say that the arguments you have examined show, for example, that the ontological argument fails, or that

direct realism is untenable in the face of the criticisms you have looked at. And make sure your conclusion does follow from your reasoning. If you look at arguments for and against, do not just plump for a conclusion without briefly explaining why, on balance, you find one side of the case more persuasive.

In the activity below there are some practice 25-mark questions. Some questions will use terms such as 'assess', 'critically discuss' and 'evaluate', which indicate that the examiners are awarding AO2 marks for evaluation and supporting a reasoned judgement (for example, *evaluate the claim that eating animals is morally wrong*). Other questions contain a less obvious request to evaluate (for example, *Is it wrong to eat animals?*) But, however the question is asked, the basic task, as outlined above, will be the same.

Practice questions

- Practice is essential as preparation for answering the most demanding questions on the paper.
- Give yourself 40–50 minutes to answer these questions.
- Plan the response so that it has a clear development.
- Start with a clear introduction which explains the question and what your judgement will be.
- In the main body explore in detail the arguments for and against and make your own position clear.
- Finish with a clear conclusion which responds to the question. Make sure your judgement is supported by the arguments you have considered.

Epistemology (25 marks)	Ethics (25 marks)
1 Do we perceive the world directly?	1 Can Aristotle's virtue ethics provide a sufficiently clear guide to moral action?
2 Does scepticism mean that knowledge is impossible?	2 Is it possible to derive an 'ought' from an 'is'?
3 In defining knowledge, can Gettier-style counter examples be avoided?	3 Is it always wrong to steal money?
4 Can reason alone provide substantive knowledge?	4 How convincing is preference utilitarianism as a theory of moral value?
5 If a tree falls in a forest and no being with hearing is present, does it make a noise?	5 Evaluate the Kantian position on the morality of telling lies.

Metaphysics of God (25 marks)	Metaphysics of mind (25 marks)
1 Is the concept of God coherent?	1 What does the knowledge/Mary argument tell us about the nature of the mind?
2 'Analysis of the concept of God reveals he must exist.' Evaluate this claim.	2 Evaluate the claim that mind is the brain.
3 Assess whether the Free Will defence succeeds in overcoming the problem of evil.	3 Can mental-state talk be reduced to behaviour talk?
4 'Talk of God is meaningless.' Critically discuss this claim.	4 Evaluate the theory of property dualism.
5 Is God the best explanation for the existence of order in the universe?	5 Is it possible that our folk psychological theory of the mind is radically mistaken?

In addition to these practice questions, you may find it helpful to look at the specification and to make up your own versions. You should also make sure you are familiar with all the terminology used in the specification as many questions are likely to be framed using this language. For other examples of the sorts of questions you might expect, look on the AQA website for specimen papers and past papers (including past papers from the previous version of the A-level).

Revision

A key aspect of our capacity for 'practical reason' is the ability to think of something in the future which we would like to achieve, and then reason backwards in a chain to work out a strategy for achieving it. Animals, it is often thought, lack this ability, and are largely, if not exclusively, driven by instinct. Now, in an exam, you want to produce a series of responses that will gain the best marks you are capable of. But to achieve this, as we have seen, you should not act instinctively and simply write on auto-pilot. Rather you must reflect on the precise nature of the end product. What exactly constitutes a successful response? And then you must work out strategies for realising this. This is what we were considering in the last section. But preparing an exam answer doesn't start in the exam. It begins as soon as you start to study the subject, and kicks into gear when you begin to revise. So we need now to consider how best to go about the revision process.

There is no official 'best way' to revise (and you may have developed your own successful systems), but a good start is to break down the A-level syllabus into chunks. In the following pages we have outlined one such way the syllabus could be 'chunked'.

- Our approach has yielded 10 chunks per section of the syllabus – making a total of 40 chunks (note that not all chunks are the same size).
- For each chunk it may be useful to go through your notes and textbooks with the aims of producing a few sides of revision notes (with a particular focus on those elements that you find harder to remember).
- This process can then be repeated on a second occasion and your revision notes reduced further (perhaps to cards).
- This is a time-consuming process, but there is no real short cut.
- To make the process more manageable, some students like to make revision timetables. A timetable might outline which days/evenings you will spend on which chunks.
- Obviously, the sooner you start the process of revising the more time you will have for this process of reading through notes, refining and memorising.

	Epistemology		✓ when you've revised this section	
			Revised once	Revised twice
What is knowledge?	1 Types	a Types of knowledge (acquaintance and so on) b Types of definition (real definitions)		
	2 JTB account	a Plato and Justified, True, Belief (JTB) b Are the three conditions individually necessary? c Are the three conditions jointly sufficient? Gettier's two examples and other types of lucky belief (barn cases, etc.)		
	3 Responses to Gettier	a Infallibilism b No false lemmas c Reliabilism d Epistemic virtue		
Perception as a source of knowledge	4 Direct realism	a Direct realism b *Counter: argument from illusion (plus possible response)* c *Counter: argument from perceptual variation (plus possible response)* d *Counter: argument from hallucination (plus possible response)* e *Counter: time-lag argument (plus possible response)*		
	5 Indirect realism	a Indirect realism and Locke's primary secondary distinction b *Counter: leads to scepticism about the existence of mind-independent objects.* c Response: (Locke's) involuntary nature of our experience d Response: coherence of various kinds of experience (Locke and Cockburn) e Response: external world is the 'best hypothesis' (Russell) f *Counter: can't know nature of independent objects as mind-dependent ideas cannot be like mind-independent objects (Berkeley).*		
	6 Berkeley's Idealism	a Arguments for: attack on the primary/secondary distinction and the 'Master' argument. b *Counter: arguments from illusion and hallucination (plus possible response)* c *Counter: leads to solipsism (plus possible response)* d *Counter: God's role in Berkeley's idealism (including how can ideas exist in God's mind if Berkeley claims that God cannot have sensations?) (plus possible response)*		
Reason as a source	7 Innatism	a Innatism: arguments from Plato (slave boy) and Leibniz b *Empiricist counter: Locke's arguments against innatism (and issues with these)* c *Empiricist counter: mind as 'tabula rasa': impressions and ideas (and issues with this)*		
	8 Intuition and deduction thesis	a Descartes: 'intuition', 'deduction' and 'clear and distinct ideas' b The cogito (*a priori* intuition) c Proofs of the existence of God (*a priori* deductions) d Proof of the external world (*a priori* deduction) e *Counter: responses to Descartes' cogito and arguments for God and external world (and responses)* f *Counter: how Hume's fork might apply (and possible responses)*		
Limits of Doubt	9 Doubt	a Philosophical doubt and ordinary doubt (including the role of philosophical doubt) b Local and global doubt c Descartes' three waves of doubt		
	10 Responses	a Descartes b Empiricist responses: Locke, Berkeley, Russell c Reliabilism		

Moral philosophy			✓ when you've revised this section	
			Revised once	Revised twice
Normative Theories	1 Utility	a Utility. Bentham and utility calculus. Act and rule b Mill: higher/lower pleasures c Mill: 'proof' of utilitarianism d Non-hedonistic utilitarianism. Preference		
	2 Issues	a Is pleasure the only good (Nozick's machine)? b Fairness and individual liberty/rights (including the 'tyranny of the majority') c Problems with calculation – including which beings should be included d Can/should we be impartial? e What about the moral integrity and intentions of the individual?		
	3 Kant	a 'Good will'. Acting in accordance with duty and acting out of duty b Hypothetical and categorical imperatives c The universal law formulation of the CI (including perfect and imperfect duties) d The humanity formulation of the CI		
	4 Issues	a Clashing and competing duties b Not all non-universalisable maxims are immoral (and not all universalisable, moral) c Consequences determine moral value d The value of certain motives such as love, friendship, kindness e Morality is a system of hypothetical, not categorical, imperatives (Foot)		
	5 Aristotle	a The 'good' for humans: Eudaimonia and its relationship to pleasure b The function argument. Virtues and function c Aristotle's account of virtues and vices d Moral responsibility: actions (voluntary, involuntary and non-voluntary) e Virtues, actions and reasons, the role of practical reasoning/wisdom		
	6 Issues	a Does virtue ethics give clear guidance about how to act? b Competing/clashing virtues c Circularity of defining virtuous acts and persons in terms of each other d Must a trait contribute to Eudaimonia to be a virtue? Relationship between the individual good and moral good		
	7 Application and comparison	a Stealing b Simulated killing (in video games, plays, films, etc.) c Eating animals d Telling lies e Comparing the three normative theories and the meanings of 'good', 'bad', 'right' and 'wrong'		
Meta-ethics	8 Origins and status	a Origins of moral principles: reasons/emotions/society b Status of moral language: cognitivism/ non-cognitivism; realism/anti-realism		
	9 Realism and Issues	a Moral naturalism (cognitivist). Utilitarianism (Bentham) and virtue ethics b Moral non-naturalism (cognitivist). Intuitionism and Moore's 'open question argument' and the Naturalistic Fallacy c *Counter: Hume's fork and Ayer's verification principle* d *Counter: (Hume) moral judgements are not beliefs (as beliefs alone cannot motivate)* e *Counter: Hume's is–ought gap* f *Counter: John Mackie's arguments from relativity and from queerness*		
	10 Anti-realism and issues	a Error theory (cognitivist) – Mackie b Emotivism (non-cognitivist) – Ayer c Prescriptivism (non-cognitivist) – Richard Hare d *Counter: how to account for how we use moral language, including moral reasoning?* e *Counter: how to account for moral progress?* f *Counter: does anti-realism become moral nihilism?*		

	Metaphysics of God			✓ when you've revised this section	
				Revised once	Revised twice
Concept	1 Concept of God	a Omniscience, omnipotence, supreme goodness (omnibenevolence) b God's relationship to time, for example, timeless (eternal) vs everlasting c Incoherence: paradox of the stone, Euthyphro dilemma d Compatibility (or not) of an omniscient God and humans with free will			
Arguments for the Existence of God	2 Ontological	a St Anselm's ontological argument b Descartes' ontological argument c Norman Malcolm's ontological argument			
	3 Issues	a Gaunilo's 'perfect island' b Empiricist objections to *a priori* arguments for existence c Kant's objection (existence not being a predicate)			
	4 Design	a Teleological/design arguments b Design argument from analogy (Hume) c Paley's argument (from spatial order/purpose) d Swinburne's argument (from temporal order/regularity)			
	5 Issues	a Hume's objections to the argument from analogy b Problem of spatial disorder (Hume and Paley) c It is an argument from a unique case (Hume) d Is God is the best or only explanation?			
	6 Cosmological	a The Kalām argument (temporal causation) b Aquinas' three ways (motion, atemporal causation and contingency) c Descartes' and his continuing existence (causation) d Leibniz's argument from the Principle of Sufficient Reason (contingency)			
	7 Issues	a Possibility of an infinite series b Objection to the 'causal principle' from Hume c Fallacy of composition (Russell) d Impossibility of a necessary being (Russell and Hume)			
	8 Problem of evil and Issues	a The nature of moral and natural evil b Problem of evil – logical and evidential forms c Responses and further issues, including: d Free Will defence (Plantinga) e Soul-making (including Hick)			
Religious Language	9 Religious language	a Cognitivism and non-cognitivism about religious language b Empiricist/logical positivist challenges to the status of religious language verification/falsification (Ayer) c Hick's response (eschatological verification) and issues arising from it			
	10 University debate	a Flew on falsification (Wisdom's gardener) b Mitchell's response to Flew (the Partisan) c Hare's response to Flew (bliks and the lunatic) d Issues with these responses			

Metaphysics of mind		✓ when you've revised this section	
		Revised once	Revised twice
1 Mental states	a All (or some) mental states have phenomenal properties b 'Qualia' as 'intrinsic and non-intentional phenomenal properties that are introspectively accessible' c All (or some) mental states have intentional properties (intentionality)		
2 Substance dualism	a Indivisibility argument for substance dualism (Descartes) b *Counter: the mental is divisible in some sense* c *Counter: not everything physical is divisible* d Conceivability argument for substance dualism (Descartes) e *Counter: cannot conceive of mind without body* f *Counter: what is conceivable may not be metaphysically possible* g *Counter: what is metaphysically possible tells us nothing about the actual world*		

3 & 4 Property dualism	3 a The 'philosophical zombies' argument (Chalmers)
	  b *Counter: a 'philosophical zombie'/'zombie' world is not conceivable*
	  c *Counter: what is conceivable might not be metaphysically possible*
	  d *Counter: metaphysical possibility tells us nothing about the actual world*
	4 a The 'knowledge/Mary' argument for property dualism (Jackson)
	  b *Counter: Mary gains no new propositional knowledge but gains ability knowledge*
	  c *Counter: Mary gains no new propositional knowledge but gains acquaintance knowledge*
	  d *Counter: Mary gains 'new knowledge' but this is 'old facts' known in a new way*		

5 Issues with dualism	a Dualism makes a 'category mistake' (Ryle) b Problems of interaction, empirical and conceptual (Princess of Bohemia) c Problem of other minds d Responses: argument from analogy, existence of other minds is the best hypothesis Issues facing epiphenomenalism: e Introspective self-knowledge f Phenomenology of our mental life (involves causal connections, psychological and psycho-physical) g Evolution		

6 Behaviourism
 	
7 Issues
	6 a 'Hard' behaviourism: mental-states talk translated into behaviour talk (including Hempel)
	  b 'Soft' behaviourism: propositions about mental states are propositions about behavioural dispositions (Ryle)
	7 a *Counter: dualist arguments applied to behaviourism*
	  b *Counter: mental states distinct from behaviour ('super-spartans' and perfect actors)*
	  c *Counter: hard to define mental states due to (a) circularity and (b) multiple realisability*
	  d *Counter: asymmetry between knowledge of self and other people's mental states*		

8 Mind–brain type identity theory	a Mental states identical to brain states ('ontological' reduction) but not synonymous (no 'analytic' reduction). b *Counter: dualist arguments applied to mind–brain type identity theory* c *Counter: issues with providing type identities (multiple realisability of mental states)*		
9 Eliminative materialism	a Some/all 'folk-psychological' mental states/properties do not exist and our current understanding is radically mistaken (Churchlands) b *Counter: certainty about our mental states trumps other considerations* c *Counter: good predictive and explanatory power of folk-psychology (best hypothesis)* d *Counter: belief in eliminative materialism is self-refuting*		
10 Functionalism	a Mental states characterised by functional roles which can be multiply realised b *Counter: possibility of functional duplicates with different qualia (inverted qualia)* c *Counter: possibility of functional duplicates without mentality/qualia (Ned Block's China mind)* d *Counter: knowledge/Mary argument applies to functional facts (no amount of facts can explain qualia)*		

Section 4 Anthology extracts

Section 1 The metaphysics of God

In the AS-level textbook we outlined five lenses that would help you to read the original (or at least translated) philosophical texts given in the AQA Anthology. You should apply these lenses to each of the extracts below, building towards the final task of putting the extract into your own words and really highlighting the structure of the extract.

When was the extract written? Who wrote it? Why did they write it?

What words are being used in a technical way? What is their meaning?

What are the recurring ideas in the extract? How would you summarise these?

Is there an argument being put forward? What are its key elements?

Write out the extract in your own words, using separate, numbered 'chunks'.

AQA have recommended the Early Modern Texts website www.earlymoderntexts.com as a free online source for some of the texts in this Anthology section. Academics on this website have 'translated' older philosophy texts into modern language so that they are more easily understood. One of the extracts below is taken from Early Modern Texts, and so will differ from the original text of the philosopher, and we have marked this extract: EMT.

Aquinas and the limits on God's omnipotence

anthology 1.1

Objection 2: Further, sin is an act of some kind. But God cannot sin, nor 'deny Himself' as it is said in 2 Tim. 2:13. Therefore He is not omnipotent …

Reply to Objection 2: To sin is to fall short of a perfect action; hence to be able to sin is to be able to fall short in action, which is repugnant to omnipotence. Therefore it is that God cannot sin, because of His omnipotence. Nevertheless, the Philosopher [Aristotle] says (Topic. iv, 3) that God can deliberately do what is evil. But this must be understood either on a condition, the antecedent of which is impossible – as, for instance, if we were to say that God can do evil things if He will. For there is no reason why a conditional proposition should not be true, though both the antecedent and consequent are impossible: as if one were to say: 'If man is a donkey, he has four feet.' Or he may be understood to mean that God can do some things which now seem to be evil: which, however, if He did them, would then be good. Or he is, perhaps, speaking after the common manner of the heathen, who thought that men became gods, like Jupiter or Mercury.

St Thomas Aquinas, *Summa Theologica*

Stump and Kretzmann on eternity

So we can characterize ET-simultaneity in this way. Let 'x' and 'y' range over entities and events. Then: (ET) For every x and for every y, x and y are ET-simultaneous if and only if

(i) either x is eternal and y is temporal, or vice versa; and

(ii) for some observer, A, in the unique eternal reference frame, x and y are both present – either x is eternally present and y is observed as temporally present, or vice versa; and present, or vice versa; and

(iii) for some observer, B, in one of the infinitely many temporal reference frames, x and y are both present – either x is observed as eternally present and y is temporally present, or vice versa. …

… On our definition, if x and y are ET-simultaneous, then x is neither earlier nor later than, neither past nor future with respect to, y – a feature essential to any relationship that can be considered a species of simultaneity. Further, if x and y are ET-simultaneous, x and y are not temporally simultaneous; since either x or y must be eternal, it cannot be the case that x and y both exist at one and the same time within a given observer's reference frame. … The propositions

(1) x is ET-simultaneous with y.

and

(2) y is ET-simultaneous with z.

do not entail

(3) x is ET-simultaneous with z.

Eleonore Stump and Norman Kretzmann, *The Journal of Philosophy*, Vol. 78, No. 8, 1981, pp.439–440

anthology 1.2

Plato's Euthyphro dilemma

anthology 1.3

Socrates:	And what do you say of piety, Euthyphro: is not piety, according to your definition, loved by all the gods?
Euthyphro:	Yes.
Socrates:	Because it is pious or holy, or for some other reason?
Euthyphro:	No, that is the reason.
Socrates:	It is loved because it is holy, not holy because it is loved?
Euthyphro:	Yes.
Socrates:	And that which is dear to the gods is loved by them, and is in a state to be loved of them because it is loved of them?
Euthyphro:	Certainly.
Socrates:	Then that which is dear to the gods, Euthyphro, is not holy, nor is that which is holy loved of God, as you affirm; but they are two different things.
Euthyphro:	How do you mean, Socrates?
Socrates:	I mean to say that the holy has been acknowledged by us to be loved of God because it is holy, not to be holy because it is loved.
Euthyphro:	Yes.
Socrates:	But that which is dear to the gods is dear to them because it is loved by them, not loved by them because it is dear to them.

Plato, *Euthyphro* 10B

St Anselm's ontological argument

God cannot be conceived not to exist. – God is that, than which nothing greater can be conceived. – That which can be conceived not to exist is not God.

AND it assuredly exists so truly, that it cannot be conceived not to exist. For, it is possible to conceive of a being which cannot be conceived not to exist; and this is greater than one which can be conceived not to exist. Hence, if that, than which nothing greater can be conceived, can be conceived not to exist, it is not that, than which nothing greater can be conceived. But this is an irreconcilable contradiction. There is, then, so truly a being than which nothing greater can be conceived to exist, that it cannot even be conceived not to exist; and this being you are, O Lord, our God.

St Anselm, *Proslogion*

Gaunilo's reply to Anselm

For example: it is said that somewhere in the ocean is an island, which, because of the difficulty, or rather the impossibility, of discovering what does not exist, is called the lost island. And they say that this island has an inestimable wealth of all manner of riches and delicacies in greater abundance than is told of the Islands of the Blest; and that having no owner or inhabitant, it is more excellent than all other countries, which are inhabited by mankind, in the abundance with which it is stored.

Now if someone should tell me that there is such an island, I should easily understand his words, in which there is no difficulty. But suppose that he went on to say, as if by a logical inference:

'You can no longer doubt that this island which is more excellent than all lands exists somewhere, since you have no doubt that it is in your understanding. And since it is more excellent not to be in the understanding alone, but to exist both in the understanding and in reality, for this reason it must exist. For if it does not exist, any land which really exists will be more excellent than it; and so the island already understood by you to be more excellent will not be more excellent.'

Gaunilo, Appendix to St Anselm's *Proslogion*

Descartes' ontological argument

I can easily believe that in the case of God, also, existence can be separated from essence, letting us answer the essence question about God while leaving the existence question open, so that God can be thought of as not existing. But on more careful reflection it becomes quite evident that, just as having-internal-angles-equal-to-180° can't be separated from the idea or essence of a triangle, and as the idea of highlands can't be separated from the idea of lowlands, so existence can't be separated from the essence of God. Just as it is self-contradictory to think of highlands in a world where there are no lowlands, so it is self-contradictory to think of God as not existing – that is, to think of a supremely perfect being as lacking a perfection, namely the perfection of existence.

René Descartes, *Meditation 5*, EMT

Malcolm's ontological argument

Let me summarize the proof. If God, a being a greater than which cannot be conceived, does not exist then He cannot come into existence. For if He did He would either have been caused to come into existence or have happened to come into existence, and in either case He would be a limited being, which by our conception of Him He is not. Since He cannot come into existence, if He does not exist His existence is impossible. If He does exist He cannot have come into existence (for the reasons given), nor can He cease to exist, for nothing could cause Him to cease to exist nor could it just happen that He ceased to exist. So if God exists His existence is necessary. Thus God's existence is either impossible or necessary. It can be the former only if the concept of such a being is self-contradictory or in some way logically absurd. Assuming that this is not so, it follows that He necessarily exists.

Norman Malcolm, 'Anselm's Ontological Argument'

Paley's argument from design

In crossing a heath, suppose I pitched my foot against a stone, and were asked how the stone came to be there; I might possibly answer, that, for any thing I knew to the contrary, it had lain there for ever: nor would it perhaps be very easy to show the absurdity of this answer. But suppose I had found a watch upon the ground, and it should be inquired how the watch happened to be in that place; I should hardly think of the answer which I had before given, that, for any thing I knew, the watch might have always been there. Yet why should not this answer serve for the watch as well as for the stone? Why is it not as admissible in the second case, as in the first? For this reason, and for no other, viz. that, when we come to inspect the watch, we perceive (what we could not discover in the stone) that its several parts are framed and put together for a purpose, for example, that they are so formed and adjusted as to produce motion, and that motion so regulated as to point out the hour of the day; that, if the different parts had been differently shaped from what they are, of a different size from what they are, or placed after any other manner, or in any other order, than that in which they are placed, either no motion at all would have been carried on in the machine, or none which would have answered the use that is now served by it. … This mechanism being observed (it requires indeed an examination of the instrument, and perhaps some previous knowledge of the subject, to perceive and understand it; but being once, as we have said, observed and understood), the inference, we think, is inevitable, that the watch must have had a maker: that there must have existed, at some time, and at some place or other, an artificer or artificers who formed it for the purpose which we find it actually to answer; who comprehended its construction, and designed its use.

William Paley, *Natural Theology*

Richard Swinburne's argument from design

Among examples of regularities of succession produced by men are the notes of a song sung by a singer or the movements of a dancer's body when he performs a dance in time with the accompanying instrument. Hence, knowing that some regularities of succession have such a cause, we postulate that they all have. An agent produces the celestial harmony like a man who sings a song. But at this point an obviously difficulty arises. The regularities of succession, such as songs which are produced by men, are produced by agents of comparatively small power, whose bodies we can locate. If an agent is responsible for the operation of the laws of nature, he must directly on the whole universe, as we act directly on our bodies. Also he must be of immense power and intelligence compared with men. Hence he can only be somewhat similar to men, having, like them, intelligence and freedom of choice, yet unlike them in the degree of these and in not possessing a body.

Richard Swinburne, *The Argument from Design*

Hume's criticism of the argument from design: Arguments from analogy are weak

Even if this world were a perfect product, we still couldn't be sure whether all the excellences of the work could justly be ascribed to the workman. When we survey a ship, we may get an exalted idea of the ingenuity of the carpenter who built such a complicated, useful, and beautiful machine. But then we shall be surprised to find that the carpenter is a stupid tradesman who imitated others, and followed a trade which has gradually improved down the centuries, after multiplied trials, mistakes, corrections, deliberations, and controversies. Perhaps our world is like that ship. It may be that many worlds were botched and bungled, throughout an eternity, before our present system was built; much labour lost, many useless trials made, and a slow but continued improvement carried on during infinite ages in the world-making trade. In such subjects as this, who can determine what is true – who indeed can even guess what is probable – when so many hypotheses can be put forward, and even more can be imagined?

David Hume, *Dialogues Concerning Natural Religion*, Part 5, EMT

anthology 1.10

Hume's criticism: The argument from design is undermined by the disorder of the universe

That is how there comes to be so much fruitless labour to account for things that appear bad in nature, to save the honour of the gods; while we have to admit the reality of the evil and disorder of which the world contains so much. What controlled the power and benevolence of Jupiter and obliged him to make mankind and every sentient creature so imperfect and so unhappy – we are told – is the obstinate and intractable nature of matter, or the observance of general laws, or some such reason. His power and benevolence seem to be taken for granted, in their most extreme form. And on that supposition, I admit, such conjectures may be accepted as plausible explanations of the bad phenomena. But still I ask: why take these attributes for granted, why ascribe to the cause any qualities that don't actually appear in the effect? Why torture your brain to justify the course of nature on suppositions which, for all you know to the contrary, may be entirely imaginary – suppositions for which no traces are to be found in the course of nature?

David Hume, *Enquiry Concerning Human Understanding*, Section 11, EMT

anthology 1.11

Hume's criticism of the argument from design: We have no experience of world-making

When two sorts of objects have always been observed to be conjoined together, custom leads me to infer the existence of an object of one sort wherever I see the existence of an object of the other sort; and I call this an argument from experience. But it is hard to see how this pattern of argument can be appropriate in our present case, where the objects we are considering don't fall into sorts, but are single, individual, without parallel or specific resemblance … To make this reasoning secure, we would need to have had experience of the origins of worlds; it isn't sufficient, surely, to have seen ships and cities arise from human artifice and contrivance … Can you claim to show any such similarity between the structure of a house and the generation of a universe? Have you ever seen nature in a situation that resembles the first arrangement of the elements at the beginning of the universe? Have worlds ever been formed under your eye; and have you had leisure to observe the whole progress of world-making, from the first appearance of order to its final consummation?

David Hume, *Dialogues Concerning Natural Religion*, Part 2, EMT

anthology 1.12

Paley anticipates two criticisms of the argument from design

Nor would it, I apprehend, weaken the conclusion, that we had never seen a watch made; that we had never known an artist capable of making one; that we were altogether incapable of executing such a piece of workmanship ourselves, or of understanding in what manner it was performed; all this being no more than what is true of some exquisite remains of ancient art, of some lost arts, and, to the generality of mankind, of the more curious productions of modern manufacture. Does one man in a million know how oval frames are turned? Ignorance of this kind exalts our opinion of the unseen and unknown artist's skill, if he be unseen and unknown, but raises no doubt in our minds of the existence and agency of such an artist, at some former time, and in some place or other. Nor can I perceive that it varies at all the inference, whether the question arise concerning a human agent, or concerning an agent of a different species, or an agent possessing, in some respects, a different nature.

anthology 1.13

Neither, secondly, would it invalidate our conclusion, that the watch sometimes went wrong, or that it seldom went exactly right. The purpose of the machinery, the design, and the designer, might be evident, and in the case supposed would be evident, in whatever way we accounted for the irregularity of the movement, or whether we could account for it or not. It is not necessary that a machine be perfect, in order to show with what design it was made: still less necessary, where the only question is, whether it were made with any design at all.

William Paley, *Natural Theology*

Hume's criticism of the argument from design: The Epicurean hypothesis

For instance, what if I should revive the old Epicurean hypothesis? This is commonly and I think rightly regarded as the most absurd system ever yet proposed; but I suspect that with a few alterations it might be given a faint appearance of probability. Instead of supposing matter to be infinite, as Epicurus did, let us suppose it to be finite and also suppose space to be finite, while still supposing time to be infinite. A finite number of particles in a finite space can have only a finite number of transpositions; and in an infinitely long period of time every possible order or position of particles must occur an infinite number of times. So this world, with all its events right down to the tiniest details, has already been produced and destroyed and will again be produced and destroyed an unlimited number of times. No-one who properly grasps the difference between infinite and finite will have any trouble with this conclusion.

anthology 1.14

David Hume, *Dialogues Concerning Natural Religion*, Part 8 EMT

Aquinas' first way

The first and more manifest way is the argument from motion. It is certain, and evident to our senses, that in the world some things are in motion. Now whatever is in motion is put in motion by another, for nothing can be in motion except it is in potentiality to that towards which it is in motion; whereas a thing moves inasmuch as it is in act. For motion is nothing else than the reduction of something from potentiality to actuality. But nothing can be reduced from potentiality to actuality, except by something in a state of actuality. Thus that which is actually hot, as fire, makes wood, which is potentially hot, to be actually hot, and thereby moves and changes it. Now it is not possible that the same thing should be at once in actuality and potentiality in the same respect, but only in different respects. For what is actually hot cannot simultaneously be potentially hot; but it is simultaneously potentially cold. It is therefore impossible that in the same respect and in the same way a thing should be both mover and moved (that it should move itself). Therefore, whatever is in motion must be put in motion by another. If that by which it is put in motion be itself put in motion, then this also must needs be put in motion by another, and that by another again. But this cannot go on to infinity, because then there would be no first mover, and, consequently, no other mover; seeing that subsequent movers move only inasmuch as they are put in motion by the first mover; as the staff moves only because it is put in motion by the hand. Therefore it is necessary to arrive at a first mover, put in motion by no other; and this everyone understands to be God.

anthology 1.15

St Thomas Aquinas, *Summa Theologica*

Descartes' cosmological argument

[T]his shows me quite clearly that I depend for my continued existence on some being other than myself. Perhaps this being is not God, though. Perhaps I was produced by causes less perfect than God, such as my parents. No; for as I have said before, it is quite clear that there must be at least as much reality or perfection in the cause as in the effect. And therefore, given that I am a thinking thing and have within me some idea of God, the cause of me – whatever it is – must itself be a thinking thing and must have the idea of all the perfections that I attribute to God. What is the cause of this cause of me? If it is the cause of its own existence, then it is God; for if it has the power of existing through its own strength, then undoubtedly it also has the power of actually possessing all the perfections of which it has an idea – that is, all the perfections that I conceive to be in God. If on the other hand it gets its existence from another cause, then the question arises all over again regarding this further cause: Does it get its existence from itself or from another cause? Eventually we must reach the ultimate cause, and this will be God.

anthology 1.16

It is clear enough that this sequence of causes of causes can't run back to infinity, especially since I am dealing with the cause that not only produced me in the past but also preserves me at the present moment.

René Descartes, *Meditation 3*, EMT

Leibniz's argument from the Principle of Sufficient Reason

31. Our reasonings are based on two great principles: the principle of contradiction, on the strength of which we judge to be false anything that involves contradiction, and as true whatever is opposed or contradictory to what is false.
32. And the Principle of Sufficient Reason, on the strength of which we hold that no fact can ever be true or existent, no statement correct, unless there is a sufficient reason why things are as they are and not otherwise – even if in most cases we can't know what the reason is.
33. There are also two kinds of truth: those of reasoning and those of fact.
    - Truths of reasoning are necessary, and their opposite is impossible.
    - Truths of fact are contingent, and their opposite is possible.

    When a truth is necessary, the reason for it can be found by analysis in which it is teased apart into simpler ideas and truths until we arrive at the basic ones.
34. That is how mathematicians use analysis, reducing theorems of mathematical theory and canons of mathematical practice to definitions, axioms and postulates.
35. Eventually their analysis comes to an end, because there are simple ideas that can't be given a definition; and their demonstrations also come to an end, because there are axioms and postulates – in a word, basic principles – which can't be proved and don't need to be proved; these are identical propositions, the opposites of which contain explicit contradictions.
36. What mathematicians do is to find sufficient reasons for the truth of mathematical propositions. But a sufficient reason must also be found for contingent truths, truths of fact – for the series of things spread across the universe of created things. For truths of this sort reasons can be given in more and more detail, because of the immense variety of things in Nature and because of the infinite divisibility of bodies. Consider the movements of pen across paper that I am making right now. Their efficient cause includes an infinity of shapes and of motions, present and past; and their final cause – that is, their end or purpose – involves an infinity of tiny inclinations and dispositions of my soul, present and past.
37. But all this detail only brings in other contingencies – ones bringing in even more detail, or ones involving events that occurred earlier – and each of these further contingencies also needs to be explained through a similar analysis. So when we give explanations of this sort we move no nearer to the goal of completely explaining contingencies. Infinite though it may be, the train of detailed facts about contingencies – running down into ever more minute detail, or back to ever earlier times – doesn't contain the sufficient reason, the ultimate reason, for any contingent fact. For that we must look outside the sequence of contingencies.
38. That is why the ultimate reason for things must be in a necessary substance which we call 'God'. The details of all the contingent changes are contained in him only eminently, as in their source.
39. This necessary substance is a sufficient reason for all this detail, which is interconnected throughout; so there is only one God, and this God is sufficient.

anthology 1.17

Leibniz, *Monadology*

Mary Midgley: How wickedness is possible

The general recipe for inexcusable acts is neither madness nor a bizarre morality, but a steady refusal to attend both to the consequences of one's actions and to the principles involved.

This is at least a part of what Socrates meant by his paradoxical insight that nobody does wrong willingly ... If the wrong-doer really understood what he was doing, Socrates said, he could not possibly do it. This sounds at first like an excuse, like saying that all wrong-doers are misinformed or mad. But Socrates certainly did not mean it as an excuse. He said it as a part of his attempt to get people to think more, in order to avoid wickedness ... He is talking about something fully in our control, something which he takes to be the essence of sin – namely, a deliberate blindness to ideals and principles, a stalling of our moral and intellectual faculties.

anthology 1.18

Mary Midgley, *Wickedness: A Philosophical Essay*, Hodder 1984, p.65

Plantinga's Free Will defence

A world containing creatures who are significantly *free* (and *freely perform more* good than evil actions) is more valuable, all else being equal, than a world containing no free creatures at all. Now God can create free creatures, but He can't *cause* or *determine* them to do only what is right. For if He does so, then they aren't significantly free after all; they do not do what is right *freely*. To create creatures capable of *moral good*, therefore, He must create creatures capable of moral evil; and He can't give these creatures the freedom to perform evil and at the same time prevent them from doing so. As it turned out, sadly enough, some of the free creatures God created went wrong in the exercise of their freedom; this is the source of moral evil. The fact that free creatures sometimes go wrong, however, counts neither against God's omnipotence nor against His goodness; for He could have forestalled the occurrence of moral evil only by removing the possibility of moral good.

Alvin Plantinga, *God, Freedom and Evil: Essays in Philosophy*

Hick on soul-making

I suggest, then, that it is an ethically reasonable judgement, even though in the nature of the case not one that is capable of demonstrative proof, that human goodness slowly built up through personal histories of moral effort has a value in the eyes of the Creator which justifies even the long travail of the soul-making process.

… For if our general conception of God's purpose is correct the world is not intended to be a paradise, but rather the scene of a history in which human personality may be formed towards the pattern of Christ. Men are not to be thought of on the analogy of animal pets, whose life is to be as agreeable as possible, but rather on the analogy of human children, who are to grow to adulthood in an environment whose primary and overriding purpose is not immediate pleasure but the realizing of the most valuable potentialities of human personality.

John Hick, *Evil and the God of Love*

Ayer on factual significance

My own version of [the verifiability principle] … was that 'a sentence is factually significant to any given person, if, and only if, he knows how to verify the proposition which it purports to express – that is, if he knows what observations would lead him, under certain conditions, to accept the proposition as being true, or reject it as being false'. Meaning was also accorded to sentences expressing propositions like those of logic or pure mathematics, which were true or false only in virtue of their form, but with this exception, everything of a would-be indicative character which failed to satisfy the verification principle was dismissed as literally nonsensical.

A.J. Ayer, *The Central Questions of Philosophy*

Ayer's modified verification principle

To test whether a sentence expresses a genuine empirical hypothesis, I adopt what may be called a modified verification principle. For I require of an empirical hypothesis, not indeed that it should be conclusively verifiable, but that some possible sense-experience should be relevant to the determination of its truth or falsehood. If a putative proposition fails to satisfy this principle, and is not a tautology, then I hold that it is metaphysical, and that, being metaphysical, it is neither true nor false but literally senseless. It will be found that much of what ordinarily passes for philosophy is metaphysical according to this criterion, and, in particular, that it can not be significantly asserted that there is a non-empirical world of values, or that men have immortal souls, or that there is a transcendent God.

A.J. Ayer, *Language, Truth and Logic*

anthology 1.22

Flew: religious statements are unfalsifiable

Now it often seems to people who are not religious as if there was no conceivable event or series of events the occurrence of which would be admitted by sophisticated religious people to be sufficient reason for conceding 'There wasn't a God after all' or 'God does not really love us then.' Someone tells us that God loves us as a father loves his children. We are reassured. But then we see a child dying of inoperable cancer of the throat. His earthly father is driven frantic in his efforts to help, but his Heavenly Father reveals no obvious sign of concern. Some qualification is made – God's love is 'not merely human love' or it is 'an inscrutable love', perhaps – and we realise that such sufferings are quite compatible with the truth of the assertion that 'God loves us as a father (but, of course …).' We are reassured again. But then perhaps we ask: what is this assurance of God's (appropriately qualified) love worth, what is this apparent guarantee really a guarantee against? Just what would have to happen … to entitle us to say 'God does not love us' or even 'God does not exist'?

Antony Flew, *Theology and Falsification*

anthology 1.23

Section 2: The metaphysics of mind

Chalmers – What is consciousness?

[T]here is something it feels like to be a cognitive agent. This internal aspect is conscious experience. Conscious experiences range from vivid color sensations to experiences of the faintest background aromas; from hard-edge pains to the elusive experience of thoughts on the tip of one's tongue; from mundane sounds and smells to the encompassing grandeur of musical experience; from the triviality of a nagging itch to the weight of a deep existential angst; from the specificity of the taste of peppermint to the generality of one's experience of selfhood. All these have a distinct experienced quality. All are prominent parts of the inner life of the mind.

David Chalmers, *The Conscious Mind*, p.4

anthology 2.1

Chalmers – The hard problem of consciousness

'The hard problem of consciousness is the problem of experience. Human beings have subjective experience: there is something it is like to be them. We can say that a being is conscious in this sense – or is phenomenally conscious, as it is sometimes put – when there is something it is like to be that being. A mental state is conscious when there is something it is like to be in that state. Conscious states include states of perceptual experience, bodily sensation, mental imagery, emotional experience, occurrent thought, and more. There is something it is like to see a vivid green, to feel a sharp pain, to visualize the Eiffel tower, to feel a deep regret, and to think that one is late. Each of these states has a phenomenal character, with phenomenal properties (or qualia) characterizing what it is like to be in the state'.

Chalmers defines 'qualia' in a footnote as 'simply those properties that characterize conscious states according to what it is like to have them'.

David Chalmers, 'Consciousness and its place in nature'

anthology 2.2

Ryle outlines what he calls the 'official doctrine' (the main tenets of substance dualism)

[E]very human being is both a body and a mind. His body and his mind are ordinarily harnessed together, but after the death of the body his mind may continue to exist and function. Human bodies are in space and are subject to the mechanical laws which govern all other bodies in space. Bodily processes and states can be inspected by external observers. So a man's bodily life is as much a public affair as are the lives of animals and reptiles and even as the careers of trees, crystals and planets. But minds are not in space, nor are their operations subject to mechanical laws. The workings of one mind are not witnessable by other observers; its career is private. Only I can take direct cognisance of the states and processes of my own mind. A person therefore lives through two collateral histories, one consisting of what happens in and to his body, the other consisting of what happens in and to his mind. The first is public, the second private. The events in the first history are events in the physical world, those in the second are events in the mental world.

Gilbert Ryle, *The Concept of Mind*

The indivisibility argument for substance dualism

There is a great difference between the mind and the body. Every body is by its nature divisible, but the mind can't be divided. When I consider the mind – consider myself purely as a thinking thing – I can't detect any parts within myself; I understand myself to be something single and complete. The whole mind seems to be united to the whole body, but not by a uniting of parts to parts, because: If a foot or arm or any other part of the body is cut off, nothing is thereby taken away from the mind. As for the faculties of willing, of understanding, of sensory perception and so on, these are not parts of the mind, since it is one and the same mind that wills, understands and perceives. They are (I repeat) not parts of the mind, because they are properties or powers of it. By contrast, any corporeal thing can easily be divided into parts in my thought; and this shows me that it is really divisible. This one argument would be enough to show me that the mind is completely different from the body, even if I did not already know as much from other considerations.

Descartes, *Meditation 6*, EMT, p.32

The conceivability argument for substance dualism

First, I know that if I have a vivid and clear [also often translated as clear and distinct] thought of something, God could have created it in a way that exactly corresponds to my thought. So the fact that I can vividly and clearly think of one thing apart from another assures me that the two things are distinct from one another – that is, that they are two – since they can be separated by God. Never mind how they could be separated; that does not affect the judgment that they are distinct. So my mind is a distinct thing from my body. Furthermore, my mind is me, for the following reason. I know that I exist and that nothing else belongs to my nature or essence except that I am a thinking thing; from this it follows that my essence consists solely in my being a thinking thing, even though there may be a body that is very closely joined to me. I have a vivid and clear idea of myself as something that thinks and isn't extended, and one of body as something that is extended and does not think. So it is certain that I am really distinct from my body and can exist without it

Descartes, *Meditation 6*, EMT, p.29

anthology 2.5

Chalmers' zombie world argument

According to this argument, it is conceivable that there be a system that is physically identical to a conscious being, but that lacks at least some of that being's conscious states. Such a system might be a zombie: a system that is physically identical to a conscious being but that lacks consciousness entirely. … These systems will look identical to a normal conscious being from the third-person perspective: in particular, their brain processes will be molecule-for-molecule identical with the original, and their behavior will be indistinguishable. But things will be different from the first-person point of view. … there is nothing it is like to be a zombie. There is little reason to believe that zombies exist in the actual world. But many hold that they are at least conceivable: we can coherently imagine zombies, and there is no contradiction in the idea that reveals itself even on reflection. As an extension of the idea, many hold that the same goes for a zombie world: a universe physically identical to ours, but in which there is no consciousness. … From the conceivability of zombies, proponents of the argument infer their metaphysical possibility. Zombies are probably not naturally possible: they probably cannot exist in our world, with its laws of nature. But the argument holds that zombies could have existed, perhaps in a very different sort of universe. For example, it is sometimes suggested that God could have created a zombie world, if he had so chosen. From here, it is inferred that consciousness must be nonphysical. If there is a metaphysically possible universe that is physically identical to ours but that lacks consciousness, then consciousness must be a further, nonphysical component of our universe. If God could have created a zombie world, then (as Kripke puts it) after creating the physical processes in our world, he had to do more work to ensure that it contained consciousness.

David Chalmers, 'Consciousness and its place in nature'

anthology 2.6

Jackson's knowledge argument. What Mary didn't know

Mary is a brilliant scientist who is, for whatever reason, forced to investigate the world from a black and white room via a black and white television monitor. She specialises in the neurophysiology of vision and acquires, let us suppose, all the physical information there is to obtain about what goes on when we see ripe tomatoes, or the sky, and use terms like 'red', 'blue', and so on. She discovers, for example, just which wave-length combinations from the sky stimulate the retina, and exactly how this produces via the central nervous system the contraction of the vocal chords and expulsion of air from the lungs that results in the uttering of the sentence 'The sky is blue'. (It can hardly be denied that it is in principle possible to obtain all this physical information from black and white television, otherwise the Open University would of necessity need to use colour television.) What will happen when Mary is released from her black and white room or is given a colour television monitor? Will she learn anything or not? It seems just obvious that she will learn something about the world and our visual experience of it. But then it is inescapable that her previous knowledge was incomplete. But she had all the physical information. Ergo there is more to have than that, and Physicalism is false.

Frank Jackson, 'Epiphenomenal Qualia'

Paul Churchland on why folk psychology (FP) might be false

When one centers one's attention not on what FP can explain, but on what it cannot explain or fails even to address, one discovers that there is a very great deal. As examples of central and important mental phenomena that remain largely or wholly mysterious within the framework of FP, consider the nature and dynamics of mental illness, the faculty of creative imagination, or the ground of intelligence differences between individuals. Consider our utter ignorance of the nature and psychological functions of sleep, that curious state in which a third of one's life is spent. Reflect on the common ability to catch an outfield fly ball on the run, or hit a moving car with a snowball. Consider the internal construction of a 3-D visual image from subtle differences in the 2-D array of stimulations in our respective retinas. Consider the rich variety of perceptual illusions, visual and otherwise. Or consider the miracle of memory, with its lightning capacity for relevant retrieval. On these and many other mental phenomena, FP sheds negligible light. …

Failures on such a large scale do not (yet) show that FP is a false theory, but they do move that prospect well into the range of real possibility, and they do show decisively that FP is at best a highly superficial theory, a partial and unpenetrating gloss on a deeper and more complex reality. Having reached this opinion, we may be forgiven for exploring the possibility that FP provides a positively misleading sketch of our internal kinematics and dynamics, one whose success is owed more to selective application and forced interpretation on our part than to genuine theoretical insight on FP's part.

Paul Churchland, 'Eliminative materialism and the propositional attitudes'

Patricia Churchland on why science rejects folk categories

Why does science tend to reject our everyday folk criteria in favor of others that are arcane and of little apparent relevance to everyday life? One answer is that the scientific categories more accurately reflect the structure of reality itself. We consider the categories more accurate because they enable more powerful explanations, predictions, and manipulations of the world. For example, our production and manipulation of fire was aided by understanding the chemical process of oxidation. But oxidation is of little use in understanding what makes the sun hot, since nuclear fusion involves events at the *subatomic* level. Additionally, the development of modern scientific categories permits scientists to connect and unify their understanding in ways that the primitive categories do not.

Patricia Churchland, *Brain-wise*, p.130

Ryle outlines how dualism may lead to the problem of other minds

There is thus a polar opposition between mind and matter, an opposition which is often brought out as follows. Material objects are situated in a common field, known as 'space', and what happens to one body in one part of space is mechanically connected with what happens to other bodies in other parts of space. But mental happenings occur in insulated fields, known as 'minds', and there is, apart maybe from telepathy, no direct causal connection between what happens in one mind and what happens in another. Only through the medium of the public physical world can the mind of one person make a difference to the mind of another. The mind is its own place and in his inner life each of us lives the life of a ghostly Robinson Crusoe. People can see, hear and jolt one another's bodies, but they are irremediably blind and deaf to the workings of one another's minds and inoperative upon them.

Gilbert Ryle, *The Concept of Mind*

anthology 2.10

Avramides on the argument from analogy

One standard response to this question [the problem of other minds] – and a very natural one – has come to be known as the argument from analogy. According to this argument, I come to know that another has a mind in the following manner: I begin by assuming the existence of my own mind and noting a correlation between my having a mind and my behaviour. I then observe similar sorts of behaviour in another, and conclude *by analogy* that the other also has a mind. Thus I reason from what I know with certainty to what I have reason to think is the case. Notice that there is a certain insecurity involved in such a form of reasoning; the conclusions of such an argument are no more than probable: given what I do know with security (the existence of my own mind), it is probable to some degree or other than there are other minds.

Anita Avramides, *Other Minds*, p.45

anthology 2.11

Ryle on category mistakes – the cricket example

A foreigner watching his first game of cricket learns what are the functions of the bowlers, the batsmen, the fielders, the umpires and the scorers. He then says 'But there is no one left on the field to contribute the famous element of team-spirit. I see who does the bowling, the batting and the wicket-keeping; but I do not see whose role it is to exercise esprit de corps.' Once more, it would have to be explained that he was looking for the wrong type of thing. Team-spirit is not another cricketing-operation supplementary to all of the other special tasks. It is, roughly, the keenness with which each of the special tasks is performed, and performing a task keenly is not performing two tasks. Certainly exhibiting team-spirit is not the same thing as bowling or catching, but nor is it a third thing such that we can say that the bowler first bowls and then exhibits team-spirit or that a fielder is at a given moment either catching or displaying esprit de corps.

Gilbert Ryle, *The Concept of Mind*

anthology 2.12

Princess Elisabeth of Bohemia outlines the conceptual interaction problem

The question arises because it seems that how a thing moves depends solely on (i) how much it is pushed, (ii) the manner in which it is pushed, or (iii) the surface-texture and shape of the thing that pushes it. The first two of those require contact between the two things, and the third requires that the causally active thing be extended. Your notion of the soul entirely excludes extension, and it appears to me that an immaterial thing can't possibly touch anything else.

Letter from Princess Elisabeth of Bohemia to Descartes

anthology 2.13

Jackson on why pain does not cause behaviour

It is supposed to be just obvious that the hurtfulness of pain is partly responsible for the subject seeking to avoid pain, saying 'It hurts' and so on. But, to reverse Hume, anything can fail to cause anything. No matter how often B follows A, and no matter how initially obvious the causality of the connection seems, the hypothesis that A causes B can be overturned by an over-arching theory which shows the two as distinct effects of a common underlying causal process. To the untutored the image on the screen of Lee Marvin's fist moving from left to right immediately followed by the image of John Wayne's head moving in the same general direction looks as causal as anything. And of course throughout countless Westerns images similar to the first are followed by images similar to the second. All this counts for precisely nothing when we know the over-arching theory concerning how the relevant images are both effects of an underlying causal process involving the projector and the film. The epiphenomenalist can say exactly the same about the connection between, for example, hurtfulness and behaviour. It is simply a consequence of the fact that certain happenings in the brain cause both.

Frank Jackson, 'Epiphenomenal Qualia'

Jackson rejects the evolution objection to epiphenomenalism

[An objection to epiphenomenalism] relates to Darwin's Theory of Evolution. According to natural selection the traits that evolve over time are those conducive to physical survival. We may assume that qualia evolved over time – we have them, the earliest forms of life do not – and so we should expect qualia to be conducive to survival. The objection is that they could hardly help us to survive if they do nothing to the physical world. The appeal of this argument is undeniable, but there is a good reply to it. Polar bears have particularly thick, warm coats. The Theory of Evolution explains this (we suppose) by pointing out that having a thick, warm coat is conducive to survival in the Arctic. But having a thick coat goes along with having a heavy coat, and having a heavy coat is *not* conducive to survival. It slows the animal down. Does this mean that we have refuted Darwin because we have found an evolved trait – having a heavy coat – which is not conducive to survival? Clearly not. Having a heavy coat is an unavoidable concomitant of having a warm coat (in the context, modern insulation was not available), and the advantages for survival of having a warm coat outweighed the disadvantages of having a heavy one. The point is that all we can extract from Darwin's theory is that we should expect any evolved characteristic to be *either* conducive to survival *or* a by-product of one that is so conducive. The epiphenomenalist holds that qualia fall into the latter category. They are a by-product of certain brain processes that are highly conducive to survival.

Frank Jackson, 'Epiphenomenal Qualia'

Hempel responds to the perfect actor objection

[I]n the case of the simulator, only some of the conditions are fulfilled which verify the statement 'This man is mentally unbalanced,' those, namely, which are most accessible to direct observation. A more penetrating examination – which should in principle take into account events occurring in the central nervous system – would give a decisive answer. If, at this point, one wished to push the objection to the point of admitting that a man could show *all the 'symptoms'* of a mental disease without being 'really' ill, we reply that it would be absurd to characterize such a man as 'really normal'; for it is obvious that by the very nature of the hypothesis we should possess no criterion in terms of which to distinguish this man from another who while exhibiting the same bodily behaviour down to the last detail, would 'in addition' be 'really ill'. (To put the point more precisely, one can say that this hypothesis contains a *logical contradiction*, since it amounts to saying, 'It is possible that a statement should be false even when the necessary and sufficient conditions of its truth are fulfilled.')

Carl Hempel, 'The logical analysis of psychology' in J. Heil (ed.), *Philosophy of Mind. A Guide and Anthology*, Oxford University Press, pp.84–95, p.91

Ryle on dispositions

When we describe glass as brittle, or sugar as soluble, we are using dispositional concepts, the logical force of which is this. The brittleness of glass does not consist in the fact that it is at a given moment actually being shivered. It may be brittle without ever being shivered. To say that it is brittle is to say that if it ever is, or ever had been, struck or strained, it would fly, or have flown, into fragments. To say that sugar is soluble is to say that it would dissolve, or would have dissolved, if immersed in water. A statement ascribing a dispositional property to a thing has much, though not everything, in common with a statement subsuming the thing under a law. To possess a dispositional property is not to be in a particular state, or to undergo a particular change; it is to be bound or liable to be in a particular state, or to undergo a particular change, when a particular condition is realised. The same is true about specifically human dispositions such as qualities of character. My being an habitual smoker does not entail that I am at this or that moment smoking; it is my permanent proneness to smoke when I am not eating, sleeping, lecturing or attending funerals, and have not quite recently been smoking.

Gilbert Ryle, *The Concept of Mind*

anthology 2.17

Putnam on mind–brain identity

Many philosophers believe that the statement 'pain is a brain state' violates some rules or norms of English. But the arguments offered are hardly convincing. For example, if the fact that I can know that I am in pain without knowing that I am in brain state S shows that pain cannot be brain state S, then, by exactly the same argument, the fact that I can know that the stove is hot without knowing that the mean molecular kinetic energy is high (or even that molecules exist) shows that it is *false* that temperature is mean molecular kinetic energy, physics to the contrary. In fact, all that immediately follows from the fact that I can know that I am in pain without knowing that I am in brain state S, is that the concept of pain is not the same concept as the concept of being in brain state S. But either pain, or the state of being in pain, or some pain, or some pain state, might still be brain state S. After all, the concept of temperature is not the same as the concept of mean molecular kinetic energy. But temperature is mean molecular kinetic energy.

Hilary Putnam, 'The nature of mental states' in Rosenthal, D.M. (ed.), 1991, *The Nature of Mind*, Oxford University Press, Oxford & New York, pp.197–203 (p.198)

anthology 2.18

Patricia Churchland on Ontological Reduction

The baseline characterization of scientific reduction is tied to real examples in the history of science. Most simply, a reduction has been achieved when the causal powers of the macrophenomenon are explained as a function of the physical structure and causal powers of the mircrophenomenon. That is, the macro-properties are discovered to be the entirely natural outcome of the nature of the elements at the microlevel, together with their dynamics and interactions. For example, *temperature* in a gas was reduced to *mean molecular kinetic energy*.

Does a reduction of a macrotheory to a microtheory require that the key words of the macrotheory *mean* the same as the words referring to the microproperties. Not at all. A common misunderstanding, especially among philosophers, is that if macrotheory about α is reduced to microtheory features β, γ, δ, then α must *mean the same as* β and γ and δ. Emphatically, this is not a requirement, and has never been a requirement, in science. In fact, meaning identity is rarely, if ever, preserved in scientific identifications. Temperature of a gas is *in fact* mean molecular kinetic energy, but the phrase 'temperature of a gas', is not *synonymous* with 'mean molecular kinetic energy.' Most cooks are perfectly able to talk about the temperature of their ovens without knowing about anything about the movement of molecules.

Patricia Churchland, *Brain-wise*, p.21

anthology 2.19

Smart defends the identity theory against a common objection

Objection 1. Any illiterate peasant can talk perfectly well about his after-images, or how things look or feel to him, or about his aches and pains, and yet he may know nothing whatever about neurophysiology. A man may, like Aristotle, believe that the brain is an organ for cooling the body without any impairment of his ability to make true statements about his sensations. Hence the things we are talking about when we describe our sensations cannot be processes in the brain.

Reply. You might as well say that a nation of slug-abeds, who never saw the morning star or knew of its existence, or who had never thought of the expression 'the Morning Star', but who used the expression 'the Evening Star' perfectly well, could not use this expression to refer to the same entity as we refer to (and describe as) 'the Morning Star'. You may object that the Morning Star is in a sense not the very same thing as the Evening Star, but only something spatiotemporally continuous with it. That is, you may say that the Morning Star is not the Evening Star in the strict sense of 'identity' that I distinguished earlier. I can perhaps forestall this objection by considering the slug-abeds to be New Zealanders and the early risers to be Englishmen. Then the thing the New Zealanders describe as 'the Morning Star' could be the very same thing (in the strict sense) as the Englishmen describe as 'the Evening Star'. And yet they could be ignorant of this fact.

There is, however, a more plausible example. Consider lightning. Modern physical science tells us that lightning is a certain kind of electrical discharge due to ionization of clouds of water-vapor in the atmosphere. This, it is now believed, is what the true nature of lightning is. Note that there are not two things: a flash of lightning and an electrical discharge. There is one thing, a flash of lightning, which is described scientifically as an electrical discharge to the earth from a cloud of ionized water-molecules. The case is not at all like that of explaining a footprint by reference to a burglar. We say that what lightning really is, what its true nature as revealed by science is, is an electric discharge. (It is not the true nature of a footprint to be a burglar.)

J.J.C. Smart, 'Sensations and brain processes'

Smart on contingent identity

Let me first try to state more accurately the thesis that sensations are brain processes. It is not the thesis that, for example; 'after-image' or 'ache' means the same as 'brain process of sort X' (where 'X' is replaced by a description of a certain sort of brain process). It is that, in so far as 'after-image' or 'ache' is a report of a process, it is a report of a process that *happens to be* a brain process. It follows that the thesis does not claim that sensation statements can be *translated* into statements about brain processes. Nor does it claim that the logic of a sensation statement is the same as that of a brain-process statement. All it claims is that in so far as a sensation statement is a report of something, that something is in fact a brain process. Sensations are nothing over and above brain processes. Nations  are nothing 'over and above' citizens, but this does not prevent the logic of nation statements being very different from the logic of citizen statements, nor does it insure the translatability of nation statements into citizen statements. (I do not, however, wish to assert that the relation of sensation statements to brain-process statements is very like that of nation statements to citizen statements. Nations do not just *happen to be* nothing over and above citizens, for example. I bring in the 'nations' example merely to make a negative point: that the fact that the logic of A-statements is different from that of B-statements does not insure that A's are anything over and above B's.)

J.J.C. Smart, 'Sensations and brain processes'

Putnam on the spatial location problem

Some philosophers maintain that 'P1 is P2' is something that can be true, when the 'is' involved is the 'is' of empirical reduction, only when the properties P1 and P2 are (a) associated with a spatio-temporal region; and (b) the region is one and the same in both cases. Thus 'temperature is mean molecular kinetic energy' is an admissible empirical reduction, since the temperature and the molecular energy are associated with the same space-time region, but 'having a pain in my arm is being in a brain state' is not, since the spatial regions involved are different. This argument does not appear very strong. Surely no one is going to be deterred from saying that mirror images are light reflected from an object and then from the surface of a mirror by the fact that an image can be 'located' three feet *behind* the mirror!

Hilary Putnam, 'The nature of mental states' in Rosenthal, D.M. (ed.), 1991, *The Nature of Mind*, Oxford University Press, Oxford & New York, pp.197–203 (p.198)

Patricia Churchland on elimination

Some theories are better than others. The theory that bubonic plague is God's punishment is not as successful as the theory that it is a rat-borne bacteria infection. The first suggests prayer as a preventative, the second predicts that hand washing, rat killing and water boiling will be more effective. As indeed they are. The theory that Zeus makes thunder by hurling luminous bolts is not as successful as the theory that lightning causes a sudden heating of adjacent air and therewith a sudden expansion. And so forth.

What about theories concerning ourselves – *our* natures? Our ideas about why people do certain things, and indeed why one does something oneself, are part of a wider network of story structures, with some cultural variability and some commonality. We explain and predict one another's behavior by relying on stories about attitudes, will power, beliefs, desires, superegos, egos and selves. For example, we explain a certain basketball player's demands for attention in terms of his big ego; we may describe a backsliding smoker as lacking will power, an actor as moody or as obsessed with popularity or as having a narcissistic personality disorder, and so on. Freud (1856–1939) urged us to explain compulsive behavior in terms of superego dysfunction. But what, in neurobiological terms, *are* these states – will power, moods, personality, ego, and superego? Are some of these categories like the categories of now-defunct but hitherto 'obvious' Aristotelian physics, categories such as 'impetus' and 'natural place'?

Patricia Churchland, *Brain-wise* p.31

anthology 2.23

Putnam on the advantages of functionalism over identity theory

[W]e *can* specify the functional state with which we propose to identify pain, at least roughly, without using the notion of pain. Namely, the functional state we have in mind is the state of receiving sensory inputs which play a certain role in the Functional Organization of the organism. This role is characterized, at least partially, by the fact that the sense organs responsible for the inputs in question are organs whose function is to detect damage to the body, or dangerous extremes of temperature, pressure and so on, and by the fact that the 'inputs' themselves, whatever their physical realization, represent a condition that the organism assigns a high disvalue to. […] this does *not* mean that the Machine will always *avoid* being in the condition in question ('pain'); it only means that the condition will be avoided unless not avoiding it is necessary to attain some more highly valued goal. Since the behaviour of the Machine (in this case, an organism) will depend not merely on the sensory input, but also on the Total State (on other values, beliefs, and so on), it seems hopeless to make any general statement about how an organism in such a condition *must* behave.

Hilary Putnam, 'The nature of mental states' in *The Nature of Mind*, Rosenthal, D.M. (ed.) (1991) Oxford University Press, Oxford & New York pp.197–203 (p.202)

anthology 2.24

anthology 2.25

Ned Block's Chinese mind

I shall describe a class of devices that are *prima facie* embarrassments for all versions of functionalism in that they indicate functionalism is guilty of liberalism – classifying systems that lack mentality as having mentality. Consider the simple version of machine functionalism already described. It says that each system having mental states is described by at least one Turing-machine table of a certain kind, and each mental state of the system is identical to one of the machine-table states specified by the machine table. I shall consider inputs and outputs to be specified by descriptions of neural impulses in sense organs and motor-output neurons. …

Imagine a body externally like a human body, say yours, but internally quite different. The neurons from sensory organs are connected to a bank of lights in a hollow cavity in the head. A set of buttons connects to the motor-output neurons. Inside the cavity resides a group of little men. Each has a very simple task: to implement a 'square' of an adequate machine table that describes you. On one wall is a bulletin board on which is posted a state card – a card that bears a symbol designating one of the states specified in the machine table. Here is what the little men do: Suppose the posted card has a 'G' on it. This alerts the little men who implement G squares – 'G-men' they call themselves. Suppose the light representing input 'I' goes on. One of the G-men has the following as his sole task: when the card reads 'G' and the 'I' light goes on, he presses output button 'O', and changes the state card to 'M'. This G-man is called upon to exercise his task only rarely. In spite of the low level of intelligence required of each little man, the system as a whole manages to simulate you because the functional organization they have been trained to realize is yours. Through the efforts of the little men, the system realizes the same (reasonably adequate) machine table as you do and is thus functionally equivalent to you.

I shall describe a version of the homunculi-headed simulation, which has more chance of being nomologically possible. How many homunculi are required? Perhaps a billion are enough.

Suppose we convert the government of China to functionalism, and we convince its officials to realize a human mind for an hour. We provide each of the billion people in China (I chose China because it has a billion inhabitants) with a specially designed two-way radio that connects them in the appropriate way to other persons and to the artificial body mentioned in the previous example. We replace each of the little men with a citizen of China plus his radio. Instead of a bulletin board we arrange to have letters displayed on a series of satellites placed so that they can be seen from anywhere in China.

The system of a billion people communicating with one another plus satellites plays the role of an external 'brain' connected to the artificial body by radio. …

It is not at all obvious that the China-body system is physically impossible. It could be functionally equivalent to you for a short time, say an hour.

Ned Block, 'Troubles with functionalism'

Glossary

Section 1 The metaphysics of God

Abductive arguments An abductive argument (which is often described as inference to the best explanation), is one that proceeds from an effect to argue for the most likely cause.

Analytic A proposition is analytic if it is true by definition. This means you can work out that it is true just by analysing the meanings of the words involved. For example, 'All sisters are female'. Analytic propositions are contrasted with 'synthetic' ones for which understanding the meanings of the words involved is not sufficient to determine whether they are true. Knowledge of such propositions therefore requires some knowledge of the way the world is as well. For example, 'All sisters are jealous of their siblings'.

Anti-realism If you are a realist about something, then you believe it exists independently of our minds. If you are an anti-realist about something you think it is mind-dependent. This is closely connected to non-cognitivism. For example, in epistemology, anti-realists about perception think that material objects exist only for minds and that a mind-independent world is non-existent. (Berkeley summed up this idealist position by saying that to be is to be perceived.) An example of anti-realism in religious language is Wittgenstein's theory that religious terms need to be understood within a religious language game.

A posteriori A Latin term that describes a belief that can only be known via experience of the world: for example, that 'snow is white' or that 'the Atlantic is smaller than the Pacific'. *A posteriori* beliefs are contrasted with *a priori* beliefs.

A priori A Latin term that usually describes a belief (or knowledge) that is known prior to or independently from experience. *A priori* beliefs are contrasted with *a posteriori* beliefs, which are ones derived from experience.

Atemporal Outside of time. It is generally agreed that God is eternal, but some theologians maintain that this means that God exists outside of time: he has no past, present or future.

Atheism In the tradition of western philosophy, atheism generally refers to the belief that there is no God in a Christian (or Jewish, or Islamic) sense.

Blik R.M. Hare's term for a foundational belief or interpretation of the world.

Cognitivism and non-cognitivism Cognitivism is the view that judgements are propositions which can be known – they refer to the world and they have a truth-value (they are capable of being true or false). Non-cognitivism is the view that judgements cannot be known, because they do not say anything true or false about the world (they do not have a truth-value). There are many different forms of non-cognitivism such as that of Hare and Wittgenstein.

Compatibilism Compatibilism is the view that free will is compatible with determinism. In other words, there is no contradiction in the idea of an action which is completely causally determined and yet still free.

Conclusion A belief or statement that an argument tries to prove. If an argument is valid and all of the premises are true, then the conclusion will also be true.

Contingent A state of affairs is contingent if it happens to be the case, but could have been otherwise. A contingent proposition is one that could be either true or false.

Cosmological argument Cosmology is the study of the universe as a whole. Cosmological arguments for the existence of God operate by claiming that there must be some ultimate cause or reason for the existence of the universe. This explanation cannot be found within the universe and so must be found in some supernatural being, namely God.

Deductive argument An argument where the truth of the conclusion is guaranteed by the truth of the premises. In other words, it is an argument in which the premises entail the conclusion. So if one accepts the truth of the premises, one must, as a matter of logical necessity, accept the conclusion. For example: either you will become a fireman or a doctor. But you can only become a doctor with a medical degree which you will never get. So you will become a fireman. A deductive argument is in contrast to an inductive argument.

Deism A belief within natural theology that a supernatural Creator, or God, created the universe but no longer interacts with its creation.

Determinism The belief that all events in the universe are the necessary consequence of physical laws, and that these laws apply to human actions as well. A determinist might claim that humans are like complex pieces of biological machinery with no free will. Some philosophers (see **compatibilism**) believe that free will is compatible with determinism.

Dualism Dualism about mind and body is the claim that humans are made of two distinct kinds of stuff: a material body and a spiritual mind.

Empiricism/empiricist An epistemological position which holds that our beliefs and knowledge must be based on experience. David Hume was one philosopher who rigorously applied his empiricist approach to questions in the philosophy of religion.

Eschatology Eschatology is the study of the 'end of things' or the 'last things' as described from a religious perspective: this includes death, what happens after we die, the end of time, the Last Judgement, and so on. Eschatological verification is a term used by John Hick to describe the process by which religious statements can (in theory) be shown to be meaningful: if they are true then they can be shown to be true (verified) after we die.

Eternality Existing forever. The claim that God is eternal was traditionally understood to mean that God is timeless or atemporal. Many theologians now argue that God is everlasting (rather than atemporal), i.e. existing in space and time but without beginning or end.

Euthyphro dilemma In the philosophy of religion this dilemma raises the question 'In what way are God's commands good?' and offers two problematic options. The first option is that whatever God commands is good, in which case his commands to commit genocide (Deuteronomy 3:2) or infanticide (Genesis 2:2), for example, are good. The second option is that God's commands are good because they conform to some external moral law, in which case we should pay attention to this moral law, rather than God.

Existentialism The name for a group of related philosophies which focus on describing and explaining what it feels like to exist as a human. Some of the key concerns revolve around the individual, the range of human experience and the significance of choice or free will.

Factual significance A statement has factual significance if it tells us something about the real world. Some theories of meaning (such as verificationism) maintain that a sentence is only meaningful if it is factually significant.

Fallacy This refers to an argument which has gone wrong, either because a mistake has been made, rendering the argument invalid; or because the argument has a form, or structure, which is always invalid.

Fallacy of composition The logical error of arguing that, because every member of a group has a property in common, the group taken as a whole also possesses that same property.

Falsificationism A philosophical theory about the nature of meaning. Closely related to verificationism, falsificationism claims that for a proposition to be meaningful we must be able to understand what would count as proving the proposition false (i.e. what would falsify it).

Hypothetical statements An 'if... then...' proposition, for example 'If you were offered a cup of tea, then you would accept.' In Ryle's analytical behaviourism, certain mental states are regarded as dispositions to act in various ways and dispositions can be translated into hypotheticals of this kind which detail what a person would do if certain circumstances were realised.

Immutable Something that can never change. God is said to be immutable, and this is bound up with the idea that God is simple (he is one thing, and his attributes such as benevolence and omnipotence cannot be separated from one another).

Incorporeal Not made of matter, non-material. God is said to be incorporeal.

Inductive arguments An argument where the truth of the conclusion is not fully guaranteed by the truth of the premises. For example, moving from particular examples (every raven I have seen has been black) to a generalisation (all ravens are black); or moving from our experience of the past (day has always followed night) to a prediction about the future (day will always follow night). Arguments from analogy are also inductive: they compare two things, and move from what these two things are known to have in common to draw a conclusion about other (unknown) things they are supposed to have in common.

Infinite regress A regress is a process of reasoning from effect to cause, or of going backwards in a chain of explanations. An infinite regress is one where the process never stops, where it is repeated endlessly. This is generally considered problematic in a philosophical argument, and a sign that a mistake has been made.

Intelligent design A modern version of the teleological argument couched in scientific terminology. It claims that certain characteristics of living things cannot be explained through evolution – they are 'irreducibly complex' – and that only the existence of an intelligent designer (God) can explain them. Although it presents itself as 'science' it is best seen as a theological argument for God's existence.

Language game The phrase used by Wittgenstein to convey the idea that language has meaning within a particular social context, and that these contexts are governed by rules (in the same way that different games are governed by different rules). The way in which a sentence is meaningful therefore varies according to the context in which it occurs.

Metaphysics One of the three main areas of philosophical study and analysis (including epistemology and moral philosophy). Metaphysics is concerned with determining what sorts of things really exist, what is the ultimate nature of reality, where the world comes from, what is the relationship of our mind to the world. (It is said that the term 'metaphysics' came about because in ancient catalogues of Aristotle's work, his books on the nature of reality came after (in Greek, *meta*) his books on physics – hence, metaphysics.)

Natural theology Gaining an understanding of God through the use of our reason. This may be through an examination of the world around us (which leads, for example, to the teleological argument), or through an analysis of concepts (which leads, for example, to ontological argument). This is in contrast to revealed theology.

Naturalism The view that we can explain the world, or a particular concept, in terms of the natural sciences.

Necessary 'Necessary' and 'contingent' are opposing terms. In the most restricted sense, a necessary truth is one which has to be true and could not be otherwise. Another way of thinking about a necessary truth is as a truth where the opposite is logically impossible; for example, that a triangle has three sides (a two-sided triangle is logically impossible and cannot be imagined). A contingent truth is one which just happens to be true, and is a truth where the opposite is logically possible, for example, it is true that Theresa May was once the prime minister of the United Kingdom (but it is entirely possible that this may never have happened).

Non-cognitivism See **cognitivism and non-cognitivism**.

Omnibenevolent All-loving or supremely good. Along with omnipotence and omniscience this is one of the main attributes of God.

Omnipotent All-powerful. Along with omnibenevolence and omniscience this is one of the main attributes of God.

Omniscient All-knowing. As with omnibenevolence and omnipotence, this is one of the attributes of God. However, some theologians have argued that these attributes cannot be separated from one another in God, because God is simple and immutable.

Ontological arguments Ontology is the study of existence. If you were to write down everything you thought existed (cats, dogs, electrons, aliens, and so on), then this list would form your own personal ontology. If aliens were present on the list then you could be said to be making an ontological commitment to the existence of aliens (in other words you claim they exist). All believers (except anti-realists) include God in their ontology. The ontological argument is a particular proof of God's existence, and tries to show that the very meaning of the concept 'God' implies that he must exist.

Physico-theological argument A term used by the philosopher Immanuel Kant to describe an argument for God's existence based on particular features of the world (for example, order, regularity, design). The phrase did not catch on, and we now refer to these arguments as teleological or arguments from design.

Predicate Many propositions can be divided into a subject and a predicate, where the subject is the thing that the sentence is about and the predicate gives us information about the subject. For example, in the sentence, 'The balloon is red', the expression 'is red' is the predicate, the term 'balloon', the subject. Some philosophers argued that in the sentence 'God exists', 'exists' is a predicate applying to 'God'. However, philosophers from Kant onwards have doubted whether existence is a genuine predicate.

Premise Any reason given (usually in the form of a statement or claim) to build or support an argument.

Problem of evil A problem recognised by both believers and atheists: how can an all-powerful, all-loving and all-knowing creator have created a world which seems to contain so much unnecessary pain and suffering?

Proposition A sentence that makes a claim about the way the world actually is. Non-cognitivists claim that judgements are not propositions; in other words, they are not making claims about the world and are neither true nor false.

Rationalism/rationalist The tendency in philosophy to regard reason, as opposed to sense experience, as the primary source of the important knowledge of which we are capable. Rationalists are typically impressed by the systematic nature of mathematical knowledge and the possibility of certainty that it affords. Using mathematics as the ideal of how knowledge should be, rationalists typically attempt to extend this type of knowledge into other areas of human inquiry, such as to knowledge of the physical world, or to ethics. Rationalism is traditionally contrasted with **empiricism**: the view that most of what we know is acquired through experience.

Reductio ad absurdum A method of argument by which you prove that a claim is false by first supposing it to be true and then drawing out the logical consequences. If these consequences can be shown to be false or absurd then the original claim cannot be true. Aquinas uses a *reductio ad absurdum* in his cosmological arguments.

Revealed theology Gaining an understanding of God through the revelations of sacred texts and prophets. This is in contrast to natural theology, although to Aquinas the two approaches are compatible with each other.

Revelation Information that is revealed, or disclosed, to humans by a supernatural source, such as God or angels. The Bible is regarded as a work of revelation, and it forms the basis of revealed theology.

Subject In grammar, the part of a proposition that picks out the main object which is being described or discussed: for example, in 'The red balloon popped', the subject is 'the balloon'. In the sentence, 'God is the greatest conceivable being', 'God' is the subject.

Syllogism A classic form of deductive logical argument in which a conclusion follows from (usually two) true premises (often a general claim and a more specific claim).

Teleological Purpose, goal or end, deriving from the Greek word telos. A teleological explanation gives an account of events by reference to their purpose or ultimate goal.

Teleological arguments Also known as arguments from design, these conclude that God exists on the basis of certain features of the universe: for example, observations concerning its ordered nature, or concerning the apparent design and purpose of the parts of living organisms.

Theodicy (From the Greek theos – 'god' – and dike – 'justice') The attempt to justify God's actions, and to show why, for example, a perfect God has created an imperfect world. The most common forms of theodicy are responses to the problem of evil that explain why God allows pain and suffering to exist.

Theology The study of God from a religious perspective. This is in contrast to the philosophy of religion, which starts from a philosophical perspective.

Transcendence To move outside, beyond or removed from something. So to say that God is transcendent is to say that he exists outside of his creation, outside of space and time.

Verification principle   The rule put forward by verificationists that a proposition is only meaningful if it can be shown to be true or false by experience or by analysis of the meanings of the terms involved.

Verificationism   A philosophical belief about the nature of meaning. Logical positivism claims that for a proposition to be meaningful it must be (hypothetically) verifiable or true by definition. Other than truths by definition most propositions make a specific claim about the universe – that it is this way or that – for example, that 'there is a cat on my mat' or that the 'leaves on my tree are green'. In such cases it is easy for us to imagine how such claims could be verified or not. 'God loves the world'. How could we verify this claim? What could we look for in the world to see whether that claim is true or not? If it is not clear how the universe would look if the claim were true or not, then it is not clear what it is asserting and thus logical positivists might claim that the proposition is not meaningful.

Section 2: The metaphysics of Mind

Acquaintance knowledge See **propositional knowledge** and **acquaintance knowledge**.

Analytic A proposition is analytic if it is true by definition. This means you can work out that it is true just by analysing the meanings of the words involved. For example, 'All sisters are female'. Analytic propositions are contrasted with 'synthetic' ones for which understanding the meanings of the words involved is not sufficient to determine whether they are true. Knowledge of such propositions therefore requires some knowledge of the way the world is as well. For example, 'All sisters are jealous of their siblings'.

Analytic reduction To reduce one **phenomenon** to another is to explain one in terms of the other. An analytic reduction is concerned with the *meaning* of the language we use to talk about phenomena and claims that all that is said about one phenomenon can be translated into talk about another without loss of meaning.

A priori *A priori* knowledge is knowledge which can be known without the need for sense experience. By contrast, *a posteriori* knowledge can only be established by reference to experience. For example, we can know that no bachelors are married without conducting a survey of bachelors' marital status and so this knowledge is *a priori*, but we could not work out what percentage of bachelors are left handed except by some sort of **empirical** investigation and so this knowledge is *a posteriori*.

Automaton (plural **automata**) A mechanism that operates and/or moves automatically, usually resembling a human being. The term is often used to refer to the idea of a being which acts without conscious awareness and so can be used as a synonym for a **philosophical zombie**. But automata may be conscious, as in Huxley's phrase 'conscious automata', used to refer to animals and humans whose actions are not controlled by conscious volitions (see **epiphenomenalism**). The term is also used to refer to a mechanism the operations of which may be described in a **machine table**.

Behaviourism Here used as short for **philosophical behaviourism**.

Cartesian dualism 'Cartesian' is the adjective deriving from Descartes' name, so it describes any doctrine expounded by Descartes. 'Cartesian dualism' refers to Descartes' version of mind–body dualism and to versions of **substance dualism** inspired by Descartes.

Chauvinism Chauvinism is the ungrounded belief in the superiority of one's own nationality, sex or race. In philosophy of mind it is used to refer to the implication one can draw from certain theories that members of other species (either real or imaginary) could not possess certain types of mental state. This implication is usually taken to represent a problem for such theories. The opposed tendency of allowing too wide a range of beings to count as minded is termed **liberalism**, and is also considered problematic.

Compatibilism Compatibilism is the view that free will is compatible with determinism. In other words, there is no contradiction in the idea of an action which is completely causally determined and yet still free.

Consciousness All that you are directly aware of, including thoughts, emotions and sensations. The contents of the mind.

Contingent A state of affairs is contingent if it happens to be the case, but could have been otherwise. A contingent proposition is one that could be either true or false.

Contingent identity Two things are identical if they are really just one thing. Angela Merkel and the Chancellor of Germany are the same thing in this sense. A contingent identity is one where two things happen to be the same, but might not have been. In other words, there is a possible world in which the two are not the same. For example, it is possible for Angela Merkel not to have become Chancellor so this identity is contingent. Mind–brain identity theorists hold that a contingent identity holds between mental states and brain states, so that while they happen to be the same, it is still conceivable that they might have been something else, meaning that there is a possible world in which the mind is some other organ, say, the heart. Such identities cannot be discovered by investigation of the meanings of the terms involved and so can only be established by empirical investigation.

Dualism In philosophy of mind, mind–body dualism (or more simply 'dualism') is the view that the mind and body are not identical (that is, they are dual) meaning that the mental cannot be reduced to the physical. Dualism is contrasted with **monism**.

Eliminativism or **eliminative materialism** The view that **folk-psychological** concepts, such as belief, desire and sensation, do not pick out real entities. Our language of the mind is therefore fundamentally misleading and so should be replaced by terminology forged by a mature **neuroscience**.

Empirical From experience or observation.

Empiricism/empiricist The philosophical tendency to regard experience as the sole or most important source of our concepts and knowledge.

Epiphenomenalism The view that mental states such as sensations and beliefs are caused by states of the brain, but that there is no reciprocal influence of mental states on the brain and body or on other mental states. Thus mental states are by-products of the physical processes that go on in the body which govern our actions.

Experimenting with ideas The 'thought experiment' is a philosophical technique employed to explore our intuitions about conceptual possibilities and implications. Because they are concerned with what is possible, rather than what is actually the case in the real world, they are conducted in the imagination. There is some controversy about how useful explorations of our intuitions are in establishing what is and is not genuinely possible.

Folk psychology Folk psychology is the theory of mind (or psychology) held by ordinary people (folk). It is claimed that our everyday picture of the mind as a private world of sensations, emotions, beliefs and so on, constitutes a theoretical framework which we use to explain and predict behaviour. The idea can be used to try to solve the problem of other minds, since if the theory that others possess minds is the best explanation of human behaviour then it is rational to believe in them. But, theories can also be refuted, and **eliminativists** claim that folk psychology will be superseded by the **neuroscience** of the future.

Functional state A state which is defined in terms of its causal role rather than in terms of what it is made of. Functionalism claims that mental states are functional states of the brain, and so that it is the causal relationship to sensory inputs, other mental states and to behaviour which determines the nature of any mental state.

Hypothetical propositions An 'if… then…' proposition, for example 'If you were offered a cup of tea, then you would accept.' In Ryle's **philosophical behaviourism**, certain mental states are regarded as dispositions to act in various ways and dispositions can be translated into hypotheticals of this kind which detail what a person would do if certain circumstances were realised.

Idealism Idealism is an anti-realist theory of perception. It is the view that matter does not exist independently of the mind and that all that exists are minds and their ideas. Physical objects are no more than collections of sensations appearing in minds.

Intentionality The quality of certain mental states which directs them beyond themselves and to things in the world. It's what makes mental states such as beliefs, desires and fears about something. For example, my belief that it is raining is about the rain, and my fear of heights it about heights.

Interactionism The common sense view that mind and body are in causal interaction, so that mental events such as acts of will or decisions, can cause actions and that events in the body, such as changes brought about by the impact of the environment on our sense organs, can cause mental events such as sensations.

Intersubjective The relationship between distinct subjects of experience. The awareness one person has of other persons and other persons' consciousnesses.

Introspection The process of looking into your own mind. The direct awareness each of us has of his or her own mental states.

Irreducible (see **Reduction**, **Reducible**) If some higher level phenomenon, such as consciousness, cannot be fully explained in terms of a lower level phenomenon, such as the operations of the brain, then the first is said to be irreducible to the second. The irreducibility of consciousness is the central tenet of dualism.

Leibniz's Law Also known as the principle of the identity of indiscernibles, the law states that no two objects can share all their properties; so that if what appear to be two objects turn out to have all the same properties, then they must be one object.

Liberalism   The tendency of a theory of mind to count as minded systems we would be reluctant to think of as conscious, such as computers or even simpler mechanisms.

Logical positivism   The twentieth-century school of thought that emphasised the necessity of an empirical basis for knowledge and rejected as meaningless 'metaphysical' claims which have no grounding in experience. Logical positivists, such as Ayer, held that all meaningful propositions must either be statements of logic or mathematics and so purely analytic, or confirmable by empirical means (that is 'verifiable').

Machine state functionalism   Machine state functionalism is the view that minded human beings are to be understood as a complex system of inputs and outputs, the inputs being sensory and the outputs behavioural. Mental states are the internal states that can be specified by a **machine table**. The mind is the software that 'runs' on the hardware of the brain.

Machine table   A representation of the set of instructions for a machine which details how it responds to different inputs.

Materialism   A synonym for **physicalism**. The view that the mind is ultimately material in nature and so is not distinct from the physical body.

Meaning and reference   Frege (in 'Über Sinn und Bedeutung', 1892) distinguished the reference (*Bedeutung*) of a term from its meaning (*Sinn*). The reference is the thing in the world that the term refers to; the meaning is the way the term presents the reference to the mind. It is possible for a term to have the same reference but different meanings. For example, the expression 'half-blood prince' has a different meaning to 'Severus Snape' and yet they refer to the same person. It is because expressions can have different meanings but the same reference that it is possible for someone not to realise that two terms refer to the same objects. According to the identity theory, the terms we use to talk about mental states have different meanings from the terms we use to talk about brain states, but they nonetheless refer to the same things.

Monism   In philosophy of mind, the view that humans are composed of just one type of substance.

Multiply realisable   Mental states are multiply realisable if the same type of mental state may be instantiated in different types of brain state. This means that a mental state, such as pain, can occur in different creatures with very different types of brain.

Neuroscience   The science of the brain.

Nomological danglers   'Nomological' concerns the formulation of a system of laws or scientific theories used to explain natural **phenomena**. A nomological dangler is a phenomenon which cannot be explained by reference to such a theory or system of laws. Smart uses the term in the Anthology article 'Sensations and brain processes' to refer to the irreducible mental properties posited by **dualists** and argues that they should be rejected because they don't fit in with the established laws of physics.

Numerical and qualitative identity   It is possible to distinguish two senses of the 'same'. Things are qualitatively the same if they share properties. Since different copies of this book share many properties they can be termed *qualitatively identical*. But one copy is still a different thing from another. They are not literally one and the same object and so are not *numerically identical*. Numerical identity is the sameness a thing has with itself and nothing else, so the copy you are holding is qualitatively identical with other copies, but can only be numerically identical with itself.

Ockham's razor   The principle that when constructing hypotheses we should avoid multiplying entities beyond necessity. So if two competing theories both explain some phenomenon equally well, it is reasonable to prefer the one that is simpler or makes fewer assumptions. **Physicalists** sometimes invoke this principle against **dualism**, arguing that the **ontological** commitment to two substances is unnecessary.

Ontological   To do with being or real existence. An ontological category is a type of being or thing, such as minds or physical substance. An ontological commitment is a commitment to the existence of some type of thing, that is the belief or assertion that a certain type of thing exists. **Dualists** have an ontological commitment to minds as a distinct type of being from matter.

Ontological reduction An ontological reduction is an explanation of one kind of **phenomenon** in terms of something more fundamental, as when chemists tell us water is H_2O, or the identity theory tries to explain the mind in terms of the brain. If one phenomenon can be ontologically reduced to another this means they are ultimately the same things under different descriptions. But it doesn't mean that the terms used to refer to them have the same meanings and so doesn't mean that the one can be analytically reduced to the other (see **analytic reduction**).

Ontology An account of what exists.

Phenomenal Concerning the way things appear. The character of what one is directly aware of in the mind.

Phenomenon (plural **phenomena**) From the Greek for 'appearance', a phenomenon is anything that appears or is shown. Here the term is mostly used to refer to what appears within the mind; or that which is revealed in conscious experience. The term may also be used more generally to refer to the aspects of things that show themselves or are apparent, but which need to be explained in terms of some theory.

Phenomenology of the mental The phenomenology of the mental refers to those properties of mental life of which we are consciously aware, including most notably, qualia. 'Phenomenology' may also be used to refer to the science which studies the phenomena of consciousness.

Philosophical behaviourism Philosophical behaviourism is a theory about the meaning of our language of the mind. It claims that our talk of mental states does not involve reference to others' internal states. Rather it is a way of talking about people's behaviour and their dispositions to behave in various ways.

Philosophical zombie See **zombie**

Physicalism (or **materialism**) The view that everything in the universe is physical. In the philosophy of mind this means that mental states must ultimately be reducible to the physical and so mentality doesn't constitute a distinct type of **phenomenon**.

Property A property is something that depends on something else for its existence (see **substance and property**).

Property dualism Unlike substance dualism, property dualism claims that humans are composed of just one kind of substance: matter. However, what makes it a dualist theory is the claim that we possess both mental and physical properties. Mental states are dependent on the physical, so that the mind cannot exist without the body, but at the same time mental states cannot be reduced to physical states.

Propositional knowledge and acquaintance knowledge Propositional knowledge is knowledge of facts or knowledge *that* something is the case. Acquaintance knowledge is the knowledge you obtain by encountering or experiencing something. The distinction is employed in an objection to Jackson's knowledge argument, 'Mary gains no new propositional knowledge'.

Qualia (singular **quale**) The subjective feel, or **phenomenal** quality of certain conscious experiences, for example what it is like to smell petrol, the way an apple tastes, or how a cat's fur feels. An important problem for **physicalism** concerns whether the subjective nature of such experiences can be accounted for in objective physical terms.

Qualitative identity See **numerical and qualitative identity**.

Reducible If some higher level phenomenon, such as consciousness, can be fully explained in terms of a lower level phenomenon, such as the operations of the brain, then the first is said to be reducible to the second. Type identity theory says that the phenomena of consciousness can be reduced to the physical properties of the brain. Property dualism denies this, saying that a complete description of the physical properties of the brain cannot account for at least some mental phenomena (such as qualia).

Reduction To reduce one type of thing to another is to explain the first in terms of the second. See **ontological reduction** and **analytic reduction**.

Reference See **meaning and reference**.

Semantics/syntax Semantics concerns the meanings of words and sentences. Syntax concerns the rules governing correct linguistic usage. Searle employs the distinction in his Chinese room argument, claiming that a computer may be programmed to follow syntactic rules, and could conceivably pass the Turing test, but it could not understand the semantics of natural language.

Solipsism The view that nothing beyond my own mind, including the external world and other minds, can be known to exist.

Subject of experience That which is conscious; the self or 'I'.

Substance and property A substance is a basic kind of stuff or thing, something which doesn't depend on anything else to exist. A property, by contrast, cannot exist on its own, but depends on a substance. While **substance dualism** claims that there are two substances and so two fundamental types of thing in the world, **physicalists** claim there is just one – matter. **Property dualists** agree with physicalists that matter is the only substance, but argue that when it is organised properly into persons with brains it also has irreducible mental properties.

Substance dualism The view that humans are composed of two types of substance: mind and matter.

Super-spartans In the Anthology extract 'Psychological predicates' (1967), Putnam develops a thought experiment as a refutation of **philosophical behaviourism** involving people who are able to suppress all outward signs of pain. He terms them super-spartans after the Spartans of ancient Greece, who were famed for their stoicism.

Supervenience The nature of the dependence relationship often said to hold between mind and brain. Mental states would supervene on brain states if there can be no difference in the mental without a difference in the brain. But at the same time a difference in the brain need not produce a difference in the mind.

Syntax See **semantics**.

Turing test A test suggested by Alan Turing in his paper 'Computing, machinery and intelligence' (1950) for determining whether a computer could be considered able to think. If a machine's linguistic competence when engaged in conversation cannot be distinguished from that of a human being then it would pass the test.

Type and token A type is a general class or kind of thing; a token is a particular instance of a type. For example, there are four tokens of the word 'a' in the previous sentence and each is a token of the same type.

Type and token identity The mind–brain identity theory claims that mental states are the same things as brain states. If mental states are type identical with brain states, then each token of a type of mental state is the same as different tokens of the same type of brain state. So pain in me and pain in you will be the same type of neurological event, say C-fibres firing. But if mental states are token identical with brain states, then each token of a given type of mental state may be identical with tokens of different types of brain state. So pain in me may be a different type of brain event than in you, or a dog or a Martian.

Verificationism Verificationism is a claim associated with **logical positivism** that a proposition is only meaningful if it is either verifiable by experience or is analytic. The idea that meaningful utterances must tell us about the world by making some difference to our experience may be used to question whether it is meaningful to speak of other minds as necessarily private, of the possibility of spectrum inversion, or of mental states with no behavioural manifestation. For claims about mental states which cannot be identified would be empty of factual significance and so meaningless. The principle may also be used to argue that the idea of **philosophical zombies** is incoherent, since no **empirical** test could be devised to distinguish them from ordinary people. Considerations inspired by verificationism may lead to **philsophical behaviourism** and the idea that to speak meaningfully about minds, we must be referring to what can be observed, namely behaviour.

Volition An act of will which leads to a bodily movement. The mental state which initiates freely chosen actions.

Will The mental power or faculty which enables us to perform acts of volition.

Zombie or **philosophical zombie** A philosophical zombie is a hypothetical being which is physically indistinguishable from a regular human being, but which has no consciousness or subjective awareness. The idea is discussed by Chalmers in Anthology extract 2.6.

Notes

Introduction

1. Locke (1690), *An Essay Concerning Human Understanding*, Epistle to the Reader.
2. Heraclitus, as attributed by Plato, *Cratylus*, 402a.

Section 1 The metaphysics of God

1.1 The concept and nature of God

1. Emerson, R.W., 1983, 'Nature', *Emerson: Essays and Lectures*, Library of America, p.9.
2. A recent exception to this is the well-reported case, in September 2013, of a man shot in Rostov-on-Don following an argument about Kant with another man.
3. Pascal, B., 1985, *Pensées* 230, Penguin, p.245.
4. For a more detailed summary of the God of Abraham see Jones, Cardinal, Hayward, 2005, *Philosophy of Religion*, Hodder Murray, pp.10–12.
5. Norman Geisler argues that the God of Abraham is the same as the God of the Philosophers, seen from two different perspectives, in his essay 'Why the God of the Bible is the One True God', in *Why I believe in God*, ed. N. Geisler and P. Hoffman, Baker Publishers, 2009, p.101.
6. St Augustine, 1984, *City of God*, Henry Bettenson (tr.), Penguin, Book 8, Chapter 2, pp.312–313.
7. St Anselm, *Proslogion*, Chapter 2 in Plantinga, A. (ed.), 1968, *The Ontological Argument*, Macmillan, p.4.
8. Descartes, Meditation 3 in *Descartes – Selected Philosophical Writings*, 1993, Cambridge University Press, p.93.
9. Swinburne, 1977, *The Coherence of Theism*, Clarendon Press, p.2.
10. Pascal, B., 1985, *Pensées*, p.150.
11. See George Mavrodes' article 'Omniscience' in C. Taliaferro and P.J. Griffiths (eds), 2003, *Philosophy of Religion*, Blackwell, pp.236–237.
12. St Thomas Aquinas, *Summa Theologica*, 1:25.3.
13. Mackie, 'Evil and Omnipotence' in Basil Mitchell (ed.), 1971, *The Philosophy of Religion*, Oxford University Press, pp.101–104.
14. Hick, J., 1968, *Evil and the God of Love*, Fontana.
15. St Augustine, *De Trinitate*, 8.3.
16. St Anselm, *Proslogion*, 19.
17. Aquinas, *Summa Theologica* 1:14:13 (reply to objection 3). Aquinas borrows this analogy from Boethius: Book 5 in his *Consolations of Philosophy*.
18. Vonnegut, K., 2000, *Slaughterhouse 5*, Vintage, p.83.
19. Nicholas Wolterstorff, 'God is everlasting, not eternal' in Brian Davies (ed.), 2000, *Philosophy of Religion: A Guide and Companion*, Oxford University Press.
20. William Lane Craig 'The Eternal Present and Stump-Kretzmann Eternity', 1999, *American Catholic Philosophical Quarterly* 73, p.521.
21. Swinburne, R., 1993, *The Coherence of Theism*, Oxford University Press, p.221.
22. Quoted in 'Eternity', E. Stump and N. Kretzmann, 1981, *The Journal of Philosophy*, Vol. 78, No. 8, p.431.
23. Kenny, A., *The God of the Philosophers*, 1974, Oxford University Press, p.38.ff.
24. This example Stump and Kretzmann take from Wesley Salmon, 1975, *Space, Time and Motion*, Dickenson, p.76.
25. See, for example, David Blumenfeld's article 'On the Compossibility of Divine Attributes', 1978, *Philosophical Studies* 34, pp.91–103.
26. Mackie, 'Evil and Omnipotence', pp.102–104.
27. George Mavrodes, 'Some puzzles concerning omnipotence', *The Philosophical Review*, 72.
28. Aquinas, *Summa Theologica*, 1:25.3.
29. C. Wade Savage, 'The Paradox of the Stone', *The Philosophical Review* 76, pp.74–79.
30. Ibid., p.78.
31. Søren Kierkegaard, *Fear and Trembling*, in Alastair Hannay (tr.), 1985, Penguin, pp.83–95.
32. Anthony Kenny, 'Divine foreknowledge and human freedom' in *Aquinas: A Collection of Critical Essays*, pp.256–257.

1.2 Arguments relating to the existence of God

1. St Thomas Aquinas, *Summa Theologica*, 1:2:2.

2. Sextus Empiricus livens his examples up by also proving that Socrates didn't have four feet: *Outlines of Scepticism*, Julia Annas & Jonathan Barnes (eds), 2002, Cambridge University Press, Book II 164.

3. Plato, *The Republic*, Desmond Lee (tr.), 1974, Penguin, 394d, p.152

4. 'Letter from Antony Flew on Darwinism and Theology', 2004, *Philosophy Now magazine*, Issue 47.

5. In eighteenth-century France, scientists and naturalists attempted to discover whether the Beast of Gevaudan (a creature that had apparently killed 140 people) really existed. For a stylish fictionalised version of their attempts see the film *Brotherhood of the Wolf*, directed by Christopher Gans (2001).

6. The philosopher J.N. Findlay argues that this definition is correct as it arises out of a genuinely religious attitude. To a believer the object of worship 'should have an unsurpassable supremacy along all avenues [and] tower infinitely above all other objects' (J.N. Findlay, 'Can God's existence be disproved?', in A. Flew and A. MacIntyre (eds), 1955, *New Essays on Philosophical Theology*, Macmillan, p.51). However, Findlay then goes on to disprove God's existence in order to show the absurdity of the ontological argument!

7. Alvin Plantinga would add to these attributes 'worthy of worship'. An imaginary God is not worthy of worship, but the supreme being must be at the very least worthy of worship, and so must exist (Alvin Plantinga (ed.), 1968, *The Ontological Argument: From St Anselm to Contemporary Philosophers*, Macmillan, p.x).

8. Gaunilo's 'On Behalf of the Fool' is reprinted in *Plantinga, The Ontological Argument*, pp.6–13. Some philosophers have had a lot of fun with the ontological argument. For example, D. and M. Haight used it to prove the existence of the greatest conceivable evil being ('An ontological argument for the devil', 1970, *The Monist*, no. 54).

9. F.C. Copleston sees Aquinas' rejection of the ontological argument as evidence of his 'empiricism' (F.C. Copleston, 1965, *Aquinas*, Penguin, p.113). Aquinas does offer five alternative proofs of God's existence, all of them based on our experience of the effects of God's existence – namely the world we see around us.

10. Descartes, 1988, *Selected Philosophical Writings*, Meditation 5, Cambridge University Press, p.107. For a more detailed expansion and analysis of Descartes' ontological argument, read Clement Dore, 'Ontological arguments', in P.L. Quinn and C. Taliaferro (eds), 1999, *A Companion to Philosophy of Religion*, Blackwell, pp.323–329.

11. Hume, D., 1998, *Dialogues Concerning Natural Religion*, Oxford University Press, p.91.

12. Ayer, A.J., 1980, *Language, Truth and Logic*, Penguin, pp.151–152.

13. Kant, I., 1980, *Critique of Pure Reason*, Norman Kemp Smith (tr.), Macmillan, pp.500ff.

14. This is also the position taken by David Hume in his *Dialogues Concerning Natural Religion*, as we have seen. For both Hume and Kant a proposition is a necessary truth if, when we reject the predicate, a contradiction results. So 'Bachelors are unmarried men' is necessarily true because when we reject the predicate, and suggest that 'Bachelors are married men', then we have a contradiction. However, Kant, following Hume, argues that no statement about existence can be necessary, as it is always possible to deny something exists, without that statement being contradictory. So to say 'God does not exist' is not a contradiction, which means 'God exists' is not a necessary truth.

15. The Dutch theologian Johan de Kater (Caterus) made a similar criticism of Descartes' argument, and this was included in the first published edition of the Meditations as 'The First Set of Objections'. See Descartes, *Selected Philosophical Writings*, p.136.

16. Kant, *Critique of Pure Reason*, p.504.

17. In making this point Kant relies on a principle already articulated by Aristotle: namely that being does not belong to the essence of things since existence is not an attribute or characteristic; in other words that questions of existence and questions of the nature of things are distinct. (Posterior Analytics Book 2 Internet Archive http://classics.mit.edu/Aristotle/posterior.2.ii.html.)

18. Russell, B., 1996, *Why I am Not a Christian*, Routledge, p.137.

19. Malcolm, N., 'Anselm's Ontological Argument' in *The Philosophical Review*, Vol. 69, No. 1 (Jan., 1960), p.45.

20. Ibid., p.47.

21. Unfortunately Roald Dahl hasn't discovered a new form of logic, but instead cheats with wordplay when he describes Wonka's square sweets that 'look round' at Charlie and Co. as they enter the room. *Charlie and the Chocolate Factory*, 2016, Penguin, Ch. 23.

22. Hick, J., 'A critique of the "second argument" in *The Many Faced Proof: Studies on the Ontological Argument for the Existence of God*, 2009, J. Hick and A. McGill (eds), Wipf & Stock, pp.353ff.

23. Ibid., p.354.

24. The character Lucilius in Cicero's *On the Nature of the Gods*, 1972, Book II, 3–5, Penguin Classics, p.124.

25. Darwin, C., 2005, *The Autobiography of Charles Darwin*, Barnes & Noble, p.261.

26. The film *Alien*, directed by Ridley Scott, uses a creature with similarly parasitic tendencies whose offspring are planted as eggs inside the human 'hosts', before exploding from the stomachs of their hosts once they've hatched.

27. Written by Cecil Alexander in 1848.

28. Kant, I., 1980, *Critique of Pure Reason*, , Macmillan, p.520.

29. Flew, A., 1978, *An Introduction to Western Philosophy*, Thames & Hudson, p.206.

30. Terence Penelhum thinks of cosmological arguments as 'Existential' arguments, and teleological arguments as 'Qualitative' arguments. See 'Divine Necessity' in Basil Mitchell (ed.), 1971, *The Philosophy of Religion*, Oxford University Press, pp.180–181.

31. Aquinas, *Summa Theologica*, 1:2:3.

32. Paley, Natural Theology, extract reprinted in Brian Davies (ed.),

2000, *Philosophy of Religion: A Guide and Anthology*, Oxford University Press, p.257.

33 Ibid., p.259.
34 Ibid., p.257.
35 Ibid., p.257.
36 Richard Dawkins devotes a whole chapter to an analysis of how complex eyes evolved from simple, light-sensing, cells in his book *Climbing Mount Improbable*, 2006, Penguin, Chapter 5.
37 Swinburne, R., 'The Argument from Design', reprinted in Davies (ed.), 2000, *Philosophy of Religion: A Guide and Anthology*, p.286.
38 See Dawkins, R., 2006, *The God Delusion*, Houghton Mifflin, pp.123–124.
39 Swinburne, R., 'The Argument from Design', reprinted in Davies (ed.), 2000, *Philosophy of Religion: A Guide and Anthology*, p.279.
40 Hume, D., 1982, *Enquiry Concerning Human Understanding*, Section X, par. 1, Oxford University Press, p.110.
41 Although Hume is usually read as an out-and-out atheist, this over-simplifies his beliefs. For a lively account of Hume's occupation of the 'borderlands between belief and unbelief' see Sutherland, S., 1984, *Faith and Ambiguity*, SCM Press, pp.28–41.
42 Hume, *Dialogues Concerning Natural Religion*, p.67.
43 Ibid., p.78.
44 For an interesting, if flawed, proof of the logical impossibility of surprise Philosophy tests see R. Martin, 1998, *There are two Mistakes in The The Title of this Book [sic]*, Broadview Press, p.60.
45 Swinburne, 'The Argument from Design', reprinted in Davies (ed.), p.276.
46 Hume, *Dialogues Concerning Natural Religion*, p.96.
47 Ibid., p.101.
48 Ibid., p.114.
49 Ibid., pp.51–53
50 Ibid., pp.51–52.
51 Paley, Natural Theology, extract reprinted in Davies (ed.), 2000, *Philosophy of Religion: A Guide and Anthology*, p.254.
52 Ibid.
53 Hume, *Dialogues Concerning Natural Religion*, p.49.
54 Ibid., pp.84ff.
55 Kant, 1980, *Critique of Pure Reason*, p.522.
56 Ibid., p.273.
57 Gerald Jones, Daniel Cardinal and Jeremy Hayward, 2005, *Philosophy of Religion*, Hodder Education, pp.150ff.
58 Quoted in De Beer, E.S., 1974, *Charles Darwin and T. H. Huxley: Autobiographies*, Oxford University Press, p.50ff.
59 Dawkins, R., 2006, *The God Delusion*, Houghton Mifflin, p.172.
60 Hume, *Dialogues Concerning Natural Religion*, p.91.
61 Kant, *Critique of Pure Reason*, p.508.
62 Hume, *Dialogues Concerning Natural Religion*, Part 9.
63 Kant, *Critique of Pure Reason*, p.508.
64 Copleston, F.C., 1965, *Aquinas*, Pelican, p.130.
65 Ibid., p.123. See also N. Geisler 'Why the God of the Bible is the One True God', in N. Geisler and P. Hoffman (eds), 2009, *Why I believe in God*, Baker Publishers, p.101.
66 Reproduced in John Hick's anthology, 1964, *The Existence of God*, Macmillan, pp.71–79.
67 Quoted in William Lane Craig, 1979, *The Kalam Cosmological Argument*, Macmillan, p.44.
68 William Lane Craig and Quentin Smith, 1993, *Theism, Atheism and Big Bang Cosmology*, Oxford University Press, Chapter 1.
69 St Anselm, Monologion III in S.D. Deane (tr.), 1994, *St Anselm, Basic Writings*, Open Court Publishing.
70 For a very clear account of the threat Aristotle posed to Christian thought and of the assimilation of Aristotelian philosophy by Aquinas into Christian theology, see Copleston, F.C., 1965, *Aquinas*, Penguin, pp.63–69.
71 Aquinas, *Summa Theologica*, 1:2:3.
72 Rowe, William L., 1998, *The Cosmological Argument*, Fordham Press, p.15.
73 Copleston, *Aquinas*, p.121.
74 Aristotle, 2017, *Physics*, Section II, Part 3, Dover Thrift, p.34ff.
75 F.C. Copleston argues that this second interpretation is the one we should take when reading Aquinas, 1965, *Aquinas*, p.122.
76 The cosmological argument of the Islamic philosopher Avicenna (937–1037) takes this form.
77 Mackie analyses these two stages very succinctly in *The Miracle of Theism*, 1986, Oxford University Press, pp.87–92.
78 Ibid., p.90.
79 Descartes, *Meditations*, p.127.
80 Hayward, Jones, Cardinal, 2017, *Philosophy for A-level Year 1 and AS*, Hodder Education p.137.
81 Hume, *Dialogues Concerning Natural Religion*, pp.63–64.
82 Lyrics by the Bare Naked Ladies for the theme of the American sitcom *The Big Bang Theory*.
83 Mackie, *The Miracle of Theism*, p.90.
84 Sadowsky, J., 'The Cosmological Argument and the Endless Regress', reprinted in Brian Davies (ed.), 2000, *Philosophy of Religion: A Guide and Anthology*, Oxford University Press, pp.239–241.
85 Hume, *Dialogues Concerning Natural Religion*, p.92.
86 Hume, D., 1982, *An Enquiry Concerning Human Understanding*, Section IV, Part 1, Oxford University Press, p.30.
87 Hume, D., *Treatise on Human Nature*, Book 1, Part iii, Section 3.
88 Anscombe, E., 'Hume's Argument Exposed', reprinted in Davies (ed.), 2000, *Philosophy of Religion: A Guide and Anthology*, p.237.
89 Ibid., p.141.
90 Hume, *Dialogues Concerning Natural Religion*, p.92.
91 Ibid., p.92.
92 Edwards, P., 'The Cosmological Argument', reprinted in Davies (ed.), 2000, *Philosophy of Religion*, pp.207–208.
93 Russell B. and Copleston, F.C., 'The Existence of God – a Debate' in *Why I am Not a Christian*, 1996, Routledge, p.140.

94 Edwards, P., 'The Cosmological Argument', p.208.

95 Hume, *Dialogues Concerning Natural Religion*, p.91.

96 Russell and Copleston, 'The Existence of God – a Debate', p.136.

97 Smart, N., 1964, *Philosophers and Religious Truth*, SCM, p.96.

98 Philosophical pedants might like to note that even this most banal example of a necessary proposition has been questioned, given the fuzziness of the concept of 'bachelor'. See Terry Winograd's article 'Moving the Semantics Fulcrum', 1985, *Linguistics and Philosophy* 8:1, pp.91–104.

99 Aquinas, *Summa Theologica*, 1:2:1.

100 Hume, *Dialogues Concerning Natural Religion*, p.92.

101 Russell and Copleston, 'The Existence of God – a Debate', p.140.

102 Capote, T., 2000, *In Cold Blood*, Penguin, p.237.

103 For a more detailed analysis of pain and suffering in relation to evil see Hick, J., 1968, *Evil and the God of Love*, Fontana, pp.328–372.

104 St Augustine, *Confessions*, Book 7, Chapter 5.

105 Capote, T., 2000, *In Cold Blood*, p.84.

106 St Augustine, *The Nature of Good*, 4.

107 St Augustine, *Confessions*, Book 3, Chapter 7.

108 See for example Hick, *Evil and the God of Love*, p.18.

109 Diamond, J., 1992, *The Rise and Fall of the Third Chimpanzee*, Vintage, Chapter 16.

110 St Augustine: 'God is good, yea most mightily better than all his works ... Where, then, is evil, and whence does it come and how has it crept in?' in *Confessions*, Book 7, Chapter 5. Aquinas: 'If, therefore, God existed there would be no evil discoverable; but there is evil in the world. Therefore God does not exist.' In *Summa Theologica*, 1:2:3.

111 This summary of Epicurus' position was made by Lanctantius, *A Treatise on the Anger of God*, Chapter 13.

112 Hick, *Evil and the God of Love*, p.3.

113 Mackie, J. L., 'Evil and Omnipotence' in 1971, *The Philosophy of Religion*, B. Mitchell (ed.), Oxford University Press, p.92.

114 Reprinted in B. Mitchell (ed.), 1971, *The Philosophy of Religion*, Oxford University Press, pp.92–93.

115 Plantinga, A., 1975, *God, Freedom and Evil*, Harper & Row, p.20.

116 Although Mary Baker Eddy, the Christian Scientist, did claim that evil is an illusion in *Science and Health*, Christian Science Publishing, 1934, p.480.

117 Quoted in De Beer, E.S., 1974, *Charles Darwin and T. H. Huxley: Autobiographies*, Oxford University Press, p.52.

118 Hume, *Dialogues Concerning Natural Religion*, p.105.

119 Rowe, W., 'The problem of evil and some varieties of atheism', in C. Taliaferro and P.J. Griffiths (eds), 2003, *Philosophy of Religion*, Blackwell, pp.306–373.

120 Sartre, J.P., 1973, *Existentialism and Humanism*, Methuen, pp.32–33.

121 Ibid., p.28.

122 See Jones, Cardinal, Hayward, 2003, *Existentialism and Humanism: Jean-Paul Sartre*, John Murray, Ch.8.

123 Midgley, M., 1984, *Wickedness*, Routledge, p.55.

124 Ibid., p.14.

125 Ibid.

126 Ibid., p.65.

127 The term 'theodicy' was first used by Gottfried Leibniz in his *Essays of Theodicy*, 1710.

128 For a succinct account of a new process theodicy as proposed by David Griffin see Hick, J., 1990, *Philosophy of Religion*, Prentice Hall, pp.48–55.

129 Hick, *Evil and the God of Love*, p.374.

130 Ibid., p.375.

131 Genesis 3:14–20.

132 Quoted in Plantinga, *God, Freedom and Evil*, p.27.

133 Hick, *Evil and the God of Love*, p.293.

134 Voltaire, 1996, *Candide*, Wordsworth Classics, p.12.

135 Flew, A., 'Divine Omnipotence and Human Freedom', in Flew and MacIntyre (eds), 1955, *New Essays in Philosophical Theology*, SCM.

136 Mackie, 'Evil and Omnipotence', pp.100–101.

137 Plantinga, A. 1974, *The Nature of Necessity*, Clarendon Press, pp.180–181.

138 Hick, *Evil and the God of Love*, p.293.

139 Rollins, H.E. (ed.), 1958, *The Letters of John Keats, 1814–1821*, Harvard, p.101.

140 Hick, *Evil and the God of Love*, p.292.

141 Ibid., pp.322–323.

142 Ibid., p.369.

143 Elim Klimov's film *Come and See* (1985) offers a compelling and graphic account of these atrocities from a child's perspective.

144 Dostoyevsky, F., 1970, *The Brothers Karamazov*, Bantam, pp.295–296.

1.3 Religious language

1. Rabelais, F., 1955, *The Histories of Gargantua and Pantagruel*, Penguin, p.231.
2. Pseudo-Dionysius, 'The Divine Names' in Lubheid, C. (tr.), 1987, *The Complete Works*, SPCK, pp.49–50.
3. Ogden, C.K. and Richards, I.A., 1989, *The Meaning of Meaning*, Harcourt.
4. From Lewis Carroll's poem 'The Jabberwocky' in *Through the Looking Glass and What Alice Found There*, 1993, Wordsworth, p.20.
5. Chomsky, N., 1957, *Syntactic Structures*, Mouton, p.15.
6. Ayer, A.J., 1980, *Language, Truth and Logic*, Penguin, p.41.
7. Hayward, Jones, Cardinal, 2017, *Philosophy for A-level Year 1 and AS*, Hachette, p.128.
8. Hick, J., 1963, *Philosophy of Religion*, Prentice Hall, p.95.
9. Ayer, *Language, Truth and Logic*, pp.151ff.
10. Ibid., p.152.
11. Sutherland, S.R., 'Language, Newspeak and Logic' in Phillips Griffiths, A. (ed.), 1992, *A. J. Ayer, Memorial Essays*, Cambridge, p.78.
12. Hick, J., 'Theology and Verification' in Mitchell, B. (ed.), 1971, *The Philosophy of Religion*, Oxford University Press, pp.59–60.
13. Flew, A., Hare, R.M. and Mitchell, B., 'Theology and Falsification', in Mitchell, B. (ed.), (ed.), 1971, *The Philosophy of Religion*, Oxford University Press, p.13ff.
14. McEwan, I., 1998, *Enduring Love*, Vintage, Appendix 2.
15. Job 19:25. For an updating of the story of Job see the Coen brothers' film *A Serious Man* (2009).
16. Flew, Hare, and Mitchell, 'Theology and Falsification', p.15.
17. Ibid., pp.18–19.
18. It is unlikely, but possible, that the film director Paul Verhoeven had read Mitchell's parable when writing the script for his gripping film about the Dutch resistance movement *Black Book* (2006).
19. Flew, Hare, and Mitchell, 'Theology and Falsification', p.16.
20. Ibid., p.17.
21. Ibid., p.22.
22. Wittgenstein, L., 1981, *Philosophical Investigations*, 43, Blackwell, p.20.
23. Ibid., 23, pp.11–12.
24. Ibid., 23, p.11.
25. Wittgenstein, L. 1970, *Lectures and Conversations on Aesthetics, Psychology and Religious Belief*, Blackwell, p.53.
26. This well-known Socratic principle is articulated in several dialogues by Plato, although never in this precise form. For example, see *The Republic* 394d (Penguin, 2003), *Euthyphro* 14a (in *Last Days of Socrates*, Penguin, 2003) and *Sophist* 224e (Dover, 2003).
27. Pascal, B., 1985, *Pensées*, Penguin, p.85.
28. Pinker, S., 1998, *How The Mind Works*, Penguin, p.561.

Section 2 The metaphysics of mind

2.1 What do we mean by 'mind'?

1. Chalmers, D., 1996, *The Conscious Mind*, Oxford University Press, p.4.
2. You may also compare your list to Chalmers' 'catalogue of conscious experiences' in *The Conscious Mind*, pp.6–10.
3. Chalmers, *The Conscious Mind*, p.4.
4. Descartes, Meditations on First Philosophy, *Meditation 2*, p.5. Early Modern Texts (EMT), Copyright ©2010–2015 All rights reserved. Jonathan Bennett. Available at: www.earlymoderntexts.com/assets/pdfs/descartes1641.pdf
5. Freud, S., *The Conscious Mind*, pp.13–15.
6. Churchland, Patricia, *Brain-wise*, pp.48–50.
7. Chalmers, D., 2003, 'Consciousness and its place in nature', in S. Stich and T. Warfield (eds), *Blackwell Guide to Philosophy of Mind*, Blackwell, pp.103–4.
8. The term 'explanatory gap' was coined by Joseph Levine in Levine, J., 1983, 'Materialism and Qualia: The Explanatory Gap', *Pacific Philosophical Quarterly*, Vol. 64, pp.354–61.
9. Other monists claim that the one ultimate reality is neither mental or physical and so is neutral about its nature; a view known as *neutral monism*.

2.2 Dualist theories

1. *Meditation 6*, EMT, p.32.
2. *Meditation 2*, EMT, p.5.
3. Descartes in the *Synopsis of the Meditations*. 1911 edition, *The Philosophical Works of Descartes*, Cambridge University Press, translated by Haldane, Elizabeth S., p.5. Available at: http://selfpace.uconn.edu/class/percep/DescartesMeditations.pdf
4. Ibid., p.5.
5. For a further philosophical discussion of this topic see Nagel, T., 1971, 'Brain Bisection and the Unity of Consciousness', *Synthese*, Vol. 22 (May), pp.396–413 and Churchland, Patricia, *Brain-wise*, pp.44–47.
6. Hume, D., *Treatise on Human Nature*, I.iv.6.
7. Ibid., I.iv.6.
8. *Meditation 2*, EMT, p.5.
9. Arnauld, A., *The Fourth Set of Objections to the Meditations*, EMT www.earlymoderntexts.com/assets/pdfs/descartes1642_2.pdf, p.56.
10. 'Objections to the Meditations with Descartes' Replies', *The Fourth Objections*, Bennett, J. (tr.), available at: www.earlymoderntexts.com/pdfs/descartes1642_2.pdf, pp.56–7.
11. *Meditation 6*, EMT p.32.
12. Ibid.
13. Ibid., p.29.
14. Churchland, Patricia, *Brain-wise*, p.44.
15. See Patricia Churchland *Brain-wise* p.44 for discussion of neural dependence as an argument against dualism.
16. Descartes, 1644, *Principles of Philosophy*, section 169.
17. See also *Meditation 6*, EMT p.33, where Descartes discusses the role of the brain and the functions of the nervous system.
18. Darwin, C., 1859, *On the Origin of Species*, John Murray.
19. Because Descartes held that the essential nature of the mind is consciousness, he was committed to the idea that a person couldn't cease to be conscious without ceasing to have a mind. Sleep, therefore, would seem to involve the destruction of the mind and with it the person you are. Rather than accept this, he argued that we remain conscious throughout sleep, that is, we dream continually even if we don't afterwards remember all our dreams. Modern brain scanning techniques again, however, appear to show that much of sleep is dreamless and anaesthesia also shows that it is possible to deactivate consciousness and this also strongly suggests that the brain needs to be active for consciousness to appear.
20. Leibniz, 1714, *Monadology*, section 17.
21. Anthology extract 2.6: Chalmers, 'Consciousness and its place in nature'.
22. Ibid.
23. Wittgenstein, L., 1953, *Philosophical Investigations*, Basil Blackwell, p.126.
24. Dennett, D., 1995, 'The Unimagined Preposterousness of Zombies', *Journal of Consciousness Studies*, Vol. 2, pp.322–6 (at p.325).
25. Ibid., p.325.
26. Jackson, F., 1982, 'Epiphenomenal Qualia', *The Philosophical Quarterly*, Vol. 32, No. 127 (April), pp.127–136 (at p.127).
27. Ibid.
28. Ibid.
29. Jackson discusses this objection from Paul Churchland in the article, 'What Mary didn't know', *The Journal of Philosophy*, Vol. 83, Issue 5, May 1986, particularly pp.292–293.
30. Lewis, D., 1988, 'What Experience Teaches', in J. Copley-Coltheart (ed.), *Proceedings of the Russellian Society*, Vol. 13, pp.29–57. Reprinted in Ludlow et al., 2004. Jackson's response is given in 'What Mary didn't know'.
31. Churchland, Patricia, 1986, *Neurophilosophy: Toward a Unified Science of the Mind-Brain*, The MIT Press, p.332.
32. Dennett, D., 1991, *Consciousness Explained*, Allan Lane Penguin Press, p.401.
33. For his brief discussion of his change of heart see his 'Postscript on qualia', 1998.
34. Dennett, D., 1988, 'Quining Qualia', in A. Marcel and E. Bisiach (eds), *Consciousness in Contemporary Science*, Oxford University Press, pp.43–77 (at p.43).

35. Churchland, Paul, 1981, 'Eliminative materialism and the propositional attitudes', *The Journal of Philosophy*, Vol. 78, No. 2 (February), pp.67–90.

36. See Churchland, Patricia, *Brain-wise*, pp.130–132.

37. You can also read Patricia Churchland's discussion of this example in *Brain-wise*, pp.22–23 which is part of the required reading from the Anthology.

38. Examples from 'Quining Qualia', p.383.

39. Wittgenstein, L., *Philosophical Investigations*, section 293.

40. Avramides, A., *Other Minds*, 2001, Routledge, London & New York, p.45.

41. See Avramides, *Other Minds*, pp.45 and 49 for this distinction.

42. Wittgenstein, L., *Philosophical Investigations*, section 293.

43. Ryle, G., 1949, *The Concept of Mind*, 2009 edition published by Routledge, p.15.

44. Ibid.

45. Mill, *Examination of Sir William Hamilton's Philosophy*, Ch. 12, cf. Hospers, *Introduction to Philosophical Analysis*, p.252.

46. Ryle, *The Concept of Mind*, 2009 edition, p.51.

47. Avramides, A., *Other Minds*, p.49

48. Wittgenstein, L., *Philosophical Investigations*, section 302.

49. Ibid., section 398.

50. Ibid., sections 243–315.

51. Avramides, *Other Minds*, p.63.

52. Descartes, *A Discourse on Method*, part v. See also Avramides pp.62–64 for a discussion of these Cartesian 'tests of real man'.

53. Ryle, G., 1949, *The Concept of Mind*, Penguin: Harmondsworth, Ch.1, sect. 2, p.19.

54. Ibid., Ch.1, sect. 2, p.17.

55. Ibid., p.17.

56. Ryle, *The Concept of Mind*, 2009 edition, Ch.1, p.7.

57. Ryle, *The Concept of Mind*, Ch.1, sect. 2, p.18.

58. Ryle, G., *The Concept of Mind*, Ch.1, sect. 3 'The Origin of the Category-Mistake'.

59. Ryle, *The Concept of Mind*, 2009 edition, Ch.1, p.7.

60. Ibid., Ch.2(i) foreword

61. 'Descartes' Myth' is the title of the first chapter of *The Concept of Mind* where Ryle attacks Cartesian dualism.

62. See *Essays on the Intellectual Powers of Man*, (1785) Essay VI, Ch. V, 8–9, EMT, pp.260–262.

63. Ibid., Ch. V, 9 EMT p.262.

64. Descartes, *Meditation 6*, EMT, p.33.

65. Letter from Princess Elisabeth of Bohemia to Descartes, 6 May 1643, available at: www.earlymoderntexts.com/pdfs/descartes1643_1.pdf, p.2.

66. Ibid.

67. Ibid.

68. Broad, C.D., 1925, *Mind and Its Place in Nature,* Ch. 3, available at: www.ditext.com/broad/mpn3.html

69. Hume, D., *Enquiry Concerning Human Understanding*, Book 1, section 4, para. 25.

70. Ibid., para. 23.

71. Ibid., para. 25.

72. Churchland, Patricia, *Brain-wise*, p.43.

73. Santayana, G., 1930, *The Realm of Matter,* Scribner.

74. Huxley, T.H., 1874, 'On the Hypothesis that Animals are Automata, and its History,' available at: http://facultypages.morris.umn.edu/~mcollier/Philosophy%20of%20Mind/huxley.pdf

75. Descartes, *Passions of the Soul*, Art. xiii.

76. Huxley, 'On the Hypothesis that Animals are Automata, and its History', p.240.

77. Ibid., p.244.

78. Ibid., p.240.

79. Ibid., p.244.

80. Libet, B., 1985, 'Unconscious cerebral initiative and the role of conscious will in voluntary action', *Behavioral and Brain Sciences*, Vol. 8, pp.529–66.

81. Huxley, 'On the Hypothesis that Animals are Automata, and its History', p.241.

82. Jackson, 'Epiphenomenal Qualia', pp.135–136.

2.3 Physicalist theories

1. Ayer, A.J., 1936, *Language, Truth and Logic*, Victor Gollancz, Ch.7.
2. Also known as logical or analytical behaviourism.
3. Hempel, C., 'The logical analysis of psychology' in J. Heil (ed.), *Philosophy of Mind. A Guide and Anthology*, Oxford University Press, pp.84–95 (at p. 90).
4. Ibid., p.87.
5. Ibid., p.89.
6. Ibid., p.91.
7. Ibid.
8. Ryle, G., 1949, *The Concept of Mind*, 2009 edition published by Routledge.
9. Ibid., p.34.
10. Ibid., p.94.
11. Ibid., p.38.
12. Ibid., p.101.
13. Ibid., p.106.
14. Hempel, 'The logical analysis of psychology', p.90.
15. Ibid.
16. Putnam. H., 2004, 'Brains and behaviour', in J. Heil (ed.), *Philosophy of Mind. A Guide and Anthology*, p.102.
17. Ibid., p.104.
18. J.J.C. Smart (2004), 'Sensations and brain processes', in J. Heil (ed.), *Philosophy of Mind*, pp.116–127 (at p.119).
19. Ibid., pp.117–118.
20. Putnam, H., 1967, 'The nature of mental states' in *The Nature of Mind*, Rosenthal, D.M. (ed.), 1991, Oxford University Press, pp.197–203 (at p.198).
21. C-fibres are nerve fibres responsible for pain.
22. The distinction is due to Gottlob Frege in his paper 'On sense and reference', *Über Sinn und Bedeutung*, 1892.
23. Putnam, H., 'The nature of mental states', p.198.
24. Block, N., 1978, 'Troubles with Functionalism', in C.W. Savage (ed.), *Perception and Cognition*, University of Minnesota Press, pp.261–325 (at p.265).
25. See Kripke, S., 1972, 'Naming and necessity', in D. Davidson and G. Harman (eds), *Semantics and natural language*, Reidel.
26. Churchland, Paul, 1981, 'Eliminative materialism and the propositional attitudes', *Journal of Philosophy*, Vol. 78, No. 2 (February), pp.67–90 (at p.67).
27. There remains some controversy over this which we can ignore for our purposes.
28. Churchland, Paul, 1981, 'Eliminative materialism and the propositional attitudes', pp.67–90.
29. Ibid., p.68.
30. Churchland, Patricia, *Brain-wise* pp.22–23.
31. Ibid.
32. Churchland, Paul, 1981, 'Eliminative materialism and the propositional attitudes', p.74.
33. Ibid.
34. Churchland, Patricia, *Brain-wise*, p.129.
35. Ibid.
36. Ibid., pp.129–130.
37. Churchland, Paul, 1981, 'Eliminative materialism and the propositional attitudes', p.70.
38. Ibid., pp.72–73.
39. A phrase Churchland borrows from the philosopher of science Imre Lakatos (1922–74), Ibid., p.75.
40. Ibid., p.89.
41. Ibid., pp.89–90.
42. Putnam, H., 'Psychological predicates', p.162.
43. Ibid., p.164.
44. Ibid., p.166.
45. Example from Block's 'flea-head' discussion in 'Troubles with functionalism', Section 1.4.
46. Putnam, H., 'The nature of mental states', p.200.
47. Ibid., p.200.
48. Block, N., 'Troubles with functionalism', section 1.6, p.293.
49. His story is dramatised in a film, *The Imitation Game* (2014).
50. Searle, J., 1980, 'Minds, Brains and Programs', *Behavioral and Brain Sciences*, Vol. 3, pp.417–57.
51. Pinker, S., 1997, *How the Mind Works*, Penguin.
52. Dennett, D., 1987, *The Intentional Stance*, The Massachusetts Institute of Technology.
53. For an influential development of this line of thought see Colin McGinn 'Can we solve the mind–body problem', *Mind* 98 (1989) republished in Heil, J. (ed.), 2004, *Philosophy of Mind: A Guide and Anthology*, Oxford University Press, pp.781–797.

Index

abductive arguments 34–5, 59
ability (practical) knowledge 222–3
Achilles and the tortoise paradox v–vii
acquaintance knowledge 221–2
actuality 98–100, 208
adaptationism 87–8
afterlife defence 139–40
analytical behaviourism, see philosophical (analytical, logical) behaviourism
analytic reduction 262
analytic statements 161
Andronicus of Rhodes viii
animal mentality 283
Anscombe, Elizabeth 122
Anselm, St 4, 56, 97, 322
    attributes of God 9, 10
    ontological arguments 40–3, 44
anti-realism 139, 181
a posteriori arguments 38, 48, 49, 59, 85, 91, 164: see also cosmological arguments; problem of evil: evidential problem of evil; teleological (design) arguments
a posteriori knowledge 161
a priori arguments 32, 38, 40, 48–9, 163–4: see also ontological arguments; problem of evil: logical problem of evil
a priori knowledge 161
Aquinas, St Thomas 25, 44, 320, 326
    attributes of God 8, 9, 10–11, 26–7
    cosmological arguments 97–108, 119
    evil 130, 132
    teleological argument 60–1
Arendt, Hannah 137
arguments
    logical forms of 31–5
    strength of conclusion 35–7
    structure of 30–1
Aristotle v, viii, 97, 102, 130, 245
    attributes of God 6, 9, 25
    cosmological argument 94–5
    theory of change (motion) 98–9
Arnaud, Antoine 203
artificial intelligence (AI) 303
as-if intentionality 303, 304
Augustine, St 4
    evil 129, 130, 131, 132
    free will defence 141–2
    theodicy 147–8
Averroes (Ibn Rushd) 19
Avramides, Anita 231, 236, 333
Ayer, A.J. 47, 48–9, 158, 178, 181, 261, 328
    Hume's fork 160, 161, 163
    verification principle 160–4, 209, 329

Barth, Karl 56
beliefs 157
Berkeley, Bishop George xi, 190
Bible references
    attributes of God 6, 7–8, 9, 10, 11, 13, 22–5
    concept of God 2, 3
    creation of world 170
    Job 151, 172
    ontological arguments 40, 41
    original sin 141
    problem of evil 129, 151
    teleological arguments 58
Big Bang theory 118
bliks 175–7, 182
Block, Ned 282, 297, 301, 302, 338
Boethius 13, 14
Broad, C.D. 248
Buddhism 198

Cantor, George 117
Capote, Truman: *In Cold Blood* 129–30
Carnap, Rudolf 163
Cartesian circle 112
Cartesian dualism, see substance dualism
causal closure of the physical 249, 255
causal principle 108–9, 120–2
causation, theory of
    chains of events 92–3, 97–8, 103–4
    Hume 79–80, 81–2, 83, 119, 120–2, 176
Celestial City parable 166
Chalmers, David 187
    consciousness 185, 186, 188, 191, 214, 329, 330
    philosophical zombies 214, 215, 217, 331
    supervenience 215–16
change v–ii, x, 98–101
Chinese room argument 303–6
Chomsky, Noam 154
Churchland, Patricia 188, 210, 223, 249, 332, 335
    eliminativism 227, 287, 288–9, 337
    physicalism 225–6
Churchland, Paul 292
    eliminativism 227, 285, 286–7, 288, 291, 293–4, 332
    physicalism 225–6
Cicero, Marcus Tullius 57

circularity 266, 271–2
Cognitive Behavioural Therapy 292
cognitivism
    about religious language 156–9
    Wittgenstein's rejection of 178–81
common sense 208, 225–6, 245–6, 254, 255, 256, 257, 258, 271, 276, 285, 286–7, 288, 294
compatibilism 141, 258
compossibility 17
computers: and consciousness 302–5
conceivability argument 199–212, 331
    Descartes 202–10
    mind/body relation 208–10
    mind/brain dependence 210–11
    possibility 201, 203–8
    theory of evolution and 211–12
conceptual interaction problem 245–8
consciousness xii, xiii, 185–91, 194, 213, 214, 252
    computers and 302–5
    and identity theory 280–1
    and mind/brain dependence 211–12
    neuroscience and 196–8
conservation of energy 250
contingency 53, 54–5, 92, 116
    contingent identity 278, 285, 298, 336
    contingent truths 114–15
    cosmological arguments and 105–8
Copenhagen Interpretation 122
Copernicus 61
Copleston, F.C. 92, 101–2, 122, 124, 126
cosmological arguments 91–128
    Aquinas 97–108, 119
    Aristotle 94–5
    Descartes 108–12
    explanation of universe 126–7
    fallacy of composition 122–4
    features of 91–2
    horizontal/vertical chains of events 92–3, 97–8, 103–4
    Hume 119–22
    impossibility of necessary being 124–6
    Kalām argument (argument from temporal causation) 96–7, 117–19
    Leibniz 112–16
    Plato 94
    possibility of infinite series 116–17
    principle of sufficient reason (argument from contingency) 112–16
Craig, William Lane 96
Cuppit, Don 177

Darwin, Charles 57, 71, 87–8, 132, 135, 211
Dawkins, Richard 88
deductive arguments 31–2, 38, 59, 91, 96
deism 13, 104
Democritus 189
Dennett, Daniel 223, 224
    philosophical zombies 216–17
    qualia 225, 228–9
    spectrum inversion 230–1
    taste, sense of 229–30
Descartes, René 4, 211, 245, 261
    causation 108–9, 120, 121, 248
    conceivability argument 199, 02–10, 331
    consciousness 187, 194, 196, 213, 252
    cosmological arguments 108–12, 326
    dualism 192–3, 202–4
    indivisibility argument 195, 196, 197, 198, 199, 330
    Leibniz's law 204–7
    ontological arguments 45–6, 322
    other minds problem 241, 243
    physicalism of animals 189
    possibility 202–3
    real man test 241
    trademark argument 108–9, 111–12
design (teleological) arguments, see teleological (design) arguments
determinism 140–1, 145: see also free will
Diamond, Jared 131
Dostoyevsky, Fyodor: *The Brothers Karamazov* 149

Edwards, Paul 123, 124
efficient causes 102–3
Einstein, Albert 15–16
eliminativism 225–6, 227, 285–94, 332
    mental states, certainty about reality of 289–90
    self-refuting nature of 293–4
Elisabeth of Bohemia, Princess 246–7, 333
emergent properties 212
Emerson, Ralph Waldo 1
emotivism 164
empirical interaction problem 245–8
Epicurean hypothesis 84–5, 89, 325
Epicurus 84–5, 132, 134, 189
epiphenomenalism 251–60, 294
    other minds problem and 259–60
eschatological verification 165–8
Euthyphro dilemma 22–5, 29, 321
evil, see problem of evil
evolution, theory of 71, 87–9, 259
    and mind/brain dependence 211–12

existentialism 136–7
fallacy of composition 122–4
falsificationism 168–82
final causes 102
Flew, Antony 37, 182
    criticism of Hare 177
    falsificationism 168–77, 329
    free will defence 144
    teleological arguments 58
    Wisdom's gardener parable 169–70
folk psychology 226, 240–1, 277, 286–93, 332
formal causes 102
free will 140–6, 256–9
    and omniscience 25–7, 29
    see also determinism
Freud, Sigmund 188
Fromm, Erich 137
functionalism 294–306, 337, 338
    and knowledge (Mary) argument 300–1
    mental states as functional states 295–9
    and qualia 299–302

Gaunilo of Marmoutier 43–4, 53, 322
al-Ghazali 96, 97
ghost in machine dogma 241–3
God, attributes of 5–17, 28–9
    eternal nature 10–12, 13–17
    everlasting nature 12–13
    immutability 6–7, 8, 10–11
    omnibenevolence 9–10, 22–5, 27
    omnipotence 7–8, 19–21, 27, 320
    omniscience 6–7, 25–7, 29
    problems associated with 18
    relationship to time 10
God, concept of 28
    incoherence of 17–27
God, existence of 30–128
    cosmological arguments 91–128
    ontological arguments 38–56
    teleological (design) arguments 57–90

hard behaviourism 263–4, 265, 267, 268
Hare, Richard 168
    bliks 175–7, 182
    falsificationism 175–7
    non-cognitivism 176–7
    paranoid student parable 175
Hawking, Stephen 117
Heidegger, Martin 244
Hempel, Carl 270, 273, 334
    hard behaviourism 263–4, 265, 267, 268
Heraclitus x

Hick, John 55–6, 181
    afterlife defence 139
    Ayer's verification principle 162
    Celestial City parable 166
    eschatological verification 165–8
    problem of evil 132, 139, 146–9
    soul-making theodicy 146–9, 166, 328
    thought experiments 166–7
Himma, Kenneth 69
Hume, David ix, 47, 49, 119–23, 197–8
    constant conjunction 80, 121, 141, 248–9
    cosmological argument 119–22
    design argument 62–5, 72–5, 324, 325
    design explained by random processes 84–5
    determinism 141
    free will 258
    infinite series 116, 120
    mind/sense experiences 209
    necessary beings 125, 126
    problem of evil 135
    problem of spatial disorder 76–8
    theory of causation 79–80, 81–2, 83, 119, 120–2, 176, 248–9
Hume's fork 48, 160, 161, 163
Huxley, T.H. 252–3, 254, 255, 258, 259
idealism 189, 190
identity theory 336, 337
    arguments for 275–7
    chauvinism of 282–3
    consciousness and 280–1
    contingent identity 278, 285, 298, 336
    introspection and 280–1
    mental life of other species 283
    mind–brain type 273–85
    necessary identity 285
    spatial location problem 278–9

impossibility 54–6
indivisibility argument 195–9, 330
inductive arguments 32–4, 59
infinite regress fallacy 119
infinite series (infinite regress of causes) 116–19, 120
intentionality xii, 186, 187, 205
    as-if intentionality 303, 304
    intrinsic intentionality 303–5
    irreducibility of 281–2
    Searle's Chinese room argument 303–6
interactionism 245–51, 271
intrinsic intentionality 303–5

introspection 185, 196, 197–8
    and identity theory 280–1
    and philosophical behaviourism 270–1
introspective self-knowledge 254–6
invisible gardener parable 169–70
Irenaeus, St 146–8

Jackson, Frank 222–3, 224, 256, 259
    qualia 220, 260, 301, 332, 334

Kalām argument (argument from temporal causation) 96–7, 117–19
Kant, Immanuel ix, 38, 58, 209
    design explained by worldly architect 85–7
    objections to ontological arguments 49–50
Keats, John 148
Kenny, Anthony 14–15, 26
Kierkegaard, Søren 24
knowledge (Mary) argument 220–31, 300–1, 332
Kretzmann, Norman 6–7, 13–17, 321

La Mettrie, Julien Offray de 189
language games 180–1, 182
laws of reality 115
laws of thought 115
Leibniz, Gottfried Wilhelm 17, 143–4, 213
    principle of sufficient reason 109, 112–16, 327
Leibniz's lapse 145
Leibniz's law 195–6, 204–7, 274, 278, 280
Libet, Benjamin 255
Locke, John ix
logical behaviourism, see philosophical (analytical, logical) behaviourism
logical positivism (logical empiricism) ix, 160, 163, 178, 264
logical possibility 200–1, 202

McEwan, Ian: *Enduring Love* 170
machine state functionalism 296–7
Mackie, J.L. 8, 108
    on free will defence 144
    and infinite series 119
    problem of evil 133–4
Malcolm, Norman 44, 52–5, 323
Manichaeism 139
masked man fallacy 204–7
material causes 102
materialism, see physicalism

Mavrodes, George 19–20
meaning
    concept of 154–5
    and reference 277–8
    theories of 178–80, 182
mental life of other species 283
mental properties 212
mental states 289–90
    distinctness from behaviour 272–3
    features of 186–91
    as functional states 295–9
    multiple realisability of 284–5, 296
    problem of definition 265–8
    Ryle's dispositional analysis 268–9
metaphysical possibility 201, 202, 203–8, 219–20
metaphysics: definition of vii–viii
Midgley, Mary 137–8, 327
Mill, John Stuart 132, 234
mind/brain dependence 210–12
mind/brain identity 273–85, 335
Mitchell, Basil 168, 174–5, 182
modality 54–6
monism 188–9
moral evil 131, 142, 148
moral responsibility 137, 257, 258
multiple realisability 265–6
    of mental states 284–5, 296

natural evil 130–1, 148
natural selection 87–9
natural theology 4–5, 28
near-death experiences 193
necessity 53–4, 55–6, 106–8
    of God 107–8
    necessary beings, impossibility of 124–6
    necessary identity 285
    necessary truths 114, 125
neuroscience
    consciousness and 196–8
    mind/brain dependence 210–11
Newton, Isaac 61, 227
nomological danglers 275, 276
non-cognitivism 156–9, 176–7, 182
numerical identity 274

objective morality 24–5
Ockham's razor 276
Ogden, C.K. 154
omnibenevolence 9–10, 22–5, 29
omnipotence 7–8, 19–21, 27
omniscience 6–7, 25–7, 29
ontological arguments 38–56
    Anselm 40–3, 44

concepts, unpacking (analysis) of 39–40
    Descartes 45–6
    empiricist objections to 47–9
    features of 38
    Gaunilo's 'perfect island' objection 43–4
    Kant's objections 49–50
    Malcolm 52–5
    Russell's objections 51–2
ontological reduction 275
Orwell, George: *1984* 164–5
other minds problem 231–45, 333
    argument from analogy 234–9
    best-hypothesis argument 239–41
    conceptual problem 236–9
    epiphenomenalism and 259–60
    epistemological problem 232–3, 239–44
out-of-body experiences 193, 209

Paley, William 65–9, 78, 82–3, 323, 325
paradox of the stone 19–21, 29
paranoid student parable 175
Parmenides v
partisans parable 174–5
Pascal, Blaise 2, 3, 4, 183, 184
phenomenology of the mental 187
philosophical (analytical, logical) behaviourism 218, 261, 262–73, 294
    arguments for 263
    criticisms of 272–3
    hard behaviourism 263–4
    introspection and 270–1
    perfect actors and 268, 273, 298, 334
    self-knowledge/knowledge of other's mental states asymmetry 271
philosophical zombies argument 213–20, 331
physicalism (materialism) 189, 213, 215, 225–6, 250, 276–7
    philosophical behaviourism 262–73
    qualia and 220–1
physical possibility 200, 201
Pinker, Steven 184, 305
Plantinga, Alvin 133, 134, 141, 142, 145–6, 328
Plato 21–3, 24, 37, 60, 94, 190, 321
    attributes of God 6, 9, 10
positivism 160, 163, 178, 264
possibility 54–6
potentiality 98–100
practical (ability) knowledge 222–3
principle of contradiction 114

principle of identity 114
principle of sufficient reason (PSR) 109, 112–16, 327
problem of evil 27, 58, 78, 129–51
    atheists' responses 136–8
    believers' responses 138–50
    definitions of evil 129–30, 137
    evidential problem of evil 132, 135
    logical problem of evil 132, 133–4
    moral/natural evil 130–2, 142
process theology 139
property dualism 212–31
    knowledge/Mary argument 220–31
    philosophical zombies argument 213–20
propositional content 186, 187
propositional knowledge 221–2
propositions (statements) 39–40, 157
    Ayer on 160–1
    Flew on 168
    religious propositions 153
Pseudo-Dionysius 153
psychology 263, 264
Ptolemy: cosmology 34–5, 227
Putnam, Hilary 277, 279, 335, 336
    functionalism 294, 295, 297, 301–2, 337
    (super-)super-spartans 272–3, 298

qualia 187–9, 260, 301, 332, 334
    existence of 225–9
    and functionalism 299–302
    physicalism and 220–1, 225
    spectrum inversion 230–1, 299–300
qualitative identity 274
quantum physics 122

Rabelais, François 152
Ratzch, Del 69–70
reactive disassociation 229
real man test 241
reductio ad absurdum arguments 94–5
reduction 285–6
reference: meaning and 277–8
regularities of co-presence 71
regularities of succession 71–2
Reid, Thomas 245
religious language 152–84
    cognitivism/non-cognitivism about 156–9
    eschatological verification 165–8
    features of 153–4
    University debate 168–82
    verification principle 160–5

revealed theology 3–5, 28
reverse engineering 82, 88
Richards, I.A. 154
Rowe, William 100–1, 135
Russell, Bertrand 51–2, 122, 123, 125, 126–7, 152
Ryle, Gilbert 199, 271, 272, 330, 333, 335
    dogma of ghost in machine 241–3
    other minds problem 233, 235, 241–4, 333
    soft behaviourism 268–9

Sadowsky, James 119
Santayana, George 251
Sartre, Jean-Paul 136, 244–5
Savage, C. Wade 20
Schopenhauer, Arthur 43
Searle, John 303–6
set theory 117
simultaneity 11, 14–16
Smart, J.J.C. 275, 276, 277, 278, 336
Socrates, see Plato
soft behaviourism 268–9
solipsism 238–9
soul-making theodicies 146–9
souls 94
spatial disorder problem 75–8
spatial location problem 278–9, 336
spatial order 65–70
spectrum inversion 230–1, 299–300
Strawson, Peter ix
Stump, Eleonore 13–17, 321
substance dualism 194–212
    conceivability argument 199–212, 331
    indivisibility argument 195–9, 330
sufficient reasons 115–16
superstition 288
supervenience 215–16, 284
supreme goodness, see omnibenevolence
Sutherland, Stewart 164–5
Swinburne, Richard 4, 70–2, 76, 89–90, 323
syllogisms 32, 96
synthetic statements 161

taste, sense of 229–30
teleological (design) arguments 57–90
    argument from spatial order and purpose 65–70
    as argument from unique case/failure of 78–83
    arguments from analogy 60–5, 72–5

    features of 58–60
    God as best/only explanation 83–90
    problem of spatial disorder 75–8
telepathy 210
terms, definition of 28
Thales of Miletus 285
theodicies 138–50
    afterlife defence 139–40
    criticism of 139, 140, 142, 143, 144, 149, 150
    free will defences 140–6
    soul-making theodicies 146–9, 166
theological anti-realism 139
time travel 219
tokens 282–3
Turing test 303–4
type identity theory: chauvinism of 282–3
types 282–3

unconscious mental states 187–8
University (journal) falsification debate 168–82
    Flew 168–70, 171–4, 175
    Hare 175–7
    Mitchell 174–5

veil of perception ix
verificationism 160–8, 209
    Ayer 160–4, 209, 329
    criticism of 164–5
    eschatological verification and 165–8
    and metaphysics of God 163–5
    strong/weak versions 162–3
Vienna Circle 160, 163, 178, 264
vitalism 293–4
volition 245, 248, 249, 252–3, 254–5
Voltaire (François-Marie Arouet) 130–1, 143
Vonnegut, Kurt 11–12

Wisdom, John 168–9
Wittgenstein, Ludwig 178–81, 230
    language games 180–1, 182
    other minds problem 233, 236, 237–8
    philosophical zombies 216–17
    private language argument 218, 238–9
    rejection of cognitivism 178–81
    theories of meaning 178–80, 182
Wolterstorff, Nicholas 12

Zeno: paradoxes v–vii